Worlds Together, WORLDS APART

WORLD · POLITICAL

NATIONAL BOUNDARIES

While man's impact is quite evident, and even striking, on many remotely sensed scenes, sometimes, as in the case with most political boundaries, it is invisible. State, provincial, and national boundaries can follow natural features, such as mountain ridges, rivers, or coastlines. Artificial constructs that possess no physical reality—for example, lines of latitude and longitude—can also determine political borders. The world political map (right) represents man's imaginary lines as they slice and divide Earth.

The National Geographic Society recognizes 192 independent states in the world as represented here. Of those nations, 185 are members of the United Nations.

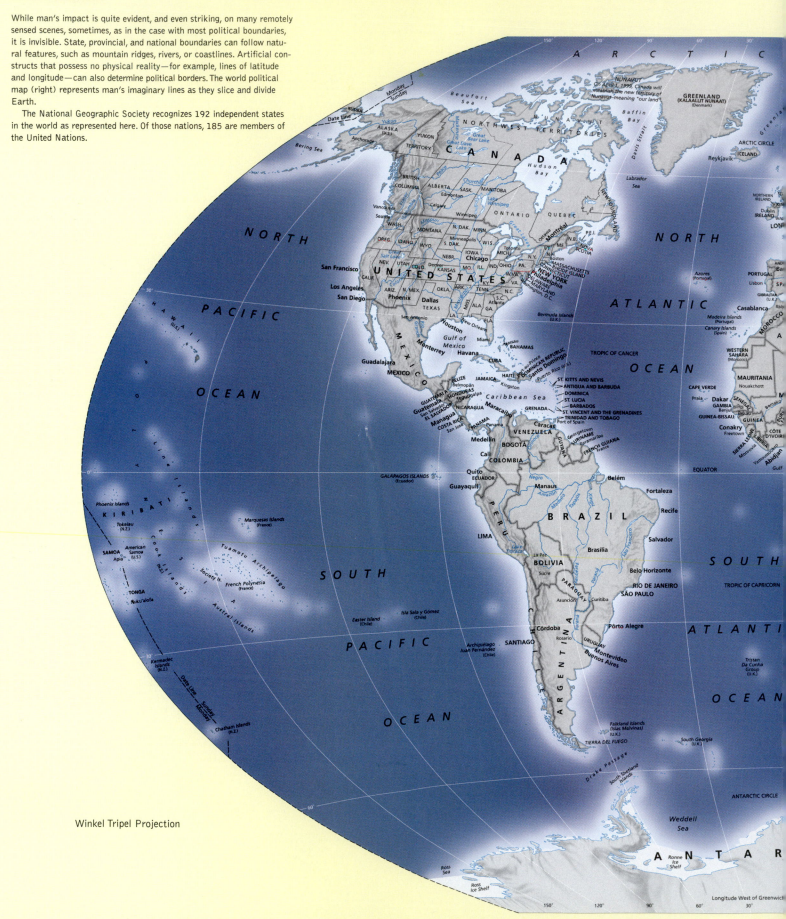

Winkel Tripel Projection

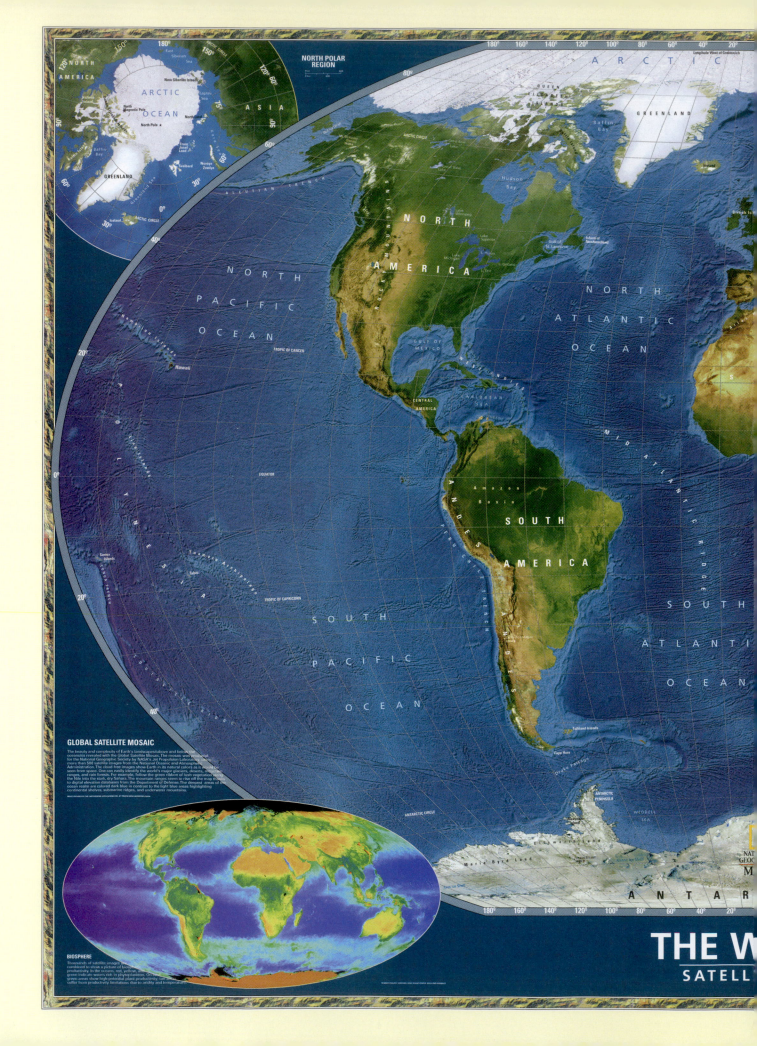

NORTH POLAR REGION

GLOBAL SATELLITE MOSAIC

The beauty and complexity of Earth's landscapes above and below the oceans is revealed with the Global Satellite Mosaic. The mosaic was produced for the National Geographic Society by NASA's Jet Propulsion Laboratory, using more than 500 satellite images from the National Oceanic and Atmospheric Administration. The cloud-free images show Earth in its natural colors as it would be seen from space. One can easily identify the world's major glaciers, deserts, mountain ranges, and rain forests. For example, follow the green ribbon of lush vegetation along the Nile into the dark, dry Sahara. The mountain ranges seem to rise off the map thanks to digital elevation databases from the Department of Defense. The deepest areas of the ocean realm are colored dark blue in contrast to the light blue areas highlighting continental shelves, submarine ridges, and underwater mountains.

BIOSPHERE

Thousands of satellite images are combined to show a picture of biospheric productivity. In the ocean, red, yellow, and green indicate waters rich in phytoplankton. On land, green areas show high potential plant productivity; tan areas suffer from productivity limitations due to aridity and temperature.

THE W
SATELL

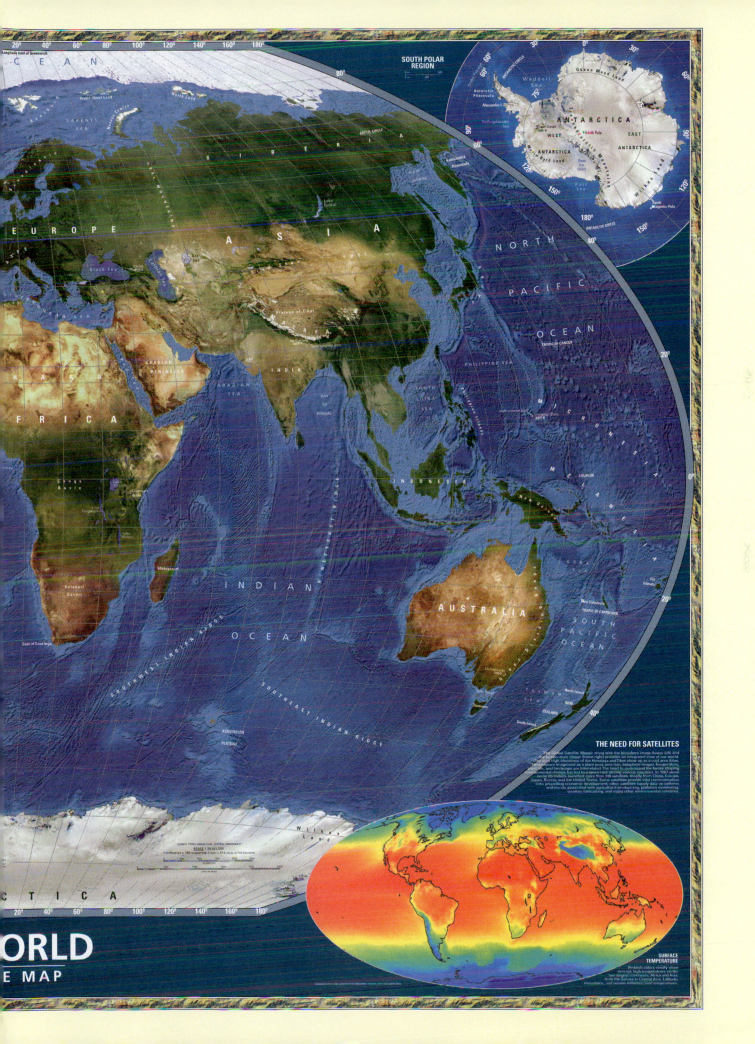

THE NEED FOR SATELLITES

The Global Satellite Mosaic along with the biosphere image (lower left) and the surface temperature image (lower right) provides an integrated view of our world. The very high elevations of the Himalaya and Tibet show up as a cold area (blue). Temperature expressed as a plant grow area than, biosphere image. Temperature, precipitation, and landscape are interrelated. The need to understand the forces shaping our planet and the changes has led to a space race among various countries. In 1997 alone some 80 rockets launched more than 110 satellites—mostly from China, Europe, Japan, Russia, and the United States. Some satellites provide vital communication links propelling economic development; other satellites supply data on patterns and trends associated with agricultural production, pollution monitoring, weather forecasting, and many other environmental concerns.

SURFACE TEMPERATURE

Reddish colors vividly show average high temperatures on the two largest continents, Africa and Asia, from the Sahara to Central Asia. Latitude, mountains, and oceans influence land temperatures.

WORLD
E MAP

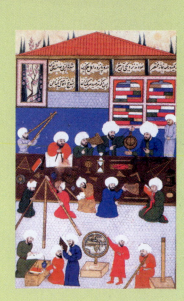

ROBERT TIGNOR

JEREMY ADELMAN

STEPHEN ARON

STEPHEN KOTKIN

SUZANNE MARCHAND

GYAN PRAKASH

MICHAEL TSIN

Worlds Together, WORLDS APART

A HISTORY OF THE MODERN WORLD FROM THE MONGOL EMPIRE TO THE PRESENT

W · W · NORTON & COMPANY
NEW YORK · LONDON

Editor: Jon Durbin
Developmental Editor: Sandy Lifland
Associate Managing Editor: Jane Carter
Editorial Assistant: Aaron Javsicas
Production Manager: Roy Tedoff
Book Designer: Rubina Yeh
Photo Researchers: Neil Hoos, Ede Rothaus
Layout Artist: Roberta Flechner
Cartographer: Carto-Graphics

The text of this book is composed in Bell, with the display set in Snell Roundhouse.
Composition by TechBooks.
Manufacturing by Courier, Kendallville.

Cover illustrations: (From front right cover to back left cover): Islamic Scientists—Topkapi Palace Museum, Istanbul; Imperial Palace, Forbidden City—Granger Collection, New York; Caravel Ship—© 1994 North Wind Pictures; Mansa Musa—Bibliothèque Nationale de France, Paris; Floating Gardens—Nicholas Sapieha/Art Resource, New York; Kabuki Theater—Réunion des Musées Nationaux/Art Resource, New York; Akbar—Reproduced by the kind permission of the Trustees of the Chester Beatty Library, Dublin; The Spice Islands—Giraudon/Art Resource, New York. View of the earth courtesy of NASA. Cover design by Spinning Egg Design Group.

Library of Congress Cataloging-in-Publication Data

Worlds together, worlds apart : a history of the modern world from the mongol empire to
the present / Robert Tignor . . . [et al.].
      p. cm.
    Includes bibliographical references and index.
    ISBN 0-393-97746-3 (pbk.)
    1. World History. 2. Civilization, Medieval. 3. History, Modern. I. Tignor, Robert L.
  D202.4.W67 2002
  909—dc21   2001044776

W. W. Norton & Company, Inc., 500 Fifth Avenue, New York, N.Y. 10110
www.wwnorton.com
W. W. Norton & Company Ltd., Castle House, 75/76 Wells Street, London W1T 3QT

2 3 4 5 6 7 8 9 0

Contents in Brief

Contents

CHAPTER 4   WORLDS ENTANGLED, 1600–1750   118

CHAPTER 7   ALTERNATIVE VISIONS OF THE NINETEENTH CENTURY   238

CHAPTER 10   OF MASSES AND VISIONS OF THE MODERN, 1910–1939   346

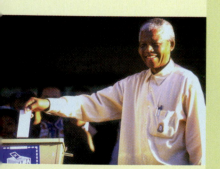

Global Connections and Disconnections Feature Boxes

Primary Source Documents

Maps

Preface

Nearly fifteen years ago, the Princeton University history department established its first course in world history. Called "The World and the West," the course surveyed the major developments in the history of the modern world from 1500 to the present. The course placed immense demands on teachers and students. The greatest challenge was how to treat the many regions of the world and the many centuries in an integrated way and in a single semester. The instructors in the course searched for a textbook that would be analytical and integrating. Unfortunately, the textbooks available at that time did not work. Some were by a single author and tended to have a clear narrative framework but to suffer from the limitations that a single individual, no matter how well read, confronted when dealing with the immensity of world history. Others were written by a team of regional experts and had authoritative treatments of regions but lacked integration and balance.

A small group of us in the Princeton history department decided to try our hand at world history, agreeing to meet together on a regular basis to plan a text that addressed the weaknesses observed in the other books. Each of us had a regional specialization as well as an interest in how our regions fitted into larger cross-regional relationships. For an entire year we met to discuss the ways in which we would craft a world history and what global themes we wanted to stress. Only after intensive and sometimes contentious discussions were we able to decide on our overarching framework, the chapter divisions, and the global themes and regional variations. As we began, we all wrote sections in each of the chapters, shared them with one another, and then gave one of our group the assignment of integrating each chapter. All of this meant that every single one of us wrote something for each of the chapters. Different individuals coordinated the chapters, after which the drafts circulated once again to all for additional thoughts and revisions. The final product is a truly collaborative work. No section, no matter how seemingly specialized, is the product of just one author.

Over the course of the five-year period of working on this book, world history has gained even more prominence in college classrooms and historical studies. Courses in the history of the world now abound, often replacing the standard surveys of European history and Western civilization overviews. Graduate history students receive training in world history, and journals routinely publish studies in this field. A new generation of textbooks is needed to help students and instructors make sense of this vast, complex, and rapidly evolving field.

From the first day that we met to discuss this book, we vowed to write a volume that would realize certain criteria. It would offer clear themes and interpretations, thus providing a synthesis of the vast body of data that often overwhelms histories of the modern world. It would integrate all of the regions of the world into thematically unified chapters. It would decenter Europe. It would also be brief, thus allowing instructors to assign other readings and develop other points of view.

Brevity has meant that *Worlds Together, Worlds Apart* is not a book of record. Readers will not encounter all of the names, dates, and places that authorities might expect to find in a standard world history reference work. Quite the contrary, we have dared to omit many specifics, no matter how colorful or interesting, so that details do not submerge general patterns. Our hope is to provide enough information to make the narrative comprehensible, easily grasped, and a platform for discussing global issues. Brevity will also permit instructors to supplement the text with readings, some of which we identify in the short primary source boxes that accompany each chapter as well in the bibliographies that follow each chapter.

As an integrated work of world history, *Worlds Together, Worlds Apart* looks at all of the regions of the world, describing events from regional and global perspectives. Readers will not find any chapter that deals exclusively with a separate region of the world. There are no freestanding discussions of China, the Middle East, or Africa, as is the case in most other works. The chapters, which are organized in the first instance chronologically, highlight those developments, like the spread of the Black Death, the influx of silver from the Americas into the world economy, and the rise of nationalism, that reverberated throughout the world, but that produced varying reactions in different regions.

Worlds Together, Worlds Apart has a central theme—one that runs through the chapters and connects the different parts of the volume. This is the theme of interconnection and divergence. While describing movements that facilitated global connectedness, this book also shows how different regions developed their own particular movements for handling or resisting connections and change. Over the last 700 years, different regions of the world and different population groups often stood apart from the rest of the world until touched by traders or explorers or missionaries or soldiers. Some of these regions welcomed global connections. Others sought to change the nature of their connections with the outside world, and yet others resisted efforts to bring them into the larger world. All, however, were somehow affected by their experience of connection. Yet, the history of the modern world has not simply been a history of increasing globalization, in which all societies eventually join a common path to the present. Rather, it has been a history of the ways in which, as people became linked, their experience of these global connections diverged.

Besides the central theme, other specific themes also stand out in this book. First, it discusses how the recurring effort of people to cross religious, political, and cultural borders brought the world together. Merchants and educated men and women traded goods and ideas. Whole communities, in addition to select groups, moved to safer or more promising environments.

The trans-regional crossings of ideas, goods, and peoples produced transformations and conflicts—a second important theme in this volume. Finally, the movement of ideas, peoples, products, and germs over long distances upset the balance of power across the world and within individual societies. Such movements changed the relationship of different population groups with other peoples and areas of the world and led to dramatic shifts that occurred in the ascendancy of regions over time. Changes in power arrangements within and between regions explain which parts of the world and which regional groups benefited from integration and which resisted it. These three themes (exchange and migration, conflict and resistance, and alterations in the balance of power) weave themselves through every chapter of this work.

In *Worlds Together, Worlds Apart*, we tell the stories of people caught in these currents of exchange, conflict, and changing power relations. We describe those historical actors, like Muslim Indian Ocean merchants in the sixteenth century and late nineteenth-century European imperialists, who sought a more closely integrated world economy and polity. Alongside those individuals, however, we also describe those individuals who led movements in defense of cherished historical and cultural heritages. The Indian prophet Tenskwatawa in North America and the religious cleric al-Wahhab on the Arabian peninsula both urged their people to return to traditional identities. Others, like Indian rebels in 1857 and advocates of a third way after World War II, sought a less unified world and used their historical and cultural traditions to favor new arrangements of world power.

OVERVIEW OF THE BOOK

This volume commences, not in 1492 as other works do, but two centuries earlier. It does so for several reasons. First, it exposes the powerful pre-1500 antecedents to globalism. Already in the late thirteenth century, peoples around the globe were linked over long distances through trading networks, the dispersal of ideals, and missionizing impulses. Second, it permits the introduction of this volume's cast of characters, so to speak, the major cultural communities of the world through which people gave meaning and purpose to their daily and often mundane activities. Third, by starting earlier than is usual, it emphasizes the strength of Asian cultures and how surprising subsequent European expansion was.

The first chapter of the book, "The Worlds of 1300," describes the different regions of the world in 1300—their political structures, their social organizations, and their religious beliefs. It draws to a close by focusing on early agents of globalization—Mongol tribesmen from the steppe-lands of East Asia who came from the margins of settled societies. The Mongols first brought turmoil to the peoples of the Eurasian land mass, then increased their political, social, and economic integration. Chapter 2, "Crises and Recovery in Eurasia, 1300s–1500s," describes how the Mongols, through their conquests and the integration of the Eurasian world, spread the bubonic plague, which brought death and depopulation to much of Eurasia. The primary agents of world connection described in this chapter were dynasts, soldiers, clerics, merchants, and adventurers who set about rebuilding the societies that disease and political collapse had laid waste. They joined the two hemispheres, as we describe in Chapter 3, "Contact, Commerce, and Colonization, 1450s–1600," bringing the peoples and products of the Western Hemisphere into contact and conflict with Eurasia and Africa. Here, too, disease and increasing trade linkages were vital. Unprepared for the advanced military technology and the disease pool of European and African peoples, the Amerindian population experienced a population decline even more devastating than that of the Black Death.

Europeans sailed westward across the Atlantic Ocean to find a more direct, less encumbered route to Asia and came upon lands, peoples, and products that they had not expected. One item, however, that they had sought in every part of the world and that they found in abundance in the Americas was precious metal. In Chapter 4, "Worlds Entangled, 1600–1750," we discuss how New World silver from Mexico and Peru became the major currency of global commerce, oiling the long-distance trading networks that had been revived after the Black Death. We also discuss the importance of sugar, which linked the economies and polities of Western Europe, Africa, and the Americas in a triangular trade, centered on the Atlantic Ocean. Sugar, silver, spices, and other products sparked expanded commercial exchanges and led to cultural flourishing around the world. In Chapter 5, "Cultures of Splendor and Power, 1600–1780," we describe Ottoman scientists, Safavid and Mughal artists, and Chinese literati, as well as European thinkers, all of whom produced notable cultural achievements that were rooted in their own cultures but tempered with a growing awareness of the intellectual activities of others.

Around 1800, transformations reverberated outward from the Atlantic world and altered economic and political relationships throughout the rest of the world. In Chapter 6, "Reordering the World, 1750–1850," we discuss how political revolutions in the Americas and Europe, new ideas about how to trade and organize labor, and a powerful rhetoric of freedom and universal rights underlay the beginning of "a great divide" in the relations between peoples who were of European descent and those who were not. Not only did these new forces of laissez-faire capitalism, industrialization, the nation-state, and republicanism attract diverse groups around the world, they also threatened groups that put forward alternative visions. In Chapter 7, "Alternative Visions of the Nineteenth Century," we present the prophets and leaders who had these visions that often drew on earlier traditions. In Chapter 8, "Nations and Empires, 1850–1914," we discuss how the political, economic, military, and ideological power that thrust Europe and North America to the fore of global events led to the era of national-

ism and imperialism. Yet, this period of seeming European supremacy was to prove short-lived. As we explain in Chapter 9, "An Unsettled World, 1890–1914," even before the catastrophe of World War I shattered Europe's moral certitude, many groups at home (feminists, Marxists, and unfulfilled nationalists) and abroad (anti-colonial nationalists) raised a chorus of complaints about European and North American dominance.

Chapter 10, "Of Masses and Visions of the Modern, 1910–1939," briefly covers World War I and then goes on to discuss how, from the end of World War I through the rest of the twentieth century, different visions of being modern competed for supremacy around the world. In the decades between World War I and World War II, proponents of liberal democracy struggled to defend their views and often to impose their will on authoritarian rulers and anti-colonial nationalists. Chapter 11, "The Three-World Order, 1940–1975," presents World War II and then goes on to describe how new adversaries arose after the war. We identify a three-world order—the First World, led by the United States and extolling the virtues of capitalism, the nation-state, and democratic government; the Second World, led by the Soviet Union and favoring authoritarian polities and economies; and the Third World, made up of former colonies and seeking an independent status for themselves in world affairs. In Chapter 12, "Globalization," we explain that, at the end of the cold war, the modern world is clearly more unified than ever before, yet cultural differences and political divisions still abound. At the beginning of the twenty-first century, capital, commodities, peoples, and ideas move rapidly over long distances. But cultural tensions and political impasses continue to exist in sharp relief.

INNOVATIVE PEDAGOGICAL PROGRAM

Worlds Together, Worlds Apart is designed for maximum readability. The crisp, clear narrative, built around stories, themes, and concepts is also accompanied by a highly useful pedagogical program designed to help the students study while engaging them in the subject matter. Highlights of this innovative program include:

PRIMARY SOURCE DOCUMENTS

Designed to add depth to the more focused narrative of *Worlds Together, Worlds Apart*, each chapter contains three or four primary sources carefully chosen to highlight the main themes of the book.

GLOBAL CONNECTIONS/DISCONNECTIONS FEATURE BOXES

Each chapter contains one thematic feature box built around key individuals or phenomena that best exemplify the main emphasis of the text. Among the many topics included: coffee drinking and coffeehouses in different parts of the world; cartography and maps as expressions of different worldviews; the growth of universities around the world; and Che Guevera as a radical visionary who tried to export revolution throughout the Third World.

Focus Question System

Ensures that the reader remains alert to key concepts and questions on every page of the text. Focus questions guide students' reading in three ways: (1) a focus question box appears at the beginning of the chapter to serve as a preview of the chapter's contents, (2) relevant questions reappear at the start of the section where they are discussed, and (3) running heads on the right-hand pages keep these questions in view throughout the chapter.

Stellar Map Program with Enhanced Captions

Sixty beautiful maps appear in the text, each accompanied by an enhanced map caption designed to engage the reader analytically, while conveying the key role that geography plays on the development of history and the societies of the world.

Pull Quotes

Lifted directly from the narrative, pull quotes appear throughout each chapter and are designed to highlight key thoughts and keen insights, while keeping students focused on larger concepts and ideas.

Chapter Chronologies

Each chapter contains one expanded chronology that highlights key events that relate to the main themes and stories of each chapter.

Outstanding Ancillaries for Both Instructors and Students

Worlds Together, Worlds Apart Online Tutor
by Jonathan Lee, San Antonio College

WWW.WWNORTON.COM/WORLDS

This online resource for students—designed specifically for use with *Worlds Together, Worlds Apart*—provides access to online review and research materials for free. Included are online quizzes, Norton iMaps, world history excursion exercises, electronic versions of the Global Connections/Disconnections feature boxes, images from the text, audio and video clips, and Norton e-Reserves.

Norton Media Library with Power Point Slides

This presentation program on CD-ROM is designed to assist students who want to make multimedia presentations. This easy-to-use program includes all the maps in the text, dynamic Norton iMaps, various images from the book.

Instructor's Manual and Test-Item File
by Jonathan Lee, San Antonio College

The Instructor's Manual includes lecture outlines, ideas for launching lectures, sample lecture topics, classroom exercises, suggested films and readings, and recommended web links. The Test-Item File contains multiple-choice, short-answer, and essay questions for each chapter of the text.

Study Guide
by Michael Murdock, Brigham Young University

This valuable guide contains chapter objectives, chapter outlines, chronologies, key terms, multiple-choice questions, and map exercises.

Acknowledgments

Worlds Together, Worlds Apart is in every sense of the word a Princeton University project. Although only one of us has a Princeton degree (Michael Tsin, Ph.D.), all of us have taught, at one time or another, in the history department. Moreover, the book grew out of two departmental courses in world history (History 213, "The World and the West" and its graduate complement, History 513); students in these two courses used (and commented on) early versions of the manuscript. The authors would like to express their gratitude to the university itself for including the project in its 250th Anniversary Fund for undergraduate teaching.

The history department's support of the effort over many years has been exceptional. Two Chairs—Daniel Rodgers and Philip Nord—made funds and departmental support available, including the department's incomparable administrative talents. We would be remiss if we did not single out the Department Manager, Judith Hanson, who provided us with assistance whenever we needed it. We also thank Eileen Kane, who provided help in tracking down references and illustrations and in integrating changes into the manuscript. We also would like to thank Pamela Long, who made all of the complicated arrangements for ensuring that we were able to discuss matters in a leisurely and attractive setting. Sometimes that meant arranging for long-distance conference calls. She went even further and proofread the entire manuscript, finding many errors that we had all overlooked.

We drew shamelessly on the expertise of the departmental faculty, and although it might be wise simply to include a roster of the Princeton history department, that would do an injustice to those of whom we took most advantage. So here they are: Robert Darnton, Sheldon Garon, Anthony Grafton, Molly Greene, David Howell, Harold James, William Jordan, Emmanuel Kreike, Michael Mahoney, Arno Mayer, Kenneth Mills, John Murrin, Susan Naquin, Willard Peterson, Theodore Rabb, Stanley Stein, and Richard Turits. When necessary, we went outside the history department, getting help from L. Carl Brown, Michael Cook, Norman Itzkowitz, Thomas Leisten, and Heath Lowry. Two departmental colleagues—Natalie Z. Davis and Elizabeth Lunbeck—were part of the original team, but had to withdraw because of other commitments. Their contributions were vital, and we want to express our thanks to them. David Gordon, now at the University of Maryland, used portions of the text while teaching an undergraduate course at the University of Durban in South Africa and shared comments with us. Shamil Jeppie, like David Gordon a graduate of the Princeton history department, and now teaching at the University of Cape Town in South Africa, read and commented on various chapters.

Beyond Princeton, we have also benefited from exceptionally gifted and giving colleagues who have assisted this book in many ways. Colleagues at Louisiana State University, the University of Florida, and the University of California at Los Angeles, where Suzanne Marchand, Michael Tsin, and Stephen Aron respectively are now teaching, pitched into this effort whenever we turned to them. Especially helpful have been the contributions of James Gelvin, Naomi Lamoreaux, and Joyce Appleby at UCLA, as well as Michael Bernstein at the University of California at San Diego, and Maribel Dietz, John Henderson, Christine Kooi, David Lindenfeld, and Victor Stater at Lousiana State University. It goes without saying that none of these individuals bears any responsibility for factual or interpretative errors that the text may contain.

The quality and range of reviews on this project were truly exceptional. The final version of the manuscript was greatly influenced by the thoughts and ideas of numerous instructors. We wish to particularly thank our consulting reviewers who read multiple versions of the manuscript from start to finish:

Hugh Clark, Ursinus College

Jonathan Lee, San Antonio College

Pamela McVay, Ursuline College

Tom Sanders, United States Naval Academy

We are also indebted to the many other reviewers from whom we benefited greatly:

Lauren Benton, New Jersey Institute of Technology

Ida Blom, University of Bergen, Norway

Major Bradley T. Gericke, United States Military Academy

Ricardo Duchesne, University of New Brunswick

John Gillis, Rutgers University

David Kenley, Marshall University

John Kicza, Washington State University

Matthew Levinger, Lewis and Clark College

James Long, Colorado State University

Adam McKeown, Columbia University

Mark McLeod, University of Delaware

John Mears, Southern Methodist University

Michael Murdock, Brigham Young University

David Newberry, University of North Carolina, Chapel Hill

Tom Pearcy, Slippery Rock State University

Oliver B. Pollak, University of Nebraska, Omaha

Ken Pomeranz, University of California, Irvine

Major David L. Ruffley, United States Air Force Academy

William Schell, Murray State University

Major Deborah Schmitt, United States Air Force Academy

Sarah Shields, University of North Carolina, Chapel Hill

Mary Watrous-Schlesinger, Washington State University

Our association with the publishers of this volume, W. W. Norton and Company, was everything that we could have asked for. Jon Durbin took us under the wing of the Norton firm. He attended all of our meetings after the first year. How he put up with some of our interminable discussions will always be a mystery, but his enthusiasm for the endeavor never flagged, even when we seemed to grow weary. Sandy Lifland was the ever watchful and careful development editor. She let us know when we were making sense and when we needed to explain ourselves more fully. Aaron Javsicas kept after us for maps and illustrations. Doug Tebay filled in with help wherever it was needed. Ede Rothaus took on the challenging assignment of finding good illustrations. Neil Hoos gave his valuable support in the photo research. Rubina Yeh created a beautiful design, and Roberta Flechner did excellent work on the page layouts. At a further distance but always within earshot were Steven Forman and Roby Harrington.

Finally, we must recognize that while this project often kept us apart from family members, their support held our personal worlds together.

The history of the modern world is not a single, sweeping narrative. On the contrary, the last 700 years have produced a series of multiple histories, moving along many paths and trajectories. Sometimes these histories merge, intertwining themselves in substantial ways. Sometimes they disentangle themselves and simply stand apart. Much of the time, however, they are simultaneously together and apart. In the place of a singular narrative, the usual one being the rise of the West, this book maps the many forks in the road that confronted the world's societies at different times and the surprising turns and unintended consequences that marked the choices that peoples and societies made, including the unanticipated and dramatic rise of the West in the nineteenth century. Formulated in this way, world history is the unfolding of many possible histories, and readers of this book should come away with a reinforced sense of the unpredictability of the past, the instability of the present, and the uncertainty of the future.

Let us begin our story!

R.T., J.A., S.A., S.K., S.M., G.P., M.T.
November 2001

About the Authors

ROBERT TIGNOR (Ph.D. Yale University) is the Rosengarten Professor of Modern and Contemporary History at Princeton University and currently chair of the history department. With Gyan Prakash, he introduced Princeton's first course in world history fifteen years ago. Professor Tignor has taught graduate and undergraduate courses in African history and world history and written extensively on the history of twentieth-century Egypt, Nigeria, and Kenya. Besides his many research trips to Africa, Professor Tignor has taught at the University of Ibadan in Nigeria and the University of Nairobi in Kenya.

JEREMY ADELMAN (D. Phil. Oxford University) is the Walter S. Carpenter III Professor of Spanish Civilization and Culture at Princeton University. He has written and edited five books, including *Republic of Capital: Buenos Aires and the Legal Transformation of the Atlantic World* (1999), which won the best book prize in Atlantic history from the American Historical Association. Professor Adelman is the recent recipient of a Guggenheim Memorial Foundation Fellowship and the Frederick Burkhardt Award from the American Council of Learned Societies.

STEPHEN ARON (Ph.D. University of California, Berkeley) is associate professor of history at the University of California, Los Angeles. A specialist in frontier and Western American history, Aron is the author of *How the West Was Lost: The Transformation of Kentucky from Daniel Boone to Henry Clay* and is completing a book on the lower Missouri Valley frontier. He has also published articles in a variety of books and journals, including the *American Historical Review*, the *Pacific Historical Review*, and the *Western Historical Quarterly*.

STEPHEN KOTKIN (Ph.D. University of California, Berkeley) teaches European and Asian history at Princeton University, where he also serves as director of Russian Studies. He is the author of *Armageddon Averted: The Soviet Collapse, 1970–2000* (2001) and *Magnetic Mountain: Stalinism as a Civilization* (1995) and is a coeditor of *Mongolia in the Twentieth Century: Landlocked Cosmopolitan* (1999). Professor Kotkin has also served twice as a visiting professor in Japan.

SUZANNE MARCHAND (Ph.D. University of Chicago) is associate professor of European and intellectual history at Louisiana State University, Baton Rouge. Professor Marchand also spent a number of years teaching at Princeton University. She is the author of *Down from Olympus: Archaeology and Philhellenism in Germany, 1750–1970* (1996) and is currently writing a book on German "orientalism."

GYAN PRAKASH (Ph.D. University of Pennsylvania) is professor of modern Indian history at Princeton University and a member of the Subaltern Studies Editorial Collective. He is the author of *Bonded Histories: Genealogies of Labor Servitude in Colonial India* (1990) and *Another Reason: Science and the Imagination of Modern India* (1999). Professor Prakash edited *After Colonialism: Imperial Histories and Postcolonial Displacements* (1995) and has written a number of articles on colonialism and history writing. With Robert Tignor, he introduced the modern world history course at Princeton University.

MICHAEL TSIN (Ph.D. Princeton University) is the director of Asian Studies and associate professor of history at the University of Florida. He previously taught at the University of Illinois at Chicago, Princeton University, and Columbia University. A specialist on modern China, Professor Tsin is also interested in the methodology of writing history from a non-Eurocentric perspective. He is the author of *Nation, Governance, and Modernity in China: Canton, 1900–1927* (1999) and is currently working on a cultural history of transformative practice in twentieth-century China.

Worlds Together, WORLDS APART

1

THE WORLDS OF 1300

In 1271, Marco Polo (1254–1324), the son of an enterprising Venetian merchant, set out with his father and uncle on a journey to East Asia. Making their way along the fabled silk route across Central Asia, the Polos arrived in Xanadu, the summer capital of the Mongol empire, after a three-and-a-half year journey. There they remained for more than two decades. When they returned to their home in Venice in 1295, fellow townsmen greeted them with astonishment, so sure were they that the Polos had perished years before. So, too, Marco Polo's published account of his travels generated an incredulous reaction. Some of his European readers considered his tales of Eastern wonders to be mere fantasy, yet others found their appetites for Asian splendor whetted by Polo's descriptions.

A half-century after Polo commenced his travels, the Moroccan-born scholar Muhammad ibn Abdullah ibn Battuta (1304–1369) embarked on a journey of his own. Then just twenty-one, Ibn Battuta vowed to visit the whole of the Islamic world without traveling the same road twice. It was an ambitious assignment, for Islam's domain extended from one end of the Eurasian land mass to the other and far into Africa as well. On his journey, Ibn Battuta eventually covered some 75,000 miles and traveled through West and East Africa, across the interior of Asia, and beyond the realm of Islam to China (see Map 1-1). Along his way, he claimed to have met at least sixty rulers, and in his book he recorded the names of more than 2,000 persons whom he knew personally.

Marco Polo and Ibn Battuta, as the best-known travelers in the late thirteenth and early fourteenth centuries, provide a wealth of information on the well-traversed lands of Africa, Europe, and Asia. What they and other travelers observed was the extreme diversity that characterized the peoples living in Eurasia, where numerous ethnicities, many political formations, and varied religious faiths and practices prevailed. In addition, they observed that the vast majority of people lived deeply localized lives, the primary goal of which was to obtain the basic necessities of everyday living. Yet, they were also aware that these very same societies, however local their orientations, welcomed and even encouraged contact, trade, and cultural exchange over long distances and between regions. In fact, they wrote most eloquently about the way in which the four major cultural systems of the Eurasian land mass—Christian, Muslim, Indian, and Chinese—each struggled to articulate definitions of themselves. Interestingly, if Ibn Battuta and Marco Polo had been able to travel in the "unknown" worlds, the African hinterlands, the Americas, and Oceania, they would have witnessed to varying degrees similar phenomena and challenges. In this chapter, we present a snapshot of the world in 1300—a period in which the world remained highly diverse and localized but was slowly becoming more unified within societies and more interconnected across regions.

CONTACT AND ISOLATION

> → *To what degree were the worlds of 1300 integrated?*

The balance between close contact and isolation among the world's peoples in 1300 was weighted decisively toward isolation. Yet, contacts were on the increase. As the world's population rose to unprecedented levels, peoples pushed out in all directions in search of new lands to cultivate and new products to trade and consume. These expansionist tendencies led political leaders, long-distance merchants, and clerics to challenge local orientations and to plan for tighter integration of these diverse societies with each other.

FRAGMENTED WORLDS

Ruling elites sought to expand their political, economic, and cultural boundaries but had to contend with populations rooted in their local activities. Indeed, across Eurasia and Africa and through all of the world's inhabited zones, most people consumed locally cultivated foods, resided in dwellings made from local materials, grew crops, herded livestock, spun cotton, and traded commodities with one another as men and women had done for centuries. Most of the world's residents rarely moved beyond or even looked beyond the localities in which they had been born. This was true for agriculturalists, who predominated around the globe, but whose work generally kept them tied to particular pieces of land. It was also the case for nomadic groups, whose migrations took them on wider circuits, but who lived as well in locales that were largely sealed off from outside influences.

The vast majority of the globe's 400 to 500 million inhabitants lived in a world of limited horizons and endured short, hard existences. In the time of Marco Polo and Ibn Battuta, life expectancies averaged only about thirty years, in part because so many died during childbirth or in the first five years of life. Most homes were sparsely furnished and were often too hot or too cold, too wet or too dark. Diets, when sufficient, were monotonous, and in times of occasional famine, they were not even that.

Not everyone struggled equally or lived so locally, however. In some places favored by nature and human ingenuity, vital resources were more abundant. Nonetheless, in almost all places, those resources were distributed unequally. Some ate tastier food, wore more opulent garments, and lodged in less spartan surroundings. Those better off consisted mostly of landowning

Focus Questions THE WORLDS OF 1300

→ *To what degree were the worlds of 1300 integrated?*

→ *What factors contributed to the cultural unity of the "worlds apart"?*

→ *What were the defining characteristics of each major Eurasian world?*

→ *How did the Middle Kingdom influence neighboring societies?*

→ *How did the Mongol empire further integrate Eurasia?*

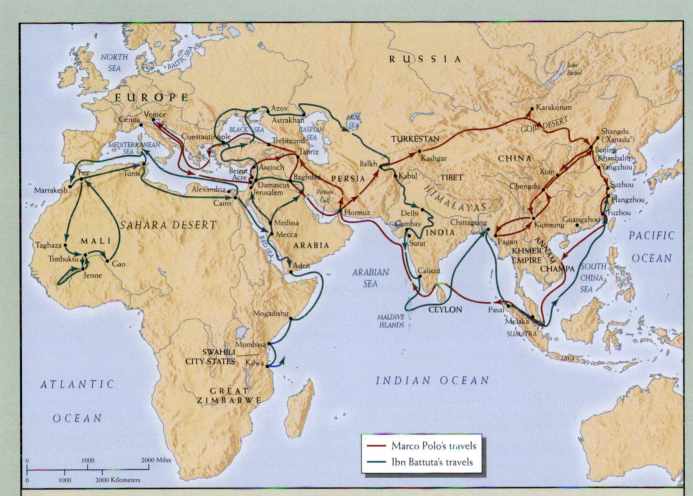

MAP 1-1   JOURNEYS OF MARCO POLO AND IBN BATTUTA

What do the long-distance travels of Marco Polo and Ibn Battuta in the thirteenth and fourteenth centuries respectively tell us about movement across the Eurasian continent at this time? Why was so much more of Marco Polo's route over land and most of Ibn Battuta's travel by sea? Why did Marco Polo not touch the African continent while Ibn Battuta crossed the Sahara?

nobility, nomadic chieftains, and entrepreneurial merchants. Combined, they took a large proportion of the goods produced within their society, and they had far greater access to imported goods and ideas.

The four large-scale and geographically separate cultural regions of Eurasia (the Islamic world, India, China, and Christendom) had overarching and enduring institutions and cultural values. Yet, even within each of these regions, great diversity and local orientations prevailed. In the four great cultural regions of Eurasia, no single language

> *Everywhere travelers went, they saw peoples separated by ethnicity and fighting for competing ruling houses and religions.*

or set of ruling and religious practices held sway. Everywhere travelers went, they saw peoples separated by ethnicity and fighting for competing ruling houses and religions. Across these great territorial expanses, political formations and ruling practices ran the gamut from empires, to kingdoms, to states, to tribal governments. Some societies were more militaristic than others, perennially plagued by incessant internal warfare or under a constant need to conquer new lands. Indeed, the same element of extreme localism and diversity existed in worlds either completely unknown or largely separated

Global Connections & Disconnections

TRADE AND CULTURAL DIVERSITY ON THE MALABAR COAST

Malabar is a narrow strip of about 360 square miles of land squeezed between the Arabian Sea on the west coast of the Indian subcontinent and the mountain chain called the Western Ghats. The Ghats serve as a barrier broken by passes leading to the southwestern and southeastern parts of the subcontinent. This geography forced the Malabar coast to always look outward to the sea. As a result, its population acquired an extraordinary diversity over the centuries. The name "Malabar" itself was given by the Arab sailors who began docking on the coast as traders in the seventh century.

By the 1300s, Malabar society was a melting pot of cultures. The Hindus formed the majority, but they, too, were internally differentiated. While the privileged groups consisted of Nambudiri Brahmans and a warrior group called the Nayars, the vast majority were the Ezhavas. Followed by the Hindus were the Christians, whose presence in Malabar, according to legend, dates back to the first century, when St. Thomas is said to have landed on the coast and preached the gospel. Whatever the truth of these legends, records establish the Christian presence by the end of the second century. During the next few centuries, Christians from Persia and Mesopotamia sought refuge here, giving rise to the group called Syrian Christians. A small number of Jews from Yemen and Babylon established an enclave in Malabar before the Christian era, and in the first century they were joined by other Jews who were fleeing from the destruction of Jerusalem by the Romans. The evidence for the first Muslim settlement on the coast dates to the ninth century, after which their presence all along the coast grew with the rising importance of Malabar in the Indian Ocean trade. The Muslims consisted of two groups: the *Pardeshis* (foreigners), and the *Mappillas* (those from the local population who had become Muslims through marriage and conversion).

Calicut was the most important port city on the Malabar coast. Its rise was due to the eleventh-century ascendance of the Zamorin, the "Ocean King," who, with Arab help, emerged as the dominant ruler over the territory and encouraged overseas trade and traders. Located at the source of pepper production, Calicut served as the hub of the spice trade. Ships set sail each year from Aden, Jiddah, and Hormuz toward the Indian subcontinent. Many came to Calicut, where they bought pepper and exchanged Western goods for the spices carried by traders who came to the port from the South China Sea and Melaka. Shops and warehouses dominated the coastline, and the port city attracted merchants from Arabia, Persia, Egypt, Southeast Asia, and China. Some lived there temporarily, while others settled permanently. The visitors to Calicut spoke glowingly of the integrity of traders, the organization of trade, and the security provided by the Zamorin.

When Ibn Battuta visited Malabar in 1342, he was impressed with the prosperity and prestige of Muslim merchants, particularly that of the *Pardeshis*. Although these merchants enjoyed the support of the Malabar rulers, they refrained from using their political influence to proselytize. Over time, many Arab merchants made Malabar their home, mixed with the local population, lost contact with the Arabic language, dress, and names, and adopted local social customs. Conversion to Islam occurred largely among the Hindus of lower ranks—those who worked as mariners and fishermen and who provided services on ships. Through these gradual processes, Islam was Indianized. The Christians, too, shared the local cultural milieu, incorporating the social distinctions and practices of Malabar. The Hindus, who were dominant in the agrarian economy, received patronage from the Zamorin who, mindful of the economic value of trade, also protected the Muslims. In the diverse world that maritime trade had built in Malabar, religious and cultural differences flourished without discord.

from the Eurasian land mass—the African heartland, the Americas, and Oceania. Around the globe, rulers and elites faced the challenge of forging the bonds that would create a common identity among diverse peoples.

CONTACT AND TRADE ROUTES

The exploits of Marco Polo and Ibn Battuta suggest that a few men and women, mainly long-distance merchants and scholars, routinely traversed immense distances. These merchants and scholars used and strengthened existing trade routes between regions and fostered contacts across cultural boundaries. Their journeys revealed a Eurasian world linked from the Mediterranean in the west to China in the east. Along the trade routes, merchants, travelers, commodities, and ideas circulated freely through great port cities such as Surat and Calicut along the Malabar coast in India, and Zanzibar and Kilwa in East Africa, and Genoa, Venice, and Alexandria along the northern and southern shores of the Mediterranean Sea.

These merchants and scholars used and strengthened trade routes between regions and fostered contacts across cultural boundaries.

Certain population groups were especially important in linking the major cultures. Many of these peoples lived in between the larger worlds in areas known as borderlands. Peoples of the borderlands did not live in isolation from the larger cultures. Quite the opposite, they were frequently visited by missionaries, settlers, and warriors from afar. In many respects, trade across the borderlands helped keep the borders of the major cultures open and blurred the sharp differences between cultural zones. These borderlands were characterized by the absence of centralized control and by the extreme ethnic and linguistic diversity of their peoples. For instance, Turkish nomads organized and led caravans across Central Asia, linking China and the Mediterranean basin. Here again, great inland cities like Baghdad in present-day Iraq and Damascus in Syria featured expansive markets and fairs, where wealthier people could come and purchase silk from China, textiles from India, spices from Southeast Asia, slaves and ivory from Africa, and fruits from Greece. Moreover, borderlands could also include island peoples. For example, Indonesians welcomed to their cities traders from around the world who were in search of spices and other exotic goods from across Eurasia.

Population pressures could lead to more interactions among peoples. Facing limited or dwindling resources, warriors burst out of their home bases to conquer and occupy new areas of the world. Chief among these during the thirteenth century were the Mongols, who emerged from the Asian north, sweeping south and west to conquer much of Eurasia. Notwithstanding their terrible destructiveness, the Mongols ended up deepening the connections among the peoples of Eurasia.

New and improved forms of transportation aided in increasing interactions. The domestication of the camel was vital for expanding commercial connections throughout the arid portions of the Middle East and bringing North Africa into contact with West Africa across the Sahara Desert. Shipping was the other key form of transportation. With varying degrees of success, oceanic trading was becoming more prominent during this period. The Chinese successfully navigated the oceanic waters of East Asia on board junks, which were ships capable of holding a fair amount of trade cargo. Likewise, Islamic traders successfully controlled the shorelines of the Indian coast through the use of land-based fortresses and ever-improving navigational devices for their ships.

Some governments and rulers were more encouraging than others in terms of trade and cross-cultural exchange. The Han dynasty in China encouraged trade with its neighbors to the west so that its people would have access to horses, alfalfa, grapes, sesame, coriander, and walnuts. Likewise, first the Greeks, then the Romans, and later the Venetians and the Genoese traders looked eastward in search of silk, pottery, paper, peaches, apricots, and spices. Elsewhere, the historical records now reveal that the nomadic peoples of the Asian steppe, the native communities in the Americas, and the island communities of Oceania were developing their own substantial trading networks and promoting cultural exchange. By 1300, the world's societies were becoming more familiar with one another.

WORLDS APART

→ *What factors contributed to the cultural unity of the "worlds apart"?*

At the end of the Ice Age, the Bering Sea submerged the land bridge that had connected North Asia and North America, thereby isolating the Americas from the Eurasian land mass. Accordingly, for more than 10,000 years, the Western Hemisphere stood on its own. So did the continent of Australia and the islands of the Pacific.

In the thirteenth century, the peoples of the Americas and Oceania knew themselves and their homelands by thousands of different names. They spoke approximately 2,000 distinct languages, and even neighboring groups had difficulty understanding one another's words. Yet, for all their local differences, each community called itself by a word meaning "the people" and believed that the place where it lived was the center of the world.

THE AMERICAS

Warfare and trade broke down the apartness of peoples by bringing neighboring groups together. In combat between North American peoples, men battled fiercely, but bloodshed was usually limited. Warriors rarely attempted frontal assaults against fortified positions. Costs were too high, especially since early American societies valued symbolic demonstrations of bravery above the conquest of territories or the obliteration of enemies. Men fought less to inflict casualties than to take captives. These prisoners were brought back to home villages, where women often decided whether captives should be executed to console mourners who had lost loved ones in battle or adopted in the place of those loved ones. Trade, too, could unite separate peoples, particularly since many groups conceived of the exchange of goods as a transfer of friendship-making gifts.

EMERGING EMPIRES   Trade could also take the form of tribute to powerful rulers. By the thirteenth century, various parts of the Americas saw the emergence and expansion of empires. One of the largest and wealthiest of these emerging empires, that of the Incas, arose in the valleys of the Andes. In Andean valleys, as in other parts of the world, agricultural surpluses provided the foundation for a large-scale political organization. To the north, in the valley of Mexico, an even more impressive imperial power was rising. Here, the stimulus to expansion came from Nahua-speaking invaders from farther north—first the Toltecs, then the Chichimec, and finally the Mexicas, the name by which the Aztecs referred to themselves. As the Mexicas settled in the valley of Mexico, they gave up their dependence on hunting and began to cultivate crops. To enhance agricultural production, the Mexicas constructed an impressive irrigation system during the early fourteenth century. Although harvests were sufficient to feed a large and growing population, the Mexicas also had to get many products and staples from neighbors. The valley of Mexico lacked some important goods, like cotton, necessary for clothing, and firewood, necessary for fuel. Needing to meet crucial demand, the Mexicas began to exert their power over neighboring peoples and towns, exacting tribute and engaging in trade with more distant regions. Large numbers of merchants (called *pochteca*) marched out of the Mexica cities bearing sacks of goods for exchange with neighbors. Mainly men, but also women, created a vast trading network that spread to the arid lands of the north (now the southwestern United States) and as far south as the isthmus (now Panama). Trade and tribute contributed to a vibrant and colorful market life in the valley of Mexico, where goods were bartered and swapped among commoners and local potentates alike.

TRADE AND SOCIETY   In the course of the fourteenth century, through trade and tribute-taking, the Mexicas became a richer and more urbanized society. Founded in 1325, Tenochtitlán started as a hamlet of mud huts built on an island, but it evolved into a major metropolis. Its markets attracted throngs of visitors from near and far, all milling about in their regional dress and speaking in dialects and tongues from around Mesoamerica.

> *The extent of market networks and cross-cultural interaction in Mesoamerica was limited compared to Eurasia.*

The extent of market networks and cross-cultural interaction was, however, limited compared to Eurasia. Mesoamericans had no domesticated beasts of burden. Nor did they possess wheeled transportation. Accordingly, the load of cargoes and the distances they could be hauled were restricted by what Mexica merchants could carry on their backs. Because they could haul only so many goods, the *pochteca* never emerged as powerful and wealthy members of the local society, though they lived one social notch above agrarian and artisanal commoners.

Trade goods, especially as displayed in dress and diet, helped to mark out local and regional social hierarchies. By drawing in the enormous wealth of Mesoamerica, the Mexicas gained access to precious metals, stones, shells, feathers, all manner of exotic commodities that became signs of their wealth to their neighbors. Mexica rulers made a habit of inviting neighboring nobles to their festivities. At these events, the rulers draped themselves in ornaments from all the corners of Mesoamerica. The jewelry and finery also served as adornments to mark internal social hierarchies, with a special code regulating who could wear what. Only nobles, for example, were permitted to wear gold earrings, jade, and turquoise, fancy plugs inserted into their pierced lips, and fine robes. Commoners wore coarse clothes of burlap-like fibers and rabbit furs, and could only wear obsidian earplugs as jewelry. Although there were women merchants, farmers, and healers, the fundamental place of women was in the family as wives and mothers. Mothers ran the household, instructing their daughters in the domestic skills of grinding maize, preparing meals, spinning, and the fine art of weaving. At the very bottom of the social ladder were slaves, fallen to this status either through impoverishment or by being captured in war. Working as domestics and cultivators, the slaves could also have families and even own other slaves.

MEXICA BELIEFS What kept this hierarchically organized society together was a shared view of the world. Like other peoples of this era, the Mexicas balanced observations of natural cycles with a faith in supernatural forces. They believed that the universe was prone to unceasing cycles of disasters that would eventually end in an apocalypse. Such an unstable cosmos exposed mortals to repeated creations and destructions. The cyclical and apocalyptic view of the cosmos shaped the daily understanding of time and Mexica religion. A powerful priesthood monitored the relationship between the people and their deities, and balanced fatalism with a faith that the gods could be honored through rituals.

The Aztec empire was a theocracy, a political regime in which the gods' emissaries enjoyed great powers and authority. In overseeing the activities of Mexica subjects, the priesthood punished wayward Mexicas and selected victims for public sacrifice to the gods. Captives faced execution because the Mexicas believed that the great god of the sun required human hearts to keep on burning and blood to replace that given by the gods to moisten the earth through rain. To fulfill this obligation, Mexica priests escorted captured warriors up the temple steps and tore out their hearts, offering their lives and blood as a sacrifice to the sun god. Allegedly, between 20,000 and 80,000 men, women, and children were slaughtered in a single ceremony in 1487, with the four-person-wide line of those who would be killed stretching for over two miles. In this marathon of bloodshedding, knife-wielding priests collapsed from exhaustion and had to be replaced by fresh executioners.

Faith governed every aspect of ordinary life. The Mexicas filled daily life with constant small gestures of obedience and sacrifice. Food was a constant preoccupation, and women were especially entrusted with treating it with proper respect. *Chinampas* (floating gardens) were used to grow crops, and the state developed an irrigation system of canals and aqueducts to enable cultivators to produce even more. Maize, above all, was an essential crop, and was given special treatment. Before cooking the kernels, women handled them with care, breathing and whispering gently into their open palms, before dropping the maize into cooking pots. These daily reminders of Mexica indebtedness to the gods were intended to ensure that the gods kept them well supplied with food.

At schools boys and girls did not learn to read and write or train for vocations. Instead, they were taught the songs, poetry, and rituals of a militaristic culture. Men of noble birth received intensive training in military skills and were showered with wealth, land, and honors for success in battle. Hope for a good afterlife depended less on how people lived than on how they died—and dying in war was the most noble activity of all.

The need for ever more blood and human offerings, coupled with the Mexicas' demand for staples and precious commodities from other peoples, compelled leaders to match commerce with conquest. For this, the Mexicas would have to create a more formal political organization. In so doing, the Mexicas founded an Aztec empire, whose fall, as we shall see in Chapter 3, reverberated around the globe.

SUB-SAHARAN AFRICA

Traveling to Africa south of the Sahara was well within the reach of the great world travelers of the thirteenth and fourteenth centuries. Ibn Battuta was known to have made several trips to Islamic Africa, for example. From earliest times, traders crossed the Sahara Desert and sailed from the east coast of Africa to Asian ports. Christian and especially Islamic influences filtered through the continent. And as in the Americas, a diverse collection of peoples, languages, belief systems, and governing institutions had developed in sub-Saharan Africa by 1300. Indeed, the term "Africa" was unknown to sub-Saharan peoples. It came from outside, originating among the Ancient Romans, who used it at first to refer to the Carthaginian empire in North Africa. Later the Romans expanded its meaning

"The Aztec World." In the centuries leading up to 1500, the most powerful empire of the Americas emerged in the Central Valley of Mexico. It relied on extensive agriculture, trade, and tribute—and engaged in constant warfare with neighboring states. This image, taken from a mural by the Mexican painter Diego Rivera, celebrates the accomplishments and portrays the violence of the Aztec empire. Rivera and other Mexican writers and artists invoked a great pre-European past as a foundation for Mexican nationalism.

to encompass all the lands south of the Mediterranean Sea. But this unifying term meant nothing to Africans, who were divided into numerous small worlds (see Map 1-2).

Although Africa south of the Sahara had been the cradle of human life, its environment and climate impeded human settlements as dense as those in North Africa or in Eurasian societies. Moreover, the Sahara Desert limited the contacts between its inhabitants and those living to the north. Most of the continent suffered from poor soils, an erratic climate, and a profuse insect and disease environment. One of these insects, the tsetse fly, carried the disease known as "sleeping sickness," which also killed animals, and thus kept domesticated animals out of the rain forests of Africa. Another insect, the anopheles mosquito, spread malaria among humans. Large cities, in contrast to sprawling village settlements, were unusual, with a handful of spectacular exceptions—Timbuktu in the West African Sahel region or the settlements of the Yoruba (in present-day Nigeria).

FOREST DWELLERS Geography and climate thus played decisive roles in the lives of Africans. Those who lived in the tropical rain forests raised different crops, had different political institutions, and worshipped different gods from those who lived in the high grasslands, often called the savannah. The tropical rain forests of western and central Africa, for example, featured small, relatively autonomous agricultural communities. For those accustomed to the climate, the rain forests offered inhabitants many advantages. They provided a huge variety of flora, especially trees, exuberant vegetation, and mighty rivers as sources of food and easy means of communication. As long as the inhabitants took care of their forests and did not alter the environment by stripping it of its trees, rain forests ensured a reasonable and varied standard of life.

For forest dwellers, the extended household—based on the family that included adopted members, protected clients, and slaves—was the basic institution. Households came together, usually in a voluntary way, to establish village settlements, and these village settlements, in turn, were linked together, through their household heads in district bodies. Since the household was the core building unit, its head was supposed to be an individual of demonstrated wisdom, leadership, and boundless energy. This individual, often called the "big man," was also expected to attract as many followers as possible. He did so by providing protection to clients, marrying numerous women, and siring many offspring, thereby adding to the size, wealth, and political power of his group. But these activities put big men in competition with one another. Rivalries were often intense and revolved around who could attract the largest crowd of followers and who could have the greatest number of children, slaves, and protected clients. The successful household—judged primarily by size—could acquire rights over larger and larger segments of land and accumulate supplies of grain and other forms of wealth.

Gender made for important differences among forest-dwelling people. In agricultural work, men cleared the soil and prepared it for planting. Because these farming communities practiced a form of shifting cultivation that required a large portion of land to be left fallow—sometimes ten times as much as was sown—clearing exerted heavy demands on the adult male population. Women, together with children of both sexes, weeded the fields. All came together for the harvesting. In addition, the division of labor sometimes varied according to crops. In the tropical rain forests of West Africa, for example, yams, which were the essential element in the diet and regarded as the most prestigious crop, belonged to men; the lesser crops were the produce of women. So, too, in trading, men dominated long-distance exchange, which was more lucrative than short-distance trading, which was the domain of women.

Men subordinated women by taking many wives, managing the cultivation of the most prestigious crops, and controlling the most lucrative trading. Nonetheless, women were able to create their own political organizations. Although these were subordinate to those of men, women's organizations were able to rally opposition to men, challenging those who exploited women in ways that exceeded the norms of the community. Moreover, "big women" did appear from time to time, and in some African societies, "queen mothers" and wives of influential men exercised considerable authority.

Like most people around the globe in the thirteenth century, Africans believed that supernatural forces and other-than-human spirits wielded enormous control over human affairs. Beliefs in witches, witchcraft, and sorcery were widespread. Africans assumed as well that behind the natural world was an active and interventionist assortment of good and bad gods, and that above these deities was likely to be a high god, perhaps the creator of the universe, perhaps even the ancestor of the mythical founder of the whole community. Ancestors were an important part of this spirit world, too. To please the ancestral spirits, who were thought capable of wreaking havoc if angered, descendants made regular ritual offerings at family shrines.

PEOPLES OF EAST, WEST, AND SOUTH AFRICA Beyond the rain forests, in the highlands of Ethiopia, the savannah lands of West Africa, the coastal areas of East Africa, and the high grasslands of southern Africa, dynastic empires emerged, ruling over large populations and extensive territories. Long-distance trade brought these polities into contact with Eurasia. African traders supplied markets in North Africa and Asia with gold, ivory, copper, and slaves. For the West African kingdoms, this commerce involved increasingly trafficked caravan routes to and from North Africa.

Along these trading routes came religious emissaries as well, whose presence contributed to the cultural unity upon which empire-building rested. In the highlands of Ethiopia, Christianity played the decisive role. Having originated in the Middle East, Christianity spread to Egypt—which by the year 400 was probably 90 percent Christian—and from Egypt southward to Ethiopia and the Sudan. The spread of Christianity and

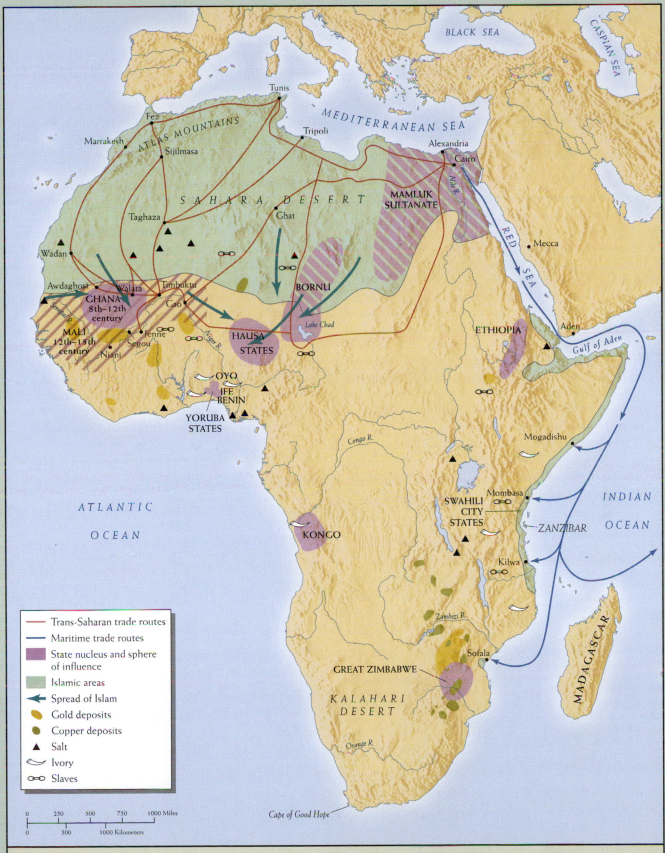

MAP 1-2   MAJOR STATES AND TRADING ROUTES IN AFRICA, 1300S

Does this map help in discovering the factors that led to the spread of Islam from the Middle East and North Africa to sub-Saharan Africa? Who would have been the likely agents for carrying out conversions in sub-Saharan Africa? What were the major commodities that tied sub-Saharan Africa to the outside world? Why did the major kingdoms of West Africa arise where they did?

its importance in Africa paled, however, next to the inroads made by Islam. In their universalist aspirations, Muslims endeavored to turn what in Arabic was called *bilad al-Sudan* (the land of the blacks) into an Islamic province. Already in the eighth century, Muslim settlements appeared along the East African coast. By the thirteenth century, a distinct Muslim culture in Africa combined the unifying force of Islam, the benefits of Indian Ocean trade, and a Bantu language (while adapting numerous Arab words). It linked the entire coast of East Africa, from Somalia in the north to the Zambezi River in the south, to the larger commercial system of the Indian Ocean. Major Swahili settlements grew up along the East African coast, such as Mogadishu, Kilwa, Pemba, and the island of Zanzibar, where African and Arab merchants congregated to trade ivory and slaves for textiles and other items.

In numerous places, Muslim traders penetrated where Islam did not. For example, the Islamic religion did not spread below the Zambezi River, but that region was nonetheless integrated into the Indian Ocean commercial network. It was in the Zambezi Valley in the years immediately after 1300 that the Kingdom of Great Zimbabwe arose. Its prosperity rested on the mining and export of gold, which the Shona-speaking inhabitants of the area exchanged for such luxury goods as silks from far-off China and highly glazed Persian earthenwares.

Both Muslim traders and Islamic missionaries spread as well into the high grass, savannah lands of West Africa. Here the kingdom of Ghana flourished from the eighth to the eleventh centuries (in present-day Mauritania). Ghana derived its wealth by acting as a go-between for trade in gold, salt, and slaves from sub-Saharan West Africa to the Arab world on the other side of the desert. After Ghana crumbled, no West African state equaled its geographical expanse, military strength, and prosperity until the thirteenth century, when the empire of Mali was consolidated. The pioneer of the Malian state was a warrior-king, Sundiata (ruled 1240–1255), who in the middle of the thirteenth century succeeded in uniting the many village groups of the Malinke peoples.

With Islam providing a common faith and language (Arabic) for its bureaucrats and merchants, the Mali empire continued to expand after Sundiata's death. By the fourteenth century, the territorial claims of his successors reached from the valley of Senegal in the west to the Middle Niger River basin in the east, more than 1,000 miles away; from north to south, Mali connected the edge of the Sahara Desert to the tropical rain forests. Its population numbered in the millions. Mali controlled the headwaters of the Niger River and a vast trading area in West Africa, which enabled its merchants to sell gold, slaves, textiles, and other goods to the peoples of North Africa. One of its rulers,

Muslims in West Africa. The great mosque of Jenne in West Africa, which demonstrates the intensity of the Islamic faith in parts of Africa far removed from the traditional Islamic centers.

Mansa Musa. The ruler of Mali was Mansa Musa, portrayed by a cartographer from the island of Majorca in 1375 and shown holding a large piece of gold. The image reveals just how widespread was the reputation of wealth that the kingdom of Mali enjoyed in the fourteenth century.

Mansa Musa (ruled 1312–1337), made clear his commitment to Islam through an elaborate pilgrimage to the holy cities of the Arabian peninsula. His stopover in Cairo on his way to Mecca actually destabilized Cairo's economy, as he spent so much gold there that it decreased in value.

Like the Americas, sub-Saharan Africa in the thirteenth century possessed a few large empires along with hundreds of polities of much smaller scale. The daily existence of most sub-Saharan Africans was affected only a little more than that of the peoples of the Americas by developments on other continents, and most Africans knew little of the outside world. Still, the penetration of Christianity and especially Islam underscored the growing connections between Africa and Eurasia.

THE FOUR MAJOR CULTURAL AREAS OF EURASIA

> → *What were the defining characteristics of each major Eurasian world?*

Describing the four major cultural zones of the Eurasian land mass is a daunting assignment. One could easily draw up a checklist of critical aspects for each culture. What were the major beliefs and value systems of each? How did each organize its polities and economies? What were the relations between men and women? But such a checklist would force each culture into predetermined and externally chosen designations. More

useful is to identify those characteristics that each of the cultures used to represent itself to its inhabitants and to the outside world. What was it that produced a sense of being Muslim to dwellers within the Islamic world? What made Christendom different from other parts of the world? Why did the people living in China regard themselves as subjects of "the Middle Kingdom"? Finally, how did the mix of peoples and traditions in India produce a conspicuous cultural mosaic?

This is a crucial undertaking. It not only enables us to understand the broader cultural patterns of the peoples of Eurasia, but it is essential to understanding the unfolding of the history of the modern world. It was, after all, these shared beliefs and institutions that the peoples of these cultural areas worked and reworked as new, more global connections impinged on their lives. As travelers like Marco Polo and Ibn Battuta recorded, the four great cultures on the Eurasian land mass met new challenges by applying quite distinctive value systems and different kinds of institutions. Islam and Christendom, for example, organized themselves for the spread of universal religious missions. By contrast, the Chinese valued a balanced and stable polity, while the dwellers on the Indian subcontinent, perhaps making a virtue of necessity, honored the great diversity of its people.

THE HOUSE OF ISLAM

The territory of the Islamic world stretched all the way from the southern part of Spain in the west to India and the borders of China in the east. It encompassed a land mass that at its widest points was more than 5,000 miles (nearly twice the length of the United States) from east to west and 3,000 miles from north to south. Within this vast expanse was immense geographic, ethnic, linguistic, and even religious diversity, but at the same time a sense of common Islamic identity, of being part of *dar al-Islam* (the House of Islam) and the *umma* (the community of the faithful). Part of that shared identity rested on the belief that these boundaries needed to be extended even further.

Islam's early warrior leaders had gone from triumph to triumph. Beginning in the seventh century, their forces had swept out of the Arabian peninsula, and through military conquests, they had seized territories that had once belonged to the Byzantine and Sasanian empires that spanned North Africa and western Asia. Thus, unlike Christianity, which shared a similar missionary zeal to convert the whole world to its faith, Islam had no formative experience as a minority religion. Islam's converts did not struggle, as early Christians had, to achieve recognition against political oppressors.

> *Islam became more diverse through the processes of conquest and conversion.*

By the thirteenth century, however, the memory of a unified Islamic state had faded. In the preceding centuries, while Islam had expanded, it had also become more diverse through the processes of conquest and conversion. Arabs dominated the first Islamic century, but over time they had to share power with other groups that had embraced Islam and now wanted to rule over Islamic territories. Fierce political rivalries, then, were the natural outgrowth of incorporating new territories, states, and peoples into the faith. These newer, distinct polities competed with each other in the quest to become the true successor state to a once-unified Islamic empire.

The core area of Islam, from North Africa to the Oxus River in Central Asia, contained the dominant ethnic and language groups of the Islamic world—Arabs, Persians, and Turks—as well as the main religious centers—Mecca, Medina, Jerusalem, Baghdad, and Cairo (see Map 1-3). Beyond this core were the outlying Islamic zones of sub-Saharan Africa, parts of the Indian subcontinent, and gradually over time, the islands of Indonesia. These areas had their own religious centers and shrines, but they looked to the Arabian peninsula, Palestine, Syria, and Egypt as containing holy places more venerable than their own. And while much of the Islamic world had come under the authority of Muslim rulers through conquest, these outlying areas owed their conversion to Islam more to the energies of Muslim clerics and merchants than to the might of warriors.

THE MUSLIM FAITH In spite of the significant regional variations of the Islamic world, Islam, as an all-encompassing religion and way of life, stamped its unifying imprint on all of the lands and peoples of *dar al-Islam*. This solidarity stemmed first and foremost from the teachings of the faith's charismatic founder, Muhammad, who was born and died in Mecca (c. 570–632), the Arabian peninsula's leading commercial center at the time. Muhammad claimed to be the Prophet whom God (Allah) had chosen for his final and most definitive revelation to mankind. Allah's revelations, as recorded in Islam's holy book,

the *Quran* (often spelled *Koran*), were thought to be a full and sufficient guide to mankind, superior to the Jewish Torah and the Christian Bible, which Muhammad recognized to be divinely inspired works but not the final revelation. When the *Quran* proved to be silent on questions of pressing importance to believers, Muslims turned for guidance to the sayings (*hadith*) of the Prophet and his early converts. This body of knowledge, supplemented by the writings, opinions, and commentaries of Islamic jurists, constituted the law of Islam, known as the *sharia*, which regulated the spiritual and secular activities of Muslims throughout the Islamic world. The *sharia*, the *Quran*, and the *hadith* were the core elements of Islam as a theology, a judicial system, and a way of life. They guided the behavior of the educated and the powerful—its *ulama* (scholarly class), rulers, and merchants. But what made common people feel that they were Muslims were the mosque, the five pillars of Islamic faith and behavior, and the Sufi brotherhoods.

No structure better reflected the Muslim belief in an all-powerful, single God than the mosque. From the largest and most elaborate of these places of worship to the most humble, mosques communicated a message of religious equality, the centrality of the *Quran*, and Muhammad as God's emissary. Their features were the same throughout the Islamic world. Their austerity befitted a religion that had no official or formal priesthood, recognized no intermediaries between Allah and the believer, and permitted any individual to lead the faithful in prayer and speech. Contributing to this uniformity were the similar layouts of mosques. All featured the minaret, or tower, from which went out the call to prayer, and the *minbar*, the pulpit from which speakers broadcast religious messages. All also had a wall point-

Muslim Worship. The kaaba is a holy rock in the center of the square at Mecca around which worshippers congregate at the time of their pilgrimage to the city.

→ *What were the defining characteristics of each major Eurasian world?*

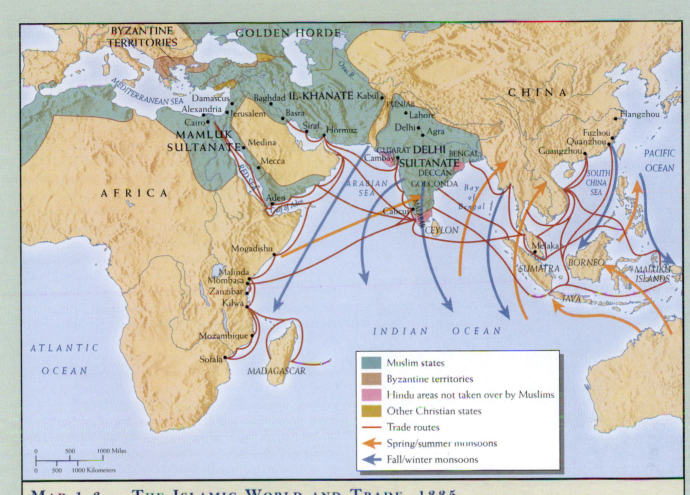

MAP 1-3   THE ISLAMIC WORLD AND TRADE, 1335
In the fourteenth century, Muslim traders dominated the commerce of the Indian Ocean. What Muslim states were they most likely to come from? Noting the trade winds of this area, plan a voyage that would take a merchant from East Africa to India and then on to China. During which months would he leave East Africa, and when would he be most likely to embark upon his return voyage? What Indian Ocean cities would have the most diverse merchant populations?

ing toward Mecca to which worshippers turned when praying. Muslim traders were able to find mosques, as well as co-religionists, throughout Eurasia and Africa.

All Muslims also accepted the faith's five pillars: (1) the belief in the affirmation that there is no God but Allah, (2) the duty to pray five times a day in certain prescribed ways, (3) the responsibility to offer alms in support of the less fortunate, (4) the obligation to fast during the month of Ramadan, with complete abstinence from food or drink during the daytime, and (5) the injunction to make the pilgrimage to Mecca at least once in one's lifetime provided

The hajj to Mecca brought together Muslims from all over the Islamic world, enabling them to exchange ideas and commodities.

one had the resources and was physically able to make the journey. (Some scholars recognized a sixth pillar, an obligation to engage in *jihad*—struggle, if need be, holy war—to advance the cause of Islam.) The *hajj*, or pilgrimage, to Mecca had far-reaching intellectual and commercial consequences. It brought together Muslims from all over the Islamic world, enabling them to exchange ideas and commodities. These weighty obligations fell on rich and poor alike. As every Muslim carried them out and felt obliged to do so, the sense of commonality intensified among co-religionists.

وكاد ينزع الجمال الشمر وانشد
ما الحج سيرك نأويا وادلاجا ولا العنا أمل الجمال اجمالاجا واخلاجا

الحج أن قصد البيت الحرام على تحرير بك لا تبغي به جابا
وطي كامل الانصاف تنجاز ادع الهوى هاديا وانحون شاجا

Caravan of Pilgrims. Muslims traveled together to visit holy shrines. The most important of these pilgrimages was to the holy city of Mecca, which all believers were obligated to visit at least once in their lifetimes.

SUNNI-SHIITE SCHISM Despite the underlying unity of Islam, in religious matters, as well as politics, conflicts did arise in the world of Islam. The most divisive schism to occur in Islam evolved out of disputes over the political succession to Muhammad. The first caliphs, or rulers, of the Islamic community and successors to Muhammad were chosen by the most powerful Arab clans at the time. Yet, some members of the original Islamic community insisted that only the descendants of Ali (the Prophet's son-in-law and fourth caliph of the Islamic polity) were the rightful rulers of the Islamic world. The proponents of Ali's line began to call themselves Shiites to distinguish themselves from the majority Sunni community. Although

by the tenth century, the Shiites had elaborated certain legal and religious ideas that were different from those of the Sunni Muslims, the main difference between the Sunni and Shiite communities revolved around political leadership. The Sunnis accepted the political authority of their caliphs and sultans, many of whom traced descent from Muhammad, but who were not thought to have special religious inspiration. In contrast, in addition to insisting that the legitimate line of succession passed only through the family of Ali, Shiites asserted that the politico-religious descendants of Ali, called *imams*, had a specially inspired relationship to Allah that other religious figures did not possess. Shiite *imams* were thought to be capable of understanding and explaining the will of God to their followers in ways not given to other Muslims. Although the last of these *imams* had long ago disappeared, he was expected to return as the *mahdi* at the time of reckoning and bring salvation to his followers. In the meantime, the Shiite clergy were given the duty of explaining the righteous ways to the believers. Although there were substantial Shiite communities in Iraq, Iran, and northern India in the 1300s, only the Shiite Fatimid dynasty (rulers of Egypt from 969 to 1171) had yet established a strong and durable state.

Along with the divide between Sunnis and Shiites, conflicts emerged between orthodox and popular creeds within *dar al-Islam*. Ordinary people, as distinct from the educated and wealthy, embraced an emotional and mystical form of Islam, called Sufism. Sufis began to appear as individual mystics, stressing inner spirituality, as early as the eighth century. The most devout of these men and women sought an intimate communion with Allah. Although the established and orthodox Islamic scholars, known as *ulama*, attempted to block the appeal of Sufism, they could not. Sufism's emphasis on a religion of feeling and its skill at establishing brotherhoods of believers in places where people congregated to worship gave this form of Islam mass appeal. In their Sufi lodges, devotees gathered to engage in religious rituals and to carry out religious training that would enable them to achieve a closer relationship with God.

AGRICULTURE AND TRADE The Islamic world was overwhelmingly agricultural. Most Muslims lived in villages and drew their subsistence from working the land. Yet, working the soil earned them little prestige within the Islamic order. The *Quran* has few references to tillers of the soil, and the Islamic lands spawned no class of "gentlemen" farmers like those soon to emerge in Europe. Large landed estates existed, but landowners preferred to live in the cities and to use peasant farmers to do the cultivating. Agricultural implements were of a rudimentary nature, hardly different from those that had been in use for centuries. The main tool remained the simple wooden, wheel-less plough.

While Islam did not venerate cultivators of the soil, it held commerce and merchants in high regard. The prophet himself came from a mercantile family, and the *Quran* and *hadith* are both full of favorable comments on the occupation of merchant.

> ❖ *What were the defining characteristics of each major Eurasian world?*

The geographical expanse and the diverse ecological zones of the Islamic world favored the long-distance traders who could exchange the produce of one locale for the products of another. As in Christian Europe, Muslims were prohibited from taking interest on loans, a practice designated as usury, but merchants found ways around these restrictions. To facilitate long-distance trade, merchants developed elaborate credit arrangements, created business partnerships, and established the equivalent of banking institutions.

Long-distance trade necessitated highly developed means of transportation, at which merchants in the Muslim world proved remarkably adept. Not surprisingly, some of the wealthiest cities of the Islamic world, notably Cairo and Baghdad, lay along rivers that linked them to oceangoing vessels. The Muslim world became expert at such transport through its use of lateen sails (triangular sails attached to masts that could be turned to catch the wind) and planks that were sewn (not nailed) together to build the ships called dhows. For overland transportation across what was basically a hot and relatively arid part of the world, the camel was the essential beast of burden. Able to carry up to 1,200 pounds, to traverse long distances each day, and to go nearly three weeks without water, camels became critical to the trans-Saharan trade. No longer did traders have to rely on wheeled transport, or roads, or on less suitable beasts of burden for land trade. Once the camel had been domesticated, probably sometime in the first or second centuries, Egypt and North Africa were able to engage in a brisk trade with sub-Saharan West Africa. The huge caravans that left from the cities of North Africa and Egypt and were bound for West Africa might have as many as 5,000 camels and would be led by expert guides and defended by armed guards.

As centers of trade and culture, cities tied the Islamic world together. Although cities such as Granada in southern Spain, Fez in Morocco, Cairo in Egypt, Isfahan in Iran, and Delhi in

VIEWS OF THE ISLAMIC WORLD

Both Ibn Battuta and Marco Polo visited parts of the Islamic world and commented on the practice of Islam. As the following excerpt from his visit to the great Islamic kingdom of Mali in West Africa indicates, Ibn Battuta celebrated the spread of Islam into black Africa, but he also observed certain practices that did not fit well with his own understanding of Islam. Marco Polo traveled extensively through the Islamic world in his journey to and from China. His comments on Muslims contained a mixture of the good and the bad, but he certainly had a high regard for their commitment to their faith and their mercantile skills.

IBN BATTUTA ON MUSLIMS IN MALI Amongst their good qualities is the small amount of injustice amongst them, for of all people they are the furthest from it. Their sultan does not forgive anyone in any matter to do with injustice. Among these qualities there is also the prevalence of peace in their country; the traveler is not afraid in it nor is he who lives there in fear of the thief or of the robber by violence. . . . Amongst the bad things which they do—their serving women, slave women and little daughters appear before people naked, exposing their private parts. . . . Also among their bad customs is the way women will go into the presence of the sultan naked, without any covering, and the nakedness of the sultan's daughters—on the night of the twenty-seventh of Ramadan, I saw about a hundred slave girls coming out of his palace with food, with them were two of his daughters; they had full breasts and no clothes on.

MARCO POLO ON MUSLIMS IN PERSIA The Saracens [Muslims] of Tabriz [in Persia] are wicked and treacherous. The law which their prophet Mahomet [Muhammad] has given them lays down that any harm they may do to one who does not accept their law, and any appropriation of his goods, is no sin at all. And if they suffer death or injury at the hands of Christians, they are accounted martyrs. For this reason they would be great wrongdoers, if it were not for the government. And all the other Saracens in the world act on the same principle. When they are on the point of death, up comes their priest and asks whether they believe that Mahomet was the true messenger of God; if they answer, "Yes," then he tells them that they are saved.

Source: *Ibn Battuta in Black Africa*, edited by Said Hamdun and Noel King (Princeton: Marcus Wiener Publishers, 1994), pp. 58–59, and *The Travels of Marco Polo*, translated and with an introduction by Ronald Latham (Harmondsworth, England: Penguin Books, 1958) pp. 57–58.

Qutb Minar, or "Pillar of Victory." This tall fluted tower is a minaret from which muezzins call the faithful to offer their prayers to God. It was erected in 1199 in Delhi by Sultan Qutb al-Din Aybak, founder of the Delhi Sultanate, as a symbol of the triumph of Islam in the Indian subcontinent.

northern India each had its own distinctive personality, the layout of the Muslim metropolis and the patterns of urban activity were similar wherever one went. The homes of the residents were relatively impermanent, made of sun-dried bricks, in contrast to the permanency of mosques, palaces, and other public buildings, which were constructed from oven-baked bricks and cut stones and designed to last through the years.

In the thirteenth century, Islam's preeminent city was Cairo, which boasted a diverse population of nearly 500,000. It was ruled by foreign-born dynasts, known as Mamluks, many of whom had entered the Islamic world during the Turkish population movements into western Asia at an earlier date and had gone to Egypt to serve the ruling elite as military and bureaucratic slaves. From 1250 to 1517, they were able to dominate the Nile River basin as a privileged, Turkish-speaking military and administrative elite that lived apart from the Arabic-speaking commoners. Cosmopolitan Cairo also included separate Christian, Jewish, and Greek quarters. Within these residential quarters, narrow, winding byways carved paths between two- and even three-story dwellings. These buildings typically jutted out over the alleys, nearly touching the upper stories of the homes on the other side of the street and providing those on the street with much-needed shade against a hot sun. Inside the homes, carpets, mattresses, hassocks, cushions, and pillows were common. Tables and chairs, however, were rare, for wood was in short supply and was mainly employed for the screens and shutters that kept houses cooler.

As befit a commercial center, Cairo had an abundance of markets, each one specializing in a particular commodity. Here were spices; there incense; further along, textiles, copperware, and foodstuffs. Shopping was meant to be a pleasurable diversion from humdrum city life. At times it could be an all-consuming activity, with buyers and sellers haggling for hours about prices as they drank cups of tea and coffee. Because shopping took time, market areas had numerous public eating places. Indeed, Cairo was said to have no fewer than 12,000 cooks to prepare its meals.

FAMILY LIFE   In Cairo and the other great cities of *dar al-Islam*, as well as in hundreds of less notable villages, Islam's bedrock was the patriarchal family. Across the world of Islam, men dominated over women, children, and slaves. Whether a household was rich or poor, located in the city or the countryside, husbands and fathers were expected to exercise power over their spouses and offspring. Islamic law permitted a man to have four wives. A husband in a poor household, however, could hardly afford to have more than one. Nor could he afford to seclude his wife or expect her to be veiled, for lower-class wives and children had to work in the fields alongside their menfolk. Men in the middling and upper classes, who had sufficient means, married multiple wives and shielded them from work outside the home. The wealthiest men also added numerous concubines to their harems.

Restrictions of the veil and the seclusion of women elevated the power of men, but they did not prevent women from having influence within the family. They acquired knowledge of the wider world through their veiled sorties into public places and their meetings with other females. In fact, the Islamic attitude toward gender relations was not exclusively patriarchal. True, as Islam spread outside of the Arabian peninsula in the seventh century, it absorbed the prevailing patriarchal views of the Persian and Christian worlds. Yet, Muhammad's life and teachings had left an ambivalent perspective on the relations of men and women. Later commentators could cite examples that favored gender equality, even as other examples seemed to extol the dominant place of men. For example, Muhammad's first wife, Khadijah, was an older, economically independent woman, who actually proposed marriage to the Prophet and to whom he remained monogamous until her death at the age of sixty-five. On the other hand, after Khadijah died, Muhammad took additional wives, whom he required to be veiled and to live secluded from male company. Elements of gender equality could be found in the *Quran*. For one, it taught that Allah spoke directly to men and women. In regard to sexual reproduction, the *Quran* affirmed that the sexual fluids of men and women were of equal importance.

The world of Islam included numerous divisions: between men and women; between rich and poor; between defenders of orthodoxy and promoters of Sufism; between Sunnis and Shiites; between urban merchants, rural cultivators, and desert herders; between Arabic, Turkish, and Persian speakers. But these cracks did not undermine the foundations of unity within the House of Islam. Ultimately, these fractures paled next to the greater divide between those inside *dar al-Islam* and those outside of it. By the end of the thirteenth century, Muslims had achieved considerable success in extending the dominion of *dar al-Islam*, and many Muslims looked confidently to the day when the peoples of all known worlds would join in facing toward Mecca for their prayers to Allah, whom they believed to be the one supreme deity.

THE MOSAIC OF INDIA

One place where Islam made significant inroads was on the Indian subcontinent, though it did not erase the region's Hindu-Buddhist culture. Indeed, it was the mixing of cultures that was the most distinctive feature of the subcontinent. This mixture of ethnic and religious groups sometimes baffled outsiders, including those who lingered for a while. Ibn Battuta, for example, spent several decades as an official in the Delhi Sultanate. His writings reflected his appreciation for the subcontinent's opulence. Yet, he found this mosaic of cultures difficult to comprehend. And like the other Muslims who came as merchants, missionaries, and conquerors, Battuta had to adapt to the heterodox traditions of the subcontinent as much as he and other agents of Islam imposed their own ways.

Like so many other parts of the world in the thirteenth and fourteenth centuries, the term we use to describe the subcontinent, "India," was not one that its inhabitants used. The origin of the word India went back to "Sindhu," the Sanskrit word for sea, and the name of the great river in the northwest of the subcontinent. The Persians transformed the initial "s" into "h," yielding the name Hindu. The term passed to the Greeks who

VIEW OF THE DELHI SULTANATE

Ibn Battuta spent many years serving as an Islamic judge or qadi *in the court of the Delhi Sultanate. The following excerpt from Ibn Battuta's travels shows how important as a unifying force the Islamic religion and Islamic law were to trading networks such as those leading into and out of India.*

On the next day we arrived at the royal residence of Dilhi [Delhi], the metropolis of the land of al-Hind, a vast and magnificent city, uniting beauty with strength. It is surrounded by a wall whose equal is not known in any country in the world, and is the largest city in India, nay rather the largest of all the cities of Islam in the East. . . . Then I went in and found the sultan [of Dilhi] on the terrace of the palace with his back leaning on the couch, the vizier Khwaja Jahan before him and the "great kin" Qabula standing there upright. When I saluted him the "great kin" said to me "Do homage, for the Master of the World has appointed you qadi of the royal city of Dilhi and has fixed your stipend at 12,000 dinars a year, and assigned to you villages to that amount, and commanded for you 12,000 dinars in cash, which you shall draw from the treasury tomorrow (if God will). . . . So

I did homage and when he had taken me by the hand and presented me before the Sultan, the Sultan said to me, "Do you think that the office of qadi of Dilhi is one of the minor functions; it is the highest function in our estimation." I understood what he said though I could not speak (in Persian) fluently, but the Sultan understood Arabic although he could not speak it fluently. . . . He replied, "I have appointed Baha al-Din al Multani and Kamal a-Din al-Bijanawri to be your substitutes; they will be guided by your advice and you will be the one who signs all the documents, for you are in the place of a son to us."

Source: *The Travels of Ibn Battuta*, translated by H. A. R. Gibb, with revisions and notes from the Arab text edited by C. Defremery and B. R. Sanguinetti (Cambridge, England: Cambridge University Press, 1958–1994), vol. 3, pp. 618, 747–48.

changed Hindu to Indus, from which the name India is derived. In the thirteenth century, however, the term "India" was neither commonly used nor did it signify a political or cultural unity. Instead, the subcontinent's people lived in a number of different—and often warring—polities. Their diverse cultural heritage included the classical languages of Sanskrit and Tamil, in which the subcontinent's elite recorded their thoughts on science, philosophy, and literature. But most people were unfamiliar with classical languages and continued to speak one of numerous, mutually incomprehensible vernaculars.

HINDUISM, THE CASTE SYSTEM, AND DIVERSITY

The subcontinent was home to a number of religions. Numerous belief systems and ritual practices, of which Hinduism was the most important, had flourished before the arrival of Islam. Hinduism, however, did not constitute a monolithic religion. Unlike Islam, which rested on one book, the *Quran*, and five pillars of faith, Hindu beliefs and practices derived from numerous texts and creeds. What united Hinduism was the ritual supremacy of the priestly caste of the Brahmans, and a society structured by a hierarchy of castes, subcastes, and outcastes.

The origin of the caste (a word derived from the Portuguese *casta*) system went back to the fourfold *varna* order established by the Vedas (the Book of Knowledge) around 600 B.C.E. The four *varna* orders consisted of Brahmans (priests), Kshatriyas (warriors), Vaishyas (merchants and artisans), and Shudras (peasants and laborers). A fifth category included those who were outside the fold altogether. Originally, *varna* functioned as a system of classifying people and organizing the division of labor. Over time, however, it became a rigid system of ranking social groups defined as *jati* (castes and subcastes), each belonging to one or another of the four great *varnas*.

The principles of purity and pollution determined caste hierarchy. The "purest" were the Brahmans who performed no physical labor. Others were ranked according to the graded scale of "pollution" entailed in their occupational tasks. If people from higher castes came into contact with those from lower castes, there were elaborate rituals to remove the taint and restore purity. Such a system of occupational classification resulted in unequal access to wealth, power, and prestige. The lowest and those deemed the most polluted were the outcastes whose very sight was considered to be polluting and who were forced to live apart from other castes in their own cluster of hamlets. These were the "untouchables." They were often classified as scavengers and tanners, a ranking that made them fit only to work as landless laborers bound to their landed patrons by a variety of servile ties.

The Brahman ideology of purity and pollution also functioned as a means of constituting and reinforcing the gender hierarchy. Brahman women could not aspire to the status of their male counterparts, for the texts considered women ineligible for Vedic studies. Yet, the caste ideology placed a premium on maintaining the purity of women. High-caste women were enjoined to refrain from physical labor. Like the wives of wealthy Muslims, they were expected to remain confined to the domestic sphere. If anything, the impulse to seclude Brahman women from contact with strangers was even greater than in the Islamic world, for the Brahmans believed that isolation was essential to maintain the woman's purity. By contrast, the women of peasant and laboring castes were considered polluted to begin with, and thus they were not prohibited from performing physical labor outside the home. As in many other parts of the world, the dominant ideology extolled women as mothers and wives, while the supreme position in the family belonged to the father-patriarch.

Learned Brahmans followed a path in which they studied and wrote religious and scientific commentaries in Sanskrit on the classic Hindu spiritual texts, like the *Upanishads*. Their writings and thinking formed the basis of Hindu spiritualism, and they developed an elaborate set of rituals around such deities as Vishnu, Shiva, Brahma, and others. While Brahmans emphasized esoteric knowledge and ritualistic practices, the people of the lower castes turned increasingly to popular cults for spiritual and secular inspiration. Adherents of these cults extolled divine love and believed that spiritual attainment was possible to ordinary mortals. The most popular cult—that of the god Krishna—inspired the composition of erotic poetry in Sanskrit and devotional songs about Krishna as a dark herdsman who formed playful and amorous relationships with adoring and indulgent milkmaids.

Popular cults challenged Brahman authority, and Brahmans responded by incorporating devotional forms into their creed. The temples, where Brahmans previously had preached an esoteric religion in Sanskrit, increasingly contained shrines for the worship of gods and goddesses. At the same time, they assimilated folk guardian spirits into the pantheon of deities. These blendings were particularly evident in the large stone temples constructed during the thirteenth century in the southern part of the Indian subcontinent.

> *What united Hinduism was the ritual supremacy of the priestly caste of the Brahmans, and a society structured by a hierarchy of castes, subcastes, and outcastes.*

The extent to which Brahmans incorporated external elements distinguished their creed from Islam (and for that matter, from Christianity). In contrast to the missionaries of Islam and Christianity, whose ambition was to convert all outsiders completely to their faiths, Brahman priests displayed more flexibility. Instead of confronting or condemning outsiders, they absorbed their deities and devotional forms of worship. In the process, Hinduism became a more diverse and more inclusive creed.

The incorporation of outside deities and worship also reflected the increasing diversity and cross-cultural mixing that characterized the subcontinent. Politically, that diversity followed from the absence of a single dominating empire from the seventh century onward. This left power in the hands of a number of more compact regional states, whose rulers secured their position by making land grants to powerful families and collecting tribute from them. In turn, grantees looked to bring their new lands into cultivation. To do this, they absorbed groups that had stood outside the *varnas* into the caste system and into the agricultural workforce.

The subcontinent's geographic location, which made it a pivot for trade across the Indian Ocean, contributed as well to its peculiar cultural mosaic. Merchants based in India exchanged the subcontinent's spices (especially pepper), sandalwood, perfumes, and textiles for silk from Egypt and China, slaves from Ethiopia, horses from Arabia and Persia, and most importantly, gold and silver from Mali to make jewelry and decorate temples and palaces. Arab and other Muslim merchants dominated the peninsula's long-distance trade, but Jewish, Chinese, and Hindu merchants also played significant roles in the Indian Ocean's commerce.

> *The development of the Indo-Islamic hybrid was a tribute to Islam's dynamism and to the strength of the subcontinent's cultures.*

TURKISH INVASIONS   Although Arab merchants were influential all over the subcontinent, it was Muslim Turkish peoples from Central Asia who carried out Islam's military penetration of the Indian peninsula in the tenth and eleventh centuries. Such invasions culminated in 1206, when Qutubuddin Aibak, a Turkish warrior of a Mamluk dynasty, conquered Delhi. Aibak then founded an independent sultanate with Delhi as its capital. The Delhi Sultanate eventually extended its political jurisdiction across the whole of northern India. Like other Turkish-speaking warrior bands, the dynasty permitted ambitious women to exercise power. Accordingly, Sultana Razziya became India's first Muslim woman ruler. She ascended the throne after her father's death in 1236, but her reign was brutally cut short in 1240, when she was murdered by Mamluk palace guards. Balban, the Mamluk leader who seized the throne, continued the expansion and consolidation of the sultanate, broadening the basis of his power by incorporating Indian-born Muslims into the ranks of the ruling nobility and subduing rebellious provincial governors.

The Muslim warriors and theologians of the Delhi Sultanate could not easily reconcile their Islamic faith with the diverse beliefs and practices of their newly conquered subjects. Calling the heterogeneous peoples of the subcontinent "Hindus" to distinguish them from Muslims, the rulers treated these communities as idolators. After all, unlike Muslims (or for that matter, Christians and Jews), the Hindus were not a people of the book. In the early years of the Delhi Sultanate, this condescension translated into a variety of discriminations. The sultanate, for example, restricted the higher levels of government office to Muslims as a way to assert their political and cultural superiority. In addition, the Turkish nobility maintained a racial exclusivity that bred resentment among the Hindu upper classes. Hindu kings and nobles refused to accept this loss of power, exploiting every opportunity to regain their lost status. Brahmans also had reasons to resent the new order as their influence in the imperial court diminished; in addition, their share of land grants declined because the Turkish sultans patronized their own theologians.

Yet, the gulf that Muslim rulers and theologians created between themselves and their subjects gave way with the passing of time. In part, the reconciliation owed to the conversion of significant numbers of Hindus to Islam. More important, however, were the ways in which the conquerors changed and adapted. The Turkish nobility began to marry into indigenous families and to adopt local customs. In addition, Muslim rulers became more flexible, allowing non-Muslims to maintain their own laws so long as they did not conflict with the interests of the state. Nor did the Turkish sultans enforce the *sharia*, or take responsibility for the spiritual salvation of their Hindu subjects. They left Hindu temples and religious institutions in peace; only outside the sultanate's frontiers did they attack Hindu establishments.

Beyond accommodation, the interactions of Muslims and Hindus led to some unique cultural fusions. Theoretically, Islam did not recognize caste, yet a caste-like hierarchy developed among Muslims. In terms of religion, the fusing of traditions involved the incorporation of Islamic ceremonies into Hindu rituals. At the same time, Sufism, with its brotherhoods and emphasis on emotional religious rituals, became quite prominent on the subcontinent, in part because it absorbed elements of Hinduism and its local, devotional cults.

Thus did Muslim Turkish conquerors blend into the intricate Indian mosaic. To be sure, the establishment of Turkish rule on the subcontinent in the thirteenth century brought India into the Muslim world. Yet, at the same time that the subcontinent's importance in the Muslim world and the Indian Ocean trade grew, Islam adapted to the region's diverse traditions and unique institutions, becoming a distinctive cultural mixture of Indian and Islamic traditions. The development of this Indo-Islamic hybrid was a tribute as much to Islam's dynamism as to the strength of the subcontinent's cultures, of which Islam now formed a part.

THE DOMAIN OF CHRISTENDOM

At the western end of Eurasia at the furthest reaches of the Asian trade was Europe. No trader or traveler, however, would have used the term Europe to describe the northwestern part of the Eurasian land mass. According to scholars, the name derives from the Assyrian-Phoenician word "ereb," which means sunset; the name Asia from "asu," which means sunrise. Thus, the terms Europe and Asia may refer to the movement of the sun, as viewed by someone on the Eurasian land mass. Whatever its etymological origins, however, Europe is an old word, but it was not in general usage in the thirteenth century. At that time, the area that would come to be called Europe was known as Christendom.

DIVISIONS WITHIN CHRISTENDOM Like the Islamic world, Christendom encompassed a vast territory and a large population. It stretched from Ireland and England in the west to Russia in the east (see Map 1-4). But even more fundamentally than in the Islamic world, the domain of Christianity was divided, most prominently between the Western Church, headed by the pope in Rome, and the Eastern Church, headed by the patriarch of Constantinople. This division arose after Emperor Constantine moved the capital of the Roman empire

MAP 1-4 EUROPE IN 1300

Compare the political map of Europe in 1300 with the map of China in this chapter (Map 1-5, page 28). Why were there so many more European political units than there were Chinese? According to this map, what were the leading European states at this time? Would you be able to predict on the basis of this map which of these units would grow and become strong and which would decline?

from Rome to Constantinople in the fourth century. His successors refused to acknowledge the supremacy of the bishops of Rome in religious matters. Many peoples, such as the Serbs and Russians, were converted to Christianity by missionaries from Constantinople; other peoples, such as the Poles and Germans, were converted by emissaries from Rome. Thus, the Christian Church began to divide between east and west. In the west, the patriarch of Rome became the pope, a single religious authority under a single Christian Church. In the east, national churches formed, such as the Serbian Orthodox Church and the Russian Orthodox Church, each with its own spiritual head who was not subordinated to the patriarch of Constantinople. And while both Eastern and Western Christianity adhered to the fundamental tenet of Jesus Christ's resurrection, their differences over doctrinal and liturgical issues kept Christendom a divided realm and led to charges from each side of the other's heresy.

Other cleavages prevented European unity. Within Christendom were many kingdoms, and indeed many non-Christians. There were Muslims (in southern France, Italy, Spain, and the Balkans), as well as Jews (in many places), while pagans lived on the Baltic Sea (in Lithuania) until the thirteenth century. Moreover, there were a bewildering number of mutually unintelligible languages and dialects spoken by the common people, who often did not speak the same languages as their rulers. Then, too, divisions between church and secular authorities went beyond mere words. While the pope served as the spiritual leader of Western Christendom, many kings and princes vied for the title of this world's emperor. The medieval German princes, in particular, insisted that they were the rightful successors to the Romans, and they tried to extend the control of the Holy Roman empire (a collection of many smaller principalities) over all of Europe. But the popes resisted, and they managed to gain backing from French and Italian princes to stave off the Germans without becoming permanent vassals of their secular protectors. Thus, the church remained a (relatively) autonomous power, entangled in, but never subsumed by, the political conflicts between European states. Indeed, an important result of the rise of the papacy was the power that the church, through its clergy, was able to wield in the lives of the common people. The church claimed papal supremacy in religious matters, arguing that only the pope could define church doctrine and rule over its own affairs. Although church and state were believed to inhabit separate realms, one spiritual, the other secular, in reality, the Christian Church intruded on all aspects of life. In addition to preparing believers for the afterlife, the church held great estates, patronized the arts, and settled political disputes.

> *The church remained a (relatively) autonomous power, entangled in, but never subsumed by, the political conflicts between European states.*

RELIGIOUS TRADITIONS AND CHALLENGES As in the Islamic world, shared religious traditions fostered a degree of cohesion among the Christian inhabitants of Western Christendom. By the thirteenth century, the Western Church had won its battles against paganism. To be sure, magical practices and folk beliefs persisted in many places, but everyday life increasingly took on Christian rhythms. As parish priests arrived in communities previously without clergy, the church began to lay the foundations for a unified Christian culture. At the Fourth Lateran Council, held in Rome in 1215, the pope and bishops established a common creed to be memorized by all Christians and said at all masses. The council also certified seven sacraments (including baptism, communion, marriage, confession, and unction) over which the clergy officiated and in which laypersons were expected to participate. Through their control over these sacraments, deemed essential to living in a state of spiritual well-being, the Christian clergy enhanced their power. Moreover, as Christian learning—theological, legal, historical, and scientific—expanded, Latin, the language of the church, increasingly became the language of Christendom's elite. Although few common folk could read or write in Latin (or any language), the sense of a common Christian way was reinforced by the sharing of the liturgy and sacraments, the increasing frequency of pilgrimages, and the new familiarity with saints' lives and remains.

Women too shared in the liturgy and sacraments, and even made pilgrimages to the shrines of saints. Moreover, they could take orders and become nuns, but they could not be priests, celebrate mass, or move up in the male hierarchy. As "brides of Christ," nuns could escape poor marriage prospects, and perhaps learn to read and write. Some women did become powerful abbesses, mystics, and seers, but inevitably women with power—political, economic, or spiritual—were seen as dangerous threats to the cohesion of the church. The fear of the power of women caused communities to bring accusations against women as witches and to burn some of them at the stake.

The cohesion of the church was also threatened by unorthodox men and women, who emphasized individual piety and challenged the church hierarchy's monopoly on interpreting the word of God. In contrast to Islam, which permitted any believer to lead prayers, the Christian Church reserved that role to accredited priests. Moreover, the austerity of mosques stood in sharp contrast to increasingly elaborate Gothic cathedrals, in which the pulpit was meant for the clergy alone, and ritual and ceremony reinforced a hierarchical order. As for the Christian religious dissenters, their teachings did not travel much beyond their local areas, although their exemplary lives—and martyred deaths—would make them highly appealing to reformers of succeeding generations.

THE FEUDAL SYSTEM The absolute authority of the Western Church faced challenges from secular elites as well as religious dissenters. During the eighth, ninth, and tenth centuries, Western Europe had been subjected to a series of assaults by Muslims, Vikings, and Hungarians (whom the Western Europeans referred to as "barbarians"). In these chaotic circumstances, a class of warriors, or knights, who were the king's vassals, emerged as a powerful presence. Some knights grew rich, and their power differed little from that of the kings or princes who claimed to rule larger territories. Indeed, kings in this era, having no standing armies or elaborate bureaucracies, depended on knights to fight their battles. In exchange for military service, the kings could offer their vassals privileges, including the title to lands, the right to tax certain commodities, the right to create and exploit their own legal and economic systems, and the right to extract forced labor and fees from their peasants.

A European Manor. This diagram shows how land was divided on a typical European manor in feudal times. Note the small size of the plots, and the large areas owned by the lord but that could be used by all (e.g., the common pasture, wood lot, barn, and oven).

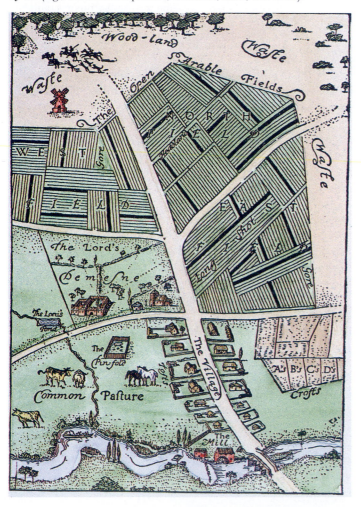

These privileged landholders thus became "lords," with their own estates—of vastly different sizes—to govern. Under this system, called feudalism, lords governed not only lands, but also the people who were tied to those lands. In exchange for the lord's protection and the right to farm some of his land, these peasants, or "serfs," paid a series of fees, determined by custom, to the lord. Many were also forbidden to leave the estate or to marry without the lord's permission. Thus, under feudalism, a set of reciprocal obligations developed across Europe: princes were obliged to offer privileges to local nobles, local nobles were obliged to provide armies or tribute to the princes, and peasants were obliged to do all the work. Yet, serfs were not slaves. They were generally tied to the land, but they could not be sold as if they were pieces of property, and they enjoyed some legal protections.

Feudalism was more fully developed and more enduring in some places than in others; it looked very different in England than it did in southern France or Bohemia. Already by the thirteenth century, labor shortages and the growth of cities made feudal obligations virtually impossible to enforce in France and England. At the same time, in Eastern Europe and Russia, feudalism was only just beginning. The effects of feudal organization, however, were similar across Europe. The doling out of land and privileges to feudal lords created a great number of local units with their own legal systems and often armies. The decentralization of power that was characteristic of Europe at this time would make the creation of unified states difficult, and the conquest of the continent as a whole an improbable, indeed, impossible venture. In regard to achieving centralized polities, Europe was similar to sub-Saharan Africa and India, but markedly different from China and parts of the Muslim Middle East, where monarchs had more success in overcoming the geographical and social barriers to political centralization.

Feudalism also left European society highly stratified between landowning noble families, commoners (who consisted of smaller landowners, merchants, and artisans), and peasants. Large landowners made up an aristocratic class, as they were allowed to pass on their privileges, titles, and land to their sons (rarely to their daughters). But birthright was not the only way to become part of the nobility. To enhance their wealth and power, kings and princes on rare occasions would bestow noble status on hard-working, extraordinary commoners. Nonetheless, upward mobility, especially the jump from commoner to noble, was the exception. Nearly unbridgeable gaps developed between nobles, commoners, and peasants during this period.

EVERYDAY LIFE Life for peasants on feudal estates, or manors, was rather bleak. Men spent the majority of their short lives engaged in farming. Women were responsible for domestic tasks, like cooking, cleaning, raising domestic animals, and brewing the family's crucially important beer (a heavy brew, full of much-needed carbohydrates). Most knew little of the world beyond the manor. Although there was some inter-estate com-

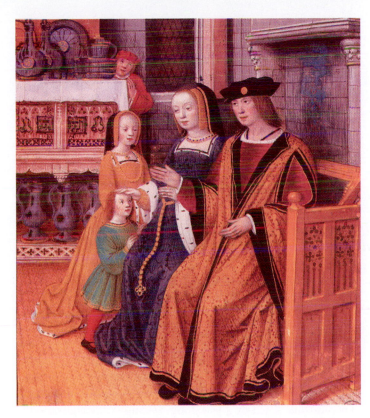

Commoners in Feudal Europe. This painting by Jean Bourdichon is one in a series called The Four States of Society, consisting of four late-medieval images of commoners: a craftsman, a poor man, a wild man, and a bourgeois. This painting of the bourgeois is a portrait of a wealthy merchant and his family and shows off both their piety and their wealth.

not, however, easy to survive in towns. The death rate generally exceeded the birthrate, and sanitary conditions were hideous. The unpaved streets served as rubbish and excrement dumps, as well as exercise grounds for pigs, dogs, donkeys, chickens, and rats.

Europe's townspeople engaged in a variety of occupations. The social hierarchy, here, too, was pronounced—though a bit more fluid than on the manors. The highest rung was occupied by the wealthiest merchants, resident aristocrats, and administrative officials (themselves usually aristocrats). Further down were smaller independent businessmen and artisans—tavern-keepers, small traders, bakers, and the like. Then came skilled craftsmen, or journeymen, who could sell their labor (as masons, cobblers, or skilled weavers) for a daily wage. Near the bottom of the heap were unskilled workers, itinerant peddlers, household servants, and the unemployed. As towns grew, they expanded their manufacturing, especially the production of wool—spinning, weaving, and dyeing. The trade in wool production fueled Europe's economic development.

Women could be found at all levels of the urban hierarchy, though their influence in economic and political matters was largely indirect. There were influential, learned women aristocrats, as well as women employed as wetnurses, midwives, or chambermaids. In Italy, France, and Flanders, "artisanal" women were employed as skilled weavers, but as the craft became more lucrative, male weavers increasingly occupied these positions. And, of course, women made up a significant proportion of the underclass—composed of beggars, orphans, widows, prostitutes, and the elderly or handicapped—individuals dependent on private charity in a world with few able to offer alms.

As in the world of Islam, European towns facilitated longer-distance trade, and they prospered where traders were most numerous and most active, on the Baltic, Flemish, and Italian coasts. In the north, lumber, fish, furs, and grain from Scandinavia and what is now northwestern Russia were shipped west, where they could be traded for high-quality woolen cloth made in Flanders (from English wool). More far-reaching trade networks radiated from the city of Venice, which imported spices, silks, porcelain, and luxury goods from the East. As some inhabitants of these towns, particularly in Italy, began to reap the profits of long-distance trade, they could afford a more luxurious lifestyle. By 1300, the consumption of sugar, spices, and books was rising steadily.

merce for locally produced goods (for example, iron for tools), salt, fine cloth, horses, spices, gems, and perfume had to be purchased at trade fairs or from itinerant peddlers. Thus, unlike the world of Islam, which boasted a large number of commercial cities, the commerce of Christendom still generally occurred at seasonal fairs in smaller crossroads.

Rural peasants made up more than 90 percent of Christendom's population, but by 1300, towns also dotted the European landscape. The largest, Paris, Florence, and Milan, perhaps claimed 100,000 inhabitants. Many of those who populated these cities and the smaller towns were peasants

> *More far-reaching trade networks radiated from the city of Venice, which imported spices, silks, porcelain, and luxury goods from the East.*

who had run away from their feudal lords. Custom decreed that those who had lived in a town for a year and a day were considered free from feudal obligations. Towns secured charters for themselves, which exempted them from many feudal obligations and guaranteed them political freedoms. It was

But for most Europeans, whether they resided in cities or on manors, life was short, luxuries were rare, and exposure to arts and sciences was quite limited. At least one of every six children died before his or her first birthday; one in four died before reaching age five. By and large, those who survived lived in cramped, dark, smoky quarters; windows were impractical, as they let in little light, and much cold in winter. Few houses had chimneys, relying instead on chinks in the roof for ventilation. Most homes included little furniture, having perhaps a table, a few stools, a chest, and a bedstead. Clothing was equally spartan. As textile production was extremely arduous—one had to spin the thread, weave the cloth, then sew the pieces together—clothes were quite expensive. A linen undershirt cost, by one estimate, about three to four days of labor. Until the fourteenth century, buttons as fasteners were unknown, and clothes had to be draped, tied on, or pinned together with straight pins.

Mealtime did not bring much in the way of variation or enjoyment. Grains and legumes, which can be stored, comprised the backbone of ordinary diets; in season, one might also have fruits and vegetables, poultry, eggs, and fish, but often these were unaffordable. Children washed their supper down not with milk but with ale or wine.

> *The few Europeans who did travel or listen to the crusaders' tales realized that Christendom's power and affluence paled next to that of the Islamic world, India, and especially China.*

The aristocracy ate a more varied diet and had meat more regularly, which they liked highly seasoned. Nobles used spices not only to prevent or disguise spoilage but also as a way of distinguishing themselves from peasants, who could not afford such expensive goods. The extremely high cost of pepper, for example, put this spice out of the reach of all but the wealthiest members of society.

EXPANSION AND CONQUEST Divisions within Christendom did not impede its external expansion. Medieval European aristocrats ranged far afield in search of new territories to conquer. Pushing out the Slavs, Germanic knights conquered great swathes of land in eastern Europe; in the centuries prior to 1300, Norman warriors seized Welsh and Sicilian lands. The most important expansions were those resulting from a series of "crusades" to the Holy Land, the first of which was launched in 1096 and the last concluded in the mid-fifteenth century. Urged to liberate Jerusalem from Muslim control by the pope, aristocrats as well as merchants and pilgrims also saw these long-distance campaigns as the means to seize estates and booty for themselves. Their travels did enrich many, as well as add to their prestige (and that of the church that sent them). Those who returned brought back eye-opening accounts of Muslim civilization. Those who stopped and set up estates along the way brought Christianity, and feudal forms, to new lands.

Still, Europeans knew very little about the world beyond Christendom, and Mediterranean sailors feared passing beyond the "pillars of Hercules" (the rocks of Gibraltar) into the Atlantic Ocean. Maps were hardly more than schematic diagrams, with Jerusalem, appropriately, at the universe's center. For many centuries, an otherworldly orientation sufficed—knowing the world seemed at best irrelevant with regard to things of real importance, at worst a threat to the church-centered social order and the soul. But the few who did travel or listen to the crusaders' tales realized that Christendom's power and affluence paled next to that of the Islamic world, India, and especially China.

Port Cities. In fourteenth-century Venice, shipping was a central part of economic and cultural life. Note here how prosperous merchants conduct business in the city center, while fantastic creatures inhabit nearby ports.

THE MIDDLE KINGDOM

The destination that drew all of the world's great travelers, including Marco Polo and Ibn Battuta, was China, known far and wide as a land of wealth and learning. Yet, in the thirteenth century, the term "China," which probably was derived from a Sanskrit word, was not used by the approximately 100 million people who lived in what they considered the world's *Zhongguo* or "Middle Kingdom." Certainly, the sense of being at the cen-

VIEW OF EUROPEANS

One of the best and most representative Arab-Muslim accounts of Europeans was written in the twelfth century by the Arab notable and adversary of the European crusaders, Usamah ibn Munqidh. Although written a century before our world history discussion begins, it represented the common thinking of Arab Muslims about Europeans at the time of the European crusades. Especially noteworthy were the observations about relations between men and women, which seemed altogether too loose to the author.

When one comes to recount cases regarding the Franks [Europeans], he cannot but glorify Allah, exalted is he!, and sanctify him, for he sees them as animals possessing the virtues of courage and fighting but nothing else; just as animals have only the virtues of strength and carrying loads. I shall now give some instances of their doings and their curious mentality. . . . Everyone who is a fresh emigrant from the Frankish lands is ruder than those who have become acclimatized and have held long association with the Moslems [Muslims]. . . . The Franks are void of all zeal and jealousy.

One of them may be walking along with his wife. He meets another man who takes the wife by the hand and steps aside to converse with her while the husband is standing on one side waiting for his wife to conclude the conversation. If she lingers too long for him, he leaves her alone with the conversant and goes away.

Source: *An Arab-Syrian Gentleman and Warrior in the Period of the Crusades: Memoirs of Usamah ibn Munqidh,* translated by Philip K. Hitti (Princeton: Princeton University Press, 1987) pp. 93–94, 159–70.

ter of the world aptly reflected the worldview of those who lived in the Middle Kingdom. True, for much of the thirteenth century, the Middle Kingdom was divided in two (see Map 1-5). In the north in the second decade of the twelfth century, the Han Chinese Song dynasty had been supplanted by invaders, the Jurchens, from what is now Manchuria. Adapting to deep-rooted patterns of rulership in the Middle Kingdom, the Jurchens established the Jin dynasty. For over a millennium, the institution of the dynasty, with its centralized bureaucratic structure and promotion of Confucian values sanctioned by the state, held the key to the coherence of the vast Chinese world. The Jin dynasty ruled over a population of 40 million until it was displaced by Mongol invaders from the north in the third decade of the thirteenth century. Meanwhile, in southern China, the Southern Song dynasty lasted until 1279, when its more than 70 million subjects also came under the rule of Mongol conquerors. Yet, in spite of political divisions and invasions, China's dynasties ruled over the richest of the thirteenth-century worlds.

EVERYDAY LIFE   As in Eurasia's other larger cultural areas, the wealth of China depended first and foremost on the production of agricultural surpluses. As elsewhere, the majority of people in China worked the land. But unlike many peasants in Europe who were serfs, most Chinese cultivators could freely buy, sell, and bequeath the lands on which they toiled. Landownership and household farming were widespread. To be sure, economic fluctuations reduced a significant number of peo-

ple to tenant farming or to hired agricultural labor, but relatively open social mobility also raised tenants and hired workers to landowning status. Peasant women contributed not only to labor in the field, but they also engaged in commerce through the silk industry. The growth of trade and the urban demand for silk cloth enabled many women to raise silkworms and to spin silk yarn.

Everyday life for these cultivators was dictated less by distant dynastic emperors than by the calendar of the agricultural year. This calendar was characterized by a variety of suggestive names, such as grain rains or excited insects. The calendar also regulated the cycles of festivals and observances: the New Year; the Festival of the Clear and Bright, during which ancestral graves were visited; the Mid-Autumn Festival, when the family got together to observe the harvest moon; and many others. The temples of China's two major religions, Buddhism and Daoism, were often major attractions for the populace on such occasions. Buddhism had entered the country around the first century C.E. It extolled the life and teachings of the saintly Indian ascetic Siddhartha Gautama (c. 563–c. 483 B.C.E.), called the Buddha, or "the enlightened one," who had taught that people should strive for liberation from all suffering through righteous living. Daoism had first appeared in China more than fifteen hundred years earlier as a philosophical school that looked back to a golden age before the onset of civilization. Later it emerged as a religious movement with its own scriptures and liturgy. While ritual observances took place within the temples

MAP 1-5   THE JIN AND SOUTHERN SONG EMPIRES

The Southern Song empire was known for its cities, its thriving commerce, and its maritime trade. Note the number of major ports under the control of the Southern Song, and contrast that with the area under the control of the Jin. What challenges and opportunities did this division present? Note the boundaries of the original Song empire. Why was the Song dynasty driven south? Why did it take the Mongols decades longer to topple the Southern Song after defeating the Jin?

of these faiths, many celebrations occurred within the confines of the family and the home. Indeed, in China, as in other worlds, large and small, the family had long been the hub of economic and social organization.

Song elites attempted to assert greater control and impose more uniformity over the ritual life of the family by producing and distributing a number of written manuals. In these pam-

phlets, they identified the institution of marriage as the key to a well-ordered society. As in other realms, the Chinese regarded marriage as a connection between families rather than individuals. Elite Chinese were particularly meticulous in arranging marriages and performing the rituals associated with the union of families. Ideally, the elite bride and groom would not even have met before their marriage. Among the common folk, by contrast, husband and wife would likely have met before their wedding, although their marriage, too, would almost surely be a union arranged by their parents. Similarly, while elite men might live up to the familial ideal of multiple secondary wives, assorted concubines, and numerous children, such a large family was beyond the means of most ordinary people.

COMMERCE AND CITIES   Although most of its people labored on the land, Song China was also a highly complex commercial society. A vibrant mercantile sector fashioned links among networks of urban centers. These ranged from small market towns, where farmers and peddlers hawked their wares, to some of the most magnificent cities in the world. The separation between the city and the countryside in the Chinese social landscape was never quite as stark as in medieval Europe. The combination in China of commercialization, urbanization, and industrialization was unprecedented in the world at the time. The key to China's robust economic development was an elaborate river transportation network. The large domestic market that owed its development to this highly developed

VIEWS OF CHINA

The Middle Kingdom (as the Chinese referred to their lands), or Cathay (as Ibn Battuta and Marco Polo often called China), was the favored destination of all travelers. No important traveler's account of the world would have been considered complete without a description of its fabled treasures and its powerful rulers. Consequently, the present-day reader cannot know for certain whether the descriptions offered by the travelers are eyewitness accounts or reports based on other people's impressions. Internal evidence would suggest that Ibn Battuta visited southern China but did not reach the court of the Yuan dynasty in Beijing, even though he reported on it. Marco Polo's descriptions have a greater ring of accuracy about them, but they, too, appear to have many embellishments. Nonetheless, the two men's accounts of the magnificent city of Hangzhou leave little doubt that it was the largest and wealthiest city in the world when these two saw it.

MARCO POLO ON HANGZHOU   Then he [the traveler] reaches the splendid city of Kinsai [Hangzhou], whose name means "City of Heaven." It well merits a description because it is without doubt the finest and the most splendid city in the world. . . . First, then, it was stated that the city of Kinsai is about 100 miles in circumference, because its streets and watercourses are wide and spacious. Then there are marketplaces, which because of the multitudes that throng them must be very large and spacious. The layout of the city is as follows. On one side is a lake of fresh water, very clear. On the other is a huge river, which entering by many channels, diffused throughout the city, carries away all its filth and then flows into the lake from which it flows out towards the Ocean. This makes the air very wholesome. And through every part of the city it is possible to travel either by land or by these streams. The streets and the watercourses alike are very wide, so that carts and boats can readily pass along them to carry provisions for the inhabitants. There are said to be 12,000 bridges, mostly of stone, though some are of wood. Those over the main channels and the chief thoroughfare are built with such lofty arches and so well designed that big ships can pass under them without a mast, and yet over them pass carts and horses; so well are the street-levels adjusted to the heights.

IBN BATTUTA ON HANGZHOU   We sailed on the river in the same way, taking our morning meal in one village and our evening meal in another, until after seventeen days we reached the city of al-Khansa. . . . It is the biggest city I have seen on the face of the earth. It takes three days to cross it, the traveler journeying on and stopping [for the night] in the city. It is laid out as we have described in the Chinese style of building, everyone having his own orchard and house.

Source: *The Travels of Marco Polo*, translated and with an introduction by Ronald Latham (Harmondsworth, England: Penguin Books, 1958) pp. 213–14, and *The Travels of Ibn Battuta*, translated by H. A. R. Gibb, with revisions and notes from the Arab text edited by C. Defremery and B. R. Sanguinetti (Cambridge, England: Cambridge University Press, 1958–1994), vol. 4, pp. 900–901.

Marco Polo in China. Marco Polo is welcomed at the court of Kubilai Khan.

internal river transportation and canal network also fostered an iron and steel industry and enabled Chinese merchants to obtain silk produced in the countryside that could be brought to the coast by river to be part of a brisk overseas trade. Also key was the use of paper money and woodblock printing to facilitate the dissemination of information.

Chinese towns and cities did not have their own charters, administrative institutions, or special privileges as did Europe's much smaller, yet rising cities. Administratively, urban centers were part of the counties and prefectures in which they were located, subject to the jurisdiction of the same imperial bureaucrats who administered the surrounding countryside. Again, in contrast to feudal Europe, China's people were free to come and go between cities and farms. Particularly during festivals, the towns came alive and filled with visitors buying and selling, or simply enjoying the fireworks, the theatrical displays, and the hustle and bustle of the crowd.

At the pinnacle of the urban networks were major cities such as the capital of the Southern Song empire, Hangzhou, which with a million plus inhabitants, was the world's largest metropolis. According to Marco Polo, Hangzhou was "without

doubt the finest and most splendid city in the world." It was a city of great wealth, ostentation, high culture, and a dazzling array of entertainment venues. It boasted a multitude of restaurants, hotels, taverns, and teahouses, where the rich and the powerful, merchants and officials alike, congregated and mingled. Teas or wines were served in cups of fine porcelain amid sumptuous décor and works by celebrated painters and calligraphers. In the arcades, singing girls, courtesans, and prostitutes invited passersby to patronize their establishments.

In Hangzhou, as in the world's other great cities, such luxuries were not available to all. In China, as elsewhere, diet and clothing marked social differences among the population. The fare of common people consisted of chicken, pork, offal, salted fish, and especially rice. To supply rice, of which the average Hangzhou resident consumed two pounds per day, barges arrived night and day at the city's riverbank markets. Meanwhile, better-off inhabitants feasted on more exotic food. In the great restaurants that catered to the wealthy, dishes such as shellfish cooked in rice wine, goose with apricots, lotus-seed soup, and fish cooked with plums were on the menu. On the streets, people of exalted rank wore long robes that reached down to the ground. For ceremonial occasions, they donned special robes with embroidered symbolic designs, such as phoenixes or dragon-claws. The costumes of wealthy women included long dresses, or blouses that came down close to the knee, jackets with long or short sleeves, and skirts—all cut from fine silk. They would also sometimes throw a "head-cover" over their shoulders. Common people, by contrast, clothed themselves in trousers and other garb of coarse hempen cloth.

THE BUREAUCRATIC TRADITION Many of China's wealthiest men owed their luxurious and comfortable lives to commercial enterprises, but most Chinese considered a career as an official the surest path to power and prestige. The bureaucratic route was officially open to males of almost any background, although members of the imperial household and their descendants were granted special access to the civil service examinations, which undermined the tradition of a meritocratic officialdom. Elaborate civil service examinations, requiring years of intensive study of the Chinese classics, provided entry at each level to the Chinese bureaucracy. Although in theory any person could sit and pass these exams, only those whose families could afford to fund long years of study could hope to have a member achieve success. The ideal of a bureaucracy open to anyone of merit was further compromised in the northern Jin empire, when the Jurchens excluded Han Chinese from the highest ranks of imperial service. Still, every effort was made to ensure that the examination process itself was rigorous, impartial, and free from corruption.

> *In the Chinese world, the bureaucracy provided the critical glue that held the vast realm together, contributing greatly to the centralization of power under the emperor.*

After spending years mastering the classical texts and surviving the grueling examination process, both anointed and potential members of the bureaucratic elite forged powerful bonds and a common identity among themselves. The dynasty placed them at the top of the social ladder; those who did well on the exams could marry well, earn a high income, and be honored with great prestige. In return, the bureaucrats were servants of the emperor, the "Son of Heaven." They could be appointed to administer distant provinces and could be put in charge of military affairs. Their service gave them an empire-wide perspective on matters of the state. Administering localities in which the population often spoke a mosaic of dialects and knew little of the outside world, they brought a unifying element to diverse communities. In the Chinese world, the bureaucracy provided the critical glue that held the vast realm together, contributing greatly to the centralization of power under the emperor.

CONFUCIAN IDEALS Officially, Confucian ideals and practices inspired the code of operation of the bureaucracy. They were traced to a minor government official and teacher named Kong Qiu (551–479 B.C.E.), whose name was Latinized to

Confucius by westerners. Kong Qiu, who lived in a period of political turmoil, was concerned with how to restore a stable social order through good government. He preached that everyone must begin by cultivating individual virtue and benevolence through learning. At the top, the ruler should lead, as the legendary sage-kings did, by exemplary moral and ethical behavior. He also taught that virtue must be expressed outwardly through the correct performance of rites appropriate to the individual's station, which differed according to context and was usually defined by age, gender, and status. Careful codification of rites anchored the moral and social order.

The Confucian ideals, however, were not always translated into practice. To the ruler, Confucian ideas formed a useful ideology to lend legitimacy to the dynasty. Thus did emperors promote an official cult of Kong Qiu. Temples were built in his honor and patronized by the elites throughout the realm. A hierarchical set of schools, headed by the Imperial Academy at the capital, was established to train loyal servants for the regime. In 1227, the Song Imperial Academy recognized a specific set of Confucian texts known collectively as the "Four Books." But contrary to the hopes of emperors, the propagation of Confucian ideas did not always solidify their legitimacy. Some scholar-officials took their roles as guardians of Confucian tradition very seriously, which meant they had the duty to maintain the proper moral or ethical order of society. If emperors failed to exemplify the ideals and to protect the realm's virtue, scholar-officials could become vocal critics. Many outspoken officials paid with their lives for adopting this course.

Song women had no chance of a public career. Men dominated government, mercantile, and literary spheres. Since women could not sit for the vaunted civil service examinations, they could not become part of the Chinese bureaucracy. For elite women, life revolved around the home. Indeed, the Song period is usually associated with the spread of footbinding (a practice believed to have been embraced first by the elites) and also with the condemnation of remarriage of widows. Despite the promotion of chastity among some elites, however, widows often did remarry. Moreover, Song women enjoyed more property rights and control of their marital assets than did their counterparts in China in later periods. Women, for example, retained control over their dowries, even taking their assets with them to their second marriages. They had the full right to inherit their husbands' property, and they were also given great latitude in selecting an heir.

Like other larger worlds, however, China was no monolith. Invasions, dynastic upheaval, and tensions between emperors and their officials introduced political instability. By 1300, both the Jin empire and the Southern Song empire would succumb to Mongol conquerors from the north—a people who in the view of the Chinese were "barbarians," inferior in all ways save one, their success as warriors. Still, China's riches were the envy of other worlds, and its impressive civilization awed visitors to the Middle Kingdom.

BORDERLANDS NEAR CHINA

> → *How did the Middle Kingdom influence neighboring societies?*

In the Chinese cosmology, the Middle Kingdom was the center of civilization. Those outside its boundaries were barbarians, arranged around China by means of the tributary system involving symbolic submission. Some of the neighboring peoples who paid tribute to the Chinese sought to reproduce the Chinese system, establishing their own tributary relations with others beside the Chinese while adopting Chinese cultural and political patterns internally. The Koreans to the north (whose land was known as Koryo) and the Vietnamese to the south (in Annam and Champa) attempted to reproduce Chinese models of domestic development and external relations. The people of the Indonesian archipelago in Southeast Asia served both as tributary and trading partners with the Chinese as silver, spices, silk, and other exotic goods changed hands between traders from across the Eurasian world. Another case of imitation could be found on the group of islands off the coast of China; the southern Chinese called these islands *jih-pen*, or Japan.

JAPAN

In the thirteenth century, Japan was a loose collection of domains ruled by powerful local lords, called *daimyo*, who had broad powers over peasants and commanded private armies of warriors, called *samurai*. They coexisted alongside a weak central government and an imperial family in a political system that had remarkable similarities with European feudalism. Geography partially accounted for this decentralization of power. Like the Italian peninsula, which is about the same size, the islands of Japan are mostly mountainous. Settlements congregated along coastal basins and in interior valleys that were largely isolated from one another.

Much of the Japanese political system and higher culture was based upon Chinese models. In the sixth and seventh centuries, the most powerful clan had imported Buddhism, Confucianism, and the Chinese systems of writing and government. As in the Middle Kingdom to its west, the Japanese rulers then created an imperial officialdom, though they restricted the qualifying examination to children of the aristocracy. But central authority, in spite of its Chinese-style system of rule, never succeeded in undercutting the power of private estate holders. Many of the functions of central administration—taxing, policing, judging, building and maintaining public works—became matters of local jurisdiction under these landholding barons. The lines of subordination between the imperial court and the local lords were ambiguous.

SOUTHEAST ASIA

In 1300, one of the most important borderland areas lay to the south and east of India in the area now referred to as Southeast Asia and consisted of the Indochina mainland, the Malay Peninsula, and the islands of the Indonesian archipelago (see Map 1-6). Defined by its dense forests and ubiquitous waterways, the region, like the Indian subcontinent, was most notable for its diversity and its openness to outside influences. Its geography made the emergence of large unified empires founded along great rivers or vast plains difficult. The result in Southeast Asia, as on the Indian subcontinent, was the emergence of numerous political communities boasting different heritages. For example, the kingdom of Angkor (889–1431), located in the Mekong Delta, drew upon Indian political institutions and encouraged the circulation of Hindu and Buddhist religious ideas. Islam began to make its influence felt as early as the eighth century, although it did not become a political force until much later. Its agents for conversion were mainly merchants and scholars, and only later, after Islam had established itself as a political force, did it compel conversions in its military conquests. In Southeast Asia, as on the Indian subcontinent, Hindu, Buddhist, and Islamic cultural systems vied against and mixed with one another. But Southeast Asia added Confucian and Chinese ideals to the political and cultural mix. These ideals were especially influential in Vietnam, where a Confucian political orthodoxy was entrenched.

Much of the Japanese political system and higher culture was based upon Chinese models.

Like India, Southeast Asia's location made the region's ports centers of trading networks that stretched from the South China Sea to the Indian Ocean and beyond. The earliest traders took sugarcane, bananas, and yams to Africa. During the era of the Roman empire, merchants brought silk from China. Later traders transported spices—

MAP 1-6 THE SPICE ISLANDS IN SOUTHEAST ASIA

Why were the territories of Southeast Asia likely to be a meeting point of merchants from all over the Eurasian land mass? Does the location of these islands enable you to guess which cities and which regions were most likely to be favorite trading areas? Despite their small size, why were the Banda Islands such a focus of mercantile attention and why were the peoples in this area able to retain their preeminence in world trade for so long? Does Southeast Asia seem to fit the definition of a borderland area as discussed in the text?

especially cloves, nutmeg, and mace, as well as cinnamon and pepper—directly from Southeast Asia. Cloves, nutmeg, and mace grew only on the smallest of islands in Maluku (the Moluccas), whose inhabitants kept the secret of the cultivation and preparation of these spices to themselves. Indian traders had visited Southeast Asia before the common era, exchanging Indian cloth, gold, and silver for spices, pearls, and aromatic wood. In later centuries, Muslim traders transported spices from Maluku to markets in the Arab world, from which they made their way to Italian, mostly Venetian, merchants and were sold throughout Europe. The largest external market for commodities from Southeast Asia was China. The growing in-

volvement of Chinese merchants, as they maneuvered their vessels around the Malay Peninsula, gave rise to new port cities, which assisted in the creation of new and often more centralized states in the region. Merchants and seamen would lodge in these ports, waiting for favorable monsoon winds to arise. As the trade between Southeast Asia and China flourished, Chinese merchants moved into the ports to commingle and even compete with Hindu, Buddhist, and Muslim newcomers, as well as with the majority population, which had its own local beliefs and cultural systems. By 1300, Southeast Asia was an archipelago of overlapping religious communities and trading networks, and one of the world's great borderland regions.

VIEWS OF SOUTHEAST ASIA

Southeast Asia was the true meeting place on the Eurasian land mass. Here, the cultures of Islam, India, and China were in a constant state of mixing. It was home to Gujarati traders, Jews from the Islamic lands, Arab and Persian merchants, and Chinese middlemen. The geographical location of its major island complexes (today's Indonesia and Malay Peninsula) made it the mandatory stopping-off place for sailors and traders either on their way to southern China or Japan or, heading in the opposite direction, to India and the Middle East. Thus, some of its cities, notably the city of Melaka, supported themselves on commerce alone, having no agricultural hinterland to feed their city dwellers. Both Marco Polo and Ibn Battuta passed through this area and agreed on the rare spices that were to be found there as well as its critical importance to traders.

MARCO POLO ON JAVA   About 100 miles southeast of Bintan lies the island of Lesser Java. You may understand that it is not so little but what it extends to more than 2,000 miles in circumference. . . . The island abounds in treasure and in costly products, including aloe wood, brazil, ebony, spikenard, and many sorts of spice that never reach our country because of the length and perils of the way but are exported to Manzi and Cathay. . . . You must also know that the people of Ferlec [Periak in northern Sumatra] used all to be idolators, but owing to contact with Saracen [Muslim] merchants, who continually resort here in their ships, they have all been converted to the law of Mahomet [Muhammad].

IBN BATTUTA ON SUMATRA   We left these peoples and after twenty-five days we reached the island of al-Jawa [Sumatra], from which Jawi incense takes its name. We saw it at a distance of half a day's sail. It is green and very well wooded with coconuts, aceca palms, cloves, and Indian aloes . . . mango, . . . orange, and camphor reeds. These people buy and sell with little pieces of tin or unrefined Chinese gold. . . . I stayed in Sumatra with him [the Sultan] for fifteen days. After that I sought permission to travel for it was the season, since the voyage to China is not organized at any time. The Sultan prepared a junk for us, stocked it with provisions, and was most generous and kind, May God reward him! He sent one of his companions with us to be host to us on the junk. We sailed along his country for twenty-one nights. Then we reached Mul Jawa, which is the country of infidels. It extends for two months' travel. It has aromatics and good aloes of Qaqula and Qamara, both places being in the country. In the country of Sultan Al-Zahir in al-Jawa, there are only incense, camphor, some cloves, and some Indian aloes.

Source: *The Travels of Marco Polo*, translated and with an introduction by Ronald Latham (Harmondsworth, England: Penguin Books, 1958) pp. 252–53, and *The Travels of Ibn Battuta*, translated by H. A. R. Gibb, with revisions and notes from the Arab text edited by C. Defremery and B. R. Sanguinetti (Cambridge, England: Cambridge University Press, 1958–1994), vol. 3, pp. 876–80.

MONGOL CONQUESTS AND CONNECTIONS

> → *How did the Mongol empire further integrate Eurasia?*

Not all the borderland areas were comprised of island pockets between the larger cultures. Sometimes borderlands could straddle large territorial expanses between major cultures. Such was the case of the northern steppe between China and western Eurasia through which the overland trade routes passed. Located between the eastern and western flanks of Eurasia, the borderlands of the steppe harbored a particular nomadic culture. These borderland peoples of the north decisively shaped the histories of peoples within the borders of the Islamic world, China, the Indian subcontinent, and Europe.

The undulating steppe, which stretched from the Manchurian plain in the Far East to the Hungarian plain in Europe, was ideal for livestock herders. Living in tents and other temporary dwellings, steppe dwellers roamed with flocks of camels, horses, oxen, and sheep. Most nomads were master horse riders who moved around with all their possessions with them; many became expert at archery and would periodically launch raids on agricultural peoples living in far-off cities, rural hinterlands, and the oases of Central Asia. It was against such raids that the Chinese, over many centuries, constructed the Great Wall.

THE COMING OF THE MONGOLS

With their swift horses and fierce fighting techniques, the borderland peoples of the steppe eventually conquered much of Eurasia. Of all the invasions launched from the steppe, that of the thirteenth-century Mongols was the most spectacular. Most significantly, their dramatic expansion and conquest served to bring the peoples of Eurasia closer together by facilitating trade and cultural exchange on a much larger scale. The Mongols' expansionist thrust began in 1206, when a cluster of tribes joined into a united force. A large gathering of clan heads acclaimed one of those present as Chinggis (Genghis) Khan, or Supreme Ruler. Chinggis (c. 1155–1227) subsequently launched a series of conquests southward across the Great Wall of China, and westward through Central Asia to Afghanistan and Persia. The armies of his son and first successor reached both the Pacific Ocean and the Adriatic Sea. His grandsons founded dynasties in China, Persia, and on the southern Eurasian steppes east of Europe (see Map 1-7). Thus, a realm took shape that was more than 6,000 miles in width and that touched all four of Eurasia's larger worlds.

> *With their swift horses and fierce fighting techniques, the borderland peoples of the steppe eventually conquered much of Eurasia.*

THE MONGOL PEOPLE Who were these conquerors of territories so much larger than their own? The Mongols were a combination of forest and prairie peoples. Residing in circular, felt-covered tents, which they shared with some of their animals, the Mongols lived by a combination of hunting and livestock herding. A mobile society, they changed campgrounds with the seasons, hunting game and herding livestock south in winter and north in summer. Life on the steppes was a constant struggle, which meant that only the strong survived. Their food, consisting primarily of animal products from their herds or from game they hunted, provided high levels of protein, which built up their muscle mass and added to their strength. Always on the march, the Mongols created a society that resembled a perpetual standing army. Their bands were organized into strictly disciplined military units led by commanders chosen for their skill. Mongol archers, using a heavy compound bow, made of sinew, wood, and horns, could fire an arrow more than 200 yards at full gallop with accuracy. Mongol horses were stocky, and capable of withstanding extreme cold. Their saddles had high

supports in front and back, enabling the warriors to ride and maneuver at high speeds. Iron stirrups permitted the riders to rise in their saddles to shoot their arrows without stopping. The Mongols were expert horsemen, who could remain in the saddle all day and night, even sleeping while their horses continued on the move. Each warrior kept many horses, enabling Mongol armies to travel as many as sixty or seventy miles per day. Between military campaigns, soldiers kept sharp by engaging in winter hunting.

Between and during their military campaigns, Mongol warriors took many wives. One Franciscan friar, sent in 1245 to the Mongols to baptize and spy on them, explained that every Mongol man "has as many wives as he can afford; some have a hundred, some fifty, some ten." The missionary added that when a Mongol died, his brother or uncle could marry his widow; a son could even marry his father's widow, provided the woman was his stepmother. Each wife had a separate tent, arranged in order of seniority. Women in Mongol society were responsible for childrearing as well as breeding and birthing the livestock, and shearing, milking, and processing pelts for clothing. But women also took part in battles, riding horses into combat alongside their fathers, husbands, and brothers. And unlike almost any other women in thirteenth-century Europe or Asia, Mongol women had the right to own property and even to divorce their husbands.

MONGOL CONQUEST AND EMPIRE Mongol success rested on a combination of ruthlessness and cleverness. The Mongols made considerable use of espionage, identifying the discontented among their enemies and using bribes to turn them into "collaborators." When they came up against fortified cities, they organized sieges, using flaming arrows and catapults. When sieges proved unsuccessful, they would fake a retreat, then suddenly return, catching their enemies off guard. Those who resisted the Mongols were usually annihilated, while those who submitted were offered a role in the ever-expanding Mongol empire. Each victory increased Mongol strength, bringing artisans, engineers, and astrologers, as well as new soldiers, slaves, and ever more wives. While warriors continued to take pride in their separate existence, they were drawn by conquest into the cultural life of Eurasia, and Buddhist, Islamic, and Christian ideas circulated within their communities.

What drove the Mongols to create one of the world's greatest empires? At least initially, Mongol conquests may have arisen from the nomads' need for grazing lands. Second, as the Mongols moved into new lands, they were able to increase their wealth massively by extracting taxes through their tributary system. Indeed, trade disputes spurred many of the Mongols' first expansions. Dependent on trade with settled peoples,

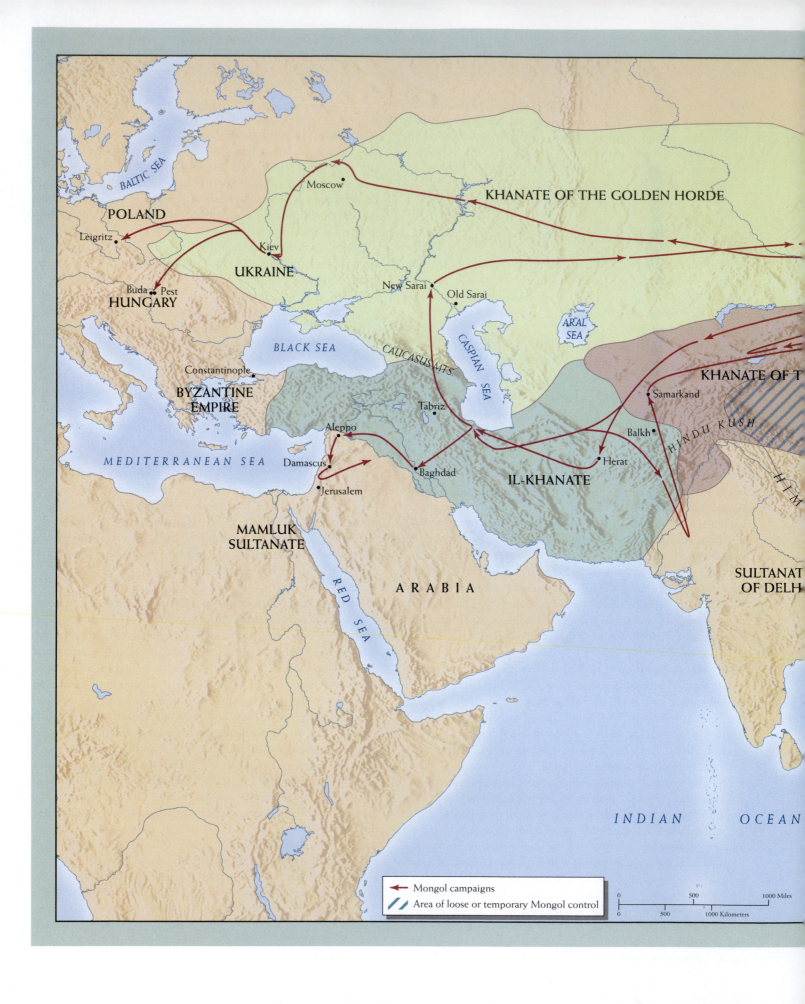

BALTIC SEA

POLAND

Leignitz

Moscow

KHANATE OF THE GOLDEN HORDE

Kiev

UKRAINE

Buda • Pest
HUNGARY

New Sarai • Old Sarai

ARAL SEA

KHANATE OF T

BLACK SEA

CAUCASUS MTS.

CASPIAN SEA

Samarkand

Constantinople

BYZANTINE
EMPIRE

Tabriz

Balkh

HINDU KUSH

Aleppo

Herat

MEDITERRANEAN SEA

Damascus

Baghdad

IL-KHANATE

Jerusalem

MAMLUK
SULTANATE

ARABIA

SULTANAT
OF DELH

RED SEA

INDIAN   OCEAN

→ Mongol campaigns

Area of loose or temporary Mongol control

0   500   1000 Miles

0   500   1000 Kilometers

S I B E R I A

MONGOL ANCESTRAL
HOMELAND

Karakorum

GOBI DESERT

GATAI

TIBET

Shangdu
(Xanadu)
Dadu

Khanbaliq (Beijing)

KHANATE OF THE
GREAT KHAN
(YUAN EMPIRE)

Kaifeng

Yangzhou

Hangzhou

KORYO

JAPAN

Kyoto

SEA
OF
JAPAN

PACIFIC

OCEAN

BURMA

Guangzhou

KHMER
EMPIRE

ANNAM

CHAMPA

SOUTH
CHINA
SEA

MAP 1-7   THE MONGOL EMPIRES, 1280

The Mongols understood their empire as a collection of conquered peoples, some of whom were nomadic tribes. What would be
the best way to represent such a nonterritorial, mobile empire on a map? What appear to be the bases for the boundaries of the
Mongol khanates? Do the boundary lines follow rivers, seas, and mountains, and to what extent do they take account of political
units, like the old Chinese empire and the conquered Islamic states? What areas of great wealth fell under Mongol control? What
wealthy areas remained beyond Mongol control?

especially for grain, but also for manufactured goods, including iron for tools, wagons, weapons, bridles, and stirrups, the first expansionist forays followed caravan routes. Here were opportunities to raid instead of trade.

Unlike many nomads, who disappeared after gathering plunder, Mongol raiders built a more permanent empire by incorporating conquered peoples and by absorbing some of their ways. They did this most directly through intermarriage. Chinggis began this process by scrutinizing newly conquered peoples, picking from them the best warriors, marrying them to Mongol women, and making them part of the Mongol armies. Before he died in 1227, he established that any succeeding Great Khan, as well as the heads of any major subsection of his lands, had to be his direct male descendant. Because succession involved a bloody conflict among all contenders to ensure strong leadership, it sometimes passed to a khan's eldest living brother, an ambiguity that could give rise to multiple claimants to the throne and deadly feuds. But despite the incorporation of many disparate peoples, and the Mongol aristocracy's partial assimilation into the cultures of the peoples they conquered, no one from a clan other than Chinggis's was recognized as ruler.

A thirteenth-century European visitor to the Mongol imperial capital at Karakorum in Mongolia was astounded that the entire encampment was smaller than the French village of St. Denis, while the Mongol imperial palace was said to be one-tenth the size of the St. Denis monastery. Mongol power derived not from permanent population centers (cities), however, but from the kinship loyalties and the extraordinary mobility of their society. In terms of population, Mongol armies, which grew to 200,000 men, were far larger than all but a handful of thirteenth-century cities. And like cities, Mongol armies took what they needed from the countryside. Indeed, by living off the land and helping themselves to everything they found, soldiers overcame problems of long-distance supply. Thus was a Mongol-speaking population, which probably numbered no more than 2 million in the thirteenth century, able to conquer much of Eurasia.

Conquest, of course, was one thing; ruling was another. Not only were the conquerors few in number compared with the peoples they subjugated, but almost all of the Mongols were illiterate. They also lacked experience in governing complex settled societies. In China, for example, just 700,000 Mongols inhabited a realm whose total population was more than one hundred times larger and whose bureaucratic officialdom could communicate in writing in a common language.

Just as they incorporated foreigners in their armies, so they brought foreigners into the administration of conquered lands. To govern China, the Mongols imported Uighurs, Tibetans, Persians, and various Turkish peoples, playing off Christians against Muslims and appointing Chinese only to subordinate

posts. They also introduced Hungarian slaves, Venetian traders, Byzantine craftsmen, Islamic merchants, and Indian holy men, making the Mongol court a true microcosm of the known world (Persian was used as the international language). To facilitate communication, the Mongols established 10,000 postal relay stations that used 300,000 horses to disseminate directives and to keep them informed of developments (messengers traveled up to 250 miles in a single day, often sleeping in the saddle). Most impressive of all, the Mongols and their multinational advisers conducted censuses of all their subjects—not just in China, but throughout Central Asia, Persia, and the Slavic principalities. Enumerated subjects were then organized into military units and taxed.

In addition to the problems of conquest and administration, the Mongols faced the question of perpetuating their rule. Chinggis handled the matter of succession by dividing his possessions among his four sons. One son claimed the oases and trading cities of Central Asia, which after 1300 adopted Islam. Another son, in the steppe east of Europe, in Slavic Russia, established what eventually became known as the Golden Horde, whose leaders also converted to Islam around 1313. To the south, in Persia and Mesopotamia, which were wealthier than the Slavic principalities, a grandson of Chinggis founded a dynasty, and took the title Il-khan (secondary khan). Around 1300, the Il-khan converted from Buddhism to Islam, changing his title to sultan.

> *Just as the Mongols incorporated foreigners in their armies, so they brought foreigners into the administration of conquered lands.*

Yet another grandson, Kubilai, completed the conquest of the grandest prize of all—China. Conquering both the Jin empire in the north and the Song empire in the south, Kubilai founded the Yuan empire in China. Moreover, he fought in a civil war with his brother, and when he won, he was named the Mongol Great Khan, or khan of khans. With China conquered, Kubilai moved the location of the Mongol court from the camping grounds at Karakorum to the site of present-day Beijing. Kubilai did not stop with the conquest of China, however. During his long reign as Great Khan (1260–1294), Kubilai and his Mongol-led armies also overran the Korean peninsula. And after a Korean scholar at the Mongol court spoke of the wealth on the Japanese islands, Kubilai twice dispatched formidable armies to subjugate Japan. Several unanticipated raging typhoons sank the Great Khan's armada, however, drowning tens of thousands of Mongol soldiers. To this day, the Japanese celebrate the "divine winds" (*kamikaze*) that saved their islands. (Nonetheless, the expenses incurred to ward off the two attempted Mongol invasions of Japan did lead to the collapse of the political order.) Nor did the Mongols enjoy markedly more success in establishing their authority over Southeast Asia. The area's reputation for spices and other forms of wealth attracted invading Mongol forces, but here, too, the sea and the dense tropical vegetation worked against the Mongol forces.

THE MONGOL LEGACY

Impressive and merciless as it was, the Mongol empire never penetrated the heart of Christendom, and it collapsed in China and Persia within about a hundred years after it was established. It collapsed because it was overstretched and forced to rely on local bureaucrats to operate the instruments of administration. The Yuan state disappeared in China in the fourteenth century. The Il-khan's Mongol state, which ruled over the old Persian empire from Azerbaijan, broke up at just about the same time. Though their reign was short-lived, the Mongols left a legacy of frightful massacres. In some areas of settled life, such as northeastern Persia, the Mongols' destructive march obliterated whole societies. Still, the Mongols' legacy was not limited to blood and terror. Throughout Eurasia, the arrival of the Mongols also fostered commercial and cultural exchanges, as the Mongol rulers protected trade routes so that merchants, travelers, and diplomats could move about safely. Those connections outlasted Mongol rule and decisively shaped the subsequent course of world history.

China, which was perhaps the most important of the Mongol conquests, displayed well the paradoxical legacy of Mongol rule. On the one hand, the Yuan dynasty that the Mongols established tried to repress some of the openness that had characterized Chinese society. Yuan laws divided China's population into a hierarchical order of Mongols, western and central Asians, northern Chinese, and southern Chinese, with legal privileges being heaped on the first two groups. The top echelon of government offices was restricted to non-Chinese, and several decades of rule passed before the Mongols instituted a pale version of the civil service examination in 1315. The Yuan also classified their subjects by occupations, which were deemed hereditary. Needless to say, these innovations generated resentment and resistance among a Chinese population that had grown accustomed to more fluid possibilities.

Even as the Mongols closed some of the paths to wealth and well-being that had been available to the Chinese, the conquerors opened and enriched Chinese civilization in other ways. In China, the Mongols introduced many Persian, Islamic, and Byzantine influences that affected architecture, art, science, and medicine. The Yuan policy of benign tolerance for foreign creeds and consistent contacts with western Asia also brought elements from Christianity, Judaism, Zoroastrianism, and Islam into the Chinese mix. Above all, the policy made possible the further development of Buddhism and Daoism, the two most powerful religious forces of the country. Indeed, the Yuan directed a substantial portion of imperial patronage to support the Tibetan strand of Buddhist belief—Tibetan Lamaism. Taking advantage of their favored status, large numbers of Tibetan clergy flocked to China, with Hangzhou being the destination of many. Yuan China also played host to Buddhist monks from Japan, who undertook the journey to establish contacts with the great masters of Chinese Chan (Zen) Buddhism.

Perhaps the Mongols' greatest impact was on the lands they began to conquer then abandoned: central and western Europe. Chinese innovations such as gunpowder and woodblock printing were carried west by released Christian slaves and merchants. For astute Muslim observers, such as the physician to the Il-khans, Rashid al-Din (1247–1318), who was born to Jewish parents, converted to Islam, and wrote a comprehensive history of the entire Mongol empire, the sophistication and wealth of the Orient, including China, was no revelation. But to Europeans such as Marco Polo, who visited and worked for the Mongol court in China, the East was a sensation.

By bringing Eurasian worlds under a more unified rule, the Mongols extended cross-cultural contacts and encouraged increased trade across longer distances. Because their armies eliminated rivals and other sources of power in their domains, the Mongols created a sort of peace that lowered the costs and risks of doing business. Merchants, using silver in Europe, gold in the Middle East, and copper in China, were able to establish partnerships and arrange for the shipment of goods to far-off places. Shared credit systems and accounting techniques enabled merchants to organize the orderly transfers of riches in a far-flung, albeit narrow, network across Eurasia. Merchants and other travelers were given *paizi*, lockets with an epigraph in Uighur script, which warned would-be bandits that the bearer had the official seal and thus the backing of the mighty Khan. In addition, the Mongols established many new, secure way stations along trade routes for caravans of merchants. These endured long after the Mongols had lost their place as rulers of much of Eurasia.

> *By bringing Eurasian worlds under a more unified rule, the Mongols extended cross-cultural contacts and encouraged increased trade across longer distances.*

 CONCLUSION

All thirteenth-century societies featured inequalities of various kinds. Within each of the time's many worlds, heredity, gender, age, learning, and wealth shaped who got more and who got less. For many people, these internal arrangements were all that mattered; local orientations left them with little if any knowledge of worlds other than their own. Such localism characterized the vast majority of people who lived during the thirteenth century, whether they resided in the Americas, Oceania, or sub-Saharan Africa, or in one of the four major cultural areas of Eurasia. Indeed, there were no true globalists during this time; no one who lived then was aware of the existence, much less the relative affluence, of all worlds.

Although no traveler crossed the Atlantic or Pacific, an increasing number ventured through the lands of Africa, Europe, and Asia. The two most famous of these thirteenth- and fourteenth-century travelers, Marco Polo and Ibn Battuta, encountered a world tied together by trade routes that crossed the Asian continent and the Indian Ocean and that often had as their ultimate destination the imperial court of the Great Khan in China.

These two men and similar, though less-celebrated travelers, observed worlds that were both highly localized and yet had culturally unifying features. Because of these unifying characteristics, long-distance travelers in the thirteenth and four-teenth centuries could easily distinguish the House of Islam from the Middle Kingdom of China, or the mosaic of India, or the domain of Christianity. In the first, the life and teachings of Muhammad and the simplicity of a creed that affirmed that "there is no God but Allah" gave disparate peoples from widely different geographical areas a powerful sense of their Islamic identity. In the same fashion, an imperial structure, centered on an emperor and a bureaucratic scholarly class and based on filial values as enshrined in the Confucian classics, led to a Chinese identity. The Indian world embraced more diversity, with its many religious, ethnic, and linguistic traditions, but this very diversity and tolerance for different cultural patterns was the hallmark of the culture of the Indian subcontinent. Finally, in Christian Europe, people derived a sense of unity from a common religious tradition and a clerical language.

Three of the Eurasian worlds aspired to enlarged, indeed, universal recognition: the Islamic world, China, and Christian Europe. Of the three, the Muslims had spread furthest by 1300. From its holy cities in the Arabian peninsula, to which all adherents looked, Islam extended from East Asia to Western Europe and reached into sub-Saharan Africa as well. In contrast to Muslim elites, the Chinese ruling elements did not have a worldwide military or religious mission, but they nonetheless expected other peoples to acknowledge the superiority of Chinese ways, by bringing tribute and by copying the institutions of the Middle Kingdom. Chinese influence radiated through East Asia, into the Korean peninsula, the Japanese islands, and Southeast Asia. By contrast, the universalist vision of Christian Europe had achieved much less by 1300. Europe had experienced great internal colonization and settlement, and had seen the conversion of its northern pagan peoples to Christianity. But Christendom's effort to reclaim the holy lands from Muslim overlords in the crusades had failed. Even within Europe itself, large numbers of Muslim peoples resisted the call for conversion.

At either end of Eurasia—in the difficult geographical and climatic circumstances of the Asian north and the sub-Saharan south—enormous territories were sparsely populated. From one of these areas, beyond the reach of the four major cultural worlds, emerged the Mongols, who swept south and west and conquered much of Eurasia. Notwithstanding their terrible destructiveness, the Mongols ended up deepening the connections between the peoples of Europe and Asia. Worlds that had been apart grew closer together, with conquest and trade establishing stronger connections between these regions.

Although death and destruction accompanied the Mongol conquests, their long-term effects were altogether more benign. The securing and expanding of long-distance trade routes and the fashioning of a *Pax Mongolica* across a large segment of the Eurasian land mass brought unprecedented prosperity and population expansion to the four great cultural domains of this part of the world. But prosperity and population growth were to prove short-lived as Eurasia encountered another of the unanticipated side effects of the Mongol conquests—the spread of the pandemic Black Death.

Chronology

889–1431	Kingdom of Angkor in Southeast Asia
1096–1270	Crusades to the Holy Land
1126	Jurchens establish Jin empire in China
1127–1279	Southern Song empire
1200	Rise of Sultanate of Kilwa in East Africa
1206	Mongol tribes unite under Chinggis Khan
1206–1290	Delhi Sultanate in India
1215	Fourth Lateran Council in Rome
1230	Consolidation of Mali empire in West Africa
1234	Fall of Jin dynasty to Mongols
1250	Mamluk dynasty established in Egypt
1258	Fall of Abbasid empire to Mongols
1265–1335	Il-khanate in Iraq and Persia
1271–1295	Marco Polo travels to East Asia
1271	Mongols found Yuah dynasty in China
1274	Mongols attempt to invade Japan
1279	End of Southern Song empire
1281	Second Mongol attempt to invade Japan
1300	Rise of Kingdom of Great Zimbabwe
1313	Last Mongol Il-khan converts to Islam
1324–1325	Mansa Musa makes pilgrimage to Mecca
1325–1369	Ibn Battuta travels the Islamic world
1325	Mexicas found Tenochtitlán
1333	Collapse of Kamakura political order in Japan

 FURTHER READINGS

Abu-Lughod, Janet, *Before European Hegemony: The World System A.D. 1250–1350* (1989). A classic work offering a challenging, sweeping interpretation.

Ahmed, Leila, *Women and Gender in Islam: Historical Roots of a Modern Debate* (1992). An admirable treatment of the place of women in the Islamic world.

Bartlett, Robert, *The Making of Europe: Conquest, Colonization and Cultural Change 950–1350* (1993). Describes how Europeans discovered their own continent, clearing its forests for agriculture and developing an identity.

Bernhardt, Kathryn, *Women and Property in China, 960–1949* (1999). Traces the changes in the property rights of women through the centuries.

Bethell, Leslie (ed.), *The Cambridge History of Latin America*, vol. 1 (1984). General essays on what is called "pre-Columbian" history of native peoples of current Latin America.

Bose, Sugata, and Ayesha Jalal, *Modern South Asia* (1998). Good for its attention to recent scholarship.

Boyle, John Andrew, *The Mongol World Empire 1206–1370* (1977). A classic overview of the Mongol empire.

Braudel, Fernand, *The Structures of Everyday Life: Civilization and Capitalism, Fifteenth–Eighteenth Centuries*, trans. Sian Reynolds (1979). A pioneering work in the field of world history. This book is a good place to begin, although Braudel has written many others that are equally noteworthy.

Bruhns, Karen Olsen, *Ancient South America* (1994). A comprehensive discussion of ancient South America.

Cambridge History of the Native Peoples of the Americas (1996). A comprehensive, three-volume synthesis of the history of Native Americans.

Carr-Saunders, A. M., *World Population: Past Growth and Present Trends* (1936). A useful book to begin with when looking for information on the population of the world in modern times.

Chattopadhyaya, B. D., *The Making of Early Medieval India* (1997). A series of excellent essays on the period.

Clendinnen, Inga, *Aztecs: An Interpretation* (1991). Brilliantly reconstructs the culture of Tenochtitlán in the years before its conquest by the Spaniards.

Coquery-Vidrovitch, Catherine, *African Women: A Modern History* (1997). An overview of the history of African women.

Ebrey, Patricia Buckley, *The Inner Quarters: Marriage and the Lives of Chinese Women in the Sung Period* (1993). An overview of the different aspects of women's lives at a time of significant social changes in China that set the stage for 1300 and beyond.

Frank, Andre Gunder, *ReOrient: Global Economy in the Asian Age* (1998). A provocative and useful work that has informed the study of world history.

Gernet, Jacques, *Daily Life in China: On the Eve of the Mongol Invasion, 1250–1276* (1962). Originally published in French in 1959, this remains an informative volume, particularly on the urban social landscape of thirteenth-century China.

Hodgson, Marshall, *The Venture of Islam: Conscience and History in a World Civilization* (1974). A useful, three-volume study of the Islamic world.

Iliffe, John, *Africans: The History of a Continent* (1995). A good general history of Africa.

Josephy, Alvin M., Jr. (ed.), *America in 1492: The World of the Indian Peoples before the Arrival of Columbus* (1993). A collection of excellent essays by leading scholars synthesizing what we know about the precolonial histories of the various regions of the Americas.

Kosambi, D. D., *An Introduction to the Study of Indian History* (2nd rev. ed., 1985). A classic, Marxist history written for the general reader.

Kulke, Herman, and Deitmar Rothermund, *A History of India* (1991). A work whose emphasis is on the pre-modern period.

Lewis, Bernard, *The Middle East: Two Thousand Years of History from the Rise of Christianity to the Present Day* (1995). A book on the Middle East in general and the Islamic world specifically.

Mass, Jeffrey P., *Antiquity and Anachronism in Japanese History* (1992). A collection of brilliant essays dissecting the modern myths projected back onto medieval Japan.

McNeill, William, *The Rise of the West: History of the Human Community* (1963). A fine work by a pioneer in the study of world history.

Miyasaki, Ichisada, *China's Examination Hell: The Civil Service Examinations of Imperial China* (1976). A classic work, first published in Japanese in 1963.

Mote, F. W., *Imperial China, 900–1800* (1999). A recent magisterial survey on politics and society over a wide span of Chinese history.

Oliver, Roland, *The African Experience: Major Themes in African History from Earliest Times to the Present* (1991). A good general history of Africa.

Robinson, Francis (ed.), *The Cambridge Illustrated History of the Islamic World* (1996). A valuable work on the Islamic world.

Rossabi, Morris (ed.), *China Among Equals: The Middle Kingdom and Its Neighbors, Tenth–Eighteenth Centuries* (1983). A superb work on the Mongols in China.

Shaffer, Lynda Norene, *Maritime Southeast Asia to 1500* (1996). A useful study of the spices of Southeast Asia that drew so many Asian merchants into this region.

Spuler, Bertold (ed.), *History of the Mongols* (1972). An excellent collection of translated thirteenth- and fourteenth-century travelers' documents.

Stein, Burton, *A History of India* (1998). A readable, general textbook, notable for its good coverage of the southern part of the Indian subcontinent.

Thapar, Romila, *A History of India* (1965). Nearly forty years old, but a classic work on the pre-Mughal period.

Wink, Andre, *Al-Hind: The Making of the Indo-Islamic World* (1990). An important work of interpretation that places the history of the subcontinent in the framework of the Islamic world.

Wolpert, Stanley, *A New History of India* (4th ed., 1993). A good book for anecdotes on India.

Chapter

2

CRISES AND RECOVERY IN EURASIA, 1300s–1500s

When Mongol armies besieged the Genoese trading outpost of Caffa on the Black Sea in 1346, they not only damaged old trading links between the Far East and the Mediterranean, they also unleashed an even more devastating, invisible force. Mongol troops entered the city and brought with them a disease picked up in the Gobi Desert: the bubonic plague. Defeated Genoese merchants and soldiers withdrew, inadvertently taking the germs with them aboard their ships. By the time they arrived in Messina, Sicily, half the passengers were dead. The rest were dying. Those who waited eagerly on shore were horrified at the sight and turned the ship away. Desperately, the ship's captain went to the next port, only to face the same fate. The Europeans were unable to keep the plague (referred to as the Black Death) from reaching their shores. As it spread from port to port, it eventually contaminated all of Europe, killing about one-third of its population.

This story exemplifies one of the many disruptive effects of the Mongol invasions on societies across the Eurasian land mass. These invasions ushered in an age in which people of dispersed worlds engaged in greater communication and contact across cultural and political borders. But in establishing and extending channels of exchange, the Mongols unwittingly created conduits for the flow of

43

microbes to follow the land trails and sea lanes of human voyagers. These germs devastated societies even more decisively than did the Mongols. They were the real "murderous hordes" of world history, infecting people from every community, class, and culture they encountered. So staggering was the magnitude of the Black Death's toll that Eurasia did not regain the population densities of the thirteenth century for another 200 years. It shook many communities to their very core. The new world of interconnectedness that the Mongols had fostered fell apart. The most severely affected were those regions and populations that the Mongols had brought together. Settlements and commercial hubs along the old silk route and around the Mediterranean Sea and the South China Sea became places of dying. While segments of the Indian Ocean trading world experienced death and disruption, the Indian subcontinent, which had escaped the Mongol conquest, was also spared the wholesale dying and political disruptions associated with the Black Death.

During the fourteenth and fifteenth centuries, following population loss, political crises, and widespread social disorders often caused by the plague, many Eurasian societies recovered their political vitality. They began to rebuild their communities and to improvise new means of ruling. Many of the Eurasians turned to well-tried and familiar dynastic ideas—rule by royal hereditary households—to restore order and stability once the microbes had done their damage. The new rulers, merchants, and scholar-bureaucrats revived the old links between communities and pioneered new commercial networks. In so doing, they created new polities, economic institutions, and social hierarchies across Eurasia—a world in which imperial dynasties became ever more important.

This chapter explores how Eurasian societies coped with and responded to the long-term impact of the Mongol invasions and the Black Death. We leave for subsequent chapters the discussions of political changes beyond Eurasia. Here, we focus on how, in the wake of political instability and devastating plague, Eurasian societies rebuilt their political orders, creating centralized power structures that lasted for centuries and that shaped their encounters with peoples and polities in Africa and the Americas.

COLLAPSE AND INTEGRATION

> → *What were the key factors in rebuilding political societies?*

While the Mongol invasions overturned political systems, the plague devastated society itself. The devastation wiped out entire populations, and in so doing, undermined the political foundations of many of Eurasia's societies. Eurasia's rulers could explain the assaults of outside "barbarians" to their people, but it was much harder for them to make sense of the invisible enemy. Many concluded fatalistically that mass death was God's wish. Following the upheaval wrought by the plague, however, Eurasians worked to rebuild their states and trading networks. To consolidate and centralize their power, rulers made dynastic matches, put in place new armies and taxes to support them, and established new systems to administer their states.

THE BLACK DEATH

The spread of the Black Death out of Mongolia and other parts of Central Asia, where it originated, was the single most significant historical development for much of the Eurasian world in the fourteenth century. The disease stemmed from a combination of bubonic, pneumonic, and septicaemic plague strains and resulted in a frightening loss of life. Among infected populations, death rates ranged from 25 to 50 percent.

How did the Black Death spread so far? One explanation seems to have been the climatic changes of this period. A drying up of the Central Asian steppe borderlands forced the pastoral peoples living there to move south into closer proximity to settled, agricultural communities. So, it is thought, began the migration of microbes. But what spread germs across Eurasia was the Mongols' economic and political grid. Breaking out first around the 1320s in Yunnan province of southwestern China,

Focus Questions CRISES AND RECOVERY IN EURASIA

→ *What were the key factors in rebuilding political societies?*
→ *What were the major differences among the three Islamic dynasties?*
→ *How did the Ming centralize their authority?*
→ *Why was Europe so disunited (compared to China and Islam)?*

Plague Victim. The plague was highly contagious and quickly led to death. Here the physician and his helper cover their noses to avoid the unbearable stench emanating from the patient; they can do little to help the victim as they do not understand what causes the boils, internal bleeding, or violent coughing that afflicts him.

the plague spread throughout China, and then traversed the major Eurasian trade routes (see Map 2-1). The main avenue of transmission was across Central Asia to the Crimea and the Black Sea, and from there by ship to the Italian city-states. Secondary routes were by sea, one from China to the Red Sea, and another across the Indian Ocean, through the Persian Gulf, and into the Fertile Crescent and Iraq. All routes terminated at the Italian port cities, where ships with dead and dying men aboard arrived in October 1347. From there, what Europeans at the time called the Pestilence or the Great Mortality spread across the western end of the Eurasian land mass.

The Black Death struck an expanding Eurasian population, made vulnerable because its members had no immunities to the disease and because its major cultural realms were now connected through more intensively used trading networks. Rodents, mainly rats, carried the plague bacilli that caused the disease. Fleas transmitted the bacilli from rodent to rodent, as

well as to humans. The epidemic was terrifying, for the disease had not been seen for centuries and its causes were unknown. The infected died quickly, sometimes overnight, and with great suffering, coughing up blood and oozing pus and blood from ugly black sores the size of eggs. Some European wise men attributed the ravaging of their continent to astrological forces; they suspected an unusual alignment of the planets Saturn, Jupiter, and Mars as the cause. Many believed that God was angry with man. The Florentine historian Matteo Villani compared the plague to the biblical Flood and believed that the end of mankind was imminent.

The Black Death wrought devastation throughout much of the Eurasian land mass. Entire populations perished. The Chinese population plunged from around 120 million to 80 million over the course of a century. Europe saw its numbers reduced by one-third. When farmers were afflicted, food production collapsed. As a result, famine often followed the disease, thereby killing off the weak survivors. But the worst afflicted were those in the crowded cities, especially in the ports along the Eurasian coast, which had been the hubs of trade and migration and where settlement was most dense. Some cities lost up to two-thirds of their population. Refugees from the cities fled their homes, seeking security and food in the countryside. The shortage of food and other necessities led to rapidly rising prices, strikes, and unrest across Eurasia. Political leaders added to their unpopularity by repressing unrest. The great Arab historian Ibn Khaldun (1332–1406), who lost his mother and father and a number of his teachers to the Black Death in Tunis, underscored the sense of desolation in the wake of the plague, saying, "Cities and buildings were laid waste, roads and way signs were obliterated, settlements and mansions became empty, dynasties and tribes grew weak. The entire world changed."

REBUILDING STATES

Starting in the late fourteenth century, Eurasians began the task of rebuilding their political order and reconstructing their trading networks. Rebuilding military and tax administrations could not be tackled without political legitimacy. In much of Eurasia, this was the challenge of the fourteenth century. In the wake of disease, rulers needed to revive confidence in themselves and their polities, which they did by inculcating among their supporters myths that stressed their legitimacy and by strengthening relationships with their subject peoples.

The basis for power was the dynasty—the hereditary ruling family that passed power from one generation to the next. Dynasties sought to establish their legitimacy in three fundamental ways: First, the ruling families insisted that they belonged in power as a calling from above. The Ming emperors in China traditionally claimed a "mandate of heaven," while European monarchs began to claim to rule by "divine right." Either way, ruling households claimed to be closer to the gods than to commoners. Second, leaders attempted to prevent

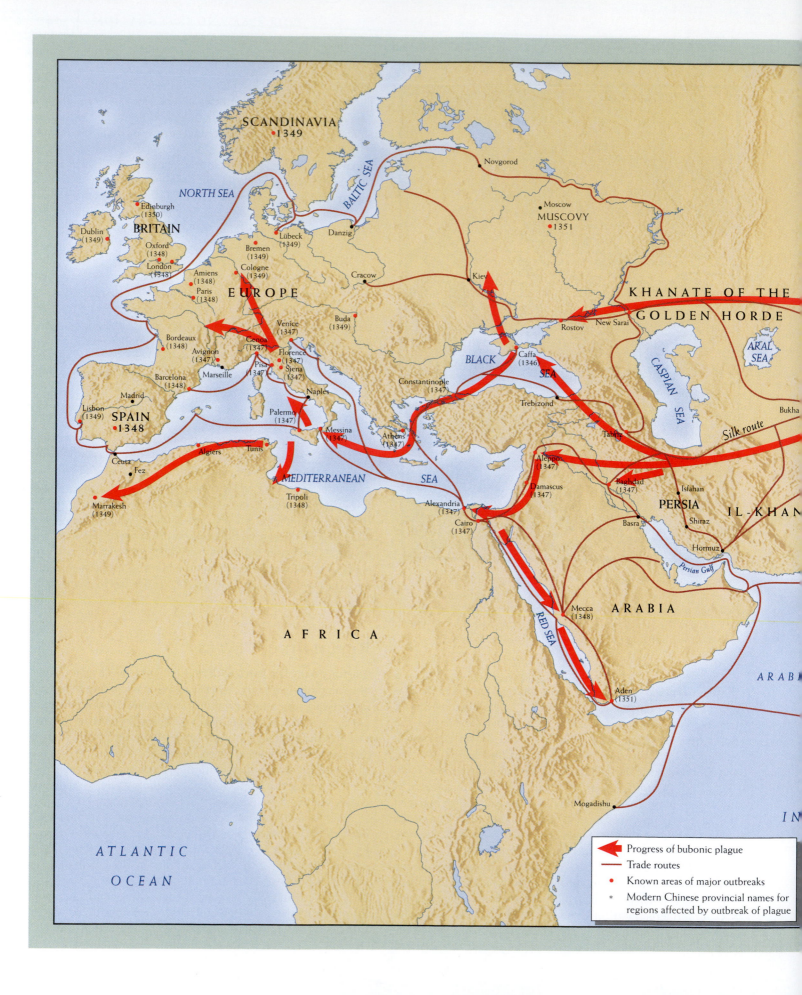

SCANDINAVIA
•1349

NORTH SEA

BALTIC SEA

Novgorod

Edinburgh
(1350)

Dublin
(1349)

BRITAIN

Oxford
(1348)

London
(1348)

Amiens
(1348)

Paris
(1348)

Bremen
(1349)

Cologne
(1349)

Lübeck
(1349)

Danzig

Cracow

Moscow

MUSCOVY
•1351

KHANATE OF THE
GOLDEN HORDE

New Sarai

Rostov

Kiev

ARAL
SEA

EUROPE

Bordeaux
(1348)

Avignon
(1347)

Barcelona
(1348)

Marseille

Venice
(1347)

Genoa
(1347)

Pisa
(1347)

Florence
(1347)

Siena
(1347)

Buda
(1349)

Naples

Constantinople
(1347)

BLACK

Caffa
(1346)

SEA

Trebizond

CASPIAN

SEA

Silk route

Bukha

Madrid

Lisbon
(1349)

SPAIN
•1348

Palermo
(1347)

Messina
(1347)

Athens
(1347)

Aleppo
(1347)

Tabriz

PERSIA

Isfahan

IL-KHAN

Ceuta

Fez

Algiers

Tunis

MEDITERRANEAN

SEA

Alexandria
(1347)

Damascus
(1347)

Baghdad
(1347)

Shiraz

Basra

Marrakesh
(1349)

Tripoli
(1348)

Cairo
(1347)

Hormuz

Persian Gulf

AFRICA

RED SEA

Mecca
(1348)

ARABIA

ARAB

Aden
(1351)

Mogadishu

ATLANTIC

OCEAN

IN

Progress of bubonic plague

Trade routes

Known areas of major outbreaks

* Modern Chinese provincial names for
regions affected by outbreak of plague

MAP 2-1   THE SPREAD OF THE BLACK DEATH

The Black Death was a Eurasian pandemic of the fourteenth century. Use the map to identify its place of origin. Can you explain why certain parts of Eurasia were more severely affected than others? Why were its major places of outbreak located in China and Western Europe? The Black Death spread across the whole of the Mongol empire. Can you offer any explanation why the Mongol states were so involved?

squabbling and fighting among potential heirs by promulgating clear rules about succession to the throne. Clear-cut succession made it difficult for contenders to challenge the authority of the heir to the throne, thereby providing stability in an age of chaos. Third, ruling families also elevated their power through conquest or alliance—sending armies to extend their domains or having princes and princesses marry the rulers of other states or members of other elite households. Once it established its legitimacy, the royal family would seek to consolidate its power by enacting coercive laws and punishments and sending royal emissaries to govern far-flung territories. It would also establish standing armies and set up new administrative structures to collect taxes and to oversee building projects that would proclaim royal power.

State-building in the wake of great devastation was a complex process. It varied around the world, since the state-builders had different experiences with the Black Death (or little or no experience at all, as in India), had been conquered by the Mongols or had avoided conquest, and drew upon quite varied political traditions. Two of the successor Islamic states, the Ottoman empire and the Safavid state, had to deal with a large influx of Turkish-speaking peoples stemming from the Mongol invasion of the Islamic world; the third Islamic state, the Mughal empire in India, replaced the Delhi Sultanate, which had been seriously weakened, not by a Mongol army, but by Turkish warriors. These three Islamic states blended pre-Islamic political and religious traditions with their interpretation of Islam. The Ottomans embraced a Sunni, or orthodox, view of Islam, while adopting pre-existing Byzantine ways of ruling. The Safavids were adherents of Shiism and ardently devoted to the pre-Islamic traditions of Persia (present-day Iran). The Mughals carried even further the already well-developed Indian religious and political traditions for assimilating Islamic and pre-Islamic Indian ways. In China, the Ming renounced the Mongol legacy, extolling their pure Han Chinese identity and repudiating the Mongol eagerness to expand.

So successful were these rebuilding efforts that many of the states that emerged out of the turmoil of the Mongol invasions and the Black Death proved remarkably durable. The Ottoman empire and the Romanov state in Russia (see Chapter 4) lasted into the twentieth century. The monarchies of Western Christendom, though they did not have the long, unbroken line of succession that the Ottomans and Romanovs enjoyed, persisted for centuries. The imperial structures established by the Ming also proved long-lived in China, as did the dynasties in Persia, where a Safavid dynasty appeared, and in India, where the Mughal state came into being. Moreover, because these regimes lasted for such a long time, their political institutions

and cultural values became deeply embedded in the fabric of their societies and influenced the actions of rulers and subjects as they came into contact with foreigners.

ISLAMIC DYNASTIES

> → *What were the major differences among the three Islamic dynasties?*

In 1258 the Mongols sacked the great city of Baghdad, capital of the Abbasid empire. In a letter to Louis IX of France, the conqueror, Hulagu (one of the sons of Chinggis Khan), boasted that his forces had put 200,000 inhabitants of the city to death and had leveled the buildings of what had been one of the world's most elegant cities. The Mongols executed the Abbasid caliph by rolling him in a rug and and then having horses trample him to death. With his death, any lingering hope of restoring the political unity of Islam evaporated.

Instead of reunifying the House of Islam, the Mongol conquest and the ravages of the Black Death left much of the Muslim world in a state of near political and economic collapse. The Mongol forces that swept out of Central Asia and across the rich agricultural lands of Persia, Iraq, and Anatolia brought with them vast numbers of nomadic peoples and massive herds of sheep and horses. The army that assaulted Baghdad in 1258 numbered 150,000 soldiers and included another 750,000 women and children.

Although the Mongols were decisive in their conquest of Muslim political regimes, they failed to establish enduring dynasties. Part of their problem was that they were unable to shed their military orientation. The original Mongol state was organized for military action; economic advancement and culture occupied a decidedly secondary status in the minds of these military men. This is not to suggest that Mongol rulers once they had achieved territorial conquest ignored merchants and failed to patronize scholars and artists. Far from it. The Mongol Il-khanate in Persia was diligent in re-creating the old trade routes of the area and went out of its way to advance the arts. But the Mongol military men were unwilling to share power with other groups. The Persian Il-khans made Maraghah in Azerbaijan their capital, even though it was little more than an enlarged military encampment, in preference to the great administrative center of Baghdad. Even their acceptance of Islam did not secure widespread popular support. They continued to employ

Because the regimes of this period lasted for such a long time, their political institutions and cultural values became deeply embedded in the fabric of their societies.

terrorizing military tactics in dealing with their opponents, leveling recalcitrant villages and intimidating their subjects by parading the heads of their enemies on pikes before sullen resisters. The Il-khans in Persia faced the daunting task of integrating massive numbers of pastoral peoples—and their enormous herds—with settled farmers, and had meager success. When Muslims in different parts of the Mongol empire began to argue and then to fight with each other, the fate of Mongol rule was sealed.

Although they did not leave behind them institutional foundations for a new order, the Mongols did clear the political slate of the old order in much of the Islamic world. The new polities that began to emerge had to build from the ground floor. Warrior chiefs and charismatic religious leaders vied with one another to fill the political vacuum, attempting to enlarge their powers through strategic marriages and their claims to religious legitimacy. The new

> *Although the Mongols did not leave behind institutional foundations for a new order, they did clear the political slate of the old order in much of the Islamic world.*

rulers who appeared as Mongol power waned in the fourteenth century, notably the Ottomans in Anatolia and the Safavids in western Persia, began on a small scale. Operating out of strategic locations in the Islamic heartland, war leaders and religious devotees at the head of bands of followers gradually gained favor and rebuilt the institutions of rulership.

Through migration, warfare, and eventually the consolidation of post-Mongol states, the boundaries of Islam's domain spread. Prior to the Mongol incursions, the political, economic, and cultural centers of the Islamic world were to be found in Egypt, Syria, and Iraq. The majority of the inhabitants of these regions spoke Arabic, the language of the Prophet, and hence the language of Islamic devotion and theology. These areas, along with the Arabian peninsula, contained Islam's most holy cities: Mecca, Medina, Jerusalem, Damascus, Cairo, and various religious cities in Iraq. Even before the Mongol invasions, Turks had begun to enter these regions, and Persian had started to emerge as a rival language of Islamic poetry and philosophy. Yet, it was the Mongol invasions of the thirteenth century, with the devastation that they brought to Persia and Iraq and the influx of nomadic peoples, that opened the door for a new Islamic world to appear. The new world of Islam, based now to a much larger extent than before on Turkish- and Persian-speaking populations, emerged in a vast geographical triangle that stretched from Anatolia in the west to Khurasan in the east and to the southern apex at Baghdad. Of course, the old Arabic-speaking Islamic world did not die out, but it had to cede some of its hegemony to the new rulers and the new religious men who now came to the fore.

By the beginning of the sixteenth century, three new and powerful dynasties dominated much of the old Islamic world. Eventually, they grew powerful enough to become empires.

Between them, the Ottoman, Safavid, and Mughal empires used and developed the rich agrarian resources of the regions of the Indian Ocean and the Mediterranean Sea basin, and benefited from a brisk seaborne and overland trade. Of these three, the Ottomans were in full flourish at the beginning of the sixteenth century; the Safavids and Mughals were just beginning to emerge.

By the middle of the sixteenth century, the Mughals dominated northern India, the Safavids Persia, and the Ottomans Anatolia, the Arab world, and large parts of southern and eastern Europe. Sharing core Islamic beliefs, each empire had unique political features. The most centralized and powerful, the Ottoman empire, occupied the pivotal expanse between Europe and Asia. The Safavids took as their mission the spread of Shiism, a variant of Islam that had begun with Muhammad's son-in-law Ali. While an internally cohesive Turkish people, Safavid rulers were less effective at expanding their mission beyond their Persian base. The Mughals ruled over the wealthy but divided realm that is much of today's India, Pakistan, and Bangladesh. Their very wealth and the decentralization of their domain made the Mughals constant targets for internal dissent and eventually for external aggression.

THE RISE OF THE OTTOMAN EMPIRE

Although the Mongols had little interest in Anatolia, a borderland region of little economic importance to them, their military forays into the area opened it up to new political forces. The ultimate victors in Anatolia proved to be the Ottoman Turks, who succeeded in transforming themselves from Islamic warrior bands operating on the borderlands between the Islamic and Christian worlds into rulers of a settled state and finally into sovereigns of a far-flung, highly bureaucratic empire.

Under their chief, Osman (ruled 1289–1326), the Turkish Ottomans developed a stern and disciplined warrior ethos, and triumphed over rival warrior bands in Anatolia. Situated on the border of the Byzantine empire, they also waged a holy war against the Christian Byzantines. Further, unlike their rivals, they succeeded in mastering the techniques of settled administration. Other warrior bands, composed of young men who lived off the land and fought for booty under the leadership of charismatic military leaders, typically had no place in their societies for artisans, merchants, bureaucrats, and clerics. By contrast, the Ottomans, based in the city of Bursa in western Anatolia, realized that their consolidation of power depended on attracting just these groups. This they did with great skill, and in time, not only did the Ottoman state win the favor of Islamic clerics, but it also became the champion of Sunni, orthodox Islam throughout the entire Islamic world.

By the middle of the sixteenth century, the Ottomans had expanded beyond their regional base in Anatolia and moved into the Balkans, as well as becoming the most powerful force in the entire Middle East. The state controlled a vast territory, stretching in the west to the Moroccan border, in the north to Hungary and Moldavia, in the south through the Arabian peninsula, and in the east to the Iraqi-Persian border (see Map 2-2). At the top of the Ottoman's elaborate hierarchy sat the sultan. Below him was a military and civilian bureaucracy, whose task was to exact obedience and revenue from subjects. The Ottoman bureaucracy allowed the sultan to expand his realm, which in turn forced him to invest in a larger bureaucracy.

THE TOOLS OF EMPIRE-BUILDING The empire's spectacular expansion was first and foremost a military affair. To recruit followers, the Ottomans promised wealth and glory to new subjects. This was expensive, but territorial expansion generated vast financial and administrative rewards. Moreover, by spreading the spoils of conquest and lucrative positions in the emerging state, rulers bought off potentially discontented subordinates. Still, without military might, the Ottomans would not have enjoyed the successes of the fifteenth century that were associated with the brilliant reigns of Murad II (ruled 1421–1451) and his aptly named successor, Mehmed the Conqueror (ruled 1451–1481). Military campaigns culminated in 1453 with the conquest of Constantinople, capital of the Byzantine empire and a city of strategic and commercial importance. The

MAP 2-2   THE OTTOMAN EMPIRE, 1300–1566

This map charts the expansion of the Ottoman state from its inception in the early thirteenth century under its founder, Osman, through the reign of Suleiman, the empire's most illustrious ruler. Against whom did the Ottomans fight? What were the limits of the empire? If you had been an Ottoman sultan, what would have been your most pressing imperial concerns? Which Ottoman policies were likely to promote unity and which would lead to dissidence?

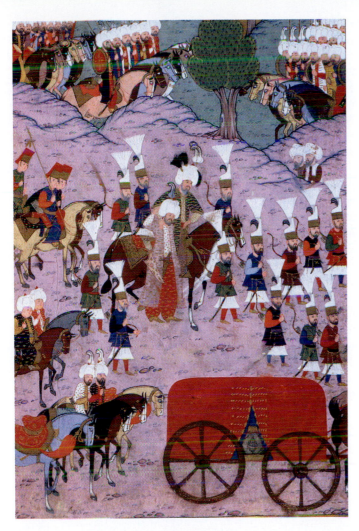

Suleiman and Territorial Expansion. Sultan Suleiman, pictured at the center of this illustration, led his army as it was about to embark on a campaign to conquer Europe.

engagements. In all, he spent ten years of his long reign away from Istanbul on military campaigns. But Suleiman was more than a brilliant military leader. He was an equally gifted administrator. He garnered accolades from his subjects, who called him "the Lawgiver" and "the Magnificent," in recognition of the attention he lavished on the arts and on civil bureaucratic efficiency. His fame spread to Europe, where he was known as "the Great Turk." Under Suleiman's administration, the Ottoman state ruled over some 20 to 30 million people. When Suleiman died in 1566, the Ottoman empire bridged Europe and the Arab world. Istanbul became a busy imperial hub, dispatching bureaucrats and military men from the capital to administer and control the vast domain.

Dynastic power was, however, not only military; it also rested on a religious foundation. At the center of this empire were the Ottoman sultans, who combined a warrior ethos with an unwavering devotion to Islamic beliefs. Describing themselves as the "shadow of God" on earth, sultans claimed to be caretakers for the welfare of the Islamic faith. Around the empire, the sultans devoted substantial resources to the construction of great mosques and to the support of Islamic schools. As self-appointed defenders of the faithful, the sultans assumed the role of protectors of the holy cities on the Arabian peninsula and of Jerusalem, defending the internal cohesion of the realm, and defining the borders demarcating heretics and infidels. Thus did the Islamic faith help to unite a diverse and sprawling imperial populace, with the sultan's power fusing the sacred and the secular.

ISTANBUL AND THE TOPKAPI PALACE Istanbul reflected the splendor of this powerful empire. After the Ottoman conquest, the sultans' engineers rebuilt the city's crumbling walls, while their architects redesigned homes, public buildings, baths, inns, and marketplaces to display the majesty of Islam's new imperial center. To crown his achievements, Suleiman ordered the construction of the Suleymaniye Mosque. This impressive structure sat on Istanbul's highest hill, across from Hagia Sophia, a domed Byzantine cathedral that Suleiman had turned into a mosque. From Suleiman's mosque, clerics broadcast the call to prayer to a burgeoning population. The Ottoman dynasts welcomed Muslims and non-Muslims to the city and revived Istanbul as a major trading center. Before its conquest, the city's population had fallen to 30,000. Within twenty-five years of its conquest by the Ottomans, its population had more than tripled, and by the end of the sixteenth century Istanbul's population numbered 400,000, making it the world's largest city outside China.

The political seat of the Ottoman empire was the Topkapi Palace. The palace neatly displayed the Ottomans' views of governance, the importance the sultans attached to religion, and the continuing influence of Ottoman household and familial traditions, even in the administration of a far-flung empire. Laid out by Constantinople's conqueror, Mehmed II, and largely completed by the middle of the sixteenth century, the palace

Ottomans converted it into an imperial Islamic capital, which they renamed Istanbul. Relying on the tools of conquest and conversion and employing Byzantine bureaucrats and administrative practices in their new state, within a century the Ottomans had transformed themselves from a small nomadic clan into the rulers of a grand empire that encroached on the heart of Christendom.

Having penetrated the heartland of Christian Byzantium in southeastern Europe in the fifteenth century, the Ottomans turned their expansionist designs to the Arab world in the next century. What Osman had begun, a sixteenth-century Ottoman successor, Suleiman (ruled 1520–1566), consolidated. During Suleiman's reign, the Ottomans reached the height of their territorial expansion. The sultan himself provided much of the military energy for Ottoman expansion, leading the army on thirteen of its major military campaigns and many of its minor complex reflected Mehmed's vision of Istanbul as the center of the world. As a way to exalt the awesomeness of the power of the sultan, the architects designed the various palaces and courtyards so that the buildings that housed the imperial household would be nestled behind layers of outer courtyards, in a mosaic of mosques, courts, and special dwellings for the sultan's harem.

The growing importance of the Topkapi Palace as the command post of empire represented an important transition in the history of Ottoman rulership. Whereas the early sultans had led their soldiers into battle personally and had met face-to-face with their kinsmen, the later rulers withdrew into the sanctity of the palace, leaving the day-to-day administration to the chief bureaucrat of the empire, the grand vizier. The sultans ventured out only occasionally for grand ceremonies. Still, every Friday, subjects queued up outside the palace to introduce their petitions, ask for favors, and seek justice. If they were lucky, the sultans would be there to greet the people—but they did so behind grated glass, issuing their decisions by tapping on the window. The palace thus projected a sense of majestic, distant wonder, a home fit for semi-divine rulers.

The palace was a training school for an elite bureaucracy. Behind its walls, young pages between twelve and fourteen, selected for their intelligence and physique, learned Arabic, the language of faith; Persian, the language of poetry; and Turkish, the language of administration. They also refined their military skills and bodily strength. These pages grew up to become the elite bureaucrats of the realm, raised to fight and rule in the name of the sultan. Some graduates of the palace's academies also went on to exceptional careers in the arts and sciences, as did the architect Sinan, who designed the Suleymaniye Mosque.

Topkapi was also, literally, the home of the sultan and his harem. Among his most cherished quarters were those set aside for women. At first, the influence of women in the Ottoman polity was slight. But as the realm consolidated and Topkapi rose to house sedentary rulers, women occupied the palace—and became a powerful political force. The harem, like the rest of Ottoman society, had its own hierarchy of rank and prestige. At the bottom were slave women; at the top were the sultan's mother and his favorite consorts. As many as 10,000 to 12,000 women lived—often they were quite cramped—in the palace. Those who had the ruler's ear conspired to have him favor their own children. This made for widespread intrigue, fueled by the practice of dispatching the entire retinue of women to a distant palace when the sultan died. Poignantly, Turks called this other palace the Palace of Tears because the women who occupied it wept at the loss of the sultan and their banishment from power.

The Suleymaniye Mosque. Built by Sultan Suleiman to crown his achievements, the Suleymaniye Mosque was designed by the architect Sinan to dominate the city and to have four tall minarets from which the faithful were called to prayer.

The Topkapi Palace. A view of the inner courtyard of the seraglio, where the sultan and his harem lived.

DIVERSITY IN THE OTTOMAN EMPIRE Ruling the realm through conquest and conversion did not entirely efface cultural differences in distant provinces. Take the example of the Ottomans' language policy. From the fifteenth century onward, the Ottoman empire was more multilingual than any of its rivals. Although Ottoman Turkish was the official language of administration, Arabic was the lingua franca of the Arab provinces, the common tongue of street life. Within the European corner of the empire, various languages also continued to be spoken.

In politics, as in language, the Ottomans showed flexibility and tolerance. The imperial bureaucracy permitted a high degree of regional autonomy. In the course of imperial expansion, the Ottoman military cadres perfected a technique for absorbing newly conquered territories into the empire by parceling out these territories as revenue-producing units among loyal followers and kin. Regional appointees could collect local taxes, part of which they earmarked for Istanbul, and part of which they kept for themselves. As we shall see, this was a common administrative device for many world dynasties trying to rule extensive domains.

The Ottoman empire was not unique among world dynasties in its awkward attempts to juggle the decentralizing tendencies of far-flung regions with the centralizing forces of the imperial capital. Like other expansive realms, the Ottoman state was perennially in danger of losing control over its provincial rulers. As provincial rulers learned to operate in-dependently from central authority, local authorities kept larger amounts of tax revenues than Istanbul deemed proper. To clip local autonomy, the Ottomans established a corps of infantry soldiers (called janissaries) and administrators who owed direct allegiance to the sultan. The system as it operated at its high point involved a conscription of Christian youths from villages in the European lands of the empire. This conscription, called the *devshirme,* required each village to turn

The *Devshirme*. A miniature painting from 1558 depicts the *devshirme* system of taking young, non-Muslim children from their families in the Balkan Peninsula as a human tribute in place of cash taxes, which the poor region could not pay. The children were educated in Ottoman Muslim ways and prepared for service in the sultan's civil and military bureaucracy.

over to the state a certain number of young males between the ages of eight and eighteen. Uprooted from their families and villages, selected for their fine physiques and good looks, these young men converted to Islam and were sent to farms to build up their bodies and learn Turkish. They were then sent to the Topkapi to learn Ottoman military, religious, and administrative techniques. Recipients of the best education available in the Islamic world, trained in Ottoman ways, instructed in the use of modern weaponry, and shorn of all family connections, the boys recruited through the *devshirme* were thus prepared for the highest administrative and military positions in the empire and owed direct allegiance to the sultan.

The Ottomans thus proved artful political jugglers. Relying on a careful mixture of faith, patronage, and tolerance, Ottoman sultans curried loyalty and secured political stability. Indeed, so strong and stable was the polity that the Ottoman empire dominated the much coveted and highly contested crossroads between Europe and Asia for many centuries.

THE EMERGENCE OF THE SAFAVID EMPIRE IN IRAN

The Ottoman dynasts were not the only rulers to extend the political domain of Islam in Eurasia. In Persia, too, a new empire arose in the aftermath of the Mongols. The Safavid empire, like the Ottoman empire, rested its legitimacy on an Islamic foundation. But the Shiism espoused by Safavid rulers was quite different from the Sunni faith of the Ottomans, and these contrasting religious visions shaped distinct political systems.

Even more so than in Anatolia, the Mongol conquest and decline brought terrible destruction and political instability to Persia. Initially, Mongol conquerors refused to embrace the Islamic faith of the area's population. Instead, from 1221 to 1295, Mongol rulers practiced a form of religious toleration. Various Mongol autocrats permitted Jews to serve the state as viziers (administrators) and employed Christians as auxiliary soldiers. But in 1295, the Great Khan of the Persian state,

QALANDAR DERVISHES IN THE ISLAMIC WORLD

The Qalandar dervish order came into being in Damascus, Syria, and Egypt in the thirteenth century and spread rapidly throughout the Islamic world into Arab and Ottoman lands in reaction to the unrest of the times. Renouncing the world and engaging in highly individualistic practices as they moved from place to place, the Qalandars were condemned by the educated elite, who believed them to be ignorant hypocrites living on alms obtained from gullible common folk. Giovan Antonio Manavino, a European observer of Ottoman society in the late fifteenth century, gives an obviously biased account of the Qalandars, whom he called the torlaks.

Dressed in sheepskins, the *torlaks* [Qalandars] are otherwise naked, with no headgear. Their scalps are always clean-shaven and well rubbed with oil as a precaution against the cold. They burn their temples with an old rag so that their faces will not be damaged by sweat. Illiterate and unable to do anything manly, they live like beasts, surviving on alms only. For this reason, they are to be found around taverns and public kitchens in cities. If, while roaming the countryside, they come across a well-dressed person, they try to make him one of their own, stripping him naked. Like Gypsies in Europe, they practice chiromancy, especially for women who then provide them with bread, eggs, cheese, and other foods in return for their services. Amongst them there is usually an old man whom they revere and worship like God. When they enter a town, they gather around the best house

of the town and listen in great humility to the words of this old man, who, after a spell of ecstasy, foretells the descent of a great evil upon the town. His disciples then implore him to fend off the disaster through his good services. The old man accepts the plea of his followers, though not without an initial show of reluctance, and prays to God, asking him to spare the town the imminent danger awaiting it. This time-honored trick earns them considerable sums of alms from ignorant and credulous people. The *torlaks* . . . chew hashish and sleep on the ground; they also openly practice sodomy like savage beasts.

Source: Ahmet T. Karamustafa, *God's Unruly Friends: Dervish Groups in the Islamic Later Middle Period, 1200–1550* (Salt Lake City: University of Utah Press, 1994), pp. 6–7.

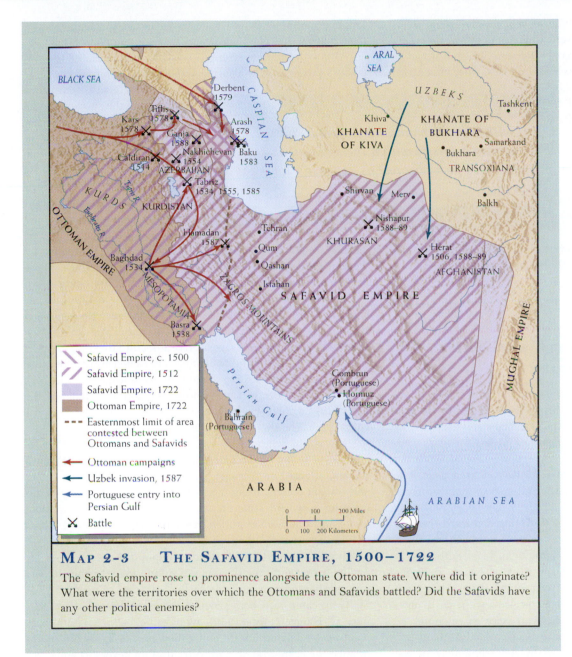

MAP 2-3   THE SAFAVID EMPIRE, 1500–1722

The Safavid empire rose to prominence alongside the Ottoman state. Where did it originate? What were the territories over which the Ottomans and Safavids battled? Did the Safavids have any other political enemies?

Turkish-speaking warrior bands. From his base in the city of Ardabil, Safi al-Din championed a Sufi version of Sunni Islam. His later successors, however, embraced Shiism.

The Safavid aspirants to power steeped themselves in the separatist sacred tradition of Shiism, rallying support from tribal groups in badly devastated parts of Persia and promising to restore good governance to the region. As a result, of the three great Islamic empires, the Safavid state became the most single-mindedly religious, persecuting those who did not follow its Shiite form of Islam. When in 1501 the most dynamic of Safi al-Din's successors, Ismail (ruled 1501–1524), acceded to power in Tabriz, he required that the call to prayer announce that "there is no God but Allah, that Muhammad is His prophet, and that Ali is the successor of Muhammad." Shiism had become the official religion of the Persian state. Ismail rejected the pragmatic counsels of his advisers to tolerate the Sunni creed of the vast majority of the city's population. Instead, he offered the people a choice between conversion to Shiism or death, exclaiming at the

Ghazan, adopted Islam as the state religion. Soon after, the Mongol order slipped into decline. When no power arose to dominate the area, the region between Konya in eastern Anatolia and Tabriz in Persia, and including Iraq, fell into even greater disorder, with warrior chieftains fighting one another for preeminence.

Adding to the volatility of the region were various populist Islamic movements that appeared at this time. These included some highly individualistic and antisocial campaigns that urged followers to withdraw from society or encouraged devotees to parade around without clothing. Among the more prominent movements was a Sufi brotherhood led by Safi al-Din (1252–1334), which gained the backing of both religious adherents and

moment of conquest that "with God's help, if the people utter one word of protest, I will draw the sword and leave not one of them alive." Under Ismail and his successors (who ruled until 1722), the Safavid shahs succeeded in restoring Persian sovereignty over the whole of the region traditionally regarded as the homeland of Persian speakers (see Map 2-3).

The Safavids employed another political tradition to enhance the legitimacy of their dynasty. Having embraced unorthodox Shiite beliefs, Safavid leaders revived the traditional Persian idea that kings had a divine right to rule—the conviction that this new lineage of rulers was ordained by God. In 1502, Ismail proclaimed himself the first shah of the Safavid empire. In the hands of the Safavids, Islam assumed an extreme and often quite militant form. Shiites believed the ruling shahs to be divinely chosen—some went so far as to affirm that there was no God but the shah. Moreover, Persian Shiism fostered an activist clergy, the so-called turbaned classes, who, in contrast to Sunni clerics, cast themselves in the role of political and religious rebels against any heretical authority. They compelled Safavid leaders to rule with a sacred purpose. Unlike the Ottomans, the Safavids did not tolerate diversity within their realm, and thus they never had as expansive an empire. Whatever territories they conquered, the Safavids ruled much more directly, based on central—and theocratic—authority.

> *Unlike the Ottomans, the Safavids did not tolerate diversity within their realm, and thus they never became as expansive an empire.*

THE DELHI SULTANATE AND THE EARLY MUGHAL EMPIRE

A quarter century after the Safavids seized power in Persia, another new Islamic dynasty, the Mughals, emerged to the east on the Asian subcontinent. Like the Ottomans and Safavids, the Mughals created a new regime destined to last for many centuries. But unlike those other Islamic empires, the Mughals did not replace a Mongol regime. Instead, they erected their state on the foundations of the old Delhi Sultanate, which had come into existence in 1206.

In 1303, when Mongol forces had moved toward the subcontinent, the Delhi Sultanate was at the height of its powers. Its formidable military force extended imperial authority to large parts of northern India, and cast a shadow over the political map of the south. The reigning sultan, Ala-ud din Khalji (ruled 1296–1316), was able to raise a sufficiently powerful army to drive the Mongols, who were threatening the northwestern cities of the sultanate, back toward Afghanistan. The Mongols never again disturbed the tranquility of the sultanate.

The sultanate's military campaigns were imperial ventures—to secure political glory and economic resources. Carried out by the imperial military, the campaigns of conquest and plunder brought additional revenue and wealth to maintain a formidable military force. The sultans also augmented their resources by increasing the tax yields from the rural economy, particularly from the core region of the empire. The access to resources not only helped to sustain a dominating military presence but also enabled the sultans to represent themselves as emperors who, like the Persians, bolstered their rule with emblems of divinity. Acting as imperial monarchs, they patronized Muslim theologians and mystics, and built impressive monuments and gardens in Delhi to commemorate their power.

Although military strength was the foundation of the sultanate's power, it was also its Achilles' heel. Toward the close of the fourteenth century, a decline in the government's revenues and a rise in expenditures on buildings and charitable institutions combined to reduce the resources for the military. Intrigues and quarreling among nobles further weakened the Delhi Sultanate and left it vulnerable to a new, Turkish rather than Mongol, invader. This was a force led by Timur (Tamerlane), a Turkish warrior from Central Asia, whose army succeeded where the Mongols had not. Sweeping down from the northwest, Timur's army sacked Delhi in 1398 and pillaged and annexed the Punjab. Death and destruction engulfed the city and much of northern India. Thousands were taken prisoner and carried off as slaves. Artisans and stonemasons who had built Delhi's beautiful buildings were carted away to beautify the conqueror's city of Samarkand (in present-day Uzbekistan). Yet, as the summer of 1399 approached, Timur abandoned the hot plains of northern India and returned home. Still, Timur's conquest accelerated the fragmentation of the Delhi Sultanate.

A wave of religious revival followed in the wake Timur's conquests. Some of the more radical movements, like Persia's Shiism, adopted an intransigent stance against central rulers and official credos. Religious reaction stood in the way of re-creating powerful state structures. Bengal broke away from Delhi and was soon engulfed in a Sufi form of mystical Islam, extolling personal union with God. Here, too, a special form of Hinduism, called Bhakti Hinduism, put down deep roots. Its devotees preached the doctrine of divine love. In the Punjab, previously a core area of the Delhi Sultanate, a new religion, Sikhism, came into being, which largely followed the teachings of Nanak (1469–1539), who while born a Hindu was inspired by Islamic ideals and called on his followers to renounce the caste system and to treat all believers as equal before God.

Following Timur's attack, rival kingdoms and sultanates asserted their independence, leaving the Delhi Sultanate a mere shadow of its former self. It became just one of several competing regional powers in northern India, ruled first by the Sayyids (1414–1451), and then by the Afghan dynasty of the Lodis (1451–1526). Surrounded by resurgent Hindu and Muslim polities, the truncated sultanate experienced something of a revival in the Lodi era. But the attempt by the last sultan, Ibrahim Lodi, to consolidate his power by clipping the wings of the Afghan nobility provoked the governor of the Punjab to invite the Turkish prince Babur (the "Tiger") to India in 1526. A great-grandson of Timur, Babur traced his lineage to both the Turks and the

NANAK'S TEACHINGS IN INDIA

Nanak, generally recognized as the founder of Sikhism, lived from 1469 to 1539 in the Punjab in northern India, where he surrounded himself with disciples and participated in the religious discussions that were such a prominent feature of the fifteenth century. This was a period, much like that in Western Europe and the Islamic Middle East, of political turmoil and intense personal introspection. As the following excerpts of hymns and poems from his writings demonstrate, Nanak exposed the failings of the age and used spiritual ideas drawn from Islamic and Hindu thought to elaborate his own unique spiritual perspective as a bulwark against the travails of the period. Nanak stressed the unity of God, an emphasis that reflected Islamic influences. Nonetheless, his insistence on the comparative unimportance of prophets ran counter to Islam, and his belief in rebirth was strictly Hindu.

There is but one God, whose name is true, the Creator, devoid of fear and enmity, immortal, unborn, self-existent; God the great and bountiful. Repeat His Name.

Numberless are the fools appallingly blind;
Numberless are the thieves and devourers of others' property;
Numberless are those who establish their sovereignty by force;
Numberless the cutthroats and murderers; Numberless the liars who roam about lying;
Numberless the filthy who enjoy filthy gain;
Numberless the slandered who carry loads of calumny on their heads;
Nanak thus described the degraded.
So lowly am I, I cannot even once be a sacrifice unto Thee.
Whatever pleaseth Thee is good.
O Formless One, Thou are ever secure.

The Hindus have forgotten God, and are going the wrong way.
They worship according to the instruction of Narad.

They are blind and dumb, the blindest of the blind.
The ignorant fools take stones and worship them.
O Hindus, how shall the stone which itself sinketh carry you across.

What power hath caste? It is the reality that is tested.
Poison may be held in the hand, but man dieth if he eat it.
The sovereignty of the True One is known in every age. He who obeyeth God's order shall become a noble in His court.

Those who have meditated on God as the truest of the true have done real worship and are contented;
They have refrained from evil, done good deeds, and practiced honesty;
They have lived on a little corn and water, and burst the entanglements of the world.
Thou art the great Bestower; ever Thou givest gifts which increase a quarterfold.
Those who have magnified the great God have found Him.

Source: William Theodore de Bary, *Sources of Indian Tradition* (New York: Columbia University Press, 1958), pp. 536–38.

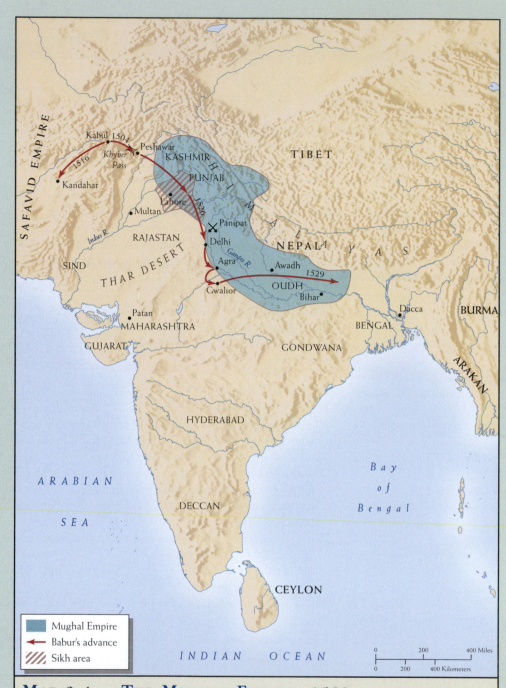

MAP 2-4   THE MUGHAL EMPIRE, 1530

Compare the Mughal state with the other major Asian empires of this period, notably the Ming, Safavid, and Ottoman states. What distinguishes the Mughal state at this time from these others? How does the Mughal state compare with its predecessor, the Delhi Sultanate, in size and location? From what part of the Eurasian land mass did the new state arise and what effect would its place of origin have on the nature of Mughal rule? To what religious traditions did the Mughals need to be sensitive?

Mongols (he was said to be a descendant of Chinggis Khan). For years, Babur had longed to conquer India. So, he accepted the invitation, and marched against Sultan Ibrahim. Massing an army of Turks and Afghans, and armed with matchlock cannons, he easily breached the wall of elephants put together by Ibrahim. Delhi fell, and the sultanate came to an end. Babur proclaimed himself emperor (ruled 1526–1530), and he spent the next few years snuffing out the remaining resistance to his rule (see Map 2-4). Thus was laid the foundation of the Mughal empire, the third great Islamic dynasty (discussed in detail in Chapter 3).

By the sixteenth century, then, the Islamic heartland had seen the emergence of three new empires. Although these states did not hesitate to go to war with each other, they shared similar styles of rule. All established their legitimacy by using military prowess, religious backing, and a loyal bureaucracy to balance sacred and secular authority. This combination of spiritual and military weaponry enabled emperors, carrying Muhammad's preachings across the Eurasian land mass, to lay claim to vast domains. Islam also bound rulers and ruled together and gave them a common cause and a singular view of the world. This shared Islamic religious culture fostered the movement of goods, ideas, merchants, and scholars across political boundaries, even across Islam's most divisive boundary, that along the border between Sunni Iraq and Shiite Persia.

MING CHINA

→ *How did the Ming centralize their authority?*

The Black Death was also ruinous on Eurasia's eastern flank and shook up political fortunes in what had appeared to be the world's most integrated and stable society. Indeed, the bubonic plague devastated the Middle Kingdom and prepared the way for the Ming dynasty to replace the Mongols in 1368.

China had been ripe for this pandemic. Its numbers had increased significantly under the Song dynasty (960–1279). Indeed, Mongol rule initially sustained Chinese prosperity and population growth. But by 1300, hunger and scarcity began to spread as China became overpopulated. A weakened population was especially vulnerable to plague. For seventy years, the Black Death ravaged China. The death and destruction brought by the disease was unprecedented and shattered the Mongol dynasty's claim to a mandate from heaven. In 1331, it may have killed 90 percent of the population in Hebei province. From there it spread throughout the Chinese provinces, reaching Fujian and the coast at Shandong. By the 1350s, severe outbreaks occurred in most of China's large cities.

The reign of the last of the Yuan Mongol rulers, Toghon Temür (ruled 1333–1368), was a time of utter chaos. Even as the Black Death was sweeping over large parts of China, bandit groups and dissident religious sects were undercutting the power of the state. In China, as in other realms desolated by the plague, popular religious movements arose and spoke of impending doom. The most prominent of these was the Red Turban Movement, which took its name from the red headbands that its soldiers wore.

The bubonic plague devastated the Middle Kingdom and prepared the way for the Ming dynasty to replace the Mongols in 1368.

The Red Turbans blended China's rich and diverse popular cultural and religious traditions, including Buddhism, Daoism, and other faiths. Its leaders imposed strict dietary restrictions on followers, engaged in penance and ceremonial rituals, in which the sexes freely mixed, and spread the belief that the world was drawing to an end.

In these chaotic times, only the emergence of a powerful military movement capable of overpowering other groups could restore order. That intervention came from a poor young man who had acquired his early training in the Red Turban Movement: Zhu Yuanzhang (ruled 1368–1398). Zhu came from the humblest of backgrounds. He was an orphan from a peasant household in an area devastated by disease and famine and a former novice at a Buddhist monastery. In 1352, the twenty-four-year-old Zhu joined the Red Turbans and rose quickly within its ranks to become a distinguished commander. Eventually, he defeated the Yuan and drove the Mongols from China.

With his ascendance, it became clear that he had a much larger design for all of China than the ambitions of most warlords. When Zhu took the important city of Nanjing in 1356, he renamed it Yingtian, meaning "In response to Heaven." With his successful military campaigns, Zhu felt strong enough by 1368 to proclaim the founding of the Ming ("brilliant") dynasty. In September of that year his troops met little resistance when they seized the Yuan capital of Beijing. The Mongol emperor fled to his homeland in the steppe. It would, however, take Zhu close to another twenty years to reunify the entire country.

CENTRALIZATION UNDER THE MING

Zhu and successive Ming emperors had to rebuild a devastated society from the ground up, for China had experienced natural catastrophes (especially flooding), depopulation, wars, and social disorganization not witnessed for centuries. The new rulers had to reconstruct the bureaucracy, rebuild the great cities, and restore respect for the ruling elites.

The rebuilding process began under Zhu, who called himself the Hongwu ("expansive and martial") Emperor and ruled in a grand style. He displayed imperial grandeur in the extravagant scale of his newly constructed capital at Nanjing. The capital city was surrounded by a city wall that measured almost twenty-four miles in total length, averaged forty feet in height, and was twenty-five feet wide at the top. The wall had thirteen gates equipped with metal barriers. Several of the gates were double, with a land gate alongside a water gate. The foundation of the wall was made with the most up-to-date technology of the age, involving enormous slabs of stone designed to withstand gunpowder charges.

When the third emperor of the dynasty, Zhu Di, known as the Yongle Emperor (ruled 1403–1424), relocated the capital to its present-day site of Beijing, he was set on a still more grandiose style. Construction in Beijing mobilized around 100,000 artisans and 1 million laborers. The city had three separate walled enclosures. Inside the outer city walls was the section known as the imperial city; inside its walls was the palace city, also often called the Forbidden City. The traffic within the walled sections navigated through boulevards leading to the different gates, which were marked by imposing towers. The palace compound, within which the imperial family resided, had more than 9,000 rooms. Anyone standing in the front courts, which measured more than 400 yards on a side and were adorned with marble terraces and carved railings, was struck by a sense of awesome power. That, of course, was precisely what the Ming emperors (just as the Ottoman sultans with the Topkapi Palace) had in mind.

Marriage and kinship buttressed the power of the Ming imperial household. The founder of the dynasty married the adopted daughter of one of the leading rebels against the Yuan Mongol regime (her father, according to legend, was a murder convict), thereby consolidating his power and eliminating a threat. She became Hongwu's principal wife, the empress, who was known for her compassion and emerged as the kinder, gentler face of the regime, tempering the harsh and sometimes cruel disposition of her spouse.

> *Instead of depending on the princes, Hongwu established an imperial bureaucracy beholden to him and to his successors (as in the Ottoman empire).*

Hongwu initially sought to rule the empire through his kinsmen. He gave imperial princes large stipends, command of large garrisons, and significant autonomy in running their own domains. His initial idea was that kinship solidarity would provide strong support for the ruling household. But when the power of the princes became too great and threatening to the court, Hongwu cut their stipends to one-fifth, reduced their overall privileges, and took over control of their garrisons. Instead of depending on the princes, he established an imperial bureaucracy beholden to him and to his successors (as in the Ottoman empire). These officials and bureaucrats were appointed based on their performance on a reinstated civil service examination.

Under this revamped system, the imperial palace not only projected the image of a power center, it *was* the center of power. Every official of the administration was appointed by the emperor through the Ministry of Personnel. All of them went to the capital to receive their appointments, and back again at the end of their terms to be reappointed or retired. Hongwu also eliminated the previously important post of prime minister in 1380 after he executed the man who held the post. Henceforth, Hongwu ruled directly. Ming bureaucrats literally lost their seats and had to kneel before the emperor. Hongwu even tried to take charge of the salaries of local officials. In one eight-day period, he reputedly reviewed over 1,600 petitions dealing with 3,392 separate matters. The drawback, of course, was that the emperor had to keep tabs on this immense

The Forbidden City. The Yongle Emperor relocated the capital to Beijing, where he began the construction of the Forbidden City, or imperial palace. The palace was designed to inspire awe in all who saw it.

THE HONGWU EMPEROR'S PROCLAMATION

This proclamation of the founding ruler of the Ming dynasty, the Hongwu Emperor (ruled 1368–1398), reveals how he envisioned the reconstruction of a devastated country as his own personal project. He distrusted his officials and berated them for their numerous shortcomings. He sought a return to a more austere world by denouncing the corrosive effect of money and material possessions on the morals of his subjects. Although frustrated in his efforts, Hongwu nonetheless set the tone for the centralization of power in the person of the emperor.

To all civil and military officials:

I have told you to refrain from evil. Doing so would enable you to bring glory to your ancestors, your wives and children, and yourselves. With your virtue, you then could assist me in my endeavors to bring good fortune and prosperity to the people. You would establish names for yourselves in Heaven and on earth, and for thousands and thousands of years, you would be praised as worthy men.

However, after assuming your posts, how many of you really followed my instructions? Those of you in charge of money and grain have stolen them yourselves; those of you in charge of criminal laws and punishments have neglected the regulations. In this way grievances are not redressed and false charges are ignored. Those with genuine grievances have nowhere to turn; even when they merely wish to state their complaints, their words never reach the higher officials. Occasionally these unjust matters come to my attention. After I discover the truth, I capture and imprison the corrupt, villainous, and oppressive officials involved. I punish them with the death penalty or forced labor or have them flogged with bamboo sticks in order to make manifest the consequences of good or evil actions. . . .

Alas, how easily money and profit can bewitch a person! With the exception of the righteous person, the true gentleman, and the sage, no one is able to avoid the temptation of money. But is it really so difficult to reject the temptation of profit? The truth is people have not really tried.

Previously, during the final years of the Yuan dynasty, there were many ambitious men competing for power who did not treasure their sons and daughters but prized jade and silk, coveted fine horses and beautiful clothes, relished drunken singing and unrestrained pleasure, and enjoyed separating people from their parents, wives, and children. I also lived in that chaotic period. How did I avoid such snares? I was able to do so because I valued my reputation and wanted to preserve my life. Therefore I did not dare to do these evil things. . . .

In order to protect my reputation and to preserve my life, I have done away with music, beautiful girls, and valuable objects. Those who love such things are usually "a success in the morning, a failure in the evening." Being aware of the fallacy of such behavior, I will not indulge such foolish fancies. It is not really that hard to do away with these tempting things.

Source: Patricia Buckley Ebrey (ed.), *Chinese Civilization: A Sourcebook* (2nd ed., revised and expanded) (New York: The Free Press, 1993), pp. 205–206.

system, and his bureaucrats were not always up to the task. Indeed, Hongwu constantly juggled personal and impersonal forms of authority, sometimes fortifying the administration, sometimes undermining it lest it become too autonomous.

In due course, Hongwu nurtured a bureaucracy that was far more extensive than those of the Islamic empires. The emperor appointed officials and put in place bureaucrats to oversee local networks of villages. These locally based officials supervised reforestation projects to prevent flooding, the rebuilding of irrigation systems, the manufacturing of porcelain, cotton, and silk products, and the collection of taxes. Hongwu reestablished the Confucian school system as a means of selecting a loyal cadre of officials (not unlike the Ottoman janissaries and administrators), who would be obedient to the emperor.

The Ming thus established the most highly centralized and rationalized system of government of all the monarchies of this period. Inspired perhaps by their Mongol predecessors, they devised an ornate classification scheme, dividing all the people under their jurisdiction into different, supposedly hereditary, categories—peasant, artisan, or soldier. The Hongwu Emperor started at the village level, envisaging a sea of self-sufficient and self-regulating village communities as the foundation for his realm. Within these village communities, the dynasty created a social hierarchy based on age, sex, and kinship. The Ming produced a more elaborate system for classifying and controlling subject peoples than did the other dynasties on the Eurasian land mass, although the system began to fall apart as early as the beginning of the fifteenth century.

RELIGION UNDER THE MING

The Ming zeal to classify went beyond its subjects and extended to the religious pantheon as well. The emperor labeled official cults as civil or military, then further distinguished them into great, middle, or minor, as well as celestial, terrestrial, or human categories. The emperor revised and strengthened the elaborate protocol of rites and ceremonies that had undergirded dynastic power for centuries. As well as underscoring the emperor's centrality, official rituals, such as those related to the gods of soil and grain, reinforced local political and social hierarchies. Under the guise of "community" gatherings, the performance of rites and sacrifices solidified the Ming order.

As in other dynasties, sacred tools of religion helped consolidate Ming rulership. Ming rulers claimed to be moral and spiritual benefactors of their subjects. On at least ninety occasions each year, the emperor engaged in rites of sacrifice, providing symbolic communion between the human and the spiritual worlds. Lavish sacred festivities were occasions for the Ming rulers to reinforce their image as mediators between otherworldly affairs of their gods and worldly concerns of their subjects. The gods were on the side of the Ming household.

Official cults, however, often collided with local faiths. Such conflicts revealed the limits to Ming centralism. Consider Dongyang, a small hilly interior region of the realm. The limits to central power are visible in the handling of this district's sacred affairs. As was common in Ming China, the people of Dongyang supported Buddhist institutions. Guan Yu, a legendary martial hero killed in the year 217, was enshrined in a local Buddhist monastery. But he was also worshiped as part of a state cult. The problem was that the state cult and the Buddhist monastery were separate entities, and according to imperial law, the demands of the state cult were supposed to prevail over those of the local monastery. In the case of Dongyang, local magistrates confined themselves to administrative concerns. Though they kept a watchful eye on local religious leaders, state officials refrained from tampering directly in Dongyang's Buddhist monastery. While the dynasty insisted that people honor their contributions to the state, people in Dongyang delivered most of their funds to the Buddhist monks. So strong were local sentiments and contributions that even officials siphoned revenues to the monastery.

MING RULERSHIP

Overall, sacred sources of political power were comparatively less essential for the Ming dynasty than for the Islamic dynasties. Secular authority was more important. Conquest and defense helped establish the realm; a bureaucracy kept it functioning. The remarkable scale of the Ming realm (see Map 2-5) meant the establishment of a complicated administration. To many outsiders, especially Europeans whose own end of Eurasia was in a state of constant war, Ming stability and centralization appeared to be political wizardry.

As we consider the political science of Ming power, we must not overlook the usual dynastic dilemmas. The emperor wished to be seen as the special guardian, or patriarch, of his subjects. He wanted their allegiance, as well as their taxes and their labor. During hard times, poor farmers were reluctant to provide resources—taxes or services—to distant officials. For these reasons alone, Hongwu preferred to entrust the management of the rural world to local leaders, whom he appointed as village chiefs, village elders, or tax captains. One popular Chinese proverb was: "the mountain is high and the emperor is far away."

The Ming empire, like the Islamic states, also had to cope with periodic unrest and rebellions. Rebels were often inspired by their own brand of religious beliefs, just as local elites resented the encroachment of central authority. Outright terror helped stymie threats to central authority. Hongwu sought to destroy political rivals. In a massive wave of carnage, Hongwu slaughtered anyone who posed a threat to his authority, from the highest of ministers to the lowliest of scribes. From 1376 to 1393, four of his purges condemned close to 100,000 subjects to execution. Purge victims included both civil and military officials, landowners, local leaders, as well as their families. Terror, Hongwu believed, would safeguard his rule.

> *To many outsiders, especially Europeans who were in a state of constant war, Ming stability and centralization appeared to be political wizardry.*

Even such terror, however, did not deter members of the scholar elite such as Fang Xiaoru (1357–1402) from looking to the Ming as the only hope of restoring proper statecraft and revitalizing Chinese society. Fang epitomized the kind of moralistic optimism that was common among Ming officials. Although he lost both his father and teacher to Hongwu's purges, he continued to support and tried to reform the new regime. Fang emphasized the need for communal cooperation at the grassroots level to rejuvenate the realm. He proposed that leaders recognized by the community rather than appointed by the government lead voluntary associations of families and households at the local level. But his ideas were never put into practice. Refusing to recognize the legitimacy of the succession of Yongle, who had come to the throne in 1403 after burning the palace and seizing the throne from his nephew, Fang was executed. Many who were only remotely associated with him were also sought out and killed.

In many ways, the Ming empire, despite the immense power of the emperor, remained undergoverned, which created problems as the number of people in the realm multiplied. By the sixteenth and the early seventeenth centuries, for example, some

MAP 2-5 MING CHINA, 1500S

The Ming state was one of the largest empires at the beginning of the sixteenth century and the most populous. It had a long sea-coast and even longer internal borders. From where did the Ming expect the greatest threat to its security to come? How did the rulers enhance the security of the state against these threats? In what part of this great empire did its largest cities tend to be located and why?

10,000 to 15,000 officials had responsibility for a population exceeding perhaps 200 million people. But Hongwu bequeathed a set of tools for ruling to his descendants, tools that enabled the Ming empire to draw on the subjects' direct loyalty to the emperor and the workings of a powerful bureaucracy. This enabled his successors to balance local sources of power with centralizing ambitions. It was of course, imperfect. But, for the times, this was a powerful dynasty.

TRADE UNDER THE MING

In the fourteenth century, China began its economic recovery from the devastation of disease and political turmoil. Gradually, political stability allowed trade to revive. China and the new dynasty's merchants reestablished their preeminence in long-distance, commercial exchange. Chinese silk and cotton textiles, as well as fine porcelains, ranked among the most coveted luxuries in the world. Wealthy families from Lisbon to Kalabar wished to wash their hands in delicate Chinese bowls, and to make fine wardrobes from the bolts of Chinese dyed linens and smoothly spun silk. When a Chinese merchant ship sailed into port, local trading partners and onlookers gathered to watch the unloading of the precious cargoes. During the Ming period, Chinese maritime traders based in ports along the southern coast, in Hangzhou, Quanzhou, and Guangzhou (Canton), were as energetic as their Muslim counterparts in the Indian Ocean. These ports were home to many prosperous merchants and the point of convergence for vast sea lanes. Leaving the mainland ports, Chinese merchants carried their wares to offshore islands, the Pescadores, and Taiwan. From there, they extended their commercial activities to the ports of Kyūshū, the Ryūkyūs, Luzon, and maritime Southeast Asia. As entrepots—commercial hubs for long-distance trade—for global goods, East Asian ports flourished. Former fishing villages evolved into major urban centers.

The Ming dynasty viewed overseas expansion with suspicion, however. Hongwu feared that too much commerce and contact with the outside world would cause instability and undermine the authority of his rule. In fact, Hongwu banned private maritime commerce in 1371. But enforcement of this prohibition was lax, and by the late fifteenth century maritime trade along the coast once again surged. Because so much of the thriving business of the South China Sea ports was conducted in defiance of official edicts, it led to ongoing friction between government officials and maritime traders. Although the Ming government, under pressure from the mercantile communities, did relax its ban and agreed to issue licenses for overseas trade in the mid-sixteenth century, it continued to vacillate in its policies. To Ming officials, the sea ultimately represented problems of order and control rather than opportunities.

The spectacular exception to the Ming government's general attitude to maritime trade was a well-known series of officially sponsored maritime expeditions in the early fifteenth century. It was the ambitious Yongle Emperor who took the initiative. One of his loyal followers was a Muslim captured by the Ming army when he was a boy. He was castrated (as a eunuch, he could not continue his family line and so theoretically owed sole allegiance to the emperor) and sent to serve at the court. The boy, Zheng He (1371–1433), grew up to be a powerful and important military leader, entrusted by the emperor in 1405 with venturing out to trade, collect tribute, and display China's power to the world. From 1405 to 1433, Zheng He commanded the world's greatest armada, and led seven naval expeditions. His larger ships reached 400 feet long (compared to Columbus's puny *Santa Maria*, which was 85 feet long), carried many hundreds of sailors on four tiers of decks, and maneuvered with sophisticated balanced rudders, nine masts, and watertight compartments. The first expedition set sail with a flotilla of 62 large ships and over 200 lesser ones. There were 28,000 men aboard, pledged to promote the cause of Ming glory.

Zheng He and his entourage aimed to establish tributary relations with far-flung territories—from Southeast Asia to the Indian Ocean ports, to the Persian Gulf, and to the east coast of Africa (see Map 2-6). A central goal of these expeditions was not territorial expansion but rather control of trade and tribute. Zheng traded for ivory, spices, ointments, exotic woods, and even some wildlife, including giraffes, zebras, and ostriches. He also used his considerable force to intervene in local affairs, exhibiting the might of China in the process. If a community refused to pay tribute to the emperor, Zheng's fleet would attack it.

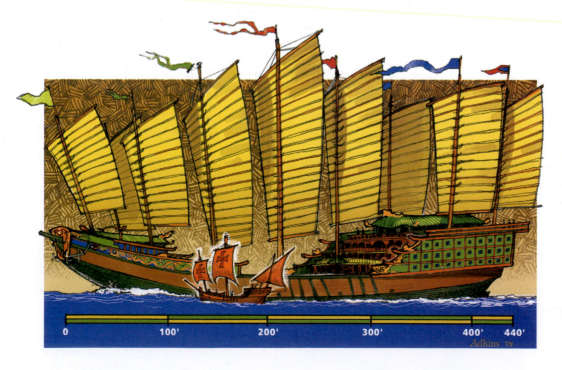

Zheng He's Ship. A testament to centuries of experience in shipbuilding and maritime activities, the largest ship in Zheng He's armada in the early fifteenth century was about five times the length of Columbus's *Santa Maria* (pictured next to Zheng's ship), and nine times the capacity in terms of tonnage. It had nine staggered masts and twelve square-shaped sails made of silk cloth, all designed to inspire awe and to demonstrate the grandeur of the Ming empire.

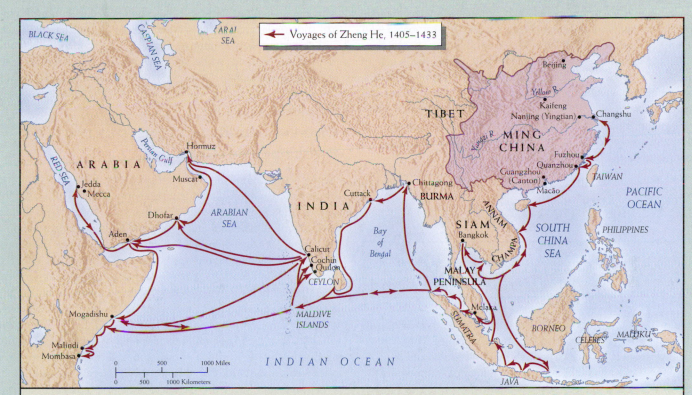

MAP 2-6   VOYAGES OF ZHENG HE, 1405–1433

Compare the voyages of Zheng He with the travels of Ibn Battuta and Marco Polo described in Chapter 1 and with the voyages of the European explorers discussed in Chapter 3. Did Zheng He travel across routes that were familiar to others at this time? Why did other state-sponsored voyages not follow these expeditions and why did the Chinese, unlike the Europeans, not establish overseas colonies?

Rulers or envoys from Southeast Asia, India, the Middle East, and Africa were encouraged to visit China. When they refused to do so, Zheng might seize them, as he did the rulers of Sumatra and Ceylon, and drag them to China to acknowledge the emperor.

Although many of the items gathered on the voyages delighted the court, most were not the stuff of everyday commerce. The expeditions were, in short, glamorous but very expensive, and they came to a rather abrupt halt in 1433. Never again did the Ming undertake such large-scale maritime ventures. In fact, as early as 1424, when the Yongle Emperor died, the official expeditions had already lost their most important and enthusiastic patron. Moreover, by the mid-fifteenth century, there was a revival of military threats from the north. In 1449, the Ming court was shocked to discover that during a tour of the frontiers, the emperor had been captured and held hostage by the Mongols. Mindful of how the maritime-oriented Song dynasty had been eventually overrun by invaders from the north, officials withdrew imperial support for maritime ventures and instead devoted their energies to overland ventures and defense. Yet, Chinese maritime commerce continued to flourish even though it lacked official patronage.

The decision to abandon imperial support for oceanic exploration did, however, lead to the decline of Chinese naval power and opened the way for newcomers and rivals. Southeast Asians took advantage by constructing large oceangoing vessels, known as "jong," which plied the regional trade routes from the fifteenth century to the early sixteenth century. These ships weighed an average of 350 to 500 tons, but could be as big as 1,000 tons, with 1,000 men on board. They carried cargoes and passengers not only to southern China, but also to the

> *The decision to abandon imperial support for oceanic exploration led to the decline of Chinese naval power and opened the way for newcomers and rivals.*

Indian Ocean as far west as Calicut and the Red Sea. Muslims also occupied the vacuum left by the Chinese, sailing from ports like Calicut across the Indian Ocean west to Mombassa and Mogadishu, and east to Melaka (Malacca). In addition, Japanese pirates took over some of the trade and made the work of Chinese overseas merchants that much more difficult. Europeans, too, made their entrance. They craved luxurious Asian silk and spices. But they had to play junior partners to the powerful Arab and Chinese merchants who already enjoyed widespread connections, substantial reserves of credit, and connections through the Asian hinterlands.

WESTERN CHRISTENDOM

> → *Why was Europe so disunited (compared to China and Islam)?*

In the wake of the Black Death, Europe entered a period of prolonged disorder, in contrast to the stable world of Ming China. On the western side of the Eurasian land mass, a period of prosperity, population growth, and cultural flowering known as the High Middle Ages ended abruptly with the coming of famine, plague, and war in the fourteenth century. By 1500, attempts were being made to found new, stable polities, but by and large, social unrest and political chaos characterized the two centuries after the appearance of the Black Death. Unlike Asia, Western Christendom saw only partial consolidations of centralized power.

The Black Death and its aftermath reversed the gains that Europe had made in the twelfth and thirteenth centuries. Between about 1100 and 1300, Europe's population had increased, and new prosperity had allowed for spectacular advances in the arts, technology, learning, building, cities, and banking. Its 80 million inhabitants still resided, overwhelmingly, on rural estates, but towns and cities were growing rapidly. Economic and social lives focused on the family, and growing households had to crowd under the same roof. Wives worked with their husbands, especially in commerce and farming. Though excluded from many crafts and professions, women were increasingly important in retail trades, weaving, and food production.

In the growing towns and cities, Europeans were widening their horizons onto the world. Universities had come into being in Bologna, Paris, Oxford, and Cambridge, and a few scholars began to appreciate the learning of the Arabs and the earlier achievements of the Greeks and Romans. Thomas Aquinas (1225–1274), the leading philosopher and theologian of the age,

> *By and large, social unrest and political chaos characterized the two centuries in Europe after the appearance of the Black Death.*

had laid out the main tenets of Western Christianity and resolved questions of faith and reason to the satisfaction of clerical and secular intellectuals. New devices like mechanical clocks and the compass had improved the accuracy of measurements on sea and on land, while spinning wheels increased the pace of cloth production.

CRISES AND REACTIONS DURING THE FOURTEENTH CENTURY

At the beginning of the fourteenth century, Europe's rising fortunes halted, with climatic changes instigating a decline. A cooling of the temperatures in Europe took much land out of cultivation. Diminished and exhausted soils no longer supplied the resources to feed and clothe growing urban and rural populations. Nobles squeezed the peasantry hard in an effort to maintain their luxurious way of life. States raised taxes to keep revenues in balance with their growing expenditures. In this context, Europe endured the first of its fourteenth-century disasters: famine. Famine appeared in 1315 and did not let up until 1322, by which time millions had died of outright starvation or diseases against which the malnourished population could offer little resistance. But this would be merely the prelude to a century and more of ceaseless warfare, epidemic disease, famine, and social unrest.

In the wake of famine came the Black Death, which appeared in Italian port cities around 1347. In Florence, which lost half of its population to the scourge, the writer Boccaccio noted in his famous work *The Decameron* that inhabitants shunned one another for fear of contracting the disease. "Tedious were it to recount how citizen avoided citizen, how among neighbors was scarce one that showed fellow feeling for another, how kinsfolk held aloof and never met, but rarely."

Even while the pandemic was ravaging the Italian peninsula, it moved on to France, the Low Countries, Germany, and England. Although no part of Europe was spared, the cities were particularly vulnerable because of their overcrowding and unsanitary conditions. London, with a population of about 60,000 residing within its walls and another 10,000 or 15,000 living outside, groaned under the weight of the death toll. Often in the poorer sections as many as twelve residents slept together on the floor in a single room. The disease spared few in these crowded quarters. Nor did it ignore their social betters if they hesitated to flee to their country estates.

No one had seen dying on such a scale. Anywhere from 25 to 50 percent of Europe's total population (between 19 and 38 million) perished within five years of the original outbreak in 1347. But the dying did not end then, for severe outbreaks occurred in 1361–1362, 1369, and then every five to ten years for the rest of the fourteenth century, as well as sporadically through the entire fifteenth century. The European population continued on a precipitous decline until by 1450 many areas had only one-quarter the number of people they had a century earlier. One historian later characterized the decline as "so vast as to border on holocaust, save for lack of intention." Indeed, it took three centuries for Europe to recover to population levels that existed prior to the Black Death.

Disaster on this scale had a number of enduring psychological, social, economic, and political effects. Many individuals, recognizing life's brevity, turned to pleasure, even debauchery, determined to enjoy themselves before it came their turn to die. Others retreated into a personal spirituality, convinced that they needed to put their lives in order before they passed on to the next life. Occasionally, like-minded individuals joined together and created eccentric groups. The Beghards or Brethren of the Free Speech claimed to be in a state of grace that allowed them to do as they pleased—from adultery, free love, and nudity, to murder. By contrast, the flagellants were so sure that man had incurred the wrath of God through his wayward ways that they whipped themselves to show their readiness to atone for human sin. But they also bullied communities that they visited, demanding to be housed, clothed, and fed in style.

For many who survived the plague, Thomas Aquinas's rational Christianity no longer appealed, and disappointment with the clergy was widespread. Famished peasants resented priests and monks for living lives of luxury in violation of church tenets. In addition, they despaired at the absence of clergy when they were so greatly needed. In fact, many clerics had perished while attending to their parishioners. Others, however, had simply deserted to rural retreats far from the ravages of the Black Death, leaving their followers to fend for themselves.

In the aftermath of famine and plague, religious authorities struggled to reclaim their power. The late medieval Western Church found itself divided at the top (at one point in the fourteenth century there were three popes!) and challenged from below, both by individuals pursuing alternative kinds of spirituality and by increasing demands on the clergy and church administration. In response to challenges to its right to define religious doctrine and practices, the church rigorously identified all that was suspect and demanded strict obedience to the true

FLAGELLANTS IN ENGLAND

*Like the Qalandar dervishes in the Islamic world, the flagellants renounced the world and engaged in violent acts of public self-punishment in reaction to the warfare, famines, and plagues of the fourteenth century. The flagellants carried whips (*flagella*) with metal pieces run through knotted thongs, which they used to beat and whip themselves until they were bruised, swollen, and bloody. Robert of Avesbury here describes the actions of flagellants in England during the reign of King Edward III.*

In that same year of 1349, about Michaelmas [29 September], more than 120 men, for the most part from Zeeland or Holland, arrived in London from Flanders. These went barefoot in procession twice a day in the sight of the people, sometimes in St Paul's church and sometimes elsewhere in the city, their bodies naked except for a linen cloth from loins to ankle. Each wore a hood painted with a red cross at front and back and carried in his right hand a whip with three thongs. Each thong had a knot in it, with something sharp, like a needle, stuck through the middle of the knot so that it stuck out on each side, and as they walked one after the other they struck themselves with these whips on their naked, bloody bodies; four of them singing in their own tongue and the rest answering in the manner of the Christian litany. Three times in each procession they would all prostrate themselves on the ground, with their arms outstretched in the shape of a cross. Still singing, and beginning with the man at the end, each in turn would step over the others, lashing the man beneath him once with his whip, until all of those lying down had gone through the same ritual. Then each one put on his usual clothes and, always with their hoods on their heads and carrying their whips, they departed to their lodgings. It was said that they performed a similar penance every night.

Source: *Robertus de Avesbury de Gestis Mirabilibus Regis Edwardi Tertii*, in *The Black Death*, translated and edited by Rosemary Horrox (Manchester, England: Manchester University Press, 1994), pp. 153–54.

Peasant Revolts. Long before the French Revolution, European peasants vented their anger against their noble masters. Lacking armaments and supplies, they usually lost—as this image of the brutal suppression of the French Jacquerie of 1358 depicts.

faith. This entailed the persecution of heretics, Jews, Muslims, homosexuals, prostitutes, and "witches." But in this period, the church was also expanding its charitable and bureaucratic functions, providing alms to the urban poor and registering births, deaths, and economic transactions.

Both persecution and administration cost money. As the church had no easy way to raise new funds, the needs as well as the extravagances of the clergy spurred the undertaking of questionable new money-making tactics. Among the most controversial of these fund-raising mechanisms was the selling of indulgences (certification that one's sins had been forgiven). It was this sort of unconventional fund raising, and the growing gap between the church's promises and its ability to actually bring Christianity into people's everyday lives, more than the persecutions, that would spark the Protestant Reformation.

Just as the mayhem of the fourteenth and fifteenth centuries unleashed a wave of popular hostility toward the church, it also undermined the legitimacy of the feudal order, especially in France and England. Since the Roman era, peasant protests and uprisings had occasionally erupted. Yet, in the wake of the catastrophes of the fourteenth century, these everyday defiances escalated into large-scale insurrections. In France and England, massive revolts broke out, in which peasant rebels expressed both their resentment against lords who failed to protect them from marauding military bands and their defiance of feudal restrictions that now seemed—for the few survivors of plague and famine—onerous. In 1358, the French revolt, or "Jacquerie"—a term derived from "Jacques Bonhomme," a name used by contemptuous masters as a blanket term for all peasants—broke out. Armed with only knives and staves, the French peasantry went on a rampage, killing a few of the hated nobles and higher clergy, and burning and looting all the property they could get their hands on. At issue was the peasants' insistence that they should no longer be tied to their land or have to make payments for the tools they used in their agricultural pursuits.

A far better organized uprising took place in England in 1381. Although what became known as the English Peasants' Revolt began as a protest against a poll tax levied to raise money for a war on France, it was also fueled by post-plague labor shortages, with serfs demanding the freedom to move about and free farm workers calling for higher wages and lower rents. When landlords balked at these demands, huge numbers of aggrieved and restless peasants joined the cause, finally assembling at the gates of London. The protesters pressed for the abolition of the feudal order, but King Richard II, assembling his nobles, ruthlessly suppressed the rebellious peasants. Nonetheless, despite these defeats in both France and England, a free peasantry gradually emerged as labor shortages made it impossible to continue to bind peasants to the soil.

STATE-BUILDING IN EUROPE

In the wake of famine, plague, and peasant uprisings, Europe's rulers (and would-be rulers) tried to rebuild their polities. Their efforts at state-building, however, paled in comparison with those of the empires rising in Asia. Although one family, the Habsburgs, provided emperors for the Holy Roman empire from 1440 to 1806, they never succeeded in restoring an integrated empire to Western Europe, as Chinese dynasts had done in the Middle Kingdom. Feudalism had left a legacy of political fragmentation and enshrined privileges, which rulers found hard to overcome. Moreover, language did not serve to unite Europeans. Although Latin was the language of the church and the learned elite, most nobles and peasants spoke local tongues. Thus, most of Western Christendom's polities in the fourteenth and fifteenth centuries were not built around speakers of one language. France, for example, included regions where people spoke Occitan, Provençal, and Breton, not to mention their rural dialects.

It took several centuries for the new states and the new monarchs of Europe to rebuild their badly torn societies. Even then, these new national monarchies did not rule over such large population groups as did the Asian rulers. Rather, regional states emerged to reintegrate political communities and define borders, although it took years for these new states to build stable foundations. To consolidate and extend their dominions, the rulers asserted their power and claimed legitimacy through a combination of force, religion, and strategic marital alliances.

To overcome the problem of regional dialects, Western European rulers chose one of the dialects to be the official state language at court. Administrators of the central government learned the official tongue in their rise up the ranks. Much later, the government would seek to create a uniform language out of the official tongue and to spread it among its subjects.

In Christendom, as in the House of Islam, rulers used religion to legitimize political regimes. Priests instructed their flocks that, after loyalty and obedience to God, loyalty and obedience were owed to legally established rulers. Sacred rituals, such as the holy oil used to anoint the king's body in France, permeated royal coronations. In both England and France, people believed that the royal touch would cure them of a skin disease called scrofula.

Divine blessings did not eliminate the need for naked force, however. Even after brutally suppressing peasant revolts in the fourteenth century, rulers still had to deal with resistance from a variety of quarters. Most threatening to those who sought to centralize power was the opposition of aristocrats, which flared whenever dynasts tried to whittle away feudal privileges. In contrast to the Ottoman and Chinese empires, where elites generally could not command sufficient resources to raise their own armies, in Europe, many could. Thanks to feudal dues, European nobles had access to their own sources of revenue.

Compounding the problems of state-builders were continuing challenges from the peasantry. In France, tax collectors might find their houses burned down by peasants claiming that the king could never have approved their gouging. In German city-states, Christian tradesmen often revolted against urban policies allowing Jewish competitors to buy and sell in their towns, and sometimes burnt down ghettoes to make their point.

Not all opposition was violent, however. After the 1460s, the printing press was available for criticisms of policies and rulers. Despite governments' attempts at censorship, clandestine presses and anonymous pamphlets circulated news and views quite different from those in newspapers sponsored by kings. Illicit publishing was an important form of political action, when consultative bodies gave no voice to most nonaristocratic men, and virtually no representation to women of any social class.

As states did form in Europe by the sixteenth century, they did so on the basis of strict hierarchies. The dynasts at the top shared some power with nobles and clergy; next came the learned lawyers, great merchants and their families; then the traders and artisans. Peasants sat at the foot of the pyramid. This hierarchical political structure was reinforced by hierarchical concepts of the family: husbands over wives, parents over children. But hierarchies could and did falter, and no single state achieved and held preeminence for long.

Despite European rulers' efforts at state-building and expansion, their populations remained quite small, and the boundaries of their states were fairly compact compared to the Ottoman and Ming empires. In the middle of the sixteenth century, Portugal and Spain, Europe's two most expansionist states at the time, had populations of 1 million and 9 million respectively. Compare these figures with Ming China's population of nearly 200 million in 1550, Mughal India's 110 million in 1600, and the Ottoman empire's 25 million in 1600. England, excluding Wales, was a mere 3 million in 1550. Only France with 17 million had a population close to that of the Ottoman empire. With such numbers, the Europeans would have far to go in asserting themselves on the world stage.

PORTUGAL   Among the earliest new dynasts to emerge in the fourteenth century were the Portuguese rulers in Lisbon. The fortunes of the newly established House of Aviz were largely tied to overseas exploits. The family patriarch, João (John) I (ruled 1385–1433), came to power after defeating an invading Castilian army, and he began his long reign by fostering maritime efforts in the North Atlantic. João enjoyed the support of many commoners, in part because he was willing to take on the Portuguese nobles. The nobles were in turn bought off through special gifts and patronage. João created a strong monarchy, making external and internal alliances, using religious unity as an instrument of national cohesion, and promoting foreign trade and territorial expansion overseas. One of the country's apparent weaknesses, its relatively small population of 1 million, proved an advantage, for the Portuguese nobility and crown had a less diverse population to instill with loyalty and obedience.

> *In contrast to the Ottoman and Chinese empires, where nobles generally could not command sufficient resources to raise their own armies, in Europe, many could.*

The death and destruction in the Mediterranean area resulting from the Black Death, as well as fear of the pirates who roamed the Mediterranean area, led the Portuguese to look to new horizons of commerce. The Portuguese had the advantage of a long tradition of fishing and seafaring in the Atlantic Ocean. Wishing to avoid the Muslim-controlled overland route through the Sahara to the gold and pepper of Africa, they decided to look for a direct seaward route that would take them to West Africa. Moreover, the fall of Constantinople to the Ottoman Turks in 1453, which threatened to close down Europe's Mediterranean trade routes (although it did not), provided a further incentive to Portuguese seamen to look for an alternate route to the Orient. Having learned how to deal with the strong Atlantic currents and winds along the coast of West Africa, Portuguese mariners pressed on along the coast of the African continent. They thus revived long-distance trade, redirecting the trade routes away from the Mediterranean and toward the Atlantic Ocean and the coast of Africa. By turning toward the Atlantic and western Africa, Portugal's royal family, nobility, and merchants showed the way to the rest of Europe.

Islam's presence on Europe's borders energized the Portuguese dynasty, for it created the illusion of a common enemy.

For centuries, Portuguese Christians had fought Muslim occupants. By the middle of the thirteenth century, they had succeeded in driving Muslims from the south in a war that consolidated an effective fighting machine. In 1415, the Portuguese crossed the Strait of Gibraltar and captured the Moorish Moroccan fortresses at Ceuta, in North Africa. They could now sail between the Mediterranean and the Atlantic without Muslim interference. With the Muslim threat diminished, the enemy was now perceived to be Portugal's neighbor, Castile, whose expansionist designs on the Iberian peninsula forced fractious Portuguese elites to draw even more closely together, first for self-defense, and later for territorial aggrandizement.

One of João's sons, Prince Henrique (1394–1460), later known as "Henry the Navigator," never ruled as king, but he further expanded the family's domain by supporting Portuguese expeditions down the coast of Africa and offshore to the Atlantic islands of the Madeiras and the Azores. The west and central coasts of Africa and the islands of the North and South Atlantic, including the Cape Verde Islands, São Tomé, Principe, and Fernando Po, soon became Portuguese ports of call.

The Portuguese monarchs allocated the Atlantic islands to nobles, granting them as hereditary possessions on condition that the grantees colonize these new lands. Soon the colonizers were establishing lucrative sugar plantations on the islands. In gratitude, noble families and merchants threw their political weight behind the king. Although the regime teetered briefly in the second half of the fifteenth century, subsequent monarchs continued to reduce the traditional power of local nobles and to ensure the smooth succession of power to members of the royal family. Political consolidation enabled Portugal to thrive in the wake of the Black Death.

SPAIN, FRANCE, AND ENGLAND Spain, the Low Countries (Belgium and the Netherlands), England, and France followed the Portuguese example and established national monarchies following the chaos of the fourteenth century. Their rebound, however, was slower and was marred by internal feuding and regional warfare (see Map 2-7).

The road to dynasty in Spain was arduous. Like France, Spain was fragmented into various kingdoms, each controlled by noble families that quarreled ceaselessly with each other. Over time, however, marriages and the formation of kinship ties among nobles and between royal lineages slowly allowed for the consolidation of a new political order. The first step came as early as 1162, when a marital union brought the Crown of Aragon and the County of Barcelona together. One by one, the major houses of the Spanish kingdoms intermarried, culminating in the most fateful wedding of Iberian royal heirs: the marriage of Isabella of Castile and Ferdinand of Aragon in 1469.

Thus, Spain's two most important provinces were joined, and Spain became a state to be reckoned with.

By the time Isabella and Ferdinand married, Spain was recovering from the miserable fourteenth century. Castile and Aragon's population, for instance, rebounded from about 6 million in 1450 to 8.5 million in 1482. This was more than just a marriage of convenience. Castile was wealthy and populous; Aragon enjoyed an extended trading emporium in the Mediterranean, including access to Italian, and especially Genoese financiers. Together, they brought unruly nobles and distant towns under their domain. They also began to root out religious heretics, renewing in 1481 the Inquisition whose aim was to identify and drive out bogus Christians, especially Jews and Muslims who had converted to Christianity. Finally, they began the last phase of recapturing Spanish lands from Muslims, culminating in the reconquest of Granada in 1492. In that year, they ordered all Jews to become Christians or to leave Spain. They topped off their achievements by marrying their children into other European royal families, especially the House of Habsburg. Such a marriage with the Habsburgs produced a grandson to Ferdinand and Isabella, who would later consolidate Habsburg preeminence in Europe and become the Holy Roman emperor, Charles V.

> *Spain, the Low Countries, England, and France followed Portugal and established national monarchies following the chaos of the fourteenth century.*

The fortunes of France and England were as closely linked with each other, as were those of Portugal and Spain. Just as the Portuguese had to fend off an invading Castilian army, so did the French have to do battle with invading English armies. When the French finally pushed the English back across the English Channel in the Hundred Years' War (1337–1453), the French House of Valois began a slow process of consolidating royal power. Once again, strategic marriages helped the French crown expand its domain, though the local nobility remained extremely powerful. It would take a further two centuries of royal initiatives and civil war to tame it. In England, even thirty years of civil war (1455–1485) between the houses of Lancaster and York did not settle which dynastic house would take the throne. Both families in this War of the Roses ultimately lost out to a new family, the Tudors, who seized the throne in 1485. Henry VII (ruled 1485–1509), a descendant of the House of Lancaster, was the first Tudor king, and he legitimized his rule by marrying Elizabeth of York, who belonged to the family that was the nominal victor of the civil war.

In France and England, the great age of European monarchy had yet to dawn. Kings were still largely considered the first among many noble knights in their domains. As late as 1559, on his deathbed, King Henry II of France graciously forgave the courtier who put his eye out during a joust; kings were still not too exalted to compete with their aristocratic henchmen, nor were they powerful enough to eliminate the privileges of

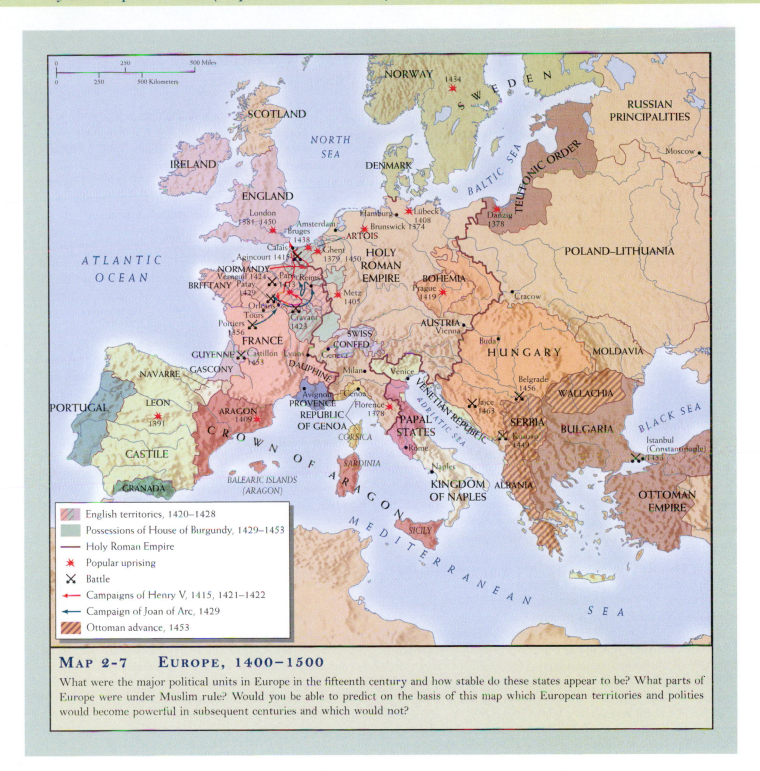

MAP 2-7   EUROPE, 1400–1500

What were the major political units in Europe in the fifteenth century and how stable do these states appear to be? What parts of Europe were under Muslim rule? Would you be able to predict on the basis of this map which European territories and polities would become powerful in subsequent centuries and which would not?

important nobles. Many states had medieval assemblies of noblemen, like the Cortes, in Castile, which advised the king on matters of great import; many towns had their own "corporate" privileges, with which kings could not tamper. And many of the great dynasts of this period—like the Jagiellons, who ruled over the medieval nations of Poland, Lithuania, Bohemia, and Hungary—did not last. Finally, in Italy and Switzerland, city-states continued to flourish despite the plague. Unlike Asia, which had created highly centralized administrations by the end of the fifteenth century, Europe at this time was only beginning to centralize, with kings seeking to establish their power over rebellious nobles, to find funds to support standing armies, and to set up administrative structures to govern the state more effectively.

THE RISE OF A CHARISMATIC LEADER IN A TIME OF SOCIAL TURMOIL: JOAN OF ARC

The immense historical impact made by a French peasant girl, Joan of Arc, demonstrates the importance given to rare and charismatic individuals, even women leaders in predominantly male-dominated societies, during periods of social turmoil. Europe in the late fourteenth and early fifteenth centuries was beset by plagues, famines, and war. Its people, thus, were willing to look for help to the special talents of women, even in areas like warfare, where women had been largely excluded. Indeed, if not for Joan of Arc, the country we know today as France might not exist. Appearing on the scene in 1429, as the English seemed to have gained the upper hand in the Hundred Years' War, she rallied the French against the English occupiers and turned the tide of the war. Although by no means a patriot in the nineteenth-century sense of the term, by giving religious sanction, as well as military succor, to the Valois monarch Charles VII, she made possible the consolidation of France and left Europe an inspiring, yet enigmatic, image of the female warrior-saint.

The world of Joan's childhood was a chaotic one, in which English lords were laying claim to various French-speaking principalities. By 1420, Valois authority had been greatly eroded. Important French lords soon began to sense the wind blowing in the English direction, and English armies gradually conquered more and more French towns. In 1428, they laid siege to Orléans, a large town in north-central France; to contemporaries, it seemed a symbolic battle: as Orléans went, they thought, so the war would go—and so would God wish it to go.

This is the point at which the paths of a seventeen-year-old peasant girl and the monarch of France crossed. Beginning at about age thirteen, the shy girl had received visions of saints who instructed her to come to rescue Orléans and conduct France's ruler to be crowned king at Reims Cathedral (he had not been crowned there, in the tradition of all French kings, because the English armies controlled Reims, Paris, and northern France). For five years, Joan resisted, but at last she agreed to obey her celestial advisers. Granted an audience with Charles VII in 1429, Joan impressed him with her piety and her passionate devotion to the Valois crown. He concluded that God really had sent her to serve France's cause—and his own. Joan was given command of 7,000 to 8,000 men and, wearing a suit of armor and brandishing a sword, she marched to relieve Orléans. Joan directed the assault with brilliance, and inspired the French forces; her charisma came not only from a tradition of female Christian "seers," but also from the peculiarity of her appearance (a young woman in male attire), and her appeal to French speakers who preferred their local French lords and customs to rule by English "outsiders." On Sunday, May 8, she drove the English from Orléans, and then pressed on to Reims; here, thanks to her military victories, Charles VII was crowned, fulfilling her visions. He was now king of France—and though the war continued, the tide now turned in favor of the French.

The tide for Joan, however, began to turn for the worse. Although she continued to direct the troops with remarkable savvy, she failed to force open the gates of Paris, and jealous courtiers around Charles began to question her divine authority. She was wounded, then taken prisoner. After a year in English captivity, she was tried by the Inquisition and found guilty—at the hands of jealous and pro-English judges—of heresy, on the grounds that her visions were false and misleading. On May 30, 1431, she was burned at the stake in the marketplace in the town of Rouen. Since that time, she has been seen as a heroic and charismatic martyr, and her name has very often been employed by the French in attempts to awaken French patriotism against foreign threats.

The fact that this young, illiterate woman played such an important role in the history of European warfare and state formation testifies to the fact that even in these spheres, male aristocrats, intellectuals, and clerics were not the only important actors. At the right place, at the right time, a woman could use courage, faith, and intelligence to make her visions prevail. Joan's followers believed that female magic could restore order to their lives, even while fearing witchcraft. They accepted her cross-dressing and personalist style of political and military leadership as proof of her calling. Yet, her death at the stake is a reminder that every charismatic heroine may be, for the opposing side, a heretic.

✦ *Why was Europe so disunited (compared to China and Islam)?*

TRADE IN EUROPE

Just as its polities suffered, European economies, especially commercial networks, also took a beating from disease. Plague killed many of Europe's traders. Mediterranean fairs, once the gathering places for merchants from Syria, North Africa, and Europe, became better known as the source of disease and vice than as markets for Eurasia's spices, fine textiles, and precious gems. Europe sank into an economic depression.

With time, as polities began to take shape, commercial ties also recovered. In some places, the revival occurred surprisingly quickly. Indeed, while Italian city-states like Genoa and Venice were decimated by the plague in the mid-fourteenth century, they also were able to spring back to mercantile life quite quickly. The Venetian merchants enjoyed a unique role in the exchange of silks and spices from the eastern edge of the Mediterranean to European ports. They also possessed cash reserves—money they could use to extend lines of credit across the Mediterranean—from Lisbon and the Algarve (in southern Portugal) at one end, to Acre, Cairo, and Constantinople on the other. European merchants sold copper, olive oil, woolens, and, in lieu of merchandise, precious metals to Syrian merchants. Italian merchants brokered the flow.

In terms of the commercial balance between the eastern and western flanks of Eurasia, Asia enjoyed vast trading advantages over the West. Europe was eager to acquire the goods of Asia, but had little that the Asians were eager to take in return. A trade deficit occurred that Europe could only cover by shipping precious metals to Asia. The need for precious metals sent the Europeans in search of new sources, and ultimately led (as we shall observe in Chapter 3) to expeditions along the coast of Africa. In central Europe, silver miners did a brisk business sending their ore to Mediterranean ports to enter the general flow of goods and money. The Portuguese also used their new toeholds in northern Africa to trade for sub-Saharan specie. Camel caravans from the western Sudan, the Upper Niger River, and Senegal carried gold from the inland mines to the coast. So opulent were the profits that the Portuguese tried to seize the port

> *Europe was eager to acquire the goods of Asia, but had little that the Asians were eager to take in return.*

Market Fair. This unusual mural depicts everyday life in a medieval marketplace. Here, women played a central role, especially in the buying and selling of food and clothing.

town of Tangier from the Moors in 1471, only to be driven back. Arab and African traders preserved their control over coveted specie. In some industries, however, Europeans did manage to wrest some control. The production of sugar, grown on slave plantations along the Syrian coast, and in Sicily, Cyprus, Crete, and Rhodes, went into decline with the Black Death. But an increased demand for refined sugar led to the search for new locations to grow sugarcane. Funded by Italian merchants, Portuguese, and later Spanish, investors adapted sugar plantations in their own territories, especially in the newfound colonies of the Azores and the Canary Islands.

Venice became the leading entrepot for the flow of commodities between the east and west of Eurasia. Merchant families contracted networks of agents and representatives around the major ports of the Mediterranean, and ensured that intermarriage among other powerful merchant families kept the competition from getting out of hand. Like the rulers of Europe's dynasties, marriage and kinship relations among the region's leading bankers and traders was a way of coping with friction and conflict as communities tried to rebuild after the destruction of the fourteenth century.

EUROPEAN IDENTITY AND THE RENAISSANCE

Europe's political and economic revival from the catastrophes of the fourteenth century also included a powerful outpouring of cultural achievements, which, too, was strongly linked to the rise of new polities. In the nineteenth century, scholars coined the word "Renaissance" (rebirth) to characterize the expanded cultural production of the Italian city-states, France, the Low Countries, England, and the Holy Roman empire in the period between about 1430 and 1550. Although the texts of Greek and Roman antiquity were not unknown in Europe, and certainly had been known in the Muslim world throughout the medieval period, the use to which Europeans put this knowledge was new. The term "Renaissance" captures contemporaries' sense that they were making a break with the church-centered medieval world and establishing a new concept of man as the center of the world. Looking back to ancient texts, scholars and artists found non-Christian models for geography and poetry, rhetoric and philosophy, medicine and natural history. In the process, they developed a new aesthetic and a secular foundation for elite education. Rather than simply learning church theology, students could now study classically based "humanities" to explore the past and present. The ancients became the yardstick against which modern ideas and arts could be

judged, and those who best knew the Latin and Greek sources became admired authorities on subjects ranging from physiology to military operations.

Economic prosperity, the increasing pace of book circulation (after Europeans made their own printing presses in the 1460s), and inter-state competition spread Renaissance culture throughout Europe by the late sixteenth century. Many princes now sought to display their wealth and power by buying paintings and sculptures. Philip II of Spain purchased more than 1,000 paintings during his reign. Courtiers followed suit, building up-to-date palaces and inviting learned scholars to live on their estates. Italian merchants, whose patronage of scholars had been very important in the Renaissance's early years, were now joined by German, French, and Dutch merchant patrons. While buying cultural goods did not make them equal to aristocrats, certainly the commercial elite was able to show, by cultivating the arts and educating their sons, that it was becoming as socially influential as those with inherited titles. Even the church found Renaissance art and scholarship appealing. The artists Raphael and Michelangelo often worked for the pope; several of the great sixteenth-century humanists—Desiderius Erasmus (1466–1536) and Philipp Melanchthon (1497–1560)—contributed much to the launching of the Reformation.

The relationship between Renaissance humanists and artists and their patrons in politics and the church was not always an easy one. Indeed, since political and religious power were not united in Europe, as they were in China and the Islamic world, scholars and artists had the opportunity to play one side off against the other, or alternatively, to suffer both clerical and political persecution. Erasmus criticized the church, but he survived happily on the patronage of English, Dutch, and French supporters; the popes had their own, very large, stable of lawyers and humanists, who ably defended the church against critics or secular claimants to church lands. As competition grew, artists and scholars could move from state to state in search of sympathetic patrons. As they did so, the educated elite became more and more cosmopolitan, as they had in China and in the Islamic empires. Scholars met one another in royal palaces and cultural centers like Florence, Antwerp, or Amsterdam. They began to correspond, asking for specialized information or rare books. Thus, gradually, a network of educated men and women formed that was not wholly dependent on either the church or the state, but which, increasingly, had the power to debunk old truths and create new beauties. If humanism often confirmed the status quo, it also would prove to be a means by which authority—political, clerical, and aesthetic—could be tested by individuals other than princes and priests.

> *The term "Renaissance" captures contemporaries' sense that they were making a break with the church-centered medieval world and establishing a new concept of man as the center of the world.*

Florence. This 1480 painting of Florence shows a bird's eye view of the city during the Renaissance. Florence expanded its territory and trade after the Black Death. Note the density of the urban area, as well as the profusion of church spires and the prominence of waterways.

In some cases, humanists and commercial entrepreneurs came together, creating strikingly new visions of governance. In Florence, a new self-image emerged after the devastation of the Black Death. As the plague subsided, the remaining residents devoted their skills and relatively enhanced fortunes to the expansion of Florentine territory, trade, banking networks, and textile production. Exporting woolens and silks to the Middle East as well as to Europe, and serving as the bankers of preference to the popes and all major European entrepots, Florentine citizens amassed new disposable wealth—and gladly embraced a legacy rediscovered for them by the scholarly elite. Emphasizing the city's origins in Roman Republican times and its success in commerce, Florentines pioneered a kind of secular, civic patriotism that inspired, for example, the production of the first secular histories and eloquent discourses on liberty and civic virtue. But it was also a Florentine, Niccolò Machiavelli, who wrote the most famous treatise on the maintenance of authoritarian power (*The Prince*) in 1513. He argued that political leadership was not about obeying God's rules but about mastering the amoral means of modern statecraft. Holding and exercising power could be ends in themselves.

Neither in Florence nor elsewhere did the Renaissance produce a consensus about who should rule: its artists and scholars simply reproduced (and sometimes exacerbated) rivalries between polities, between church and state, and increasingly between wealthy merchants and titled aristocrats. Instead, it produced a culture of critics and competitive individuals, who looked to many sources of authority and power—ancient texts as well as modern princes, wealth as well as blood—for support. It also produced an image of the "good Europe," one in which all these rivalries would produce, not warfare, but legitimate, stable government, not patrons who protected intellectuals because they were useful to them, but real freedom of thought. It was this dream of a good, "civilized" Europe, in combination with the crusaders' desire to spread the true faith, that would, in the following centuries, be endlessly contrasted to the "barbarism" of the rest.

CONCLUSION

Comparisons help us to understand complex institutions and historical events like those that took place in Eurasia in the two centuries after the Black Death. There have been other eras of feverish state-building and other empires that exercised military might over large expanses of territory. But anyone viewing these two centuries would have to concede that a small number of quite powerful, expansive, and centralized dynasties had thrust themselves or were beginning to thrust themselves onto the world stage. The ascent of each, except for the Mughals, stemmed, in the first instance, from the impact of the Mongol invasions and the Black Death. To these factors must be added numerous local developments—the ambition of a Ming warlord, the military expansionism of Turkish households on the edge of the Christian empire of Byzantium, and the unifying vision of Mughal rulers in the northern part of India. An eagerness to reestablish and expand trade networks following the

Mongol invasions and the Black Death and the desire to convert unbelievers to "the true faith" set many of the peoples of the world in motion.

The great dynasties that came to the fore in this period all had to deal with a common set of problems. They had to create legitimacy for themselves, had to ensure smooth procedures of succession to the throne when a monarch died, had to come to terms with religious groups, and had to establish working relationships with the nongovernmental elements in society, especially nobles, townspeople, merchants, and peasants. Yet, the states developed distinctive traits. The new Eurasian polities were a combination of outright political innovation, the use of well-known ways of ruling handed down within their own communities, and avid borrowing from nearby polities. The Ottoman rulers perfected techniques for ruling a far-flung and ethnically and religiously diverse empire. They were able to move military forces swiftly, to allow local identities a degree of autonomy, and at the same time to train a civil and military bureaucracy dedicated to the Ottoman and Sunni Islamic way of life. The Ming fashioned an imperial system based on a Confucian-trained bureaucracy and intense subordination, if not loyalty, to the emperor so that it could cope with the mammoth task of ruling over 200 million subjects. The monarchies of Europe were in the process of achieving a high degree of internal unity, although this unity was often brought about through warfare with neighbors. The rising monarchies of Europe, the Shiite regime of the Safavids in Persia, and the Ottoman state were all fired by religious fervor and sought to eradicate or subordinate the beliefs of other groups.

Eurasian societies and states recovered from the Mongols and the Black Death with greater political and economic powers than before. The Islamic states, the Ming empire, and the new monarchies that were coming into prominence in Europe were all founded on military prowess, and each of them was expansionist. Each recognized the importance of vigorous commercial activity. Each used dynastic marriage and succession, religion, and administrative bureaucracies to legitimize its rule. By the sixteenth century, societies across Eurasia were seeking to expand trade with their neighbors or to conquer them. The Muslim regimes especially, and their far-flung traders, engaged in increasing world trade. Their ascendance in turn provoked Europeans to find alternative trade routes to Africa and the Orient. Scarcely a century after the devastation of the plague, Europeans were exploring commercial connections east, south, and most unexpectedly, west. This surprising turn will be the theme of the next chapter.

Chronology

1289–1326	Osman begins to build Ottoman empire
1295	Great Khan makes Islam the state religion in Persia
1303	Delhi Sultanate army repulses Mongols
1315–1322	Famine in Europe
1320	Black Death begins in China
1328–1529	Valois Dynasty in France
1337–1453	Hundred Years' War in France
1347	Black Death reaches Italian port cities
1358	Jacquerie Revolt in France
1361–1362	New outbreaks of Black Death
1368–1398	Reign of Hongwu Emperor in China
1381	English Peasants' Revolt
1398	Timur sacks Delhi
1403–1424	Reign of Yongle Emperor in China
1405–1433	Zheng He's voyages from China
1415	Portuguese capture Ceuta in North Africa
1421–1451	Murad II expands the Ottoman empire
1429	French recapture Orléans from English
1451–1481	Mehmed II expands the Ottoman empire
1453	Ottoman armies conquer Constantinople
1455–1485	War of the Roses in England
1469	Castile and Aragon united
1485	Tudors seize English throne
1492	Christians take Granada from Muslims
1501	Shiism becomes Safavid state religion
1501–1524	Shah Ismail reigns over Safavid empire
1520–1566	Suleiman consolidates Ottoman empire
1526	Babur founds Mughal empire in India

FURTHER READINGS

Bois, Guy, *The Crisis of Feudalism: Economy and Society in Eastern Normandy, c. 1300–1550* (1984). A good case study of a French region that illustrates the turmoil in fourteenth-century Europe.

Brook, Timothy, *Praying for Power: Buddhism and the Formation of Gentry Society in Late Ming China* (1994). An analysis of the role of a significant religious force in the political and social developments of the Ming.

Dardess, John, *A Ming Society: T'ai-ho County, Kiangsi, Fourteenth to Seventeenth Centuries* (1996). A work that covers the different changes and developments of a single locality in China through the centuries.

Dols, Michael W., *The Black Death in the Middle East* (1977). One of the few scholarly works to examine the Black Death outside Europe.

Dreyer, Edward, *Early Ming China: A Political History, 1355–1435* (1982). A useful account of the early years of the Ming dynasty.

Hale, John, *The Civilization of Europe in the Renaissance* (1994). A beautifully crafted account of the politics, economics, and culture of the Renaissance period in Western Europe.

Hodgson, Marshall, *The Venture of Islam: Conscience and History in a World Civilization*, vol. 3 (1974). A good volume on the workings of the Ottoman state.

Itzkowitz, Norman, *Ottoman Empire and Islamic Tradition* (1972). Another good book on the Ottoman state.

Jackson, Peter, *The Delhi Sultanate* (1999). A meticulous, highly specialized, political and military history.

Jackson, Peter, and Lockhart, Lawrence (eds.), *The Cambridge History of Iran*, vol. 6 (1986). A volume that deals with the Timurid and Safavid periods in Iran.

Jones, E. L., *The European Miracle* (1981). A provocative work on the economic and social recovery from the Black Death.

Kafadar, Cemal, *Between Two Worlds: The Construction of the Ottoman State* (1995). A thorough reconsideration of the origins of one of the world's great land empires.

Karamustafa, Ahmed, *God's Uunruly Friends: Dervish Groups in the Islamic Later Middle Period, 1200–1550* (1994). A book that describes the unorthodox Islamic activities that were occurring in the Islamic world prior to and alongside the establishment of the Ottoman and Safavid empires.

Levathes, Louise, *When China Ruled the Seas: The Treasure Fleet of the Dragon Throne, 1405–33* (1994). A book that provides a lively account of the Zheng He expeditions.

McNeill, William, *Plagues and Peoples* (1976). A pathbreaking work with a highly useful chapter on the spread of the Black Death throughout the Eurasian land mass.

Morgan, David, *Medieval Persia, 1040–1797* (1988). Contains an informative discussion of the Safavid state.

Pierce, Leslie, *The Imperial Harem: Women and Sovereignty in the Ottoman Empire* (1993). A work that describes the powerful place that imperial women had in political affairs.

Pirenne, Henri, *Economic and Social History of Medieval Europe* (1937). A classic study of the economic and social recovery from the Black Death.

Reid, James J., *Tribalism and Society in Islamic Iran, 1500–1629* (1983). A useful account of how the Mongols and other nomadic steppe peoples influenced Iran in the era when the Safavids were establishing their authority.

Russell, Peter, *Prince Henry "the Navigator"* (2000). A close examination of the formation of the Portuguese kingdom of the House of Aviz.

Singman, Jeffrey L. (ed.), *Daily Life in Medieval Europe* (1999). An introductory description of the social and material world experienced by Europeans of different walks of life.

Tuchman, Barbara W., *A Distant Mirror: The Calamitous Fourteenth Century* (1978). A book that shows, in a vigorous way, how war, famine, and pestilence devastated Europeans in the fourteenth century.

Wittek, Paul, *The Rise of the Ottoman Empire* (1958). A work that contains vital insights on the emergence of the Ottoman state amidst the political chaos in Anatolia.

Contact, Commerce, and Colonization, 1450s–1600

On September 20, 1519, a fleet of five ships under the command of Ferdinand Magellan set out from the Spanish port of Sanlúcar de Barrameda. Nearly three years later, a single vessel returned home, having successfully circumnavigated the globe. This achievement had come at a high cost. Four ships had been lost, and only eighteen men, from an original complement of two hundred and sixty-five, staved off scurvy, starvation, and stormy seas to complete the journey. Magellan himself had died in a battle with inhabitants of the Philippines. But the survivors of Magellan's voyage had become the first true world travelers. In contrast to Ibn Battuta, Marco Polo, and earlier adventurers who confined their primarily overland treks to Eurasia and Africa, Magellan's transoceanic passage connected these worlds with those that had been apart—the Americas.

The voyages of Magellan and other European mariners did more than create contacts among cultures across the Atlantic, Pacific, and Indian Oceans. They also altered the economic and political relationships among all worlds. Crucial to this reconfiguring was the unexpected "discovery" of what European explorers proclaimed to be the "New World." Finding the Americas was not what Christopher Columbus had in mind when he headed west across the Atlantic. In his wake, however, Europeans set out to pray for and prey on the peoples of the Americas. In the conquest and colonization of the Americas, Europeans also drew heavily on connections with West Africa. During the sixteenth century, through trade in agricultural products and precious metals that were increasingly extracted from the Americas by African laborers, European merchants became more prominent participants in the vibrant commercial circuits of Eurasia.

By no means did this greater prominence translate immediately into imperial dominance for Europeans in Asia. Through the sixteenth century, the mightiest Asian empires—the Ming in China, the Mughal on the South Asian subcontinent, and the Ottoman straddling West Asia, North Africa, and southeastern Europe—maintained their economic prowess and retained control over all but small pockets of their expansive realms. Still, by 1600, the impact of the European conquest and colonization of the Americas was being felt around the globe, tipping the balance of military and economic power in Eurasia from east to west.

REVIVAL OF TRADE

> → *Why was silver critical to revitalizing sixteenth-century world trade?*

Even before the products of the Americas entered the circuits of Eurasian trade, long-distance commerce had staged an impressive recovery from the destruction wrought by the Black Death. Just as political leaders had rebuilt their states by mixing traditional ideas with innovative ones, so, too, merchant elites in Europe and Asia revived old trade patterns while establishing new networks. Increasingly, traffic across seas supplemented, if not supplanted, the overland transportation of goods across long distances. In the fifteenth century, the Indian Ocean and China Seas were the focal points of Eurasia's maritime commerce. Across these waters, an assortment of goods moved from one point to another, their shipment and exchange directed by a mixed group of merchants. Searching for new routes to South and East Asia, European mariners and traders began exploring the Atlantic coast of Africa. Lured by spices, silks, and slaves, and aided by advances in maritime technology, Portuguese expeditions made their way around Africa and to India in the last decade of the fifteenth century. At almost the same time, neighboring monarchs in Spanish kingdoms sponsored Christopher Columbus's bid to reach Asia by sailing west across the Atlantic. Both Portuguese and Spanish ventures shared similar motivations: to convert "heathen" peoples to Christianity and to reap the riches to be found in ports along the Indian Ocean and China Sea. But traders and rulers on the other end of Eurasia were not waiting around for Europeans to come to them. Indeed, through the fifteenth century, Europeans had little to offer their would-be trading partners.

THE REVIVAL OF THE CHINESE ECONOMY

Crucial to Eurasia's growing economies and populations was the dynamism of China. In the fifteenth century under the Ming dynasty, commerce rebounded from the devastation of Mongol invasions and the Black Death, and the Chinese achieved impressive economic growth rates. China's internal development, in turn, stimulated the other economies across the Eurasian land mass.

China's vast internal economy, not external trade, was the mainspring of the country's progress. The Ming transferred their capital city from the coastal settlement of Nanjing to the interior city of Beijing, from whence the Yongle Emperor had originally come. Here the Ming believed they could better defend themselves against the Mongols. With the scale of the domestic market, this move had no adverse impact on the economy. Chinese merchants, artisans, and cash crop farmers took advantage of a rapidly growing population. Over the three centuries of Ming rule, the Chinese populace doubled and increasingly congregated in large cities. The reconstruction between 1411 and 1415 of the Grand Canal, which stretched from Hangzhou in the south to Beijing in the north, opened a major artery that enabled food and riches from the lower Yangzi region to provision Beijing and the northern border cities. China's

Focus Questions CONTACT, COMMERCE, AND COLONIZATION

> → *Why was silver critical to revitalizing sixteenth-century world trade?*
> → *What military and maritime technologies advanced Portuguese exploration?*
> → *Why were Spanish conquistadors able to dominate in the New World?*
> → *How was Europe transformed politically and spiritually?*
> → *Why did trade expand and wealth increase in sixteenth-century Asia?*

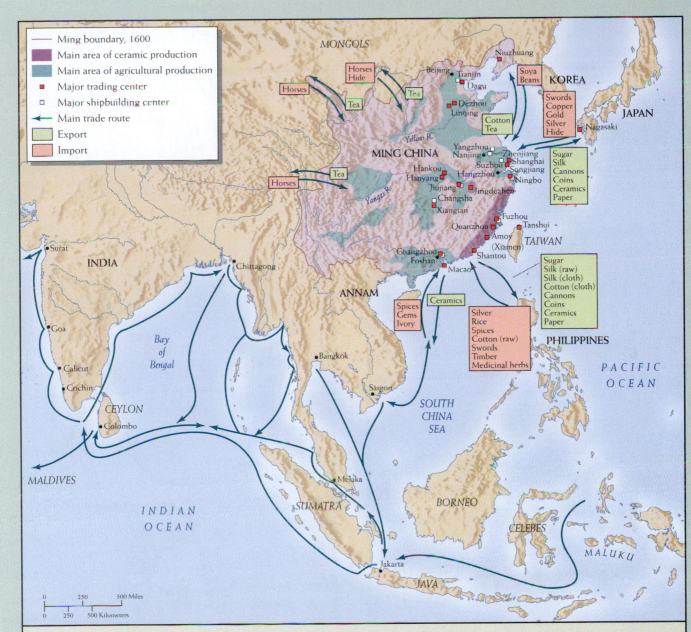

Legend:
— Ming boundary, 1600
▨ Main area of ceramic production
▨ Main area of agricultural production
■ Major trading center
□ Major shipbuilding center
← Main trade route
▨ Export
▨ Import

MAP 3-1   TRADE AND PRODUCTION IN MING CHINA

The Ming Empire at the beginning of the seventeenth century was the world's most populous state and arguably its wealthiest. What were the main items involved in China's export-import trade? Why was China the world's leading importer of silver in the seventeenth and eighteenth centuries? What were the main overland items of trade and what were the main overseas items of trade? Why were there such great differences in the commodities involved in these two avenues of trade?

cities themselves, such as Nanjing with a population approaching a million and Beijing at half a million, became massive and lucrative markets. In addition to Nanjing, the growth of other urban centers in the lower Yangzi area such as Suzhou and Yangzhou further challenged, and then eclipsed, Hangzhou's preeminence. Further south, the sister cities of Guangzhou (Canton) and Foshan together had as many residents as the whole of Europe's urban population around 1600.

China's elaborately developed trading networks distributed silk and cotton textiles, rice, porcelain ceramics, paper, and many other products all over the country. The Ming state's concerns about the autonomy of the merchant classes did not dampen internal trade, and its efforts to curb overseas commerce, following Zheng He's voyages (see Chapter 2), were also largely unsuccessful. As long as merchants did not disturb the Ming order, they were ignored and tolerated. In spite of the government's strictures on engaging in overseas trade, coastal cities remained active harbors (see Map 3-1).

The Chinese alone manufactured brocaded silks and porcelain ceramics to the highest standards of workmanship. Many

Making and Painting Porcelain. The production of porcelain, for both the domestic and external markets, became a highly sophisticated enterprise during the Ming dynasty. The most famous center was the cluster of workshops at Jingdezhen, where there was a clear division of labor among the artisans, each specializing in a particular part of the production process, including decorating and glazing porcelain cups and bowls as shown here.

Chinese cities produced silk textiles, but the city that acquired the reputation for producing the best quality was Suzhou, south of the Yangzi River. So important were the products of the Suzhou artisans to the Ming budget that taxes on their silks often provided one-tenth of the state's revenues. The second of the most prized commodities of the Ming period was porcelain, the first pieces of which were found in the town of Jingdezhen. The biggest single consumers, with the deepest of pockets, were the Ming rulers themselves. Potentates of the Ming court developed an almost insatiable appetite for porcelains of high quality. With their access to the fiscal reserves of the govern-

ment, they purchased nearly all of its most beautiful products, leaving the rougher and more durable of Jingdezhen's output for the less discerning foreign buyers.

Although the Chinese kept the best for themselves, their silks and porcelain were coveted by wealthy persons across Eurasia. But buyers outside of China faced a severe problem. What did they have to trade with the Chinese?

The answer was silver, which became essential to the smooth functioning of the Ming monetary system. Ming predecessors had used paper money and copper coinage, but Ming consumers and traders mistrusted anything but silver or gold for their commercial transactions, though coins of varying quality continued to circulate for ordinary market exchanges. Silver also became a mainstay of the Ming fiscal system. Especially once the rulers adopted the precious metal as a means of tax payment in the 1430s, silver became the predominant medium for larger commercial transactions.

Fortunately for foreigners, China did not produce silver in sufficient quantities. Indeed, silver and other precious metals were about the only commodities that China needed to import and for which the Chinese were willing to trade their highly valued manufactures. Foreigners learned to exploit this need. China's main supplier of silver in the sixteenth century was Japan, which one Florentine merchant referred to as the "silver islands." During the sixteenth century, however, China turned increasingly to the Americas for its silver supplies. With American silver, as we will see later in this chapter, Europeans gained much greater access to China's precious goods, especially silk and porcelain.

> *Silver and other precious metals were about the only commodities that China needed to import and for which the Chinese were willing to trade their highly valued manufactures.*

a single overarching political authority. This gave them considerable autonomy from political affairs and allowed them to occupy strategic positions in the long-distance trade of Eurasia.

Of the many port cities that connected the peoples and commodities of the Indian Ocean, none was more important than Melaka, located at a choke point on the Malay Peninsula between the Indian Ocean and the South China Sea. Unlike other trading places in this region, it had no hinterland of farmers to support it. Instead, Melaka thrived exclusively as an emporium for world traders, thousands of whom resided in the city or passed through it. Indeed, Melaka's merchants were a microcosm of the Indian Ocean's diverse community of traders. Arabs, Indians, Armenians, Jews, East Africans, Persians, and eventually Western Europeans established themselves there to participate in and profit from the commerce that moved in and out of Melaka's port.

REVIVAL OF INDIAN OCEAN TRADE

Chinese economic expansion was part of a broader revival of Indian Ocean trade in the fifteenth century. Although merchants sought to trade with China, they also developed a brisk commerce that tied the whole of the Indian Ocean together. Once again ports in East Africa and the Red Sea were linked with the coastal cities of the Indian subcontinent and the Malay Peninsula. Muslims dominated the Indian Ocean trade, and Islam provided a unifying religion and a judicial system, but by no means were all merchants followers of Allah.

The Indian subcontinent was the geographic and economic center of these trade routes. Its population expanded as rapidly as that of China, and it also had large cities, such as Agra, Delhi, and Lahore, each of which had nearly half a million residents. India's manufacturing center was Bengal, which exported silk and cotton textiles and rice to the rest of the subcontinent and throughout Southeast Asia. There was a parallel then between Indian trade and Chinese commerce. Like China, India had a favorable trade balance with Europe and West Asia, exporting textiles and pepper, the spice most coveted by Europeans, in exchange for silver.

But in dealing with China, Indian merchants faced the same problem as Europeans and West Asians: they had to pay for Chinese silks and porcelains with silver. This made Indian merchants as dependent on gaining access to silver as the rest of those seeking advantage in Chinese commerce. What is more, unlike Chinese merchants, Indian and Islamic traders in the commercial hubs from the Red Sea to Melaka did not obey

OVERLAND COMMERCE AND OTTOMAN EXPANSION

The growth of seaborne commerce eclipsed but did not destroy overland caravan trading. To the contrary, along some routes,

Chinese Porcelain Box. The shape, coloring, and texture of this Chinese porcelain writing box are a tribute to the exquisite craftsmanship that went into its production. It was also a symbol of the flourishing world trade, and a typical example of what the French then called "chinoiserie," the possession of which was considered a hallmark of taste and cultivation among the rich and the status-conscious in Europe.

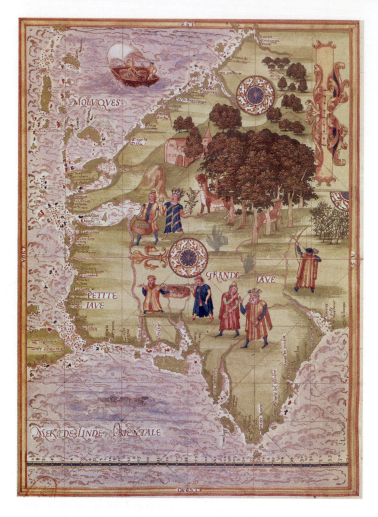

The Spice Islands. This watercolor by the French artist, Guillaume Le Testu, painted in 1555 and titled *Commerce of Spices at the Molucca Islands*, indicates the attraction these Southeast Asian islands (now collectively called Maluku) had for Europeans in the sixteenth century. The important island of Java is identified in the painting, and some of the individuals are portrayed carrying nutmeg nuts.

overland commerce thrived anew. One of these well-trafficked routes ran across northern Eurasia, linking the Baltic Sea, Muscovy, Central Asia, and China. Southern routes, connecting China and Indian Ocean ports to the Ottoman empire's heartland and then on to Europe, also saw an increase in commercial traffic.

Of the many great entrepots that grew up along caravan routes, none enjoyed a more spectacular economic success than Aleppo in Syria. Thanks to its prime location at the end of the caravan routes from India and Baghdad, Aleppo came to overshadow its other Syrian rivals, Damascus and Homs. It became a vital supply point for Anatolia, Syria, and the Mediterranean cities. Indeed, by the end of the sixteenth century, it had become the most important commercial center, particularly for silk, in the whole of the Middle East.

The Aleppans, like others within the Ottoman empire, revered successful merchants. Rich merchants were extolled as "paragons" and celebrated, in popular stories such as *The Thousand and One Nights*, as shrewd men who had amassed enormous wealth by mastering the intricacies of the caravan trade. Those close to the trade recognized how difficult the merchant's task was. The caravans gathered on the edge of the city, where

Overland Caravans and Caravanserais. Muslim governments and merchants associations constructed inns, or caravanserais, along the major trading routes. These areas were capable of accommodating a large number of traders and their animals in great comfort.

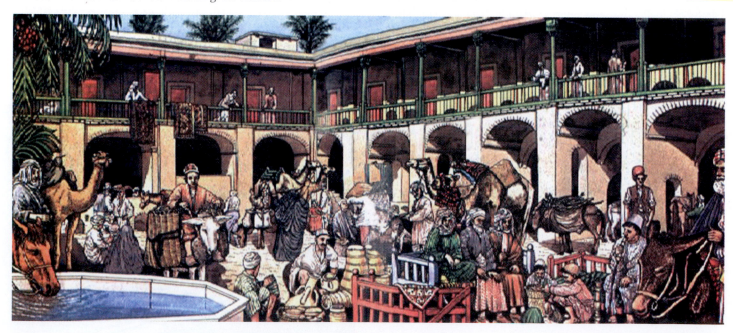

animals were hired, tents sewn, and saddles and packs arranged. Large caravans involved 600 to 1,000 camels and as many as 400 men; smaller parties required no more than a dozen animals. Whatever the size, a good leader was essential, for only someone who had knowledge of difficult desert routes and the confidence of the Bedouin tribes that provided safe passage for a fee could hope to make the journey profitable.

Ottoman authorities also took a keen interest in the caravan trade, since the state gained considerable revenue from taxes on it. To facilitate and secure the movement of caravans, the government maintained refreshment and military stations along the route. Some of these stations or caravansarais, were quite elaborate. The largest and most ornate were made of stone and had individual rooms set aside to accommodate the chief merchants. Some were so vast that they provided overnight lodging for 800 travelers and could feed and care for all their animals. Gathering so many traders, animals, and cargoes could also attract marauders. The main security threat came from Bedouin tribesmen who could not resist the temptation to plunder the caravanserais. To placate the marauders and stop the raids, authorities and merchants offered large cash payments to tribal chieftains as "protection money."

Revenue from the overland caravan trade helped finance the Ottoman empire's expansion. These taxes contributed to the support of Ottoman armies, which pushed the frontier of the empire westward across North Africa and northward into the Balkans. They also helped the Ottomans to develop a powerful navy that controlled the sea lanes of the eastern Mediterranean.

By the middle of the fifteenth century, Ottoman land forces had closed in on one of the great commercial centers of the Eurasian trade and the European gateway to the East: Constantinople. The Ottoman sultan, Mehmed II, had vowed to capture the capital of the Byzantine empire, and shortly after his coronation as emperor in 1451, he hatched his plan. First he built a fortress of his own, overlooking the heavily fortified city of Constantinople. He trained his artillery—including massive cannonry—against the great walls of the city. Until then, Constantinople had withstood many assaults; indeed, it had kept the Turks at bay for almost a century. But now the Turks amassed a huge army, outnumbering the defending force of 7,000 by more than tenfold. The sultan promised his soldiers free access to booty if they triumphed. Portraying himself as the agent of Allah, and the conquest of Constantinople as a holy cause, Mehmed led his soldiers into battle. After a heavy bombardment that lasted forty days, on May 29, 1453, Ottoman troops overwhelmed the surviving soldiers and took the ancient capital of Byzantium. Many inhabitants fled in terror. Mehmed, called "the Conqueror," made the city (which he renamed Istanbul) the capital of his own ascending empire. One of his first acts after the conquest of the city was to enter the most sacred of the Christian cathedrals, the largest house of worship in all Christendom, Hagia Sophia. There, he ordered one of his men to pronounce the Muslim creed that "there is no God but Allah and Muhammad is His Prophet." Mehmed continued his

The Conquest of Constantinople. Constantinople withstood an Ottoman siege for many months because of the strength of its fortifications, notably its huge walls, and because Venetians and Genoese supplied its population from the sea. But the huge manpower superiority and continuous bombardment of the walls finally enabled the Ottoman forces to overrun the city.

expansion from Istanbul, eventually seizing all of Greece and the Balkan region. From the former Christian capital, the Ottomans were poised to penetrate central Europe.

The Muslim conquest of Constantinople sent shock waves through Christendom. According to one monk, "nothing worse than this has happened nor will happen." When news reached the far-off Scandinavian world, Christian I, king of Norway and Denmark, declared that the triumph of the Turk was a signal of the forthcoming apocalypse. For him it represented the rise of the beast from the waters as described in the Bible. Italy braced itself for an invasion, and Europeans shuddered at reports that Mehmed longed to conquer the world and shed more Christian blood. Ottoman armies now menaced one of Europe's great capitals, Vienna, while Ottoman navies choked the Mediterranean sea lanes.

European merchants worried that the fall of Constantinople would mean that the Ottoman sultans would deprive them of safe passage to the East through the now-defunct Byzantine empire. The city's incorporation within the Ottoman empire, already expanding into eastern and central Europe, raised the unpleasant prospect that European merchants would be shut out

Hagia Sophia. After conquering Constantinople in 1453, Mehmed II, the Muslim Ottoman sultan, made Hagia Sophia, Byzantium's greatest cathedral, into a mosque, which he renamed Aya Sophia.

EUROPEAN EXPLORATION AND EXPANSION

> ✦ *What military and maritime technologies advanced Portuguese exploration?*

Somehow, new networks had to be created in the face of Ottoman power, prompting Europeans to probe unexplored links to the East. Some opted for territorial expansion against weaker neighbors. Muscovite tsars, for instance, presided over both defensive and commercial expansion across the Urals into Siberia. This stretched Christendom's eastern flank overland (see Chapter 4). Other Europeans looked south and west—and to the seas. With the Ottomans in control over land routes to the East, Western Europeans sought new sea lanes to sustain their access to the Asian goods. But instead of finding the desired maritime passage to Asia, European sailors accidentally discovered the Americas.

Before European monarchs could explore new avenues to Asia, they had to consolidate their control at home (see Chapter 2). For the rulers of the Iberian kingdoms, that meant reconquering the lands on the Iberian peninsula that were under Muslim rule.

IBERIAN RECONQUEST

Prior to 1492, the southwestern flank of Christendom was not an exclusively Christian domain. Indeed, even within those parts of present-day Spain and Portugal where Christian monarchs had asserted control, Muslims, Jews, and Christians lived side by side in relative harmony. But the royal families in Castile and Portugal were determined to drive Muslim armies from the Iberian peninsula. By the early fifteenth century, Portuguese forces had driven Muslims from their domains. In Spain, as well, Christian armies pushed Muslim forces further and further south, so that by the middle of the fifteenth century, only Granada, a strategic lynchpin overlooking the straits leading from the Mediterranean to the Atlantic, remained in Muslim hands. After a long and costly siege, the Christian forces entered the fortress of Granada. Iberia, indeed all of Western Europe, as of 1492 was under Christian rule.

When Granada fell, many in Western Christendom celebrated. It was a victory of enormous symbolic importance, as joyous as the fall of Constantinople was depressing. Pope Alexander recognized the triumph and praised the monarchs of Spain. In Spain proper, people thumped their chests in pride and indulged in a wave of intense patriotism.

In this moment of triumph, Isabella and Ferdinand sought to eliminate all traces of heterodoxy and infidelity from Spain. Already in 1481, they had launched the Inquisition, taking aim

of the lucrative Asian markets just as Asian economies were experiencing new dynamic growth.

These fears were not unfounded. Based in Tripoli and Algiers, Islamic merchants competed with European merchants. Ottoman allies in North Africa equipped their own corsairs to fight and plunder Christian vessels, especially Venetian and Genoese ships. In 1560, to defend their commerce, Europeans gathered a massive force of ninety ships and 12,000 men. On the island of Djerba, however, Turkish forces devastated the massive fleet (sinking half the ships) and captured the army of 10,000 survivors. The defeated soldiers were marched through the streets of Istanbul. With the Mediterranean increasingly insecure and the overland routes to Asia increasingly in the hands of powerful Ottomans, how were the Europeans to acquire the spices and textiles that had been coming to them from Asia? Europeans would have to find alternative routes to Asia.

especially against the *conversos*, converted Jews and Muslims, whom they suspected were unfaithful believers. When the walls of Granada fell, the crown ordered the expulsion of all Jews from Spain. By the terms of the treaty ending the war, the Moors were allowed to remain and to practice their religion. But, in 1609, they too would be formally expelled. All told, almost half a million people were forced to pack what possessions they could carry and flee the Spanish kingdoms. Those who converted and stayed behind faced torture and mass burnings before jeering crowds if they were found to be heretics or secret Jews or Muslims. Fueling this giant expulsion was a conviction that the struggle against Islam and Judaism constituted a just war. Both the Portuguese and Spanish believed that the reconquest was nothing less than the defense of a creed and that the Christians' victory was a form of divine justice. In some cases, the freed territories were seen as long-lost lands being restored to their legitimate lords.

The reconquest of Granada was marked by another fateful event—though one without the same immediate fanfare. In 1487, a Genoese navigator, Christopher Columbus (1451–1506), had appeared before Isabella and Ferdinand to ask for Spanish royal patronage to support a voyage into the "Ocean Sea" (the Atlantic) and to thereby open a more direct—and more lucrative—route to Japan and China. Columbus promised them the riches that could pay for their military campaigns and that could bankroll a final and decisive crusade to liberate Jerusalem from Muslim hands. Initially, Ferdinand and Isabella turned Columbus away, as had the Portuguese rulers and

Unlike Columbus, who planned to sail west across the Atlantic, Portuguese explorers headed south, looking to get to Asia by going around Africa.

merchants before them. But in late 1491, Columbus followed the Spanish monarchs to their camp below the besieged walls of Granada. Such was the tide of Spanish optimism and fervor after the reconquest in early 1492 that the monarchs at last agreed to back Columbus's modest but daring venture into the unknown. Off he sailed with a royal patent that guaranteed the Spanish monarchs a share of all he discovered.

THE PORTUGUESE IN AFRICA AND ASIA

Before the Ottomans had taken Constantinople, before the Spanish kingdoms of Castile and Aragon had cleansed their portion of the Iberian peninsula of Muslim armies, and before Isabella and Ferdinand sent Columbus on his way, neighboring Portugal had taken the lead in searching for a new maritime route to Asia (see Chapter 2). Unlike Columbus, who planned to sail west across the Atlantic, Portuguese explorers headed south, looking to get to Asia by going around Africa. Like Columbus, these Portuguese mariners combined a religious am-

bition to convert unbelievers to the true faith with the economic motive of gaining a cut, if not control, of the rich trade of the Indian Ocean.

The Portuguese decision to sail along the African coast and then into the Indian Ocean was not entirely determined by Asian economic developments, for Africa, too, was seen as a place from which to profit. During the Black Death and in its aftermath, Europe suffered from an acute shortage of precious metals. The price of gold had skyrocketed, enticing ambitious men to go out in search of this commodity and its twin, silver. Africa was thought to be a storehouse of precious metals. A fourteenth-century map of Africa, the Catalan Atlas from 1375–1380, illustrated a single black ruler, depicted as controlling a vast quantity of gold, in the interior of Africa. So, too, the fifteenth-century cartographic depiction of Africa, the so-called map of Columbus, also placed gold in the middle of the African land mass.

MARITIME TECHNOLOGY The Portuguese led the European ventures into oceanic voyaging because they were the most advanced maritime nation in Europe. Having absorbed the maritime knowledge of the Greeks and Arabs, the Portuguese added to it their navigational experiences in two of Europe's main sailing areas: the Mediterranean Sea and the North and Baltic Seas. The Portuguese used hybrid ships for their long-distance trips. One kind of ship, called a carrack, worked well on bodies of water like the Mediterranean, while the second, the caravel, was more suited for nosing in and out of estuaries and navigating in waters with unpredictable currents and winds. Often, vessels blended elements of carrack and caravel, which allowed Portuguese mariners to overcome some of the hazards that oceanic voyages had always presented. Only by using highly maneuverable caravel vessels and perfecting the technique of tacking (sailing into the wind rather than before it) were the Portuguese able to advance far along the West African coast. In addition, the Portuguese had become expert in the use of the compass and the astrolabe, which enabled them to determine their latitudes. More precise maps allowed Portuguese mariners to gain a better sense of where they were in the ocean. As they piloted their ships into new waters, especially as they crossed the equator and sailed into the Southern Hemisphere, their records of the stars and their maps permitted successors to make the same journeys more rapidly and more safely. Using these navigational skills and equipment, the Portuguese gradually advanced along the western coast of Africa and soon sailed into the Indian Ocean.

Sailing into new waters was not just a matter of making use of new technology, however. It was also about facing the unknown, or more precisely, facing what they believed they already

The Catalan Atlas. This 1375 map shows the world as it was then known. Not only does it depict the location of continents and islands, it also includes information on ancient and medieval tales, regional politics, astronomy, and astrology.

knew and greatly feared about distant areas. The Portuguese and Spanish mariners of the fifteenth century were, in many respects, still medieval men. They held to a set of commonly accepted notions about lands inhabited by giants and Amazons, and about seas of darkness in the great beyond, where high winds destroyed any vessel that entered. They also took with them views of faraway peoples: visions of Africans and Asians, whom they believed to husband great stores of wealth, and visions of others, whom they believed to be savage and primitive, given over to cannibalistic orgies.

SUGAR, SLAVES, AND GOLD　Africa and the islands along its coast proved to be far more than a stop-off en route to India

or a source of precious metals. The continent became a valued trading area, and its islands became prime locations in which to grow sugarcane, a crop that had exhausted the soils of Mediterranean islands where it had been cultivated since the twelfth century. Along what they called the Gold Coast, the Portuguese established many fortresses and ports of call. Having taken over islands off the West African coast, notably São Tomé, Principe, and Fernando Po, they introduced the cultivation of sugarcane on relatively large-scale plantations and used slave labor brought in from the African mainland. The Madeira, Canary, and Cape Verde archipelagos in particular became laboratories for plantation agriculture. Their rainfall and fertile soils made these islands ideally suited for growing sugarcane. Moreover, large numbers of workers were needed to cultivate, harvest, and process the sugarcane; hence, the availability of a supply of slave labor in the vicinity enabled Portugal and Spain to build sizeable plantations in their first formal colonies. Thus, in the fifteenth century, these islands off the coast of West Africa saw the beginnings of a plantation model that included a system of slavery that was to be transported across the Atlantic in the following century.

The Portuguese did not restrict the export of slaves to these West African possessions. As early as 1441, Portuguese merchants had brought a shipload of African slaves back to Portugal, where they were pressed into service as domestic workers. The slave trade to Portugal increased throughout the fifteenth and into the sixteenth century, so that by 1551 the city of Lisbon, with a population of over 100,000, was reported to have 10,000 African slaves.

COMMERCE AND CONQUEST IN THE INDIAN OCEAN

Having explored the African coast and established plantation colonies off it, Portuguese seafarers ventured into the Indian Ocean and inserted themselves into its thriving commerce (see Map 3-2). The first of these Portuguese mariners to reach the Indian Ocean was Vasco da Gama (1469–1524). Like Columbus, Da Gama was a relatively unknown sailor before he commanded four ships around the Cape of Good Hope in 1497. He then spent four months exploring the east coast of Africa but did not encounter either friendly traders or great riches. What he did encounter was a vast network of existing commercial ties spanning the Indian Ocean and skilled men who knew the currents, winds, and ports of call. Vasco da Gama took on board a Muslim pilot at Malindi, on the coast of East Africa, to instruct him on how to navigate in the winds and currents of the Indian Ocean. Indeed, throughout Portugal's exploration, European seamen relied on the aid and information furnished by seasoned Arab and Chinese mariners.

With his newfound partnership, Vasco da Gama sailed straight for the Malabar coast in southern India, one of the most important trading areas in the whole region, arriving there in 1498. Da Gama, for all his pioneering spirit, was still a cautious man, and he feared attack from the ports and capitals of rich Asian kingdoms. As he approached the west coast of India, he hesitated offshore, waiting for boats to greet him. Finally, he dispatched one of his convict-sailors to lead a party into Calicut, where the envoy proclaimed that the Portuguese were searching for Christians and spices. Two Tunisian traders replied: "You should give thanks to God for having brought you to a land where there are such riches." At Calicut, despite the disdain of the Indian traders for Portuguese goods and the reluctance of local rulers to per-

The Caravel Ship. As Europeans began to explore the Atlantic, they tinkered with maritime technology. In the sixteenth century, they figured out how to combine the bulk of old square-rigged ships with the maneuverability of lateen sails in their "caravels." Portrayed here is the caravel *Santa Maria*, which carried Christopher Columbus from Spain to the New World.

mit the Portuguese to trade, Da Gama was finally able to load his ships with a valuable cargo of spices and silks. Although he lost more than half of his crew on the difficult voyage back to Lisbon in 1499, he did prove the feasibility—and profitability—of trade via the Indian Ocean.

Da Gama's efforts laid the bases for Europe's first seaborne presence in Asia and promoted Lisbon into a major entrepot. With the aid of their Muslim guides, the Portuguese mapped out in detail the commercial opportunities scattered across the Indian Ocean. Once there, European vessels sailed directly for the most important commercial and strategic locations in the region. Indian Ocean commerce had three great

> *The islands off the coast of West Africa saw the beginnings of a plantation model that included a system of slavery that was to be transported across the Atlantic in the following century.*

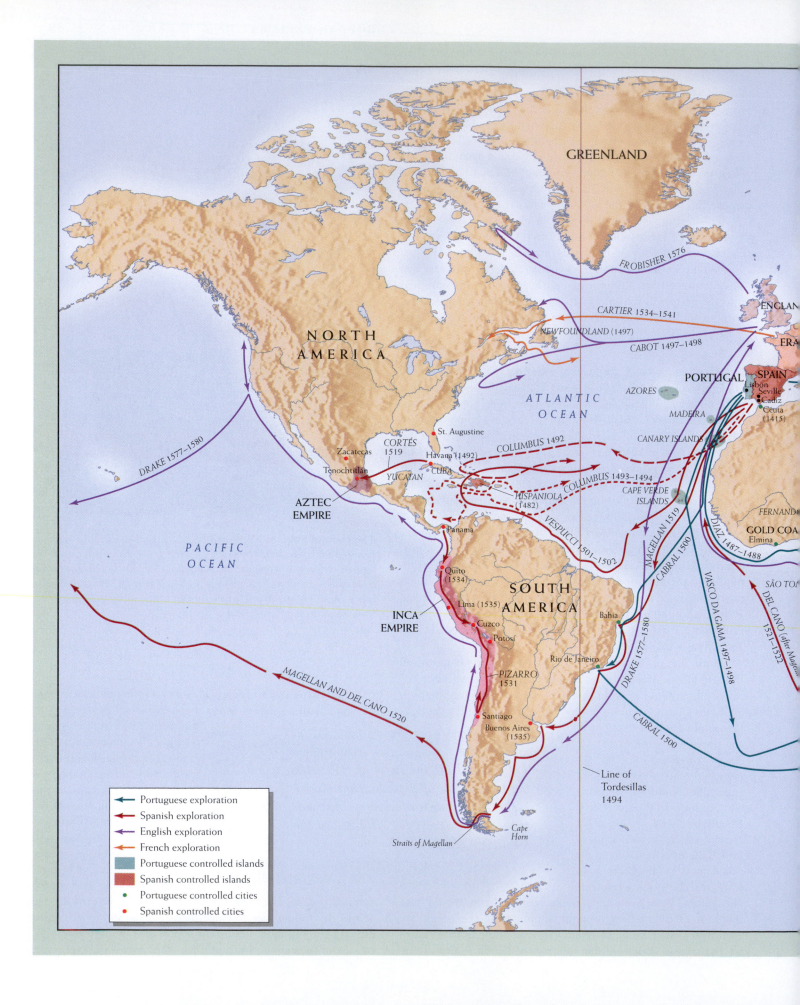

GREENLAND

NORTH
AMERICA

ATLANTIC
OCEAN

FROBISHER 1576

CARTIER 1534–1541

NEWFOUNDLAND (1497)

CABOT 1497–1498

ENGLAN

FRA

PORTUGAL SPAIN

Lisbon
Seville
Cadiz
Ceuta
(1415)

AZORES

MADEIRA

CANARY ISLANDS

*CAPE VERDE
ISLANDS*

FERNAND

GOLD COA

Elmina

SÃO TOM

St. Augustine

COLUMBUS 1492

Zacatecas

*CORTÉS
1519*

Havana (1492)

Tenochtitlán

YUCATAN

CUBA

*HISPANIOLA
(1492)*

COLUMBUS 1493–1494

AZTEC
EMPIRE

DRAKE 1577–1580

VESPUCCI 1501–1502

MAGELLAN 1519

CABRAL 1500

DIAZ 1487–1488

VASCO DA GAMA 1497–1498

*DEL CANO
1521–1522*

PACIFIC
OCEAN

Panama

Quito
(1534)

Lima (1535)

INCA
EMPIRE

Cuzco

Potosí

SOUTH
AMERICA

Bahia

Rio de Janeiro

DRAKE 1577–1580

CABRAL 1500

MAGELLAN AND DEL CANO 1520

*PIZARRO
1531*

Santiago

Buenos Aires
(1535)

Line of
Tordesillas
1494

Straits of Magellan

*Cape
Horn*

Portuguese exploration
Spanish exploration
English exploration
French exploration
Portuguese controlled islands
Spanish controlled islands
Portuguese controlled cities
Spanish controlled cities

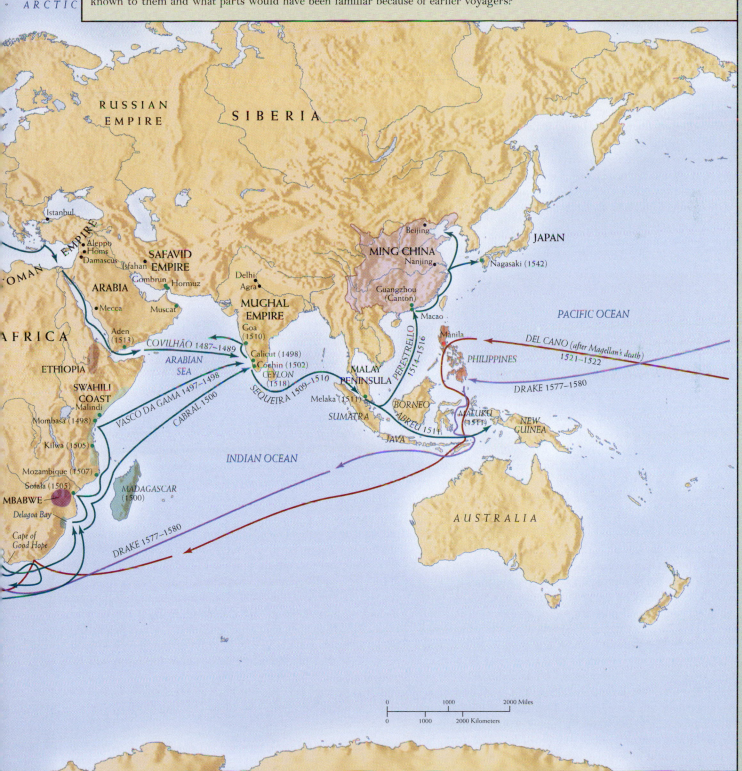

MAP 3-2   EUROPEAN EXPLORATION, 1420–1580

In the fifteenth and sixteenth centuries, sailors from Portugal, Spain, England, and France explored and mapped the coastline of most of the world. What areas of the world formed the core of the Spanish overseas empire? Why did Spain establish its American colonies where it did? How did the Portuguese overseas empire differ from the Spanish? Follow the voyage of the first Europeans to circumnavigate the world (Magellan and Del Cano). What route did they take? What parts of the route would have been unknown to them and what parts would have been familiar because of earlier voyagers?

ARCTIC

RUSSIAN
EMPIRE

SIBERIA

Istanbul

Aleppo
Homs
Damascus

OTTOMAN EMPIRE

SAFAVID
EMPIRE

Isfahan

ARABIA

Gombrun   Hormuz

Mecca

Muscat

Aden
(1513)

AFRICA

ETHIOPIA

SWAHILI
COAST

Malindi

Mombasa (1498)

Kilwa (1505)

Mozambique (1507)

Sofala (1505)

MBABWE

Delagoa Bay

Cape of
Good Hope

MADAGASCAR
(1500)

COVILHÃO 1487–1489

ARABIAN
SEA

Delhi
Agra

MUGHAL
EMPIRE

Goa
(1510)

Calicut (1498)
Cochin (1502)
CEYLON
(1518)

VASCO DA GAMA 1497–1498

CABRAL 1500

SEQUEIRA 1509–1510

MALAY
PENINSULA

Melaka (1511)

SUMATRA

JAVA

BORNEO

ABREU 1511

Beijing

MING CHINA

Nanjing

Guangzhou
(Canton)

Macao

JAPAN

Nagasaki (1542)

PERESTRELLO 1514–1516

Manila

PHILIPPINES

MALUKU
(1511)

NEW
GUINEA

PACIFIC OCEAN

DEL CANO (after Magellan's death)
1521–1522

DRAKE 1577–1580

INDIAN OCEAN

AUSTRALIA

DRAKE 1577–1580

0   1000   2000 Miles

0   1000   2000 Kilometers

naval choke points: Aden at the base of the Red Sea, Hormuz in the Persian Gulf, and Melaka at the tip of the Malay Peninsula. Between 1508 and 1511, the Portuguese used their cannons to blast their way into these Asian ports and to establish defensible toeholds. Having ensconced themselves in the area's main choke points and chief commercial ports, they attempted to take over the trade themselves, or failing this, to tax local merchants. Although they failed to hold Aden for long, they did solidify their trading networks by establishing their control in Sofala, Kilwa, and other important port cities on the East African coast, Goa and Calicut in India, and Macao in southern China. From these strongholds, the Portuguese soon commanded the most active sea lanes of the Indian Ocean, allowing them to issue levies on traders, and to introduce goods of their own into the commercial circuits of the region. As the products of the Indian Ocean made their way back to Lisbon, that city eclipsed the Italian ports that had previously been the prime entry point for Asian imports.

In the sixteenth century, the Portuguese managed to create an empire based on both territorial and trading port models. In the Atlantic islands, they established colonies boasting sugarcane plantations. At the same time, along the African coast, the Indian Ocean, and the China Sea, they sent their merchants and navies to maintain posts and attempt to control trade. Thus, theirs was a seaborne empire that circled around the Islamic heartland in the Indian Ocean and established commercial routes up and down Africa and in the South China Sea. This mode of expansion, it should be clear, involved Europeans in Eurasian commerce—but their presence in Asia remained restricted to exploiting the commercial ports of the Indian Ocean and Chinese trading systems. Neither territorial acquisition nor formal takeovers of distant productive colonies were yet part of the European expansionist impulse. Only with the discovery of the Americas and the conquest of Brazil did Portugal become an empire with large overseas colonies. For this to transpire, the Atlantic Ocean itself had to be traversed.

PORTUGUESE VIEWS OF THE CHINESE

When the Portuguese arrived in China in the early sixteenth century, they encountered a vast empire whose organizational structure and ideological orientation were quite different from their own. Written in 1517, this Portuguese report is replete with misrepresentations that were to characterize many Europeans' views of China for centuries to come. It also signaled a new and aggressive phase of European expansionism, in which the use of brute force was celebrated as a legitimate means to destroy and conquer those who stood in the way.

God grant that these Chinese may be fools enough to lose the country; because up to the present they have had no dominion, but little by little they have gone on taking the land from their neighbors; and for this reason the kingdom is great, because the Chinese are full of much cowardice, and hence they come to be presumptuous, arrogant, cruel; and because up to the present, being a cowardly people, they have managed without arms and without any practice of war, and have always gone on getting the land from their neighbors, and not by force but by stratagems and deceptions; and they imagine that no one can do them harm. They call every foreigner a savage; and their country they call the kingdom of God. Whoever shall come now, let it be a captain with a fleet of ten or fifteen sail. The first thing will be to destroy the fleet if they should have one, which I believe they have not; let it be by fire and blood and cruel fear for this day, with-

out sparing the life of a single person, every junk being burnt, and no one being taken prisoner, in order not to waste the provisions, because at all times a hundred Chinese will be found for one Portuguese. And this done, Nanto must be cleared, and at once they will have a fortress and provisions if they wish, because it will at once be in their power; and then with the whole fleet attack Aynācha, which lies at the bar of Tãcoam, as I have already said above having a good port. Here the ships, which cannot enter the river, will be anchored, and whatever craft they may have will be burnt; and after it has been taken if it seem good the town can be burnt, in order to terrify the Chinese. . . .

Source: Letters from Canton, translated and edited by D. Ferguson, *The Indian Antiquary* 31 (January 1902), in J. H. Parry, *European Reconnaissance: Selected Documents* (New York: Walker, 1968), p. 140.

MILITARY DEVELOPMENT AND EUROPEAN EXPANSION

The success of Portuguese ships in the Indian Ocean was in part the result of a revolution in military technology and tactics that had been gathering momentum for a long time—and owed much to borrowings from Asia. This began with the adaptation of a Chinese technology: gunpowder. Making use of this technology, the Ottomans employed enormous cannons filled with gunpowder and 800-pound cannonballs to conquer Constantinople in 1453. In like fashion in 1492, Christians used cannons to breach the walls of Granada. Europeans also used the explosive to fire projectiles from smaller cannons, which were more mobile and could propel iron balls in relatively flat trajectories. These proved effective in laying ruin to old fortifications. They could also be mounted against the gunwales of warships to bombard ports and rival navies.

Within Europe, the main beneficiaries of this revolution in warfare were the dynastic rulers, who were the only political powers with the financial resources to equip large fighting forces with new armaments. In 1492, what was then a huge force of 60,000 Christian soldiers drove Islam's army out of Granada; two centuries later, such an army would have been dwarfed by the hundreds of thousands of men fielded by the most powerful European states. So, too, tactics shifted. In medieval Europe, a day of combat or a short siege of castles often settled matters. By the middle of the sixteenth century, battles often involved protracted, and usually inconclusive struggles. This way of war, more costly in terms of money and manpower, gave an advantage to larger, centralized states.

The transformation of military hardware and tactics had effects well beyond Europe. As Europeans took to the seas to find new routes to Asia, and to defend sea lanes in the Mediterranean, rulers began to mount cannonry aboard ships, including merchant vessels. Thus, for example, as Portuguese ships entered the Indian Ocean, these merchant vessels could double as warships; their cannons could be trained against unsuspecting Asian ports, whose defenses were unprepared for such artillery.

> *New technologies certainly aided European expansion, but diseases made the difference.*

but diseases made the difference. In their encounters with the peoples of the Americas, Europeans introduced more than new cultures to this isolated world; they also brought devastating new pathogens and illnesses. The catastrophic decline of Amerindian populations enabled Europeans to colonize the Americas and take advantage of their natural resources.

Most of the people who made the Atlantic voyage after 1500 were not Europeans but Africans. The decimation of Indians in many areas deprived Europeans of an indigenous labor force and drove them to seek workers elsewhere. As a supplier of slave labor, Africa became the third corner in an emerging triangular order. Born of the links between the peoples and resources of Europe, Africa, and the Americas, this emerging "Atlantic Ocean system" enriched Europeans. Through conquest and resettlement in the New World, Europeans gained access to the precious metals of the Americas. New World silver provided Europeans with the means to offer something to their trading partners in Asia.

The crossing of the Atlantic Ocean was a feat of monumental importance in world history. But it was not accomplished with an aim to discover new lands. It was an accident that grew out of the search for new routes to the East. Notably, it was the two most western European powers, Portugal and Spain, that led in exploration of the Americas and in the subsequent creation of an Atlantic world system. Still, while the idea of creating an entirely new system of trade and expansion was unintended, it took scarcely a generation for Europeans to realize the significance of the event. By 1550, all of Europe's powers were scrambling, not just for a share in the Indian Ocean action, but also for the spoils of the Atlantic. In the process, they began destroying the societies, even the great dynasties, of the New World. The effects of expansion included both the sharpening of European rivalries and the devastation of the people of the Americas.

 ## THE ATLANTIC WORLD

→ *Why were Spanish conquistadors able to dominate in the New World?*

Western European Christendom, in opening new sea lanes in the Atlantic, set the stage for an epochal transformation in world history. New technologies certainly aided European expansion,

WESTWARD VOYAGES OF COLUMBUS

Few figures in history have come to embody their age more than Christopher Columbus. His little fleet of three ships set sail from Spain in early 1492, stopped in the Canary Islands for supplies and repairs, and cast off into the unknown. When he walked onto the beach of San Salvador (in the Bahamas) on October 12, 1492, Columbus ushered in a new era in world history. He did not, however, return with the precious commodities of Asia. In this, and in three subsequent voyages, Columbus kept searching in vain for the valuable products of the South China Sea and the Indian Ocean.

It is important to see Columbus as a man of his time. Like other expansion-minded Europeans, he may be characterized as a mystical man on the make; his oceanic voyages aimed to

Christianize the world while enriching himself (and his backers). These twin goals, to save souls and to make money, inspired the European colonization of the Americas and resulted in the formation of an Atlantic world system. It is worth reminding ourselves, however, that while the effects of his voyage ushered in a new future, he was a man who in many ways looked backward. The aim of his voyage was not to create new colonies but to realize commercial profits, which could be used to pay off debts incurred in the conquest of Granada and in the reconquest of the Holy Land. To his dying day, Columbus never believed that he had discovered anything new.

Although Columbus did not realize what he had found, the news of his voyage spread quickly through Europe. Especially in the Iberian ports, ambitious mariners prepared their vessels to sail west. Other ships on the way to the East also found the New World by accident. For example, in 1500, Pedro Alvares Cabral and his Portuguese fleet, on a voyage originally intended for India, were blown west in the Atlantic and landed instead on the bulge of South America that is now Brazil. For Cabral and others, it became clear that these discoveries were not the outer edges of Asia, but that an entire hemisphere lay between Europe and Asia. For the peoples of the Americas, the encounters with the European explorers soon had devastating consequences.

> *The twin goals, to save souls and to make money, inspired the European colonization of the Americas and resulted in the formation of an Atlantic world system.*

FIRST ENCOUNTERS

When Columbus made landfall in the Caribbean, he unfurled the royal standard of Ferdinand and Isabella and claimed the "many islands filled with people innumerable" for Spain. Meeting the peoples whom he would mislabel "Indians," Columbus offered them his sword. Fittingly, the first encounter with Caribbean inhabitants, in this case the Tainos, drew blood. As Columbus noted in his journal, "I showed them swords and they took them by the edge and through ignorance cut themselves." The Tainos were unable to forge steel—and thus such sharp edges were unknown to them.

For Columbus, the naiveté of the Tainos in grabbing the sword symbolized the child-like primitivism of these people. In Columbus's view, the Tainos had no religion, but they did have gold (found initially hanging as pendants from their noses). Likewise, Pedro Alvares Cabral wrote to his own king about the soils of Brazil which, "if rightly cultivated would yield everything." The people had all "the innocence of Adam" and were ripe for conversion. But, as with Africans and Asians, Europeans also developed a contradictory view of the peoples of the Americas. From the Tainos, Columbus learned of another people, the Caribs, who, according to his informants, were savage, warlike cannibals. For centuries, these contrasting images provided the two competing visions of Indians that structured European (mis)understandings of the indigenous peoples of the Americas as innocents or savages.

We know less about what the Indians thought of Columbus or other Europeans whom they first encountered. Certainly the appearance of Europeans and their technologies often inspired awe. The Tainos of San Salvador fled into the forest at the approach of three giant monsters. For others, European ships were likened to floating islands, and European metal goods, in particular their weaponry, were assumed to be otherworldly. The strangely dressed white men seemed godlike to some, although many Indians soon abandoned this view. Many found the newcomers different, not so much for their skin color (only Europeans drew the distinction based on skin pigmentation), as for their hairiness. Indeed, the beards, the breath, and the bad manners of Europeans repulsed their Indian hosts. Moreover, the inability of European voyagers to live off the fruit of the land showed the limits of their wondrous new technologies.

In due course, the image of a strange, hairy people bearing beads and metal soon evolved into a fear of conquerors. The Indians realized that these newcomers were not just odd trading partners, but that they meant to stay and that they also meant to force the native population to work for them. By the time Indians were aware of the dislocations and upheaval brought by the Spaniards, however, it was too late. The explorers had become conquerors.

FIRST CONQUESTS

After the first voyage, Columbus claimed "he had found what he was looking for" on the island of Hispaniola (present-day Haiti and the Dominican Republic): gold. The glitter of gold transformed the scale of oceanic expeditions. The Spanish crown immediately endorsed larger and larger expeditions. Whereas Columbus first sailed with three small ships and 87 men, ten years later the Spanish outfitted an expedition with 2,500 men.

Between 1492 and 1519, the Spanish experimented with institutions and practices of colonialism on Hispaniola, creating a model to be modified and applied in the rest of the New World colonies. Here, the Spaniards faced problems that would recur. The first was Indian resistance. As early as 1494, starving Spaniards raided and pillaged Indian villages. When the Indians revolted, Spanish soldiers replied with punitive expeditions and began enslaving the native population to work extracting gold.

With time, the crown began to systematize the practice of granting the conquerors control over the labor services of Indian communities. These grants of labor were called *encomiendas*. Those who were granted the labor rights were called *encomenderos*, and they soon grew rich while the Indians toiled as virtual slaves. Although the placer gold mines soon ran dry, the model of granting favored settlers the right to coerce Indian labor survived. In return, those granted the labor rights paid special taxes on the precious metals that were extracted. Thus, both the crown and the *encomenderos* shared in the benefits of the extractive economy. The same cannot be said of the Indians. By 1518, due to disease, dislocation, and malnutrition, there were but 30,000 Indians left alive on the island (in contrast to a population of up to 1 million in 1491).

This model of conquest spawned quarrels over the spoils. The family of Columbus, in particular, had been granted a commercial monopoly on his discoveries, but some of the settlers objected and challenged Columbus's authority. To prevent insurrection, the crown granted more *encomiendas* to other Spanish claimants. Special grants became a common feature of Spanish colonialism. Yet, less favored settlers soon grew disenchanted. When Indians began to die off in massive numbers and the gold supplies evaporated, many settlers pulled up their stakes and returned to Spain. Others looked further afield, for new untapped territories that might be rich in precious metals.

Not all joined the rush for riches or celebrated what conquistadors (Spanish conquerors) and *encomenderos* did to the Indians. Dominican friars protested the abuse of Native Americans, seeing them as potential converts, equal to the Spaniards in the eyes of God. In 1511, Father Antonio Montesinos accused the settlers of barbarity: "By what right do you wage such detestable wars on these people who lived idly and peacefully in their own lands, where you have consumed infinite numbers of them with unheard-of murders and desolations?" Dissent and debate would be a permanent feature of Spanish colonialism in the New World.

THE AZTEC EMPIRE AND THE SPANISH CONQUEST

As Spanish colonists saw the bounty of Hispaniola begin to dry up, they hankered to move on. Setting out to discover and conquer new countries, they found their way to the mainlands of the American continents. There, they encountered larger, more complex, and more militarized societies than the ones they had quickly overrun in the Caribbean.

MEXICA SOCIETY   In Mesoamerica, the ascendant Mexicas had created an empire, and named it "Aztec" after the foundational story of the people who migrated from the mythic town of Aztlan. Around Lake Texcoco, Mexica cities grew and formed a three-city league in 1430, which then expanded outward through the Central Valley of Mexico to incorporate neighboring peoples. Over the course of the fifteenth century, the Aztec empire united numerous small independent states under a single monarch who ruled with the help of counselors, military leaders, and priests. By the end of the fifteenth century, the Aztec realm may have embraced 25 million people and Tenochtitlán, the primary city of the Aztecs, situated on an island in Lake Texcoco, ranked among the world's largest with a population estimated at between 200,000 and 300,000.

Extended kinship provided the scaffolding for Aztec statehood. Villages of households chose elders from among the community's most prestigious men. These chieftains managed diplomatic relations with neighboring towns. Marriage of men and women from different villages solidified alliances and created clan-like networks. In the Aztec capital city of Tenochtitlán, in particular, powerful families married their children to each other or found appropriate nuptial partners among the prominent families of other important cities. Not only did this concentrate power in the great capital, it also ensured a pool of potential successors to the throne. In this fashion, a fictive lineage emerged to create a corps of "natural" rulers. Upon taking the throne, priests legitimized a new emperor in elaborate rituals to convey among his subjects the image of a ruler closer to the gods, and to distinguish between the elite and the lower orders.

A hierarchy already present at the village level provided the bedrock for layers of increasingly centralized political authority. Local elders developed representative bodies and councils, which selected delegates to a committee responsible for electing the dominant civil authority, known as the "chief speaker." As Aztec power spread, the chief speaker became a full-blown emperor. He was, however, not supreme, but competed increasingly with rival religious and especially military power-wielders. Thus, at the top of the Aztec social pyramid, was a small but antagonistic nobility.

By the end of the fifteenth century, Aztec power had spread to much of Mesoamerica, but the empire's constant wars and conquests of neighboring territories deprived it of stability. In successive military campaigns, the Aztecs subjugated their neighbors, feeding first off plunder, and then forcing subject peoples to pay annual tribute of crops, gold, silver, textiles, and other goods. The tribute financed Aztec grandeur. Conquest of Aztec neighbors also provided imperial rulers with the constant supply of victims for human sacrifice to the gods (see Chapter 1).

The peoples whom the Aztecs sought to dominate did not submit peacefully. From 1440 onward, the empire was in a state of constant turmoil as subject peoples rebelled against the oppressive hand of their Aztec overlords. In particular, Tlaxcalans and Tarascans along the Gulf of Mexico waged a relentless war for freedom, pinning down entire divisions of Aztec armies. To pacify the realm, the empire diverted more and more men and money into a mushrooming military. By the time the electoral committee chose Moctezuma II as emperor in 1502, the Aztec

Tenochtitlán. At its height, the Aztec capital Tenochtitlán was as populous as Europe's largest city. *(Left)* As can be seen from this map, it spread in concentric circles, with the main religious and political buildings in the center, and residences radiating outward. *(Right)* As the city was built on an immense island, its outskirts connected a mosaic of floating gardens producing food for urban markets. Canals constantly irrigated the land, waste was used as fertilizer, and the tremendously high yields were easily transported to markets. Observe how entire households worked: men, women and children all had roles in Aztec agriculture.

empire was already under stress both from divisions at the apex of power and pressure from the periphery.

Cortés and Conquest   Not long after Moctezuma became emperor, news arrived of strange sightings off the eastern coast of large floating mountains (ships) bearing pale,

bearded men and monsters (horses and war dogs). Moctezuma consulted with his ministers and soothsayers over the news, wondering if these men were the god Quetzalcóatl and his entourage. The people of Tenochtitlán saw omens of impending disaster. Moctezuma sank into despair, hesitating as to what course of action to take. He sent emissaries bearing jewels and feathers; later he sent sorcerers to confuse and bewitch the new-comers. But he did not prepare his city for any military engagement—Mesoamericans had no idea of the forces behind these interlopers, nor of the destructive potential of their weaponry and germs.

Aboard one of the ships was Hernán Cortés (1485–1547), a former law student from the Spanish province of Estremadura. Cortés was to become the model conquistador, just as Columbus was the model explorer. For a brief while, he was an *encomendero* in Hispaniola, but when news arrived of a potentially even more wealthy land to the west, he mustered an expedition and set sail with over 500 men, eleven ships, sixteen horses, and some artillery. When they arrived near present-day Veracruz, Cortés acquired two translators, including the daughter of a local Indian noble family. Doña Marina, as she became known, was crucial for Cortés as she and her fellow-translator guided the Spaniards through local customs and geography. From his beachhead, Cortés marched his troops to Tenochtitlán. Entering the city, he gasped in wonder that "this city is so big and so remarkable" that it was "almost unbelievable." One of his soldiers also wrote, "it was all so wonderful that I do not know how to describe this first glimpse of things never heard of, seen or dreamed of before."

How was this tiny force to overcome an empire of many millions with an elaborate warring tradition? Crucial to Spanish conquest was their alliance, negotiated with the help of the translators, with Moctezuma's enemies, especially the Tlaxcalans. After decades of yearning for release from the Aztec yoke, the Tlaxcalans and other Mesoamerican peoples embraced Cortés's promise of help. The second main advantage was the

CORTÉS APPROACHES TENOCHTITLÁN

When the Spanish conquered the Aztec empire, they defeated a mighty power. The capital, Tenochtitlán, which was immensely rich, was probably the same size as Naples, Europe's biggest city at the time. Glimpsing the Aztec capital in 1521, Hernán Cortés marveled at the magnificence of the city. But to justify his acts, he claimed that he was bringing civilization and Christianity to the Aztecs. Note the contrast, however, between Cortés's admiration for Tenochtitlán and his condemnation of Indian beliefs and practices, as well as his claim that he abolished cannibalism, something the Aztecs did not practice (although they did sacrifice humans).

This great city of Tenochtitlán is built on the salt lake. . . . It has four approaches by means of artificial causeways. . . . The city is as large as Seville or Cordoba. Its streets . . . are very broad and straight, some of these, and all the others, are one half land, and the other half water on which they go about in canoes. . . . There are bridges, very large, strong, and well constructed, so that, over many, ten horsemen can ride abreast. . . . The city has many squares where markets are held. . . . There is one square, twice as large as that of Salamanca, all surrounded by arcades, where there are daily more than sixty thousand souls, buying and selling . . . in the service and manners of its people, their fashion of living was almost the same as in Spain, with just as much harmony and order; and considering that these people were barbarous, so cut off from the knowledge of God and other civilized peoples, it is admirable to see to what they attained in every respect. . . .

It happened . . . that a Spaniard saw an Indian . . . eating a piece of flesh taken from the body of an Indian who had been killed. . . . I had the culprit burned, explaining that the cause was his having killed that Indian and eaten him which was prohibited by Your Majesty, and by me in Your Royal name. I further made the chief understand that all the people . . . must abstain from this custom. . . . I came . . . to protect their lives as well as their property, and to teach them that they were to adore but one God . . . that they must turn from their idols, and the rites they had practised until then, for these were lies and deceptions which the devil . . . had invented. . . . I, likewise, had come to teach them that Your Majesty, by the will of Divine Providence, rules the universe, and that they also must submit themselves to the imperial yoke, and do all that we who are Your Majesty's ministers here might order them. . . .

Source: *Letters of Cortés*, translated by Francis A. MacNutt (New York: G.P. Putnam, 1908), pp. 244, 256–57.

The Conquest of the Aztecs. *(Left)* This is Diego Rivera's idealized account of the Spanish defeat of the Aztec warriors. It portrays Spanish soldiers with muskets and horses mowing down brave, but technologically outgunned Indians. Of course, Rivera's efforts to accentuate Spanish brutality led him to exclude important factors in the fall of Tenochtitlán: Aztec rivals who joined with Spaniards, and diseases. In fact, guns and horses were important, but not decisive in the Spanish conquest. *(Right)* This image of the conquest was drawn by a converted Indian later in the sixteenth century and relied on indigenous oral histories and familiar artistic forms. Observe the importance of Indians fighting Indians, and the conventional frontal images of bodies with profiles of heads.

Spanish method of warfare. The Aztecs were seasoned fighters, but they fought to capture, not to kill. Nor were they familiar with gunpowder or sharp steel swords. Outnumbered, the Spaniards killed their foe with abandon, using their superior weaponry, and horses and war dogs. The Aztecs, still unsure who these strange men were, allowed Cortés to enter their city. With the aid of the Tlaxcalans and a handful of his own men, Cortés was able in 1519 to capture the Aztec ruler, Moctezuma, who then ruled as a puppet of his Spanish conqueror.

Within two years, the Aztecs realized that these newcomers were not gods, and that Aztec warriors too could fight to kill. What precipitated the fighting was the Spanish troops' massacre of an unarmed crowd in Tenochtitlán's central square, which occurred while Cortés was away from the city. This led to a massive uprising, during which Spanish men led Moctezuma to one of the palace walls to plead for a truce. The Aztecs kept up their barrage of stones, spears, and arrows—striking and killing Moctezuma. Cortés returned to the city to try to reassert Spanish control, but realizing that this was not possible, he took his loot and escaped. Left behind were hundreds of Spaniards, many of whom were dragged up the steps of the temple and sacrificed by Aztec priests.

With the help of the Tlaxcalans, Cortés regrouped. This time he chose to defeat the Aztecs completely. He ordered the building of brigantines to sail across Lake Texcoco to besiege the capital and bombard it with artillery. Even worse from the Aztec viewpoint was the spread of smallpox, brought by the Spanish, which ran through the ranks of soldiers and commoners like wildfire. "Sores erupted on our faces, our breasts, our bellies; we were covered with agonizing sores from head to foot. The illness was so dreadful that no one could walk or move." Still, led by a new ruler, Cuauhtémoc, the Aztecs rallied their forces and nearly drove the Spaniards from Tenochtitlán. But starvation, disease, and lack of artillery ultimately vanquished the Aztec forces. In the end, more Aztecs died from disease than from fighting—the total number of casualties in two years of confrontation reached, it is said, 240,000. As Spanish troops entered the capital, they found a city in ruins, with a population that was too weak to resist. Cuauhtémoc himself was executed in 1524, thereby ending the royal Mexica

> *Starvation, disease, and lack of artillery ultimately vanquished the Aztec forces; in the end, more Aztecs died from disease than from fighting.*

lineage. The Aztecs lamented their defeat in verse: "We have pounded our hands in despair against the adobe walls, for our inheritance, our city, is lost and dead." In 1522, Cortés became the governor of the new Spanish colony which, by royal order, was renamed "New Spain." He quickly set about allocating *encomiendas* to his loyal followers and dispatching expeditions to conquer the more distant Mesoamerican provinces.

The Mexica experience taught the Spanish an important lesson in conquest: it did not take long for Indians to figure out that the intruders were not gods but enemies. Thus an effective conquest had to be swift—and it had to remove completely the symbols of legitimate authority. But one ally that preceded them, without their knowing it, was disease. Having established their toehold in the Americas, the Spaniards also introduced germs, which soon spread faster than humans. As the germs spread, they crippled the societies they encountered. This made subsequent military conquests all that much easier.

THE INCAS

In addition to Cortés's victory over the Aztecs, the other great Spanish conquest was in the Andes, where the Incas had established an impressive polity stretching from present-day Colombia to Argentina. From their base in the valley of Cuzco, Quechua-speaking rulers, called Incas, governed an empire of 4 to 6 million. But the Incas were internally split. Bereft of a clear inheritance system, the empire suffered repeated convulsions. In the early sixteenth century, the fight over who would succeed Huayna Capac, the Inca ruler, was especially fierce. Huascar, his "official" son, took Cuzco (the capital of the empire), while Atahualpa, his favored son, governed the province of present-day Ecuador. Open conflict might have been averted were it not for Huayna's premature death. His killer was probably smallpox, which along with other epidemics was sweeping down the trade routes from Mesoamerica into the Andes (not unlike the bubonic plague's spread through the trade routes of Eurasia in the mid-fourteenth century). With the father gone, Atahualpa declared war on his brother, and after crushing his rival, forced him to witness the execution of all his supporters, before he too was killed and his skull used as a vessel for Atahualpa's maize-beer.

When the Spaniards arrived in 1532, they ran into an empire that was already internally divided, and they quickly learned to exploit this situation. Francisco Pizarro, who led the Spanish campaign, had spent time in Hispaniola and, inspired by Cortés's victory, yearned for his own moment of glory. Pizarro commanded a force of about 600 men and invited

Machu Picchu. Nestled at 8,000 feet among towering mountains, the citadel of Machu Picchu is located in present-day Peru. Although we do not know why the Incas abandoned this fortress, its ruins testify to the complexity of the architecture and civilization of the Incas.

THE VOICE OF THE CONQUERED: GUAMAN POMA DE AYALA

After defeating the Inca armies in the sixteenth century, the Spanish conquerors tightened their hold over the central Andes. They created new political authorities, invited victors to set up silver mines and trading networks using forced Indian laborers, and licensed missionaries to go out into Andean communities to consolidate a more difficult "spiritual conquest." In reaction, Andean peoples resisted Spanish conquerors. They fled the mines, plundered trade routes, and kept fighting, now with the use of Spanish weaponry. The conquered Andeans also used techniques of the conquerors themselves, like the Spanish language and Spanish books, to resist Spanish control.

One of the most polemical voices of the conquered was a native Andean, Felipe Guaman Poma de Ayala (c. 1535–c. 1615). His illustrated history of the Inca kingdoms, *Primer nueva crónica y bien gobierno* (c. 1615), fiercely criticized colonial rule, while urging the Spanish king, Philip III, to adopt a new model of "good government." The book itself, like the idea that Spain could govern the colonized peoples benevolently, disappeared, and was only discovered in a library in Copenhagen in 1908. As a polemical testimony against European conquest, however, *Primer nueva crónica* offers readers a voice of colonized peoples.

The author's native tongue was Quechua, but he was schooled, possibly by missionaries, in Spanish language and culture. With his bilingual skills, he was drafted as an interpreter in the Christian campaigns to wipe out heresy and idol worship in the Andes. In this capacity, he read books belonging to missionaries and learned of the religious, political, and historical traditions of the Spaniards. Guaman Poma also served as an interpreter for Indians who challenged the land claims of the conquistadors, and in this capacity he eventually earned himself a reputation as a minor nuisance and was evicted from several jurisdictions. Frustrated that the Spanish conquerors refused to live by their spiritual and political proclamations, he grew increasingly bitter, and delivered his illustrated text of 1,188 pages and 398 pen and ink drawings to the viceroy in Lima to defend the Indians. Rebuffed, he wrote the king on February 14, 1615. Thereafter, Guaman Poma disappeared from the historical record.

Guaman Poma narrated the history of the Inca empire, recounted the arrival and victory of the Spanish, and then described the misery of everyday life under colonial authority. Relying on his own first-hand experiences and centuries of oral culture, the author told an epic tale—very much in a Spanish mode—of the tragic fate of a non-Spanish people. Indeed, the book accepted in many ways the Andean destiny, while denouncing colonialism. He was pro-Andean, but he celebrated Catholicism and Spanish monarchical rule.

As a chronicler of the Andean peoples before the Spanish conquest, Guaman Poma argued that his people were innocents, a Christian people, well before the conquest. They lived, according to the author, by Christian principles and knew but one God, "though they were barbarous, knowing nothing." Indeed, his history of the Incas begins with biblical creation, the arrival in South America of one of Noah's sons, and ends with the rule of Inca Huayna Capac. While much of his historical account was his own fabrication, claiming Christian roots enabled the Andean author to denounce the conquistadors as treasonous usurpers. They had killed the natural and legitimate Inca rulers, and were thus eternally doomed.

Primer nueva crónica culminated in a detailed account of everyday life in the colony. It charted the system of forced labor in the mines, the burdens of Spanish taxes, and the hypocrisy of missionaries who seized Indian property and failed to defend Indian lives. Guaman Poma wrote that the colonists violated Christian precepts of justice and their own laws. He added that, given the origins of the Andean peoples and their colonial fates, the king of Spain had a moral as well as a political duty to protect his Christian subjects in the Andes: he should free them from sinful authorities and create a sovereign Andean state as a universal Christian kingdom ruled from Madrid. Guaman Poma simultaneously denounced colonialism, while affirming his loyalty to the king.

For all his skills at crossing the large cultural and political divide between Andeans and Spaniards, conquered and conquerors, Guaman Poma was not optimistic. Near the end of his work, he asked forlornly, "Where are you, our lord king Philip?" His prose invoked many of the conventions of Spanish treatises, and his strong visual representations were meant to stir the reader's Christian sentiments. But at the same time, his images portrayed the irreconcilable differences between Spaniards and Andeans. Isolation, and not understanding, was what characterized the colonial experience for Guaman Poma. As he doubted the potential for cross-cultural communication, he concluded that "there is no resolution in this world."

Atahualpa to confer at the town of Cajamarca. There he laid a trap for the Inca ruler. As the columns of warriors and servants, covered with colorful feathers and decorated with plates of silver and gold, marched into the main square of Cajamarca, the Spanish soldiers were awed at the mighty spectacle. One recalled that "many of us urinated without noticing it, out of sheer terror." But Pizarro's plan worked. His guns and horses shocked the Inca forces. Atahualpa himself fell into Spanish hands, later to be decapitated. Pizarro's conquistadors overran Cuzco in 1533 and then went about mopping up the rest of the Inca forces, a process that took decades in some areas of the Andes.

In the intervening years, Spaniards began to arrive in droves, landing at the new coastal capital of Lima. They began to stake their own claims for *encomiendas*, outdoing each other with greed, and by 1538, they were at war with one another. In 1541, one armed faction managed to capture Pizarro himself and assassinated the conquistador. Rival factions kept up a brutal war until the Spanish king dispatched a viceroy and issued a new set of laws in 1542 to prevent the *encomiendas* from being heritable. This act was to prevent the establishment of a powerful aristocracy, to deter the outbreak of uncontrollable civil war, and to reinforce loyalty to Madrid, since once an *encomendero* died, his title would now revert to the crown.

The defeat of the two great empires of the New World had enormous repercussions for world history. It meant first that Europeans had access to the human and material wealth of Native Americans. Second, it gave Europeans a market for their own products—goods that other Eurasians seemed less inclined to consume. Finally, it opened a vast new frontier, which could be colonized and made into staple-producing provinces. The conquest of the New World allowed Europeans to become imperialists. While the Russians in Siberia and the Portuguese in Africa and Asia had begun this process, the conquest of the New World introduced Europe to a whole new scale of imperial expansion and enterprise—whose outcome would destabilize Europe itself.

"THE COLUMBIAN EXCHANGE"

The Spanish came to the Americas for its mineral riches, but the Indians offered Europeans a variety of hitherto unknown crops, especially potatoes and corn. Europeans also took away tomatoes, beans, cacao, peanuts, tobacco, and squash. Combined, these staples transformed European diets and contributed to the explosion of population growth across Eurasia.

What did the Indians get from this hemispheric transfer that historians have come to call "the Columbian exchange"? The Spanish brought wheat, grapevines, and sugarcane. They and other Europeans also transported livestock, such as cattle, swine, and horses, which would have an equally revolutionary impact on the New World. Without natural predators, these animals reproduced with lightning speed. Indeed, these large animals soon destroyed entire landscapes with their hooves and their foraging. Over the ensuing centuries, the flora and fauna of the Americas took on an increasingly European appearance—a process that the historian Alfred Crosby has called "ecological imperialism."

But the most profound and destructive effect of the Columbian exchange was not immediately visible. For millennia, the isolated populations of the Americas were cut off from Eurasian microbe migrations. In other corners of the world, Europeans, Africans, and Asians had at least some contact. It was of course this shared

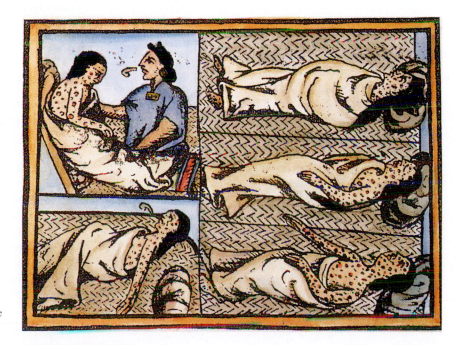

Disease and Decimation of Indians. The real conqueror of American Indians was not so much guns as germs. Even before Spanish soldiers seized the Aztec capital, germs had begun decimating the population. The first big killer was in fact smallpox, recorded here by an Indian artist, covering the bodies of victims.

pool of germs that spread the bubonic plague. Accordingly, the peoples of Africa and Eurasia shared disease pools and gained some immunities, while the Amerindians did not. Arriving in these former "worlds apart," Europeans and Africans unwittingly brought the pathogens that would spread epidemics of an unprecedented scale and scope.

Disease ravaged the New World. Sickness started from almost the moment the Spaniards arrived. One Spanish soldier noted, as he entered the Aztec capital after its fall, that "the streets were so filled with dead and sick people that our men walked over nothing but bodies." Native American accounts of the fall of Tenochtitlán recalled the epidemic of smallpox more vividly than the fighting. What made matters worse was that no sooner had smallpox done its work than Indians were visited by a second pandemic: measles. Then came pneumonic plague and influenza. As each wave retreated, it left behind a population more emaciated than before, even less prepared for the next wave. All told, the foreign pathogens wiped out up to 90 percent of the Native American population (between 80 and 100 million in 1492). A century after smallpox arrived on Hispaniola in 1519, no more than 5 to 10 percent of the island's population, once numbering close to 1 million, was left standing. Here and in other places ravaged by epidemics, Indians were so diminished and weakened by disease that they could not prevent their lands from becoming outposts of European settlement. Thus were Europeans the unintended beneficiaries of a horrifying catastrophe.

> *In its architecture, its economy, and even its most intimate facets, the Spanish adapted as much as they transformed the worlds they encountered.*

SPAIN'S TRIBUTARY EMPIRE

In the territories its conquistadors overran, Spain forged the model tributary empire. In Mexico and Peru, where the Inca empire suffered the same fate as the Aztecs, the Spanish decapitated native polities while leaving much of their structure intact. In both the valley of Mexico and the Andes, Spanish conquerors took over existing tributary networks. Like the Europeans who sailed into the Indian Ocean to tap into extant commercial systems, the Spaniards sought to exploit the wealth of indigenous empires without fully dismantling them. But unlike the European penetration of the Indian Ocean, the occupation of the New World was not restricted to control of commercial outposts. Instead, European colonialism in the Americas involved the control of large amounts of territory—and evolved into formal control over the entire land mass (see Map 3-3).

Across the heartlands of the new Spanish empire, villagers delivered goods and services to their new masters. As they had done in their earlier conquests, the Spanish continued to give *encomiendas* to favored individuals. Such rights enabled the *encomenderos* to demand labor from subject Indian inhabitants for work in mines, landed estates, and public works. Aztec and Inca rulers had used labor conscription systems to build up their public domains; Spaniards did so for private gain.

Most Spanish migrants were men; only a few Spanish women accompanied the conquistadors and early settlers. One, Inés Suárez, reached the Indies to find her husband dead. Nonetheless, as the mistress of the conquistador Pedro de Valdivia, she assisted in the conquest of Chile, and she later helped to rule it as wife of Rodrigo de Quiroga, governor of the province. A handful of other female voyagers foraged for food, tended wounded soldiers, and set up European-style settlements, but there were always too few to go around. The sexual imbalance spurred Spanish men to consort with local women. Although the crown did not smile on the taking of concubines, the practice was widespread. From the onset of colonization, Spaniards also actively married into Indian families. After conquering the Incas, Francisco Pizarro wedded an Inca princess, thereby (or so he hoped) inheriting the mantle of local dynastic rule. As a result of intermarriages, *mestizos*, that is, mixed-blood offspring, became the fastest-growing segment of the population of Spanish America.

For the most part, Spanish migrants and their progeny preferred towns to the countryside. Except for ports (such as Veracruz, Havana, or Portobelo), the major cities of Spanish America were the former centers of Indian empires. Mexico City was built on the ruins of Tenochtitlán; Cuzco arose from the foundations of the razed Inca capital. In its architecture, its economy, and even its most intimate facets, the Spanish adapted as much as they transformed the worlds they encountered.

SILVER

For the first European adventurers in the Americas, the foremost measure of wealth and power was the store of gold and silver that they could accumulate for themselves and the monarchs they served. On the surface, this seemed to benefit Spanish merchants and the Spanish crown. It was, after all, the Spanish who discovered, and then plundered, the vast riches of the Aztecs and the Incas. In the twenty years after the fall of Tenochtitlán, the conquistadors took more specie from Mexico and the Andes than all the gold accumulated by Europeans over the previous centuries.

Having looted Indian coffers, the Spanish quickly entered the business of mining directly, opening the Andean Potosí mines in 1545. Between 1560 and 1685, Spanish America sent 25,000 to 35,000 tons of silver annually to Spain. From 1685 to 1810, this sum doubled. The two great mother lodes were

MAP 3-3   THE SPANISH AND PORTUGUESE EMPIRES IN THE AMERICAS, 1492–1750

The Spanish empire arose where the great Aztec and Inca states had once existed. What were the major export commodities from Spanish America and where were they found? Sugar was one of the New World's most important export crops. How important was the export of sugar to Spanish Americans? The Portuguese empire in America arose where Pedro Alvares Cabral and his fleet made land in present-day Brazil when blown off course on the way to India. How important was the export of sugar to the Portuguese?

Silver. *(Left)* An important discovery for Spanish conquerors were veins of silver in Mesoamerica and the Andes. Conquerors expanded the customs of Inca and Aztec labor drafts to force Indians to work in mines, often in brutal conditions. *(Right)* By the middle of the sixteenth century, a vibrant trade developed between the Americas and Asia, carrying silver, dyes, and foodstuffs. The conquest of the Americas helped give Europeans trade goods for sale in Asian markets. This image shows a fleet of Spanish galleons on the Pacific coast of Mexico as they are being loaded with the silver extracted from the mines.

Potosí in present-day Bolivia and Zacatecas in northern Mexico. Potosí was the greater fount in the sixteenth century, but the silver veins of Mexico proved the more lucrative over the centuries. Silver brought bounty not only to the crown, but to a small coterie of families based in Spain's colonial capitals—a private wealth to fund the formation of local aristocracies.

Colonial mines were perhaps the first mass production systems in the Atlantic world. They relied on an extensive network of recruited Indian labor, at first enslaved, subsequently drafted. Here again, the Spanish adopted existing Inca and Aztec practices of requiring labor from subjugated villages. Each year, under the traditional system, village elders selected a stipulated number of men to toil in the shafts, refineries, and smelters. Under the Spanish, however, the burdens grew more onerous. The digging, hauling, and smelting of rocks taxed human limits to their capacity—and beyond. By one conservative estimate, 50,000 workers moved to Potosí each year; mortality rates were appalling. The system pumped so much silver into the networks of European commerce that it transformed Europe's relationship to all of its trading partners, especially those in China and India. It also shook up trade and politics within Europe itself.

PORTUGAL'S NEW WORLD COLONY

By papal edict (the Treaty of Tordesillas of 1494), Spain initially shared its New World with its neighbor, Portugal. Having pio-neered the European exploration of Africa, the Portuguese turned to the western side of the Atlantic. No less interested in immediate riches than the Spanish, the Portuguese were disappointed by the absence of tributary populations and precious metals in Brazil. What they did find in Brazil, however, was abundant, fertile land on which favored persons received massive royal grants. These estate owners governed their plantations like fiefdoms.

COASTAL ENCLAVES Hemmed in along the coast, the Portuguese created enclaves. By the end of the seventeenth century, Brazil's white population was 300,000. Unlike the Spanish, the Portuguese rarely intermarried with Indians, most of whom had fled or had died from imported diseases. Failing to find already established cities in Brazil, the colonists chose to remain in more dispersed settlements.

The problem for the settlers, though, was where to find the labor to work these rich lands. Unlike the Spanish in Mexico or the Andes, the Portuguese in Brazil did not encounter a centralized polity of the dimensions of the Aztecs or the Incas. Initially, the Portuguese tried to enlist the efforts of Brazil's fragmented and dispersed aboriginal population, but when recruitment became increasingly coercive, Indians quickly turned on interlopers. Some, especially the Tupi, fought. Others fled to a vast interior rather than submit. Reluctant, indeed scared, to pursue the Indians inland, the Portuguese hugged their beach-heads, extracting brazilwood (the source of a beautiful red dye) and sugar from their coastal enclaves.

The Portuguese found the solution to the labor problem in the importation of African slaves to Brazilian plantations. What had worked for the Portuguese on sugarcane plantations in the Azores and other Atlantic islands was now brought to Brazil. Especially in the northeast, in the Bay of All Saints, the Atlantic world's first vast sugar emporium appeared.

SUGAR PLANTATIONS   The cultivation of sugarcane had originated in Bengal on the Indian subcontinent, from where it spread to the Mediterranean region, and then to the islands off the coast of West Africa. There, sugarcane plantations, tended by African slaves, flourished. This model was then transported by the Portuguese to Brazil and by other European powers to the Caribbean. By the beginning of the seventeenth century, sugar had become a major new export from the New World. Its full development did not, however, occur until the eighteenth century (as described in Chapter 4). Eventually, as sugar production boomed, its value surpassed that of silver as an export from the Americas to Europe.

Most Brazilian sugar plantations were fairly small, employing between 60 and 100 slaves. But they were efficient enough to create an alternative model of empire, one that resulted in full-scale colonization and dislocation of the existing

> *The Portuguese found the solution to the labor problem in the importation of African slaves to Brazilian plantations.*

population. The slaves lived in wretched conditions. Their barracks were miserable, and their diets were insufficient to keep them alive under back-breaking work routines. Moreover, slaves working on Brazilian sugar plantations were disproportionately men. As the slaves rapidly died off, the only way to ensure a supply of labor for the Brazilian plantation complex was to import more Africans. This model of agrarian settlement, then, relied to a very high degree on the transatlantic flow of slaves.

BEGINNINGS OF THE TRANSATLANTIC SLAVE TRADE

The Atlantic slave trade began in a modest way in the late fifteenth century. It was inextricably linked to a single commodity, sugar. As the European demand for this commodity increased, so slavery and the slave trade expanded. With this expansion, the Atlantic system came into being. By themselves, Europe and the Americas were a triangle with only two corners. Africa became the third corner, supplying five times as many peoples to the Americas as people of European descent, from the time of Columbus until 1820 (approximately 2 million Europeans to 10 million Africans made the crossing).

Having taken the lead in the exploration of the African coast, the Portuguese also pioneered the taking of human cargo. The trade in slaves grew steadily through the rest of the fifteenth and sixteenth centuries, then expanded by leaps and bounds in the seventeenth and eighteenth centuries (see Chapter 4 for a

map and further discussion). During the first two centuries of the slave trade, all European powers participated in the business—Portuguese, Spanish, Dutch, English, and French. Eventually, New World merchants in both North and South America also set up direct trade links with Africa.

Although the impact of the Atlantic slave trade on Africa can hardly be minimized, Africans had been involved in long-distance slave trading well before European merchants arrived off the coast of West Africa. Beginning in the seventh century, Arab and Muslim slavers transported large numbers of Africans across the Sahara or from the Red Sea and East African ports to Muslim centers of civilization. Some became domestic servants; others toiled as agricultural, industrial, and mining workers. Owing to the long duration of this trade, the number of Africans sold into captivity in the Muslim world exceeded that of the Atlantic slave trade.

Not only did Africans engage in long-distance slave trading, they also maintained slaves themselves. The African practices of slaveholding were as diverse as anywhere else in the world. African slavery, like its American counterparts, was a response to labor scarcities. Compared with other continents, Africa was underpopulated. Its harsh climate, poor soil, and profusion of diseases meant that land was abundant, while labor was scarce. For many Africans, the solution was coerced labor. In many parts of Africa, however, slaves were not consigned to permanent servitude. Instead, slaves were assimilated into families, gradually losing their servile status and swelling the size and power of lineage groups.

With the additional demand of Europeans for slaves to work New World plantations, the pressure on African supplies intensified. Combined with the ongoing Muslim slave trade, little of Africa was free from the impact of this commerce in human beings. Only a narrow band, stretching down the spine of the African continent in a north-south direction from present-day Uganda and the highlands of Kenya to Zambia and Zimbabwe, escaped the influence of Oriental and Occidental slave traders.

If the Atlantic slave trade and plantations enriched Europeans, what effects did this commerce have on Africans? The social and political consequences of the trade were not fully felt until the great age of the slave trade in the eighteenth century (discussed in Chapter 4), but already some of the economic aspects of the trade were clear. The overwhelming economic consequence was to further limit the population of Africa. African laborers fetched high enough prices to more than cover the costs of their capture and transportation across the Atlantic.

By the end of the sixteenth century, several important pieces had fallen into place to create a new, Atlantic-centered world, one that did not exist at all a century earlier. This was a three-cornered system, with Africa supplying labor, the Americas land and minerals, and Europeans the technology and military power to keep the system together. None of these changes could have been predicted a century earlier. They produced unintended effects in Africa and the Americas, but also profound disruptions within Europe itself.

THE TRANSFORMATION OF EUROPE

> → *How was Europe transformed politically and spiritually?*

Instead of uniting Europeans, the development of the new Atlantic system deepened divisions within Europe. In particular, the growing wealth of the Spanish empire tilted the weight of European power toward the Habsburg dynasty, and toward the West. Europe was transformed by Atlantic rivalries, as well as by the Reformation, which resulted in religious divisions and led to warfare among states that adhered to different beliefs.

THE HABSBURGS AND THE QUEST FOR UNIVERSAL EMPIRE IN EUROPE

The European dream of universal empire had persisted since the fall of Ancient Rome, and it was almost realized by the Habsburg dynasts. Charles V was the grandson of the Spanish monarchs Isabella and Ferdinand and of Maximilian I, head of the Austrian Habsburg family and Holy Roman emperor from 1493 to 1519. Charles was elected Holy Roman emperor in 1519 and became the ruler of the largest empire known in European history. His realm encompassed territories in the Americas, as well as Spain, Belgium, the Netherlands, Burgundy, Austria, southern Italy, and most of central Europe. It was an amalgamation of states that maintained their local rulers and laws but contributed soldiers, paid taxes, and recognized the sovereignty of Charles V. The Habsburgs expanded and became dominant within Europe, mostly through dynastic marriages, and secondarily as a result of the endemic warfare of the times. But their loose-knit empire could not put together a unified administrative structure, and religious and political divisions persisted even at the empire's height. Moreover, Charles had to defend his eastern flank from the encroachments of the Ottomans. Sultan Suleiman's Ottoman armies took Habsburg Belgrade in Serbia in 1521, Mohács in Hungary in 1526, and three years later laid siege to Vienna (failing to capture it). Charles counterattacked in Hungary in 1531,

Europe was transformed by Atlantic rivalries, as well as by the Reformation, which resulted in religious divisions and led to warfare.

and his successors ultimately regained Hungary from the Ottomans at the end of the seventeenth century.

Overstretched by the challenges of trying to keep such an ambitious empire intact, Charles abdicated in 1556 and formally divided his empire between his younger brother Ferdinand and his son Philip. Ferdinand (ruled 1556–1564) took the Austrian, German, and central European parts of the empire that straddled the Danube and was elected Holy Roman emperor in 1556. (The crown of the Holy Roman empire was held continuously by Habsburgs from 1452 until 1801, with the exception of only five years.) Philip II (ruled Spain 1556–1598) took Spain, Belgium, the Netherlands, southern Italy, and the New World possessions. Moreover, in 1580, he inherited the Portuguese throne (his mother had been a Portuguese princess), adding Portugal and its colonial possessions to his empire; this gave him a virtual monopoly on Atlantic commerce. Yet, he had to defend his half of the empire from attack from both within and without. Unrest in the Netherlands began in 1566, followed by a full-scale Dutch revolt in 1568, as well as by Ottoman harassment on land and on sea. Philip sent troops to put down the revolt in the Netherlands, and he directed the Spanish fleet to set up defenses against the Ottomans and North African Muslim pirates in the Mediterranean Sea. In 1571, the Spanish fleet defeated the Ottoman fleet at Lepanto. Yet, while Philip controlled a wide-ranging empire, the power and wealth of this sprawling empire had become the source of enormous tension within late sixteenth-century Europe.

The French, English, and Dutch rulers envied the riches of the Portuguese and Spanish colonial possessions. These rivals yearned for their own profitable colonies. But in their explorations of the New World, the French, English, and Dutch had not yet found their own "El Dorados," nor had they discovered a new and easier route to Asia. Still, they were able to claim a share of the wealth of the Americas by stealing it on the high seas. Some of the plunderers were pirates, who raided for their own benefit; others were privateers, who did their stealing with official sanction and shared the profits of their thefts with their monarchs. Often the distinction between pirate and privateer was blurred.

The most famous of the raiders was Sir Francis Drake, who was commissioned by the British crown to plunder Spanish ships and ports. From the 1570s to 1596, Drake was a singular menace to Spanish galleons sailing from the Caribbean to Cádiz. Circling the globe between 1577 and 1580, Drake plundered one Spanish port after another. Through his privateering career, his favorite hunting ground was the Caribbean, where Mesoamerican and Andean silver, loaded onto Spanish vessels, made lucrative targets. Besides, the many islands provided a natural shelter. While Drake's exploits were undertaken for per-

The Reformation. Reformation images played an important role in the often violent polemics of the period. In this rather tame image, Luther preaches to Christ and the godly *(left)*, while the pope *(right)* doles out indulgences to wealthy sinners.

sonal gain, his monarch, Queen Elizabeth, also profited and so approved of his crippling of the Spanish empire that she rewarded him with a knighthood.

Queen Elizabeth called Drake back to England to prepare for the impending naval battle between the world's commercial powerhouse, Spain, and the emerging naval power, England. In 1588, in the English Channel, the Spanish Armada took on the Royal Navy and suffered a devastating defeat. In the retreat, the Spanish king lost many of his most prized battleships. Following the battle, the conflict between England and Spain continued in other seas, and Drake returned to his career of privateering. When the news of Drake's death in the Caribbean (from yellow fever in 1596) arrived in Madrid, the Spanish court erupted in jubilation. The old, infirm King Philip declared that this news would allow him to recover quickly. Alas, two months later, an English fleet of 40 warships and over 100 smaller vessels sailed into Spain's premier port of Cádiz, and occupied the city for two weeks, burning 200 Spanish ships and seizing the massive treasure of the Indies that was sitting in warehouses. Spain, the powerhouse of the

Atlantic world, had its honor and reputation severely humbled. Two years later, a despondent King Philip died.

THE REFORMATION

This Protestant Reformation arose out of the same internal political conflicts and pursuit of individual aims that characterized European activities in the New World. But it was spurred by the spiritual concerns of those, like the Dutch Brethren of the Common Life in the fourteenth century, who despaired of the Catholic Church's ability to satisfy longings for deeper, more individualized religious experience. Movements like the Brethren had inspired Christians to adopt devotional practices, like the Stations of the Cross, and to form reading groups among the laity. When sixteenth-century reformers took up the call for change, they were hopeful that an already reforming church would respond to their criticisms. They had no notion that their complaints would split Christendom for good.

What seemed to reformers to be constructive criticism was, in the eyes of church officials, heresy. And the clergy were right to be worried about the claims of critics like the German monk Martin Luther (1483–1546), who in 1517 proclaimed "Salvation by faith alone" and pronounced the Bible as the sole source of Christian truth. Luther circulated ninety-five "theses" for disputation with his learned colleagues. In this declaration and in subsequent debates, Luther denounced the corruptions of the church and the repression of Germanic freedoms by far-away Latin authority. In *On the Freedom of the Christian Man* (1520), he upbraided "the Roman Church, which in past ages was the holiest of all" for having "become a den of murderers beyond all other dens of murderers, a thieves' castle beyond all other thieves' castles, the head and empire of every sin, as well as of death and damnation." His doctrine struck at both the spiritual and the social authority of the clergy over laity, undermining its claims to control the channels for salvation and to determine Christian truth. He also translated the New Testament into German so that laypersons could have direct access, unmediated by the clergy, to the word of God.

Spread by printed books and ardent preachers in all the vernacular languages of Europe, Luther's doctrines won widespread support. Many of the German princes embraced the new faith as a means of asserting their independence from the Holy Roman emperor. For many, the new ideas, known by 1529 as "Protestantism," promised not just the renewal of Christianity, but attention to individual spiritual needs, and a new moral foundation for community life. Across Western Europe, reformed ideas established a powerful presence, especially in the German states, France, Switzerland, the Low Countries, and Britain. There was no special class appeal to the new Christian creed. It was a faith restricted neither to commoners nor to elites. It appealed to all, although it enjoyed more popularity among communities resentful of the rule of Catholic "outsiders" (like Habsburg Philip II, who ruled the Netherlands from his palace in Spain).

Some zealous reformers, like Jean Calvin (1509–1564) in France, made their own modifications to Luther's ideas. Calvin added to Luther's emphasis on the individual's relationship to God an emphasis on moral regeneration through church discipline and the autonomy of religious communities. He laid out, and his successors underscored, the doctrine of predestination—the notion that each person was already "predestined" for damnation or salvation even before birth. The "elect," he thought, should also be free to govern themselves, a doctrine that ratified both radical political dissent (as in the case of the Puritans in England) and the rule of the clergy (as in the Swiss city-state of Geneva). Calvinism proved especially popular in Switzerland, the Netherlands, northeastern France, and Scotland (where it was called Presbyterianism).

In England, Henry VIII (ruled 1509–1547) and his daughter Elizabeth (ruled 1558–1603) crafted a moderate reformed religion—a "middle way"—called Anglicanism. Neither rigidly Catholic nor predestinarian, Anglicanism sought to include the majority of Englishmen. Although Anglican rule was imposed in Ireland, most nonelite Irishmen adhered to Catholicism, while the Scots maintained a fierce devotion to their Presbyterian Church, insuring a measure of religious diversity within the British Isles. Indeed, in the British Isles, as on the continent, more radical sects, like the Anabaptists and the Quakers, survived within mainstream Protestant polities. While all Protestants were opposed to Catholicism, members of these different communities also quickly developed animosities toward one another, as well as distrust of the papal hierarchy (see Map 3-4).

The Catholic Church responded to the challenges of Luther and Calvin by embarking on a successful reformation of its own (which became known as the Counter-Reformation). At the Council of Trent (1545–1563), it reaffirmed its doctrines, sacraments, the importance of acts of charity, papal supremacy, and the distinctive role of its clergy. But it also enacted reforms to answer the Protestants' assaults on clerical corruption. In contrast to their predecessors, the popes who headed the Catholic Church during the second half of the sixteenth century were renowned for their piety and asceticism. These pontiffs also installed bishops and abbots, who generally steered clear of the unscrupulous practices that had been so fervently attacked by Protestant critics. Taking on the Protestant theological challenge, reformed Catholicism gave greater emphasis to individual spirituality. Like Protestants, reformed Catholics carried their message overseas, especially through the activities of an order established in 1534 by a former soldier named Ignatius Loyola (1491–1556). Loyola founded a brotherhood of priests, the Society of Jesus, or Jesuits, that was dedicated to the revival of the Catholic Church. The Jesuits grew rapidly, becoming a powerful organization devoted to missionizing and educating around the world.

In addition, the Vatican continued to use repression and persecution to combat what it considered to be heretical beliefs. The Index of Prohibited Books (a list of books and theological treatises banned by the Catholic Church) and the Inquisition remained weapons to be used against the church's enemies. But the proliferation of printing presses and Protestantism's remarkable successes made it impossible for the Catholic Counter-Reformation to turn back the tide.

> *The Catholic Church responded to the challenges of Luther and Calvin by embarking on a successful reformation of its own (which became known as the Counter-Reformation).*

RELIGIOUS WARFARE IN EUROPE

The religious fervor of the sixteenth century led the European continent into another round of wars that were as disruptive and ferocious as those of the fourteenth century. Their ultimate

MAP 3-4   RELIGIOUS DIVISIONS IN EUROPE AFTER THE REFORMATION, 1590

The Protestant Reformation divided Europe religiously and politically. Yet, in nearly every European state there were minority religious communities, including the Anabaptists, who were a socially radical Protestant sect that often emerged with the backing of artisan groups and practiced adult baptism. In what countries would you expect Protestant-Catholic tensions to be the most intense? Can you explain why Protestantism triumphed where it did and why it did not prevail over all of Europe?

effect was to weaken the Spanish and strengthen the English, French, and Dutch. The circulation of Luther's ideas—between 1518 and 1525, one-third of all books sold in the German states were written by Martin Luther—precipitated a series of brutal peasant revolts across central Europe. These revolts often broke out when princes or town councils that had decided to accept or reject the Reformation tried to force religious uniformity on their subjects. Often this entailed burnings, beatings, and drownings to persuade those who were reluctant to change their beliefs. As religiously defined polities took up arms to defend themselves against dissenting neighbors, guns and armies to wield them became more and more central to the security of states. In contrast to the small armies of earlier wars, in which one noble's retinue fought a rival's followers, the defense of the Catholic mass and the Protestant Bible brought a large number of simple folk to arms. In 1555, after nearly forty years of religious warfare, the Holy Roman emperor Charles V was compelled to allow the German princes the right to choose whether

Protestantism or Catholicism would be the official religion within their domains. This did not mean, however, that Europe's religious wars were over.

These internal conflicts both weakened European dynasties and made them all the more eager for conquest abroad. Spain, with its massive empire and its silver mines in the New World, spent much of its new fortune waging war in Europe. Most debilitating to Spain was its costly, and eventually futile, effort to subdue its recently acquired Dutch territories. After a series of wars that continued in fits and starts from 1568 to 1648, Catholic Spain finally conceded the Protestant Netherlands its independence.

Wars took their toll on the Spanish empire, which was soon wallowing in debts; not even the riches of the American silver mines could bail out the empire. In the late 1550s, Philip II had to renege on obligations to the empire's creditors. Within two decades, Spain was onto its third declaration of bankruptcy. As the Spanish empire declined, the Dutch and the English extended their trading networks into Asia and the New World. Competition between the two soon led to trade wars, proving that religious differences were not the only sources of inter-European strife.

If religious conflicts drew Spain into costly struggles with the Netherlands and England, they also created civil wars within countries. In France, religious violence took an enormous toll. The internal divide between Catholics and Protestants exploded in the St. Bartholomew's Day Massacre in 1572. Catholic crowds, shouting "kill, kill, kill," rampaged through the streets of Paris murdering Huguenot (Protestant) men, women, and children, and dumping their bodies into the Seine River; parades of rioters displayed the heads of Protestants on pikes. The number of dead reached 3,000 in Paris and at least 10,000 in provincial towns. Mass murder on this scale did not break the Huguenots' spirit. But it did bring more disrepute to the monarchy for failing to ensure peace. Indeed, this was the beginning of the end of the Valois dynasty. Another round of warfare exhausted the French, who yearned for peace, and brought Henry of Navarre, a Protestant Bourbon prince, to the throne. To become king, Henry IV converted to Catholicism, and in 1598, he issued the Edict of Nantes. This proclamation declared France a Catholic country, but it at least temporarily diffused the tensions by tolerating some public Protestant worship.

Europe entered its age of overseas dominance as a collection of increasingly powerful yet competitive rival states.

As dynastic rulers resolved religious questions within their own dominions—by peaceful or bloody means—and built up their armies in order to respond to outside threats, a sense of national identity began to take root. A feeling of being English or French became discernible, although Europeans still had many kinds of identities—ethnic, religious, provincial, and local—which did not coincide with national borders. This was especially true in central Europe. Nor did the emergence of more clearly defined states solve the riddle of how to establish peace within and between Europe's political communities. On the contrary, the religious strife, which propelled the process of nation formation, created grander struggles on the continent and more ferocious rivalries for wealth and territory overseas. Thus, Europe entered its age of overseas dominance as a collection of increasingly powerful yet irreconcilably competitive rival states.

GROWTH OF TRADE IN ASIA

> ⇝ *Why did trade expand and wealth increase in sixteenth-century Asia?*

While Europe was being devastated by religious warfare that left a fragmented and exhausted region of the world, in Asia empires were expanding and consolidating their power, and trade was flourishing.

CHANGING EUROPEAN RELATIONS WITH ASIA

Europe's overseas expansion had originally been directed to Asia. The conquest and colonization of the New World now gave Europeans the means to reshape their relations with Asia. The Portuguese led the way with their existing outposts there. Portuguese merchants and administrators profited greatly from being the first Europeans to establish themselves in the Indian Ocean. They inserted themselves into the overseas trading networks bridging East Africa to China, and within a short while they became either important commercial intermediaries or collectors of customs duties from Asian traders. In 1557, their arrival at Macao, a port city along the southern coast of China, enabled them to penetrate China's expanding import-export trade. To be sure, they did not dominate Chinese commerce, but they did become important shippers of China's most prized manufactures, its porcelains and silks, throughout Asia and to Europe. They also took over much of the silver trade from Japan.

Seeing how much the Portuguese were earning on Asian trade, other Europeans also attempted to enter into the commerce with China and ports in the Indian Ocean. The Spanish, English, and Dutch sailed into areas whose trade was hitherto controlled by the Portuguese. With monopolistic access to American silver,

Spain took the early competitive lead. In 1565, the first Spanish trading galleon reached the Philippines, and in 1571, after the Spanish captured the city of Manila and made it a colonial capital, they established a brisk trade with China. Each year, ships from New Spain crossed the Pacific to Manila, bearing cargoes of American silver. The annual galleon shipments from China carried away vast quantities of porcelain and silks for an avid European consumer population, now supplied with Chinese wares by ships arriving from eastbound and westbound trading lanes. Merchants of Manila also procured silks, tapestries, and feathers from the China Seas for direct shipment to New Spain, where the mining potentates waited eagerly for their imports from China.

The year 1571, therefore, proved to be a decisive date in the history of the modern world, for in that year Spain inaugurated a trade circuit that made good on Magellan's achievement of a half-century prior. As Spanish ships circumnavigated the globe from the New World to China, and from China eventually back to Europe, the world was commercially interconnected. And it was silver that solidified the linkage, for it was the only foreign commodity for which the Chinese had a constant and unquenchable demand. From the massive mother lodes of the Andes and Mesoamerica, silver made the commerce of the world go round.

Anxious to share in the profits of the Asia trade, other European states were not content to allow the Iberians a free hand in the Indian Ocean and China Seas. Just as they began to prey on Portuguese and especially Spanish business in the New World, so too the English, Dutch, and French aimed to take a cut of Spain's world trade. Francis I of France was outraged when the pope decreed in the Treaty of Tordesillas of 1494 that the non-European world would be divided into spheres of interest between Spain and Portugal. If this treaty were honored, then only Spain and Portugal would have colonization and trading rights in the Americas, Africa, and Asia. Francis asserted that no one, not even the pope himself, had the right to deny the French monarch and his heirs their rightful share of overseas possessions. Yet, the treaty did not stop other nations from

COMMENTARY ON FOREIGNERS FROM A MING OFFICIAL

Although China had a long history of both overland and maritime trade with the outside world, Ming officials were often hostile toward contact with foreigners. Urging that the foreign presence must be brought under strict government control, the bureaucrat He Ao (Ho Ao) portrayed the Europeans (whom he called Feringis) as unruly, untrustworthy, and a threat to the security of the country in this commentary from around 1520. Such sentiments were also often found among Chinese officials in subsequent centuries, even as China thrived in the growing commercial exchanges of an increasingly connected world.

The Feringis are most cruel and crafty. Their arms are superior to those of other foreigners. Some years ago they came suddenly to the city of Canton, and the noise of their cannon shook the earth [these were cannon shots fired as a salute by the fleet of Fernão Peres]. Those who remained at the post-station [places where foreigners were lodged] disobeyed the law and had intercourse with others. Those who came to the Capital were proud and struggled [among themselves?] to become head. Now if we allow them to come and go and to carry on their trade, it will inevitably lead to fighting and bloodshed, and the misfortune of our South may be boundless. In the time of our ancestors, foreigners came to bring tribute only at fixed periods, and the law provided for precautionary measures, therefore the foreigners who could come were not many. But some time ago the Provincial Treasurer, Wu T'ing-chü, saying that he needed spice to be sent to the Court, took some of their goods no matter when they came. It was due to what he did that foreigner ships have never ceased visiting our shores and that barbarians have lived scattered in our departmental cities. Prohibition and precaution having been neglected, the Feringis became more and more familiar with our fair ways. And thus availing themselves of the situation the Feringis came into our port. I pray that all the foreign junks in our bay and the foreigners who secretly live (in our territory) be driven away, that private intercourse be prohibited and that our strategical defence be close, so that that part of our country will have peace.

Source: Tien-tse Chang, *Sino-Portuguese Trade, From 1514 to 1644: A Synthesis of Portuguese and Chinese Sources* (Leyden: E. J. Brill, 1934), pp. 51–52.

trying to insert themselves into world trade. Thus, the English and the Dutch arrived as the first competitors of the Portuguese in Asia, sailing into the South China Sea in the last decade of the sixteenth century. Captain James Lancaster made the first English voyage to the East Indies between 1591 and 1594. Five years later, in 1599, 101 English subscribers pooled their funds and formed a joint-stock company. With an initial capital of £30,000, the English East India Company was given a royal charter the following year. The charter granted the company exclusive rights to import East Indian goods. Rapidly, the company displaced the Portuguese in the Arabian Sea and the Persian Gulf. Doing a brisk trade in indigo, saltpetre, pepper, and cotton textiles, the company would eventually acquire control in villages on both coasts of the Indian subcontinent—Fort St. George (Madras; 1639), Bombay (1661), and Calcutta (1690).

> *Military campaigns consolidated Akbar's control over the Indian subcontinent, and favors and intermarriage contributed to the growth and stability of his empire.*

It is tempting to see the arrival of Europeans in the waters of the Indian Ocean as the beginning of the end of Asian autonomy from Europe. This was hardly the case, however. Through the sixteenth century, Europeans forged only very weak connections to Asian societies. For the moment, the opportunity to trade and the acquisition of silver enhanced the wealth and might of Asian dynasties.

MUGHAL INDIA AND COMMERCE

Illustrative of Asia's economic flourishing was the Mughal empire, which became one of the world's wealthiest and most powerful at the very moment that Europeans were establishing their first sustained connections with India. These connections, however, only touched the outer layer of Mughal India. Indeed, connections to Europe were nearly irrelevant to the emergence of one of Islam's greatest regimes. Established in 1526, the Mughal empire was a vigorous, centralized state whose political authority extended over most of the Indian subcontinent. During the sixteenth century, its realm encompassed a population between 100 and 150 million.

The strength of the Mughals rested on their impressive military power. The dynasty's founder, Babur, brought horsemanship and, most notably, trained artillery men and field cannons from Central Asia. Babur's gunpowder secured swift military victories and control over northern India. Not until the reign of his grandson, Akbar (ruled 1556–1605), however, did the empire experience a vast expansion and consolidation that would continue under Akbar's grandson Aurangzeb until the empire encompassed almost the whole of India (see Map 3-5). Known as the "Great Mughal," Akbar extended the military campaigns of his predecessors. These campaigns consolidated Akbar's control over the subcontinent. But the key to Akbar's success was not might alone. Akbar was a skilled practitioner of the art of alliance-making. Deals with Hindu chieftains through favors and intermarriage among notables also contributed to the growth and stability of his empire.

Mughal rulers were even more flexible in their dealings with the subcontinent's various peoples than their predecessors had been. This was especially true in spiritual affairs. Though its primary commitment to Islam was never in doubt, the imperial

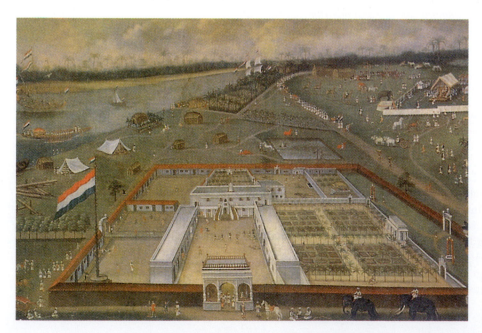

Dutch Trading Post in Bengal. A painting from 1665 shows the layout of Dutch warehouses in its Hooghly trading post in Bengal. Established in 1610, this trading post was an important part of the Dutch trading network in Asia. The painting shows the trading post protected by high walls, indicating that trade and fortification went hand in hand at this time.

Babur's domain, 1526

Akbar's domain, 1556–1605

Areas added by Aurangzeb to 1707

■ Trading port

MAP 3-5   EXPANSION OF THE MUGHAL EMPIRE, 1556–1707

Under Akbar and Aurangzeb the Mughal empire expanded throughout most of the Indian subcontinent. Can you speculate on why present-day India does not include the whole of the Mughal empire? By looking at the trading ports along the Indian coast, can you determine the areas where Portuguese, Dutch, French, and English influences predominated? Which parts of India served as the building blocks for the establishment of English and French colonial presences?

court patronized a variety of beliefs, earning it legitimacy in the eyes of diverse subjects. The contrast with sixteenth-century Europe, where religious differences created deep fractures within and between states, could not have been starker. Unlike European monarchs, who tried to enforce religious uniformity, Akbar engaged in a systematic study and discussion of comparative religion. He hosted regular disputations in his famous *Din-i-Ilahi* (House of Worship), where Hindu, Muslim, Jain, Parsi, and Christian theologians debated the merits of different religions. Akbar had both a Hindu and a Christian wife (besides having a Muslim wife, as well as numerous concubines of many different nationalities and religions), and his palace boasted temples to each faith. Akbar's pragmatic tolerance did not always

Akbar Hears a Petition. In keeping with the multiethnic and multireligious character of Akbar's empire, the image reflects the diversity of peoples seeking to have their petitions heard by the Mughal emperor.

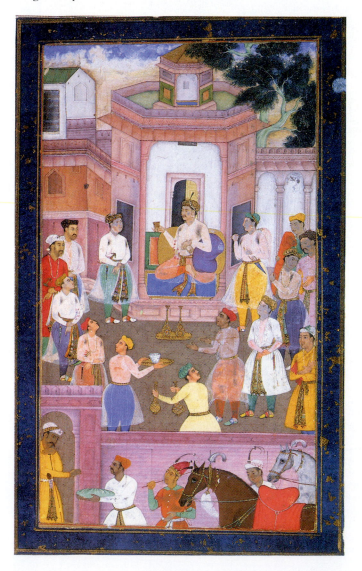

keep theologians happy—especially those who advocated orthodox beliefs—but it kept a sprawling and diverse spiritual kingdom under one political roof.

Akbar's regime enjoyed the fruits of the commercial recovery and expansion in the Indian Ocean. Indeed, increasing trade brought in more and more commercial wealth and reinforced the use of money in the Mughal economy. In this context, European trading connections contributed to the formation of the Mughal polity by adding to the increasing traffic and flow of money.

The strength of the Mughals limited European incursions, while enabling the empire to profit from trade with a variety of partners. Although the Portuguese occupied Goa and Bombay on the subcontinent's coast, they had little presence beyond these ports and, in fact, they did not dare to antagonize the Mughal emperor. In 1578, Akbar recognized the credentials of a Portuguese ambassador and allowed a Jesuit missionary to enter his court. In the ensuing years, the commercial ties between the Mughals and Portuguese intensified, but the latter's merchants were still effectively confined to a few ports on the fringes of the Mughal domain. More Portuguese ships entered those harbors, but many of these were manned by Indian seamen. In addition, the Mughals ended the Portuguese monopoly on the oceanic trade with Europe. In the 1580s and 1590s, to the chagrin of the Portuguese, Dutch and English merchantmen started to arrive in Indian ports.

Akbar seized on the commercial boom to overhaul his empire's revenue system. Until the 1560s, the Mughal empire relied on a vast network of decentralized tribute collectors called *zamindars*. These collectors possessed rights to claim a share of the harvest from the region's peasants, while earmarking part of their earnings for the emperor. The imperial state itself did not penetrate deeply into regional societies and could not rely on regular sources of cash. Moreover, sharing the spoils between the emperor and cooperative local leaders created underlying problems, for high levies did not always sit well with peasants. All across the peripheries of Mughal rule, local populations mounted prolonged and fierce resistance against dynastic power. But as trade flourished, the supply of money rose. Akbar's officials, and especially the Hindu revenue minister Todar Mal, monetized the tax assessment system and curbed the political and fiscal power of the *zamindars* over the peasantry. The emperor undertook a variety of other reforms that further rationalized and centralized the revenue system. The result: imperial revenues began to rise markedly, and these helped cover the cost of Akbar's military expeditions and his extravagant spending on the beautification of his court.

These fiscal policies reinforced the commercialization of the empire. To generate the cash to pay taxes, peasants had to sell their produce in the market. Market towns and ports flourished. Dealers in grain and money became more prominent in the countryside as they helped peasants get their produce to market. Between one-fifth and one-third the value of all this burgeoning rural produce flowed into state coffers. The *zamindars* evolved from private tribute lords into servants of the state, though they continued to enjoy their share of the peasants' income.

When it came to luxuries, the imperial household set lofty standards. Every year, Akbar ordered 1,000 new suits stitched of the most exquisite material. His harem was attired in fine silks dripping with gold, brocades, and pearls. Carpets, mirrors, and precious metals decorated noble households and camps, while perfume and wine flowed freely. Retainers, even horses and elephants, were garbed in elaborate attire. The splendor of the realm was perhaps most evident in the field of fine arts. In architecture, for instance, Akbar's temporary capital at Fatehpur Sikri, near Agra, combined the fort's flat stone beams and sense of immensity from the Hindu tradition with the arches and the feathery lightness of Islamic art.

Babur and Akbar's empire in India seized upon the wealth of the subcontinent and channeled resources—military, architectural, and artistic—to glorify the state. Some of this commercial bonanza could be traced to greater commerce with Europeans. At the same time, this wealth created potential divisions between Indian regions, and even between merchants and rulers. So long as merchants

> *The Chinese population probably accounted for a higher proportion of the total world population than at any other time in the history of the world—more than one-third.*

relied upon rulers for their commercial gains, and so long as rulers carefully balanced local and imperial interests, however, the Mughal realm remained unified and kept Europeans on the outskirts of society.

PROSPERITY IN MING CHINA

In the late sixteenth century, China's Ming dynasty also prospered from the commerce with silver-bearing European traders. As with the Mughals, the Ming seemed relatively unconcerned with the more regular appearance of foreigners in its ports. After all, as in India, the Ming retained the power to confine Europeans to port cities.

Until the 1570s, China's main source of silver was Japan. Both Chinese and European merchants plied the routes from Japanese ports to the Chinese mainland. From the 1570s onward, however, Manila became a gateway for silver from the New World. The influx of American silver enabled the Chinese economy to continue its expansion. Silver flowed into China, as Chinese merchants conducted a brisk business in silks and porcelains. Although some officials protested, most looked the other way to protect the wealth that percolated into their pockets. Despite modest official attempts to control trade, precious metals reached China in large quantities. Indeed, China was the final repository for much of the world's silver from the beginning of the sixteenth century until the end of the eighteenth

century. According to one estimate, fully one-third of all of the silver mined in the Americas wound up in Chinese hands.

The influx of silver spurred commercial and monetary changes in sixteenth- and early-seventeenth-century China that enhanced the prosperity of the country. As in Mughal India, the availability of silver facilitated the spread of market activities across the Ming realm. Employers paid their workers with money rather than in kind (with produce or goods). Agriculture and handicraft production soared. The injection of money eased the constraints of borrowing and lending. Rural industries also flourished. A cotton boom, for example, helped make spinning and weaving into China's largest single industry.

A clear measure of China's prosperity was the surge in its population. By the middle of the seventeenth century, the Chinese population probably accounted for a higher proportion of the total world population than at any other time in the history of the world—more than one-third, or approximately 250 million out of 750 million. Although fully 90 percent of the people lived in the countryside, this still left large numbers to swell the ranks of the urban dwellers. Beijing, the Ming capital, saw its population grow to over 1 million, and Nanjing, the secondary capital, grew to nearly the same number of inhabitants. There were another half dozen cities with populations of 500,000, and another twenty or so with 100,000 or more residents.

Chinese cities were not squalid havens for the desperate and destitute. Quite the contrary, urban life allowed people of means to find all manner of diversions, ranging from literary and theatrical societies, to schools of learning, religious societies, and urban associations. Here, too, the diverse manufactures from all over the Ming empire were available to satisfy the taste of the discerning consumer. The elegance and material prosperity of Chinese cities dazzled European visitors. Consider, for instance, Matteo Ricci, a Jesuit missionary, who described Nanjing in 1600 as a city that surpassed all others in the world "in beauty and grandeur. . . . It is literally filled with palaces and temples and towers and bridges. . . . There is a gaiety of spirit among the people who are well mannered and nicely spoken."

What had changed in China over the previous century was the appearance of Europeans in larger and larger numbers. Some, like Ricci, were there to evangelize, others came to trade. By 1563, the number of Portuguese in Macao neared 1,000. Still, the Portuguese contingent in Macao was dwarfed by the far larger number of Melakans, Indians, and Africans milling about the port. Moreover, while Ming authorities finally permitted a Portuguese presence in Macao, the government in Beijing remained unwilling to establish an official relationship with European traders there. Like the Mughals, the Ming confined Portuguese merchants to a coastal enclave. Indeed, in 1574, the

Chinese built a wall at the isthmus connecting Macao with the mainland. This barrier, and the soldiers who guarded it, served to restrict the movement of the Portuguese and their access to inland trade.

Through the sixteenth century, then, Europeans hovered on the margins of Chinese life. But slight though their presence was, it nonetheless symbolized how the world had grown more interconnected and how contact between cultures was altering economic and political systems.

CONCLUSION

In the middle of the fifteenth century, the world had many different regional trading spheres. In this sense, it was multicentered, with Islam occupying the pivotal place. In an Indian Ocean system straddling Africa, the eastern Mediterranean, and South and East Asia, merchants plied their wares along overland—and increasingly seaborne—routes, while intermingling in multiethnic urban centers. To the extent that Asian empires expanded, they sought tribute and trade. Conquest and colonial settlement were scarcely considered. Exchange, or better yet, tributary relations among newfound subject peoples drove imperial agendas.

In this multicentered world of the fifteenth century, Europe was a poor cousin. A new spirit of adventure and achievement, however, animated European peoples, stirred up by the rediscovery of antiquity (the Renaissance), the ambitions of a rising mercantile elite, and later by the spiritual energy let loose by the Reformation. Learning much from Arab seamen, European sailors perfected techniques for sailing into dangerous waters. Desiring Asian goods, especially for luxury consumption, European merchants and mariners were eager to exploit existing trade routes leading eastward. But Europe's location gave its people another direction into which to expand, across the still largely unknown Atlantic Ocean. With the Ottoman conquest of Constantinople and control over the eastern Mediterranean, the Atlantic sea lanes offered an alternative route to Asia. As the Europeans searched for alternative routes around Islam, they first sailed down the coast of Africa and then across the Atlantic.

Encountering America was an accident of monumental significance. There, Europeans found riches. Mountains of silver and rivers of gold gave Europeans the currency they had lacked in dealing with Asian traders. In the Americas, Europeans also found opportunities for exchange and settlement. And here, unlike in Asian empires, European rivals were able to supplement their drive for commerce with conquest and colonization. Yet, establishing these transatlantic empires heightened tensions within Europe, as rivals fought over the spoils, and as a religious schism turned into a political and spiritual struggle that divided Europe. It is for this reason that two conquests in particular characterize this age of increasing world interconnections. The Islamic conquest of Constantinople drove Europeans to search for new connections to Asia and demonstrated the centrality of Islam in the making of modern world history. In turn, the conquest of Tenochtitlán, some seventy years later, gave Europeans access to silver, which enabled them to increase their presence in Asian trading circuits. In this era of growing interconnectedness, these two conquests were decisive turning points in the making of the modern world.

American Indians also played an important role in the making of the modern world, as Europeans sought to exploit their labor, conquer their lands, and confiscate their gold and silver. Sometimes Indians worked with Europeans, sometimes they worked under Europeans, sometimes they worked against Europeans, and sometimes there were none left to work at all. In this last all too common case, the Europeans made Africans do what Indians could not, thereby compounding the calamity of the encounter with the tragedy of slavery. Out of the catastrophe of contact, a new oceanic system arose, linking the peoples and products of Africa, America, and Europe. This was the Atlantic world, one that gave new meaning to the notion of

Chronology

1453	Ottomans sack Constantinople
1492	Christians complete reconquest of Granada
1492	Columbus discovers the New World
1497	Da Gama sails to the Indian Ocean
1508–1511	Portuguese establish Indian Ocean bases
1517	Luther posts 95 theses
1519–1522	Magellan's ship circumnavigates the globe
1519–1522	Cortés conquers the Aztecs
1525	Peasant wars in Holy Roman empire
1533	Pizarro conquers the Incas
1540	Portuguese arrive at Macao (China)
1545	Opening of Potosí mines
1556–1605	Consolidation of Mughal empire
1568	Dutch revolt against Spanish rule
1571	Spanish capture city of Manila
1571	Spanish fleet defeats Ottomans at Lepanto
1574	Ming erect wall to Macao to restrict European movement
1588	English defeat Spanish Armada

oceanic systems. In contrast to the tributary and trading orders of the Indian Ocean and China Seas, the Atlantic Ocean became a system of formal imperial control and settlement of distant colonies.

 **FURTHER READINGS**

Axtell, James, *Beyond 1492: Encounters in Colonial North America* (1992). A wonderfully informed speculation about Indian reactions to Europeans.

Brady, Thomas A., et al. (eds.), *Handbook of European History 1400–1600: Late Middle Ages, Renaissance, and Reformation. Structures and Assertions* (1996). A good synthetic survey of recent literature and historiographical debates.

Chaudhuri, K. N., *Trade and Civilisation in the Indian Ocean: An Economic History from the Rise of Islam to 1750* (1985). An excellent and comprehensive work that deals with changes in the Indian Ocean economy and charts the appearance of European merchants in that part of the world from the sixteenth century onward.

Clendinnen, Inga, *Aztecs: An Interpretation* (1991). Brilliantly reconstructs the culture of Tenochtitlán in the years before its conquest.

Crosby, Alfred W., *The Columbian Exchange: Biological and Cultural Consequences of 1492* (1972). A provocative discussion of the ecological consequences that followed the European "discovery" of the Americas.

Crosby, Alfred W., *Ecological Imperialism: The Biological Expansion of Europe, 900–1900* (1986). Another important work on the ecological consequences of European encounters with other cultures.

Curtin, Philip, *Cross-Cultural Trade in World History* (1984). A work stressing the role of trade and commerce in establishing cross-cultural contacts.

Febvre, Lucien, *The Problem of Unbelief in the Sixteenth Century: The Religion of Rabelais* (1982). A tour de force of intellectual history by the man who moved the study of the Reformation away from great men to the broader question of religious revival and mentalities.

Flynn, Dennis, and Arturo Giráldez (eds.), *Metals and Monies in an Emerging Global Economy* (1997). Contains several articles relating to silver and the Asian trade.

Frank, Andre Gunder, *ReOrient: Global Economy in the Asian Age* (1998). A reassessment of the role of Asia in the economic development of the world from around 1400 onward.

Gruzinski, Serge, *The Conquest of Mexico* (1993). An important work on the conquest of Mexico.

Habib, Irfan, *The Agrarian System of Mughal India* (1963). One of the best studies on the subject.

Hodgson, Marshall, *The Venture of Islam*, vols. 2 and 3 (1974). A magisterial work that includes the Indian subcontinent in its careful study of the political and cultural history of the whole Islamic world.

Hulme, Peter, *Colonial Encounters: Europe and the Native Caribbean, 1492–1797* (1986). Presents an interesting interpretation of the encounters of Europeans and Native Americans.

Kishlansky, Mark, *A Monarchy Transformed: Britain 1603–1714* (1996). An insightful treatment of one of the early modern European dynasties during a period marked by crises.

Lockhart, James, and Stuart Schwartz, *Early Latin America* (1983). One of the finest studies of European expansion in the late fifteenth century.

Mignolo, Walter D., *The Darker Side of the Renaissance: Literacy, Territoriality, and Colonization* (1995). Uses literary theory and literary images to present provocative interpretations of the encounter of Europeans and Native Americans.

Pagden, Anthony, *European Encounters with the New World* (1993). A complex look at the deep and lasting imprint of the New World on its conquerors.

Parker, Geoffrey, *The Military Revolution: Military Innovation and the Rise of the West, 1500–1800* (1996). Traces the changes in technology and tactics in the early modern period and discusses the political significance of this "revolution."

Pelikan, Jaroslav, *Reformation of Church and Dogma (1300–1700)* (1988). An important overview of major religious controversies.

Phillips, William D., and Carla Rahn Phillips, *The World of Christopher Columbus* (1992). One of the finest studies of European expansion in the late fifteenth century.

Russell-Wood, A. J. R., *The Portuguese Empire, 1415–1808* (1992). An important survey of early Portuguese exploration.

Von Glahn, Richard, *Fountain of Fortune: Money and Monetary Policy in China, 1000–1700* (1996). Includes an excellent analysis of the history of silver in Ming China.

4

WORLDS ENTANGLED, 1600–1750

*I*n 1720, a devastating financial panic swept across Europe, making rich men into paupers and ruining many political careers. The panic was rooted in a speculative mania surrounding anticipated high profits flowing from trade with the Americas. A group of British merchants set up the South Sea Trading Company to compete with French trading firms and obtained privileged trading rights with all of Spanish America. Most coveted of all was the exclusive right to sell African slaves to Spanish colonies. Enthusiasm for these and other less substantial companies soared, and investors rushed in, sending share prices skyrocketing. But rumors of fantastic spoils gave way to word that the original investors were dumping their shares and that many of the companies were worthless. The speculative bubble burst. Share prices plummeted, with nearly all the companies created at the time going bankrupt, and even many solid firms in Europe going under. The South Sea Bubble, as it came to be called, reflected the euphoria of overseas trading ventures and the greater interconnections across the world. But it also stood as a vivid example of the perils that could accompany global trade and investment.

From 1600 to 1750, the circuits of world trade expanded as commerce continued to flow across the world's oceans. Ships laden with sugar from Brazil, spices from Southeast Asia, cotton textiles from India, silks from China, and increasingly, silver from Mesoamerica and the Andes made their way from port to port. In these global trading networks, New World silver played a decisive role. It gave Europeans a commodity to exchange with Asian partners and began to tilt the balance of wealth and power in a westerly direction across Eurasia.

During this period, increasing economic connection along with the territorial expansion of various empires produced dramatic, if sometimes unintended, effects around the world. In the Atlantic basin, European colonial powers consolidated their control over larger portions of the Americas. England and France joined Spain and Portugal in the full-scale colonization of American possessions. In addition, the number of African slaves shipped to the Americas rose dramatically during the seventeenth and eighteenth centuries, drawing the peoples and products of Africa, Europe, and the Americas more closely together. By no means was this growing expansion of empires limited to the Atlantic world. European empires also established colonies in Southeast Asia and, with New World silver, sought to extend their trade with Asian societies. At the same time, rulers in India, China, and Japan enlarged the borders of their empires, while Russia's tsars incorporated vast Siberian territories into their domain.

Predictably, economic linkages and territorial expansion were tempestuous processes. Commercial, colonial, and religious rivalries provoked bitter and bloody conflicts between and within European states. In Asia, too, increasing global trade and political expansion produced political and economic instability. In particular, the increased flow of silver posed a stiff challenge to the centralized control of the Ottoman and Mughal empires, and contributed to the toppling of the Ming dynasty. In this chapter, we will examine the processes of economic interdependence and territorial expansion and their effects, both intended and unintended, on the peoples of the world.

INCREASING ECONOMIC LINKAGES

> → *How did economic integration affect political systems?*

Increasing economic ties changed the relations between different parts of the world. New places and new products entered world markets: furs from French North America, sugar from the Caribbean, tobacco from the British mainland American colonies, and coffee from Southeast Asia and the Middle East, to name only the more obvious items. So important did the products of world trade become during the seventeenth and eighteenth centuries that interruptions in their availability, most notably of silver, but of other items as well, destabilized regional economic and political systems.

SOCIAL AND POLITICAL EFFECTS

The increasing economic interdependence that followed the search for oceanic routes to Asia had dramatic and unexpected repercussions on social and political systems. Although transoceanic trade most directly affected the mercantile groups who financed and directed these expensive undertakings, the deepening connections between the economies of distant places also affected rulers and common peoples. For example, the output of the new gold and silver mines of the Americas was vital to the commercial networks that linked the markets of the world. The supply of precious metals might fall because political disturbances brought work stoppages or increase greatly when new mines opened. The prices of commodities could soar or drop, bringing prosperity to some and poverty to others. Such shifts in economic fortunes, in turn, produced major political and social upheavals, both within and between societies. And because greater wealth could finance the purchase of more weaponry and larger standing armies, these conflicts had even more destructive consequences.

Focus Questions WORLDS ENTANGLED

The benefits of closer economic contact could—and did—enhance the power of some states. It could bolster the legitimacy of existing holders of power, as it did for the rising new states of England and France. It could also encourage local power groups to throw their weight behind new rulers, as happened in Japan and in parts of sub-Saharan Africa. Old or new, however, the challenges of a more closely linked world introduced problems. In England, France, Japan, and Russia, and across Africa, the linkages of the seventeenth and eighteenth centuries were accompanied by civil wars and large-scale social unrest.

For other regimes and economies, the impact of trade and closer global connections was even more destabilizing to the existing systems of rule and to the old social order. Large empires, notably the Ottoman state, found outlying provinces slipping from central control. To the east of the Ottoman empire's borders, the Safavid regime foundered in 1722, and it came to an end in 1773; the once mighty Ming dynasty gave way to a new dynasty, the Qing, in 1644. In India, internal rivalries among princes and powerful merchants whittled away at the central authority of the Mughals, compounding the instability caused by peasant uprisings. In many of these great Asian monarchies, European traders and their political backers, at first operating only on the fringes, were only too eager to enter the fray and enhance their own preeminence at the expense of their Asian counterparts.

EXTRACTING WEALTH: MERCANTILISM

Transformations in relations between different parts of the world began in the Atlantic, where the extraction and shipment of gold and silver siphoned wealth from the New World to the Old. Mined by Indian workers and delivered into the hands of merchants and monarchs, precious metals from the Andes and Mesoamerica accounted for a rising share of the world's supply of silver. Added to the output of these regions, a boom in gold production made Brazil the world's single largest producer of that metal in the eighteenth century.

So lucrative was American mining that other European powers wanted a share in the bounty that Spain and Portugal were reaping from mineral-rich possessions. Looking for their own areas in the Americas from which to take gold and silver, a number of European rivals launched colonizing ventures in the seventeenth century. In contrast to the first century of European colonialism, latecomers failed to find much in the way of minerals. But they came to realize that there were other means to extract wealth from colonies. The New World, it became apparent, had an abundance of resources and fertile lands on which to cultivate sugarcane, cotton, tobacco, indigo, and rice, as well as fur-bearing wildlife, whose pelts were much demanded in Europe (see Map 4-1). Better still from the perspective of new colonizers, New World crops and skins could be produced and

THE PRINCIPLES OF MERCANTILISM

In 1757, a British commercial expert by the name of Malachy Postlewayt published a commercial dictionary, which he called The Universal Dictionary of Trade and Commerce. *Under the entry "trade," he set forth "some maxims relating to trade that should seem to be confirmed in the course of this work." The first five provide a succinct statement of the economic philosophy of mercantilism and the importance that countries attached to the acquisition of precious metals.*

I. That the lasting prosperity of the landed interest depends upon foreign commerce.

II. That the increase of the wealth, splendour, and power of Great Britain and Ireland depends upon exporting more in value of our native produce and manufactures than we import of commodities from other nations and bringing thereby money into the kingdom by means of freight by shipping.

III. That domestic and foreign trade, as they are the means of increasing national treasure, of breeding seamen, and of augmenting our mercantile and royal navies they necessarily become the means of our permanent prosperity and of the safety and preservation of our happy constitution.

IV. That the constant security of the public credit and the payment of interest and principal of the public creditors depend upon the prosperous state of our trade and navigation.

V. That gold and silver is the measure of trade, and that silver is a commodity and may be exported, especially in foreign coin as well as any other commodity.

Source: Malachy Postlewayt, *The Universal Dictionary of Trade and Commerce*, vol. 2, p. 792.

GREENLAND

ALASKA

ICELAND

DENMAR
NETHERLANDS

RUPERT'S
LAND

ENGLAND

Amsterdam
London

NEWFOUND-
LAND

Québec

Tobacco
Rice
Furs
Indigo
Meat
Timber
Grain
Taxes

Sugar
Gold
Hides
Coffee
Diamonds
Calico
Taxes

FRAN

NOVA
SCOTIA

PORTUGAL

NEW
FRANCE

Boston

Manufactures

Lisbon

SPAIN

New York
Philadelphia

Seville

LOUISIANA

THIRTEEN
COLONIES

Cadiz

Silk
Spices

VICEROYALTY
OF
NEW SPAIN

Sugar
Coffee
Indigo
Cotton

Sugar
Indigo
Hides
Taxes

ATLANTIC
OCEAN

Timbuktu

Zacatecas

New Orleans

MEXICO

ASANTE

Mexico City

Veracruz

Accra

Lago

Acapulco

FERNANDO P

Cartagena

SURINAM

Panama

VICEROYALTY
OF
GRANADA

Slaves

Iron
Copper
Textiles
Cutlery
Firearms

Quito

DUTCH
BRAZIL

VICEROYALTY
OF BRAZIL

Recife

PACIFIC
OCEAN

Lima

Bahia

Slaves

VICEROYALTY
OF PERU

Potosí

Tobacco
Sugar

Rio de Janeiro

Pepper
Spices
Silk
Coffee

Buenos Aires

Spices

Line of
Tordesillas
1494

Silk
Calico

Silk
Calico
Coffee
Pepper
Indigo
Drugs

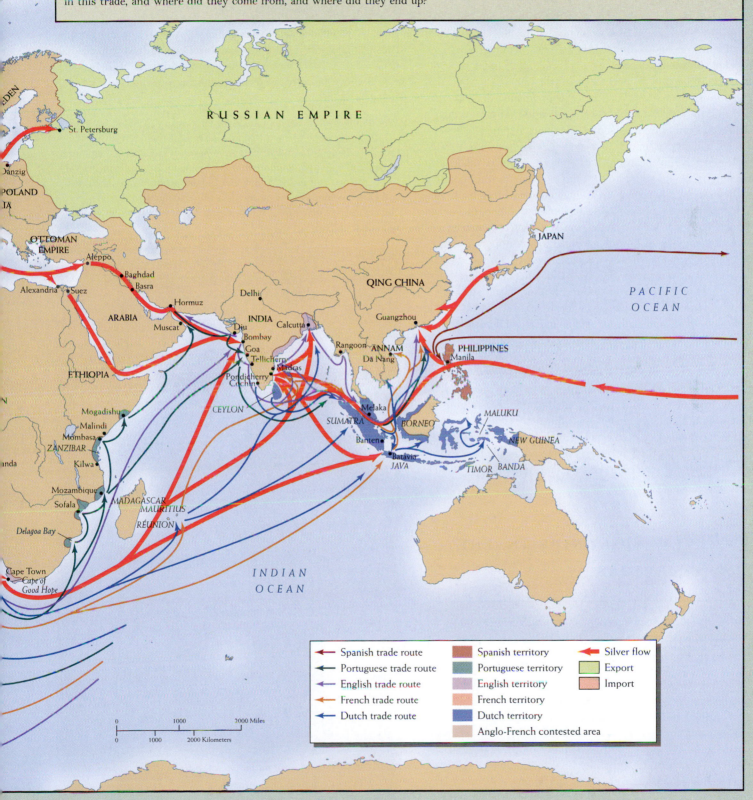

The seventeenth and eighteenth centuries were the first centuries of true global commerce. Silver was the one item that was traded all over the world. Can you trace the flows of silver from the Americas around the globe and identify the commodities that silver was exchanged for in different parts of the world? What continents were involved in the triangular trade, what were the major commodities in this trade, and where did they come from, and where did they end up?

RUSSIAN EMPIRE

St. Petersburg

Danzig

POLAND

OTTOMAN
EMPIRE

Aleppo

Baghdad

Basra

Alexandria

Suez

Hormuz

Delhi

JAPAN

QING CHINA

PACIFIC
OCEAN

ARABIA

Muscat

INDIA

Diu

Bombay

Goa

Tellicherry

Calcutta

Guangzhou

PHILIPPINES

Manila

ETHIOPIA

Pondicherry

Cochin

Madras

Rangoon

ANNAM

Da Nang

Mogadishu

CEYLON

Malindi

Mombasa

Melaka

MALUKU

ZANZIBAR

SUMATRA

BORNEO

NEW GUINEA

Kilwa

Banten

Mozambique

Sofala

MADAGASCAR

MAURITIUS

Batavia

JAVA

TIMOR

BANDA

Delagoa Bay

RÉUNION

Cape Town

Cape of
Good Hope

INDIAN
OCEAN

Spanish trade route	Spanish territory	Silver flow
Portuguese trade route	Portuguese territory	Export
English trade route	English territory	Import
French trade route	French territory	
Dutch trade route	Dutch territory	
	Anglo-French contested area	

0   1000   2000 Miles

0   1000   2000 Kilometers

transported more easily and cheaply than had been previously imagined. No longer, then, was the quest for specie to pay for Asian commodities the only rationale for European expansion in the Atlantic world.

In the process of extending their domains in the Americas, Europeans created a new philosophy of wealth to buttress their colonial ventures and to finance their dynastic struggles on the European continent. Coined by a French economist in 1763, what came to be called "mercantilism" described a system that had developed over several centuries. Mercantilist doctrine presumed that the world's wealth was fixed, and that one country's wealth could only be increased at another's expense. The system's proponents assumed that overseas possessions existed solely to enrich European motherlands. In practice, this meant that colonies should ship more "value" to their mother country than they received in return. In addition to providing trade surpluses, colonies were supposed to be closed to competitors, lest foreign traders drain precious resources from an empire's exclusive domain. As the mother country's monopoly over the trade of its colonial territories generated wealth for royal treasuries, European monarchs acquired the wherewithal to wage almost unceasing wars against one another. Ultimately, mercantilists believed that rich kings made strong states. In the words of the philosopher of the modern state, Thomas Hobbes (1588–1679), "wealth is power and power is wealth."

The mercantilist system rested on an alliance between the state and its merchants. Mercantilists believed economics and politics were interdependent, with the merchant needing the monarch to protect his interests, and the monarch relying on the merchant's trade to enrich the state's treasury. The chartered royal company, created by wealthy merchants and granted monopoly rights by the European monarchs, is the best example of the alliance between merchants and monarchs.

NEW COLONIES IN THE AMERICAS

> → *How did European mercantilism and colonialism transform the Americas?*

One by one, rulers in England, France, and Holland granted monopolies to merchant companies, giving to them a monopoly over the trade and settlement of new colonies in the Americas (see Map 4-2). If old motives—finding stores of specie or water routes to Asia—initiated many of these enterprises, the Dutch, French, and English learned that only by exploiting other resources could their claims in the Americas be made into profitable colonies. That the latecomers met with New World societies very different from those in Mesoamerica or the Andes

also necessitated fresh thinking about the appropriate character of colonial regimes.

WOODLANDS INDIANS

In the woodlands of eastern North America, for example, European colonizers did not encounter centralized empires like those of the Aztecs or Incas. Instead, the Indians of the eastern woodlands generally lived in small-scale polities, with kinship

Woodlands Indians. This late sixteenth-century drawing by John White, a pioneer settler on Roanoke Island off the coast of North Carolina, depicts the Indian village of Secoton in eastern Virginia. In contrast to the great empires that the Spanish conquered in the valley of Mexico and in the Andes, the Indians whom English, French, and Dutch colonizers encountered in the woodlands of eastern North America generally lived in villages that were politically autonomous entities.

MAP 4-2   COLONIES IN NORTH AMERICA, 1607–1763

France, England, and Spain laid claim to much of North America in the seventeenth and eighteenth centuries. Where was each one of these colonial powers strongest before the outbreak of the French and Indian War in North America? Who gained the most North American territory and who lost the most at the end of the war in 1763? How do you imagine that Indian peoples reacted to the territorial arrangements agreed to by Spain, France, and England at the Peace of Paris, which ended the war?

Map legend:
- English claims 1756
- French claims 1756
- Spanish claims 1756
- Dutch claims until 1664
- English acquisitions 1763
- Spanish acquisitions 1763
- French possessions 1763
- Anglo-French contested area

connections providing the basis for political and social organization. For the most part, villages were independent of one another; indeed, they were often engaged in endemic, if generally low-intensity, warfare against one another. In places, villages joined together in loose confederations, creating larger-scale organizations. One such powerful grouping was the alliance of villages known as Iroquoia, which emerged in what is now upstate New York sometime in the middle of the fifteenth century. Intervillage diplomacy stitched together this "Great League of Peace and Power," uniting previously warring hamlets. Outside the "five nations" of the Iroquois Confederation, however, warfare remained pervasive. Moreover, the Iroquois Confederation did not create a centralized state, and certainly its grandeur did not approach that of the Aztecs or the Incas. And yet because the woodlands boasted no single, centralized empire, the conquest of the Iroquois and their woodland neighbors proved more difficult for the English, French, and Dutch than subjugating the Aztecs and Incas had been for the Spanish.

HOLLAND'S TRADING COLONIES

The Dutch first established a settlement in North America at the mouth of the Hudson River. The river was named for an Englishman, Henry Hudson, who had been hired by the Dutch East India Company to explore the Atlantic coast of North America. The company hoped that Hudson might find a "northwest passage" through North America and on to Asia. Of particular promise was the broad river, which was given Hudson's name after he entered it in 1609. When his backers realized that the Hudson River did not lead to the Pacific Ocean, however, their interest in the area diminished. Still, Dutch merchants found that the waterway did provide access to a region filled with fur-bearing animals and with Indian peoples, including the Iroquois, able to trap and ready to trade. In 1624, thirty Dutch families settled on an island at the Hudson's mouth (Manhattan); many, however, soon abandoned the town for upriver locations where they could engage in exchanges with the Iroquois.

Trading furs with Indians was not the original idea behind Dutch colonization. In the sixteenth and seventeenth centuries, the Dutch were pleased to be the carriers for other colonizers. They happily used their vessels to transport the cargo of other nations to any corner of the world. Dutch merchants made considerable profits from handling the slaves, spices, textiles, and silver of others. At the same time, these traders recognized the importance of a direct North Atlantic passage to Asia to their shipping business: hence, the Dutch East India Company's sponsorship of Hudson's explorations. They also coveted the riches that the Spanish and Portuguese took from their possessions. Especially tempting were some of the lesser Spanish island possessions in the Caribbean. In the beginning, Dutch seamen sought to pillage Spanish ships, particularly silver convoys bound for Spain. But their main Caribbean thrust was to create plantation settlements. In 1621, Amsterdam merchants founded the Dutch West India Company to regulate commerce, promote settlement, and maintain the flow of slaves to the Caribbean. The Dutch laid claim to St. Eustatius and two other islands in 1632, captured Curaçao from Spain in 1634, and a few years later claimed Aruba and St. Martin (see Map 4-3). Unfortunately for its backers, these colonies never yielded the plantation fruits that were expected of them, leading to bankruptcy for the Dutch West India Company in 1674.

In search of an immediate boon, the Dutch took aim at the Portuguese sugar bastions in Brazil. In the first half of the seventeenth century, Brazil was the world's largest producer of sugar. But it was an underdefended outpost of the Portuguese seaborne empire and vulnerable to attack. The Dutch West India Company went after the Brazilian sugar belt, beginning in Bahia in the 1620s, and gradually expanded its control as far as Recife. For several decades, the Dutch firm controlled the New World's main sugar zone. Again, however, Dutch designs did not produce the desired profits. Local Brazilian planters, most of whom were Portuguese Catholics, resisted the control of Dutch Protestants. By 1654, Brazilian settlers drove out the last of the company officials, and the firm was left with the puny outpost on the South American mainland, Surinam, where it tried to introduce plantation agriculture, but with only meager results.

Although the Dutch efforts to establish colonies in the Americas were largely unsuccessful, their businessmen continued to profit from financing foreign merchants, lending vessels to other nations, and handling slaves, silver, and textiles. They were, in fact, often referred to as the world's "universal carriers." It is well to remember, too, that the most important Dutch colonial possessions were not in the Americas. More significant for the Dutch were their lucrative colony in the East Indies and a small colonial possession in South Africa (Cape Town), which was founded in 1652 as a refreshment station for ships going between the Atlantic and Indian Oceans.

In the first half of the seventeenth century, Brazil was the world's largest producer of sugar.

FRANCE'S FUR-TRADING EMPIRE

Like the Dutch, the French began their colonizing exploits in North America with a search for a northern water route to the Pacific that turned into a fur-trading enterprise. The initial French explorations were conducted by Jacques Cartier (1491–1557), and the chief French route into the interior of North America was the St. Lawrence River. Sailing up the St. Lawrence, Cartier and subsequent French explorers, most notably Samuel de Champlain (1567–1635), found not a waterway to the Pacific but huge bodies of fresh water (the Great Lakes) in the midst of a massive continent. In the wake of this discovery, Champlain founded the colony of New France, with its base in Québec, in 1608. From Québec, French traders and missionaries penetrated deep into the interior of North America, eager to engage its Indian inhabitants in commercial exchange and to convert them to the Catholic faith.

At the center of the trade between the French and the Indians in northern North America was the beaver, an animal for which Indian peoples previously had little use. But Europeans coveted the barbed underfur of the beaver and were willing to give Indians a variety of goods in return. For the Indians, as one native hunter proclaimed, "the beaver does everything perfectly well; it makes kettles, hatchets, swords, knives, bread, in short it makes everything." As long as there were beavers to be trapped, trade between the French and their Indian partners flourished. Almost unique for this age of encounter, the fur trade wove an enduring, if not always peaceable, alliance between the French and the Indians.

→ *How did European mercantilism and colonialism transform the Americas?*

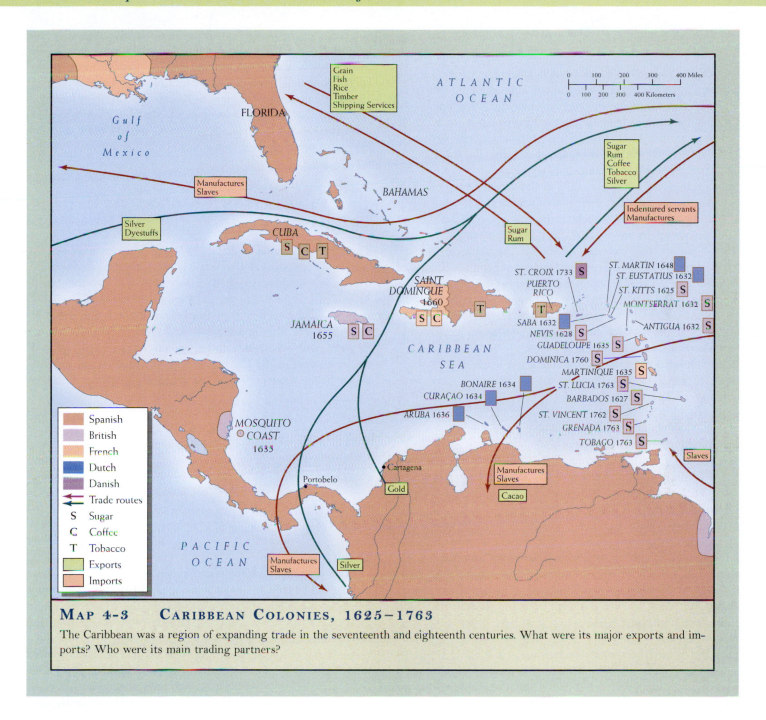

MAP 4-3   CARIBBEAN COLONIES, 1625–1763

The Caribbean was a region of expanding trade in the seventeenth and eighteenth centuries. What were its major exports and imports? Who were its main trading partners?

The distinctive aspect of the fur trade was the Europeans' utter dependence on Indian know-how. Trapping required close familiarity with the habits and habitats of the beaver—a skill that Europeans lacked. This reliance forced the French to adapt to Indian ways. Such accommodation is easily seen in the pattern of exchange. Although the French had wanted to make the export of beaver pelts a purely commercial venture, their Indian partners insisted on their own protocols. For the Indians, exchange was governed by more than material concerns. Trade

cemented familial bonds. For the most part, the French obeyed by giving gifts and partaking in Indian diplomatic rituals.

To solidify their trade networks, Frenchmen often married into Indian families. As a result of these unions, *métis*—French-Indian offspring—became important players in the landscape of New France. Interpreters, traders, and guides, the *métis* brokered French relations. Compared to all other empires, the French accomplished colonization without conquest, stretching their trading empire deep into North American forests.

ENGLAND'S LANDED EMPIRE

Part of the rationale for the French alliance with the Indians was strategic: the French and Indians alike shared a deep mistrust of the other major North American interlopers, the English. From their beginnings, the English colonies in North America, unlike their French counterparts, were expansive agrarian settlements that encroached on more and more Indian lands. Accordingly, relations between English colonists and Indian inhabitants were generally far less cordial than relations between the French and their native trading partners.

Along the Atlantic seaboard, the English colonies differed from one another, but their settlers shared a hunger for land that came at the expense of Indian inhabitants. Around Massachusetts Bay, one group of Protestant refugees (Puritans) founded a colony whose population rose substantially after 1630. As the colonial population of New England increased, so did the colonists' demand for fresh farmlands. The result was a souring of relations between natives and newcomers, which led to ferocious wars in the 1630s and 1670s.

A similar cycle unfolded further south around Chesapeake Bay. In Virginia, the impulse for colonization was more commercial and less religious than among the Puritans of Massachusetts, but the pattern of intercultural relations was remarkably similar. From the founding of the settlement at Jamestown in 1607, Chesapeake colonists aimed to make money. Their initial experiences were disastrous, however. The first winters wiped out large numbers of settlers, many of whom were gentlemen adventurers with little interest in labor. Like the Puritans, Chesapeake colonists would not have survived their "starving times" had local Indians not provided them with food and other assistance. But within a few years, the colony began to thrive, especially once the colonists found a suitable staple that could be profitably exported. In the Chesapeake, the crop of choice was a weed that Indians cultivated called tobacco. In Virginia, the tobacco boom of the 1620s transformed a failing colony into a commercial phoenix. Prosperity induced thousands of Englishmen to migrate to Virginia, compounding the pressures on Indian lands. As in Massachusetts, this hunger for plantations led to a series of wars and to the dispossession of Indians from their Chesapeake homelands.

As Indians were evicted, European men and women, along with African slaves, occupied the Atlantic seaboard. By 1700, the European population of the English mainland colonies approached 250,000, with an additional 33,000 settled in the West Indies. At the same time, the African population of England's American possessions was close to 150,000, of whom three-quarters lived in the Caribbean islands.

This pattern of colonialism had a distinctive impact on the English North American colonies. While the French intermixed freely with their trading partners and the Spanish married into Indian societies, the English steered clear of marital-political alliances. Like the Portuguese in Brazil, cultivation of land was the foundation for England's empire in the New World; yet, unlike Brazilian settlers, English colonists pushed the borders of European property ever deeper into Indian country.

THE PLANTATION COMPLEX IN THE CARIBBEAN

The English colonies in mainland North America were not the only land-intensive colonial settlements. Indeed, as late as 1670, the most populous English colony was not on the North American mainland, but on the Caribbean island of Barbados. From the mid-seventeenth century onward, the sugarcane plantations of the Portuguese in Brazil were replicated on the English- and French-controlled islands of the Caribbean. All was not sweet in the Caribbean, however. Because no colonial power held a monopoly over the sugarcane-growing islands of the Caribbean, the competition to control the region—and to profit from the production of sugar—was especially fierce. Florida was perhaps the most chaotic place on the borderlands of the Caribbean. Initially colonized by the Spanish, the peninsula at one time or another fell to Dutch, French, and English forces.

> *Silver and sugar were the dominant commodities flowing from west to east across the Atlantic, and slaves filled the ships on their return.*

The turbulence of the Caribbean was not simply a matter of imperial rivalry. It was also the result of the labor arrangements in the colonies. Unlike the rest of the Americas, where indigenous workers initially sustained staple production, the populations of the Caribbean were decimated in Columbus's wake. Bereft of a local labor force, the owners of Caribbean estates followed the Portuguese to Africa to obtain workers for their plantations. Silver and sugar were the dominant commodities flowing from west to east across the Atlantic, and slaves filled the ships on their return.

Sugar, whose cultivation employed the most slaves, was a killing crop. So deadly was the tropical environment in which sugarcane flourished—hot and humid climates were as fertile for disease as they were for tropical commodities—that many sugar barons spent little time on their plantations. Management fell to overseers who supervised crop production, and in short order worked their slaves to death. Despite having immunities to yellow fever and malaria, Africans could not withstand the regimen. Poor food, atrocious living conditions, and filthy sanitation added to the miseries of life on Caribbean sugarcane plantations. Here, especially, Europeans treated their slaves as nonhumans.

During the first day on the plantation, all recently bought slaves were branded with the planter's seal. In the words of one English gentleman, Negro slaves were like cows, "as near as beasts may be, setting their souls aside." Indeed, in the 1680s, one Barbados planter domiciled his slaves and cattle in two sheds of the same dimensions and construction. His slaves subsisted on a meager ration of corn, plantains, beans, and yams.

On a good day, like Saturday, the planter offered rum to drown the taste of what was often rancid meat. In all, most English planters spent less than 2 pounds sterling per annum to clothe and feed each slave.

More than disease, the work process itself decimated the enslaved. The numbers are ghoulish: the survivors of the passage from Africa to the Americas could look forward to worse on the

SILVER, THE DEVIL, AND THE COCA LEAF IN THE ANDES

When the Spanish forced thousands of Andean Indians to work in the silver mines of Potosí, they also condoned the spreading habit of chewing coca leaves (which are now used to extract cocaine). Chewing the leaves gave Indians a mild "high," alleviated their hunger, and blunted the pain of hard work and deteriorating lungs. But the habit also spread to some Spaniards. In this document, Bartolomé Arzáns de Orsúa y Vela, a Spaniard born in Potosí in 1676, expresses both how important coca was to Indian miners, and how pernicious it was for Spaniards who fell under its spell.

I wish to declare the unhappiness and great evil that, among so many felicities, this kingdom of Peru experiences in possessing the coca herb. . . . No Indian will go into the mines or to any other labor, be it building houses or working in the fields, without taking it in his mouth, even if his life depends on it. . . .

Among the Indians (and even the Spaniards by now) the custom of not entering the mines without placing this herb in the mouth is so well established that there is a superstition that the richness of the metal will be lost if they do not do so. . . .

The Indians being accustomed to taking this herb into their mouths, there is no doubt that as long as they have it there they lose all desire to sleep, and since it is extremely warming, they say that when the weather is cold they do not feel it if they have the herb in their mouths. In addition, they also say that it increases their strength and that they feel neither hunger nor thirst; hence these Indians cannot work without it.

When the herb is ground and placed in boiling water and if a person then takes a few swallows, it opens the pores, warms the body, and shortens labor in women; and this coca herb has many other virtues besides. But human perversity has caused it to become a vice, so that the devil (that inventor of vices) has made a notable harvest of souls with it, for there are many women who have taken it—and still take it—

for the sin of witchcraft, invoking the devil and using it to summon him for their evil deeds. . . .

With such ferocity has the devil seized on this coca herb that—there is no doubt about it—when it becomes an addiction it impairs or destroys the judgment of its users just as if they had drunk wine to excess and makes them see terrible visions; demons appear before their eyes in frightful forms. In this city of Potosí it is sold publicly by the Indians who work in the mines, and so the harm arising from its continued abundance cannot be corrected; but neither is that harm remediable in other large cities of this realm, where the use and sale of coca have been banned under penalties as severe as that of excommunication and yet it is secretly bought and sold and used for casting spells and other like evils.

Would that our lord the king had ordered this noxious herb pulled up by the roots wherever it is found. . . . Great good would follow were it to be extirpated from this realm: the devil would be bereft of the great harvest of souls he reaps, God would be done a great service, and vast numbers of men and women would not perish (I refer to Spaniards, for no harm comes to the Indians from it).

Source: Bartolomé Arzáns de Orsúa y Vela, *Tales of Potosí*, edited by R. C. Padden and translated by Frances M. López-Morillas (Providence: Brown University Press, 1975), pp. 117–20.

Slaves Cutting Cane. Sugar was the preeminent agricultural export from the New World for centuries. Owners of sugarcane plantations relied almost exclusively on African slaves to produce the sweetener. Labor in the fields was especially harsh, as slaves worked in the blistering sun from dawn until dusk. This image shows how women and men toiled side by side, and how European overseers whipped those who resisted.

plantation. Average life expectancy on some sugarcane plantations in the Caribbean—irrespective of the European power—was a mere three years. Six days a week, slaves rose before dawn, labored continuously until noon, ate a short lunch, and then worked until dusk. At harvest time, however, the workday often included extended shifts, sometimes seven days per week. Average harvest days of sixteen hours saw hundreds of slaves—men, women and children alike—doubled over to cut sugarcane and transport it to large factory-like refineries that housed massive cauldrons of boiling water. Under this brutal schedule, slaves occasionally dropped dead from exhaustion in the fields. Moreover, this system of production lent itself to gang labor, depriving slaves of any control over their own work.

Amidst disease and toil, the enslaved resisted as they could. The most dramatic expression of slave resistance was violent insurrection. In the early sixteenth century, slave revolts were so frequent in Panama that the crown banned the slave trade to the region altogether. In the early seventeenth century, in parts of coastal Mexico, the viceroy had to negotiate an armistice to pacify the region. Still, these instances of large-scale uprisings were sporadic.

A more common form of resistance was flight. Thousands of slaves took to the hills to seek refuge from overseers. In the remote highlands of Caribbean islands, runaway slaves found sanctuary in "maroon" communities—named after the Spanish word *cimarron*, meaning people from the heights. But the largest of these refuge havens were in Brazil, where the vast interior sheltered communities of fugitive slaves. In the group of villages that made up Palmares, for instance, there were over 20,000 Africans in the late seventeenth century. Finally, for those who remained as slaves on the plantations, by far the most common, if least dramatic, form of resistance was the everyday pattern of foot dragging, pilfering, and sabotage, which slaves employed to soften the inhumanity of their condition.

Sugar Mills. After cutting the cane, slaves transported it to sugar mills. *(Left)* At the mills, the sugarcane would be bruised or crushed between horizontal rollers so that the cane juice would run down a trough and collect in a basin. The juice would then be poured into cauldrons and boiled down. The crushing machines were powered by the labor of slaves, as here, or oxen. *(Right)* Horizontal rollers gave way to vertical ones in the eighteenth century.

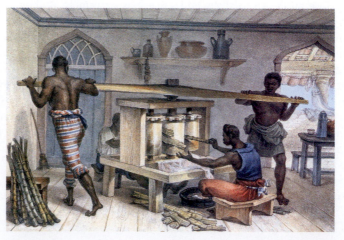

The settlements and slaveholdings of Caribbean plantations were not restricted to any single European power. But it was the latecomers, the Dutch, the English, and especially the French, who concentrated on slave plantations in the Antilles. The English took Jamaica from the Spanish and made it the premier site of Caribbean sugar by the 1740s. When the French seized half of the island of Santo Domingo in the 1660s (renaming it Saint Domingue, which is present-day Haiti), they created one of the wealthiest societies based on slavery of all time. This single French colony's exports eclipsed those of all the Spanish and English Antilles' exports combined. The capital, Port au Prince, was one of the richest cities in the Atlantic world. The great merchants and planters of Saint Domingue, known as "big whites," built immense mansions worthy of the highest of European nobles. In Paris, where the "big whites" returned to shop or rub shoulders with the metropolitan elites, they were frequently envied for the wealth and ostentation they displayed.

Together, these variations on conquest, colonization, and commercialization joined the Americas and Europe. By contrast, Europeans only touched the surface of the cultures of East Asia and the Indian Ocean. The Atlantic system, due in large part to contingencies like accidental contact and disease, utterly disrupted indigenous ways and transformed European lives. It also built fabulous new fortunes for elites in the colonies and in Europe.

THE SLAVE TRADE AND AFRICA

→ *How did the slave trade reshape African societies and polities?*

During the seventeenth and eighteenth centuries, far more Africans than Europeans crossed the Atlantic. Although the beginnings of the slave trade can be traced back to the mid-fifteenth century, only in the seventeenth and eighteenth centuries did the numbers of forced human exports from Africa begin to soar (see Map 4-4). By 1800, two slaves had crossed the Atlantic for every European. Those numbers were essential to the prosperity of Europe's American colonies. At the same time, the departure of so many inhabitants depopulated parts of Africa and destabilized many of the continent's polities.

CAPTURING AND SHIPPING SLAVES

European slave traders grafted onto an existing system of slave commerce, much of it flowing north and east to the Red Sea

Captured Africans. *(Left)* Africans were captured in the interior and then bound and marched to the coast. *(Right)* After reaching the coast, the captured Africans would be crammed into the holds of slave vessels, where they suffered grievously from overcrowding and unsanitary conditions. Long voyages were especially deadly. If the winds failed or ships had to travel longer distances than usual, more of the captives would die en route to the slave markets across the ocean.

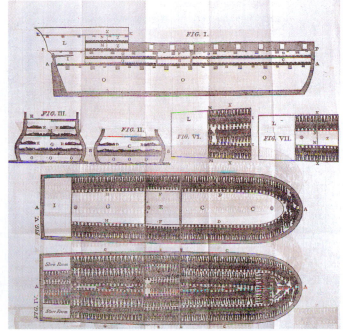

NORTH AMERICA 400,000

Hudson Bay

New York

Charleston

New Orleans

Gulf of Mexico

Zacatecas

Havana

CUBA

SAINT DOMINGUE 860,000

ATLANTIC OCEAN

Mexico City •
Veracruz

Acapulco •

PACIFIC OCEAN

MEXICO AND SPANISH CARIBBEAN c. 1,000,000

JAMAICA 750,000

CARIBBEAN SEA

ANTIGUA
GUADELOUPE 290,000
DOMINICA
MARTINIQUE 360,000
ST. VINCENT
BARBADOS 360,000

GRENADA 67,000

Cartagena •

NEW GRANADA AND VENEZUELA c.320,000

GUIANA AND SURINAM 500,000

Lima •

PERU 95,000

• Potosí

Recife •

BRAZIL 3,600,000

Bahia

SOUTH AMERICA

Rio de Janeiro •
São Paulo •

Buenos Aires

Legend:
- Main sources of African slaves
- Main areas of slave importation in the New World
- European slave trader routes
- Muslim slave trader routes
- Slave factory

Inset map:

OYO
Niger R.
YORUBA
Benue R.

ASANTE

Kumasi •
Winneba
Accra

Cape Coast Castle
Commenda
Shama

Keta

Ada
Christiansborg

Whydah

SLAVE COAST

Old Calabar •

Axim

Elmina

GOLD COAST

Dixcove

Butri

Bight of Benin

FERNANDO PO

Bight of Biafra

Gulf of Guinea

SÃO TOMÉ

0   100   200 Miles
0   100   200 Kilometers

Legend (inset):
- British town
- Dutch town
- Danish town
- Portuguese town

MAP 4-4   THE AFRICAN SLAVE TRADE, 1440–1867

The Atlantic slave trade flourished in the seventeenth, eighteenth, and nineteenth centuries, linking many parts of Africa with the Americas. Where were the largest groups of African slaves found in the Americas, why were they taken to these areas, and what parts of Africa did they come from? Given that the longer the crossing the greater the loss of life on the slave ships, which of the Atlantic crossings were likely to be the most deadly, and which the least? How did the trans-Saharan slave trade and the Indian Ocean slave trade differ from the Atlantic slave trade?

EUROPE
50,000

OTTOMAN EMPIRE

BLACK SEA

ARAL SEA

CASPIAN SEA

Lisbon
Seville

MEDITERRANEAN SEA

Tangiers
MOROCCO

Algiers
Tunis

Tripoli

Alexandria
Cairo
EGYPT

Baghdad

PERSIA

ARABIA

RED SEA

TRANS-SAHARAN
SLAVE TRADE
TO NORTH AFRICA
1,250,000

SAHARA

Arguin

TRANS-SAHARAN
SLAVE TRADE
TO OTTOMAN EMPIRE
AND OTHER PARTS
OF MIDDLE EAST
550,000

Aden

ARABIAN
SEA

St. Louis

Timbuktu

Gao

EAST
AFRICAN
SLAVE TRADE
700,000

SIERRA
LEONE

ASANTE
Kumase
Elmina Accra
Whydah
DAHOMEY
OYO

Inset area

ARO

Old Calabar

AFRICA

ETHIOPIA

MIDDLE PASSAGE

FERNANDO PO

SÃO TOMÉ

BOBANGI

Mogadishu

CONGO

Mombasa

ZANZIBAR

ANGOLA
Luanda

Benguela

Mozambique
MOZAMBIQUE

Sofala

MADAGASCAR

MAURITIUS

INDIAN

OCEAN

Cape Town

0   500   1000   1500 Miles
0   500   1000   1500 Kilometers

African Trade with Europeans. *(Left)* People living along the Congo coast engaged in a vigorous trade with European merchants. Portuguese slave traders are depicted on this late sixteenth- or early seventeenth-century plaque that decorated the doors of the Obas, or Kings of Benin, one of the West African kingdoms deeply involved in the Atlantic slave trade. *(Right)* The kings and other high-ranking individuals in the Kongo kingdom in central Africa embraced Christianity as a result of their contacts with European traders. Here King Alvaro II, an active slave trader, is receiving a deputation of Dutch officials in 1642.

and toward the Swahili coast of East Africa. From these destinations, merchants, most of them Muslim, but also some Hindus, shipped slaves to ports around the Indian Ocean. Although the number of these slaves was significant, they could not match the volume destined for the Americas once extensive plantation agriculture began to spread.

In the western flow, 12 million Africans survived forcible enslavement and shipment to Atlantic ports from the 1440s until 1867 (when the last ship carrying slaves reached Cuba). Far more slaves were in fact loaded onto the vessels in Africa and perished en route. Most of these captives were adult men. Only one-third of Atlantic slaves were women, and 10 percent were children. Although this reflected European preferences for male laborers, it also was the result of African slavers' desire to keep female slaves, primarily for household work. The imbalance of sex ratios made it difficult for slaves to reproduce in most places in the Americas. Accordingly, planters and slavers had to return to Africa to procure more captives, especially as the sugar economy boomed.

Merchant capitalists in Europe and the New World prospered as the slave trade soared, but their commercial fortunes depended on alliances with African trading and political networks. Indeed, European slavers in African ports knew little if anything about the happenings in the interior. They were not themselves involved in the lucrative capture of slaves in Africa. This was a business left to their African partners and their commercial networks of money lending, commodity sales, and alliances with traders in the African hinterland. In the West

African Bight of Biafra, for instance, English merchants relied on traditional African practices of "pawnship," the use of human "pawns" to secure European commodities in advance of the delivery of slaves. According to the custom of the region, a secret male society called Ekpe enforced payments of promised slave deliveries. If a trader failed to deliver on his promise, his "pawns" (quite often members of his kin group) were sold and shipped to the Americas. Ekpe divided its members into various ranks, from chief priests or officers all the way down to common members. By the middle of the eighteenth century, Ekpe was a powerful institution with networks stretching deep into African hinterlands and supplying the expanding slave trade in the port of Old Calabar.

The slave ports along the African coast became vast, gruesome entrepots. Indeed, the highest rates of slave mortality occurred on the African side of the shipping, with most slaves who perished doing so before ever losing sight of Africa. Stuck in vast holding camps, where disease and hunger ravaged the captives, they were then forced aboard slave vessels in cramped and wretched conditions. These ships waited for weeks to fill their holds while their human cargoes wasted away below deck. Dead Africans were tossed overboard as other Africans were brought from the shore. When the cargo was finally complete, the ships weighed anchor and set sail. In their wake, crews continued to dump scores of dead Africans. Annual average losses on board reached 20 percent. Most died of gastrointestinal diseases, leading to dehydration. Smallpox and dysentery were also scourges. Either way, death was slow and agonizing. Because high mortality led to losses of profits, slavers learned to carry better food and more supplies of fresh water as the trade became more sophisticated in the eighteenth century. Mortality rates began to dip. Still, when slave ships finally reached New World ports, they reeked of disease and excrement.

AFRICA'S NEW SLAVE-SUPPLYING POLITIES

Africa's participation in the world economy through the slave trade profoundly reshaped the continent's political and social structures. Africans did not stand at the sidelines, passively letting captives fall into the arms of European slave buyers. Instead, African political leaders and merchants played an active role in supplying slaves for transatlantic shipment. This participation in the Atlantic slave trade contributed to the growth of centralized polities, particularly in the rain forest areas of West Africa. The trade also shifted control of wealth away from households that commanded large animal herds or land to those who profited from the capture and exchange of slaves—urban merchants and warrior elites. In Luanda and Benguela (in present-day Angola), where the Portuguese had established slave trading centers in 1575, African merchants erected impressive homes to emulate fashions in Lisbon.

In some parts of Africa, the booming slave trade wreaked only havoc. To get their share of the spoils, African leaders feuded over control of the traffic. In the Kongo kingdom, civil wars raged for over a century after 1665, and captured warriors were sold as slaves. As members of the kingdom's royal family fought one another, entire provinces saw their populations vanish. Most important to the conduct of war and the control of trade were firearms and gunpowder. With this weaponry, capturing slaves became a highly efficient enterprise. Large numbers were also kidnapped. So prevalent was kidnapping in certain forest areas and among some of the stateless people that cultivators went out to their fields bearing weapons, leaving their children and wards behind in guarded stockades.

As some African merchants and warlords became active vendors of other Africans, their commercial windfall enabled them to consolidate their political power. Through the taking and trading of slaves, West African kingdoms like the Oyo empire in present-day Nigeria and the Asante state in present-day Ghana, as well as wealthy mercantile groups like the Aro peoples in southeastern Nigeria and the Bobangi canoemen in the Central Congo River grew wealthy. That wealth enabled them to purchase additional weapons, with which they subdued their neighbors and extended their political control. These emerging dynasties in turn converted long-established patterns of domestic slavery into vast slave plantations in Africa itself, using especially the female captives to produce grains, leather, and cotton.

Among the most durable of the new polities was the Asante state, which arose in the West African tropical rain forest. This state grew in power because of its access to gold, which its Akan

The Port of Loango. The export of African captives was especially profitable, and partly as a result of the profits of the slave trade, African rulers and merchants were able to create large and prosperous port cities such as Loango, pictured here, which was on the west coast of south-central Africa.

speakers used to acquire firearms from European traders. They employed their arms to raid nearby communities for servile workers. At first, different village groups competed with one another for preeminence, but at the beginning of the eighteenth century, the Asante triumphed over their rivals. From its capital city at Kumasi, the state eventually encompassed almost the whole of present-day Ghana, an area of 250,000 square miles. A network of main roads spread out from the capital like spokes of a wheel, each of which was approximately twenty days' travel from the center. Thus, the empire acquired territorial definition, even clear boundary lines, which were established through the common-sense notion that the state could control territories within twenty days' march from the capital, but no more. Through the Asante trading networks, African traders bought, bartered, and sold slaves, who eventually wound up in the hands of European merchants waiting in coastal ports with vessels loaded with manufactures and weaponry.

Another regime that was active in the organization of the slave trade was the Yoruba-speaking Oyo empire. The Oyo territory, which was strategically located astride the main trade routes, enjoyed easy transportation that linked tropical rain forests with interior markets of the savannah areas to the north. In the absence of the tsetse fly, this empire supported large cavalry forces. It grew rich from the export of slaves and expanded its political reach. The king of the Oyo, called the *Alafin*, was in theory an absolute ruler, but he needed the support of powerful Yoruba families to remain in power. These families deposed or endorsed *Alafins* at will, which often led to turmoil during times of succession. The strength of the empire rested on its ability to field an impressive army bristling with weaponry secured from trade with Europeans. Straddling the boundary between the savannah and the rain forest, the Oyo used cavalry units in the savannah and infantry units in the rain forest. Military campaigns became annual incursions, only suspended so that the warriors could return for their agricultural duties. Every dry season, Oyo armies marched on their neighbors to capture entire villages.

African slavery and the emergence of new political organizations enriched and empowered some Africans, but it cost Africa dearly. For the princes, warriors, and merchants who organized the trade in Africa, their business, not unlike that of Amerindian fur suppliers, enabled them to obtain European goods, especially alcohol, tobacco, textiles, and guns. The Atlantic commercial system also tilted wealth away from rural dwellers and village elders, and increasingly toward the port cities that handled the traffic in and out of Africa. Across the continent, the slave trade thinned the population. True, the continent was spared a demographic catastrophe equal to the devastation of American Indians. The introduction of new American food crops, notably maize and cassava, capable of producing

many more calories per acre than the old staples of millet and sorghum, blunted the depopulating aspects of the trade. Yet, some areas, such as Angola, suffered grievously. Three centuries of heavy involvement in the trade caused depopulation and disintegration. With this human plunder, West African kingdoms rose and fell. Over the long run, commerce in chattel slavery fused mercantile and political power and enhanced the strength of warrior classes. The slave trade also reinforced the practice of polygyny—allowing relatively scarce men to take several wives.

Three centuries of heavy involvement in the slave trade caused depopulation and disintegration in West Africa.

ASIA IN THE SEVENTEENTH AND EIGHTEENTH CENTURIES

→ *How did global trade affect the Asian dynasties?*

Long-distance trading networks blossomed as vigorously in Asia as they did in the Americas. Here, however, the Europeans were less dominant than they were in the Atlantic world. With American silver, Europeans could open Asian markets, but they could not conquer powerful Asian empires or colonize vast portions of the continent as they were doing in the Americas. Nor were Europeans able to enslave Asian peoples as they were enslaving Africans. But in some places, the balance of power had begun to tilt in Europe's direction. By the middle of the eighteenth century, parts of India and much of Southeast Asia had begun to experience European military and political power and had come under European colonial domination. The Ottomans experienced a contraction of their borders. The Mughals continued to expand their empire, and the Qing dynasty, which had wrested control of China from the Ming dynasty, initiated a vast expansion of the empire's borders. China remained the richest state in the world at the time.

THE DUTCH IN SOUTHEAST ASIA

In Southeast Asia the Dutch already enjoyed a dominant position by the seventeenth century. Although the Portuguese had seized the vibrant port city of Melaka in 1511 and the Spaniards had taken Manila in 1571, neither was able to monopolize the

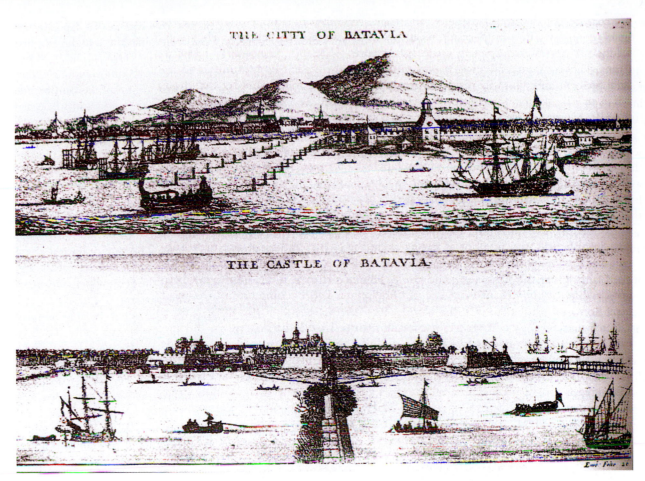

THE CITTY OF BATAVIA

THE CASTLE OF BATAVIA.

Batavia. At the beginning of the seventeenth century, Dutch traders established a base at the Javanese coastal settlement of Jakarta, which became Batavia, the capital of a Dutch Asian empire. Dutch traders and officials became familiar with island customs and consorted with native women, who were crucial for supplying local knowledge and translation. Many Eurasian children were born to Dutch men and Javanese women. The Batavian fortress projected Dutch power, as did the numerous warehouses for shipping the many riches coveted by Europeans.

lucrative spice trade. To challenge the Portuguese and the Spaniards, the Dutch government took the initiative in pulling its merchants together to charter the Dutch East India Company (abbreviated as VOC) in 1602. Making full use of Amsterdam's position as the most efficient money market with the lowest interest rates in the world, the VOC raised ten times the capital of its English counterpart—the royal chartered English East India Company, established two years earlier. The advantages of chartered companies could be seen in the VOC's scale of operation. At its peak in the 1660s, the company had 257 ships at its disposal and went on to employ directly 12,000 persons. In the two centuries of its existence, it sent ships manned by a total of a million men to Asia, although the toll of the Asian trade was such that only a third of them ever returned to Europe.

Much of the impact of the VOC was felt in Southeast Asia, where spices, coffee, tea, and teak were grown and exported.

The objective of the VOC was to secure a monopoly in trade wherever it could, to fix prices, and to replace the native population with Dutch planters. In 1619, under the militant leadership of Jan Pieterszoon Coen, who once said that trade could not be conducted without war nor war without trade, the Dutch swept into the Javanese port of Jakarta (renamed Batavia by the Dutch). In defiance of its local rulers and their English rivals, the Dutch burned all the houses, drove out the population, and proceeded to construct a fortress from which the VOC could control the Southeast Asian trade. Two years later, Coen and his fleet of twelve ships took over a cluster of five small nutmeg-producing islands known collectively as Banda. The traditional chiefs and almost the entire population of the islands, some 15,000 people, were killed outright, left to starve in isolation, or otherwise taken into slavery in Jakarta. Dutch planters and their slaves replaced the decimated local population and sent their produce to the VOC. The motive for such rapacious action was the huge profits that could be made by buying nutmeg at a small price in the Bandas and selling it at many times that price in Europe.

With their monopoly of nutmeg secured, the Dutch went after the market in cloves. The VOC's strategy was to control the clove-growing in one region and then destroy the rest, which entailed, once again, wars against both producers and traders in other areas. Portuguese Melaka fell to the Dutch in 1641 and became an outstation of the VOC. Resistance to this aggressive Dutch expansion was widespread among the local population as well as among Muslim, Chinese, and other European merchants involved in the Southeast Asian trade. Nevertheless, with a combination of ruthlessness and ability in taking advantage of local political divisions, the Dutch had the whole of the lucrative Malukan (Moluccan) spice trade in their hands by 1670.

Next, the VOC set its sights on another of the important spices of Southeast Asia, pepper, which was a rather more difficult target to monopolize since its trade was scattered across a dozen major and minor ports. In this gambit, the VOC gained control of Banten (present-day Bantam), the largest pepper-exporting port, but the Dutch could not fully reserve the commerce in this spice to themselves. Chinese and English merchants continued to be competitors. Moreover, since there was virtually no demand for European products in Asia, the Dutch were forced to become more involved in inter-Asian trade as a way to reduce their payments in bullion. They purchased, for example, calicoes in India or copper in Japan for resale in Melaka and Java. They also diversified their trade to include silk, cotton, tea, and coffee, in addition to spices.

One of the significant side effects of the Dutch enterprise, however, was reducing old cosmopolitan cities such as Banten, which had once served as centers of political power, economic life, and cultural creativity in Southeast Asia, to a subsidiary position, eclipsed by newer European outposts such as Dutch Batavia or Spanish Manila. As Europeans penetrated and competed for supremacy in the borderlands of Southeast Asia, they harnessed local societies to their commercial ambitions and began replacing what were once the crossroads of Eurasian trading with European outposts.

> *As Europeans penetrated and competed for supremacy in the borderlands of Southeast Asia, they began replacing what were once the crossroads of Eurasian trading with European outposts.*

THE SAFAVID EMPIRE UNDER ASSAULT

Compared to Southeast Asia, Eurasia's Islamic empires were as yet not directly affected by European intrusion; they faced increasing difficulties on a variety of other fronts, however. The Safavid empire, for instance, could no longer ward off neigh-

boring enemies and rivals. Safavid rule had always depended on a powerful, religiously inspired ruler, like the founding figure, Shah Ismail, and his most noteworthy successor, Abbas I. When such a figure was not present to enforce Shiite religious orthodoxy and to hold together the tribal, pastoral, mercantile, and agricultural factions, the state foundered. A series of weak successors to Abbas left the state in a chaotic condition. By 1722, it was under assault from within and without. Afghan clansmen, who had never been subdued by imperial armies, invaded Safavid territory. They overran the inept and divided armies and besieged Isfahan, the Safavid capital. The city's inhabitants began to perish from hunger and disease. Some survivors ate the corpses of the deceased. Finally the shah abdicated. The invading Afghan fighters executed thousands of Safavid officials and members of the royal household. The empire limped along until 1773, when a revolt toppled the last puppet ruler from the throne.

The other Islamic empires did not fare as badly, but they, too, faced increasing stress. Some of these difficulties were entirely internal. But the problems of Islamic empires also stemmed from the new trade links with the world, which gave rise to competitive centers of economic and political power within the Ottoman and Mughal empires.

THE TRANSFORMATION OF THE OTTOMAN EMPIRE

Having attained a high point in the reign of Suleiman (ruled 1520–1566), the Ottoman empire faced numerous problems, many of which stemmed from Ottoman successes. After Suleiman's reign, Ottoman armies and navies continued to try to expand the empire's borders but were defeated. On the empire's western flank, the European Habsburgs finally reversed Ottoman military expansion. Financing military campaigns pressed upon the realm's limited resources, as did the needs of a growing population. Already at the end of the sixteenth century, Ottoman intellectuals were concerned that the empire had entered a period of "decline," comparing the military triumphs and political expansion of early sultans to the difficulties of later rulers. During the seventeenth century, the sense of decline became a preoccupation of the Ottoman elite, whose essays were increasingly devoted to identifying causes of this supposed decline and proposing remedies for it.

A series of unimpressive successors to Suleiman did not help matters. Suleiman the Great, for example, passed the crown to Selim, whom his detractors dubbed the Sot (ruled 1566–1574). He was succeeded by a string of incompetent sultans. Indeed, of the nine individuals who became sultans in the 1600s, only three were both adult and sane when they ascended to the throne. Such were the weaknesses of monarchy.

Competent or not, seventeenth-century sultans confronted the problems of a commercially more connected world. As silver flowed from the mines of Mesoamerica and the Andes, it entered Ottoman networks of commerce and money lending, and eventually destabilized the empire. The early Ottoman rulers had endeavored to create an autonomous economy that did not depend for its well-being on trade with the outside world. The lure of silver broke through state regulations, however, drawing commodities like wheat, copper, wool, and other items in demand in Europe away from Ottoman areas. Merchants figured out how to sidestep imperial regulations and exported these commodities in return for silver. Because these goods were illegally exported, their sale did not generate tax revenues, which led to a shortfall in money to pay administrative and military expenses. Ottoman rulers were then forced to rely on merchant loans of silver to sustain their civilian and especially military administration. Financial dependency meant that rulers could ill afford to impose their own official rules on those who bankrolled them.

More silver and budget deficits were a recipe for inflation. Indeed, prices doubled between 1550 and 1600, and then tripled in the first half of the seventeenth century. The surge in the price of goods especially hit hard the artisans and peasants living in Anatolia. Fed up with high food prices and shortages—and increasing taxes to pay off dynastic debts—they joined together in a series of popular uprisings, called the Celali revolts, which threatened the stability of the Ottoman state between 1595 and 1610. By the time of Sultan Ibrahim's reign (1640–1648), the cycle of spending, taxing, borrowing, and inflation was so bad that his own officials toppled and murdered him.

The Ottoman empire also faced growing pressures for commercial and political autonomy from its outlying regions. In 1517, Egypt became the Ottoman state's greatest conquest. As the wealthiest of the Ottoman territories, it was an imperial plum for any administrator. Egypt was also a great source of revenue, and its people shouldered heavy tax burdens. Moreover, trading routes continued to run through Egypt, and as commerce grew, many merchants began to resent Ottoman control. By the seventeenth century, the Ottoman administrator of Egypt had become a mere figurehead, funneling increasingly limited revenues to Istanbul but unable to control the military groups around him. When the sultan dispatched Mamluk military and administrative personnel from the Caucasus to rule over Egypt, the newcomers forged alliances with Egyptian merchants and catered to the Egyptian *ulama*. As they became a new provincial ruling elite, the Mamluks kept much of the fiscal wealth for themselves,

at the expense not only of imperial coffers but also of the local peasantry.

Yet, there was great resilience in the Ottoman system. Decaying leadership provoked demands for reform from administrative elites. Toward the end of the seventeenth century, the Koprulu family took control of the powerful office of grand vizier and spearheaded changes to revitalize the empire. Mehmed Koprulu, the first of the family to assume office, had been born into an obscure Albanian family. Taken as a slave in the *devshirme*, he slowly made his way up the bureaucratic ladder until he became grand vizier when he was eighty years old, in 1656. Pragmatic and incorruptible, Mehmed not only rooted out his venal peers, but he also balanced the budget and reversed the misfortunes of the Ottoman armies. His death in 1661 did not bring a halt to the reforms, for Mehmed had groomed his son, Fazil Ahmed Koprulu, for the task. Indeed, Fazil Ahmed was, if anything, more successful than his father. Better educated and even more shrewd, the young grand vizier continued trimming the administration and strengthening the Ottoman armies until he died after fifteen years in charge.

Known as the "Koprulu reforms," the changes in public administration gave the state a new burst of energy and enabled the military to reacquire some of its lost possessions. Thanks to these reforms, revenues again began to rise, and inflation abated, reviving expansionist ambitions. Emboldened by its new energy, Istanbul decided to renew its assault on Christianity. Fazil Ahmed's brother-in-law, Kara Mustafa Pasha, rekindled old plans to seize Vienna. Outside the Habsburg capital, the Ottomans gathered between 200,000 and 500,000 soldiers in July 1683. An all-out attack on September 12, 1683, inflicted heavy losses on both sides, after which Kara Mustafa withdrew his forces, intending to renew his assault in the spring. The sultan, however, worried about bringing even more disgrace to the realm, ordered his followers to have Kara Mustafa strangled. Thereafter, the Ottomans ended their military advance, never again threatening Vienna. With the end of conquest, the empire was deprived of the booty that had been theirs after taking over new regions. Worse still, the Treaty of Carlowitz with Austria in 1699 resulted in the Ottomans' loss of major European territorial possessions, including Hungary, prompting further soul-searching for the causes of "decline."

> *Known as the "Koprulu reforms," the changes in public administration gave the Ottoman state a new burst of energy and enabled the military to reacquire some of its lost possessions.*

THE ZENITH AND DECLINE OF THE MUGHAL EMPIRE

In contrast to the Ottoman empire's territorial setbacks, the Mughal empire reached its height in the 1600s. By the end of the seventeenth century, Mughal rulers had extended their domain over almost all of India, and the Mughal empire prospered from an increase in domestic and international trade. But as they expanded their empire, the Mughals eventually faced the difficulties of governing dispersed and not always loyal provinces. Indeed, though nominally in control of wide areas, the Mughals had a limited impact on many villages, whose inhabitants retained their own religions and cultures.

Before the Mughals, the subcontinent had never had a single political authority. Akbar took over much of the subcontinent, but conquest and expansion did not stop after his death in 1605. Throughout the seventeenth century, his successors continued the work of expanding the empire and extending administrative control over conquered territories (see Map 3-5, p. 113). With the north of the subcontinent already under their jurisdiction, the Mughals turned to the south. Though the advances were slow and frustrating, the Mughals controlled most of the region by 1689. The new, outlying provinces of the empire provided the state with resources and local lords, warriors, and tributary chiefs, from whom the state could extract service and demand loyalty.

The revival and flourishing of the Indian Ocean trading system was not the mainstay of the state's wealth. Indeed, the Mughals showed little interest in becoming a naval power; they were willing to profit from seaborne trade, but they never undertook overseas expansion. Still, the empire's economy benefited from the growing demand for Indian goods and services by Europeans. For example, the English East India Company's purchase of textiles rose from 4.2 million square meters in 1664 to 26.9 million square meters in 1684. Similar trends existed in the Dutch trade. As specie flowed in from Japan and the New World to finance this growing trade, the imperial mint struck increasing amounts of silver coins, which, in turn, contributed to the growth of trade and the use of specie as a medium of exchange. The rural economy also grew under the Mughals. New lands came under cultivation, agricultural production grew, and peasants in India quickly adopted New World crops like maize and tobacco.

To a considerable extent, the Mughals were victims of their own success. More than a century of imperial expansion, commercial prosperity, and agricultural development placed an increasing amount of resources in the hands of local and regional magnates. Using these resources, powerful local warrior elites, always looking for opportunities to evade imperial demands, became increasingly autonomous. By the late seventeenth century, many of these regional leaders were well positioned to resist Mughal authority.

As in the Ottoman empire, then, distant provinces began to challenge central rulers. Under Aurangzeb (ruled 1658–1707), the Mughals had pushed the political frontier of the empire deep into southern India. There, however, the Mughals encountered fierce opposition from the powerful Marathas in the northwestern Deccan plateau. The military effort cost the imperial treasury a small fortune, and pinned down Mughal armies. To

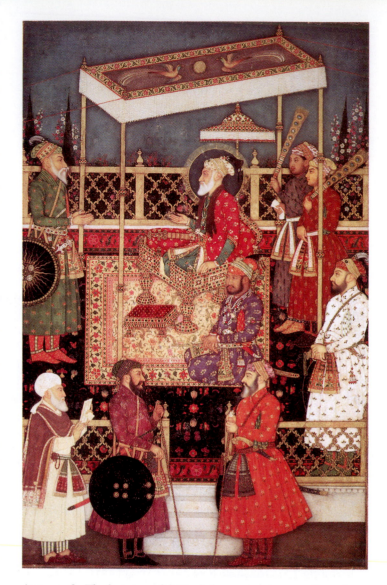

Aurangzeb. The last powerful Mughal emperor, Aurangzeb continued the conquest of the Indian subcontinent. Pictured in his old age, he is shown here with his courtiers.

finance these expansionist operations, Aurangzeb raised taxes on the empire's peasants. Resentment and alienation spread through the population, and even the Mughal elite grew restive at the continuing drain on imperial finances. In an effort to win the support of the orthodox *ulama*, the monarch abandoned the toleration of heterodoxy and of non-Muslims practiced by his predecessors. But ultimately only the strong hand of Aurangzeb kept order in the empire.

When Aurangzeb died in 1707, a war of succession broke out almost immediately. The revenue system eroded as local tax collectors kept more of the returns for themselves. Prosperous and powerful local elites used their growing fiscal autonomy to rally military forces of their own, annexing neighboring lands to their fiefdoms and chipping away at imperial authority.

Indian peasants, like their counterparts in Ming China, Safavid Persia, and the Ottoman empire, capitalized on the breakdown in central authority to assert their independence from state authority. Many rose in rebellions; others took up banditry. Bonds of caste and religion were critical in the revolt of the Jat peasant caste in northern India in the late seventeenth century. Refusing to pay taxes, the Jat people killed a Mughal official and then seized lands and plundered the region. A half century later, peasant cultivators of the Punjab in northern India turned their closely knit community into a military power that was able to keep the Mughal forces off balance. Peasants were also critical in the rise of the Marathas of western India. Their legendary leader, Shivaji (1627–1680), threatened Mughal prestige in the south. Though no peasant himself, Shivaji used the peasantry's hatred of imperial oppression to mount fierce resistance to Mughal hegemony.

The Mughal emperors had to reconcile themselves to their diminished power. The empire now existed as a loose unity of provincial "successor states." While the Marathas based in Poona and the Sikhs in the Punjab stood outside the imperial system, the successor states of Bengal, Awadh, and Hyderabad accepted Mughal paramountcy in name only. They administered semiautonomous regimes based on their access to local economic, political, and cultural resources.

Although local elites hollowed out the structure of the empire, India still flourished. Imperial expansion and the rising power of landed elites brought new territories into agrarian production. Cotton, for instance, became a major staple crop to supply a thriving textile industry. In many parts of India, peasant households complemented agrarian production with weaving and artisanal cloth production. Much of this industry was destined for export as the subcontinent deepened its integration into world trading systems.

The Mughals themselves paid scant attention to commercial matters, but local potentates, recognizing the benefits of exchange with foreign traders, encouraged the Europeans to establish posts at Indian ports. As more and more European ships arrived in Indian harbors, provincial magnates struck special deals with rival merchants from Portugal, and increasingly from England and Holland. Some Indian merchants created trading companies of their own to control the sale of regional produce to competing Europeans; others set up vast trading networks that reached as far north as Russia, straddling west and east between Iraq and the South China Sea. One of these companies was the house of Jagat Seths in eastern India. The Jagat Seths built a huge trading and banking empire, involving extensive shipments of Bengal cloth and commercial relations with Asian and European merchants. Increasingly, however, a large part of their business in the provinces of Bengal and Bihar was tax-farming, whereby the Jagat Seths took responsibility for collecting taxes for the imperial coffers. The Jagat Seths maintained their own retinue of agents to gather levies from farmers, while pocketing substantial profits for themselves. Thus did mercantile houses grow ever richer and gain greater political influence over financially strapped emperors. As a result, local economic and social prosperity undercut the Mughal dynasty.

FROM MING TO QING IN CHINA

China prospered enormously during the Ming period, but prosperity also led to a splintering of central control. As in Mughal India, local power holders in China often defied the authority of the Ming central government. Because Ming sovereigns turned inward and away from the possibilities of overseas commerce, forbidding the Chinese to travel abroad and prohibiting coastal shipping, the emperors did not reap the rewards of long-distance exchange. Rather, most of the profits went to traders and adventurers who successfully evaded imperial edicts. Together, the persistence of local autonomy and the challenge of defiant merchants weakened imperial structures until finally, in 1644, the Ming empire collapsed.

ADMINISTRATIVE PROBLEMS How did a dynasty that in the early seventeenth century governed perhaps a third of the world's population and was the most economically advanced society fall from power? As in the Ottoman empire, bad rulers played a big role. Take, for example, the disastrous reign of Zhu Yijun, the Wanli Emperor (ruled 1573–1620). During his long reign, Wanli's major claim to fame was his reputation for degrading the image of a wise and just emperor. For years, he avoided any involvement with the administration of the realm, to the point that he refused to meet with his officials or preside over the routine state ritual performances. A mountain of reports and petitions piled up in his study unattended.

Reputedly a precocious young boy, Wanli ascended to the throne at age nine. Like his predecessors, he grew up within the confines of the Forbidden City (see Chapter 2). The Forbidden City, an area of a quarter of a square mile, was covered with blocks of glazed tile palatial buildings, ceremonial halls and gates, and magnificent marble terraces. To those secluded within the precinct, however, life could be oppressively monotonous. The emperor was the most secluded of them all, despite being surrounded by a staff of 20,000 eunuchs and 3,000 women to serve him. The "Son of Heaven" rarely ventured outside the palace compound in Ming times, and when he moved within it he was accompanied by a large retinue led by eunuchs clearing his path with whips. (Senior eunuchs at times wielded great

> *China prospered enormously during the Ming period, but prosperity also led to a splintering of central control.*

The Emperor's Concubines. Under the Qing, the emperor's consorts were headed by the empress, while the concubines were classified into seven different ranks. Jewelry, stipends, maids, clothing, and even food were allocated according to rank. Unlike the Ming, the Qing did not limit succession to the throne to sons of the empress. Even low-ranking consorts could be promoted to empress and be treated with the same privileges as those invested with the title at marriage.

power in the Ming court, particularly in the absence of a competent emperor.) Everything the emperor did was an event watched by many, designed to reinforce the awesome majesty of the office.

Despite his secluded existence, the emperor still had to fulfill his duties as the chief administrator. He had to get up before dawn to meet with his officials, who gathered outside the palace each morning waiting patiently for the gates to open, before lining up in designated rows in the courtyard in front of the ceremonial hall. His day was filled with state functions, during which he had to change clothes to suit each occasion. Ming emperors did not wear metal crowns. Instead, their most formal headgear was a rectangular black mortarboard, with the shorter edges facing front and rear. Dangling from each of the two edges were twelve strings of beads. The uncomfortable, curtain-like beads forced the emperor to move solemnly and deliberately. Ming emperors like Wanli quickly found out that while all the elaborate arrangements and ritual performances

affirmed their position as the Son of Heaven, the rulers actually exercised little direct control over the vast bureaucracy. An emperor frustrated with his officials could do little more than punish them or simply refuse to cooperate. Such was the situation of the Wanli Emperor. Unable to change or reshape the Ming administration, he ignored his bureaucrats altogether, while some of them took advantage of his neglect to accumulate private wealth.

ECONOMIC PROBLEMS The timing of administrative breakdown in the Ming government was unfortunate. While rulers dithered, the economy was feeling the effects of commercial integration with the rest of the Eurasian trading system. Expanding trade induced many to circumvent official regulations. From the mid-sixteenth century, bands of supposedly "Japanese" pirates, or *wokou*, ravaged the Chinese coast. Indeed, the Ming government had great difficulties regulating its official trade relations with Japan. Japanese missions, often armed

HUANG LIUHONG ON ELIMINATING AUTHORIZED SILVERSMITHS

The influx of silver into China had profound effects on both its economy and government. In the seventeenth century, silver, for instance, gradually became the medium through which taxes were assessed. In his magistrate's manual from around 1694, Huang Liuhong (Huang Liu-hung) indicated the problems and abuses posed by the use of authorized silversmiths in the payment process, demonstrating clearly how silver had become an integral part of the lives of the Chinese people.

The purpose of using an authorized silversmith in the collection of tax money is twofold. First, the quality of the silver delivered by the taxpayers must be up to standard. The authorized silversmith is expected to reject any substandard silver. Second, when the silver is delivered to the provincial treasury, it should be melted and cast into ingots to avoid theft while in transit. But, to get his commission, the authorized silversmith has to pay a fee and arrange for a guarantor. In addition, he has to pay bribes to the clerks of the revenue section and to absorb the operating expenses of his shop—rent, food, coal, wages for his employees, and so on. If he does not impose a surcharge on the taxpayers, how can he maintain his business?

There are many ways for an authorized silversmith to defraud the taxpayers. First, he can declare that the quality of the silver is not up to standard and a larger amount is required. Second, he can insist that all small pieces of silver have to be melted and cast into ingots; hence there will be wastage in the process of melting. Third, he may demand that all ingots, no matter how small they are, be stamped with his seal, and of course charge a stamping fee. Fourth,

he may require a fee for each melting as a legitimate charge for the service. Fifth, he can procrastinate until the taxpayer becomes impatient and is willing to double the melting fee. Last, if the taxpayer seems naive or simple minded, the smith can purposely upset the melting container and put the blame on the taxpayer. All these tricks are prevalent, and little can be done to thwart them.

When the silver ingots are delivered to the provincial treasury, few of them are up to standard. The authorized silversmith often blames the taxpayers for bringing in silver of inferior quality although it would be easy for him to reject them at the time of melting. Powerful official families and audacious licentiates often put poor quality silver in sealed envelopes, which the authorized silversmith is not empowered to examine. Therefore, the use of an authorized silversmith contributes very little to the business of tax collection; it only increases the burden of small taxpayers. . . .

Source: Huang Liu-hung, *A Complete Book Concerning Happiness and Benevolence: A Manual for Local Magistrates in Seventeenth Century China* (Tucson: University of Arizona Press, 1984), pp. 190–91.

and several hundred people strong, raided and looted Chinese coastal villages. Yet, while Ming officials labeled all pirates as Japanese, most of the *wokou* were in fact Chinese subjects.

Operating out of coastal towns of the empire, as well as from Japanese and Southeast Asian ports, these maritime adventurers deeply disturbed Ming authorities. In tough times, pirates became roving gangs, terrorizing sea lanes and harbors. In better times, some of them functioned much like mercantile groups; their leaders often mingled with gentry elites, foreign trade representatives, and imperial officials. What made these commercial predators so resilient—and their business so lucrative—was their ability to move among and between the mosaic of East Asian cultures.

The Chinese economy was, moreover, further stimulated and commercialized by the influx of silver from the New World and

from Japan. As noted in Chapter 3, Europeans used New World silver to pay for their purchases of Chinese goods. During the second half of the sixteenth century, silver imports contributed at least eight times more bullion to China's domestic stock of money; in the first half of the seventeenth century, silver imports exceeded domestic bullion production by some twenty-fold. Increasing monetization of the economy bolstered market activity and state revenues at the same time.

As silver became the primary medium of exchange in the Chinese economy, peasants came under pressure to convert the copper coins that circulated widely in the local economy into silver. With this silver, they could pay off their taxes and purchase locally traded goods. But the need to acquire silver created hardships for the peasants. When silver supplies were abundant, peasants had to deal with price inflation. When silver supplies were interrupted, peasants faced problems discharging their obligations to state officials and merchants. Peasants thus often seethed with resentment, which quickly turned to rebellion.

Market fluctuations in trading centers as far off as Mexico now also affected the Chinese economy, introducing new sources of unpredictability and instability. After 1610, Dutch and English assaults on Spanish ships headed to Asia cut down silver flows into China. Then, in 1639, Japanese authorities clamped down on foreign traders, thereby curbing the outflow of Japanese specie to China. All these blows to the Asian trading system destabilized the supply of money in China and contributed to a downturn in the Chinese economy in the 1630s and 1640s.

THE COLLAPSE OF MING AUTHORITY By the seventeenth century, the administrative and economic difficulties of the Ming government had a visibly negative impact on the daily lives of its subjects. This became particularly evident when the regime failed to cope with the devastation caused by natural disasters in outlying provinces such as Shaanxi, where social unrest was already rising. Crop failures sent the price of grain soaring in Shaanxi. Without relief from the government, the poor and the hungry fanned out to find food by whatever means they could muster. Officials wrote of abandoned babies and noted signs of cannibalism. Meanwhile, the financial problems of the government led to additional tax levies and cutbacks in the military budgets. A large contingent of young, mobile, and able-bodied males, including mutinous soldiers and demobilized government couriers, swelled the ranks of the desperate and the discontented. Many of them were instrumental in organizing the multitude of uprooted peasants into rebels, turning the late Ming world upside down in the process.

After 1600, increasingly large bands of dispossessed and marginalized peasants vented their anger at local tax collectors. At the core of these armed peasant bands, former soldiers and transport workers became leaders. Outlaw armies terrorized vast areas. Led by charismatic leaders whose appeals often contained messianic and religious overtones, half a dozen or so such large mobile armies—the so-called "roving bandits"—appeared in the 1620s. The most famous of these rebel leaders, the self-anointed "dashing prince" Li Zicheng, arrived at the outskirts of the capital, Beijing, on April 23, 1644. The capital's twenty-one miles of walls were defended by only a few companies of soldiers and a few thousand eunuchs, allowing Li Zicheng to take Beijing easily. Two days later, the emperor hanged himself. On the following day, the triumphant "dashing prince" rode into the capital and claimed the throne.

The news of the fall of the Ming capital sent shock waves around the empire. One hundred and seventy miles to the northeast of the capital, at the point where northeast China meets Manchuria, the commander of the Ming army, Wu Sangui, received the news in late April of the death of the emperor and of Li Zicheng's triumph. Wu's task in the area was to defend the Ming against its increasingly menacing neighbor, a group who began to identify themselves as "Manchu" around 1635, but who were descendants of the Jurchens (see Chapter 1). In May 1644, Wu found himself in a very precarious position. Caught between an advancing rebel army on the one side, and the Manchus on the other, Wu made a fateful decision. He appealed for the cooperation of the Manchus to fight the "dashing prince," promising his newfound allies that "gold and treasure" awaited them in the capital. Thus, without shedding a drop of blood, the Manchus crossed the strategic pass and joined Wu's army. After years of coveting the Ming empire, the Manchus were finally on their way to Beijing (see Map 4-5).

THE QING DYNASTY ASSERTS CONTROL At the time that they defeated Li Zicheng and seized power in Beijing, the Manchus numbered around 1 million. Assuming control of a domain that then included perhaps 250 million people, the conquerors were keenly aware of their minority status. Taking power, they understood, was one thing; keeping it was another. But keep it they did. In fact, in the eighteenth century, the Qing (which means "pure") dynasty (1644–1911) embarked on impressive economic expansion, incorporated new territories, and experienced substantial population growth. All this happened without provoking the kind of economic and political turmoil that rocked the societies of the Atlantic world.

> *The key to China's stable economic and geographical expansion can be found in the shrewd and flexible policies of its rulers.*

The key to China's relatively stable economic and geographical expansion can be found in the shrewd and flexible policies of its rulers. The early Manchu emperors were able and diligent administrators. They also knew that to govern a sprawling and diverse population they had to adapt to local mores. To promote continuity with the earlier regime and draw upon the social and cultural practices of their predecessors, they respected Confucian ideas, codes, and ethics. The classic texts remained the basis of the prestigious civil service examinations. Social hierarchies of age, gender, and kin—indeed, the entire image of the family as the bedrock of social organization—endured. In some areas, like Taiwan, the Manchus consolidated new territories into existing provinces. Elsewhere, they gave newly acquired territories, like Mongolia, Tibet, and Xinjiang, their own distinct form of local administration. In these regions, imperial envoys presided, but they administered through staffs of locals and relied on indigenous institutions. Until the late nineteenth century, the Qing dynasty showed little interest in integrating those regions into "China proper."

MAP 4-5   FROM MING TO QING CHINA, 1644–1760

Qing China commanded a much larger territorial expanse than its Ming predecessor. How can we explain the ways in which the Qing empire expanded? Compare and contrast the expansionism of the Europeans in this period with that of the Qing. How should we characterize the vast areas beyond the Ming boundaries that were incorporated into the Qing empire in the seventeenth and eighteenth centuries? What states were tributaries of the empire?

At the same time, Qing rulers and their minions were determined to convey a clear sense of their own majesty and legitimacy. Rulers relentlessly promoted patriarchal values. Widows who remained "chaste" were publicly praised, and women in general were exhorted to lead a "virtuous" life serving their male kin and family. To the majority Han, the Manchu emperor represented himself as the worthy upholder of famil-

ial values and classical Chinese civilization; to the Tibetan Buddhists, by contrast, the Manchu state offered plenty of imperial patronage. So, too, with otherwise disgruntled Islamic subjects. Although the Islamic Uighurs, as well as other Muslim subjects, might not have approved the Manchus' easygoing religious attitude, they accepted the emperor's favors and generally endorsed his claim to rule.

But merely insinuating themselves into an existing order or simply appeasing subject peoples did not wholly satisfy the Manchu yearning to leave their imprint on the governed. They also introduced measures that extolled their authority, emphasized their distinctiveness, and ensured the submission of their mostly Han Chinese subjects. Qing officials composed or translated all important documents into Manchu and banned intermarriage between Manchu and Han (although this was difficult to enforce in practice). Other edicts imposed Manchu ways on Han subjects. The day after the Manchus entered Beijing in 1644, a decree required all Han Chinese males to follow the Manchu practice of shaving their foreheads and braiding their hair at the back in a queue. This met with immediate and vociferous protests from the Chinese, and led to temporary shelving of the policy. A year later, however, feeling somewhat more secure, the new dynasty reissued the order, and presented its subjects with the stark choice of cutting their hair or losing their heads. This time, the policy stuck. In a similar vein, the Qing also decreed that Han males adopt Manchu garb: instead of the loose Ming-style robes, they now had to wear high collars and tight jackets.

Manchu impositions fell mostly on the peasantry, for the Qing financed their administrative edifice by extracting surpluses from peasant households through taxation and surcharges. In response, the peasants spread out to border areas to find new lands to cultivate. Often they planted these newly occupied lands with New World crops that grew well in less fertile soils. This resulted in an important change in Chinese diets. While rice was the staple diet of wealthy Chinese, peasants increasingly relied on corn and sweet potatoes for their subsistence. As the realm expanded, however, the government failed to keep pace with the administrative demands posed by a rising population and the settlement of frontier lands. This would ultimately lead to problems for the dynasty.

Although the Chinese people found ways to contest official Qing values, the Manchus sought to suppress dissent by assuming a role as guardians of moral rectitude, decrying the evidence of decadence and extravagance. Nothing earned the regime's opprobrium more than the urban elites' display of conspicuous consumption and indulgence in sensual pleasure. But a gulf began to open between the government's aspirations and its ability to police society. For example, the urban public continued to flock to performances by female impersonators in defiance of Qing efforts to ban this and other sexually provocative forms of theater.

EXPANSION AND TRADE UNDER THE QING Despite the public's disregard for some imperial edicts, the Qing dynasty enjoyed something of a heyday during the eighteenth century.

Territorial expansion extended the realm far beyond the frontiers of the Ming into Central Asia, Tibet, and Mongolia. Tributary relations were established with Korea, Vietnam, Burma, and Nepal. While officials emphasized and redoubled their reliance on their agrarian base, trade and commerce flourished as they had done in the late Ming era. Chinese merchants continued to ply the waters stretching from Southeast Asia to Japan, exchanging textiles, ceramics, and medicine for spices and rice. In the early years of the dynasty, the Qing authorities vacillated about whether to permit trade with foreigners in China. Meanwhile, in 1720 in Canton (Guangzhou), a group of merchants formed a monopolistic guild, known as the Cohong, to trade with European merchants, whose numbers rose as they vied for coveted Chinese goods and tried to peddle their wares to the vast Chinese market. Although the guild disbanded after a year in the face of opposition from both foreign and other local merchants, it was revived after the Qing decided to restrict the Europeans to trading in Canton and ordered that Chinese merchants guarantee the good behavior and the payment of fees by the Europeans. This "Canton system," as it came to be known, would be formalized by decree of the emperor in 1759.

Trading monopolies dealing with the outside world were marginal to the overall commercial life of the Qing era. The production and circulation of most daily commodities remained in local hands. If anything, the Qing government was ineffective at tapping the burgeoning commercial wealth of China. The Qing, like their Ming predecessors, cared much more about the agrarian health of the empire, believing it to be the foundation of social tranquility and prosperity. As long as China's vast peasantry could keep the dynasty's coffers filled with revenue, the government was content to squeeze the merchants simply on an irregular basis.

China, in sum, negotiated a century of upheaval without dismantling established ways of arranging politics or economics. For the peasantry, popular faiths continued to govern their belief systems, and most peasants continued to cultivate their crops and stay close to their fields and villages. For merchants, the Qing were just one more Beijing-based dynasty with whom they had to negotiate. Some historians have labeled this China's failure to adapt to a changing world order. In time, these historians assert, this left China vulnerable to outsiders, especially Europeans. But this view puts the historical cart before the horse. By the middle of the eighteenth century, it was still clear that Europe needed China more than the other way around. For the vast majority of Chinese, no superior model of belief, politics, or economics was conceivable. Indeed, although the Qing had taken over a crumbling empire in 1644, a century later it realized a new level of splendor.

> *By the middle of the eighteenth century, it was still clear that Europe needed China more than the other way around.*

TOKUGAWA JAPAN

Integration with the Asian trading system also exposed Japan to new external pressures, even as the islands grappled with internal turmoil. But the Japanese dealt with these pressures far more successfully than did the four great mainland Asian empires (the Ottomans, the Safavid, the Mughal, and the Ming), where political fragmentation and even the overthrow of an existing dynasty took place. In Japan, rivalry among powerful clans did not produce autonomous regimes. Instead, a single ruling family emerged, and this dynastic state, known as the Tokugawa Shogunate, managed to do something that eluded most of the regimes around the world at this time: regulate foreign intrusion into its islands. While Japan played a modest role in the expanding world economic system, it remained free of outside exploitation.

> *The Tokugawa shoguns ensured a flow of resources from the working population to rulers and from the provinces to the capital.*

UNIFICATION OF JAPAN During the sixteenth century, Japan had suffered from chronic political instability, as rampant banditry and civil strife spread disorder across the countryside. Regional ruling households, called daimyos, had commanded private armies made up of skilled warriors known as samurai. The daimyos held sway over local populations and sometimes succeeded in bringing a measure of order to their domains. But no one daimyo family could establish its preeminence over others. Although Japan did have an emperor, who ruled from Kyoto, his authority did not extend beyond the court.

At the end of the sixteenth century, several military leaders attempted to unify Japan. One general loomed above his rivals: Toyotomi Hideyoshi (1535–1598). He not only conquered his rivals, but with the imprimatur of the Kyoto emperor, he became the supreme minister, and proceeded to arrange marriages among the children of the local magnates to solidify political bonds. He also ordered that the wives and children of the daimyos be kept within reach as semi-hostages, thereby coaxing cooperation from powerful regional rulers. After

Hideyoshi died, one of the daimyos, Tokugawa Ieyasu (1542–1616), took power for himself. This was a decisive moment. In 1603, Ieyasu assumed the title of "shogun" (military ruler). He also solved the problem of succession, declaring that thereafter rulership was hereditary and that his family would be the ruling household. Ieyasu passed the shogunate to his son in 1605, though he continued to rule behind the scenes. This hereditary Tokugawa Shogunate lasted until 1867.

The source of administrative authority shifted from the imperial capital of Kyoto to the site of Ieyasu's new domain headquarters: the castle town called Edo (later renamed Tokyo). The Tokugawa built Edo out of a small earthen fortification that was in bad repair and clinging to a coastal bluff. Behind Edo lay a village in a swampy plain. In a monumental work of engineering, the rulers ordered the swamp drained, the forest cleared, many of the hills leveled, canals dredged, bridges built, the seashore extended by landfill, and a new stone castle completed. By the time Ieyasu died, in 1616, Edo had a population of 150,000.

The Tokugawa shoguns ensured a flow of resources from the working population to rulers and from the provinces to the capital. Villages paid taxes to the daimyos, who in turn transferred resources to the seat of shogunate authority. No longer engaged in constant warfare, the samurai became administrators. Peace brought prosperity. Indeed, agriculture thrived. Improved farming techniques and land reclamation projects enabled the country's population to grow from 10 million in 1550 to 16 million in 1600 and 30 million by 1700.

FOREIGN AFFAIRS AND FOREIGNERS Having consolidated a national regime based on power sharing with the regions, Japanese rulers tackled foreign affairs. Hideyoshi launched a grandiose but ultimately failed scheme to conquer and displace China as the main power of East Asia. Toward that goal, the shogun dispatched an army to the Korean peninsula. Although the Japanese force overran Korea, it failed to subdue the local populace. Armored Korean wooden boats (dubbed tur-

Portuguese Arriving in Japan. In the 1540s, the Portuguese arrival on the islands of Japan sparked a fascination with the strange costumes and the great ships of these "southern barbarians" (so-called because they had approached Japan from the south). Silk screen paintings depicted Portuguese prowess in exaggerated form, such as in the impossible height of the fore and aft of the vessel pictured here. The Portuguese introduced the musket, which Japanese artisans began to replicate in large quantities. Its accuracy and reach greatly affected the wars that culminated in Japan's new political system under the Tokugawa in 1603.

tle boats) harassed their long supply lines and set up bottlenecks in interior waterways. Moreover, Japanese forces eventually faced Ming troops at the Chinese border. Unable to secure control in Korea, Hideyoshi's imperial ambitions foundered and dissolved with his death in 1598.

The more pressing concern for Hideyoshi's successors was what to do about the intrusion of foreigners, especially Christian missionaries and European traders, who had begun to arrive in Japan at the end of the sixteenth and beginning of the seventeenth centuries. Spanish Franciscan friars had come via the Philippines (in 1592). These missionaries were followed by Dutch (in 1609) and English (in 1613) merchants, who set up trading posts at Hirado (an island off Kyūshū) in competition with the Portuguese at Nagasaki. Initially, Japanese officials welcomed trade and Christianity because of their eagerness to acquire muskets, gunpowder, and other new technology. But once the ranks of the converted had swelled into the hundreds of thousands, Japanese authorities came to see that Christians were intolerant of other faiths, believed Christ to be superior to any authority, and fought among themselves. Trying to stem the tide, the shoguns issued decrees to stop conversion to Christianity and attempted to ban its practice. After a 1637 rebellion, in which peasants in southwestern Japan who had converted to Christianity rose up in protest against high rents and taxes, the government cracked down, suppressing Christianity and driving European missionaries from the country.

Even more troublesome for the shogunate was how to handle the lure of trade with Europeans, whose record of conquest of Manila and Melaka was well known. The Tokugawa knew that trading at different ports in Japan threatened to pull the commercial regions in various directions, away from the capital. When it became clear that European traders preferred the ports of Kyūshū, the shogunate restricted Europeans to trade only in ports under Edo's direct rule. Then, one by one, Japanese authorities expelled all European competitors. Only the Protestant (and non-missionizing) Dutch were permitted to remain in Japan, but they were confined to a small island near Nagasaki. The Dutch were allowed to unload just one ship each year, and only under strict supervision by Japanese authorities.

These measures did not close Tokugawa Japan to the outside world, however. Trade with the Chinese and Koreans flourished, and the shogun received Korean and Ryūkyū missions. Beyond these embassies, Edo gathered reports and publications about the outside world from the resident Dutch and Chinese (who included monks, physicians, and painters). A select few Japanese were permitted to learn Dutch and to learn about European technology, shipbuilding, and medicine (see Chapter 5). By setting the terms on which encounters with out-

By setting the terms on which encounters with outsiders would occur, Japanese authorities ensured that foreigners would not threaten Japan's security.

siders would occur, however, Japanese authorities ensured that foreigners would not threaten Japan's security.

Ruling over three islands, Tokugawa Japan was surrounded by "vassals" that were neither completely part of the realm nor entirely independent (see Map 4-6). The most important peripheral areas were the Ryūkyūs in the south and the island of Ezo to the north, neither of which the Japanese attempted to annex, preferring to maintain them as buffers. Establishing dependent buffer areas facilitated the strengthening of a distinct Japanese identity for all the peoples living "on the inside" and limited outside influence. When, beginning in 1697, the Russians approached Japan from the north, the Japanese rebuffed entreaties to open relations and instead sought to manage contacts with the Russians through their northern buffer zone. As the Russians became more aggressive in trying to "open" Japan to trade, the Japanese annexed and began to colonize Ezo. Ezo became Hokkaidō, the country's fourth main island, and a strong barrier to European penetration. In regulating outside contacts, Japanese rulers suppressed sources of upheaval and consolidated a dynasty that lasted well into the nineteenth century.

TRANSFORMATIONS OF EUROPE

> ⤳ *Why did the centers of European dynamism shift northward in the seventeenth century?*

Between 1600 and 1750, religious conflict, commercial expansion, and the consolidation of dynastic power transformed Europe. Commercial centers shifted northward, and Spain and Portugal lost ground to England and France. Waged chiefly over religion, the Thirty Years' War (1618–1648) changed the nature of warfare and political authority.

Russia was one of the few European countries not touched by the devastation of the Thirty Years' War. In this period, indeed, the Russian empire expanded in all directions to become the world's largest-ever state, gaining positions on both Europe's Baltic Sea and the Pacific Ocean. Russia established political borders with the western-expanding Qing empire and with Japan—the first time in history Japan created a border with another state. These momentous shifts involved the elimination of the steppe nomads, who had roamed through Russia and China, as an independent force in world history, and recast the problem of the Europe-Asia frontier. For China and Japan,

→ *Why did the centers of European dynamism shift northward in the seventeenth century?*

Legend:
- Outer daimyos
- Hereditary daimyos
- Tokugawa domains

RUSSIAN EMPIRE

CHINA

KOREA

YELLOW SEA

EAST CHINA SEA

SEA OF JAPAN

SEA OF OKHOTSK

EZO (HOKKAIDŌ)

JAPAN

Edo (Tokyo)

HONSHŪ

Kyoto
Osaka

SHIKOKU

KYŪSHŪ

PACIFIC OCEAN

Shimabara 1638: Uprising of Christian converts put down

Hirado 1609: Dutch trading post

Nagasaki 1570: opened to European trade

DESHIMA ISLAND: 1641 Dutch traders confined there

TANEGASHIMA: 1542 Portuguese trading post

MAP 4-6   TOKUGAWA JAPAN, 1603–1867

What does the map of Tokugawa Japan reveal about the nature of the Japanese polity during this period? In what ways does its geographical location help us to understand its history and relations to the outside world? Note the locations of the trading ports marked on the map. Why were they concentrated in the southwestern part of the country?

Europe (in the form of predominantly Christian Russia) stretched right up to their states. By contrast, Western Europeans placed the geographical boundary of Europe and Asia at the Ural Mountains. Culturally, Europeans as well as Russians debated whether Russia belonged more to Europe or to Asia. The answer was both.

EXPANSION AND DYNASTIC CHANGE IN RUSSIA

Muscovy, like Japan and China, used territorial expansion and extended commercial networks to consolidate a powerful political order, the Russian empire, the new name given to Muscovy by Tsar Peter the Great around 1700. But Russia was more internally heterogeneous than its Asian neighbors, both in its core and as a result of its annexation of adjacent lands. In the four centuries after 1480, the weak principality of Muscovy, a mixture of

Slavs, Finnish tribes, Turkic-speakers, and many others, expanded at the rate of about fifty square miles per day. Despite setbacks and long defensive periods, this new Russian empire grew to occupy one-sixth of the earth's land surface, spanning parts of Europe, much of northern Asia, numerous islands in the North Pacific, and even a corner of North America. Territorial expansion, together with natural population growth, increased Russia's population from about 6 million in 1550 to 20 million by 1750.

Like Japan, Russia emerged out of turmoil. Muscovy's security concerns, the ambitions of private individuals, and religious conviction inspired the regime to seize territory. For the Muscovite grand prince Ivan III (ruled 1462–1505), expansion was inseparable from security. Because the steppe, which stretches deep into Asia, remained a highway for horse-riding peoples, especially descendants of the Mongols, Muscovy sought to dominate the areas south and east of Moscow. By marrying the niece of the last Byzantine emperor, Ivan added a strong religious dimension to his expansionist claims. Now he could as-

Celebration in Red Square. Russian nobles gathered to celebrate in Red Square, which originally meant "Beautiful Square" and was a processional and market space just outside the walls of the Kremlin fortress where the Muscovite tsars lived, ruled, and prayed. The Russian nobles wore long beards and caftans, or gowns, often lined with Siberian furs, which were much coveted both at home and abroad. Many Russian nobles were descended from Tatar (Turkish) Muslims, conquered peoples who converted to Christianity and loyally served the tsar.

→ *Why did the centers of European dynamism shift northward in the seventeenth century?*

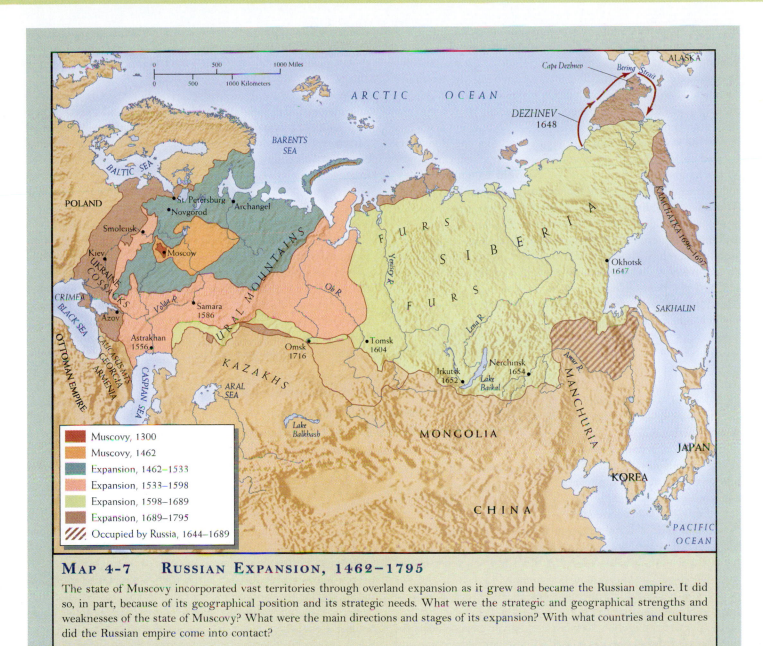

MAP 4-7 RUSSIAN EXPANSION, 1462–1795

The state of Muscovy incorporated vast territories through overland expansion as it grew and became the Russian empire. It did so, in part, because of its geographical position and its strategic needs. What were the strategic and geographical strengths and weaknesses of the state of Muscovy? What were the main directions and stages of its expansion? With what countries and cultures did the Russian empire come into contact?

sert that Moscow was the center of the Byzantine faith and heir to the conquered city of Constantinople. Territorial expansion continued under Ivan III's successors, especially his grandson, Ivan IV (ruled 1533–1584), who adopted the title of "tsar" in 1547. To secure Muscovy's eastern borders, Ivan IV permitted private armies to extend the domain of the Russian state into Siberia. Beginning in the 1590s, Russian authorities built forts and trading posts along the great Siberian rivers for defensive purposes and to facilitate the taxation of aboriginal peoples. The rulers' efforts to control tribute and trans-Eurasian trade, however, could not prevent privateers, enticed by the large profits that could be made from the sale of furs, from pushing the

Russian domain outward. In this fashion, Muscovy's frontier expanded eastward, reaching the Pacific, more than 5,000 miles from Moscow, in 1639. In just over a century, Moscow had created a landed empire straddling Eurasia from west to east, incorporating peoples of many languages and religions (see Map 4-7).

Much of this expansion occurred despite the dynastic chaos that followed the death of Ivan IV. Tsar Ivan was succeeded by a feeble-minded son, who died in 1598, leaving no heir. During the ensuing period (known as the "Time of Troubles"), the regime slipped into internal feuding. "False pretenders" claimed to be the grandson of Ivan IV, and Catholic Poles invaded and occupied Muscovy. Finally, a group of prominent families gathered in 1613 to reestablish central authority and threw their weight behind a new family of potentates. These were the Romanovs, court barons who set about reviving the Kremlin's fortunes. Like the Ottoman and Qing dynasts, Romanov tsars and their aristocratic supporters would retain power into the twentieth century.

In the seventeenth and eighteenth centuries, the Romanovs created an "absolutist" system of government, clustering power in the hands of the ruling family. The right to make war, tax, judge, and coin money was limited to the tsar and his retinue. To transcend old sources of tension and friction, the Romanovs made the nobles serve as bureaucrats. Russia, following the Byzantine preference for a monarch, embraced a despotic version of rulership. Moscow had no political assemblies for nobles or any other sectors of society. Powerful families at the court referred to themselves as "slaves of the tsar." Away from Moscow, local aristocrats exercised nearly unlimited authority in exchange for fealty and tribute to the tsar.

Russia's peasantry bore the burden of maintaining the wealth of the small nobility and the monarchy. Most of Muscovy's peasant families gathered into "communes," enclosed rural worlds in which people helped each other to deal with the everyday strains of the harsh climate and the periodic travails of poor harvests and severe masters. Communes were not based on kinship, but they functioned like extended kin networks in that members reciprocated favors and chores for survival. Even with mutual support, the peasants lived poorly, their huts usually consisting of a single chamber heated by a wood-burning stove and no chimney. Livestock and humans often shared the same quarters. In 1649, peasants were legally "bound" as serfs to the nobles and the tsar, meaning they had to perform obligatory services and deliver part of their produce to their lords, who exercised almost complete command over the life and death of their minions. Serfdom grew directly out of the state's ever-increasing military ambitions and challenges.

Having consolidated an internal order, Russian leaders redoubled their pursuit of imperial expansion. With their sovereignty established over a bewildering variety of native peoples in the east, all the way to the Pacific Ocean and the borders of China and Japan, Russia pushed southward, deeper into the steppe during the eighteenth century; and westward, on to the Baltic Sea. Peter the Great (ruled 1682–1725) symbolized this westward push by founding, and building with forced labor, a new capital, St. Petersburg, in 1703. By the late eighteenth century, Russian sovereignty stretched from the Baltic Sea through the heart of Europe, Ukraine, the Crimea on the Black Sea, and into the ancient lands of Armenia and Georgia in the

Caucasus Mountains, bordering on the Ottoman empire. As the Russians sought to secure their southeastern steppe frontier, they signed border treaties with the Qing in 1689 and again in 1727.

With a territorial empire secured, more people started to migrate eastward, some to escape being serfs and to settle their own land. The steppe nomadic redoubts that once threatened Muscovy's heartland became the staging ground for Russia's conquest and colonization of Siberia. At the beginning of the migration eastward, more than 90 percent of Siberia's approximately 200,000 inhabitants were indigenes. By 1750, the number of Slavs in Siberia had almost caught up to the native population and soon surpassed it. Battling astoundingly harsh circumstances, peasant migrants traveled on horseback and foot to resettle in the east. Religious schismatics, known after 1667 as Old Believers because of their refusal to accept changes in the Eastern Orthodox liturgy, were deported to uninhabited areas. But the difficulties of clearing forested lands or planting crops in boggy Siberian soils, combined with extraordinarily harsh winters, made for very high attrition among settlers. To this was added the problem of isolation. There was no established land route back to Moscow until the 1770s, when the Great Siberian Post Road finally cut through the swamps and peat bogs of western Siberia. The writer Anton Chekhov called it "the longest and ugliest road in the whole world."

> *The Romanovs created an "absolutist" system of government with the right to make war, tax, judge, and coin money limited to the tsar and his retinue.*

Russia's territorial acquisitions produced complex, mixed societies that bridged eastern and western ends of Eurasia, producing many children of mixed parentage. Perhaps half the inhabitants of Siberia in the 1750s were runaway serfs. Russian authorities also resettled in Siberia unwanted families and people banished by the tsar because they were considered politically dangerous or undesirable. These exiles, though they never approached in number the legions of hardy peasant settlers, would later make Siberia infamous as a land for prisoners, overshadowing its reputation as a destination of freedom. "The road to Siberia is wide," went the saying, "the way back, narrow."

ECONOMIC AND POLITICAL FLUCTUATIONS IN WESTERN EUROPE

During the seventeenth and eighteenth centuries, the commercial integration of different parts of the world shook up old regimes in Mughal India, Ming China, and the Ottoman empire, while spawning new dynasties like the Tokugawa in Japan and the Romanovs in Russia. At the same time, European economies grew and became more commercialized. As in Asia, happenings in distant parts of the world shaped upturns and

STIMULANTS, SOCIABILITY, AND COFFEEHOUSES

As the world's trading networks expanded, the great merchants of Europe, Asia, Africa, and the Americas also globalized and popularized many new commodities. None were more enthusiastically received around the world than a group of stimulants—coffee, cocoa, sugar, tobacco, and tea—all of which, except for sugar, were slightly or highly addictive and had the added feature of producing a sense of well-being. Previously, many of these products had been grown in isolated parts of the world. Yemen had been the only location in the fifteenth century for the distribution of the coffee bean. Tobacco and cocoa were New World products, and sugar, while it originated in Bengal, did not become a product with a vast global market until it began to be cultivated on a large scale on American plantations. Yet, by the seventeenth century, in nearly every corner of the world, the well-to-do classes began to congregate in coffeehouses, consuming these new products and engaging in sociable activities.

Although sugar was probably consumed in larger amounts than any other product in this group, coffee and coffeehouses gained the greatest notoriety among the well-to-do. Coffeehouses everywhere served as locations for social exchange, political discussions, and business activities. Yet, they also varied from cultural area to cultural area, reflecting the values of the society in which they arose.

The coffeehouse first appeared in Islamic lands toward the end of the fifteenth century. As its consumption caught on among the well-to-do and leisured classes in the Arabian peninsula and the Ottoman empire, local growers protected their advantage by monopolizing its cultivation and sale and refusing to allow any seeds or cuttings from the coffee tree to be taken abroad.

Despite some religious opposition, coffee spread into Egypt and throughout the Ottoman empire in the sixteenth century. Ottoman bureaucrats, merchants, and artists assembled in coffeehouses to trade stories, to read, to listen to poetry, and to play chess and backgammon. Indeed, so deeply connected were the coffeehouses with the literary

Turkish men drinking coffee at a banquet.

and artistic lives of many people that they were referred to as schools of knowledge.

From the Ottoman territories, the culture of coffee drinking spread to Western Europe. The first coffeehouse in London opened in 1652, and such establishments soon proliferated. By 1713, there were no fewer than 500 coffeehouses in London. The Fleet Street area of London was filled with so many of these establishments that the English essayist Charles Lamb commented "that the man must have a rare recipe for melancholy who can be dull in Fleet Street."

Drinking coffee in an English coffeehouse.

Although the coffeehouses attracted people from all levels of society, they especially appealed to the new mercantile and professional classes as locations where stimulating beverages like coffee, cocoa, and tea easily led to lively conversations. Here, too, there were opponents, some of whom claimed that an excessive drinking of coffee destabilized the thinking processes and even resulted in conversions to Islam. But against such opposition, the pleasures of coffee, tea, and cocoa prevailed. These bitter beverages in turn required liberal doses of the sweetener, sugar. A smoke of tobacco topped off the experience. In this environment of pleasure, patrons of the coffeehouses indulged their addictions, engaged in gossip, conducted business, and talked politics.

The most ardent European exponents of coffee even suggested that its consumption would moderate another of the addictions that beset many people—the use of beer, wine, and spirits, often to excess. But this was destined not to be. Samuel Johnson, one of England's most astute observers, wryly observed that "a man is never happy in the present unless he is drunk."

downturns in European economies. Compounding the pressures of economic change in Europe was the continuation of dynastic rivalries and religious conflicts.

WESTERN EUROPEAN ECONOMIES Silver from the Americas and the emergence of new commodities in world trade exposed Europe's increasingly monetized economies to the booms and busts associated with short-term money supply cycles. For instance, as the inflow of precious metals dipped around 1619 (due to the exhaustion of Andean mining and before Mesoamerican mines could compensate for the shortage of silver), economies around Europe faced a severe downturn. But, in general, silver and gold helped support commercial expansion throughout the seventeenth and eighteenth centuries. Powerful new merchant classes arose. Amsterdam and London became important trading and financial hubs for the Atlantic economy and local business. Cities grew, and population expanded across Europe, from 70 million to 86 million between 1600 and 1750—this despite the political conflicts of the period. Indeed, after 1600, the region's population density surpassed for good the levels reached before the Black Death of the 1300s.

Economic expansion was uneven, however. In particular, areas that had pioneered commercial connections in earlier centuries began to face new threats. Silver created problems for Spain as inflation and the costs of defending the empire soared. Even worse, Spain's empire was a great magnet for merchants from the rest of Europe, who sought to profit from Spanish trading networks. Spain began to lose ground to its rivals. In the seventeenth century, its trade and agriculture stagnated. But it

was not only Spain that felt the effects of new competition; many of the economies that had flourished in the sixteenth century now had difficulty adapting to the pressures of greater economic connection. The economy of Venice, which before the era of transoceanic shipping had been Europe's chief gateway to Asia, fell into decline.

During the seventeenth century, the centers of European dynamism shifted northward. The Dutch were at the forefront, creating new commercial practices and a new mercantile elite. They specialized in shipping and in financing regional and long-distance trade. Their famous *fluitschips* could carry heavy bulky cargoes, like Baltic wood, with relatively small crews over long distances. The cost of shipping goods around the Atlantic world dropped significantly as Dutch ships transported their own goods as well as cargoes of other countries. Amsterdam's merchants founded an exchange bank in 1609 and even a rudimentary stock exchange in 1611—with a weekly publication of price quotations in 1613. They also pioneered systems of underwriting and insuring cargoes. Other mercantile centers in Europe followed suit, and soon began to compete with Dutch merchants. The Dutch began to lose their share of the commercial activity and eventually fell behind the larger European commercial and military powers. But their pioneering ways set an early example for new trading and financing practices that helped integrate the Atlantic economies even further.

England and to some extent France emerged as the commercial powerhouses in the seventeenth century. Each was backed by aggressive state policies that aimed to promote national business and drive out competitors. The English Navigation Act of 1651, which stipulated that only English ships could carry goods between the mother country and its colonies, sought to protect English shipping and merchants, especially from the Dutch. The English subsequently launched a series of effective trade wars against Holland between 1652 and 1672. The French, too, especially under King Louis XIV's finance minister, Jean-Baptiste Colbert, aggressively applied mercantilist policies and joined forces with England to invade Holland in 1672. These European powers also perfected the use of official monopoly trading companies to organize commerce and drive away competitors.

Monopolistic trading flourished until the eighteenth century, when it was eventually superseded by a much more diversified range of trade and networks far beyond the controlling powers of any single firm. England, in particular, began to loosen formal controls and restrictions on trade. As it did so, its capacity to create new markets and commercial networks grew even more. By the early part of the century, 85 percent of England's exports were manufactured products, especially woolens. But increasingly, new industries such as cotton textiles, housewares, and iron products accounted for a larger share of exports and were sold to a wide network of ports all around the Atlantic, including the New World colonies. What made Holland, France, and England so responsive to the changing commercial order was the ability of public policies to support

Amsterdam Stock Exchange. Buying and selling shares in the new joint-stock companies was daily business at the Stock Exchange in seventeenth-century Amsterdam. This image depicts gentlemanly negotiations between prosperous merchants and investors, but panics could also occur, as during the South Sea Bubble.

new ventures and the power of merchant groups to make the best of their opportunities.

Economic development was not limited to port towns. In the countryside, too, new techniques for organizing production led to breakthroughs. Most important was the expansion in the production of food. In northwestern Europe, especially, new crop rotations, investments in water drainage, larger livestock herds, and the refinement of cultivation practices all helped farmers produce more and more food. This increased output supported a growing urban population. By contrast, in Spain and Italy, agricultural change came more slowly, and agrarian backwardness checked population growth.

Production rose most where farming underwent profound changes in the way rural property was organized. The sharpest transformation came in England. For generations, leading up to the end of the eighteenth century, landowners redefined their relations with their workforces. In a movement known as "enclosure," landowners took control of lands that local customs had treated as the common property of residents, built fences, and claimed exclusive rights. Within their enclosed properties, landowners planted new crops or pastured sheep with the aim, not of satisfying local needs, but of selling the products in distant markets—especially cities. At the same time, large landowners put their farms in the hands of tenants, who in turn hired wage laborers to till the land and collect harvests. In England, peasant agriculture gave way increasingly to farms

> *England was at the forefront of a European-wide process of commercializing the countryside.*

run by families who made their money from buying and selling what they needed (including labor) and what they produced in the marketplace. But England was not alone; it simply was at the forefront of a European-wide process of commercializing the countryside.

THE WAYS OF WAR Commercial integration was a major factor in aggravating Europe's political tensions after 1600. But it was not the only one. Religious and political struggles engulfed much of the region, focusing especially on central Europe and the remnants of the old Holy Roman empire.

Germany, in particular, the nursery of the Reformation, was a seething battleground from the 1520s to the 1640s, and a location central to the last and greatest of the religious wars, the Thirty Years' War (1618–1648). Protestant princes and the Habsburg Catholic emperor struggled to establish their control over the divided region. For the first phase of the war, it seemed as if the Holy Roman empire might triumph; Protestant forces were on their heels by 1630. When it seemed as if Protestantism would be wiped off the central European map, the Swedish king, Gustavus Adolphus II (ruled 1611–1632), came to the rescue. Though he died from battle wounds, his intervention allowed the Protestant forces to survive. The most notorious battle in this conflict occurred in 1631 at Magdeburg, where Catholic forces sacked and destroyed the city of 40,000. Three-quarters of the civilian inhabitants died. In total, fighting, disease, and

The Thirty Years' War. The mercenary armies of the Thirty Years' War were renowned for pillaging and tormenting the civilians of central Europe. Here, the townsfolk extract revenge on some of these soldiers, hanging, as the engraving's caption claims, "damned and infamous thieves, like bad fruit, from this tree."

famine wiped out a third of Germany's urban population and two-fifths of its rural population. The war also depopulated Sweden and Poland. By 1648, the remnants of the Holy Roman empire had 8 million fewer subjects than it had prior to the war. Exhausted from the long conflict, the primary belligerents signed the Treaty of Westphalia in 1648.

The Thirty Years' War was the religious war to end all major European religious wars, ushering in a new era of war-making and state-building. Old medieval struggles between nobles had been mainly sieges, and the belligerents had fielded small armies capable of prolonged engagements. The Thirty Years' War began a slow transformation in European war-making and enhanced the powers of larger centralized states. After 1648, with the increase in the size of standing armies, rulers had to wage decisive, grand-scale campaigns. The Thirty Years' War changed the nature of being a soldier, too— enlisted men from among the local population who were defending their king, country, and faith were replaced by criminals who were forced into service or mercenaries who were hired to fight. Even officers, previously granted their stripes by purchase or royal fiat, now earned them and became more professional. Finally, gunpowder, cannons, and handguns became standardized and more efficient. By the eighteenth century, Europe's wars were increasingly fought by huge standing armies, boasting a professional officer corps and bristling with effective artillery. To keep these armies going, rulers had to organize and sustain long supply trains and make sure that food and ammunition got to the front. The costs—material and human—of war in Europe began to soar. In Holland, the public debt, mostly for supporting armies, soared from 140 million guilders in 1650 to over 400 million a century later. French rulers increased their debt sevenfold to 2 billion livres by 1715.

As war costs rose, rulers also recognized the need to avoid unnecessary squabbles. Wars did not disappear, but they were laced with a new style of statecraft run increasingly by diplomats. The crucial ingredient to the system established by the Treaty of Westphalia was the general recognition that no single European power could be dominant, and that any threat from one power would face the combined powers of the rest. In so doing, the Treaty of Westphalia established the boundaries between Protestantism and Catholicism in Europe.

After the Thirty Years' War, struggles for supremacy in Europe focused less on religious divisions and more on the territorial and commercial ambitions of the region's monarchs and merchants. In the seventeenth and eighteenth centuries, two states in particular emerged as the main military and economic powers in Europe, and each had contrasting systems for organizing their political affairs—France and England.

> *The Thirty Years' War was the religious war to end all major European religious wars, ushering in a new era of war-making and state-building.*

DYNASTIC MONARCHIES: FRANCE AND ENGLAND

European monarchs had various degrees of success in their attempts to centralize state power. Louis XIII of France (ruled 1610–1643), and especially his chief minister Cardinal Richelieu, concentrated power in the hands of the king. By the time of Louis XIV's reign (ruled 1643–1715), the Bourbon family had established a monarchy where succession passed strictly to the oldest male in the male line. After 1614, kings refused to convene the Estates-General, a medieval advisory body. Once composed of representatives of three groups—the clergy (the First Estate, those who pray), the nobility (the Second Estate, those who fight), and the unprivileged remainder of the population (the Third Estate, those who work)—the Estates-General was seen as an obstacle to the full empowerment of the king. The idea of the king and his counselors was to create a monarchy that was "absolute." By this they did not mean tyrannical rule, but complete and thorough rule, free of bloody disorders such as the religious wars that shattered France during the sixteenth century. The king's rule was to be lawful, but it was he, not his jurists, who dictated the last legal word. If he—the king—made a mistake, only God could call him to account. This was the "divine right of kings."

In French absolutism, privileges and state offices flowed from the king's grace. All patronage networks, even those headed by dukes and princes, ultimately went back to the king's grants and treasury. The great palace Louis XIV built at Versailles teemed with noblemen and noblewomen from all over France, seeking benefits, dressing according to the king's expensive fashion code, and attending the latest tragedies, comedies, and concerts. Just as the Japanese shogun monitored the daimyos by keeping them in Edo, so, too, could Louis XIV and his retainers keep a watchful eye on the French nobility at Versailles.

The French dynastic monarchy provided a model of "absolute" rule for other European dynasts, like the Habsburgs of the Holy Roman empire, the Hohenzollerns of Brandenburg, and the Romanovs of Muscovy. Public power was clustered in the hands of the king and his ministers, while the various groups in society, from the nobility to the peasantry, were deprived of formal means to represent their interests. Nonetheless, French absolutist government was not as "absolute" as the king would have wished. Pockets of stalwart Protestants practiced their religion secretly in the plateau villages of central France. Peasant disturbances continued. Criticism of court life and of Louis's wars and religious policies flowed from pens in anonymous printed pamphlets, jurists' notebooks, and the private journals of courtiers. The nobility also grumbled about their political misfortunes, but since the king would not call the Estates-General, they had no formal way to express their political concerns.

Versailles. Louis XIV's Versailles, just southwest of Paris, was a hunting lodge that was converted at colossal cost in the 1670s–1680s into a grand royal chateau with expansive grounds. Much envied and imitated across Europe, the palace became the epicenter of a luxurious court life that included entertainments such as plays and musical offerings, state receptions, royal hunts, boating, and gambling. Thousands of nobles at Versailles vied with each other for closer proximity to the king in the performance of court rituals.

England might also have evolved into an absolutist regime. Queen Elizabeth (ruled 1558–1603) and her successors in the early seventeenth century employed many of the same policies of the "absolute" monarchy in France, such as control of patronage and elaborate court festivities. But there were important differences. In England, the system of succession allowed women to rule as queens in their own right. In addition, in England, Parliament remained an important force. Importantly,

Queen Elizabeth of England. This portrait (c. 1600) depicts an idealized Queen Elizabeth near the end of her long reign. The queen is pictured riding in a procession in the midst of an admiring crowd composed of the most important nobles of the realm.

The Execution of Charles I. This famous image of the beheading of Charles I of England in 1649 conveys something of the shock Europeans felt at this first public execution of a monarch. The four inset pictures depict (counter-clockwise): the king at his trial, the king's march to the block, citizens collecting blood and relics after the execution, and one of the leading Cromwellians with Charles's severed head.

while the French kings did not need the consent of the Estates-General to enact taxes, the English monarchs were required to call Parliament if they wanted to raise money.

Under Elizabeth's successors, fierce quarrels broke out over taxation, religion, and royal efforts to rule without parliamentary consent. Tensions ran high between the Puritans, with their relatively simple form of worship and more egalitarian church government, and the Anglicans, supporters of the Church of England, with its more ornate ceremonies and its hierarchy of bishops and archbishops headed by the king. Social and economic grievances fanned the flames further. Civil war erupted in the 1640s, ending in a victory for the parliamentary army (which was largely Puritan) and the beheading of King Charles I (ruled 1625–1649). Twelve years of government as a Commonwealth without a king ensued, during which time the middle and lower classes enjoyed political and religious power, but the Commonwealth culminated in a military dictatorship.

In 1660, the monarchy was restored, but the issues of the king's relation to Parliament and of religious tolerance were unresolved. Charles II (ruled 1660–1685) and his successor James II (ruled 1685–1688) aroused opposition by their autocracy and clandestine efforts to bring England back into the Catholic fold. The conflict between an aspiring absolutist throne and a Puritan struggle for "liberty" and parliamentary defense of autonomy finally culminated in the Glorious Revolution of 1688–1689. In a bloodless upheaval, James II fled to France, and Parliament offered the crown to William of Orange and his wife Mary (a Protestant daughter of James II). The outcome of the conflict established the principle that monarchs must rule in conjunction with Parliament. The Church of England was reaffirmed as the official church, but Presbyterians and Jews, though saddled with many civic disabilities (they were not welcome at the universities, for instance), could at least practice their religions. Catholic worship was still officially forbidden, but was in fact tolerated as long as the Catholics kept quiet. By 1700, then, England's powerful nobility and merchant classes were permanently guaranteed a say in public affairs and ensured that state activity would operate to the advantage of propertied classes and not just the ruler.

Events in both France and England stimulated much political writing. In England, Thomas Hobbes published his *Leviathan* in 1651, a reasoned defense of the absolute power of the state over all competing forces as a necessary remedy against the natural "war of all against all." Nearly forty years later, John Locke published his *Two Treatises of Civil Government*, which laid out an argument based on the natural rights to liberty and property and on the rights of peoples to agree to form government and to disband and reform it when it did not live up to the contract. French theorists, like Jean Bodin, also wrote about new forms of conducting politics and making law. More and more, writers began to discuss the costs of unchecked state power. What differed was the extent to which these elites could demand and win the right to check the king. As the eighteenth century unfolded, the question of where sovereignty lay grew ever more pressing.

MERCANTILIST WARS The ascendance of new powers in Europe, especially France and England, intensified commercial rivalries for control of the Atlantic system. In the eighteenth century, a new type of conflict replaced earlier religious and territorial struggles: mercantilist wars for control of commercial colonies and sea lanes. Commercial struggles, then, evolved into worldwide wars. Across the world, European empires engaged in constant skirmishing over control of trade and territory. The English and Dutch trading companies took aim at the Portuguese outposts in Asia and the Americas. Then they took aim at each other. Ports in India were the target for repeated assaults and counterassaults. In response, European powers built huge navies to protect their colonies and trade routes and also to attack their rivals.

Smuggling across the mercantilist lines became rampant. English and French traders, sometimes with the open support of their political authorities, violated the sovereign claims of rival colonies. Curaçao, for instance, became an entrepot for traders from England and the Low Countries to sell illegal goods in South America. French and English traders set up shop in southern Brazil to smuggle goods into the River Plate in return for Andean silver. All around the Gulf of Mexico and the Caribbean, merchants sought to introduce their goods into their enemies' colonies.

After 1715, mercantilist wars were mainly conducted outside Europe, as empires feuded over colonial possessions. They were especially bitter in border areas, where the lines between empires blurred. In the Caribbean and North America, in particular, mercantilist wars made the borderlands into battlegrounds. Each round of peripheral warfare ratcheted up the scale and cost of fighting, culminating in the first world conflict, which was known as the French and Indian War in the United States, but as the Seven Years' War (1756–1763) everywhere else. For the first time in history, a war was fought simultaneously across many hemispheric fronts: not just in Europe, but also in India and across the Americas. American Indians, African slaves, and European settlers were all dragged into the conflict.

The Seven Years' War marked the triumph of the British empire over its rivals, especially France and Spain. Britain captured one of Spain's prime Caribbean defensive bastions, Havana, as well as Florida and Manila, Spain's prize in Asia. Later, the British returned Havana and Manila, but they kept Florida, leaving little doubt that Spain's main rival in the New World was definitely Britain. France lost Canada and several outposts in India, but hung on to its Caribbean possessions. While Britain emerged as the dominant overseas power in the world, the struggle left all the European empires in deep debt.

 **CONCLUSION**

Between the beginning of the seventeenth century and the middle of the eighteenth century, the corners of the world went from being loosely connected to becoming more economically linked. Traders shipped ever more goods over longer distances. And they exchanged a wider variety of commodities, from Baltic wood to Indian cotton. The world's commercial linkages could

be seen in people wearing clothes manufactured elsewhere, consuming beverages made from products cultivated in far-off locations, and using imported guns to settle local conflicts. Colonization in the Americas provides an obvious example of

Chronology

1600–1644	Political and economic problems in China
1600–1800	Massive expansion of the Atlantic slave trade
1600	English East India Company established
1602	Dutch East India Company established
1603	Tokugawa Shogunate founded in Japan
1607	English establish Jamestown colony
1608	French establish colony of New France
1613	Romanov dynasty established in Russia
1618–1648	Thirty Years' War in Europe
1620s	Roving bandits destabilize China
1621	Dutch West India Company founded
1624	Dutch settle New Amsterdam
1637	Japanese expel European missionaries
1639	Russian state's frontier reaches Pacific
1641	Dutch seize Melaka from Portuguese
1642–1649	English Civil War
1643–1715	Reign of France's Louis XIV
1644	Ming dynasty falls to the Qing
1652	Dutch seize Cape Town
1656–1676	Koprulu reforms revitalize Ottoman empire
1658–1707	Aurangzeb expands Mughal empire
1682–1725	Peter the Great rules Russia
1683	Ottomans defeated at Vienna
1688–1689	Glorious Revolution in England
1690s–1713	Oyo empire expands to coast of Africa
1701–1750	Asante state expands in Africa
1722–1773	Safavid empire under assault
1756–1763	Seven Years' War

this growing interdependence. European decisions to settle new colonies meant an increase in the Atlantic slave trade from Africa and the expulsion of Indians from their lands, clear cases of global connectedness—and glaring inequalities.

Economic integration had destabilizing and fragmenting political consequences for many of the great dynasties of Eurasia. The Mughals, the Ming, and the Ottomans all confronted rivals to their authority—both inside and out. Local magnates challenged the imperial centers, while European newcomers knocked with greater frequency at imperial doors, for royal favor, for rights to trade, and for permission to convert souls.

Politically, certain societies coped with increased commercial exchange more successfully than others, although everywhere greater linkages and new wealth shook up existing orders. The Safavid and Ming dynasties could not cope with these pressures. Both collapsed. The Spanish and Mughal dynasts managed to survive, but they were harried by aggressive rivals. For the newcomers to the integrating world, the opportunity to trade helped create new dynasties. Japan, Russia, and England emerged on the world stage. But even in these newer regimes, competition and conflict created enormous internal pressures, some of which sparked domestic upheaval. Were these changes to be celebrated or condemned? This was the central question that intellectuals as well as rulers confronted in the years after 1750, and will be, accordingly, the theme of our next chapter.

FURTHER READINGS

Alam, Muzaffar, *The Crisis of Empire in Mughal North India* (1993). Represents the best of the new interpretation on the subject.

Blackburn, Robin, *The Making of New World Slavery: From the Baroque to the Modern, 1492–1800* (1997). A good place to begin when studying African slavery and the Atlantic slave trade, it compares the early expansion of the plantation systems across the Atlantic and throughout the Americas.

Crossley, Pamela, *A Translucent Mirror: History and Identity in Qing Imperial Ideology* (1999). The author historicizes the formation of identities such as "Manchu" and "Chinese" during the Qing period.

Dennis, Matthew, *Cultivating a Landscape of Peace: Iroquois-European Encounters in Seventeenth-Century America* (1993). An excellent discussion of the relations of the Iroquois and the European colonists.

De Vries, Jan, *The Economy of Europe in an Age of Crisis, 1600–1750* (1976). A useful discussion of the European economy.

Dvornik, Francis, *The Slavs in European History and Civilization* (1962). Thorough analysis of Muscovy as well as other Slavic dynasties that did not achieve the power of the Russian one.

Flynn, Dennis O., and Arturo Girladez (eds.), *Metals and Money in an Emerging World Economy* (1997). A collection of articles about the place of silver in the world economy.

Forsyth, James, *A History of the Peoples of Siberia: Russia's North Asian Colony 1581–1990* (1992). A narrative overview of a violent history reminiscent of the western expansion of the United States.

Glahn, Richard von, *Fountains of Fortune: Money and Monetary Policy in China, 1000–1700* (1996). A discussion of the place of silver in the Chinese economy.

Halperin, Charles J., *Russia and the Golden Horde: The Mongol Impact on Medieval Russian History* (1985). A book on the rise of Muscovy, forebear of the Russian empire, from within the Mongol realm.

Hattox, Ralph S., *Coffee and Coffeehouses: The Origins of a Social Beverage in the Medieval Near East* (1985). This work shows how widespread and popular coffee consumption and coffeehouses were around the world.

Huang, Ray, *1587, A Year of No Significance: The Ming Dynasty in Decline* (1981). An insightful analysis of the problems confronting the late Ming.

Katz, Stanley N., John M. Murrin, and Douglas Greenberg (eds.), *Colonial America: Essays in Politics and Social Development* (5th ed., 2001). Brings together many of the most important interpretations of seventeenth- and eighteenth-century life in North America.

Klein, Herbert S., *The Atlantic Slave Trade* (1999). A recent study of the African slave trade.

Lensen, George, *The Russian Push Toward Japan: Russo-Japanese Relations 1697–1875* (1959). A discussion of why and how Japan established its first border with another state and how Russia pursued its ambitions in the Pacific.

Lockhart, James, *The Nahuas After the Conquest* (1992). A landmark study of the social reorganization of Mesoamerican societies under Spanish rule.

Lovejoy, Paul, *Transformations in Slavery: A History of Slavery in Africa* (1983). An excellent discussion of African slavery.

Nakane, Chie, and Shinzaburo Oishi (eds.), *Tokugawa Japan: The Social and Economic Antecedents of Modern Japan* (1990). First-rate essays on Japanese village society, urban life, literacy, and culture.

Pamuk, Sevket, *A Monetary History of the Ottoman Empire* (2000). A discussion of the place of silver in the Ottoman empire.

Parker, Geoffrey (ed.), *The Thirty Years' War* (1997). The standard account of the conflict and its outcomes.

Platonov, S. F., *Ivan the Terrible* (1986). Covers the controversies over Russia's infamous tsar.

Rawski, Evelyn, *The Last Emperors: A Social History of Qing Imperial Institutions* (1998). This volume explores the mechanisms and processes through which the Qing court negotiated its Manchu identity.

Reid, Anthony, *Charting the Shape of Early Modern Southeast Asia* (1999). A collection of articles by a leading historian of Southeast Asia.

Richter, Daniel, *The Ordeal of the Longhouse: The Peoples of the Iroquois League in the Era of European Colonization* (1992). A superb analysis of the Iroquois and their relations with Dutch, English, and French colonists.

Spence, Jonathan, and John Wills (eds.), *From Ming to Ch'ing: Conquest, Region, and Continuity in Seventeenth-Century China* (1979). Covers the various aspects of a tumultuous period of dynastic transition.

Thornton, John, *Africa and Africans in the Making of the Atlantic World, 1400–1800* (1998). A wonderful discussion of how African slaves played a large role in the formation of the Atlantic world.

Toby, Ronald P., *State and Diplomacy in Early Modern Japan: Asia in the Development of the Tokugawa Bakufu* (1984). A demolition of the myth of Japanese isolationism with a subtle alternative view.

Vilar, Pierre, *A History of Gold and Money* (1991). An excellent study of the development of the early silver and gold economies.

CULTURES OF SPLENDOR AND POWER, 1600–1780

Silver from the New World coursed through the arteries of world trade in the seventeenth and eighteenth centuries. Its dispersal often resulted in political fragmentation, causing widespread disruptions in the world's economy. Yet, the flow of silver also created wealth for states and individuals and financed cultural flourishing in many parts of the world. Ruling elites in China, the Islamic empires, and Europe used their newfound prosperity to patronize the arts and to build architectural masterpieces like the Palace of Versailles just outside Paris and the Taj Mahal in India, often as a means to legitimate vulnerable political positions. Book production and consumption soared, with some publications even finding their way across the world. Artists and writers in distant places reveled in their cultural attainments and celebrated the vitality of their ways of life.

World prosperity supported cultural splendors and fostered knowledge of foreign ways, but the intellectual developments of these two centuries still remained rooted in the cultural soil of each of the different regions of the world. Ottoman, Safavid, and Mughal architecture reflected Islamic precepts, and Chinese writing and painting continued to be based on their particular beliefs and traditions. Chinese and Muslim scholars remained convinced that their forms of knowledge and art were superior to those of others.

Europeans invented what they believed was a series of universal principles—to the perplexity of people from other parts of the world, who largely stuck to their own arts and sciences. Despite familiarity with other cultures, the real cultural battles of this period, just like the struggles to achieve political autonomy, were waged inside polities, as centralized dynasties and new states struggled to dominate the cultural production of their intellectuals.

TRADE AND CULTURE

> → *How did world trade begin changing world cultures?*

Knowledge of different cultures spread throughout the world with trade and conquest, but the ideas had varying effects in different polities. Narratives of cultural flourishing and diversification can be told for China, the Islamic world, and Europe. They demonstrate how the educated and artistic groups in each of these areas became increasingly aware of other cultures and yet at the same time affirmed the validity of their own ways. In contrast, the Japanese were able to appropriate ideas from foreign cultures in their cultural flowering. In the Americas and the South Pacific, conquest and trade undermined many aspects of indigenous cultural life, and although Europeans and native peoples often borrowed ideas and practices from one another, these were not free and equal exchanges. Native Americans, for example, adapted to European missionizing efforts in resourceful ways, by creating mixed forms of religious worship, but they did so in response to external pressure. And as the Europeans grew richer and swallowed new territories, it was their culture, not that of the local populations, that spread and diversified, absorbing ideas and practices from Native Americans and African slaves, but offering these contributors little share of either expanding sovereignty or increasing prosperity.

By the late eighteenth century, Europe's cultural curiosity, like its commercial ambitions, propelled some of its members into the rest of the world in search of information. Europeans were busily collecting information on everything from Sanskrit grammar to Polynesian wind currents. Based on the data they gathered, they created pragmatic principles for commercial and even colonial use, as well as a kind of empirical knowledge they felt could be extended to the rest of the world. In this era, the Europeans, internally divided and anxious to assert themselves culturally as well as economically, believed that they could understand all of nature and that European modes of thinking had universal applicability.

The three scientific-colonizing voyages of Captain James Cook (1728–1779) in the South Pacific epitomized the search for knowledge about the unknown (see p. 189). In a few years, between 1768 and 1779, this virtually uncharted world suddenly became the subject of plays, poems, scientific treatises, and political rivalries. It is worth emphasizing how bizarre the desire to make this long, arduous trip would have seemed to Europeans in 1300, and how impossible, both technically and fiscally, launching it would have been. Cook's voyages certainly signal, then, just how much Europe's wealth and aspirations had expanded.

The cultural flourishings of the seventeenth and eighteenth centuries took place in a world much changed since 1300. There were new dynasties. There were also many more people. By 1750, the world's population had doubled from its level in 1300. There was also a much greater volume of long-distance trade, which generated a level of prosperity that would have amazed even the wealthiest dynast 500 years earlier. Yet, despite the unifying aspects of world trade, each culture flourished in its own way and was shaped by local educational institutions and local artistic conventions. Ruling classes disseminated values that drew from their cherished classical texts, crafted their visions of the world on the basis of long-established moral and religious principles, mapped their geographies according to their traditional visions of the universe, and wrote their separate histories. They could still celebrate their achievements in politics, economics, and culture without worrying about threats from within or from without.

Focus Questions CULTURES OF SPLENDOR AND POWER

→ *How did world trade begin changing world cultures?*

→ *How did the Islamic empires foster vibrant and syncretic cultures?*

→ *How did the Chinese and Japanese governments control culture and knowledge?*

→ *What were the major tenets of Enlightenment thought?*

→ *How did hybrid cultures develop in the New World?*

→ *What role did race play in how Europeans viewed others, especially those from Oceania?*

CULTURE IN THE ISLAMIC WORLD

> → *How did the Islamic empires foster vibrant and syncretic cultures?*

For centuries, Muslim elites had put significant resources into cultural development. As the three great "gunpowder empires"—the Ottoman, the Safavid, and the Mughal—extended their control, dominating territories from the Balkans to Bengal, new resources were available for the funding of cultural pursuits. Rulers used the vast agrarian and commercial wealth at their disposal to patronize new schools and building projects, and the elite produced and consumed new books, artworks, and luxury goods. Cultural life was clearly connected to the politics of empire-building, as emperors and elites sought to gain prestige from their patronage of intellectuals and artists.

> *The Ottoman world achieved its cultural unity above all by its system of administrative law, known as* kanun.

Forged under contrasting imperial auspices, the cultural and intellectual life of the Islamic world was organized in three distinct, regional worlds. In place of an earlier Islamic cosmopolitanism, a specific pattern of cultural flourishing prevailed within the boundaries of each empire. Though the Ottomans, the Safavids, and the Mughals were united by a common faith, each developed a relatively autonomous form of Muslim culture.

THE OTTOMAN CULTURAL SYNTHESIS

By the seventeenth century, the Ottoman empire had developed a remarkably rich and syncretic culture. Its blend of ethnic, religious, and linguistic elements, in fact, exceeded in diversity and depth those of previous empires of the Islamic world. The Ottomans' creative and flexible cultural synthesis accommodated both Sufis (mystics who stressed contemplation and ecstasy through poetry, music, and dancing) and ultra-orthodox *ulama* (Islamic jurists who stressed tradition and religious law). It also balanced the interests of military men and administrators with the desires of clerics. Finally, it allowed autonomy to the minority faiths of Christianity and Judaism.

The Ottomans permitted religious diversity, allowing *dhimmis* (followers of religions permitted by law: Armenian Christians, Greek Orthodox Christians, and Jews) to organize themselves into *millets*, minority religious communities, as long as they acknowledged the political superiority of the Sunni and Sufi Muslims. Drawing on Islamic law, the Ottomans allowed the *dhimmis* to worship as they pleased, to send their children to their own religious schools, and to cultivate the arts and sciences as they wished. For this cultural autonomy, the *dhimmis* paid a special tax (*jizya*) that applied to all non-Muslims.

The Ottoman world achieved its cultural unity, above all, by what many regarded as the supreme intellectual achievement of the Ottomans, its system of administrative law, known as *kanun*. As the sultans gained control over diverse cultures and territories, they realized that the *sharia* (Islamic holy law) by itself would not suffice; it was silent on many crucial, secular matters. Moreover, the far-flung Ottoman state needed a comprehensive and well-understood set of laws to bridge differences between the many different social and legal systems that had come under Ottoman rule. Under Mehmed II, conqueror of Constantinople, administrative reform began, and the *devshirme* became the means of recruiting young boys who would be trained to be administrators or military men accountable directly to the sultan. Mehmed's most illustrious successor, Suleiman the Magnificent and the Lawgiver, revised and improved upon Mehmed's work, overseeing the codification of a comprehensive legal code. The code included laws on the rights and duties of

Suleiman the Lawgiver. The most illustrious ruler of the Ottoman empire was Suleiman, who began his reign in 1520 and brought the empire to its military and political height. This miniature painting shows Suleiman giving advice to the crown prince.

subjects, on what clothes they could wear, and on how Muslims were to relate to non-Muslims. The code reconciled many differences between administrative and religious law.

A highly developed educational system was crucial for the religious and intellectual integration of the Ottoman empire. Here, too, the Ottomans displayed a talent for flexibility and showed their tolerance of difference. They encouraged three distinct educational systems that produced three streams of talent—civil and military bureaucrats, *ulama*, and Sufi masters. The Ottoman administrative elite received its training at a hierarchically organized set of schools, culminating in the palace schools at Topkapi. The boys and young men who passed through these institutions staffed the civil and military bureaucracy of the Ottoman state and accepted posts all across the empire. In the religious sphere, an equally elaborate series of schools took students from elementary schools, where they received basic instruction in reading, writing, and numbers, on to higher schools (*madrassa*s), where they learned law, religious sciences, the *Quran*, and the regular sciences. Graduates became *ulama*. Some entered the court system as *qadis* (judges); others became *muftis* (experts in religious law) or teachers. Yet another set of schools (*tekkes*) taught the devotional strategies and the religious knowledge for students to enter Sufi orders and ultimately to become masters of these brotherhoods. Each of these sets of schools created linkages between members of the Ottoman ruling elite and the orthodox religious elite that lasted throughout their lifetimes. The *tekkes* were particularly effective in promoting empire-wide social and religious solidarity and creating frameworks of integration for the Muslim peoples living under Ottoman rule.

The Ottomans attached great prestige to education and scholarship. Scholars claimed that "an hour of learning was worth more than a year of prayer." Schools stressed training in law, language, religious commentary, rhetoric, logic, and theology over the natural and mathematical sciences. Yet, teachers did not ignore the sciences, and Ottoman scholars carried out important work in the fields of astronomy and physics, as well as in the fields of history, geography, and politics.

In the seventeenth and eighteenth centuries, scholars tended to focus on defects and decline in the Ottoman system. Thus, Katip Celebi, author of *The Guide to Practice for the Rectification of Defects* (1643), created an impression—accepted by many later writers—that the empire was sinking into decay. Mustafa Naima, a son and grandson of janissary officers and the most distinguished historian of the period, claimed that there was still hope for the empire. In his book, *The Garden of Hussein, Being the Choicest of News of the East and the West* (1734–1735), Naima wrote that while the Ottoman state had already experienced a stage of youthful optimism, the decline of the civilization could be delayed, if not prevented, if every individual understood his proper place in the universe and social change remained limited.

While scholars argued about whether or not the empire was in decline, a cultural obsession with tulips came to dominate the sultan's court in the 1720s. The Ottoman elite had long been

Islamic Scientists. This fifteenth-century Persian miniature shows a group of Islamic scholars working with sophisticated navigational and astronomical instruments and reflects the importance that the educated classes in the Islamic world attached to observing and recording the regularities in the natural world. Indeed, many of Europe's advances in sailing drew upon knowledge that passed to Europe from the Muslim world.

fascinated with the bold colors and delicate blooms of the tulip. For centuries, the flower served as the symbol of the Ottoman sultans. Mehmed the Conqueror and Suleiman the Lawgiver grew tulips in the most secluded and prestigious courtyards of the Topkapi Palace in Istanbul. Many Ottoman warriors had worn undergarments embroidered with tulips into battle as a means to ensure victory. But the flower's great age was the early eighteenth century, which contemporaries dubbed "the tulip period." At this time, the Ottomans developed the same sort of infatuation that the Dutch had developed a century earlier. Interest in the flower spread from the sultan and his household to the wealthy classes, and estate owners began to specialize in growing tulips. They used tulip designs to decorate tiles and fabrics and to adorn public buildings, and they celebrated the beauty of the flower every spring by holding elaborate tulip festivals.

Fascination with the tulip was one manifestation of a widespread delight in the things of this world, encouraged by Grand Vizier Damat Ibrahim (ruled 1718–1730). As well as restoring order to the empire after the military defeats of the seventeenth century, Ibrahim loosened customary *ulama* controls over the

The Ottomans and the Tulip. From the earliest times, the Ottomans admired the beauty of the tulip. (*Left*) Sultan Mehmed II smelling a tulip, symbol of the Ottoman sultans. (*Right*) The Ottomans used tulip motifs to decorate tiles in homes and mosques and pottery wares, as on the plate shown here. The most skilled pottery makers and painters were those who collected in the Turkish city of Iznik.

social activities of the people, and he sanctioned elite consumption of luxury goods. The working classes, too, were drawn into this celebration of life's pleasures as coffeehouses and taverns became centers of popular entertainment.

Some of the things in which Ottoman subjects delighted were imports from Europe. The interest in European ways was on display at social events, where wealthy men donned trousers and women wore evening gowns. For everyday living, house owners replaced the traditional pillows and divans in their homes with imported European furniture.

Under the patronage of the grand vizier, Ottoman intellectuals also took an interest in works of European science, some of which appeared in Turkish translation for the first time. The most impressive of these efforts occurred when a Hungarian convert to Islam, Ibrahim Muteferika (1674–1745), set up a printing press in Istanbul in 1729 and published works on science, history, and geography. In one of his published essays, printed in 1731, he included sections on geometry, a discussion of the works of Copernicus, Galileo, and Descartes, and a plea to the Ottoman educated classes to learn from Europe. Yet, when the grand vizier was killed in 1730, the *ulama* moved vigorously to close off this promising avenue of contact with Western learning.

SAFAVID CULTURE

The Safavid empire in Persia was not as long-lived as the Ottoman empire, but it was significant in the history of Central Asia for giving the Shiite version of Islam a home base. Previously, there had been Shiite governments, the most powerful being the Fatimid state in medieval Egypt. But once the Mamluks overthrew the Fatimids in the thirteenth century, Shiism became overwhelmingly a religion of opposition and a faith embraced by those seeking to overthrow established rulers. This, of course, made for a great dilemma for Shiite groups; once they came to power they were likely to face opposition from other dissatisfied groups—who also drew on the tenets of Shiism. Rather like Protestant sectarianism, Shiism created a culture of criticism with the potential to undermine dynastic stability.

The Safavids faced just such dilemmas, for they owed their rise to the support of Turkish-speaking tribesmen, the *kizilbash* ("red heads," so-called because of the red color of their turbans), who espoused a populist and charismatic form of Islam. In power, the Safavid shahs endeavored to cultivate the more conservative elements of Iranian society: Persian-speaking landowners and orthodox *ulama*. They turned away from the

Turkish-speaking Islamic brotherhoods with their mystical and Sufi qualities, in spite of the fact that these groups had facilitated their rise to power.

Just as the great achievement of the Ottomans was the ability to blend Sufism and clerical orthodoxy, so the Safavid triumph was to create a political-religious system based on Shiism and loyalty to the Safavid royal family. Also like the Ottomans, the Safavids used well-established institutions like the *madrassas* and brotherhood lodges (*takkiyas*) and the *ulama* to inculcate the new Shiite orthodoxy. Even after the Safavids were swept from power in the eighteenth century, Shiism remained the fundamental religion of the Iranian people.

Under the Safavids' most successful and energetic ruler, Shah Abbas I (ruled 1587–1629), Persia enjoyed a cultural revival stimulated by royal patronage and the great prosperity during his reign. Once Abbas had solidified his power, he sought to make a grand gesture to display his power, wealth, and artistic sensibility. In 1598 he moved the capital of the state to Isfahan and hired elite artists and architects from all corners of Persia (as well as beyond) to design a city that would dwarf even Delhi and Istanbul, the other showplaces of the Islamic world. His centerpiece was the great plaza next to his palace and the royal mosque at the heart of the capital; when completed, the plaza, surrounded by elaborate public and religious buildings, was seven times as large as that of San Marco in Venice.

Other aspects of Safavid intellectual life also reflected a culture dominated by the ideals, aspirations, and wealth of the court and of its landed and commercial classes. Safavid artists perfected the design of the illustrated book, the outstanding example being *The King's Book of Kings*, which contained 250 miniature illustrations. They mastered the technique of three-dimensional representation and were skilled in harmonizing colors. Master weavers continued to produce the silks and carpets long traded throughout the world. Artisans painted tiles in vibrant colors and created tile mosaics that adorned mosques and other buildings. The Safavids also developed an elaborate calligraphy that was the envy of artists throughout the whole of the Islamic world.

POWER AND CULTURE UNDER THE MUGHALS

Like the Safavids and the Ottomans, the Mughals fostered a courtly and prosperous high culture. Because the Mughals, like the Ottomans and unlike the Safavids, ruled over a large non-Muslim population, the Islamic high culture that developed on the Asian subcontinent was a broad and open one. This culture attached high value to works of art and learning, making it possible to overlook the religious identity of non-Muslim artists and to admit them into the world of the arts and learning. Thus, while Islamic traditions were structurally dominant, the Hindus shared with the Muslims the aristocratic culture of learning, music, painting, and architecture; the realm of high culture functioned as an arena in which religious differences could be bridged by aesthetic refinement and philosophical sophistication.

The promise of an open Islamic high culture found its greatest fulfillment under the Mughal emperor Akbar. He remained a devout Muslim and a believer in Islamic monotheism, but he also searched for universal truths outside the strict limits of the *sharia*. In keeping with the tone that Akbar set, Mughal intellectuals cultivated Muslim legacies, particularly Sufi thought, while also studying the Sanskrit classics that they translated into Persian. Akbar valued Hindu literary works, art, and music. During his reign, Muslim piety did not inhibit cultural experimentation.

The most important example of the intellectual mood under Akbar and the most creative thinker of the entire Mughal era was Abulfazl (1551–1602). Acutely aware of the historical accomplishment that the Mughal empire represented, Abulfazl sought to reconcile the traditional Sufi interest in the inner life with the worldly context of a great empire. In his famous composition, the *Akbarnamah* (the Book of Akbar), written between 1587 and 1602, he described Akbar as a philosopher-king, someone who had received kingship as a gift from God because he was a true philosopher and who was born a perfect person in the Sufi sense.

Isfahan Palace Grounds. The Safavid ruler, Abbas I, made the capital city of his empire, Isfahan, a showpiece of elegance and power. The central plaza in Isfahan was laid out on a grand scale and contained gardens and trees of great beauty.

ISLAMIC VIEWS OF THE WORLD

Although maps attempt to give the impression of objectivity and geographic precision, the way in which they arrange the world, the names that they give to locations, the areas that they place in the center or at the peripheries, and the text that accompanies them show the mapmakers' view of the world around them. Thus, in most cultures, official maps located their own major administrative and religious sites at the center of the universe and reflected local elites' speculations about how the world was organized. The two maps below, which are taken from the Islamic world, are interesting in this regard. The famous map of al-Idrisi, dating from the twelfth century, was a standard one of the period. It showed the world as it was known to peoples on the Eurasian land mass at that time and thus featured only three continents—Africa, Asia, and Europe. The second Islamic map, made in Iran around 1700, was unabashedly Islamic, for it offered a grid that measured the distances from any location in the Islamic world to the holy city of Mecca.

Al-Idrisi map, twelfth century

Iranian map, seventeenth century

Though the brilliance of Akbar and Abulfazl was not equaled under later emperors, Mughal culture remained vibrant. François Bernier, a seventeenth-century French traveler to the Mughal empire, wrote admiringly of the broad philosophical interests of Danishmand Khan, a prominent intellectual whom the Emperor Aurangzeb had appointed as the governor of Delhi. According to Bernier, Khan avidly read the works of the French philosophers Gassendi and Descartes and studied Sanskrit treatises to understand different philosophical traditions. Later, under Aurangzeb, intellectuals debated whether metaphysics, astronomy, medicine, mathematics, and ethics were of any use in the practice of Islam.

The Mughal patronage of intellectuals produced a courtly high culture in the fine arts that achieved notable successes in

Akbar Leading Religious Discussion. This miniature painting from 1604 shows Akbar receiving Muslim theologians and Jesuits. The Jesuits (shown in the black robes on the left) hold a page relating, in Persian, the birth of Christ. A lively debate will follow the Jesuits' claims on behalf of Christianity.

who had been—like many other women in the Mughal court—an important political counsel. Designed by an Indian architect of Persian origin, this structure, known as the Taj Mahal, took twenty years and 20,000 workers to build. The forty-two-acre complex included a main gateway, garden, minarets, and a mosque; the mausoleum for Mumtaz Mahal was built of translucent white marble and lay squarely in the middle of the structure, enclosed by four identical facades and crowned by a majestic central dome rising to 240 feet. The stone inlays of different types and hues, organized in geometrical and floral patterns, and *Quranic* verses inscribed in Arabic calligraphy, gave the white marble surface an appearance of delicacy and lightness. Blending Persian and Islamic design with Indian materials and motifs, this poetry in stone represented the most splendid example of Mughal cultural efflorescence and the combining of cultural traditions. Like Shah Abbas's great plaza, the Taj Mahal lent a sense of refined grandeur to this Islamic empire's formidable political, military, and economic power.

Well into the eighteenth century, the Mughal nobility exuded confidence and lived in unrivaled luxury. The presence of foreign scholars and artists only added to the luster of courtly culture, and the elite eagerly consumed foreign luxuries. Traders who carried goods from China or Europe were welcome. Besides, foreign trade brought increasing supplies of silver to the subcontinent, helping to advance the money economy and support the sumptuous urban lifestyles of the nobility. The Mughals were also quick to assimilate European military technology and resources. They hired the Europeans as gunners and sappers in their armies, employed them to forge guns, and bought guns and cannons from them. Their appreciation for European knowledge and technology, however, was limited. Thus, when Thomas Roe, the representative of the English East India Company, presented an edition of Mercator's *Maps of the World* to Emperor Jahangir in 1617, the emperor returned it a fortnight later with the remark that no one could read or understand it. Supremely confident of their own cultural world, the Mughals saw limited use for European knowledge and culture.

The cultural life of the Islamic world was centered in Istanbul, Cairo, Isfahan, and Delhi, and thus drew on intellectual currents that spanned the Eurasian–North African land mass. But from Islam's founding, Muslims had looked eastward, to India and China, not to Europe, for external inspiration. While the crusades had proved that Europeans could be worthy military rivals, most

the seventeenth century. The emperors and great nobles patronized painters who specialized in scenes of court life. These paintings owed much to the Persians, who were famous for their exquisitely detailed and brilliantly colored miniatures. But Indian artists added naturalistic details to these portraits, and modified the horizon to establish a more direct relationship between the viewer and the painted objects. Both of these innovations gave their images a humanistic orientation, bringing the world of art a little closer to the lives and interests of the emperor's subjects.

A similar story can be told of the imperial patronage of architecture. Here, the high point was reached under Shah Jahan

> *Supremely confident of their own cultural world, the Mughals saw limited use for European knowledge and culture.*

(ruled 1628–1658), who poured enormous resources into the enhancement of Agra, the imperial capital, into rebuilding Delhi, and into the erection of an enormous royal palace there. In 1630, Shah Jahan ordered the building in Agra of a magnificent tomb of white marble for his beloved wife, Mumtaz Mahal,

Muslims continued to regard Europeans as rude barbarians, who had little to teach Islamic scholars. Thus, the world histories that Muslim intellectuals had composed in the fourteenth century had said little about Europe, and the Islamic elites in Persia, India, and the Ottoman empire in the seventeenth and

The Taj Mahal. A symbol of Mughal splendor, the Taj Mahal was a mausoleum that was built of white marble. Often described as poetry in stone, it was constructed under Shah Jahan as an homage to his deceased wife, Mumtaz Mahal.

eighteenth centuries continued to view Europeans as less than their cultural and political equals.

CULTURE AND POLITICS IN EAST ASIA

→ *How did the Chinese and Japanese governments control culture and knowledge?*

Like the Ottomans, Safavids, and Mughals, the Chinese did not need to prove to anyone the richness of their scholarly and artistic traditions. China had long been a venerable and renowned center of learning, its emperors and elites serving as patrons to a large number of artists, poets, musicians, scientists, and teachers. But the cultural flourishing that characterized late Ming and early Qing China owed less to imperial leadership than to a robust internal market. Driven by a growing population and extensive mercantile networks, expanding commerce proved instrumental in enhancing the circulation and exchange of ideas as well as goods. As a result, China's cultural sphere underwent significant diversification and expansion, predating similar changes elsewhere. If the dynasty managed to remain at the center of this expanding cultural sphere, it had to exert increased control over new consumers and producers.

In Japan, too, economic prosperity created favorable conditions for cultural dynamism in this period. The looming presence of its giant neighbor across the sea had rendered the Japanese historically amenable to recognizing outside influences. Like the Chinese dynastic government, the ruling Tokugawa Shogunate tried to disseminate a cultural orthodoxy based on Confucian notions of order and hierarchy and to shield the country from potentially subversive ideas. But the forces that worked to undermine the government's control of knowledge in China proved stronger still in Japan. Its decentralized political structure further facilitated the spread of different cultural currents, including European ideas and practices. By the eighteenth

ROYAL ARCHITECTURE IN THE AGE OF SPLENDOR AND POWER

By the seventeenth century, all of the great imperial monarchies of the Eurasian land mass had elaborate architectural structures that projected the power and the values of their individual states. All were ornate and splendid. All were expensive to construct and involved the best craftsmen and artists available to the monarchs. While they seem not to have consciously borrowed from one another, they all arose or were elaborated on in an age when imperial and monarchical power was at a high point. In the case of the Ottoman, Safavid, and Mughal royal structures, the emperors brought in skilled artisans and craftsmen from outside their empires, and, through the work of these skilled people, they indirectly borrowed from the achievements of other cultures. Yet, each reflected unique elements of its own culture as well as the vision of the ruler or rulers who paid for the projects.

We start with the Forbidden City of Beijing, which was the earliest of these sites of royal power and, because of its worldwide reputation, an inspiration to other powerful monarchs and emperors. Beijing became the capital of a unified Chinese empire for the first time under the Mongols in the thirteenth century, although it had enjoyed some prominence in earlier times. Chinggis Khan had razed the old city to the ground, but his Sinocentric successor, Kubilai Khan, restored the city and made it the capital of his empire. He did more than that, however. He rebuilt the city, calling it Khanbaliq, along the lines of early imperial Chinese capitals. Following the classical ideal of a capital city, Khanbaliq was laid out on strict north-south and east-west axes. It was surrounded by high walls, and the inner part of the city housed the emperor and his court. The Ming successors, who overthrew the Mongols, at first made Nanjing their capital, but the Yongle Emperor reinstated Beijing as the imperial capital. The inner areas of the city, known as the Imperial City and the Forbidden City, were aligned on a firm north-south axis and were thought to be the very center of the Chinese state and indeed of the whole universe. Here, government took place, and it was to here that those who sought the favor of the emperor journeyed. Indeed, only those who had business with the state were permitted to enter the imperial domain. They did so, bowing and scraping ("kowtowing"), as indications of the great respect they felt for the awesome power of the emperor. As befit a powerful figure, the ruler was expected to stay within the confines of the imperial quarters (although Qing emperors—who succeeded the Ming in the seventeenth century—did travel with more regularity) and

had to rely on envoys and chief ministers for information about the rest of his kingdom and the outside world. So effective were these arrangements that the Qing rulers retained Beijing as their capital and, despite changes and renovations, the Qing kept the Ming structures mostly in place.

The center of Safavid power in the seventeenth century was the great plaza at Isfahan, the inspiration of Shah Abbas, who ruled from 1587 to 1629. It reflected Shah Abbas's notion that trade, government, and religion should be brought together under the authority of the supreme political leader. A great public mosque, called the Shah Abbas Mosque, dominated one end of the plaza, which measured 1,667 feet by 517 feet. At the other end were the trading stalls and markets, which made Iran wealthy. On one side of the rectangular mosque were the offices of the government, and on the other side was an exquisite mosque, called the Mosque of Shaykh Lutfollah, set aside for the personal use of the shah. Many of Shah Abbas's most proficient craftsmen came from India and were familiar with the architecture of the Mughal empire.

The Palace of Versailles, which Louis XIV built in the 1660s, has many similarities with the Isfahan plaza, although the French builders had no knowledge of Isfahan. Here, too, the great royal palace opens outward onto a large courtyard. The buildings adjoining the central palace housed the great notables and clergy, whom the French monarchs wanted to keep an eye on.

The Topkapi Palace was in Istanbul, the capital of the Ottoman empire. Topkapi began to take shape in 1458 under Mehmed II and was steadily added to over the years. As described in detail in Chapter 2, it projected royal authority in much the same way as the Forbidden City emphasized the power of the Chinese emperors. Here, too, the governing officials worked enclosed within massive walls, and the monarchs rarely went outside their inner domain. By isolating the rulers from the rest of society the Ottomans and the Chinese made even more awesome the power of their monarchs.

Yet another advocate of royal architecture was the Mughal emperor, Shah Jahan, who ruled from 1628 until 1658. He is best known for his peacock throne; for the Taj Mahal, which he built as a magnificent tomb for his wife, Mumtaz Mahal; and for his building program for the state's capital at Delhi.

century, in struggling to define its own identity through these different contending currents, the cultural scene in Japan was rather more lively, open, and varied than its counterpart in China.

CHINA: THE CHALLENGE OF EXPANSION AND DIVERSITY

TRANSMISSION OF IDEAS In the sixteenth and seventeenth centuries, China witnessed significant expansion in both the publication and circulation of books and ideas. The phenomenon had less to do with technological innovations—both woodblock and moveable type printing had been known in China for centuries—than with the gradual decentralization of cultural production. At the outset, the state provided the initiative for book production—sponsoring and printing

> *By the late Ming era, a burgeoning commercial publishing sector had emerged, catering to the diverse needs of the educated elites and the growing urban population.*

particular editions of Confucian texts—but as the years passed, the increasing commercialization of the economy eroded governmental controls.

Schools acquired books not officially sanctioned by the state as early as the fifteenth century. As an observer proudly remarked when a school in Shanghai built a library in 1484, its collection included "the six classics, the imperially produced books issued by the Ming court, plus the philosophers of the hundred schools and the histories, there isn't a title they don't have!" The holdings, in other words, clearly exceeded the corpus of official publications. Although local magistrates still backed library expansion, seeing this as part of a government effort to control the production of knowledge, the state could not dictate the way in which all books were produced and consumed. While officials could and did clamp down on unorthodox texts, the empire had no centralized system of censorship, and many unauthorized opinions circulated freely.

By the late Ming era, a burgeoning commercial publishing sector had emerged, catering to the diverse social, cultural, and religious needs of the educated elites and the growing urban population. European visitors were struck by the vast collections of printed materials housed in Chinese libraries, describing them as "magnificently built" and "finely adorn'd." In fact, the latter part of the Ming was an age of collections of other sorts as well. Many members of the elite in this increasingly affluent society cultivated a passion for acquiring physical objects for display as a sign of their status, refinement, and taste. Connoisseurship of all the arts reached unprecedented levels. Consumers could build their collections by purchasing artworks from multiple sources, from roadside peddlers to monasteries to gentlemen dealers whose proclaimed love of art masked the commercial orientation of their passions.

Perhaps more importantly, books and other luxury goods were now more affordable. A low-quality commentary on the Confucian classics—the Four Books—published in Nanjing in 1615 cost only half a tael of silver. Even a low-level private tutor could earn more than 40 taels from tuition in a year. And, increasingly, publishers offered diverse wares: readers could purchase guidebooks for patrons of the arts, travelers, or merchants; handbooks for those performing rituals; manuals on how to choose dates for ceremonies or on how to write proper letters. Other book choices included almanacs, encyclopedias, morality books, and medical manuals. Demand was especially high for study aids for the civil service examination. By the late fifteenth century, examinees were required to submit their answers in the so-called "eight-legged" style, a highly structured form of essay in eight parts. Model essays, written either by examiners or successful candidates, flooded the market. In 1595, a scandal broke out in Beijing as the second-place graduate at the metropolitan examination reproduced verbatim a series of model essays published by commercial printers. Just over twenty years later, the top graduate was found to have plagiarized a winning essay submitted years earlier. Ironically, then, the increased circulation of knowledge led critics to bemoan a decline in real learning; instead of mastering the classics, they charged, the candidates were simply memorizing the work of others.

Chinese Civil Service Exam. Lining the sides of this Chinese examination compound were cells in which the candidates would sit for the examination. Other than three long boards—the highest served as a shelf, the middle one as a desk, and the lowest as a seat, the cell had neither furniture nor a door. Indeed, the cells were little more than spaces partitioned on three sides by brick walls and covered by a roof; the floors were packed dirt. Generations of candidates spent three days and two nights in succession in these cells as they strove to enter officialdom.

Examination hopefuls were not the only beneficiaries of the booming book trade. Elite women also took advantage of widening access to China's literary culture. As readers, writers, and editors, educated women now assumed a limited but visible presence in what was hitherto an exclusively male domain. Anthologies of poetry produced by women were particularly popular. Besides producing for the market, some collected works of individual women were issued by their families for limited circulation to celebrate the refinement of the family. Men of letters were quick to recognize the market potential of women's writings; some also saw the less regularized style of women—who usually acquired their skills through family channels rather than through state-sponsored schools—as a means to challenge what was perceived as the stifling stylistic conformity of the sixteenth century. The promotion of new styles opened up opportunities for women writers. On rare occasions, women even served as publishers themselves.

> *Elite women also took advantage of widening access to China's literary culture.*

POPULAR CULTURE AND RELIGION Important as the development of the book trade was, its impact on the majority of men and women in late Ming China was indirect. To those excluded from the literary culture because they could not read or could not read well, the transmission of cultural norms and values occurred through oral communication, ritual performance, and daily practices. The Ming government tried to control these channels, too. It appointed village elders as guardians of local society and instituted a system of "village compacts" to ensure communal social responsibility for proper conduct and observation of the laws.

Still, the everyday life of rural and small-town dwellers existed mostly outside these official networks. Apart from toiling in the field, the villagers' social milieu was typically shaped by a variety of popular cultural and religious practices. Most villages had shrines honoring the guardian spirits of the locality as well as Buddhist and Daoist temples, not all of which were officially approved.

Villagers often undertook group pilgrimages to religious sites. They might attend periodic markets in adjacent towns, which during good times would be filled with restaurants, brothels, and other venues of entertainment. Otherwise, their links to the outside world were forged by gathering news and gossip in the teahouses or marketplaces, listening to the tales of itinerant storytellers and traveling monks, or by watching performances by touring theater groups on portable stages or in the courtyards of temples. Despite official vigilance, the open-ended nature of such a process of cultural transmission meant that village audiences were quite capable of appropriating and reinterpreting official norms and values to serve their own purposes and to challenge the dictates of the government.

The popular religions of the late Ming period were syncretic in nature, and religious practices remained diffused and decen-tralized. Sectarian lines were usually of minimal significance; at the grassroots level there was often little distinction between Buddhist, Daoist, or local cults. Thus, China avoided the sectarian or religious warfare of post-Reformation Europe. This was largely because the Chinese believed in cosmic unity and, although they recognized and venerated spiritual forces, they did not consider any of them a Supreme Being who favored one faction over another. It was the emperor, rather than any religious group, who was supposed to have the Mandate of Heaven. The enforcement of orthodox norms and values and the suppression of popular resistance to them was more a matter of political than of religious control. And unless sects posed an obvious threat, the emperor had no real reason to regulate

Jesuit Missionary. Shown in the garb of a Qing official, Father Johann Adam Schall von Bell was in Beijing when the Ming fell in 1644. Recognizing his scientific expertise, the new Qing government appointed him the director of the Imperial Bureau of Astronomy. Schall von Bell was close to the young Shunzhi Emperor, who called the Jesuit "Grandpa" and regularly discussed religion and politics with the missionary.

their spiritual practices. This situation made for, in effect, a unique kind of religious tolerance.

TECHNOLOGY AND CARTOGRAPHY Belief in cosmic unity did not prevent members of the Chinese elite from devising technologies to master and control nature's operations in this world, however. China was well known for its invention of the magnetic compass, gunpowder, and the printing press. Chinese technicians had mastered iron casting and produced mechanical clocks centuries before Europeans managed such feats. Chinese astronomers were historically the most accurate observers of celestial phenomena in the pre-modern period, and they had compiled records of eclipses, comets, novae, and meteors. Their interest in astronomy and calendrical science was driven, in part, by the needs of the emperor—it was his job as the Son of Heaven, and thus mediator between heaven and earth, to determine the dates for the beginning of the agrarian seasons, festivities, mourning periods, and judicial assizes. The Chinese believed that the very stability of the empire depended on correct calculation of these dates. Thus, even by modern standards, the Chinese were quite precise.

European missionaries and traders who arrived in China were greatly impressed by Chinese technological expertise, eloquence, and artistic refinement. Nonetheless, convinced of the

CHINESE VIEWS OF THE WORLD

The Chinese developed cartographical skills at an early stage in their history. A third-century map, no longer extant, was designed to enable the emperors to "comprehend the four corners of the world without ever having to leave their imperial quarters." The Huayi tu *map from 1136 depicted the whole world on stone stele and included 500 place names and textual information on foreign lands. The Jesuit missionary Matteo Ricci modified his original map of the world in response to Chinese concerns and placed China more in the center. Chinese maps devoted more attention to textual explanations that carried moral and political messages than to locating places. One such map is a Chinese wheel map, which is from the 1760s and is full of textual explanations.*

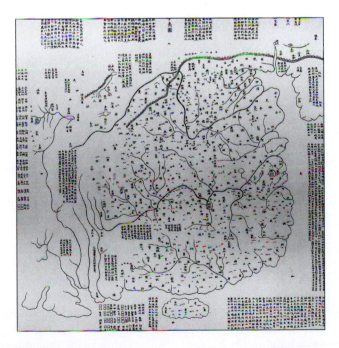

The *Huayi tu* map, 1136

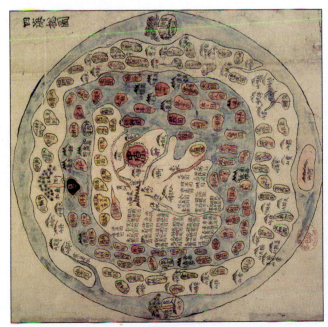

Chinese wheel map, 1760s

superiority of their sciences, Christian missionaries sought to impress the Chinese with their knowledge in areas such as astronomy and cartography. Possessing sophisticated sciences of their own, the Chinese were selective in their appropriation of these novel European practices. To be sure, members of the Jesuit order served in the astronomy bureau within the imperial bureaucracy. In the early eighteenth century, they also undertook a series of monumental surveys of the Qing empire for the emperor. Taken as a whole, however, the cultural impact of the Europeans in China in this period was decidedly limited.

Nowhere was this more evident than in the realm of cartography. Here, the Chinese demonstrated most clearly their understanding of the world. Significantly, Chinese maps were meant to encompass elements of history, literature, and art, not simply to offer technical detail. It was not that the necessary "scientific" techniques were lacking; a map made as early as 1136 reveals that Chinese cartographers were fully capable of producing maps drawn to scale. Yet, operating within a cultural context in which the written text was often privileged over visual and other forms of representation, Chinese elites did not always treat geometric and mathematical precision as the principal objective of cartography. Rather, these maps offered vivid testimony to the worldview of the Chinese elites. The realm of the Chinese emperor, as the ruler of "all under Heaven," typically occupied the very center of the map surrounded by foreign countries. As such, the physical scale of China and the actual size and distances to other lands were generally distorted. Still, some of the maps do manage to cover a vast expanse of territory. One fourteenth-century map includes an area stretching from Japan to the Atlantic, encompassing Europe and Africa.

While Europeans might understand resistance to Christianization—they had, after all, long experience with heretics, infidels, and sectarian intransigence at home—they were puzzled by the Chinese resistance to the adoption of European science. In 1583, the Jesuit missionary Matteo Ricci brought European maps to China, hoping to impress the local elite with European learning. Ricci challenged the conventional wisdom of the Chinese elites, who held that the world was flat. His maps demonstrated the sphericity of the earth—and that China was just one country among many other similar ones. Chinese critics complained that he treated the Ming empire as just "a small unimportant country." As a concession, Ricci actually modified his projection and placed China closer to the center of the maps. He also followed the practice of Chinese cartographers in providing additional textual information. Still, the long-term impact of Ricci's maps was negligible. The makers of "Complete Maps of All under Heaven," who provided Qing China's images of the world until the mid-nineteenth century, did not consider sphericity of the earth or precise mathematical scale particularly important. The European regime of spatial ordering, as represented through its cartography, was rejected as mostly irrelevant.

In China, prior to the nineteenth century, knowledge regarding foreign lands, despite a long history of contacts, remained rather partial. Like many other civilizations, the Chinese empire cultivated an image of its own superiority and tended to see others through its own prism. From antiquity onward, Chinese elites glorified their own "white" complexions against the dark skin of the peasants, the black, wavy-haired "devils" of Southeast Asia, and the "ash-white" pallor of the Europeans. Chinese writers often identified groups of people as oddities, to be scrutinized with a mixture of curiosity and revulsion. A Ming geographical publication, for example, portrayed the Portuguese as "seven feet tall, having eyes like a cat, a mouth like an oriole, an ash-white face, thick and curly beards like black gauze, and almost red hair." In a ten-volume compendium put together as late as the mid-eighteenth century, the authors vaguely described the "Great Western Ocean Country" as somewhere in the Atlantic region. They did not distinguish European countries from their Asian counterparts. They confused France with the Portugal known during Ming times, and they characterized England and Sweden as dependencies of Holland. During this period of cultural flourishing, in short, the Qing empire did not yet feel any compelling reason to revise its view of the world.

> *Taken as a whole, the cultural impact of the Europeans in China in this period was decidedly limited.*

CULTURAL IDENTITY AND TOKUGAWA JAPAN

Chinese cultural influence had long crossed the Sea of Japan. But during the Tokugawa Shogunate, there was also a renewed interest in a competing cultural model from Europe. Japanese interest in Europe grew via the Dutch presence in Japan and more limited contacts with Russians. In addition to such foreign influences, however, there was also a surge in "native learning," or the study of Japanese traditions and culture in the late seventeenth and especially eighteenth centuries. Thus, Tokugawa Japan found itself engaged in a three-cornered conversation among time-honored Chinese ways (transmitted via Korea), distinctly Japanese traditions, and European teachings. Increased trade, new prosperity in the land, and a long period of domestic and international peace were, in turn, accompanied by a remarkable cultural flowering that provided the background for debates over competing cultural models.

Until the sixteenth and seventeenth centuries, cultural patronage remained the preserve of the imperial court in Kyoto (which did not rule), the hereditary shogunate, religious insti-

Artist and Geisha at Tea. The erotic, luxuriant atmosphere of Japan's urban pleasure quarters was captured in a new art form, the *ukiyo-e*, or "pictures from a floating world." In this image set in Tokyo's celebrated Yoshiwara district, several geisha flutter about a male artist.

tutions, and the upper class, about 5 percent of the population. Samurai (former warriors turned bureaucrats) and daimyo (the regional lords) favored a masked theater, called Nō, and an elegant ritual for making tea and engaging in contemplation. In their gardens, the lords built teahouses with stages for Nō drama. There arose hereditary schools of actors, tea masters, and cultivated flower arrangers. The upper classes also used the services of commoner-painters, who decorated tea utensils and other articles made of lacquer (dried sap of the sumac tree), and painted the brilliant interiors and standing screens in grand stone castles. Some upper-class men did their own painting, called "literati" painting, which was supposed to convey philosophical thoughts. Calligraphy was also proof of cultivation.

Alongside this elegant elite culture of theater and stylized painting arose a new, rougher urban culture, one that was patronized by artisans and especially merchants. Urban dwellers, consisting of 10 percent of the population by 1800, delighted in an array of popular entertainment; consumers could purchase works of fiction and colorful prints made from carved wood blocks—also used to make books—that were often risqué. A new class of female entertainers appeared who were known as geisha because they were artistically skilled (*gei*) in the three-stringed instrument (*shamisen*), storytelling, and performing, though some were also prostitutes. Geisha could be found in officially approved pleasure quarters of the big cities, which were famous for their geisha houses, public baths, brothels, and theaters. *Kabuki*, a type of theater that combined song, dance, and skillful staging to dramatize conflicts between duty and passion, became a wildly popular diversion and art form characterized by bravura acting, brilliant makeup, and sumptuous costumes.

Kabuki **Theater.** *Kabuki* originated among dance troops in the environs of temples and shrines in Kyoto in the late sixteenth and early seventeenth centuries. The characters used to denote *kabuki* mean "song, dance, and skill," though some scholars believe the term derives from a related word (*kabuku*) meaning eccentric, rakish, deviant, outlandish, or erotic. As *kabuki* quickly spread to the urban centers of Japan, the theater designs enabled the actors to enter and exit from many directions and to step out into the audience, lending the skillful, raucous shows great intimacy.

In 1629, the shogunate, concerned for public order, banned female actors, and so men began to play women's roles. These male actors sometimes maintained their impersonations of females offstage, and inspired trends in fashion for urban women.

Much Japanese popular entertainment chronicled the world of the common people rather than politics or high society. The pleasure-oriented culture of urbanites was known as "the floating world" (*ukiyo*), and the woodblock prints depicting it as *ukiyo-e* (*e* meaning picture). Here, the normal order of society was temporarily turned upside down. The wealth of the socially low-ranked merchant trumped the official highly ranked samurai. Those who were otherwise looked down upon—actors, musicians, courtesans, and rakes—became idols and objects of dedicated imitation. To a degree, upper-class samurai partook of this "lower" culture. But to enter the pleasure quarters, samurai had to leave behind their swords, a prime mark of rank, since commoners were not allowed to carry such weapons.

Literacy in Japan approached a remarkable one-third of the population (it was far higher for men). The most popular novels sold 10,000 to 12,000 copies. In the late eighteenth century, Edo had some sixty booksellers and also had hundreds of book lenders, who provided an alternative to the relatively high cost of buying books, and thereby spread them to a wider public. By the late eighteenth century, as books proliferated and some criticized the government, officials made arrests and sought to exercise control over publications.

In the realm of higher culture, China, the largest and wealthiest of Japan's neighbors, loomed large in the Tokugawa world. Japanese scholars wrote imperial histories of Japan in the Chinese style. Chinese law codes and other books attracted a significant readership, and many Japanese wrote exclusively in Chinese. Some Japanese traveled south to Nagasaki just to meet Zen Buddhist masters and Chinese residents of cosmopolitan Nagasaki. Some Chinese monks were even allowed to found monasteries outside Nagasaki and to travel to Kyoto and occasionally to Edo to give lectures and construct temples.

Chinese Confucianism offered the Tokugawa Shogunate a set of politically useful teachings. Initially, Zen Buddhists and monks had nurtured the study of Confucian teachings, but in the seventeenth century, some devotees of Confucianism, encouraged by the political authorities, brought Buddhism outside monasteries and developed the doctrines into a lay school of thought. After 1640, all Japanese were required to register at a Buddhist temple. Buddhist temples grew in number, but they did not displace the indigenous Japanese practice of ancestor veneration and worshipping gods in nature, later called Shintō (the way of the gods), which boasted an extensive network of shrines throughout the country. Japanese Confucianism stipulated that the government existed to facilitate the attainment of a moral order among men. A text called *The Greater Learning for Women* elaborated rules of female subservience to parents, parents-in-law, husbands, and, if widowed, to sons. By the early eighteenth century, neo-Confucian teachings of filial piety and loyalty to superiors had become the de facto official credo of the state. The new philosophy legitimated the social hierarchy and the absolutism of the political order, but it also instructed the shogun and the upper class to provide "benevolent administration" (*jinsei*) for the people's benefit.

> *Chinese intellectual authority in Japan was competing with a new native learning and by the late seventeenth century with other imported sources of knowledge.*

In partial reaction to the official credo that adapted Chinese traditions to Japanese circumstances, but also out of a desire to venerate the greatness of Japan, some creative Japanese thinkers promoted nativist intellectual traditions drawn from Japan's past. After 1728, for example, Kada Azumamaro (1668–1736), a Shintō priest, initiated a movement stressing "native learning" and the celebration of Japanese texts. Subsequent proponents of native learning, such as Motoori Norinaga (1730–1801), emphasized Japanese uniqueness, helped codify the elements of a Japanese religious and cultural tradition, and denounced Confucianism and Buddhism as foreign contaminants from a country of disorder and deceit. A few also looked to the nonruling, but uninterrupted imperial line in Kyoto, for validation of Japan's intellectual lineage and cultural superiority. While some who called for the revival of rule by the dormant Japanese emperor were arrested, others went on to develop Japanese poetry, one of the art forms popular with both upper and lower social groups.

Not only did Chinese intellectual authority in Japan have to compete with a new native learning, but by the late seventeenth century, Japan was also tapping other imported sources of knowledge. In East Asia in the late seventeenth century, Portuguese was the lingua franca and even the Dutch used it in communicating with the Japanese. By 1670, however, there was a guild of Japanese interpreters in Nagasaki who could speak and read Dutch and who accompanied Dutch merchants on trips to Edo. European knowledge also spread to high circles in Edo in 1709. In 1720, the shogunate lifted its ban on foreign books. Thereafter, European ideas, called "Dutch learning," circulated more openly. Scientific, geographical, and medical texts, such as *The New Book of Dissection*, were translated into Japanese and in some cases displaced Chinese texts, particularly for the calculation of important celestial phenomena. A Japanese-Dutch dictionary appeared in 1745, and the first official school of Dutch learning followed. Students of Dutch or European teachings remained a limited, if enthusiastic segment of Japanese society, but the demand for translations rose appreciably.

One of the strong proponents of a European orientation was Honda Toshiaki (1744–1821), who traveled to Ezo to examine

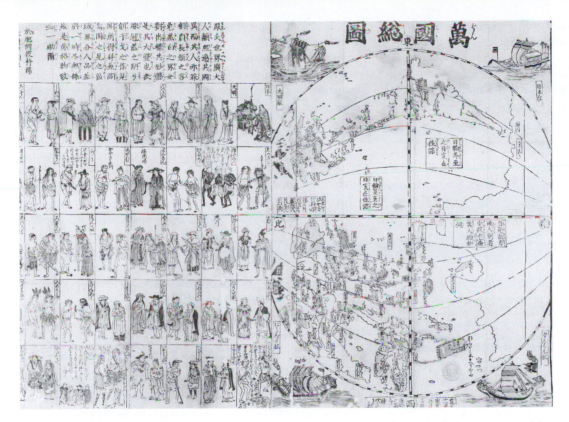

Japanese Map of the World. Japanese maps underwent a shift in connection with their encounters with the Dutch. Here, in a map dated 1671, much information is incorporated about distant lands, both cartographically on the globe and pictorially, to the left, in two-person images representing various peoples of the world in their purported typical costumes.

the frontier, studied European texts, and set his thoughts down in late-eighteenth-century unpublished manuscripts. Toshiaki believed that Japan should learn about and adapt European advances in science, especially geography and astronomy, which helped in ocean trade. He also praised European economic progress, while extolling the vastness and might of Japan's new neighbor to the north, the Russian empire. For Toshiaki, the greatness of Japan depended on its ability to modernize. Nonetheless, despite his admiration for European advances, Toshiaki did not reject Confucianism. Nor did he repudiate Japan's system of social ranks, based on Confucianism, and he showed Confucian contempt for unethical businessmen. What comes across most clearly in his celebrations of European prowess are his pragmatism about adaptation and his aspirations for Japan.

Japanese deliberations about what and how to borrow from the Europeans and the Chinese illustrate the vast changes that the world had undergone since 1300. If, in that era, products and ideas did travel, they usually did not travel very far, or make significant inroads into local cultural practices. By the eighteenth century, new networks of exchange and communication and new prosperity made the integration of foreign ideas into local cultures feasible and sometimes desirable. The Japanese

were especially eager to choose among useful new ideas and practices and often to transform them. This selective openness to the ideas of foreigners stemmed from Japan's long historical relationship to outside influences, particularly its receptivity to Chinese thought and institutions. The Japanese did not consider embracing learning from overseas as a mark of inferiority or subordination, particularly when they knew that they could put new ideas to good use at home. This was not the case for the great Asian land-based empires, which were eager lenders but hesitant borrowers.

THE ENLIGHTENMENT IN EUROPE

→ *What were the major tenets of Enlightenment thought?*

An extraordinary cultural flourishing, often defined in intellectual terms as the Enlightenment but in fact a much broader series of developments, took place in Europe in the seventeenth and eighteenth centuries. Unlike previous episodes in the history of thought, the individuals who championed the new ideas of the Enlightenment sought not simply to develop these ideas but to diffuse them as widely as possible. They wanted, in effect, to change people's worldviews and political institutions. Crucial for the success of their endeavor were widening patronage networks that extended beyond the traditional ecclesiastical and monarchical supporters of arts and sciences to include the new men and women of wealth, the rising business classes. Equally important was an expansion in the methods and networks of communication that now included cafes and intellectual salons, newspapers, extensive exchanges of correspondence, public theaters, and book publishing. The men and women of letters of this period, although their ideas frequently clashed, nonetheless shared a desire to "spread light" and to change the way their societies were governed.

A new sense of culture emerged in Europe as these literate, middle-class men and women gained confidence in their own worthiness to create culture and rule states.

The cultural dynamism of the Enlightenment was more ambitious and expansive than earlier learning had been. To begin with, Enlightenment thinkers aspired to universal and objective knowledge, to the creation of forms of knowledge that would not be dependent on the knower's religion, political views, class, or gender. Their quest for knowledge knew no territorial boundaries, and the seekers after information gathered it to formulate natural laws, which they presumed applied everywhere and to all peoples. Most of these thinkers were quite unaware of the extent to which their "objective" knowledge was colored by European, upper-class male perspectives.

ORIGINS OF THE ENLIGHTENMENT

Europe's remarkable diffusion of ideas is inconceivable without the increasing contacts between Europeans and the wider world that had occurred in previous centuries. In turn, it greatly affected the further development of Europe's relations with other lands. From the fourteenth century onward, Europeans had been consumers of the cultural goods of other peoples. From the trapping methods of Native Americans to the crop cultivation techniques of African slaves, from Chinese porcelain to New World tobacco and chocolate, Europe in the seventeenth and eighteenth centuries continued to be shaped by its contact with others. Yet, European intellectuals became more and more critical of other cultures—and more confident that their culture was unique and superior and that it should be the standard against which others were judged.

Well into the seventeenth century, European culture continued to be defined by two major institutions: the Catholic Church (unchallenged until the Protestant Reformation of the

sixteenth century) and the dynastic court system. But by the late seventeenth century, the experiences of traveling, conquering, and trading with a vastly increased number of the world's peoples had begun to affect European culture. Increased prosperity, derived from trade and conquest, led to new curiosity about other cultures and to new confidence in European commercial practices and secular culture. But prosperity also created new cultural forms and social tensions at home. Though dynastic courts and established churches continued to dominate cultural production in most states, by about 1750 a whole new class of nonaristocrats (including doctors, lawyers, entrepreneurs, and journalists) had begun to participate in the production and consumption of the arts and sciences. A new sense of culture emerged as this new group of literate, middle-class men and women gained confidence in their own worthiness—to create art, to write books, to observe the world accurately, and perhaps even to rule their states.

Europe's cultural outpouring was a product both of new wealth and of persistent social, religious, and political tensions. After the Reformation, Europeans were, more than ever, divided into hostile states. While the sixteenth century brought new prosperity, the seventeenth century produced grand-scale disasters: civil and religious wars, dynastic conflicts, plague, and famine. Seventeenth-century crises and conflicts left behind a host of opponents to established religious and political authorities. The opponents ranged from downwardly mobile aristocrats, to heavily taxed peasants, to dissenting minorities. This disenchantment with the old order in turn helped to create a longing for impersonal, or "objective" knowledge of the world. The seventeenth century's upheavals also allowed for great increases in private wealth, particularly in the newly successful commercial nations of Britain, France, and the Netherlands. Intellectuals could find private patrons among these wealthy individuals. No longer beholden to the king for a livelihood, these intellectuals could challenge social and political hierarchies. A few even displayed a keen interest in foreign learning, although familiarity with other cultures did not supplant a commitment to their own well-established traditions. The combination of a new longing for useful, objective knowledge and the proliferation of cultural centers created the conditions for a distinctive new relationship between creators of culture and wielders of power.

The search for objective knowledge is most apparent in the post-Reformation flourishing of natural science. Before the Reformation, the church had opposed new scientific findings that threatened basic assumptions about the earth, God, and the church itself. Slowly, however, as the role of the church was questioned during the Reformation, so too was there a questioning of old scientific certitudes. New scientific visions of men

EUROPEAN VIEWS OF THE WORLD

As the Europeans became world travelers and traders, they needed accurate information on places and distances that they had reached so that they could get home as well as return to these sites. This meant forsaking their own tradition of placing Jerusalem at the world's core. Europe's first printed map to show the New World, the Waldseemüller map, was produced in 1507 and portrayed the Americas as a long and narrow strip of land, its unexplored land mass dwarfed by Asia and Africa. By the mid-seventeenth century, maps were seemingly more objective, yet European maps invariably grouped the rest of the world around the European countries. Moreover, Europeans favored maps, like the popular Mercator projection of 1569, which by giving more space to the poles than to lands at the equator made the lands in the Northern Hemisphere, including Europe, appear much larger than those around the equator. Had they had a map, like the Peterson projection, only developed much later, in which the land masses of the world were in correct geographical proportion to one another, Europe would have seemed quite small. Moreover, it was still at the discretion of the mapmaker as to which territories would be at the center of the map and which on the edges. Maps made in Europe invariably grouped the rest of the world around the European countries.

Waldseemüller map, 1507

Mercator projection, 1569

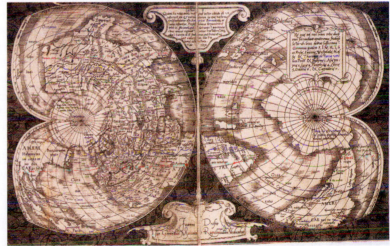

like the astronomer Galileo Galilei (1564–1642) and the anatomist Andreas Vesalius (1514–1564) began to catch on. Galileo's findings in mathematics, physics, and astronomy contradicted age-old assumptions. His belief that the earth revolved around the sun led to his publication of *Dialogue on the Two Chief Systems of the World* (1632) and to his subsequent trial (1633) for heresy. Vesalius's studies based on dissecting human cadavers overturned long-held beliefs about human anatomy. For a small, but influential group of these new scientists, theories were to be built on experiment and observation; the skepticism of the philosopher Sir Francis Bacon (1561–1626) became their unwritten code of conduct. According to Bacon, in such works as *The Advancement of Learning* (1605) and the *Novum Organum* (1620), the duty of the scientist was to observe and to test nature himself following the inductive method. By means of carefully controlled, empirical testing, Bacon believed that modern man could gradually comprehend the general principles of nature's manifold operations and thus bend nature to man's will. Experiments, Bacon believed, should be conducted, samples collected, variables isolated; traditional authorities should not be trusted! Of course, Bacon was chiefly concerned that classical and medieval authorities be distrusted, but the principle would be the same when European scientists confronted traditional knowledge in the rest of the world. Similarly, René Descartes (1596–1650) discarded ancient traditions in mathematics, and in such works as his *Discourse on Method* (1637), he stressed the importance of logic and rational thought. Confident of their own calculations, scientists like Isaac Newton (1642–1727) defined what they believed were the universal laws that applied to all matter and motion, and disparaged all older conceptions of nature—from Aristotelian ideas to folkloric and foreign ones—as absurd and obsolete. Thus, in his *Principia Mathematica* (1687), Newton set forth the laws of motion, including the famous law of gravitation, which explained falling bodies on earth and planetary motion.

Yet, it is no longer fashionable to speak about the changing views of sixteenth- and seventeenth-century Europeans regarding nature and the universe as a scientific revolution. European thinking about nature and the universe did not change overnight. Only gradually and fitfully did a group of European thinkers come to see the natural world as operating according to inviolable laws that experimenters could fathom. And only over a lengthy period of time did wealthy individuals and states see practical advantages in these studies and begin to set up research institutions and technical training schools, such as schools of engineering and war colleges. Indeed, scientific inquiry did not establish itself as the reigning mode of inquiry until the late nineteenth century.

BASES OF THE NEW SCIENCE

The new science was produced essentially by the confluence of two factors: Europeans' post-Renaissance fascination with the Greek and Roman classics, and their expanding commerce with and knowledge of the non-European world. The classics provided the impulse to describe nature's varieties and, at the same time, to seek its regularities. Expanding commerce brought wealth with which European merchants and government officials supported scientific inquiry, but it also opened Europe up to the wider non-European world of plants, animals, peoples, and historical experiences. And, once again, intra-European competition played a role in the development of the new science. Innovative thinkers who might have been executed for heresy in a culturally unified realm here managed to find the refuge, and often the patronage, that they required to develop iconoclastic ideas.

Although the new sciences did not immediately appeal to many Europeans, by the late seventeenth century monarchs and oligarchs, particularly in Protestant countries, had developed a new interest in science's discoveries, and many established royal academies of science to encourage local endeavors. This patronage, of course, was not purely disinterested; in incorporating the British Royal Society in 1662, for example, Charles II hoped to show not only that the crown backed scientific progress but also that England's great minds backed the crown. Similar reasoning was shown in the founding of the French Royal Academy of Sciences in 1666. Support for artistic monuments had a similar political function. In France, Louis XIV's erection of the fabulously expensive new palace complex at Versailles beginning in 1661 was meant not only to show that he had taste but also that he had power. The nobility, he meant to say, needed to look to him for both cultural and political guidance.

Gradually, science began to expand beyond court circles around 1700. By the early eighteenth century, the new science was becoming popular in elite circles; the upper-crust Marquise de Châtelet (1706–1749) built a scientific laboratory in her home and translated Newton's *Principia* into French. Groups of well-to-do landowners formed societies, like the Society for the Improvement of Knowledge in Agriculture—founded in Edinburgh in 1723—to discuss the latest methods of successful animal breeding. Military schools increasingly stressed engineering methods and thus produced graduates with refined technical skills. By about 1750, even artisans and journalists, especially in England, could be found applying Newtonian mechanics to their practical problems and inventions. Moreover, many Europeans now believed that useful knowledge came from collecting data and organizing it into universally valid systems, rather than from revered classical texts. As we will see in the next chapter, Europe's industrial revolution owed much to this increasingly broad familiarity with mechanics and the new mathematics—just as new kinds of political and social criticism also owed much to the new science's defiance of received wisdom.

By no means, however, was the scientific worldview the only one held by Europeans; most still understood their relationships with God, nature, and fellow humans by reference to Christian doctrines on the one hand and local customs on the other.

Although literacy was increasing, especially in northern Europe, it was by no means universal; schools remained elite, male institutions. All governments employed censors, and punished, often severely, radical thinkers; peasants still suffered under arbitrary systems of taxation, and judicial regimes had hardly improved since medieval times. It certainly cannot be said that science and rationality pervaded all spheres of European life by 1700. Indeed, if it had been so, there would have been no need for the movement we now call the Enlightenment.

ENLIGHTENMENT THINKERS

Enlightenment thinkers like Voltaire (1694–1778), Denis Diderot (1713–1784), and Adam Smith (1723–1790) believed in the power of human reason and the perfectibility of mankind; they rejected the medieval belief in man's helplessness and God's remoteness. But while these writers affirmed the ultimate rationality of the universe, they also observed with unprecedented acuity the evils and flaws of human society in their day. Voltaire wrote scathing critiques of the torture of criminals; Diderot denounced the despotic tendencies of Louis XIV and Louis XV; Smith detailed the inefficiency of mercantile economics.

In general, Enlightenment thinkers trusted nature and individual human reason and distrusted institutions and traditions. "Man is born good," Jean-Jacques Rousseau (1712–1778) wrote in *Émile* (1762), "it is society that corrupts him." In *The Social Contract* (1762) Rousseau wrote about government as the expression of the general will and how the people could withdraw their support if the government violated this social contract. Moreover, in *Candide* (1759), Voltaire warned against undue optimism in a world containing inequality and injustice. Like Rousseau and Voltaire, other Enlightenment thinkers believed that improvements could be made to human society, but that there was a great deal that needed to be improved. Their critiques of tradition, of religious and secular customs and authorities, and of barriers to social mobility were largely directed at contemporary European conditions, and they were often imprisoned or exiled as punishment for writing about what they considered to be superstitious beliefs and corrupt political structures.

The Enlightenment can be described as a pan-European movement, but the extent of its reach varied in different countries: in France and Britain, enlightened learning spread rather widely; in other places, like Spain, Poland, and Scandinavia, enlightened circles were small and had little influence either on the rulers or on the population at large. Enlightened thought flourished in commercial centers, like Amsterdam and Edinburgh, and it also spread to colonial ports like Philadelphia and Boston.

> *Enlightenment thinkers trusted nature and individual human reason and distrusted institutions and traditions.*

As education and literacy became more widespread in these commercial cities, book sales and newspaper circulation expanded. By 1770, approximately 3,500 different books and pamphlets were being produced each year in France alone, as compared to 1,000 in 1720. By 1776, something like 12 million copies of newspapers were being issued in Britain.

In the emerging marketplace for new books, new ideas, and new visions, some of the most popular works were not from the high intellectuals of the period. Pamphlets alleging rampant corruption circulated widely wherever reading publics flourished; charges of stock-jobbing and insider trading provided raw material for popular literary slander. Sex, too, sold well. While the works of Voltaire, for instance, enjoyed a respectable readership among France's increasingly literate population, some of the real best-sellers of the age came from the pens of cruder and more sensationalist essayists. Works like *Venus in the Cloister or the Nun in a Nightgown* (anonymous, with at least twenty-two editions between 1682 and 1782) sold as well as many of the now-classical works of the Enlightenment and were full of bawdy and irreligious material. These vulgar best-sellers took advantage of consumer demand—but they also seized the opportunity to mock icons of authority. In many of these works, nuns often came across as lascivious, priests as fornicators. Some were daring enough to go after the royal family, portraying Louis XV as a king fond of being spanked, or Marie Antoinette copulating with her court confessor. In these cases, pornography—some of it even philosophical—spilled into the literary marketplace for political satire. These works display the seamier side of the Enlightenment. But they too spoke of the willingness of intellectuals—high and low alike—to explore new and iconoclastic modes of thought.

Those who were part of the growing reading public also participated in the creation of a whole new set of cultural institutions and practices. In Britain and Germany, book clubs proliferated and coffeehouses sprang up to cater to sober men of business and learning; here, aristocrats and well-to-do commoners could read some of the first news sheets or discuss stock prices, political affairs, or technological novelties. The same sorts of noncourtly socializing were available in Parisian salons and cafes, where witty gossip could turn into criticism of state policies. Libraries began to open their doors to the public. It must be understood, however, that aristocratic, royal, and even ecclesiastical patronage remained the major source of funding for intellectuals in this age; female aristocrats were central in supporting salon life in France, and Germany's Enlightenment thinkers were chiefly university professors, bureaucrats, and pastors. Art collecting boomed—primarily because local aristocrats found it a means to display their good taste, wealth, and distance from the rabble.

Salon of Madame Geoffrin. Much of the important work—and wit—of the Enlightenment was the product of private gatherings known as salons. Often hosted, like the one depicted here, by aristocratic women, these salons also welcomed down-at-the-heels writers and artists, offering everyone, at least in theory, the opportunity to discuss the sciences, the arts, politics, and the idiocies of their fellow men on an equal basis.

While they took the aristocracy's money, many Enlightenment thinkers nonetheless sought to overturn the status distinctions that defined the worth of individuals in Europe at this time. They emphasized merit rather than birth as the basis for status. John Locke (1632–1704) claimed that man was born with a mind that was a clean slate (*tabula rasa*), and acquired all his ideas as a result of experience. Locke's *Essay Concerning Human Understanding* (1690) stressed that cultural differences were the result, not of unequal natural endowments, but rather of unequal opportunities to develop men's faculties. Similarly, in *The Wealth of Nations* (1776), Adam Smith remarked that there was little difference (other than education) between a philosopher and a street porter. Both had been endowed with reason, and were (or should be) free to rise in society according to their talents. Yet, Locke and Smith still believed that a mixed set of social and political institutions would be needed to regulate relationships between ever imperfect humans. Moreover, they did not believe that women could act as independent, rational individuals in the same way that all men, presumably, could. Although educated women took up the pen to protest these inequities, the Enlightenment actually did little to change the subordinate status of women in European society.

Inspired by the new science, many Enlightenment thinkers sought to discover the "laws" of human behavior, an endeavor

> *Inspired by the new science, many Enlightenment thinkers sought to discover the "laws" of human behavior, an endeavor closely bound up with criticism of existing governments.*

closely bound up with criticism of existing governments. Explaining the laws of economic relations was chiefly the work of Adam Smith. His *The Wealth of Nations*, in which he described universal economic laws, was one of the most influential and long-lived of enlightened treatises. Smith claimed that unregulated markets in a laissez-faire economy best suited mankind because they allowed our "trucking and bartering" nature full expression. In Smith's view, the "invisible hand" of the market, rather than the regulations of government, would lead to general prosperity and social peace. Interestingly, Smith was quite conscious of growing economic gaps between the "civilized and thriving" and the "savage" nations, which remained so miserably poor as to be regularly reduced to infanticide, starvation, and euthanasia. Yet, he believed that until these nations learned to play by what he called nature's laws, they could not expect a happy fate. Smith was just one of many Enlightenment thinkers to paint a picture of what they believed to be universal laws that offered non-Europeans no other solution but that of imitation.

One of the most controversial realms for the application of universal laws was that of religion. Although few Enlightenment thinkers were actually atheists, most advocated some kind of religious toleration, insisting that reason, not force, was the means to create a community of believers and moral actors. For European audiences, these critiques of church authorities and practices were highly controversial. States often reacted to radical critiques by censoring books or exiling writers, but some princes were convinced by these arguments. In response, acts of toleration were passed in the late eighteenth century by governments from Denmark to Austria offering religious minorities some degree of freedom of worship. Toleration did not mean, however, that full civil rights were bestowed on, for example, Catholics in England or Jews anywhere in Europe. Toleration simply meant a loosening of religious uniformity, and the population as a whole often resented even this. The "No Popery" riots in Edinburgh and Glasgow in 1779, for example, compelled the British government to withdraw its proposed moderation of restrictions on Catholics.

The Enlightenment produced numerous works that purported to encompass universal knowledge, the most important of which was the French *Encyclopedia*, which began to be published in 1751 and would run to twenty-eight volumes by 1772. Nearly 200 intellectuals, including Voltaire and Rousseau, contributed essays; it was extremely popular among the elite, despite its political, religious, and intellectual radicalism. Its purpose, claimed Diderot, its editor and energizing force, was "to collect all the knowledge scattered over the face of the earth" and to make it useful to men and women in the present and future. Although critics almost forced the discontinuation of the *Encyclopedia*'s publication, their attacks only whetted public interest in it. Advance orders, or subscriptions, jumped to almost 5,000. The publishers advertised ownership of the book as a way to proclaim one's status as a true person of knowledge. Mostly representatives of upper layers of society bought the multi-volume work: a diverse group of administrative, cultural, and ecclesiastical elites, including those of provincial centers. All told, an astonishing 25,000 copies were published before 1789; a little less than half that total sold in France.

Title Page of the *Encyclopedia*. Originally published in 1751, the *Encyclopedia* was the most comprehensive work of learning of the eighteenth-century French Enlightenment. The title page features an image of light and reason being dispersed throughout the land. The title itself identifies the work as a dictionary, based on reason, that deals not just with the sciences but also with the arts and occupations. It identifies two of the leading men of letters (*gens de lettres*), Denis Diderot and Jean le Rond d'Alembert, as the primary authors of the work.

The *Encyclopedia* offered a wealth of information about the rest of the world, including more than 2,300 articles (constituting 4 percent of the total word space) that treated Islam. Here, quite typically, the authors praised Arab civilization for preserving and even extending Greek and Roman science, and in doing so, preparing the way for scientific advances in Europe. But, predictably, too, the *Encyclopedia* writers portrayed Islam with the same malevolence that they applied to all organized religions, condemning Muhammad as the apostle of a bloodthirsty religion, and Muslim culture in general for its inability to renounce superstition.

Enlightenment thinkers also evolved a new cultural hierarchy that extolled commerce and rationality and placed those regions of the world that lacked these ingredients at the bottom of the world's cultures. While praising certain of the world's cultures like the Chinese for having achieved much in these areas, Enlightenment thinkers were confident that Europe was advancing over the rest of the world in its acquisition of goods and universal knowledge.

Absolutist governments were not entirely hostile to enlightened ideas, recognizing the virtues of universality (as in a universally applicable system of taxation) and precision (as in a well-drilled army). After all, social mobility allowed more skilled bureaucrats to rise through the ranks, while commerce provided the state with new riches. Knowledge collection, too, appealed to states that had begun to exert greater and greater dominion over their subjects; Louis XIV was persuaded to establish a census, though he never carried it out, so that he could "know with certitude in what consists his grandeur, his wealth, and his strength." Some enlightened princes, like Frederick II of Prussia and Joseph II of Austria, even instituted impressive legal reforms and backed innovations in the arts and agriculture and

The *Encyclopedia* on Pin Making. Contributors to the *Encyclopedia* included craftsmen as well as intellectuals. This detailed illustration of a pin factory and the processes and machinery employed in pin making is from a plate in the fourth volume of the *Encyclopedia* and demonstrates its emphasis on practical, this-worldly information.

were accordingly idolized by Enlightenment thinkers. In theory, at least, enlightened ideas could form the basis for the most successful sort of absolutist rule.

HYBRID CULTURES IN THE AMERICAS

> → *How did hybrid cultures develop in the New World?*

In the Americas, mingling between European colonizers and native peoples (as well as African slaves) produced new, hybrid cultures. But this syncretism, or mixing, of cultures grew increasingly unbalanced as Europeans imposed their political and cultural authority over more and more of the Americas. For Native Americans, the pressure to adapt their cultures to those of the European colonists began with their first encounters (indeed, in some places, such as North America's Great Plains,

where horses spread ahead of European colonizers, borrowing and cultural adaptations preceded human contacts). Over time, Indians faced mounting pressure to accept the ways of Europeans, who insisted that their conquests and colonizations were not simply military endeavors, but also spiritual errands. In addition to their guns and germs, all of Europe's colonizers brought their bibles, prayerbooks, and crucifixes. With these, they set out to Christianize and "civilize" the Indian and African populations of the Americas. Still, even with the imbalance of military power, the efforts of Christian missionaries to convert Indians and slaves produced uneven and often unpredictable outcomes. Indian and African converts adopted Christian beliefs and practices, but they also often retained older religious practices.

European colonists, too, adapted to their new cultural environments, borrowing from the peoples they subjugated and enslaved. This was especially true in the sixteenth and seventeenth centuries, when the survival of Europeans in the New World often depended on such adaptations. By the middle of the eighteenth century, however, many American settlements had achieved a level of stability and prosperity, and colonists became less and less likely to admit their past dependency on others. New sorts of hierarchies emerged, and elites in Latin and North

America began increasingly to set their cultural standards according to the tastes and fashions of European aristocrats. And yet, even as they imitated Old World ways, these colonials also forged identities that separated them from Europe.

Spiritual Encounters

In the New World, unlike in other European colonial outposts, settlers not only tried to impose their culture and especially their religion on indigenous peoples, but they had the military and economic power to do so on an unprecedented scale. Although the Jesuits had relatively little impact in China and the Islamic world, Christian missionaries in the Americas had armies and officials to support their insistence that indigenous peoples and African slaves abandon their own deities and spirits for Christ.

European missionaries, especially Catholics, employed a vast range of techniques to bring and keep Indians within the Christian fold. Dominicans, Jesuits, and Franciscans learned what they could about Indian beliefs and rituals and used their knowledge in their efforts to make conversions to Christianity. To this effect, many of the missionaries found it useful to demonize native gods, subvert indigenous spiritual leaders, and transform Indian iconography into Christian symbols. Nonetheless, the missionaries were responsible for much of the historical information that was preserved on these communities. In sixteenth-century Mexico, the Dominican friar Bernardino de Sahagún compiled an immense ethnography of Mexican ways and beliefs. In seventeenth-century Canada, French Jesuits prepared dictionaries and grammars of the Iroquoian and Algonquian languages and translated Christian hymns into Amerindian tongues. Yet, smashing idols, razing temples, whipping backsliders, and burning "witches" were also part of the missionaries' arsenal.

Neither gentle persuasion nor violent coercion produced the results that missionaries desired. When conversions did occur, the Christianity practiced was usually a hybrid form in which indigenous deities and rituals merged with newly adopted Christian ones. Among Andean mountain people, for example, priestesses of native cults were given the name of Maria to mask their secret worship of the traditional deities of local kinship groups. In other cases, indigenous communities made no secret of their disdain for missionaries. They simply turned their backs on Christianity and accused missionaries of bringing plague and death. New converts tended to see Christian spiritual power as an addition to, not as a replacement for, their own religions.

More distressing to missionaries than evidence of syncretic beliefs and outright defiance were the successes of Indians in converting colonists. Many Indian groups had long practiced

> *When conversions did occur, the Christianity practiced was usually a hybrid form in which indigenous deities and rituals merged with newly adopted Christian ones.*

adoption of captives. Such adoptions were a common means to replenish numbers and replace lost kin. That many colonists adjusted to their captivity and accepted their adoptions, refusing to return to colonial society even when given the chance, was deeply troubling to missionaries. So were those Europeans who chose to live among the Indians. Comparing the records of cultural conversion, one eighteenth-century colonist in British America suggested that "thousands of Europeans are Indians," yet, "we have no examples of even one of those Aborigines having from choice become European." While this calculation exaggerated the imbalance in rates of intercultural borrowing, it points to the fact that Indianized Europeans, like Christianized Indians, lived in a mixed cultural world. Indeed, their familiarity with both Indian and European ways made them ideal cultural brokers, acting as intermediaries to facilitate diplomatic arrangements and economic exchanges.

Beyond the attractions of Indian cultures, Europeans were inclined to mix with Indians because of the demography of colonization. Almost all of the early European traders, missionaries, and settlers were men, and the preponderance of male colonists remained true in all but the British North American settlements. In response to the scarcity of women and as a means to acculturate native peoples, the Portuguese crown authorized intermarriage between Portuguese men and local women. In truth, colonizing men needed no official encouragement to consort with native women; indeed, these relations often amounted to little more than rape. But in those places where Indians retained their independence, longer-lasting relationships were common, as among French fur traders and Indian women in Canada, the Great Lakes region, and the Mississippi Valley. And whether by coercion or consent, sexual relations between European men and native women created new, hybrid peoples—the *mestizos* of Spanish colonies and the *métis* of French outposts, who soon outnumbered settlers of wholly European ancestry.

The increasing numbers of Africans who were forcibly transported to the Americas added to and complicated the mix of New World cultures. European masters coerced sex from African slave women. The children who were born from such unions swelled the ranks of mixed ancestry people in the colonial population. Again, too, Europeans initiated campaigns to Christianize slaves, though many slave owners expressed doubts about the wisdom of converting persons they regarded as mere property. Protestants had more difficulty than Catholics in reconciling the belief that Africans could be both slaves and Christians, and they were less aggressive than Catholics in mounting missionary efforts.

Sent forth with papal blessing, Catholic priests went to work among the slave populations of the American colonies of Portugal, Spain, and France. Employing many of the same techniques that had been used with Indian "heathens," missionaries produced similarly syncretic results. Often converts blended Islamic or indigenous African religions with Catholicism. Converted slaves wove remembered practices and beliefs into their American Christianity, transforming both along the way. In the northeast of Brazil, for example, slaves combined the Yoruba faiths of their ancestors with Catholic beliefs, and they frequently attributed powers of African deities to Christian saints. Sometimes Christian and African faiths were practiced side by side, as in the case of *candomblé*, a Yoruba-based religion in northern Brazil, where slaves from the Oyo and Dahomey kingdoms were shipped in large numbers. In Saint Domingue, slaves and free blacks practiced *vodun* (meaning "spirit" in the Dahomey tongue) and in Cuba, *santería*, a faith of similar origins.

Just as slaveholders feared, Christianity, especially in its syncretic forms, could inspire resistance, even revolt, among slaves. A major maroon (runaway slave) leader in mid-eighteenth-century Surinam was a Christian. In the English colonies, those held in bondage drew inspiration from Christian hymns that promised deliverance and embraced as their own the Old Testament's story of Moses leading the Israelites out of Egypt. By the end of the eighteenth century, freed slaves like the Methodist Olaudah Equiano were saying in their own voices that slavery was unjust and incompatible with Christian brotherhood.

THE MAKING OF COLONIAL CULTURES

In Spanish America, widespread ethnic and cultural mixing led to the emergence of a powerful new class, the "creoles," persons of full-blooded European descent who were born in the Americas. By the latter part of the eighteenth century, creoles had become increasingly restive about the control that "peninsulars"—men and women born in Spain or Portugal—had over colonial society. Mercantilist restrictions, which gave peninsular merchants exclusive privileges and forbade creoles from trading with other colonial ports, fired local resentments. So, too, did the practice of royal ministers who dished out most official posts to peninsulars. While the Spanish and Portuguese rulers did occasionally soften the discriminatory blows for fear of angering the creoles, their reforms often aggravated tensions with peninsulars.

The growing sense of creole identity also stemmed from the dissemination of new ideas in the colonies, especially many of the notions circulating in the rest of the Atlantic world under the umbrella of the Enlightenment. Abbé Raynal's *History of the Settlements and Trade of the Europeans in the East and West Indies*

> *By the latter part of the eighteenth century, creoles had become increasingly restive about the control that peninsulars had over colonial society.*

(1770), for example, was one of the favorite texts among the colonial reading circles in Buenos Aires and Rio de Janeiro. As a history of colonization in the New World, it was unkind to Iberian emperors and conquerors—and often helped creoles justify their dissatisfaction. Other French works were also popular, especially those of Rousseau. So were some English texts, like Adam Smith's *The Wealth of Nations*. Although Smith's treatise was not translated into Spanish until the 1790s (the Portuguese translation came even later), educated creoles read it with ease in English. Smith's reformist spirit contributed to creole impressions that mercantilist Iberian authorities were political and economic laggards.

In many of the cities of the Spanish and Portuguese empires, reading clubs and salons provided environments where fresh ideas and concepts could be deliberated. Even among Catholic circles, Rousseau was made to fit a Christian critique of Spanish exploitation of Indians. In one university in Upper Peru, Catholic scholars taught their students that Spanish labor drafts and taxes on Andean Indians were more than a violation of divine justice; they offended the natural rights of free men. The Spanish crown, recognizing the importance of printing presses in the spread of insidious ideas, kept a strict control over the number and location of printers in the colonies; in Brazil, the royal authorities banned them altogether. In spite of these controls, books, pamphlets, and simple gossip allowed new notions of science, history, and politics to circulate widely among literate creoles.

Wealthy colonists in British America were similar to the creole elites in Spanish and Portuguese America. They, too, strove to emulate European ways, using their profits to construct "big houses" in Virginia modeled on the country estates of English gentlemen, to import opulent furnishings and fashions from the finest British stores, and to exercise more control over colonial assemblies. Becoming like the English also involved a solidification of patriarchal authority at all levels, but especially among the colonial elite. In seventeenth-century Virginia, men had vastly outnumbered women, which gave women a measure of power, with widows in particular gaining hold of substantial property. During the eighteenth century, however, sex ratios became more equal, and women's property rights diminished as they reverted to English norms. Symbolically, the new order was displayed in countless family portraits, where husband-patriarchs were customarily pictured above their wives and children.

Intellectually, too, British Americans were linked to Europe, importing enormous numbers of books and journals. Indeed, Americans played a big role in the Enlightenment, serving as both producers and consumers of political pamphlets, scientific treatises, and social critiques. Drawing on the words of Montesquieu

(1689–1755), Locke, and Rousseau, genteel American intellectuals created the most famous of enlightened documents, the Declaration of Independence (1776), which announced that all men were endowed with equal rights and created to pursue this-worldly happiness. Here, Anglicized Americans showed themselves, like the creole elites of Latin America, to be both European and products of New World encounters.

IMPERIALISM IN OCEANIA

> ➔ *What role did race play in how Europeans viewed others, especially those from Oceania?*

Not only in Europe and the Americas, but also in the South Pacific, especially in Australia, a new, enlightened form of cultural aggrandizement was underway in the eighteenth century. Though in centuries past, Hindu, Buddhist, Islamic, and Chinese missionaries and traders had brought their cultures to Malaysia and nearby islands, they had not ventured beyond Timor. Europeans began to do so in the years after 1770. Using their new wealth—public and private—to fund voyages that were both scientific and political, Europeans invaded these remaining aboriginal areas. The results were mixed: while some islands maintained their autonomy, through resistance or European disinterest, the biggest prize, Australia, underwent thorough Anglicization.

Until Europeans colonized it in the late eighteenth century, Australia was truly a world apart. Separated by water and sheer distance from other regions, it was characterized primarily by its generally harsh natural conditions and sparse population. At the time of the European colonization, the island was home to around 300,000 people, mostly hunter-gatherers. While seafarers from Java, Timor, and particularly the port of Makassar were likely to have ventured into the area in the past, there was little evidence that either Chinese or Muslim merchants ever strayed that far south despite their active involvement in the Southeast Asian trade.

Europeans had visited Oceania before the eighteenth century. Spices drew the Portuguese and Dutch into the South Pacific (see Chapter 4). The Spanish had regularly plied the Pacific waters on their travels between Manila and Acapulco, but they had made habitual stops only in Guam and the Mariana Islands. In the 1670s and 1680s, they attempted to conquer these islands, and despite considerable resistance, finally succeeded in doing so by 1700. The Dutch visited Easter Island in 1722, and the French arrived in Tahiti in 1767. The Portuguese (in the sixteenth century) and the Dutch (in the seventeenth century) had seen the northern and western coasts of Australia, but they had found only sand, flies, and Aborigines.

Not until the late eighteenth century did Europeans see Australia's verdant eastern coast, or find grounds for serious interest in colonization.

THE SCIENTIFIC VOYAGES OF CAPTAIN COOK

In Oceania and the South Pacific, Europeans experimented with a scientific form of imperialism. The story of the region's most famous explorer, Captain James Cook, shows how intimately related science and imperialist ventures could be and how cultural exchange became unequal even before the onset of the industrial age. As Columbus was a man of a mystical age, Cook was a man of science—but both served the cause of European expansion. Cook's voyages and his encounter with the South Sea Islanders opened up the Pacific, and particularly Australia, to European colonizers. Captain Cook has become a legendary figure in European cultural history, portrayed as one of the saintly scientists of enlightened progress. Charged by the Royal Society

Captain James Cook. During his widely celebrated voyages to the South Pacific, Captain James Cook kept meticulous maps and diaries. Although he had little formal education, he became one of the great exemplars of enlightened learning through experience and experiment.

with the scholarly task of observing the transit of the planet Venus from the Southern Hemisphere, and by the British government with the more pragmatic, if secret, mission of finding and claiming "the southern continent" for Britain, he set sail for the Pacific in 1768. This voyage proved so fruitful that Cook was sent back on two more scientific-political adventures. The extremely popular accounts of his discoveries, and the engravings that accompanied them, opened up the exotic worlds of Tahiti, New Zealand, Australia, and Hawaii to European scrutiny. They also prepared the way for a new, more intensive sort of cultural colonization.

Cook was chosen to head the first expedition because he, like many of his British contemporaries, was scientifically inclined. Although he had little schooling, Cook had gone to sea early and, through long experience in navigating the uncharted waters of Newfoundland, had developed excellent surveying skills. Besides Cook, the Royal Society sent on the expedition one of their members, Joseph Banks, a gentlemanly but serious botanist; Daniel Solander, a doctor and student of the renowned Swedish botanist Linnaeus; and a number of artists and scientists. The crew also took along sophisticated instruments, and they were asked to keep extensive, detailed diaries. This was to be a grand data-collecting odyssey, a heroic, scientific response to recent French expeditions to the same regions.

Cook's voyages surpassed even the Royal Society's hopes. It is said that on his three voyages to the South Pacific between 1768 and 1779, the scientists made about 3,000 drawings of Pacific plants, birds, landscapes, and peoples never seen before in Europe. Naturally, the flora and fauna were described according to the new Linnean classificatory system, and the geographical features were given English designations, like the Bay of Good Success, where Cook's ship the *Endeavour* anchored in 1769. Cook and his crew kept meticulous diaries and records, which fascinated scholars, travelers, missionaries, and government officials across Europe. Just as many poems and plays were written in celebration of the great navigator, Cook's expeditions were also considered state-of-the-art scientific practice. They inspired many a later scientific reconnaissance trip, including Napoleon's expedition to Egypt in 1798 (see Chapter 6).

More than a mere trading area, Australia was intended to supply Britain with raw materials. But the hunter-gatherer Aborigines of Australia could not be for the British what American Indians or African slaves had been for the Spanish or Portuguese. Thus, plans were developed for grand-scale conquest and resettlement by and for British colonists. On his third voyage, Cook took with him a veritable Noah's ark of animals and plants with which to turn the South Pacific into a European-style garden. Cook's lieutenant, William Bligh, later brought apples,

Engraving from Cook's *Voyage Round the World in the Years 1768–1771*. Kangaroos were unknown in the West until Cook and his colleagues encountered (and ate) them on their first visit to Australia. This engraving of the animal (which unlike most animals, plants, and geographical features, actually kept the name the Aborigines had given it) from Cook's 1773 travelogue lovingly depicts the kangaroo's environs and even emotions.

quinces, strawberries, and rosemary to Australia; the seventy sheep imported in 1788 laid the foundations for the region's wool-growing economy. The domestication of Australia was born both from certainty about Europeans' superior know-how and a desire to make the continent as a whole serve British interests.

In 1788, a British military expedition took official possession of the whole eastern half of Australia. The intent was, in part, to set up a prison colony far from home. This plan, too, belonged to the realm of enlightened dreams: that of ridding "civilized" society of all evils by resettling the lawbreakers among the "uncivilized" (previously convicts had been sent to Georgia in the Americas). The continent, too, was to be exploited for its timber and flax and used as a strategic base against Dutch and French expansionary endeavors. In the next decades, immigration—free and forced—increased the Anglo-Australian population from an original 1,000 to about 1.2 million by 1860. Importing their customs and their capital, British settlers turned Australia into a frontier version of home, just as they had done in British America. Yet, as in the Americas, such large-scale immigration had disastrous consequences for the Aborigines. Like the Native Americans, the original inhabitants of Australia were killed in large numbers by European diseases and increasingly forced westward by European settlement.

In one important way Cook had not departed so decisively from the practices of the past. Earlier travelers had developed an efficient means of studying foreign peoples and their languages: taking certain of them to Europe, by kidnapping if necessary. On his first voyage to the New World, Columbus captured six Amerindians and took them back to Spain, both to show off these exotic people and so that they could learn Spanish and thus serve as intermediaries between the two cultures. Other explorers did the same, seizing local peoples, taking them to Europe, and even putting them on display. This was not the way that Europeans learned the languages of peoples they considered to be civilized, the Chinese and Arabs, for example—here texts stood in for living bodies. But it continued to be a crude means of ethnography for peoples they considered to be uncivilized. Right through the nineteenth century, exhibitions of Laplanders, Africans, and Polynesians traveled, circus-like, from town to town through Europe. Cook himself captured and transported to England a highly skilled Polynesian navigator, Omai. Arriving in 1774, Omai quickly became the talk of London society and symbolized for some people the innocence and beauty that was being lost as Europe developed complicated machines and stock exchanges. Cook's return of Omai to his home on his third voyage was a sensation of equal proportions, seen as a colossally generous act by the revered British explorer.

CLASSIFICATION AND "RACE"

Cook's description of the South Sea Islanders underscores the large place that race had come to occupy in eighteenth-century

Carolus Linnaeus. The Swedish naturalist Carolus Linnaeus remained safely in Uppsala while his students undertook perilous voyages to collect new species for the master to classify. In this 1805 image, the twenty-five-year-old Linnaeus is portrayed as a proto-nationalist, wearing Lapland dress.

Europeans' views of themselves and others. Previously, the word "race" referred to a swift current in a stream or a trial of speed, and on occasion meant a lineage, mainly that of a royal or noble family. By the end of the seventeenth century, a few writers were beginning to expand the definition of race to designate a European ethnic lineage, identifying, for example, the indomitable spirit and freedom-loving ethos of the Anglo-Saxon race. François Bernier, who had traveled in Asia, may have been the first European to attempt a racial division of the globe in his 1684 *New Division of the Earth by the Different Groups or Races Who Inhabit It*. Carolus Linnaeus (1707–1778); Georges Louis LeClerc, the comte de Buffon (1707–1788); and Johann Friedrich Blumenbach (1752–1840) would be the first to use racial principles to classify humankind.

Europe's most accomplished naturalist, Carolus Linnaeus, took his passion for classifying and naming all the plants and

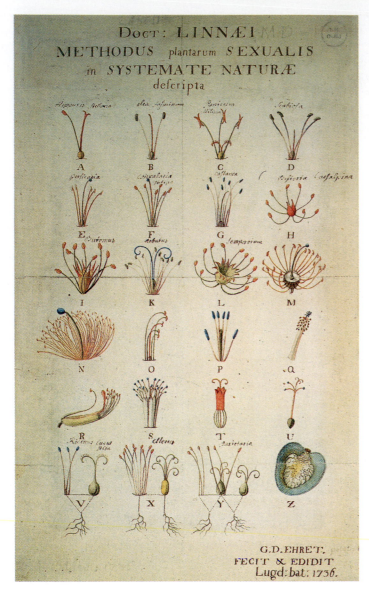

Linnaeus and Classification. Linnaeus's famous system of plant and animal classifications, which depended on sexual forms (such as the stamen and pistil in plants), was in wide use by the end of the eighteenth century.

animals in the world to identify several species within the genus *Homo*—*Homo sapiens*, *Homo caudatus* (tailed man), and *Homo troglodytes*—in his *Systema Naturae* (1735). The latter two species—the tailed man and troglodyte man—were groups Linnaeus defined on the basis of classical texts, travelers' accounts, rumors, freak show exhibits, and misunderstandings. Within *Homo sapiens*, he identified five groups, or races, using a combination of physical characteristics, including skin pigmentation and social qualities. Linnaeus characterized the Europeans as light-skinned and governed by laws. He believed that the peoples of Asia, whom he called "the sooty people," were regulated by opinion. He said that copper-skinned, indigenous American peoples were governed by custom. He

wrote that Africans, whom he consigned to the lowest rung of the human ladder, were ruled by little other than personal whim. Later eighteenth-century natural historians dismissed Linnaeus's troglodyte and tailed men, but the habit of ranking races and lumping together physical and cultural characteristics stuck. In time, some would even question the unity of the human species.

In inventorying the peoples of the world and assigning each group a place on the ladder of human achievement, the long-standing idealization of classical sculpture played a role: those who most resembled Greek nudes were believed to be the most beautiful, as well as the most civilized and suited for world power. In his *Natural History* (1750), a noted French scientist, the comte de Buffon, insisted that proper proportion for the human form had been established by classical sculptures. Having divided the human genus into distinct races, he determined white peoples to be the most admirable, and Africans the most contemptible.

The father of physical anthropology, Johann Friedrich Blumenbach, crystallized much of Enlightenment thought about race in his authoritative book *De Generis Humani Natura*, published in 1775. He divided humanity into four races: Europeans, Asians, Africans, and Americans, with these classifications based largely, although not exclusively, on physical characteristics, like skin color, cranial size, hair, and the like. Blumenbach introduced the word "Caucasian" to denote Europeans, but he believed Caucasians and "Ethiopians" (his word for Africans) belonged to the same species because they had the same physical characteristics. Blumenbach, in fact, asserted a rough racial equality, maintaining that there were beautiful Ethiopians just as there were ugly Caucasians.

South Sea Islanders, like Omai, fell somewhere between the Caucasians and the Ethiopians. They retained an aura of mythical similarity to the Greek gods, but in succeeding decades Europeans would cease to view them as "noble savages," a phrase coined by Rousseau to describe the virtues of the uncivilized. The waning of appreciation for their innocence and simplicity may indeed have begun with the final act in the Cook legend: his killing by the Hawaiians in 1779.

In their first encounters, Cook had greatly impressed the Hawaiians; some commentators believe the Hawaiians recognized in him the embodiment of their god Lono; others simply think they treated him as an important chief. He had, in any event, deeply offended them by destroying one of their sacred shrines, ostensibly for firewood, but possibly because he wished to destroy symbols of their religion. When he then tried to take several chiefs hostage in order to force the return of a boat, tensions rose. In unclear circumstances, his men killed several important Hawaiians, and the islanders, incensed and frightened by the violence, closed in on the captain, stabbing him repeatedly. The news, of course, scandalized Cook's homeland; the king himself, it is said, shed tears. Now the "darker side" of South Pacific cultures also came clearly into European perceptions. *Ode to the Memory of the Late Captain James Cook*

(1780) depicted the sullen, vengeful savage "Whose darken'd mind in mercy found no joy." A French traveler, who had seen the explorer Marion de Fresne killed by Maoris on New Zealand's coast, similarly denounced "the passions of rapacity, violence, and treachery" common to the South Pacific "Children of Nature."

CONCLUSION

The new wealth produced by increasing intercontinental exchange created the conditions for a kind of global cultural renaissance in the period between 1600 and 1780. Book production and consumption soared; grand new monuments arose; luxury goods became available for wider enjoyment. Knowledge of the world's cultures was more available than ever before. Yet, the Chinese and Islamic cultural flourishings were largely generated by social and cultural forces from within rather than from the outside. Their artists and essayists celebrated the prosperity that their indigenous institutions seemed to have fostered.

Perhaps the most striking thing about this cultural renaissance was its unevenness. While elites and sometimes the middle classes benefited, the poor did not. They remained illiterate, undernourished, and often subjected to brutal treatment by rulers and landowners. In Europe and China, elite women increasingly joined literate society, writing, reading, and publishing books, acting as patrons and translators, but they gained no new rights. Urban areas also profited much more from the new wealth than rural ones, and those seeking refinement flocked to the cities. Some regions, which had once been cultural meccas, like the Italian peninsula, lost their luster as new, more commercially and culturally dynamic centers took their place.

Between states, too, cultural inequalities were now glaring. Although the Islamic and Chinese worlds confidently retained their own systems of knowing, believing, and representing, the Americas and Oceania were increasingly subjected to European cultural pressures. Here, while syncretic practices were widespread by the later eighteenth century, clearly European ideas, beliefs, and habits had become the standards by which degrees of "civilization" were judged.

As the Oceania example shows, by the late eighteenth century, Europeans had an expansive view of the world and their place in it. They were gleefully classifying the plants, animals, and peoples of the world, and seeking ways to make new worlds more and more useful and comfortable for themselves. It is important to recognize, however, that Europe's categories and descriptions did not win easy acceptance beyond Europe's self-created borders. Not only did the Chinese, Ottomans, Safavids, and Mughals remain largely unaware of or unimpressed by European endeavors, resistance from Native Americans as from South Sea Islanders remained stiff.

The world in the seventeenth and eighteenth centuries was commercially more tightly integrated. Populations moved around with increasing ease and frequency, and mercantile transactions involving very distant groups took place more frequently and easily. In general, well-established cultural groups and traditional institutions were able to deal effectively with increasing interaction and borrowing. In some respects, borrowing and exposure only reconfirmed established ways. The Chinese, for instance, still believed in the superiority of Chinese

Chronology

1587–1602	Abulfazl's *Akbarnamah* in Mughal India
1598–1629	Building of palace and plaza in Isfahan, Iran
1600s	Growing circulation of books and ideas in China
1600s	*Kabuki* theater appears in Japan
1620	Francis Bacon's *Novum Organum*
1630–1650	Building of Taj Mahal in Agra, India
1632	Galileo Galilei's *Dialogue on the Two Chief Systems of the World*
1637	René Descartes's *Discourse on Method*
1661	Building of Versailles begins outside Paris
1662	Incorporating of British Royal Society
1687	Isaac Newton's *Principia Mathematica*
1690	John Locke's *Essay Concerning Human Understanding*
1720s	Tulip period in Ottoman empire
1728	Movement for "native learning" begins in Japan
1735	Carolus Linnaeus's *Systema Naturae*
1750	Comte de Buffon's *Natural History*
1751–1772	Denis Diderot's *Encyclopedia*
1762	Jean-Jacques Rousseau's *Émile* and *Social Contract*
1768–1779	Voyages of Captain James Cook
1775	Johann Blumenbach's *De Generis Humani Natura*
1776	Adam Smith's *The Wealth of Nations*
1776	American Declaration of Independence
1788	First British settlement in Australia

knowledge and customs, and regarded those who had not mastered their ways as lesser peoples.

Islamic rulers, too, claimed universality on behalf of Islam as a body of revealed, not objective knowledge. Confident of the superiority of Islam, the dynasts allowed others to form their own—though clearly subordinate—cultural communities. At the elite level, they accommodated non-Muslim subjects and knowledge by constructing a realm of courtly culture and philosophy, where the superiority of Islam was not in question but where other systems of knowledge could be discussed and debated. Within these imperial Islamic cultures, the Europeans were useful, decorative pieces, and their knowledge, to the extent considered helpful for imperial purposes, was taken into account.

Only the Europeans were constructing knowledge that they believed was both universal and objective, a kind of knowledge that could be used to master nature and all its inhabitants. It was this approach to cultural differences that separated the 1700s from the 1300s and was to prove consequential in the centuries to come.

FURTHER READINGS

Axtell, James, *The Invasion of America: The Contest of Cultures in Colonial North America* (1985). Discusses the strategies of Christian missionaries in converting the Indians, as well as the success of Indians in converting Europeans.

Berlin, Ira, *Many Thousands Gone: The First Two Centuries of Slavery in North America* (1998). Surveys the development of African-American culture in colonial North America.

Brook, Timothy, *The Confusions of Pleasure: Commerce and Culture in Ming China* (1999). An insightful survey of Ming society.

Clunas, Craig, *Superfluous Things: Material Culture and Social Status in Early Modern China* (1991). A good account of the late Ming elite's growing passion for material things.

Collcutt, Martin, Marius Jansen, and Isao Kumakura, *A Cultural Atlas of Japan* (1988). A sweeping look at the many different forms of Japanese cultural expression over the centuries, including the flourishing urban culture of Edo.

Darnton, Robert, *The Business of the Enlightenment: A Publishing History of the Encyclopédie, 1775–1800* (1979). The classic study of Europe's first great compendium of knowledge.

Dash, Mike, *Tulipomania: The Story of the World's Most Coveted Flower and the Extraordinary Passions It Aroused* (1999). A global perspective on and lively account of the spread of the tulip around the world as a flower signifying both beauty and status.

Eze, Emmanuel Chukwudi (ed.), *Race and the Enlightenment: A Reader* (1997). Readings examining the idea of race in the context of the Enlightenment.

Fleischer, Cornell, *Bureaucrat and Intellectual in the Ottoman Empire: The Historian Mustafa Ali (1540–1600)* (1986). Offers good insight into the world of culture and intellectual vitality in the Ottoman empire.

Grafton, Anthony, April Shelford, and Nancy Siraisi, *New Worlds, Ancient Texts: The Power of Tradition and the Shock of Discovery* (1995). A concise discussion of the impact of the New World on European thought.

Gutierrez, Ramon, *When Jesus Came, the Corn Mothers Went Away: Marriage, Sexuality, and Power in New Mexico, 1500–1846* (1991). A provocative dissection of the spiritual dimensions of European colonialism in the Americas.

Hannaford, Ivan, *Race: The History of an Idea in the West* (1996). A study of how race began to take on critical importance in Western thinking in the seventeenth and eighteenth centuries.

Harley, J. B., and David Woodward (eds.), *The History of Cartography.* Vol. 2, Book 2: *Cartography in the Traditional East and Southeast Asian Societies* (1994). An authoritative treatment of the subject.

Horton, Robin, *Patterns of Thought in Africa and the West: Essays on Magic, Religion, and Science* (1993). Reflections on African patterns of thought and attitudes toward nature, which can help us to understand African-American religious beliefs and resistance movements.

Keene, Donald, *The Japanese Discovery of Europe: Honda Toshiaki and Other Discoverers, 1720–1798* (1952). A study of the ways Japan managed to incorporate knowledge from the outside world with the development of national traditions.

Ko, Dorothy, *Teachers of the Inner Chambers: Women and Culture in Seventeenth-Century China* (1994). Explores the lives of elite women in late Ming and early Qing China.

Lewis, Bernard, *Race and Color in Islam* (1979). Examines the Islamic attitude toward race and color.

Morgan, Philip D., *Slave Counterpoint: Black Culture in the Eighteenth-Century Chesapeake and Lowcountry* (1998). Describes the development of African-American culture in colonial North America.

Munck, Thomas, *The Enlightenment: A Comparative Social History, 1721–1794* (2000). A wonderful survey, with unusual examples from the periphery, especially from Scandinavia and the Habsburg empire.

Necipoglu, Gulru, *Architecture, Ceremonial and Power: The Topkapi Palace in the Fifteenth and Sixteenth Centuries* (1991). A magnificently illustrated book that shows the enormous artistic talent that the Ottoman rulers poured into their imperial structure.

Publishing and the Print Culture in Late Imperial China (Special Issue). *Late Imperial China*, Vol. 17:1 (June 1996). Contains a collection of important articles with a forward by the French cultural historian Roger Chartier.

Qaisar, Ahsan Jan, *The Indian Response to European Technology, AD 1498–1707* (1998). A meticulous, scholarly work on this little-studied subject.

Rizvi, Athar Abbas, *The Wonder That Was India.* Vol. 2: *A Survey of the History and Culture of the Indian Sub-continent from the Coming of the Muslims to the British Conquest, 1200–1700* (1987). A deeply learned work in intellectual history.

Shapin, Stephen, *The Scientific Revolution* (1998). An overview that is informed by innovative new thinking on the subject.

Smith, Bernard, *European Vision and the South Pacific* (1985). An excellent cultural history of Cook's voyages.

Smith, Richard J., *Chinese Maps: Images of "All under Heaven"* (1996). Provides a good introduction to the history of cartography in China.

Welch, Anthony, *Shah Abbas and the Arts of Isfahan* (1973). Describes the astonishing architectural and artistic renaissance of the city of Isfahan under the Safavid ruler, Shah Abbas.

Whitfield, Peter, *The Image of the World: Twenty Centuries of World Maps* (1994). A good introduction to the history of cartography in different parts of the world.

Zilfi, Madeline C., *The Politics of Piety: The Ottoman Ulema in the Post-Classical Age (1600–1800)* (1988). Explores the cultural flourishing that took place within the Islamic world in this period.

Chapter

6

REORDERING THE WORLD, 1750–1850

At the end of the eighteenth century, the commander of a French army, Napoleon Bonaparte, led an expedition to Egypt. For many Europeans, Egypt was an exalted territory—the cradle of a once-great civilization, home to fertile lands along the Nile River, a land bridge to the Red Sea and trade with Asia, and a provincial outpost of an old rival, the Ottoman empire. Introducing the principles of the recent French Revolution, of liberty, equality, and fraternity, to distant lands would bring glory to France. Occupying the country would also represent a strategic victory over Great Britain for the control of trade routes to Asia. Most important to Napoleon, however, defeat of the Ottomans would catapult him to historic greatness.

But, the revolutionary crusade of 1798 did not go as Napoleon planned. After landing his troops in Egypt and defeating the Mamluk army of Egypt beneath the pyramids just outside Cairo, his troops bogged down in the country and faced the wrath of the local population. Eager to play a larger role in Europe, Napoleon returned to France a little more than six months after he had stepped on Egyptian soil, leaving his troops vulnerable to inevitable counterattacks. But the invasion of Egypt did shake up Ottoman rule as well as play a role in altering the European balance of power and the old European order. Indeed, more than any other event, Napoleon's actions in Africa, the Americas, and especially in Europe, combined with the principles of the French Revolution, laid the foundations for the era of the nation-state. What gave these political events added impact were a number of equally disruptive changes in social and economic arrangements around the world.

The period 1750–1850 witnessed a fundamental reordering of the balance of power in the world. The reordering began in the Atlantic world, where political upheavals destroyed the colonial domains of Spain, Portugal, Britain, and France in the Americas and established a number of new nations. To these political events were added far-reaching economic changes that propelled Western Europe to global preeminence. These reorderings, in turn, forced Asian and African governments to come to terms with the new economic and political might of Europe. In Egypt and the Ottoman empire, reform-minded leaders undertook desperate modernizing efforts to deal with Europe's threatening power. In China, too, by the 1830s the ruling Manchus were faced with European gunboats insisting that the Chinese permit expanded trade with the Europeans.

TRANSFORMATIONS IN THE ATLANTIC WORLD

> → *How did Enlightenment ideas transform the Atlantic world?*

In the eighteenth century, the increasing circulation of goods, people, and ideas created new pressures for reform around the Atlantic world. As economies expanded, many men and women felt that the restrictions of the mercantilist system stood in the way of their aspirations. They clamored for changes that would enable them to partake in this wealth and power. Similarly, as enlightened ideas spread through an increasingly literate public, new voices called for their states to adopt rational, humane, and just practices, including the abolition of torture and the accountability of the governors to the people they governed. Demanding more freedom to trade and more influence in governing institutions, these reformers did not, at first, aim at revolution; but their new set of concepts for organizing politics and economics ran up against the resistance of aristocratic elites. It is a testimony, indeed, to the weakness of these elites, as well as to the power of these new forces, that those in power could not stamp out these demands before they became—in a number of places—full-scale revolution. Reformers began to advance concepts of popular sovereignty (of power residing in the people themselves) and to argue that unregulated economies would produce more rapid economic growth. In denouncing commercial privileges and monopolies, as well as arbitrary rulers, reformers employed a rhetoric of freedom, which would alter the course of world history. They argued that free trade, free markets, and free labor would yield more just and more efficient societies. With time, proponents of the new order argued that this new social order would benefit everyone everywhere in the world.

The struggle to create new political and economic relationships gave rise to languages and identities of nationalism (that people belonged to a shared community called a "nation") and democracy (that these people, by virtue of their membership in the nation, enjoyed public rights to representation). In the thirteen British colonies and in France, the democratic rights of a nation mobilized sufficient opposition to topple old rulers.

As democratic and nationalist ideas emerged in the American and French Revolutions, the question arose as to how far freedom should be extended, even within the Atlantic world. Should women, Native Americans, and slaves be given the rights of citizens? Should people without property be given the vote? Moreover, should freedom be extended to non-Europeans? By and large, European and Euro-American elite groups answered no to these questions, and often they backed their answer with violence. The very same elites who championed a freer world often exploited slaves and those in the lower orders, still restricted colonial economies, and were prepared to use force to expand further the markets of Asia and Africa to European trade and investment.

> *Reformers began to advance concepts of popular sovereignty and to argue that unregulated economies would produce more rapid economic growth.*

Focus Questions REORDERING THE WORLD

→ *How did Enlightenment ideas transform the Atlantic world?*
→ *What major changes in government and society grew out of the Atlantic Revolutions?*
→ *Why did the abolition of the slave trade have unintended effects on African society?*
→ *How did the industrial and commercial revolutions reorder society?*
→ *How did the Atlantic Revolutions affect Eurasian societies?*

POLITICAL REORDERINGS

→ *What major changes in government and society grew out of the Atlantic Revolutions?*

The second half of the eighteenth century witnessed the spread of revolutionary ideas across the Atlantic world (see Map 6-1). In part, this spread followed the trail of Enlightenment ideas about freedom and reason. By the late eighteenth century, the number of newspapers, pamphlets, and books in circulation had soared, drawing readers in European mother countries and American colonies into a discussion of their society's problems—and how to fix them. Many more people began to believe that they had the right to participate in governance. Gradually and unevenly and on both sides of the Atlantic, politics became a noisier activity, involving a wider group (though chiefly of middle- and upper-class males), rather than a matter reserved for kings, court advisers, and landed magnates. Increasingly, too, those who made or wished to make political revolutions claimed that they were acting for the good of "the people."

> *The slogans of the era—independence, freedom, liberty, and equality—were especially powerful terms that seemed to promise an end to oppression, hardship, and inequities of all kinds.*

The slogans of the era—independence, freedom, liberty, and equality—were especially powerful terms that seemed to promise an end to oppression, hardship, and inequities of all kinds. While colonists in British America demanded independence and freedom for themselves, they tuned out—or at least tried to tune out—Indian and slave demands for the same. Likewise, when French aristocrats called for *liberté* from a king who was encroaching on their privileges, they meant immunity from the king's demands. This differed from the meaning that insurrectionary Haitian slaves attached to the same word. For slaves, liberty meant complete exemption from the master's demands. During the French Revolution, more moderate reformers sought *égalité* for all (white males) before the law, while radicals insisted that social and economic conditions be equalized. As women, workers, peasants, and colonized peoples employed these terms, they became fighting words that challenged the whole of the Atlantic world order.

Fired by these new ideas, political revolts spread throughout the Atlantic world, starting first in Britain's North American colonies and spreading to France's absolute monarchy. In both, revolutions ultimately caused monarchies to be replaced with republics. The examples of the United States and France soon encouraged others in the Caribbean and Central and South America to seek king-less polities. In all of these revolutionary environments, new representative institutions such as permanent parliaments, enshrined in written constitutions, came into being.

By the end of the eighteenth century, the liberals had largely acquired the legal and commercial freedoms they desired, and they were eager to stop the revolution. In the Americas, they were largely successful; the slaves and Native Americans who rose up met stiff resistance from the elites of European descent who restricted the fruits of freedom to white male property owners alone. In France, a brief period of radical rule terrified the liberals; but even the Jacobins did not extend citizenship to women, and when their reign was over, Napoleon secured the interests of propertied males in a new set of French laws called the Napoleonic Code. In Africa, the third corner of the Atlantic world, the upheavals resulted not in the emergence of free and sovereign peoples but in intensified enslavement. Still, the radicalism of eighteenth-century reorderings should not be too quickly dismissed. The rhetoric of revolution—freedom, liberty, and equality—once unleashed, proved difficult to contain in later generations.

THE NORTH AMERICAN WAR OF INDEPENDENCE, 1776–1783

By the mid-eighteenth century, Britain's mainland colonies swelled with people and prosperity. Through bustling port cities like Charleston, Philadelphia, New York, and Boston, African slaves, European migrants, and manufactured goods flowed in, while agrarian staples flowed out. A colonial "genteel" class, composed of merchants and landowning planters, came to dominate the affairs of these colonies, and aspired to the status of English gentlemen. But with settlers arriving from Europe and slaves from Africa, land was a constant source of dispute. Big planters collided with independent farmers (yeomen). Sons and daughters of farmers, unable to inherit or acquire real estate near their parents, spilled into the continent's interior, and their land-seeking put them in conflict with Indian peoples. To defend their lands, many Indians allied with Britain's rival, France, but after the Seven Years' War (1756–1763), France ceded its Canadian colony to Britain. Without French support and overwhelmed by settlers, many Indians continued to mount a spirited resistance, but they often died in battle or of disease. A large number of survivors fled west.

By the mid-1760s, the British empire stood supreme in eastern North America. A political revolution seemed unimaginable. And yet, a decade later, that is precisely what occurred. Why did colonists sever their ties with England? They acted, paradoxically, in defense of their rights as "freeborn Englishmen." The

RUSSIA

Hudson Bay

BRITISH NORTH AMERICA

OREGON
(Claimed by Spain,
Russia and Britain)

LOUISIANA

Quebec

Boston
New York
Philadelphia
UNITED
STATES
✸ 1776
(independence recognized
by Great Britain 1783)
Washington, D.C.

Santa Fe

MEXICO
✸ 1821

FLORIDA

Charleston

A T L A N T I C

O C E A N

*Gulf
of
Mexico*

Mexico City

CUBA

PUERTO RICO

BELIZE

JAMAICA

REPUBLIC
OF HAITI
✸ 1804

GUADELOUPE (Fr.)

MARTINIQUE (Fr.)

UNITED PROVINCES
OF CENTRAL AMERICA
✸ 1823

Cartagena

Caracas

TRINIDAD (Br.)

P A C I F I C

REPUBLIC OF
COLOMBIA
✸ 1819

GUIANA

Quito

O C E A N

PERU
✸ 1821

Lima

BRAZIL
✸ 1822

BOLIVIA
✸ 1825

PARAGUAY
✸ 1811

Rio de Janeiro

CHILE
✸ 1818

PROVINCES
OF LA PLATA
✸ 1816

URUGUAY
✸ 1828

Buenos Aires

Montevideo

British possessions
Spanish possessions
French possessions
Portuguese possessions
Dutch possessions
✸1776 Date of political independence
from European (or Ottoman)
colonial rule

| 0 | 1000 | 2000 Miles |

| 0 | 1000 | 2000 Kilometers |

MAP 6-1   REVOLUTIONS OF NATIONAL INDEPENDENCE IN THE ATLANTIC WORLD, 1776–1829

Colonies gained independence from European powers (and in the case of Greece from the Ottoman empire) in the late eighteenth and early nineteenth centuries under the influence of Enlightenment thinkers and the French Revolution. What were the first two American colonial territories to gain their independence? Why was the United States reluctant to recognize the political independence of the second independent American republic? Why did colonies in Spanish and Portuguese America obtain their political independence decades after the United States gained its independence?

The Boston Massacre. Paul Revere's idealized view of the "Boston Massacre" of March 5, 1770. In the years after the Seven Years' War, Bostonians grew increasingly disenchanted with British efforts to enforce imperial regulations. When British troops fired on and killed several members of an angry mob in what came to be called the "Boston Massacre," the resulting frenzy stirred revolutionary sentiments among the populace.

spark was provided by King George III, who proposed to end the policy of benign neglect of the colonies and to make the colonists pay for Britain's war with France and for the benefits of being subjects of the empire. Colonial merchants, particularly in New England, protested the Revenue Act of 1764, intended to end the lucrative smuggling by many colonists. Even more vexing to the colonists was taxation without representation, for no colonists sat in the British House of Commons. Agitation for freedom turned to open warfare between a colonial militia and British troops at Lexington and Concord, Massachusetts, in the spring of 1775. One firebrand, Thomas Paine, a recent immigrant from England, captured the mood in *Common Sense*, a pamphlet published in January 1776, in which he argued to an increasingly literate public that it was common sense for people to govern themselves. Paine's pamphlet had sold more than 100,000 copies by July 1776, when the Continental Congress adapted part of it in the Declaration of Independence.

The Declaration—written primarily by the Virginia tobacco planter Thomas Jefferson—drew on themes of the European

The prospect of a social revolution of artisans, women, and slaves, rather than a narrower liberal revolution, generated a reaction against what American elites called the "excesses of democracy."

Enlightenment. It championed the "natural rights" of people to govern themselves and the contract theory of government. "We hold these truths to be self-evident," it proclaimed, "that all men are created equal, that they are endowed by their Creator with certain inalienable Rights, that among these are Life, Liberty and the Pursuit of Happiness. That to secure these rights, Governments are instituted among Men, deriving their just powers from the consent of the governed. That whenever any Form of Government becomes destructive of these ends, it is the Right of the People to alter or abolish it." These principles went beyond English constitutionalism, but neither the Declaration of Independence nor *Common Sense* provided a blueprint for how a nonmonarchical government might be organized, or how thirteen tenuously connected states might win a war against the world's most powerful empire.

Through the War of Independence, Americans began to work out new political arrangements. Much of that work occurred in the individual states, where elections were held to select delegates to constitutional conventions. These elections were unprecedented, as was the decision to put the constitutions in writing. Constitution-writers exhibited a revolutionary faith in representative government. Dispensing with royal authority, all the new state constitutions assigned sweeping powers to legislative bodies, whose members were to be elected by "the people." But who constituted the people? Except for a small number of widows in New Jersey, who headed households and paid taxes, no women qualified as voters. Property qualifications also continued to limit the franchise to a percentage of adult white men, though the constitutions generally reduced the landholding requirements that had prevailed during the colonial era.

The notion that all men were created equal flew in the face of established hierarchies in which people supposedly knew—and kept—their place. Taking this rhetoric to heart, common men no longer automatically deferred to gentlemen of higher rank. Many women, too, claimed that their contributions to the patriots' cause, managing farms and shops in the absence of husbands, merited greater respect and equality in marital relations, including property rights. In letters to her husband, John Adams, Abigail Adams stopped referring to the family farm as "yours." In a telling substitution of pronouns, she started writing of the farm as "ours." Most revolutionary of all, tens of thousands of slaves from the Carolinas to Maryland fled plantations to join the war effort, though these runaways sometimes sided with the British, believing that loyalty to the crown would win them freedom from their masters.

The prospect of a social revolution of artisans, women, and slaves, rather than a narrower liberal revolution, generated a reaction against what American elites called the "excesses of democracy." Their fears grew after farmers in western Massachusetts, led by Daniel Shays, interrupted court proceedings in which the state sought to foreclose on properties for nonpayment of taxes. The farmers who joined Shays in the fall of 1786 also denounced illegitimate taxation, this time by the American government. Massachusetts militiamen easily defeated the ragtag rebel army, but to save the nation from falling into "anarchy," propertied men convened a Constitutional Convention in Philadelphia in the summer of 1787.

Amid fierce debate among the assembled merchants, planters, physicians, governors, military officers, and lawyers (common farmers were not in attendance), the Constitutional Convention drafted a charter for a republican government. The new Constitution substantially enlarged the power of the federal government and, compared to the state constitutions of a decade earlier, reduced the stature of the legislature, the branch of government most responsive to popular will. The Constitution also included a system of checks and balances to prevent any of the three branches of government from becoming too powerful, and to deter majorities from trampling on the rights and property of a wealthier minority. Submitted to the states for approval, the Constitution proved controversial. Its critics, known as Anti-Federalists, echoing Shays, claimed to be defending the people against the growth of a potentially tyrannical federal government. Anti-Federalists also insisted on the inclusion of a Bill of Rights to protect individual liberties from abusive government intrusions. After a series of closely contested campaigns, the Constitution won ratification, though a Bill of Rights was soon amended to it.

From the 1780s onward, the Federalists and Anti-Federalists disagreed fervently over the new design of the United States, as the new country was called, but they confined their jousting to the constitutional arena. In an uneasy truce, property owners agreed not to convert the debate over whether to abolish slavery, brewing since the 1770s, into a cause for disunion. As the frontier expanded westward, the question of which new states would be free states and which would be slave states led to a series of contentious compromises. Only the existence of ample land postponed a confrontation. By 1800, the election of Thomas Jefferson as the third president of the United States signaled the triumph of a model of sending pioneers out to new lands to defuse conflict on old lands. In the same year, however, a Virginia slave named Gabriel Prosser hatched a plan to raise an army of slaves to seize the state capital at Richmond and win support from white artisans and laborers for a more inclusive republic. Gabriel's dream of an egalitarian revolution fell victim to white terror and black betrayal, however. Twenty-seven slaves, including Gabriel, went to the gallows. With them, for the moment, died the dream of a multiracial republic in which all men were truly created equal.

THE FRENCH REVOLUTION

The rhetoric of freedom and rights also shook up social and political hierarchies in Europe's capitals. Partly inspired by the American Revolution, French men and women soon began to issue their own calls for liberty—and the result was a series of events that, even more than the American Revolution, shook the continent's established dynasties and social hierarchies. In France, the Revolution changed its course so suddenly, involved so many participants, and was so extensively reported in books, pamphlets, journals, and songs across the globe that it had a riveting effect on all who heard of it. That the Revo-

> *That the French Revolution's ideas inspired so many other rebels around the world into the twentieth century made it an event of global importance.*

lution's ideas—and its violent course of events—inspired so many other rebels around the world, beginning in 1789 and lasting long into the twentieth century, made it an event not only of European, but also of global importance.

For decades before the outbreak of the Revolution, enlightened thinkers had attacked the inefficiencies, inequalities, and cruelties of France's old regime. In widely read pamphlets and books, satirists poked fun at the corruptions and prejudices of the church, the court, and the aristocracy, and offered suggestions on how the system might be reformed. Their criticisms often resulted in their imprisonment or exile, but by the mid-eighteenth century, discontent with France's ruling elite had already spread beyond the educated few. In the countryside, peasants had grumbled for centuries about paying taxes and tithes to the church, and had suffered periods of deprivation (while the nobility and clergy paid almost no taxes). Compounding the opposition to taxes, crop yields had been poor for several years in the 1780s, and the extremely cold winter and poor grain harvests of 1788–1789 brought real suffering to many. By the close of the eighteenth century, in part as a result of the American Revolution, there was a growing sense that inheritance need not dictate people's place in the world. But revolutions do not occur simply because people are oppressed, hungry, and angry, or even because some begin to imagine alternatives to the order of things. It took a unique combination of these pressures, and the opportunity provided by a fiscal crisis, to unleash the French Revolution of 1789.

Interestingly, it was the king himself who opened the door to revolution. Eager to weaken his arch-rival, England, Louis XVI (ruled 1774–1793) spent huge sums in support of the American rebels; by doing so, he greatly increased France's state debt, which consumed some 50 percent of France's national budget by 1788. In and of itself, this was not disastrous—the Dutch and the English at the time had even larger debts. But in France, the king could not raise taxes on the privileged classes without calling a meeting of the Estates-General, a medieval advisory body that had last met in 1614. Like American colonists, French nobles argued that taxation

Women March on Versailles. On October 5, 1789, a group of market women, many of them fishwives (traditionally regarded as leaders of the poor), marched on the Paris city hall to demand bread. Quickly, their numbers grew, and they redirected their march to Versailles, some twelve miles away and the symbol of the entire political order. In response to the women, the secluded king finally appeared on the balcony and agreed to sign the revolutionary decree and return with the women to Paris.

gave them the right or privilege of representation. When the king reluctantly agreed to summon the Estates-General in 1788, he did so knowing that the clergy and aristocracy would have a long list of grievances to air, and that he would probably have to institute reforms. Nonetheless, Louis still believed that this body would remain advisory and that the delegates of the clergy (the First Estate) and the aristocracy (the Second Estate) would overrule the delegates who represented everybody else (the Third Estate). Although the constituencies of the first two groups numbered about 500,000 and that of the last numbered about 25 million, each estate voted as one body rather than as individuals, which meant that the Third Estate could be outvoted.

The king did not realize the extent of discontent with his rule and the Third Estate's unwillingness to agree to reforms that benefited only the upper classes. When the delegates finally assembled in the spring of 1789, the Third Estate refused to be outvoted by the other two, insisted that those who worked and paid the taxes *were* the nation, and demanded that the delegates sit together in one chamber and vote as individuals. The privileged few, some began to say, were simply parasites. As arguments raged and pamphlets poured out of Paris in the spring and early summer of 1789, in the countryside peasants began to sack castles—yet another indication that "the people" now believed the time had come to throw off the old system of inequalities. In June 1789, the delegates of the Third Estate simply declared themselves to be the "National" Assembly, the body fit to determine France's future.

On July 14, 1789, a Parisian crowd, angered at the king's dismissal of a favorite minister, attacked a medieval armory in search of weapons. Not only did this armory, the Bastille, hold gunpowder, it was also an infamous prison for political prisoners—though in 1789 it held only five forgers and two lunatics.

Enraged at the commanding officer's refusal to open the doors, the crowd stormed the prison and murdered the officer, then cut off his head and paraded it through the streets of Paris, stuck on a pike. On this day, subsequently celebrated as Bastille Day, the king made the fateful decision not to call out the army, and the capital city belonged to the crowd. The news from Paris quickly spread to the countryside, emboldening peasants to burn down manor houses and destroy municipal archives, where the records of the hated feudal dues were kept. Reformist sentiment—and middle-class fear that the Revolution would get out of hand—ran so high that on August 4, 1789, at a special night session, the deputies declared the abolition of the feudal privileges of the nobility and the clergy and the opening of a new era of liberty, equality, and fraternity.

A "Declaration of the Rights of Man and Citizen" followed on August 26. Its seventeen articles echoed Jefferson's Declaration of Independence—but the grander promises of the French document and its different context made it a more radical document. It endowed all citizens of the French nation with inviolable liberties, and gave all men, at least, equality under the law. The French document also proclaimed in Article 3 that "the principle of all sovereignty rests essentially in the nation." Thus, the French Revolution not only trumpeted individual rights and the principle of equality, but it also connected more closely the concept of a people with a nation. Both the rhetorical and real war against feudal privileges marked the beginning of the end of dynastic and aristocratic rule on the continent.

Altering social hierarchies affected the relations among men and women. Some women felt that the new principles of citizenship should also include the rights of women. Radical republican ideology spawned an early feminist movement. In 1791, a group of women circulated a petition demanding the right to bear arms to defend the revolution, but they stopped short of

THE RIGHTS OF WOMEN

In the late eighteenth century, revolutionaries extolled the rights of "man" across the Atlantic world. But what about women? Mary Wollstonecraft (1759–1797), an Englishwoman, writer, teacher, editor, and proponent of spreading education, grew exasperated at her male colleagues' celebration of newfound liberties for men. In 1792, she published A Vindication of the Rights of Woman, *one of the founding works of modern feminism. In this work, she argued that the superiority of men was as arbitrary as the divine right of kings. For this, she won the opprobrium of male progressives. The author is a "hyena in petticoats," noted one critic. In fact, she was arguing that women had the same rights to be reasonable creatures as men, and that especially education should be available equally to both sexes.*

I love man as my fellow; but his sceptre, real or usurped, extends not to me, unless the reason of an individual demands my homage; and even then the submission is to reason, and not to man. In fact, the conduct of an accountable being must be regulated by the operations of its own reason; or on what foundation rests the throne of God?

It appears to me necessary to dwell on these obvious truths, because females have been insulated, as it were; and while they have been stripped of the virtues that should clothe humanity, they have been decked with artificial graces that enable them to exercise a short-lived tyranny. Love, in their bosoms, taking the place of every nobler passion, their sole ambition is to be fair, to raise emotion instead of inspiring respect; and this ignoble desire, like the servility in absolute monarchies, destroys all strength of character. Liberty is the mother of virtue, and if women be, by their very constitution, slaves, and not allowed to breathe the sharp invigorating air of freedom, they must ever languish like exotics, and be reckoned beautiful flaws in nature. Let it also be remembered, that they are the only flaw.

As to the argument respecting the subjection in which the sex has ever been held, it retorts on man. The many have always been enthralled by the few; and monsters, who

scarcely have shown any discernment of human excellence, have tyrannized over thousands of their fellow-creatures. Why have men of superior endowments submitted to such degradation? For, is it not universally acknowledged that kings, viewed collectively, have ever been inferior, in abilities and virtue, to the same number of men taken from the common mass of mankind—yet have they not, and are they not still treated with a degree of reverence that is an insult to reason? China is not the only country where a living man has been made a God. *Men* have submitted to superior strength to enjoy with impunity the pleasure of the moment; *women* have only done the same, and therefore till it is proved that the courtier, who servilely resigns the birthright of a man, is not a moral agent, it cannot be demonstrated that woman is essentially inferior to man because she has always been subjugated.

Brutal force has hitherto governed the world, and that the science of politics is in its infancy, is evident from philosophers scrupling to give the knowledge most useful to man that determinate distinction.

Source: Mary Wollstonecraft, *A Vindication of the Rights of Woman*, edited by Miriam Brody (New York: Penguin Books, 1792/1993), pp. 122–23.

demanding equal rights for both sexes. Women would become citizens by being good revolutionary wives and mothers, not by virtue of enjoying their own natural rights. In that same year, Olympe de Gouges (1748–1793) composed a "Declaration of the Rights of Woman and Citizen," in which she repeated the sev-

enteen articles of the Rights of Man, adding to each one the word "woman," and proposed female rights to divorce, to hold property in marriage, and to be educated and have public careers. The all-male Assembly did not take up these proposals, despite the claims that "liberty and equality" were universal rights. For them it was self-evident that a "fraternity" of free *men* composed the nation.

As the Revolution gained momentum between the fall of 1789 and the winter of 1792, the radicals gained more and more power, and more and more nobles and clergy fled the country. In late 1790, all clergy were forced to take an oath of loyalty to the new state. This action created enormous opposition among pious Catholics and spurred a major counterrevolutionary movement. Meanwhile, the revolutionary ranks began to splinter, as men and women discussed the proper aims and ends of the Revolution. In this period, two crucial political associations took shape. The liberal revolutionary group, known as the Girondins, supported the creation of a constitutional monarchy, while the radical Jacobins wanted to do without the king and to remake French culture as a whole. In 1791, it seemed that the Girondins had the upper hand, and France was set to become a constitutional monarchy. But when Louis XVI and his family were caught trying to escape from France, the Jacobins gained the advantage. Fearing the king would join the emigré nobles and religious opponents who were trying to raise an army to overthrow the Revolution, the radicals confined the king under house arrest. Now the Jacobin calls to purge the Assembly of counterrevolutionary elements grew more shrill, and the Girondins lost control of the government. In September 1792, a new National Convention was elected by universal

> *In the wake of the king's execution, radicals launched a campaign to purge the nation of its enemies and to extend the Revolution beyond France's borders.*

manhood suffrage (the first such election in Europe), and the first French Republic was proclaimed. Thereafter, seized by a combination of panic and exhilaration, the Jacobins began to call for a revolutionary war, both inside and outside France, to destroy the counterrevolution. By early 1793, Louis XVI had been tried, found guilty of treason, and guillotined, and France was at war with many of its neighbors. The events in France, especially the execution of the king, shocked Europeans accustomed to fixed social hierarchies and a world in which the king was presumed to rule as God's representative on earth, answering to no one.

In the wake of the king's execution, radicals launched a campaign, known as the Reign of Terror, to purge the nation of its enemies and to extend the Revolution beyond France's borders. Jacobin leaders, such as the lawyer Maximilien Robespierre (1758–1794), oversaw the execution of as many as 40,000 persons who were judged enemies of the state—most of whom were peasants and urban laborers. The institution of universal conscription allowed radicals to create an army large enough to spread the Revolution to Europe. By the spring of 1794, France's army numbered some 800,000 soldiers, making it the world's largest. In a startling departure from older practice, most of the French officers came from the middle classes, and some even had lower-class origins; foot soldiers identified with the French *patrie*, or fatherland, and demonstrated their solidarity with revo-

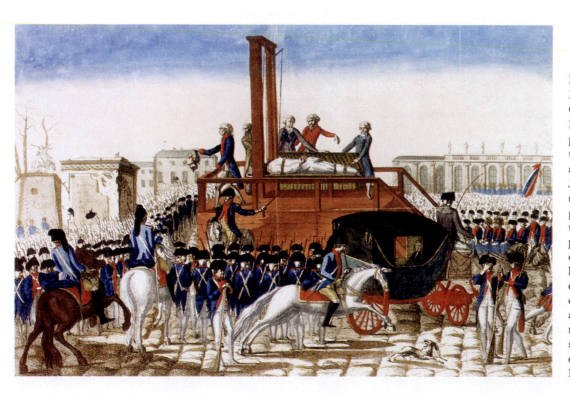

Execution of Louis XVI. In December 1792, the National Convention under the lawyer Robespierre and other Jacobins put Louis XVI on trial for treason after he tried to escape abroad and raise an army. On January 15, the monarch was unanimously pronounced guilty. The next day a resolution calling for execution passed by a single vote (361 out of 721), and Louis was beheaded by guillotine. Regicide eliminated the possibility of constitutional compromise among opposing radical and moderate factions, and more sharply delineated the supporters and enemies of the Revolution abroad.

lutionary songs like "The Marseillaise," which soon became the French national anthem. Though it suffered horrible deprivations in 1794–1795, the army remained loyal to the revolutionary government and a critical means by which revolutionary ideology was spread, not just throughout France, but throughout Europe as well. This enormous conscript army also was a major means by which ordinary Frenchmen learned to identify themselves with the goals of the nation as a whole.

> *The revolutionaries understood that to make fundamental social change really stick they would have to do away with the symbols and rituals of the old regime.*

The revolutionaries understood that to make fundamental social change really stick they would have to do away with the symbols and rituals of the old regime. They changed street names and took down monuments to the royal family, substituting for religious and dynastic names the names of revolutionary heroes or of natural phenomena. They adopted a new flag, eliminated titles, and insisted that everyone be addressed as "Citizen." The revolutionaries' passion for rationalizing the world and their exhilaration at the prospect of creating a new world should not be forgotten or underestimated. Indeed, they were so exhilarated by the new world they were bringing into being that they changed time itself. Time was now reckoned not from the birth of Christ but from the moment that the French Republic was proclaimed: September 22, 1792, became day 1 of year 1 of the new age. The radicals also attempted to supplant the Catholic faith, since they believed that it smacked of corruption and inequality, with a religion of Reason. The French people could, they were told, worship a rational Supreme Being on days prescribed by the state. This did not go over very well, however. In 1794, in the town of Saint Vincent, the unveiling of a statue of the Supreme Being invited characteristic derision from townspeople. The occasion was interrupted by an old woman who motioned to all the women in the crowd to rise, turn their backs to the secular altar, raise their skirts, and expose their buttocks to the Supreme Being.

By mid-1794, enthusiasm for Robespierre's measures had lost popular support, as had the perpetrators of the Terror. Robespierre himself and other Jacobins were guillotined. Reaction spread to the provinces, where many others were killed. In 1795, a temporary junta known as the Directory took over the affairs of state and rounded up many remaining radicals. In 1799, following more political turmoil, a coup d'état unexpectedly resulted in the rise to power of a thirty-year-old general from the recently annexed Mediterranean island of Corsica, Napoleon Bonaparte (1769–1821). Napoleon first was a member of a three-man consulate, then became first consul, and in 1804 proclaimed himself emperor of the French nation.

Napoleon checked the excesses and chaos of radical rule, while letting some revolutionary changes continue. Retreating from the anti-Catholicism of the Jacobins, Napoleon signed a Concordat with the Vatican in 1804, which allowed religion to be freely practiced again in France. A dictator, he retreated from republican principles and declared himself emperor. Napoleon nonetheless prepared a constitution, which he submitted to a vote of approval known as a plebiscite. Maintaining the Revolution's enthusiasm for a more rational order, he centralized government administration (appointing local prefects who reported to the central government) and revamped finances by eliminating tax exemptions and centralizing tax collection. Most important, he codified the nation's laws, including those for property and contracts, thereby providing a legal framework for business and commerce. The new "Code Napoleon" eliminated a baroque system of old laws and privileges and created a uniform law code for all of France. By emphasizing the equality of all men and the protection of individual property across France, Napoleon's reforms revolutionized European legal history.

NAPOLEON'S EMPIRE

Napoleon shared with the radicals a determination to extend the geographic reach of the French Revolution. He dreamed of reinventing the Roman empire on new foundations. Everywhere that French armies advanced, they claimed to be introducing the principles of liberty, equality, and fraternity, and in many places local populations embraced the French, regarding them as liberators from the old order.

Napoleon believed that the entire world would greet his cause with open arms. But such was not always the case, as he had learned in Egypt. After defeating Ottoman troops at the Battle of the Pyramids in 1798, Napoleon had thought the French would be welcomed as liberators, but he soon found himself faced with uprisings by the local Egyptian population.

In Portugal, Spain, and Russia, French troops also faced fierce national resistance. Portuguese and Spanish soldiers and peasants formed bands of resisters called "guerrillas" (after the French word *guerre*), and they were joined by British troops to fight the French in what became known as the Peninsular War (1808–1813). In the Germanies and in Italy, French occupiers quickly wore out their welcome, as they plundered resources, imposed taxes, and conscripted young men. As the locals in these areas tired of being told that French ways were better in all spheres of life, many looked backward to their past for comfort and for inspiration to oppose the French. In so doing, they discovered something that had only barely been visible before: *national* traditions, borders, and character types. It is one of the great ironies of Napoleon's attempt to bring all of Europe un-

Battle of the Pyramids. The French army invaded Egypt with grand ambitions and high hopes. Napoleon brought a large cadre of scholars along with his 36,000-man army, intending to win Egyptians to the cause of the French Revolution and to establish a French imperial presence on the banks of the Nile. This idealized portrait of the famous Battle of the Pyramids, fought on July 21, 1798, shows Napoleon and his forces crushing the Mamluk military forces.

der French rule that it did not create continental unity, but rather laid the foundations for nineteenth-century nationalist strife.

The revolutionary conflicts of the 1790s became, after 1800, a world war, with troops fighting in Africa, across Europe, in the Americas, and in Southeast Asia. Napoleon extended his empire from the Iberian peninsula in southwestern Europe all the way to Moscow (see Map 6-2). By 1812, when he invaded Russia, however, his forces were overstretched and lacked food supplies to survive the harsh Russian winter. Napoleon had been aided by divisions among his enemies; only Great Britain had been continuously at war with France (except for 1803–1804). But in 1813, after Napoleon's attack on Russia, all the major European powers (Austria, Prussia, Russia, and Great Britain) united against the French. Forced to retreat from Russia and now confronted by a united force of all his enemies, Napoleon and his army were finally vanquished in Paris in 1814. Exiled to the island of Elba by the allies, Napoleon escaped to lead his troops one last time. At the Battle of Waterloo in Belgium in 1815, however, a coalition of armies from Prussia, Austria, Russia, and Britain decisively crushed Napoleon and his troops as they made their last stand.

At the Congress of Vienna (1814–1815), convened to restore peace, the victorious European monarchies agreed to respect each other's borders and to cooperate in guarding against future revolutions and war. Delegates to the Congress understood that the world had changed, but they were determined to manage those changes as best they could. France became a

> *At the Congress of Vienna, convened to restore peace, the victorious European monarchies agreed to respect each other's borders and to cooperate in guarding against future revolutions and war.*

monarchy once more, under Louis XVIII (the Bourbon brother of executed Louis XVI). Great Britain and Russia—one a constitutional monarchy, the other an autocracy—cooperated to prevent a revival of French or other attempts to assert hegemony over the continent.

The impact of the French Revolution and Napoleon's conquests, however, proved to be far-reaching. They had decisive effects on Spain and Portugal's links to their colonies in the Americas. In many of the smaller German principalities (states) between Prussia and France—which Napoleon reduced from around 300 to around 30—the changes introduced under French revolutionary occupation, such as the abolition of serfdom, remained in place after Napoleon's defeat. Napoleon's occupation of the Italian peninsula also sparked a number of underground movements for liberty and for Italian unification, much to the chagrin of Austrian and French monarchs.

REVOLUTIONS IN THE CARIBBEAN AND IBERIAN AMERICA

From North America and France, revolutionary enthusiasm spread through the Caribbean and Spanish and Portuguese America. But while men of property directed the war of independence that gave birth to the United States, the political upheaval in the rest of the Americas started from the bottom up, with uprisings by subordinated people of color, whose desire for

MAP 6-2   NAPOLEON'S EMPIRE, 1812

During the first decade of the nineteenth century, Napoleon controlled almost the whole of Europe. He tried to create a continental political and economic system that would undermine the British economy, and to this effect instituted the continental system, a blockade whose purpose was to keep British goods out of continental Europe. How were the British able to defeat Napoleon's efforts? What parts of Europe were most deeply affected by French revolutionary and Napoleonic culture and what parts were least affected?

freedom from exploitation antedated the French Revolution's slogan of freedom.

Even before the French Revolution, Andean Indians had risen against Spanish colonial authority to protest onerous taxes and labor obligations. In a spectacular uprising in the 1780s, Andean Indians called for freedom from the forced labor draft and compulsory consumption of Spanish wares. Led by a local political chieftain who took the name of an early anti-Spanish rebel, Tupac Amarú, an Indian army of 40,000 to 60,000 besieged the ancient capital of Cuzco and nearly vanquished Spanish armies. It took the Spanish many years to eliminate the insurgents.

This uprising shook the confidence of Iberian-American colonial elites whose fear of their Indian or slave majorities caused them to renew their loyalty to the Spanish or Portuguese crown. For a time, these elites hesitated to follow the example of independence-seeking Anglo-American colonists, lest the struggle for political power unleash a more radical and uncontrollable social revolution. Ultimately, however, Iberian-American elites joined their counterparts in the United States in severing colonial ties, but they responded to the revolts from the lower orders by seeking to establish regimes that interpreted the principle of liberty to mean freedom for the property-owning classes. Only in the French colony of Saint Domingue (modern-day Haiti) did slaves carry out a successful insurrection. This sent shivers down the spine of white elites throughout the Americas, and made them even more determined to secure property and order.

REVOLUTION IN SAINT DOMINGUE (HAITI) The French Revolution had its most immediate reverberation in the most precious of all French colonies, Saint Domingue. It led to the loss of the colony and the emancipation of its slaves. For Saint Domingue's slaves, the road to independence and emancipation was a bloody one. The island's black slave population numbered 500,000, compared with 40,000 white French settlers and about 30,000 free "people of color" (free mulattoes, who were of mixed black and white ancestry, as well as freed black slaves). After the events of 1789 in France, white settlers in Saint Domingue campaigned for self-government, while slaves borrowed the revolutionary language to denounce their masters. As whites clashed with people of color

Toussaint L'Ouverture. In the 1790s, Toussaint L'Ouverture led the slaves of the French colony of Saint Domingue in the world's largest and most successful slave insurrection. Toussaint embraced the principles of the French Revolution and demanded that universal rights be applied to people of African descent.

Revolution in Saint Domingue. In 1791, slaves and people of color rose up against the white planters. This engraving was based on a contemporary German report on the uprising, and depicted the fears of the whites in the face of slave rebellion as much as the actual events themselves.

and slaves in 1791, the island descended into civil war. Dominican slaves fought French forces dispatched in 1792 to restore order. The National Convention in France abolished slavery in 1793. The former slaves took control of the island, but they joined with French troops to fight British and Spanish forces sent to Saint Domingue to stir up trouble. When Napoleon took power, he decided to reassert French authority in the island, and he restored slavery in 1802. Napoleon sent an army of 58,000 under his brother-in-law, General Victor-Emmanuel Leclerc, to quash the forces led by Toussaint L'Ouverture (1743–1803), a former slave. Leclerc's army, perhaps the most fearsome in Europe, was decimated by guerrilla fighters and yellow fever. After eighteen months, the French surrendered and left, having lost over 50,000 of their finest soldiers. Toussaint died in a French jail, after treachery led to his capture while he was trying to negotiate a settlement. Nonetheless, in January 1804, General Jean-Jacques Dessalines declared "Haiti" independent.

Independence, however, did not bring international recognition from fellow revolutionaries. To the victorious Haitians, it seemed clear that the French commitment to empire overrode their commitment to the ideals of republican citizenship. Toussaint, the "black Jacobin," and the slaves of Saint Domingue had shown a greater fidelity to ideals of liberty than the French themselves. Yet, Thomas Jefferson, the author of the Declaration of Independence and the U. S. president, refused to recognize Haiti. Like many other American slave owners, Jefferson worried that the example of a successful slave insurrection might inspire slave revolts in the United States.

INSPIRATIONS FOR SLAVE REBELLION ON HAITI

The ideals of the French Revolution spread rapidly beyond France through the rest of Europe and even overseas. In few places did they produce a more radical effect than on the island of Saint Domingue, renamed Haiti after it acquired independence. By the 1780s, Saint Domingue was France's richest colony and its most valuable overseas trading possession. Its wealth came from sugar plantations that depended on a vast, highly coerced slave population. About 40,000 whites ruled over and ruthlessly exploited 500,000 enslaved Africans, approximately two-thirds of whom had recently arrived from Africa. The lives of the slaves were short and brutal, lasting on average only fifteen years; hence the need for the wealthy planter class to replenish their labor supplies from Africa at frequent intervals. White planters from the island had the reputation of great wealth. Those who dressed ostentatiously as they strode the streets of Paris in the late eighteenth century were said to be as wealthy as a "creole," meaning a Caribbean planter. But the white planters also knew their privileges were vulnerable, which made them eager to amass quick fortunes so that they could sell out and return to France. These men and women were vastly outnumbered by the enslaved, who were seething with resentment, at a time when abolitionist sentiments were gaining ground in Europe and even circulating among the slaves in the Americas.

Yet, the planters greeted the onset of the French Revolution in 1789 with enthusiasm. They saw an opportunity to gain internal political power and to engage in wider trading contacts with North America and the rest of the world. They ignored, at their peril, the fact that the ideals of the French Revolution, and especially its slogan of liberty, equality, and fraternity, could inspire the island's free blacks, free mulattoes, and slaves. Indeed, no sooner had the white planters thrown in their lot with the Third Estate in France than a slave rebellion broke out in their midst in Saint Domingue. From its inception in August 1791, it led, after great loss of life to African slave dissidents and French soldiers, to the proclamation of an independent state in Haiti in 1804, ruled by African Americans. Haiti became, in fact, the Americas' second independent republican government.

The revolution had many sources of inspiration. It was both French and African. According to a later West Indian scholar, a group of black Jacobins, determined to carry the ideals of the French Revolution to their logical end point— the abolition of slavery—made up the revolutionary cadre. Their undisputed leader was a freed black by the name of Toussaint L'Ouverture, who had learned about the French abolitionist writings of the age. But it is hardly surprising, given how recently most of the slaves had arrived from Africa, that African cultural and political ideals also fomented slave resistance. At a secret forest meeting held on August 14, 1791, the persons who were to lead the initial stage of the revolution gathered to affirm their commitment to one another at a voodoo ritual, presided over by a tall, black priestess, "with strange eyes and bristly hair." Voodoo was a mixture of African and New World religious beliefs that existed among slave communities in many parts of the Americas (see Chapter 5). According to one description of the forest ceremony, the priestess arrived "armed with a long pointed knife that she waved above her head [as] she performed a sinister dance singing an African song, which the others, face down against the ground, repeated as a chorus. A black pig was then dragged in front of her, and she split it open with her knife. The animal's blood was collected in a wooden bowl and served still foaming to each delegate. At a signal from the priestess, everyone threw themselves on their knees and swore blindly to obey the orders of Boukman, who had been proclaimed supreme chief of the rebellion." Boukman was a voodoo chief himself, and he initiated the revolution against the planters, though it was Toussaint L'Ouverture who later assumed leadership of the revolt.

Inspired by both voodoo and the French Revolution, the rebellion in Saint Domingue resulted in a series of dramatic ruptures. European slavery came to an end. White planters yielded to a black political elite. Hundreds of thousands of slaves and French soldiers perished or were maimed, and the old sugar export economy could no longer be sustained. No slave shipments arrived, and no sugar was exported.

BRAZIL AND CONSTITUTIONAL MONARCHY The French Revolution and Napoleonic Wars shattered the ties between Spain and Portugal and their colonies in the Americas. Brazil offers an example of a colonial society whose road to independent statehood minimized political revolution and squelched social revolution. In late 1807, French troops stormed Lisbon, but they were too late to capture the royal Braganza family. The royal family and their extensive retinue fled to Rio de Janeiro, the capital of Portugal's prize colony, Brazil. Upon arrival, they instituted reforms in administration, agriculture, and manufacturing, and established schools, hospitals, and a library. The migration of the royal family to Brazil preempted colonial claims for autonomy, for Brazil was now the center of the Portuguese empire. Further dampening revolutionary enthusiasm was the royal family's willingness to share power with the local planter aristocracy. Over the ensuing years, the economy prospered and slavery expanded. In 1821, the exiled Portuguese king agreed to return to Lisbon, leaving instructions to his son Pedro to preserve the family lineage in Rio de Janeiro. It did not take long, however, before Brazilian elites rejected Portugal altogether. Faced with the threat that colonists might topple the dynasty in Rio de Janeiro, and concerned that such upheaval might cascade into regional disputes and rivalries, Pedro declared Brazil an independent empire that was free from Portugal in 1822. Shortly thereafter, he signed a charter establishing a constitutional monarchy that would last until the late nineteenth century.

Brazilian business elites and bureaucrats collaborated to minimize their conflicts, lest an insurrection of slaves erupt. Regional insurrections, like the creation of the fledgling Republic of the Equator in 1817, were crushed. In the south, a campaign by cowboys, known as gauchos, who wanted a decentralized federation with a great deal of autonomy, also proved to be no match for the central government's powerful army and navy. Even the largest urban slave revolt in the Americas, led by African Muslims in the Brazilian state of Bahia in 1835, was put down in a matter of days. By the 1840s, Brazil had achieved a political stability unmatched in the Americas. Indeed, Brazil's socially controlled transition from colony to nation proved to be the exception in Latin America.

MEXICO'S INDEPENDENCE When Napoleon occupied Spain, he sparked a crisis in the Spanish empire. In the Spanish colonies the dynasty did not manage change, as had the Portuguese. Most political independence movements in Spanish America evolved into noisy social revolutions or civil wars. Unlike the Portuguese Braganza family, which managed to elude French troops, the Spanish Bourbons fell captive to Napoleon in 1807, and spent many years under comfortable house arrest.

Colonial elites in Buenos Aires, Caracas, and Mexico City, grappling with the problem of self-rule without an emperor, came to enjoy autonomy from Madrid. Creoles (American-born Spaniards) resented it when the mother country reinstated peninsulars (officials from Spain) once the Spanish Bourbons returned to power in 1814. The creoles disliked the economic regulations and taxation of the mother country and chafed under the rule of the peninsulars. Inspired by Enlightenment thinkers and revolution in North America, the creoles wished to retain their elite privileges and to rid their lands of the peninsulars.

> *Like the creoles of South America, those of Mexico were beginning to identify themselves more as Mexicans, and less as Spanish Americans.*

In Mexico, the royal army prevailed as long as there was any hope that the emperor in Madrid could keep a firm grip on political authority. But from 1810 to 1813, two rural priests, Father Miguel Hidalgo (1753–1811) and Father José María Morelos (1765–1815), galvanized an insurrection that incorporated a broad alliance of peasants, Indians, and artisans. They called for an end to elite abuses, denounced bad government, and called for redistribution of wealth, return of land to the Indians, and respect for the Virgin of Guadalupe (who would become Mexico's patron saint). Eventually they demanded a full break from Spain. The rebels sent shock waves across the viceroyalty and nearly encircled Mexico City itself, the capital of Spain's richest colony. This horrified peninsulars and creoles alike, who overcame internal disputes to plead with Spanish armies to rescue them from the rebels. It took years, but the royal armies eventually crushed the uprising.

Despite the military victory, the Spanish crown's hold on its colony gave way. In these years of conflict, colonists started to enjoy measures of autonomy and even began electing representatives to local assemblies. Moreover, like the creoles of South America, those of Mexico were beginning to identify themselves more as Mexicans, and less as Spanish Americans. So, when Ferdinand VII, the Spanish king, appeared unable to handle affairs, not only abroad, but within Spain itself, the colonists began considering home rule. The critical factor was the army, which remained faithful to the crown. When anarchy seemed to spread through Spain in 1820, however, Mexican generals, with the support of the creoles, cut their losses, proclaiming Mexican independence in 1821.

OTHER SOUTH AMERICAN REVOLUTIONS The process of uncoupling Spain's grip on mainland America was far more prolonged and militarized than was Britain's separation from its American colonies. The struggle for independence from Spain completely refashioned the nature of political leadership in South America. Venezuela's Simón Bolívar (1783–1830), the son of a wealthy merchant-planter family who was weaned on European Enlightenment texts, dreamed of a land governed by reason. In Napoleonic France, he found a compelling model of a new state, one forged by military heroism and constitutional proclamations. The same held true for the less aristocratic Argentine leader, General José de San Martín (1778–1850). Men like Bolívar, San Martín, and their many generals waged an extended war between 1810 and 1824. In some areas, like present-day Uruguay and Venezuela, the carnage depopulated entire provinces.

What in South America started as a political revolution against Bourbon authority escalated into social struggle. Warfare mobilized Indians, *mestizos*, and slaves. The militarized populace threatened the fortunes of planters and great merchants. Rural folk from the grasslands rode into battle against aristocratic creoles. Andean Indians fled the mines and occupied great estates. On the Caribbean coast of South America, graffiti announced the end of colonial slavery. "Death to shitty little whites," cried one

> *The contradictory legacy of the revolutions of Spanish America was the triumph of wealthy elites under the banner of liberty, yet at the expense of poorer, ethnic, and mixed populations.*

Colombian slogan. As the struggle for self-rule evolved into social revolution, Indians fought whites. Provinces fought their neighbors. Popular armies, having defeated Spain by the 1820s, engaged in civil wars over the new postcolonial order in South America. By the 1840s and 1850s, the old viceroyalties had broken up.

In Latin America, new states, common myths of sacrifice, and collective identities of nationhood emerged, but the people active in these political communities made up a narrow social elite, and the myths were contradictory. Simón Bolívar, for instance, repeatedly urged his followers to become "American," to identify with a larger, pan-creole ideal. He tried to get the liberated countries to unite into a Latin American confederation, urging Peru and Bolivia to join Venezuela, Ecuador, and Colombia in the "Gran Colombia." But the confederation quickly fell apart as local identities continued to take precedence over Spanish-American unity. Bolívar's dream of a United States of South America, possibly even governed by a hereditary king or dictator, gave way to unstable national republics. Bolívar met his end surrounded and hounded by his enemies; San Martín died in exile. The real heirs to independence were not slaves, Indians, or even republican national leaders, but local military chieftains called *caudillos*, who often forged alliances with landowners. The contradictory legacy of the revolutions of Spanish America was the triumph of wealthy and powerful elites under a banner of liberty, yet at the expense of poorer, ethnic, and mixed populations.

Simón Bolívar. The son of a wealthy creole family, Simón Bolívar fought Spanish armies from Venezuela to Bolivia, securing the independence of five countries. Bolívar wanted to transform the former colonies into modern republics, and used many of the icons of revolution from the rest of the Atlantic world—among his favorite models were George Washington and Napoleon Bonaparte. Notice how this image portrays Bolívar in a quintessential Napoleonic pose on horseback.

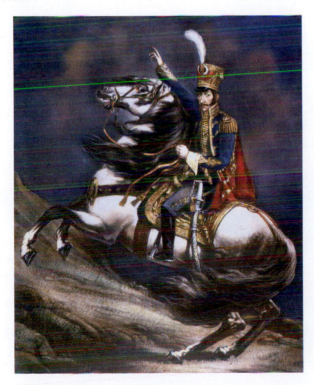

CHANGE AND TRADE IN AFRICA

→ *Why did the abolition of the slave trade have unintended effects on African society?*

Along with Europe and the Americas, Africa, the third corner of the Atlantic world, was also swept up in revolutionary tides. Increased domestic and world trade, particularly but not exclusively in African slaves, shifted the terms of state-building across the continent. Around the edges of Lake Victoria, in the highlands of present-day Rwanda and Burundi, and in southern Africa, new, more powerful kingdoms emerged in the first half of the nineteenth century. Burgeoning commerce created new sources of wealth for ruling groups, who began to assert their power over other peoples. Some regimes, however, fell apart as a result of internal rivalries. The main commercial catalyst for Africa's political shake-up was the rapid growth and then the demise of the Atlantic slave trade.

ABOLITION OF THE SLAVE TRADE

Even as it enriched and empowered some Africans and many Europeans, the slave trade became a subject of fierce debate in the late eighteenth century. Some European and American revolutionaries wanted trade and production to be governed, not by the laws of compulsion, but by the laws of supply and demand. Alongside these advocates of free trade emerged a small but committed group of abolitionists who insisted that traffic in slaves was immoral. In London, they created committees, often led by Quakers, to lobby Parliament for an end to the slave trade. Quakers in Philadelphia followed suit. Pamphlets, reports, and personal narratives denounced the heinous traffic.

In response to abolitionist campaigns, North Atlantic powers moved to ban the international slave trade. Denmark acted first in 1803, with Great Britain following in 1807, and the United States banning it in 1808. Over time, the British persuaded the French and other European governments of the rightness of this

> *Even as it enriched and empowered some Africans and many Europeans, the slave trade became a subject of fierce debate in the late eighteenth century.*

position, with France abolishing it in 1814, the Netherlands in 1817, and Spain in 1845. To enforce the ban, Britain posted an anti-slave-trade naval squadron off the coast of West Africa to cut off traders operating above the equator, and compelled the emperor of Brazil to respect earlier promises to end slave imports. After 1850, Atlantic slave-shipping dropped sharply. In 1867, the last slave vessel entered a New World harbor, Havana.

Until the 1860s, slavers continued to ply the waters of the West African coast to buy captives and illegally transport them as slaves. The British naval squadrons stopped as many smugglers as they could and took the captives they freed to the British base at Sierra Leone, where they were resettled. Liberia, first settled in 1821 by free black Americans, also became a refuge for freed captives and for former slaves returning to Africa from the Americas.

NEW TRADE WITH AFRICA

While eventually choking off the Atlantic slave trade, Europeans endeavored to promote new forms of commerce with Africa. European traders, who had previously thought of Africa only as a source of human captives, now wanted Africans to supply Europe with raw materials and for them to purchase

Chasing Slave Dhows. From being the major proponents of the Atlantic slave trade the British became its chief opponents, using their naval forces to suppress those European and African slave traders who attempted to subvert the injunction against slave trading. Here a British vessel chases an East African slaving dhow trying to run slaves from the island of Zanzibar.

FREDERICK DOUGLASS ASKS "WHAT TO THE SLAVE IS THE FOURTH OF JULY?"

Born in 1818, Frederick Douglass spent the first twenty years of his life as a slave. After running away in 1838, Douglass toured the northern United States delivering speeches that attacked the institution of slavery. The publication of Douglass's autobiography in 1845 cemented his standing as a leading abolitionist. In the excerpt below, taken from an address delivered on July 5, 1852, Douglass contrasts the freedom and natural rights extolled in the American Declaration of Independence and celebrated on the Fourth of July with the dehumanizing condition—and lack of freedom—of African-American slaves.

Fellow-Citizens—pardon me, and allow me to ask, why am I called upon to speak here to-day? What have I, or those I represent, to do with your national independence? Are the great principles of political freedom and of natural justice, embodied in that Declaration of Independence, extended to us? and am I, therefore, called upon to bring our humble offering to the national altar, and to confess the benefits, and express devout gratitude for the blessings, resulting from your independence to us? . . .

But, such is not the state of the case. I say it with a sad sense of the disparity between us. I am not included within the pale of this glorious anniversary! Your high independence only reveals the immeasurable distance between us. The blessings in which you this day rejoice, are not enjoyed in common. The rich inheritance of justice, liberty, prosperity, and independence, bequeathed by your fathers, is shared by you, not by me. The sunlight that brought life and healing to you, has brought stripes and death to me. This Fourth of July is *yours*, not *mine. You* may rejoice, *I* must mourn. . . .

. . . Must I undertake to prove that the slave is a man? That point is conceded already. Nobody doubts it. The slaveholders themselves acknowledge it in the enactment of laws for their government. They acknowledge it when they punish disobedience on the part of the slave. There are seventy-two crimes in the state of Virginia, which, if committed by a black man (no matter how ignorant he be) subject him to the punishment of death; while only two of these same crimes will subject a white man to the like punishment. What is this but the acknowledgment that the slave is a moral, intellectual, and responsible being. The manhood of the slave is conceded. It is admitted in the fact that southern statute books are covered with enactments forbidding, under severe fines and penalties, the teaching of the slave to read or write. When you can point to any such laws, in reference to the beasts of the field, then I may consent to argue the manhood of the slave. When the dogs in your streets, when the fowls of the air, when the cattle on your hills, when the fish of the sea, and the reptiles that crawl, shall be unable to distinguish the slave from a brute, then will I argue with you that the slave is a man!

Source: David W. Blight (ed.), *Narrative of the Life of Frederick Douglass: An American Slave, Written by Himself* (Boston: Bedford Books, 1993), pp. 141–45.

European manufactures. European publicists dubbed the new trade "legitimate" commerce to distinguish it from the "illegitimate" trade in human beings. It was intended to raise the standards of living of Africans by substituting trade in produce for trade in slaves. West African cultivators responded by beginning a brisk export in palm kernels and peanuts. The real bonanza was in vegetable oils to lubricate machinery and to be made into candles, and especially palm oil to produce soap. European merchants argued that by becoming vibrant export societies, Africans would earn the wealth also to become potentially profitable importers of European wares.

The gradual abolition of the slave trade and the emergence of legitimate commerce gave rise to a new generation of West African merchants. Inserting themselves between African producers in the interior or plantations on the coast, and the European export-import firms, they amassed fortunes. The Sierra Leonean merchant, William Heddle, was said to be worth a half million pounds sterling at mid-century. There were many rags-to-riches stories, like that of Jaja of Opobo (1821–1891), who was kidnapped and sold into slavery as a youngster. Jaja was initially one of the many slaves who paddled the canoes that carried palm oil from inland markets to coastal ports. He rose to become the head of a coastal canoe house. As a powerful merchant-prince and chief, he founded the new port of Opobo and could summon a flotilla of war canoes on command. Another freed slave, a Yoruba, William Lewis, made his way back to Africa and settled in Sierra Leone in 1828. Starting with only a few utensils and a small plot of land, Lewis became a successful merchant who was able to send his son Samuel to England for his education. There, Samuel studied law, attended University College in London, and eventually became an important political leader in Sierra Leone, whereupon Queen Victoria recognized him with a knighthood.

> *No longer the supplier of slaves, Africa, in the wake of Atlantic world revolutions, had turned into the largest slaveholding continent.*

Just as the slave trade shaped the rhythms of African political communities, its demise forced African polities to ad-

King Jaja of Opobo. Among the many influential and powerful merchant-princes who rose to prominence along the West African coast in the nineteenth century was King Jaja of Opobo, who rose out of slavery to become the head of a canoe house that transported and traded palm oil. In 1869, Jaja established an independent trading state based around the city of Opobo.

just. For some, it was a boon because it ended the constant drainage of people from an already underpopulated continent. For others, especially if they had positioned themselves as the commercial brokers between African slave supply and Euro-American demand, the demise of the traffic was a disaster, cutting off income necessary to buy European arms and luxury goods. The Asante state, however, endured even as the slave trade declined and despite British military efforts to destroy it. To be sure, the regime wavered when its supply of slaves could find no legal outlet. But it soon recovered. Other West African regimes, like the Yoruba kingdom, did not. There, civil strife broke out once chieftains could no longer use the spoils of the slave trade to support retinues and armies.

The rise of free labor in the Atlantic world and the dwindling of the foreign slave trade also had unintended and perverse effects in Africa: it strengthened slavery in Africa itself. In some African locales by the mid-nineteenth century, more than half of the population were slaves. No longer were slaves mainly to be found in domestic employment, sharing the same table with their masters, eating the same foods, and likely to be assimilated into that society. Instead, slaves worked on palm oil plantations or, in East Africa (especially in Zanzibar), on clove plantations owned by Arabs or Swahili big men. They also served in the military forces, and carried palm oil and ivory to markets as porters or as the oarsmen on the canoes that plied the rivers leading to the coast. In the Fulani emirates of northern Nigeria, slaves comprised a large proportion of the total population. In 1850, the Fulani had as many as 2.5 million slaves, more than the slaves in independent Brazil and second only to the number of slaves in the United States. No longer the supplier of slaves, Africa, in the wake of Atlantic world revolutions, had turned into the largest slaveholding continent.

ECONOMIC REORDERING

> → *How did the industrial and commercial revolutions reorder society?*

The political upheavals in the Atlantic world shattered the old mercantilist system and encouraged economic transformations that placed Western Europe at the hub of an increasingly interconnected world economy. These economic transformations are often referred to collectively as the industrial revolution. They also marked the opening of what many scholars regard as "the great divide" in world history between the economically developed areas of the world and less developed areas. Certainly by 1850 people living in Western Europe and North America were wealthier and healthier than their counterparts elsewhere—a statement that probably could not have been made about the world's population a century earlier. In addition, the Western Europeans, notably the British, were able to translate their economic prowess into political power and were in the process of altering the global balance of power.

BRITAIN'S ECONOMIC LEADERSHIP

The presence of a variety of institutional and economic factors enabled the British to pioneer the innovations that have ever since characterized economic modernity. To begin with, Britain had large and accessible supplies of coal and iron, two of the most important raw materials used to produce the goods of the first industrial revolution. In addition, its manufacturers benefited from a cascade of technological innovations, notably in steam power and textile production, which they put to practical use to produce cheaper goods in larger quantities. But none of these physical or technological factors alone propelled an economic revolution. What was crucial also was that political and social conditions enabled merchants and industrialists to mobilize capital for investment while expanding internal and international markets for their commodities. Finally, Britain's colonies provided it with sources of capital accumulation, raw materials, and markets for manufactured goods. These factors, which were all favorable to far-reaching economic change, all came together in Britain and drove the British economy into continuous and self-sustaining economic growth.

A crucial aspect of economic progress also involved a remarkable expansion in agricultural production for the market, and here, too, British farmers led the way. By exploiting new lands and making existing lands more productive (through enclosing fields and pastures and draining swamp land), farmers in Western Europe and North America could feed more mouths and support a large increase in population. In Great Britain, for example, the population rose from about 5 million in the early 1700s to 9 million by 1800 and to 18 million by 1851. Population growth, in turn, generated pressure on the land, and forced many people to migrate to the cities, creating a supply of urban laborers for

> *Economic growth in Britain was fueled by its supplies of coal and iron, technological innovations, political and social conditions that enabled merchants and industrialists to mobilize capital and expand markets.*

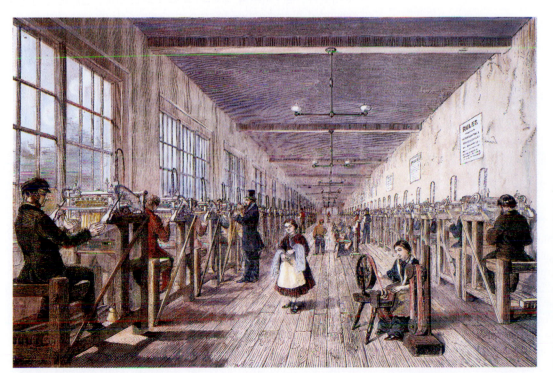

A Model Textile Mill. In the nineteenth century, the English industrialist and reformer Robert Owen tried to create humane factories. Worried about the terrible conditions in most textile mills, Owen created clean and orderly working environments in his mills and had the work rules posted on the walls. Owen still shared most of his contemporaries' employment of children, as can be seen in this image.

the new manufacturing industries. Also adding to the growth of the labor force was the appropriation of common lands as private property by English landowners in the eighteenth century. This threw a large number of small farmers who depended on common lands into the ranks of the landless, compelling them to earn their livelihood as wage workers.

As Britain outdistanced its European rivals in manufacturing, claiming for itself the designation "the workshop of the world," a new economic world order began to emerge. Britain's industrial capitalists increased productivity by organizing a new division of labor around the world. In British workplaces, wage laborers turned the raw cotton grown by peasants in India and slaves in North America into cloth, which was then sold in the home market or exported abroad in exchange for agricultural products from India and Argentina. Thus, Great Britain and the other industrializing states exported manufactures to colonies and dependencies, all under the banner of free trade and free (wage) labor. In return, these colonies and dependencies shipped raw materials to industrial societies.

The economic reordering of the late eighteenth and early nineteenth centuries transformed virtually all aspects of the lives of people who were caught up in it. It required people to alter the way they traded with one another and what they consumed. It also required new methods for mobilizing capital, as well as changes in the rhythms and work routines of merchants, wage laborers, and farmers. Furthermore, changes affected where people worked, where they lived, whom they married, how many children they had, and how they regarded people whose lives were different from their own.

TRADING AND FINANCING

Economic reordering involved dramatic expansions and alterations in patterns of commerce and consumption. By the eighteenth century, sugar and silver, the pioneering commercial commodities of world trade, were joined by other products. Tea became a beverage of international commerce. Its leaves came from China, the sugar to cut its bitterness from the Caribbean, the slaves to harvest the sweetener from Africa, and the ceramics from which to drink a proper cup from the English Midlands. Soap was another truly international commodity. In the 1840s, the American entrepreneur William Colgate was importing palm oil from the slave states of West Africa, coconut oil from Malabar and Ceylon, and poppy seed oil from colonial South Asia, all to make aromatic bars of soap, which were then sold around the world.

So widespread was the economic reordering that ordinary people were able to purchase imported goods with their earnings. Thus, even the poor expanded their diets to include coffee, tea, and sugar—all tropical goods, and all goods that had to be purchased on the market with cash. European artisans as well as farmers purchased tools, furnishings, and home decorations on the market. Slaves and colonial laborers also used their meager earnings to buy imported cotton cloth made in Europe from the raw cotton they picked.

Merchants reaped the greatest rewards of international trade, earning more money than previous traders ever had and enjoying higher social status than they had under dynastic regimes. To be sure, merchants faced great risks. Bad weather, unexpected price fluctuations, and inept handling turned many promising deals into bankrupting disasters. But successful merchants accumulated immense fortunes. Also profiting were accountants and lawyers, who assisted with insurance, bookkeeping, and the recording of legal documents. The new class of commercial men and women, known as the "bourgeoisie," took up residence in thriving ports and other centers of trade. The bourgeoisie formed a new elite, not of birth and titles, but of property and capital. They increasingly assumed positions of authority to match their growing wealth. Indeed, if the bourgeoisie sometimes strove to marry their sons and daughters into old aristocratic families as a way to establish legitimacy for their new wealth, aristocrats just as often sought such marriages for the money and property they brought.

The greatest fortunes—and considerable political power—flowed to those who bankrolled world trade. Some financiers, like many merchants, emerged not from long-established noble families but from the common people. Consider, for example, Mayer Amschel Rothschild (1744–1812). Born the son of a money changer in the Jewish ghetto of Frankfurt, Rothschild expanded his activities from coin dealing to money changing, from trading textiles to lending funds to kings and governments, especially to those at war. By the time of his death, his five sons were running operations in London, Paris, Vienna, Naples, as well as in Frankfurt. Theirs was the world's biggest banking operation, upon which governments became semidependent.

By extending credit for a fee, families like the Rothschilds also enabled traders to ship goods across long distances without having to worry about immediate payment. All these financial changes eased the way for world integration through the flow of goods as well as the flow of money. In the 1820s, sizeable funds amassed in London flowed out to Egypt, Mexico, and New York to support trade, public investment, and even speculation. Some eager British financiers, for example, jumped at the promise of untold fortunes in the silver mines of La Rioja in South America. They invested some of their own capital and, even more, the capital of others in the mines, but they never saw a return. Thus was born a de-

> *The economic reordering of the late eighteenth and early nineteenth centuries transformed virtually all aspects of the lives of people who were caught up in it.*

THE OTHER REVOLUTION OF 1776

The year 1776 is mainly known as the year American colonists declared their independence from the British empire, but it also was the year of the publication of Adam Smith's An Inquiry into the Nature and Causes of the Wealth of Nations, *the most important book in the history of economic thought. Smith, a Scottish philosopher, felt that constraints on trade, by governments or private monopolies, deprived people of their ability to realize their full potential and as such impoverished nations. Although he was not opposed to colonies per se, in this short selection, he warns British authorities that the exclusions placed on their colonies, which bear the brunt of mercantilist controls, are not only unjust, they are counterproductive. Thus, "free trade" is tied up with the fate of Europe's colonies.*

The exclusive trade of the mother countries tends to diminish, or, at least, to keep down below what they would otherwise rise to, both the enjoyments and industry of all those nations in general, and of the American colonies in particular. It is a dead weight upon the action of one of the great springs which puts into motion a great part of the business of mankind. By rendering the colony produce dearer in all other countries, it lessens its consumption, and thereby cramps the industry of the colonies, and both the enjoyments and the industry of all other countries, which both enjoy less when they pay more for what they enjoy, and produce less when they get less for what they produce. By rendering the produce of all other countries dearer in the colonies, it cramps, in the same manner, the industry of all other countries, and both the enjoyments and the industry of the colonies. It is a clog which, for the supposed benefit of some particular countries, embarrasses the pleasures, and encumbers the industry of all other countries; but of the colonies more than of any other. It not only excludes, as much as possible, all other countries from one particular market; but it confines, as much as possible, the colonies to one particular market: and the difference is very great between being excluded from one particular market, when all others are open, and being confined to one particular market, when all others are shut up. The surplus produce of the colonies, however, is the original source of all that increase of enjoyments and industry which Europe derives from the discovery and colonization of America; and the exclusive trade of the mother countries tends to render this source much less abundant than it otherwise would be.

Source: Adam Smith, *An Inquiry into the Nature and Causes of the Wealth of Nations,* Book 4, edited by Edwin Cannan (Chicago: The University of Chicago Press, 1776/1977), pp. 105–106.

sire to exert political pressure over countries where money was invested.

Merchants and financiers soon recognized that a new commercial order was emerging and wanted new laws to support it. Through the eighteenth century, and especially with the political shake-up of old regimes, these emerging urban elites gained more political power. By the early nineteenth century, they began to press for free trade, the right to trade freely across borders. This idea dated back to the sixteenth century and had been extensively elaborated in the writings of Adam Smith. But it took decades for the doctrine to become practice, partly because so many domestic interests benefited from special tariff protections and exclusive access to certain markets. For example, Europe's landed interests ensured that laws obstructed the entry of cheaper foodstuffs; in Great Britain, the Corn Laws imposed a tariff on imported grain and thereby kept the price of bread artificially high. Old mercantilist laws likewise protected national shipping interests. As long as more businesses profited from commercial protection, free trade was a pipe dream.

The first region to embrace free trade practices and policies was in fact the New World. Merchants in the former colonies wanted access to obstructed markets. But it was especially in Iberian America that merchants wanted to export raw materials and import needed European, and especially British, manufactured goods—all with a minimum of hurdles and taxes. After 1810, Latin American countries abolished most tariffs protecting local producers and removed all special laws covering Spanish and Portuguese commerce. The United States also sought to promote its raw materials, but never went as far as Latin America in dismantling protection of local producers against competitive imports. Rather, in the United States, local industries clamored for laws to stop cheap British goods from entering the domestic market.

The rise of free trade in the Americas offered European consumers access to cheap foodstuffs and other primary staples, like timber, cotton, leather, and minerals. The British were the first to seize on the opportunity of free trade with New World societies. Indeed, with fewer formal ties, restricted only to a handful of Caribbean islands and Canada, free trade became the de facto guiding principle of Atlantic commerce between Britain and the Americas. In the 1840s, old protectionist laws gave way to open markets. Under the Conservative British prime minister Robert Peel (1788–1850), new budgets slashed the duties on all kinds of imported staples. Moreover, when famine hit Ireland in the mid-1840s, the British government repealed the Corn Laws (in 1846) to allow grains to enter duty-free from around the world. Finally, the succeeding Liberal government abolished many of the remaining obstacles and preferences, especially the Navigation Acts, which had been originally designed to prevent Dutch merchants from taking over English trade routes. Free trade then became the guiding commercial policy of Great Britain as it embraced the idea that domestic wealth depended on imports of basic goods and exports of new industrial commodities to the world's consumers.

> *Free trade then became the guiding commercial policy for Great Britain as it embraced the idea that domestic wealth depended on imports of basic goods and exports of new industrial commodities.*

MANUFACTURING

Bankers and merchants facilitated not only the development of trade, but also of industries. Industrial development was due to several interlocking changes, however. The accumulation and diffusion of technical knowledge necessary for manufacturing began in the countryside, where handicraft operations were gradually enlarged and mechanized. Often it was small- and medium-sized producers, and the occasional crackpot in a barn, who were the inventors and innovators. Numerous little inventions, applied and diffused across the Atlantic world, gradually built up a stock of technical knowledge and practice that was widely available.

Most famous of these inventors was James Watt (1736–1819) of Scotland, who succeeded in making steam engines more efficient. Steam engines burned coal to boil water, which condensed into steam that was used to drive mechanized devices. Watt devised a way to separate steam condensers from piston cylinders so that pistons could be kept hot, and therefore running constantly. This set the stage for a fuel-efficient engine. Early prototypes of Watt's engine were used to pump water out of mines. After moving to Birmingham in 1774, Watt joined forces with the industrialist Matthew Boulton (1728–1809), who marketed the steam engine, won an extension of the patent for another twenty-five years, and set up a special laboratory for Watt so that he could refine his device. Thus, technical exploration joined forces with the interests of business; collaboration between inventors and entrepreneurs was a sign of the new times. Moreover, perhaps the most important aspect of Watt's engineering feat was that it was subject to a stream of improvement and adaptation, not just from Boulton and company, but from its competitors as well.

The steam engine, driven by burning coal, provided vastly increased power and catalyzed a revolution in transportation. Steam-powered ships and railroads, built once inventors were able to construct lighter engines that required less coal to run, slashed the time and cost of long-distance travel. Steam power's diffusion accelerated when iron-making improved, allowing for the production of railroad track and cables used to hang suspension bridges. The first public rail line opened in 1830 in England between Manchester and Liverpool. During the next twenty years, railway mileage increased from less than 100 to almost 25,000 in England, France, Russia, and the German-speaking countries. Steamships appeared in the 1780s in France, Britain, and the United States, and in 1807 Robert Fulton inaugurated the first commercially successful route between New York City and Albany on the Hudson River. A century of toying with boilers and pistons culminated in the radical reduction of distances. Moreover, steam-powered engines also improved sugar refining, pottery making, and many other industrial processes. Mechanizing processes that would have taken much longer and been subject to human error if done by hand enabled manufacturers to make more products at cheaper cost.

Textile production was one of the areas that benefited from both technical changes and the consolidation of different stages of the work in a factory. With new machinery, a single textile

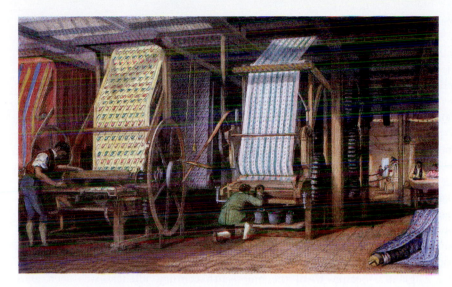

A Cotton Textile Mill in the 1830s. The region of Lancashire became one of the major industrial hubs for textile production in the world. By the 1830s, mills had made the shift from artisanal work to highly mechanical mass production. Among the great breakthroughs was the discovery that cloth could be printed with designs, such as paisley or calico (as in this image), and marketed to middle-class consumers.

operator could handle many looms and spindles at once, and could produce bolts of cloth with stunning efficiency. Gone were the hand tools, the family traditions, and the loosely organized and dispersed systems of households producing cloth in their homes for local merchants to carry to markets. The material was also stronger, finer, and more uniform. Thanks to such innovations, British cotton output increased tenfold between 1770 and 1790, leading to a 90 percent decline in the price of cloth between 1782 and 1812.

Most raw cotton for the British cloth industry had come from colonial India until 1793, when the American inventor Eli Whitney (1765–1825) patented a device called a "cotton gin" that separated cotton seeds from fiber. Cotton farming quickly spread from South Carolina into Georgia, Alabama, Mississippi, and Louisiana, as the United States came to produce more than 80 percent of the world cotton supply by the 1850s. Thus, the American South became a supplier of raw cotton to Britain. In turn, every black slave in the Americas, as well as many Indians in British India, could be consumers of cheap, British-produced cotton shirts. Between 1816 and 1848, cotton goods amounted to 40 percent of British exports.

Manufacturing was not only developing in England, however; it had a place in other Western European economies as well. Thus, coal mining and textile and iron industries could also be found in various parts of northern Europe in the middle of the nineteenth century, although only England at this time had half its labor force employed in manufacturing. In the rest of Europe, manufacturing accounted for between 5 and 10 percent of employment, most of it still in rural domestic workshops. Except for Great Britain, the quantity and quality of the agrarian harvest remained by far the most important economic concern for most people throughout the world.

> *While the industrial revolution did not mean a wholesale shift to factory labor, industrialization did alter both where people worked and how they worked.*

WORKING AND LIVING

While the industrial revolution did not mean a wholesale shift to factory labor, industrialization did alter both where people worked and how they worked. People had to work harder and had more demanding work routines. This was true both in the industrializing economies of Western Europe and North America as well as on the farms and plantations of Asia and Africa. The European side of the story is better known, more fully documented, but it had its counterpart in intensified agrarian routines throughout the rest of the world.

Increasingly, Europe's workers dwelled and made their livings in cities. London, already Europe's largest city in 1700, saw its population nearly double over the next century to almost 1 million. The rate of population growth was even greater in the industrial hubs of Leeds, Glasgow, Birmingham, Liverpool, and Manchester. By contrast, in the Low Countries and France, where the pace of industrialization was more gradual and small-scale rural-based manufacturing flourished, the shift to cities was less marked.

For most urban dwellers, cities were not healthy places. No European city in the early nineteenth century had as clean a water supply as the largest towns of the ancient Roman empire once had. Water had to be taken from polluted sources, like

Manchester's filthy Irk River, or carried long distances. Disease, not surprisingly, was widespread.

As families moved to cities and found jobs in small and large factories, they earned wages, which they brought home and added to the family's revenues. Children, wives, and husbands, who ordinarily had worked at home and sold the goods they produced, increasingly worked outside the home for cash (though many members of most families continued to work at least part of the time at making handicrafts inside the home). Urban employers experimented with various ways of paying workers according to tasks performed or the number of goods produced per day (piece rates). Employers imposed no ceiling on the number of hours children could work. To earn subsistence wages, men, women, and children frequently remained on the job for twelve or more hours. In 1851 in England, in the cotton and woolen industries, the most mechanized industries, there were 811,000 workers, about two-thirds of whom were women and children. England also had 1 million domestic servants, almost all of whom were women, and 1.8 million agricultural laborers, many of whom were women.

Changes in work affected the understanding of time. Whereas most farmers had adapted tasks and workloads to seasonal demands and constraints, employers and master artisans had always asked workers to obey some form of schedule. After about 1800, a more rigid concept of work discipline began to spread in industrial settings. To keep new machinery operating, factory and mill owners fastened huge clocks at the top of towers over work sites, using bells or horns to signify the beginning or end of the workday. Employers also used clocks to measure output per hour and to compare one worker's performance to that of others. Josiah Wedgwood (1730–1795), a maker of

teacups and other porcelain, had a manufactory called Etruria and, having installed a Boulton & Watt steam engine, ensured respect for time from his workers. He rang a bell at 5:45 in the morning so that employees could get to work as day broke. At 8:30 the bell rang for breakfast, 9:00 to call them back, 12:00 for a half-hour lunch, and it last tolled when darkness put an end to the workday. Sometimes, however, the clocks at factories were put back in the morning and forward at night, falsely extending the workday and cheating workers. In response, some workers smashed the timekeeping instruments.

Industrialization meant greater levels of production, but it established numbing work routines and provided paltry wages. Real wages did not begin to rise for most workers until after 1850. Worse than the drudgery or low pay, however, was having no work at all. As families moved off farmland and became dependent on wages, being idle meant having no source of income. Until the nineteenth century, idleness was seen as a problem of individual maladjustment. Poverty and involuntary unemployment became real concerns by the 1790s. The spectacle of riotous crowds and strikers haunted Europe's propertied sectors. In 1834, the British Parliament centralized the administration of all poor relief under a national board and deprived able-bodied workers of any relief unless they joined a workhouse, where working conditions resembled those of a prison. Work routines in these houses were intended to be more heinous than working for an employer.

Even as much new literature celebrated "entrepreneurs" who accumulated private wealth through diligence and enterprise, the effects of the industrial revolution on working-class families became a cause of widespread concern. In the 1810s in England, groups of jobless craftsmen, who called themselves

Capital and Labor. By the 1840s, many people in Europe were growing worried about the effects of industrialization. This English cartoon from 1843 depicts the terrible laboring conditions for coal miners and satirizes the lazy and idle owners of mining capital. Around this time, writers invented the term "capitalist" to deride this class.

Luddites, smashed the machines that had rendered them unemployed. In 1849, the English novelist Charlotte Brontë published a novel, *Shirley*, which depicted the misfortunes wrought by the power loom. Yorkshire weavers lost their jobs, leading to, in Brontë's words, a moral earthquake and forcing the poor to drink the waters of affliction. Charles Dickens described a mythic Coketown to evoke pity for the proletariat in his 1854 classic, *Hard Times*. Friedrich Engels, the son of a Manchester factory owner, published *The Condition of the Working Class in England* in 1844, cataloguing the inhumane practices of his fellow capitalists. These social advocates added to the pressures to promulgate protective legislation for workers, including curbing child labor.

PERSISTENCE AND CHANGE IN EURASIA

> → *How did the Atlantic Revolutions affect Eurasian societies?*

While the ideas that originated in the Enlightenment and stimulated the American and French Revolutions spread across the Eurasian continent, Western Europe's military might, its technological achievements, and its economic strength represented the clearest threat to the well-being of the remaining Eurasian empires. Everywhere on the Eurasian land mass, Western European merchants and industrialists, often backed up by military power, sought to forge tighter economic and sometimes even political ties. They did so in the name of securing "free" access to Asian markets and produce. In response, ruling elites in the Russian and the Ottoman empires, where French forces had soundly defeated local armies, moved rapidly to modernize their military organizations and to emulate Europe's economic accomplishments. At the same time, they distanced themselves from the liberal, egalitarian, and democratic principles of the French Revolution. The Chinese empire, at a long distance from the revolutionary epicenter in the Atlantic world, remained largely unaffected by Europe and America's revolutionary transformations, until the first Opium War of the early 1840s forced the Chinese to face up to their military weaknesses. Thus, changes in the Atlantic world unleashed new political and economic pressures around the world, but in varying degrees of intensity.

REVAMPING THE RUSSIAN MONARCHY

Western European ascendance did not always mean the downfall of dynasties elsewhere in Eurasia. Some dynasties responded to European economic and political pressures by bolstering the strength of traditional rulers—enacting modest reforms combined with the suppression of domestic opposition. This was how Russian rulers responded in the nineteenth century. Tsar Alexander I (ruled 1801–1825) was fortunate that Napoleon committed a number of blunders and lost the world's most modern army in the snow and cold of Russia. Yet, even though Russia was among the victors at Vienna in 1815, the French Revolution and the massive French armies motivated by patriotism struck at the heart of Russian political institutions, which were based upon the enserfment of the peasantry. The autocratic tsars could no longer justify their absolutism by claiming that enlightened despotism was the most advanced form of government, since a new model, rooted in popular sovereignty and the concept of the nation (or the people), had taken its place. One response was to make much of the heroic resistance of the Russian people that culminated in the great victory over the French. Tsar Alexander glorified patriots who had either fought in the war or grown up hearing about it, but he offered few concessions for any new political order.

In December 1825, when Alexander died unexpectedly and childless, there was a question as to which of his brothers would be the next tsar. In the confusion, some members of the Russian officer corps launched a patriotic revolt, hoping to convince one of Alexander's brothers, Constantine, to take the throne (and to guarantee a constitution) in place of another, more conservative brother, Nicholas. The "Decembrists," as they were called, came primarily from elite families. Many had first-hand knowledge of European life and institutions, some from the campaigns against Napoleon. A few Decembrists called for a constitutional monarchy to replace Russia's despotism; others favored a tsar-less republic and the abolition of serfdom. But they failed to win over the peasantry, who continued to believe in the divine right of the tsar to rule without constraints. Constantine supported Nicholas's claim to power. Nicholas (ruled 1825–1855) became tsar and brutally suppressed the insurrectionists. For the time being, the influence of the French Revolution was quashed.

Still, Alexander's successors had to meet the challenges of a world in which powerful European states had constitutions and national armies of citizens, not subjects. One way Russian tsars tried to reinvigorate absolute rule in the new circumstances was by idealizing the monarch's family as the historical embodiment of the nation with direct ties to the people. But in addition to cultivating this image of the tsar as the head of the family of Russia, Nicholas sought to keep thoughts and acts of rebellion under control by expanding the Third Section (a political police force), enforcing censorship, having his army engage in military exercises, and maintaining serfdom.

Not all subjects were susceptible to Russian national feeling or could be kept under control by the secret police, however. It took the government more than a year to suppress a

Decembrists in St. Petersburg. Russians energetically participated in the coalition that defeated Napoleon, but the ideas of the French Revolution exerted great appeal to the educated upper classes, including aristocrats of the officer corps. In December 1825, at the death of Tsar Alexander I, some regimental officers staged an uprising of about 3,000 men, demanding a constitution and the end of serfdom. But Nicholas I, the new tsar, called in loyal troops and brutally dispersed the "Decembrists," executing or exiling their leaders.

revolt that began in November 1830 in the empire's Polish provinces. The special constitution granted in 1815 for Russian Poland was abrogated, and Nicholas sought a closer alliance with the conservative monarchies of Austria and Prussia. In the 1830s, Nicholas introduced a conservative ideology with the slogan of "Orthodoxy, Autocracy, and Folk Nationality," which stressed religious faith, hierarchy, and obedience, and idealized but did not enfranchise, the people. And while some reformers continued to call for more far-reaching changes, these as yet led nowhere.

REFORMING EGYPT AND THE OTTOMAN EMPIRE

The Napoleonic invasion of Egypt shook the Ottoman empire and led European merchants to press Ottoman rulers for increased commercial concessions. True, unlike in Russia, where Napoleon's army had reached Moscow, the Ottoman capital in Istanbul was never threatened by French troops. Still, Napoleon's attack on Egypt shook the confidence of Ottoman rulers at the empire's center. Even before this trauma, imperial authorities faced the challenge that increased trade with Europe—and the increased presence of European merchants and missionaries—posed. Many of the non-Muslim religious communities in the sultan's empire openly looked to the European powers to advance their interests. In the wake of Napoleon, who had promised to remake Egyptian society, re-

formist energies swept from Egypt to the center of the Ottoman domain.

The decisive victory that Napoleon's infantry won over Mamluk cavalry at the Battle of the Pyramids (1798) boosted the cause of reform, with European ways inspiring many proponents of change. In Egypt, far-reaching changes came with Muhammad Ali, the most adept of the area's modernizing rulers. During his long rule (1805–1848), he initiated a series of reforms that sought to make Egypt competitive with the great powers. Having made himself the most powerful ruler in the area, he threatened the integrity of the slower-moving Ottoman empire, which was only saved from extinction through European intervention.

After the French withdrawal in 1801, Muhammad Ali emerged victorious in a chaotic struggle for supreme power in Egypt. After defeating Mamluk generals, he defied his Ottoman superiors. For support, he aligned himself with influential Egyptian merchant and scholarly families. Once he seized full power in 1805, he looked to revolutionary France for a model of modern state-building. As with Napoleon and Simón Bolívar, the key to his rise and hold on power was the army. Muhammad Ali understood that without a strong military apparatus, Egypt remained vulnerable to Ottoman forces from Istanbul. Accordingly, he turned to French advisers to help revamp the Egyptian military. Among these first French advisers was an officer, Colonel Seve, who had served with Napoleon and now lent his talents to Egypt. Seve married an Egyptian woman, took an Egyptian name, Suleiman Pasha, and converted to

AN EGYPTIAN INTELLECTUAL'S REACTION TO THE FRENCH OCCUPATION OF EGYPT

In the invasion of Egypt in 1798, the French commander, Napoleon Bonaparte, attempted to win rank and file Egyptian support against the country's Mamluk Turkish rulers by portraying himself as a liberator and by invoking the ideals of the French Revolution as he had done with great success all over Europe. His campaign did not succeed, and the French met with bitter local opposition. The Egyptian chronicler, Abd al-Rahman al-Jabarti, has left one of the most perceptive accounts of these years.

On Monday news arrived that the French had reached Damanhur and Rosetta [in the Nile delta].... They printed a large proclamation in Arabic, calling on the people to obey them.... In this proclamation were inducements, warnings, all manner of wiliness and stipulations. Some copies were sent from the provinces to Cairo and its text is:

In the name of God, the Merciful, the Compassionate. There is no God but God. He has no son nor has He an associate in His Dominion.

On behalf of the French Republic which is based upon the foundation of liberty and equality, General Bonaparte, Commander-in-Chief of the French armies makes known to all the Egyptian people that for a long time the Sanjaqs [its Mamluk rulers] who lorded it over Egypt have treated the French community basely and contemptuously and have persecuted its merchants with all manner of extortion and violence. Therefore the hour of punishment has now come.

Unfortunately, this group of Mamluks, imported from the mountains of Circassia and Georgia, have acted corruptly for ages in the fairest land that is to be found upon the face of the globe. However, the Lord of the Universe, the Almighty, has decreed the end of their power.

O ye Egyptians . . . I have not come to you except for the purpose of restoring your rights from the hands of the oppressors and that I more than the Mamluks serve God....

And tell them also that all people are equal in the eyes of God and the only circumstances which distinguish one from the other are reason, virtue, and knowledge. . . . Formerly, in the lands of Egypt there were great cities, and wide canals and extensive commerce and nothing ruined all this but the avarice and the tyranny of the Mamluks.

[Jabarti then undertook to challenge the arguments in the French proclamation and to portray the French as godless invaders, inspired by false ideals.] They follow this rule: great and small, high and low, male and female are all equal. Sometimes they break this rule according to their whims and inclinations or reasoning. Their women do not veil themselves and have no modesty. They do not care whether they uncover their private parts. Whenever a Frenchman has to perform an act of nature he does so where he happens to be, even in full view of people, and he goes away as he is, without washing his private parts after defecation.... They have intercourse with any woman who pleases them and vice versa. . . .

His saying "[all people] are equal in the eyes of God" the Almighty is a lie and stupidity. How can this be when God has made some superior to others as is testified by the dwellers in the Heavens and on Earth? . . .

So those people are opposed to both Christians and Muslims, and do not hold fast to any religion. You see that they are materialists, who deny all God's attributes.... May God hurry misfortune and punishment upon them, may He strike their tongues with dumbness, may He scatter their hosts, and disperse them.

Source: Abd al-Rahman al-Jabarti, *Napoleon in Egypt: al-Jabarti's Chronicle of the French Occupation, 1798*, translated by Shmuel Moreh (Princeton: Markus Wiener Publishing, 1993), pp. 24–29.

Islam. Reorganizing the army along French lines and drilling them in French techniques, Suleiman Pasha drafted peasants and expanded the force to 100,000 men. Before long, the Egyptian army was the most powerful fighting force in the Middle East.

Along with modernizing the military, Muhammad Ali pushed for reforms in education and agriculture. He established a school of engineering, and opened the first modern medical school in Cairo under the supervision of a French military doctor, A. B. Clot. During an autopsy, an enraged student attacked the French doctor, claiming that the dissection of human cadavers violated Islamic norms. Afterwards, Clot accustomed his students to anatomical lessons, first employing dog cadavers, then wax models, before again dissecting a human corpse, al-

Muhammad Ali. The Middle Eastern ruler who most successfully assimilated the educational, technological, and economic advances of nineteenth-century Europe was Muhammad Ali, ruler of Egypt from 1805 until 1848. He brought in European military and industrial advisers, sent Egyptian educational missions to Europe, and carried out an industrialization program. Unfortunately, his ambition to extend his political influence into Syria and even perhaps into the heart of the Ottoman empire in Anatolia aroused European concerns, and the Europeans forced him to limit the size of his army and to give back some of the lands he had taken from the Ottoman empire.

ways conducting his classes in secret. In the countryside, Muhammad Ali made Egypt one of the world's leading cotton exporters and the primary region for the cultivation of the highly prized long-staple cotton. A summer crop, cotton required steady watering during the low Nile season when irrigation waters were in short supply. To meet those needs, Muhammad Ali's Public Works Department, acting under the advice of European irrigation engineers, deepened the irrigation canals and began the construction of a series of dams across the Nile.

Muhammad Ali's modernizing reforms, however, disrupted the local peasantry. Incorporation into the new industrial world economy, whether as wage laborers in English factories or peasants on Egyptian cotton estates, entailed harder and more demanding work, often with little additional compensation. Because irrigation improvements permitted year-round cultiva-

tion, peasants now had to plant and harvest three crops instead of one or two. Moreover, the Egyptian state controlled the prices at which cultivators sold their products, so peasants saw little profit from their added exertions. Young men also now faced conscription into the state's enlarged army, while whole families had to engage in unpaid public works projects. To evade military service, some men maimed themselves. Many more fled so as not to be drafted into the army or as public workers. Those who had to work on Egypt's irrigation canals often contracted *bilharzia*, a water-borne illness that debilitated its hosts. Egypt's ruler also sought a state-sponsored program of industrialization that would put Egypt on a par with Europe. Within the short span of a decade and a half, the state had set up textile and munitions factories that employed 200,000 workers. But Egypt had few skilled laborers or cheap sources of energy. By the time of Muhammad Ali's death in 1849, few of the factories still survived.

External forces also checked Muhammad Ali's ambitious plans. At first, his new army enjoyed spectacular success. At the bidding of the Ottoman sultan, the Egyptian military fought creditably against Greek nationalists, although Egyptian forces were unable to prevent the Greeks from acquiring independence in 1829. Egyptian soldiers also carried out conquests in the Sudan. Muhammad Ali overplayed his hand, however, when he sent his forces into Syria in the early 1830s and later in the decade when he threatened to launch expeditions into Anatolia, the heart of the Ottoman state. The prospect that an Egyptian ruler might march into Istanbul and supplant the Ottoman sultan alarmed the European powers. Led by the British foreign minister, Lord Palmerston, European diplomats compelled Egypt to withdraw from Anatolia and in 1841 to reduce its army to 18,000 soldiers. In the name of free trade, European merchants pressed for unobstructed access to Egyptian markets, just as they did in Latin America and Africa.

Under political and economic pressures that were similar to those facing Muhammad Ali in Egypt, Ottoman rulers also began to change their ways. Already in the eighteenth century, the more forward-looking sultans were well aware of the rising power of Europe. Military defeats and humiliating treaties with Europe provided ample reminders of the Ottoman rulers' vulnerability. This vulnerability deepened as Europe's economic and military might increased. Stunned by Napoleon's defeat of the Egyptian Mamluks and disenchanted with conservative and privileged janissaries who resisted efforts to impose discipline and reforms, in 1805 Sultan Selim III tried to create a new and effective source of military strength. He founded the New Order infantry, trained by Western officers. But before he could bring this new force up to fighting strength, the janissaries rose in revolt, storming the palace, killing New Order officers, and sticking their heads on poles outside the palace. They overturned the New Order army and deposed Selim in 1807. Over the next decades, janissary military men and clerical scholars (*ulama*) cobbled together an alliance that continuously thwarted reformers.

Why did reform falter even before it had a chance to be implemented? After all, in France and Spain, the old regimes were also inefficient and saddled with accumulated debts and military losses. But reform or revolution was only feasible if the forces of restraint—especially in the military—were weak and the reformers strong; in France, a domestic coalition toppled the ruling bloc; in Spain, colonists allied to reject absolutism and mercantilism. In the Ottoman empire, the janissary class had grown powerful, providing the bulwark of resistance to change. Also, Ottoman authority aligned with and depended upon clerical support, and the clergy also resisted change. Blocked at the top, Ottoman rulers were loath to appeal for popular support in a struggle against anti-reformers. Such an appeal, in the new age of popular sovereignty and national feeling, was always dangerous for an unelected dynast in a multiethnic and multireligious realm.

The political deadlock was broken by Mahmud II (ruled 1808–1839), who spoke no European languages but was painfully aware of the need to deal with Europe's rising power. He was also a shrewd tactician, able to manipulate his conservative opponents. Convincing some clerics that the janissaries neglected old laws and customs of discipline and piety, and promising that a new corps would pray fervently, the sultan won the support of the *ulama* and in 1826 established a new European-style army corps. When the janissaries plotted their inevitable mutiny, Mahmud rallied clerics, students, and his subjects. The schemers retreated to their barracks, only to be shelled by the sultan's artillery and then destroyed in flames. Thousands of janissaries were rounded up and executed.

> By the nineteenth century, the ties of trade and financial dependency bound the Ottomans to Europe on terms that the Europeans controlled.

The sultan was now freer to follow the example of Muhammad Ali in Egypt and pursue reform within an autocratic framework. Like Muhammad Ali, Mahmud brought in a group of European officers (in 1835) to advise his forces. Here, too, military reform spilled over into nonmilitary areas. The Ottoman modernizers created a medical college, then a school of military sciences. To understand Europe better and to create a first-rate diplomatic corps, the Ottomans schooled their officials in European languages and encouraged the translation of European classics into Turkish. Mahmud's successors kept up the reforms and extended them into civilian life. This era, referred to as the *Tanzimat*, or Reorganization period, saw legislation that guaranteed equality for all Ottoman subjects, regardless of religion.

The reforms, however, stopped well short of revolutionary change. For one thing, reform relied too much on the personal whim of rulers. The bureaucratic and religious infrastructure remained wedded to old ways. Moreover, any effort to reform the rural sector encountered the resistance of the rich landed interests. Finally, the merchant classes profited from business with a debt-ridden sultan. By staving off the fiscal collapse of the empire, the bankers alleviated the pressure for reform and removed the spark that had fired the revolutions in Europe. Together, these factors impaired the cause of reform in the Ottoman empire. Yet, by failing to make greater reforms, the empire lost economic and military ground to its European neighbors. For centuries, European traders had needed Islam's goods and services more than the other way around. By the nineteenth century, however, the ties of trade and financial dependency bound the Ottomans to Europe on terms that the Europeans controlled.

COLONIAL REORDERING IN INDIA

The largest and most important of Europe's Asian colonial possessions between 1750 and 1850 was British India. Unlike in North America, the changes that the British fostered in Asia at this time did not lead to political independence. Quite the contrary, India was increasingly dominated by the East India Company, a private company that had been chartered by the crown in 1600. The Company's increasing control over India's imports and exports in the eighteenth and nineteenth centuries, however, flew in the face of British professions about their allegiance to a world economic system based on "free trade."

Initially, the British, through the East India Company, sought to control the commerce of India by establishing trading posts along the coast, but without taking complete political control. After conquering the princely state of Bengal in 1757 and placing a puppet on Bengal's throne, the East India Company began to fill its coffers, and Company officials began to amass personal fortunes. In 1760, several senior officials were making the astonishing sum of £500,000 a year through illicit and predatory business ventures. None other than Robert Clive, the governor of Bengal, accrued a huge private fortune by forcing the ruler to cede him a portion of the tax revenues. The unbridled abuse of power caused the Bengal ruler to start hostilities against the Company. In 1764, the forces of the Mughal emperor and the ruler of Awadh joined with his army to battle against British troops. They were defeated, but instead of decapitating the empire, British officials elected to leave the emperor and most provincial leaders in place—at least as nominal rulers. Nonetheless, in 1765, the British extracted a proclamation from the Mughal emperor that granted the East India Company the right to collect the tax revenues in Bengal as well as in Bihar and Orissa. In addition, the Company also secured the right to trade free of duties throughout the Mughal territory. In return, the Company agreed to pay the emperor an annual pension of £260,000. The Company went on to annex other territories, bringing much of the subcontinent and its estimated 200 million inhabitants under Company rule by the early 1800s (see Map 6-3).

To carry out its responsibilities, the Company needed to establish a civil administration. Rather than place Britons in these positions, the Company preferred to enlist Hindu kings and Muslim princes. The Company allowed them to retain their royal symbols and privileges while depriving them of their autonomy. And though the Mughal emperor proclaimed in 1765 that the Company was his "servant," the roles were in fact reversed. Previously weakened by the rise of provincial rulers, the emperor became little more than a paper ruler under the thumb of the Company's administrators. Still, the Company did not depend entirely on local leaders to enforce its dictates, for it also maintained a large standing army. By 1805, this army included 155,000 soldiers, more than a third of whom were native recruits or sepoys (a corruption of the Urdu term *sipahi* for soldier). It employed a centralized bureaucracy that by the 1780s was trained to rule colonial subjects. Together, the military force, bureaucracy, and an array of local rulers enabled the Company state to maintain security and assure the stability of revenue collection.

To rule with a minimum of interference and cost, however, required knowing the conquered society. This requirement provided the impetus for what became known as "Orientalist" scholarship. English scholar-officials wrote the first modern histories of the subcontinent, translated and published Sanskrit and Persian texts, identified philosophical writings, and compiled Hindu and Muslim law books. The most famous of these scholars was William Jones who, while serving as a judge in Calcutta between 1783 and 1794, founded the Asiatic Society. While Jones and like-minded Orientalists admired Sanskrit language and literature, they still approved of English colonial rule. Thanks to their efforts, the Company state presented itself as a force for revitalizing authentic Hinduism and recovering India's literary and cultural treasures. Nonetheless, the views of Orientalist scholars did not always accord with the actual Indian village beliefs in local deities and the importance of local vernacular tongues.

Maintaining a sizeable military and civilian bureaucracy compelled the Company to intrude on the lives of Indians in many ways, especially through taxation. Landholding arrangements were of vital importance to the Company because taxes on land were its largest source of revenues. From 1793 onward, a series of land settlements bolstered state revenues and

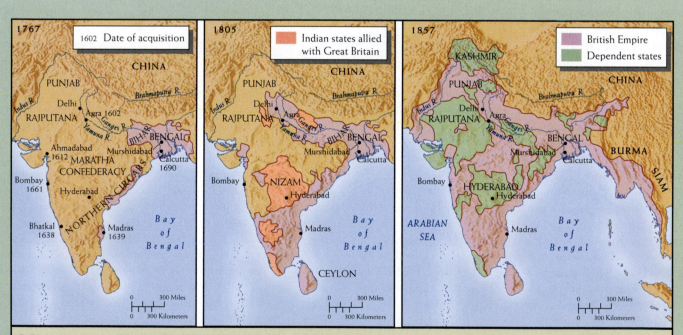

MAP 6-3　THE BRITISH IN INDIA, 1767–1857

Starting from locations in eastern and northeastern India, Britain extended its authority over much of the Indian subcontinent prior to the outbreak of the Indian Rebellion of 1857. Referring back to Map 3–5 of Mughal India (p. 113), compare the geographic centers of power of these two empires. Can you explain why British influence began where it did and why the British moved into certain territories and not into others?

Indian Resistance to Company Rule. Lord Cornwallis taking charge of Tipu Sultan's sons as hostages in 1792. Tipu Sultan, the Mysore ruler, put up a determined resistance against the British. The painting by Robert Home shows Cornwallis, the East India Company's governor, receiving Tipu's two sons as hostages after defeating him in the 1792 war. The boys remained in British custody for two years. Tipu returned to fighting the British and was killed in the war of 1799.

undercut the autonomy of villagers. These policies made large and small landowners responsible for paying taxes to the Company—in so doing, tax policies helped spread private property at the expense of traditional landowning rights. In particular, large estate owners gained more power and joined with the Company in determining who could own property. The old flexible tax system gave way to one in which all landholders had to pay, irrespective of means. When proprietors defaulted on their taxes, the Company put their properties up for auction, with the firm's own employees and large estate owners often obtaining title. Some took out loans to save their property or to make rental payments, exposing themselves to rural moneylenders.

Company rule altered India's urban geography as well. By the early nineteenth century, colonial cities, like Calcutta, Madras, and Bombay, became the new and growing centers at the expense of older Mughal cities like Agra, Delhi, Murshidabad, and Hyderabad. As trade boomed, colonial cities attracted British merchants and Indian clerks, artisans, and laborers. Calcutta's population reached 350,000 in 1820, and Bombay's jumped to 200,000 by 1825. In these cities, Europeans lived in enclaves around the Company's fort and trading stations, while migrants from the Indian countryside clustered in crowded quarters called "black towns."

Back in Britain, the debts of rural Indians and the conditions of black towns generated little concern. Instead, calls for reform focused on the Company's monopoly. Criticism of colonial methods, but not of colonialism, mounted as the Company's arbitrary rule in India became better known in London. British critics of the Company objected to its monopoly over access to Indian wealth, and British industrialists resented the protection afforded to the Company's shareholders and investors. In 1813, the British Parliament, responding to the wishes of merchants and traders to participate in the Indian economy, abolished the East India Company's monopoly over trade with India.

Criticism of colonial methods, but not of colonialism, mounted as the East India Company's arbitrary rule in India became better known in London.

No longer the preserve of a single company, India was now expected to serve the interests of an industrializing Britain. In pursuit of this goal, India became an important market for British textiles, as well as an exporter of raw cotton. This was a new trading arrangement, entailing a reversal of India's traditional trade. In the past, even under early Company rule, India had been an important textile manufacturer, exporting fine cotton goods throughout the Indian Ocean and to Europe. But the Indian business elites had difficulty resisting the import of cheap British textiles. As a result, a long-term partial deindustrialization took place on the subcontinent. In addition, Indian imports of British manufactures led to unfavorable trade balances that changed India from a net importer of gold and silver to an exporter of these precious metals.

Nor were the British content simply to alter the Indian economy. The colonial rulers also advocated far-reaching changes in traditional Indian society and culture so that its people would place a high value on British goods and culture. In 1817, James Mill, a philosopher and an employee of the East India Company, condemned the backwardness of indigenous social practices and cultural traditions. He and his son, John Stuart Mill, who was also employed by the Company, argued that only dictatorial, illiberal rule could bring good government and economic progress to Indians, who were deemed unfit for autonomy, self-rule, or liberalism.

> *The Chinese were largely unaware of the revolutionary events taking place in the Atlantic world, and they felt no great compulsion to alter the fundamentals of their society.*

Evangelicals and liberal reformers also agitated for a thorough transformation of Hindu and Muslim social practices through legislation and the introduction of European education. For example, they sought to stop the practice of *sati*, wherein a woman was burned to death on the funeral pyre of her dead husband. The mood swung away from the Orientalists' respect for India's classical languages, philosophies, cultures, and texts. In 1835, Lord Macaulay, entrusted with the task of making recommendations on educational policies, declared that a single shelf in any decent Western library contained more valuable knowledge than all the accumulated Sanskrit and Persian texts. English was to replace Persian as the language of administration, and European education was to displace training in Oriental learning. The result, reformers hoped, would be the raising of a class that was Indian in blood and color, but English in tastes and culture.

This was a new colonial order, but it was not a stable one. While some European-educated Indians thanked the British rulers for their benevolent reforms, most landed magnates, facing dispossession and loss of their authority, grumbled with disaffection. Peasants, thrown to the mercy of the market, moneylenders, and landlords, were in turmoil. The so-called tribals, or non-Hindu forest dwellers and shifting cultivators, faced with the hated combination of the colonial state and moneylenders, revolted. Dispossessed artisans brought unrest to towns and cities. Merchants and industrialists resented the fact that they could now make money only by working as subordinates in a British-dominated economy. Undeterred, the British persevered in extending and refining the reach of the colonial state, combining reform with autocracy, advancing free trade with colonial dictates. India participated in an increasingly interconnected world and contributed to Europe's industrialization, but it did so as a colony. Expanding freedom in Europe was paralleled by exploitation in India.

PERSISTENCE OF THE QING EMPIRE

In contrast to the declining fortunes of the other dynasts, the Qing dynasty, which had taken power in China in 1644, was still enjoying considerable economic prosperity and territorial expansion as the nineteenth century dawned. The Chinese were largely unaware of the revolutionary events taking place in North America, France, and Britain, and they felt no great compulsion to alter the fundamentals of their society. Their sense of imperial splendor continued to rest upon the political structure and social order inherited from the Ming. Although some Chinese felt that the Manchu Qing were foreign occupiers, the Qing carefully adapted Chinese institutions and philosophies. Thus, Chinese elites at court did not challenge the prerogatives of the dynasty—unlike the delegates to the Estates-General in France in 1788–1789.

EXPANSION OF THE EMPIRE The Qing demonstrated a special talent for extending the boundaries of the empire and fostering settlement in frontier lands. Before 1750, they conquered Taiwan (the stronghold of remaining Ming forces), pushed westward into Central Asia, and annexed Tibet. In the 1750s, the Qianlong Emperor (ruled 1736–1796) marched a quarter million men against the powerful West Mongol Oirats, who were utterly decimated. The Qing victory put an end to Russian efforts to take southern Siberia. Subsequent treaties with Russia established the limits of Chinese westward expansion into Turkic- and Mongol-speaking lands. To secure these territorial gains, the Qing encouraged settlement of frontier lands. New crops from the Americas aided this spread of China's population into recently acquired lands. Corn and sweet potatoes, which could grow well in less fertile soils, became more prominent. Crops were seeded methodically in neat rows, unlike in Europe, where the broadcast method of seeding involved much wastage.

Thanks to rising agricultural productivity and population growth, rural life became more commercialized and state revenues increased. In the eighteenth century, rural markets multiplied, making possible an increasing volume in interregional trade in grain, cotton, tea, and silk. Rural industries also proliferated. As in Europe, peasant households became the backbone of early manufactures, especially in textiles. Like the Europeans, the Chinese espoused an ideal in which women stayed home while men worked in the field. But in China as in

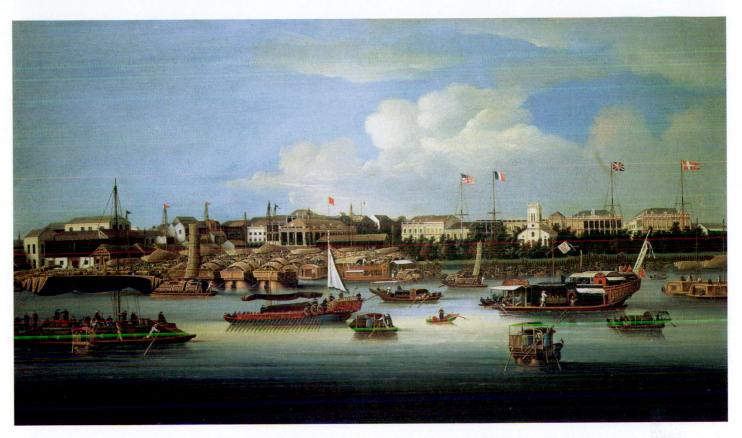

Trade in Canton. In this painting, titled *A View of the Hongs*, we can see the hongs, the buildings that made up the factories, or establishments, where foreign merchants conducted their business in Canton. From the mid-eighteenth century to 1842, Canton was the only Chinese port open to European trade.

ments of silver. Fortunately for the Company, the Chinese showed an eagerness for Indian goods—first cotton and opium, and subsequently mostly opium—permitting the British to export very little or no silver after 1804. Given the importance of opium, the Company extended its cultivation by offering loans to Indian peasants who, in return, agreed to grow opium and sell it to the Company's agents at a predetermined price.

The illegal opium traffic could not have flourished without the connivance of corrupt Chinese bureaucrats and a network of local brokers and distributors. Yet, a Qing decree of 1799 reiterated the official ban. Until 1821, no more than 5,000 chests of opium per year found their way into China, but the number increased to 16,500 chests in 1831–1832 and 40,000 in 1838–1839. The import explosion resulted primarily from an influx of private British merchants in 1834, when the British government revoked the East India Company's monopoly over trade with China, which meant that anyone could now enter the trade.

> *The impact of opium on the Qing's trade balance was devastating; silver began to flow out of instead of into China.*

The impact of opium on the Qing's trade balance was devastating. In a clear reversal from earlier trends, silver began to flow out of instead of into China. About 2 million taels of silver left the country each year in the 1820s. The figure jumped to 9 million taels a decade later. China experienced silver shortages, and ordinary peasants saw their tax burden surge (remember that taxes had to be paid in silver; see Chapter 4). Unrest in the countryside, on the rise since the 1790s, spread and gained momentum. At the Qing court, some officials wanted to legalize the opium trade both to stamp out corruption and to channel revenues into the treasury (as long as it remained officially an illegal substance, the government could not tax the traffic). Others wanted stiffer prohibitions, though they did not specify how they would be enforced. The emperor followed the latter tack, and in 1838 sent a specially appointed commissioner, Lin Zexu, to the main entrepot, Canton (now called Guangzhou, it was the only port, besides the Portuguese settlement of Macao, where foreigners could trade

Steamer *Nemesis* Destroying Junks. The Opium War was fought between a newly industrialized power and an established landed empire. One of the major disparities between the two sides was military technology. Here is a scene of British steam-powered warship, the *Nemesis*, sailing up the Pearl River toward the city of Canton, bombarding areas along the river at will, and destroying Chinese ships that attempted to block its way.

with the Chinese), to eradicate the influx of opium. In a letter to Queen Victoria of Britain, Lin claimed that China exported its goods such as tea and silk for no other reason than "to share the benefit with the people of the whole world," asking why the British inflicted harm on the Chinese people through opium imports.

Lin demanded that foreigners surrender their opium stocks to the Chinese government for destruction and stop the trade in opium. When British merchants in Canton balked at Lin's instructions, he ordered the arrest of Lancelot Dent, head of the second largest foreign firm in Canton and president of the British Chamber of Commerce, in March 1839. Dent refused to comply with the arrest order, and 350 foreigners were blockaded inside their own quarters. Lin scored an apparent victory when the foreign community in Canton, after forty-seven days of blockade, gave up 20,283 chests of opium, with an estimated value of $9 million, an enormous sum in those days. But merchants had overstocked their supplies in anticipation of the legalization of the trade, and the British government representative in Canton promised to

compensate the merchants for their losses. For Lin, however, the surrendering of the opium, which the Chinese flushed out to sea, was proof that foreigners accepted submission. The Chinese victory, however, was short-lived. As a member of the British Parliament put it, the opium merchants in Canton "belonged to a country unaccustomed to defeat, to submission or to shame."

A British fleet, including four newly armed steamers, entered Chinese waters in June 1840. For the Chinese, a steam-powered battleship was a new sight. British warships bombarded Chinese coastal regions near Canton and even sailed in shallow water upriver for a short way. On land, Qing soldiers commanded by hereditary bannermen—the Chinese equivalent to the equally out-of-date Ottoman janissaries—used spears and clubs, and a few imported matchlock muskets, against the modern artillery of British troops, many of whom were Indians supplied with percussion cap rifles. Still, along the Yangzi River, outgunned Chinese forces fought fiercely. Rather than surrender, many Qing soldiers killed their own wives and children before committing suicide.

The British prevailed, as the Qing preferred to sue for peace rather than risk all-out war. The British seized the tiny island of Hong Kong and, with the 1842 Treaty of Nanjing, they received the right to trade in five treaty ports and forced the Chinese to pay an "indemnity" for the war and compensation for the opium destroyed by Lin. British traders were now given the right to trade directly with the Chinese (and not only through the Cohong; see Chapter 4) and to reside in the treaty ports.

That the British government would go to such lengths merely to force trade struck many Chinese as barbaric. In addition, subsequent treaties guaranteed the principle of extraterritoriality, which meant that the British and other foreign nationals would be tried in their own courts for crimes, rather than in Chinese courts, and would be exempt from Chinese law; this humiliated the Chinese. Of further threat to Chinese autonomy, the British insisted that any privileges granted to future treaty signatories would also apply to them. Accordingly, if one European country acquired special rights, others would, too, which insured all Europeans and North Americans a privileged position in China.

Still, China did not suffer India's fate and become a formal colony. To the contrary, in the mid-nineteenth century Europeans and North Americans were trading only on the outskirts of China and restricted their presence to a few coastal cities. Most Chinese did not encounter the Europeans, and daily life for the majority of the Chinese went on as it had before the Opium War and the Treaty of Nanjing. It was only the political leaders and urban dwellers who were beginning directly to feel the foreign presence and to ponder what steps, if any, China might take to acquire European technologies, goods, and learning.

 ## Conclusion

During the second half of the eighteenth century and into the early nineteenth century, changes wrought by politics and ideas, on the one hand, and commerce, industry, and technology, on the other, resulted in unprecedented upheaval in the Atlantic world. The reordering of the Atlantic world occurred against the background of several centuries of trade and imperial conquests, and it reverberated, to varying degrees, elsewhere around the world. By 1850, the world was more integrated economically, with Europe more than ever before at the center of global affairs.

The political crises and the economic and social revolutions in Western Europe and the Americas disrupted polities around the world, though less so in China than anywhere else. In the Americas, colonial ties were severed; in France, the people toppled the monarchy, and dissidents threatened the same in Russia. Political upheavals did not rewrite the rules of state completely, but they did introduce a new public vocabulary that would enjoy increasing power as the nineteenth century unfolded: the language of the nation. Equally important, they made the idea of revolution—that societies could be changed in radical ways—empowering. In the Americas and parts of Europe, nation-states, with new symbols of authority, national armies, and a mystique of self-governing communities took shape around redefined social hierarchies of class, gender, and color. Western Europe, particularly Britain and France, emerged from the political crises of the late eighteenth century with determination to expand their influence beyond their borders. Their drive forced older empires such as Russia and the Ottoman state to undertake state-led reforms. Egypt broke free from Ottoman rule under the banner of reform, although ultimately European governments intervened in Egypt, leading to an end to state-sponsored reforms.

Commerce and industrialization played a decisive role in the reshuffling of economic and political power. Through the end of the seventeenth century, commerce bridged distant cultures; thereafter, as trade deepened and diversified, it began to transform those cultures. European governments and their armies compelled various countries—including Egypt, India, and China—to expand their trade with European merchants. Ultimately this meant that these and other countries were not free to pursue whatever economic policies they wished. Rather, they were expected to participate in a European-centered economy as exporters of raw materials and importers of European manufactures.

By the 1850s, the density and strength of trading ties had helped create a more interconnected world order. More of the world's peoples produced less for themselves and more for distant markets. Thanks to changes in the organization and technology of manufacturing, some areas of the world also made more goods than ever before. Although the world remained multicentered, economic power in the early nineteenth century was shifting to the western end of the Eurasian land mass. With manufactures to sell in Asia and a new ideology of free trade, Europe began to force open new markets, even to the point of colonizing them. Gold and silver, which had poured into China and India in the sixteenth and seventeenth centuries, were now flowing out to pay for European-dominated products like opium and textiles.

Nonetheless, the reordering of the world did not mean that Europe's rulers had uncontested control over other people, or even over their own people. Nor did it mean that the institutions and cultures of Asia and Africa ceased to be dynamic. Some countries became informal dependencies, like the Ottomans; others, like India, became outright European colonies. China escaped colonial rule, but was forced into unfavorable trade relations with the Europeans. In sum, changes in commerce, manufacturing, technology, politics, and ideas combined to unsettle systems of rulership and to alter the economic and military balance between Western Europe and the rest of the world.

Chronology

1736–1796	Chinese expansion under Qianlong Emperor
1765	British establish Company rule in India
1769	James Watt invents steam engine
1776–1783	American Revolution
1780s	Andean Indian revolts
1789–1799	French Revolution
1791–1804	Haitian Rebellion
1793	Eli Whitney invents the cotton gin
1796–1804	White Lotus Rebellion, China
1798–1801	French invasion of Egypt
1803–1867	Abolition of Atlantic slave trade
1804–1815	Napoleon's Empire
1805–1848	Reign of Muhammad Ali, Egypt
1807	Robert Fulton launches first commercial steamship
1808–1839	Reign of Mahmud II, Ottoman empire
1810–1824	Revolutions in South America
1810–1813	Insurrection in Mexico
1810–1848	Rise of free trade in the Atlantic world
1813	Abolition of Company trade monopoly in India
1821	Mexican independence
1821	Free blacks begin to settle Liberia
1822	Brazil declares independence
1825	Decembrist Revolt in Russia
1826	Revamping of Ottoman army
1829	Greek independence
1830	First railway launched in England
1835	Urban slave revolt in Bahia, Brazil
1839–1842	Opium War, China
1846	Repeal of Corn Laws, England

 ## FURTHER READINGS

Anderson, Fred, *Crucible of War: The Seven Years' War and the Fate of Empire in British North America, 1754–1766* (2000). The best synthesis of the "great war for empire" that set the stage for the American Revolution.

Bayly, C. A., *Indian Society and the Making of the British Empire* (1998). A useful work on the early history of the British conquest of India.

Blackburn, Robin, *The Overthrow of Colonial Slavery, 1776–1848* (1988). Places the abolition of the Atlantic slave trade and colonial slavery in a large historical context.

Brook, Timothy, and Bob Tadashi Wakabayashi (eds.), *Opium Regimes: China, Britain, and Japan, 1839–1952* (2000). Examines the role of opium in the various aspects of modern Chinese history.

Cambridge History of Egypt: Modern Egypt from 1517 to the End of the Twentieth Century, Vol. 2 (1998). Volume 2 contains authoritative essays on all aspects of modern Egyptian history, including the impact of the French invasion and the rule of Muhammad Ali.

Chaudhuri, K. N., *The Trading World of Asia and the East India Company, 1660–1760* (1978). An authoritative economic history of the East India Company's operations.

Crafts, N. F. R., *British Economic Growth During the Industrial Revolution* (1985). A pioneering study that emphasizes a long-term, more gradual process of adaptation to new institutional and social circumstances.

Doyle, William, *The Oxford History of the French Revolution* (1990). A highly detailed discussion of the course of events.

Fick, Carolyn E., *The Making of Haiti: The Saint Domingue Revolution from Below* (1990). Provides a detailed account of the factors that led to the great slave rebellion on the island of Haiti at the end of the eighteenth century.

Findley, Carter, *Bureaucratic Reform in the Ottoman Empire: The Sublime Porte, 1789–1922* (1980). A useful guide to Ottoman reform efforts in the nineteenth century.

Hevia, James, *Cherishing Men from Afar: Qing Guest Ritual and the Macartney Embassy of 1793* (1995). Offers a new interpretation of the nature of Sino-British conflict in the Qing period.

Hobsbawm, Eric, *Nations and Nationalism since 1780* (1990). Charts how the French Revolution generated a tradition of imagined realities of nationhood.

Hunt, Lynn, *Politics, Culture and Class in the French Revolution* (1984). Examines the influence of sociocultural shifts as causes and consequences of the French Revolution, emphasizing the symbols and practice of politics invented during the Revolution.

Jones, E. L., *Growth Recurring* (1988). Discusses the controversy over why the industrial revolution took place in Europe, stressing the unique ecological setting that encouraged long-term investment.

Kinsbruner, Jay, *Independence in Spanish America* (1994). A fine study of the Latin American revolutions for independence that argues that the struggle was as much a civil war as a fight for national independence.

Mokyr, Joel, *The Lever of Riches* (1990). An important study of the causes of the industrial revolution that emphasizes the role of small technological and organizational breakthroughs.

Naquin, Susan, and Evelyn Rawski, *Chinese Society in the Eighteenth Century* (1987). A survey of mid-Qing society.

Neal, Larry, *The Rise of Financial Capitalism* (1990). An important study of the making of financial markets.

Nikitenko, Aleksandr, *Up from Serfdom: My Childhood and Youth in Russia, 1804–1824* (2001). One of the very few recorded life stories of a Russian serf.

Pomeranz, Kenneth, *The Great Divergence: Europe, China, and the Making of the Modern World Economy* (2000). Offers explanations of why Europe and not some other place in the world, like parts of China or India, forged ahead economically in the nineteenth century.

Rudé, George, *Europe in the Eighteenth Century* (1972). Emphasizes the rise of a new class, the bourgeoisie, against the old aristocracy, as a cause of the French Revolution.

Wakeman, Frederic, Jr., "The Canton Trade and the Opium War," in John K. Fairbank (ed.), *The Cambridge History of China*, Vol. 10 (1978), pp. 163–212. The standard account of the episode.

Wong, R. Bin, *China Transformed: Historical Change and the Limits of European Experience* (2000). Draws attention to the relative autonomy of merchant capitalists in relation to dynastic states in Europe compared to China.

Wood, Gordon, *The Radicalism of the American Revolution* (1991). Makes a persuasive case for the revolutionary consequences of American independence and nationhood.

Wortman, Richard, *Scenarios of Power: Myth and Ceremony in Russian Monarchy*, 2 vols. (1995–2000). Examines how dynastic Russia confronted the challenges of the revolutionary epoch.

Chapter 7

ALTERNATIVE VISIONS OF THE NINETEENTH CENTURY

By the last decades of the nineteenth century, the territorial expansion of the United States left almost all Indians confined to reservations. Across the American West during the 1880s, many on the reservations fell into despair. Among the downtrodden was a Paiute Indian named Wovoka. But on January 1, 1889, Wovoka had a vision that proposed an alternative, and much brighter, future. In his dream, the "Supreme Being" told Wovoka that if Indians lived harmoniously, shunned white ways (especially alcohol), and performed the cleansing Ghost Dance, the buffalo would return and multiply to their former numbers, and all Indians, including the dead, would be reborn to live in eternal bliss. As word spread of Wovoka's vision, Indians from hundreds of miles around made pilgrimages to the lodge of this new prophet. Many came away proclaiming him the Indians' messiah or the "Red Man's Christ," an impression fostered by the scars on Wovoka's hands, which he maintained had resulted from his centuries-old crucifixion. Especially among the Shoshone, Arapaho, Cheyenne, and Sioux peoples of the northern Plains, Wovoka's message inspired new hope. In the fall of 1890, increasing numbers joined in the ritual Ghost Dance, hoping that it would restore, as Wovoka claimed, the good life that colonialism had seemed to extinguish. Among those given hope by the Ghost Dance was Sitting Bull, the revered Sioux chief, who was himself famous for his visions. Yet, rather than heralding the return of the buffalo and the retreat of white people, the Ghost Dance culminated in the murder of Sitting Bull and the bloody massacre of Sioux Ghost Dancers at a South Dakota creek called Wounded Knee.

Less than two years separated Wovoka's initial vision from the crushing of the Ghost Dancers at Wounded Knee on December 29, 1890. Yet, this movement was connected to a much longer and larger history of prophetic crusades that challenged an emerging nineteenth-century order based on the ideals of the French and American Revolutions, the worldwide spread of laissez-faire capitalism, the nation-state organization, new technologies, and industrial organizations. This emerging new order provided a set of answers to the questions of who should govern and what beliefs should prevail. But it did not stamp out other answers. Equally important if less influential during this period were alternative ideas for organizing life. A diverse assortment of political radicals, charismatic prophets, peasant rebels, and anti-colonial insurgents developed these perspectives. Animated by a sense of the impending loss of their existing worlds and energized by visions of utopian futures, these seers put forward striking counterproposals to those that capitalists, colonial modernizers, and nation-state builders had developed.

REACTIONS TO SOCIAL AND POLITICAL CHANGE

> → *What did radical alternative movements have in common?*

The transformations of the late eighteenth and early nineteenth centuries had upset polities and economies around the globe. In Europe, the old order had either been swept aside or severely battered by the tide of political and economic revolutions. In North America, the newly independent United States began an expansion across the continent. Territorial growth led to the dispossession of hundreds of Indian tribes and the acquisition of nearly half of Mexico by conquest. In Latin America, fledgling nation-states, which had replaced the Spanish empire at the beginning of the nineteenth century, struggled to maintain control over their subject populations. And in Asia and Africa, rulers and people confronted the growing might of Western military and industrial power. At stake throughout the world were questions of how territories were to be defined and ruled and what social and cultural visions they were to embody.

The alternatives varied considerably. Some called for the revitalization of traditional religions; others sought to strengthen village and communal bonds; still others imagined a society where there was no private property and where the material world was meant to be shared equally. The actions of these rebels and dissidents depended on their local traditions and the degree of contact with the emergent power of industrial capitalism, European colonialism, and centralizing nation-states.

In this era of flux and rapid social change, when differing visions of power and justice vied with each other, we have unique opportunities to hear the voices of the lower orders—the peasants and workers, whose perspectives the elites so often ignored or suppressed. While there is scant documentation or written records that capture the views of the illiterate and the marginalized, folklore, dreams, rumors, and prophecies, spread and handed down from generation to generation through oral tradition, illuminate the visions of common folk.

In this chapter, we highlight the emergence of three distinct alternative perspectives. The first comprised movements in regions not colonized by Europeans, but where European ideas and European commerce had disrupted the existing order: the Islamic Middle East and Islamic Africa, non-Islamic Africa, and China. Some of these areas were quite distant from industrial capitalism and European colonialism but were feeling the effects of these forces in more indirect ways. Others, like China, were being drawn rapidly into a European commercial world but had managed to stay free of outright colonization. Here, popu-

Focus Questions ALTERNATIVE VISIONS OF THE 19th CENTURY

→ *What did radical alternative movements have in common?*
→ *How did prophets and big men tap into Islamic and African traditions?*
→ *Why did the Taiping Rebellion arise in the 1850s in China?*
→ *What forces fueled European radicalism?*
→ *How were the alternative movements in America and India similar and different?*

lation growth, new patterns of world trade, and the growing power of Europe disrupted the old order. Accordingly, during the first half of the nineteenth century, these regions witnessed the rise of leaders who believed that their traditions required rejuvenation. Dynamic religious prophets and charismatic military leaders seized the historical stage and went on to reorganize their communities into powerful polities.

A second pattern appeared in Europe and the Americas, in what were the heartlands of industrial capitalism, colonialism, and the new nation-states. Here, there was no turning back, especially following the collapse of old regimes under the onslaught of revolutions, wars, and the rising power of the bourgeoisie in the first half of the nineteenth century. Yet, here, too, utopians, romantics, and radicals dreamed of new, more far-reaching changes to the order that economic and political revolutions had created. The most thoroughgoing radical conceptions envisioned an end to private property and a socialist alternative to capitalism.

The third pattern of alternative visions took shape in the fierce struggle to defend traditional worlds under attack from imperialist nation-states in areas where European colonizers and settlers already dominated. Under this pattern, we find Indian prophets in North America who produced compelling visions to mobilize their people against the westward expansion of the newly established American republic. So, too, the Mayans in the Yucatan, confronted with the domineering power of the Mexican state, fought wars until the end of the nineteenth century to defend their cultural and political autonomy. And finally, peasants and old elites in British India advanced their conceptions of a just order that led to a fierce revolt to replace colonial rule in 1857.

Much separated one movement from another in the three patterns identified above, but together they offered radical alternatives to a world that was being structured by industrial capitalism and centralized modern states—national and colonial. Although these movements happened in different places and times, they shared four characteristics. First, whether presented by secular intellectuals or religious prophets, by ordinary peasant rebels or charismatic elite leaders, all of them opposed some form of established authority. Second, in giving voice to these visions, they steeped themselves in their own historical and cultural traditions, regarding their local communities as the source of political and cultural legitimacy. Third, and paradoxically, these movements authorized new social and political arrangements. Fourth, the movements in favor of alternatives either took place in regions far from the center of the developing world or were led by men and women who were themselves on the margins of political and social power.

PROPHECY AND REVITALIZATION IN THE ISLAMIC WORLD AND AFRICA

→ *How did prophets and big men tap into Islamic and African traditions?*

Our first category of alternative visions appeared in the part of the world that had felt the effects of European and American commercial and cultural influence but that had not fallen under direct colonial rule. In such regions, alternative perspectives took on their most forceful expression in areas distant from the main trade and cultural routes and were led by persons who were outside the emerging capitalist world order. In the Islamic world, the margins played an especially important role in articulating these views because, in the Islamic heartland (the Ottoman empire) and the most Western-influenced regions of sub-Saharan Africa (the west coast and the southern tip of the continent), reformers were trying to adapt to Europe—that is, to reform their societies along European lines.

Even though much of the Islamic world and non-Islamic Africa had not been colonized and were only partially integrated into a European-dominated set of trading networks, these regions had reached turning points at the end of the eighteenth century. By then, the era of Islamic expansion and the flowering under the Ottomans, Safavids, and Mughals was over. The dominance of these empires had extended Muslim trading orbits, facilitated cross-cultural communication, and led to the formation of common knowledge over vast territories. Their political and military decline, however, confronted the faithful with new challenges. The sense of alarm grew as the power of Christian Europe spread from the edges of the Islamic world to its centers. While this perception of danger motivated military men in Egypt and the Ottoman sultans to modernize their states (see Chapter 6), it also fomented the emergence of religious revitalization movements throughout the Islamic world. Led by prophets who were convinced that the Islamic faith was in trouble, these movements spoke the language of revival and restoration as they sought to establish new theocratic governments across the Islamic lands.

Prophecy also surfaced and exerted a powerful influence in non-Islamic Africa as it, too, experienced social change brought about by long-distance trade and population growth. Just as Muslim clerics and political leaders sought solutions to desta-

> *Each movement offered radical alternatives to a world that was being structured by industrial capitalism and centralized modern states—national and colonial.*

bilizing changes in their world by re-reading Islamic classics, so, too, African communities, caught up in a world of changing trade relations and new ideas, looked to charismatic leaders. Drawing strength from the spiritual and magical traditions of African communities, the new leaders often succeeded in uniting previously disparate and dispersed communities around their dynamic leadership and their spiritual and cultural themes.

ISLAMIC REVITALIZATION

Movements to revitalize Islam took place on the peripheries—in areas that seemed more distant and thus immune from the intense and potentially threatening repercussions of the world economy. In the peripheral zones, religious leaders rejected westernizing influences (see Map 7-1). Instead, the leaders of Islamic revitalization movements looked back to Islamic traditions and modeled their revolts on the life of Muhammad. But even as they looked to the past, they also strove to establish something new: full-scale theocratic polities. The new generation of Islamic reformers conceived of the state as the primary instrument of God's will and as the vehicle for purifying Islamic culture.

The leaders of Islamic revitalization movements looked back to Islamic traditions and modeled their revolts on the life of Muhammad.

WAHHABISM One of the most powerful of these purifying reformist movements arose on the Arabian peninsula, the birthplace of the Muslim faith. In the Najd region of the peninsula, an area surrounded by mountains and deserts, and located just north of one of the most barren places in the world—the Empty Quarter—a religious cleric, Muhammad Ibn abd al-Wahhab (1703–1792), galvanized the local population by attacking what he regarded as lax religious practices. His message found a ready response among the local inhabitants, who felt their lives threatened by the new commercial activities and new intellectual currents stirring around them. Abd al-Wahhab demanded a return to the pure Islam of Muhammad and the early caliphs. Although Najd was as far removed from the currents of the expanding world economy as an area could be, Abd al-Wahhab himself was not. He had been educated in Iraq, Iran, and the Hijaz before returning to the Arabian peninsula. His belief was that Islam had fallen into a degraded state, particularly so in its birthplace. He railed against the polytheistic beliefs that had taken hold of the people, complaining that men and women, in defiance of the tenets of Muhammad, were worshipping trees, stones, and tombs, and making sacrifices to false images. Abd al-Wahhab's movement stressed the absolute oneness of Allah (hence his followers were referred to as *Muwahhidin*, or Unitarians) and directed its most severe criticism against Sufi sects for extolling the lives of saints over the worship of God.

As Wahhabism swept across the Arabian peninsula, the movement posed less of a threat to European power than it did to the Ottomans' hold on the region. Wahhabism gained a powerful political ally in the Najdian House of Saud, whose followers, inspired by the religious zeal of the Wahhabis, went on a militant religious campaign. They sacked the Shiite shrines of Karbala in southern Iraq, and in 1803 they overran the holy cities of Mecca and Medina, where they damaged the tombs of the saints. Frightened by the Wahhabi challenge, the Ottoman sultan persuaded the breakaway provincial ruler of Egypt, Muhammad Ali, to send troops to the Arabian peninsula to suppress the movement. The Egyptians defeated the Saudis, but Wahhabism and the House of Saud continued to represent a pure Islamic faith that attracted clerics and common folk throughout the Muslim world.

DAN FODIO AND THE FULANI In West Africa, as in the Arabian peninsula, Muslim revolts erupted from Senegal to Nigeria in the late eighteenth and early nineteenth centuries, responding in part to Western inroads. In this region, the Fulani people played the decisive role in religious uprisings that sought, like the Wahhabi Movement, to recreate a supposedly purer Islamic past. Although the Fulani originated in the eastern part of present-day Senegal (and retain a powerful presence there today), they moved outward in an easterly direction, particularly when drought conditions caused a deterioration in their home territory. Over time, the Fulani set down roots in strategic locations across the savannah lands of West Africa. The majority were cattle-keepers, practicing a pastoral and nomadic way of life. But some were sedentary, and it was people in this group who converted to Islam, read the Islamic classics, and put themselves in touch with holy men of North Africa, Egypt, and the Arabian peninsula. They came to the conclusion that the peoples of West Africa were violating Islamic beliefs and were engaging in irreligious practices.

The most powerful of these Islamic reform movements flourished in what is today northern Nigeria. It was led by a Fulani Muslim cleric, Usman dan Fodio (1754–1817), who succeeded in creating a vast Islamic empire. Dan Fodio's movement had all the trappings of the Islamic revolts of this period. It sought inspiration in the life of Muhammad and demanded a return to early Islamic practices. It attacked false belief and heathenism and called upon its followers to wage holy war (*jihad*) against unbelievers. Usman dan Fodio's adversaries were the old Hausa rulers, whose commitment to Islam, in his view, was less than absolute. To register his aversion to apostates, dan Fodio withdrew from his original habitation in Konni. He then set up a new community of believers at Gudu, citing the precedent of Muhammad, who had withdrawn from Mecca

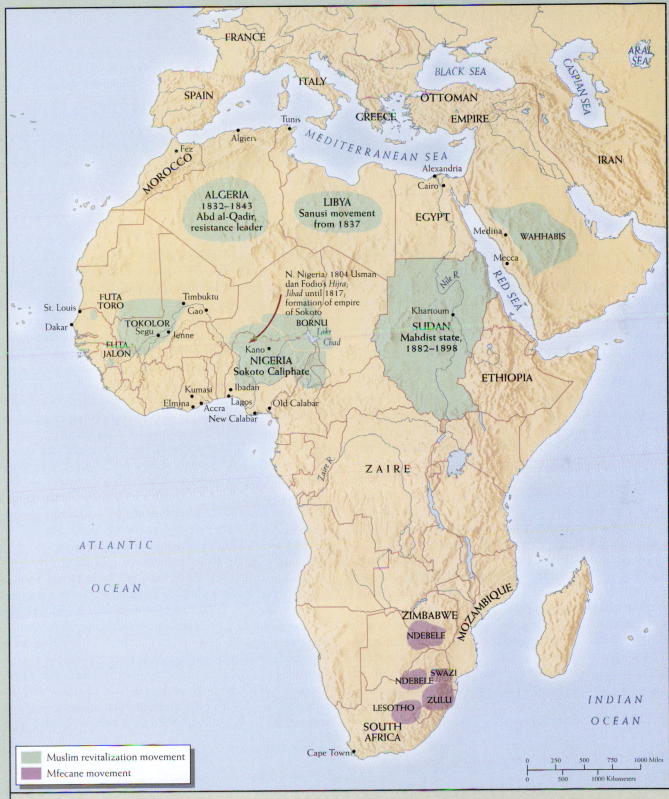

FRANCE

SPAIN

ITALY

GREECE

OTTOMAN EMPIRE

BLACK SEA

CASPIAN SEA

ARAL SEA

IRAN

MOROCCO

Fez

Algiers

Tunis

MEDITERRANEAN SEA

Alexandria

Cairo

EGYPT

Medina

Mecca

RED SEA

WAHHABIS

ALGERIA
1832–1843
Abd al-Qadir,
resistance leader

LIBYA
Sanusi movement
from 1837

FUTA
TORO

St. Louis

Dakar

TOKOLOR

Timbuktu

Gao

Segu

Jenne

FUTA
JALON

N. Nigeria, 1804 Usman
dan Fodio's *Hijra*;
Jihad until 1817;
formation of empire
of Sokoto

BORNU

Kano

*Lake
Chad*

Nile R.

Khartoum

SUDAN
Mahdist state,
1882–1898

NIGERIA
Sokoto Caliphate

ETHIOPIA

Kumasi

Ibadan

Elmina

Accra

Lagos

Old Calabar

New Calabar

Zaire R.

ZAIRE

ATLANTIC

OCEAN

ZIMBABWE

NDEBELE

MOZAMBIQUE

INDIAN
OCEAN

SWAZI

NDEBELE

ZULU

LESOTHO

SOUTH
AFRICA

Cape Town

| | Muslim revitalization movement |
| | Mfecane movement |

0   250   500   750   1000 Miles

0   500   1000 Kilometers

MAP 7-1   MUSLIM REVITALIZATION MOVEMENTS IN THE MIDDLE EAST AND
AFRICA AND THE *MFECANE* MOVEMENT IN SOUTHERN AFRICA

The nineteenth century saw a series of Muslim revitalization movements take place throughout the Middle East and North Africa.
Can you explain why they occurred in certain parts of the Islamic Middle East and Africa, like the Arabian peninsula, North Africa,
and West Africa, and not in other Islamic centers, like Egypt, Syria, and Turkey, the heartland of the Ottoman empire? Why did
one of the first of these movements occur in the Arabian peninsula, and why did the Wahhabi Movement there have such an influence in other parts of the Islamic world? Were any of the same factors that led to Islamic revitalization involved in the *Mfecane*
developments in southern Africa?

Global Connections & Disconnections

ISLAMIC REBELS: ABI AL-QASIM AND ZAYNAB

Reformist ideas swirled through the Islamic world throughout the nineteenth century, producing new visions and powerful new communities across the Middle East and Africa. In no part of the Islamic world was opposition to European colonial and capitalist encroachment more strongly articulated than in Algeria, over which France claimed jurisdiction beginning in 1830. Algerians rose in bold and bloody revolts. The most violent of these uprisings were the rebellion of Abd al-Qadir in the 1830s and the revolt of 1849. The French repressed these movements ruthlessly, resulting in heavy losses to combatants and to many civilians. The military lessons took hold. Algerian Muslims, living on the edges of French authority, learned to use more subtle means to preserve their autonomy, fearing to challenge the French authorities overtly.

A master in the art of protecting his community's religious and political autonomy in the face of France's constantly encroaching power was Shaykh Muhammad ibn Abi al-Qasim (1823–1897), a religious notable who lived in southern Algeria at the foothills of the Saharan Atlas Mountains. He gained a large circle of religious devotees because his Sufi brotherhood served as a safe haven for those who did not want to live under direct French rule. When, however, his health deteriorated, in the late 1870s, the French became embroiled in an internal struggle over his succession. Accepting the conventional wisdom that Islam was a patriarchal religion, the French supported the candidacy of the shaykh's male cousin over his daughter, Zaynab (1850–1904). Unfortunately, their calculations proved utterly wrong, having failed to account for Zaynab's powerful personality and her religious legitimacy. When al-Qasim passed away in 1897, the French found themselves in a situation for which their traditional dealings with Islamic leaders had not prepared them. They stood in opposition to a dynamic female religious personage.

Zaynab laid claim to her father's legacy because of her exemplary piety, her understanding of her father's teachings, her vow of celibacy, and her independence from the French. Her descent from the family of the Prophet Muhammad and the many miracles attributed to her soon elevated her to the status of a religious holy person and gave her a legitimacy that women did not frequently attain in Islamic religious affairs. But as we have seen in other settings (see the box on Joan of Arc in Chapter 2), at times when communal values are under great pressure, as they were because of the French advance into the southern part of Algeria and France's interference in local religious succession, people were prepared to turn to a woman. Indeed, Zaynab was willing to contest French power more vigorously and directly than her father would have considered prudent, realizing that the French had never faced a woman leader before. Zaynab's actions revealed a vulnerability, only occasionally, however, tested in colonial affairs—in their uncertainty about how to respond to opposition from women, a group whom the colonial authorities claimed they were protecting from male exploitation. Nonetheless, the French turned against Zaynab, describing her as "passionate to the point of hatred and bold to the point of insolence and impudence." But their opposition only heightened her appeal and her legitimacy among her followers.

to establish a community of true believers at Medina. The practice of withdrawal, called *hijra* in Muhammad's time, was yet another of the Prophet's inspirations invoked by the religious reformers.

Dan Fodio was a member of a Sufi brotherhood, the Qadiriyya, one of the many Sufi orders that, from the sixteenth century onward, had facilitated the spread of Islam into West Africa. Sufism, the mystical and popular form of Islam, sought an emotional connection with God and extolled the achievements of devoted religious men. Usman dan Fodio had studied Sufi religious writings and was already adept in Sufi practices by his early twenties, employing the traditional Sufi techniques of a strict regimen of prayers, fasting, and religious exercises to obtain mystical states.

Dan Fodio's visions led him to challenge the ruling classes of West Africa. In one of his visions, the founder of the Qadiriyya order came to him and ordered him to unsheathe the sword of truth against the enemies of Islam. Dan Fodio won the support of devout Muslims in the area, who agreed with his message that Islam was not being properly practiced. He also gained the backing of his Fulani tribesmen and many of the Hausa peasantry, who had suffered under the rule of the Hausa landlord class. The revolt, initiated in 1804, resulted in the overthrow of the Hausa rulers and the creation of a confederation of Islamic emirates, almost all of which were in the hands of the Fulani allies of dan Fodio.

Usman dan Fodio considered himself a cleric first and a political and military man second. Although his political leadership was decisive in the success of the revolt, once military success was assured, dan Fodio retired to a life of scholarship and writing. He delegated the political and administrative functions of the new empire to his brother, Abdullahi, and his son, Muhammad Bello. The two built a solid and stable empire. They forged an enduring decentralized state structure, which became known as the Sokoto Caliphate in 1809 and fostered the spread of Islam through the region. In 1800, on the eve of dan Fodio's revolt, Islam was the faith of only a minority of people living in northern Nigeria; a century later, it had become the religion of the vast majority. Although the Fulani of northern Nigeria were on the fringes of the world economy, they nonetheless were drawn into enlarging economic and cultural connections through their contacts with the religious centers of the Middle Eastern Islamic world and through expanding long-distance trade.

CHARISMATIC MILITARY MEN AND PROPHETS IN NON-ISLAMIC AFRICA

In non-Islamic Africa, revolts, new states, and prophetic movements arose from the same combination of factors that were at work in the rest of the world, particularly long-distance trade and population increase. Local communities here also looked to religious traditions and new political leaders for solutions. In southern Africa, during the first three decades of the nineteenth century, a group of political revolts, called in Zulu the *Mfecane* ("the crushing"), reordered the political map. Its epicenter was a large tract of land lying east of the Drakensberg Mountains, an area where population pressures and land resources existed in a precarious balance (see Map 7-1). In this region, trade with the Portuguese in Mozambique and with other Europeans at Delagoa Bay had disrupted the traditional social order. Compounding the disorder was the pressure that growing populations put on various vital resources. This set the stage for a political crisis for the northern Nguni (Bantu-speaking) peoples, a branch of whom, the Zulus, produced a fierce war leader and state-builder, Shaka (1787–1828).

The Bantu people had inhabited the southern part of the African continent for centuries. At the end of the eighteenth century, however, their political organizations still operated on a small scale, revolving around families and clans and modest chieftaincies. These tiny polities could not cope with the problems of overpopulation and competition for land that had become prevalent in southern Africa at that time. The Zulus under Shaka stole an advance on their neighbors by creating a ruthless war-

Shaka, King of the Zulus. This illustration, which is the only one from the time, may be an exaggeration, but it does not exaggerate the view that many had of the awesome strength and power of Shaka, the leader who united the Zulu peoples into an invincible warrior state.

rior state that drove other populations out of the region, and forced them to emulate Shaka by fashioning similarly large, centralized monarchies throughout southern and central Africa. At no previous moment in African history had the evolution from small clan communities to centralized monarchies occurred so rapidly or over such a wide area.

Shaka was the son of a minor chief who managed to emerge as the victor in the struggle for cattle-grazing and farming lands that arose during a period of severe drought. A muscular and physically imposing figure, Shaka was also a violent man who did not hesitate to use terror to intimidate his subjects or to overawe his adversaries. His enemies knew that the price of opposition would be a massacre, which would include the killing of women and children. Nor was he much kinder to his own people. Following the death of his mother, who was the only person with whom he had a close personal relationship, Shaka took out his feelings of grief on his own people. He executed those who were not properly contrite and who did not weep profusely. Reportedly, it took 7,000 lives to assuage his grief.

Shaka built his new state around his own military and organizational skills and the fear that his personal ferocity produced. He drilled his men relentlessly in the use of short stabbing spears and in discipline under pressure. Like the Mongols, he had a remarkable ability to incorporate defeated communities into the state and to absorb young men into his ultra-dedicated warrior forces. His army numbered 40,000 men and was organized into regiments that lived, studied, and fought together. Whether his warriors came from the core of Shaka's original community or from newly conquered peoples, he forbade them from marrying until he discharged them from the army. They developed an intense esprit de corps, took pride in their fighting abilities, and

Zulu Regiments. Shaka's Zulu state owed its political and military successes to its young warriors, who were deeply loyal to their ruler and whose military training and discipline were exemplary. Shown here is a regimental camp in which the warriors slept in huts massed in a circular pattern and trained in military drill and close combat in the inside circle.

regarded no sacrifice as too great in the service of the state. So overpowering were Shaka's forces that other peoples of the region fled from their home areas, and Shaka laid claim to their estates for himself and his followers.

Shaka's defeated foes were themselves to adopt many of the Zulu state's military innovations. They did so first to defend themselves, and then to take over new land as they were driven away from their old areas. The new states of the Ndebele in what later became Zimbabwe and of the Sotho of South Africa came into existence in the middle of the nineteenth century in this way and proved long-lasting.

Thus did the Zulus under Shaka create a ruthless warrior state that conquered much territory in southern and central Africa, assimilating some peoples, and forcing others to fashion their own similarly centralized polities. In turning southern Africa from a region of smaller polities into an area with larger and more powerful ones, Shaka seemed very much a man of the modern, nineteenth-century world. And yet, he was in his own unique way a familiar kind of African leader. He shared a charismatic and prophetic style with others who emerged during periods of acute social change. He was, in this sense, only the latest of "big men" to seek dominance. Like others, Shaka's rise depended on his ability to resolve a community crisis—in this case, a drought and a shortage of arable land. Also, like other big men, past and present, Shaka drew on a tradition of hand-to-hand combat to buttress his authority, although he was perhaps unique in the combination of military prowess, political skills, and the considerable terror he inspired. By successfully integrating young men from conquered territories into his regiments, he succeeded in enlarging communal and ethnic ties. Other rulers were able to draw strength from long-standing religious and cultural symbols as well. They adopted the rituals of those they conquered, and even succeeded in creating totally new ethnic communities out of the fragments of African polities.

PROPHECY AND REBELLION IN CHINA

> → *Why did the Taiping Rebellion arise in the 1850s in China?*

The prophetic and charismatic movements in the Islamic world and Africa appeared in areas relatively distant from Western influences. Yet, China, which had seen its trade surplus with Europe turned into a deficit in the first half of the nineteenth century through a brisk trade in opium, was no longer isolated. Up until 1842, the Chinese had confined trade with Europeans to the port city of Canton (Guangzhou). After the Opium War, westerners forced Qing rulers to open up a number of other ports to trade. Moreover, foreigners were given the right to reside in the five open ports and the right to be tried for crimes in their own consular courts rather than in Chinese courts (see Chapter 6). To be sure, the dynasty retained its authority over almost the whole realm, and Western influence remained confined to a small minority of merchants and missionaries. Nonetheless, the appearance of an occasional gunboat reminded the Chinese of the power of the West. The resulting humiliation of Qing authorities diminished the state's capacity to govern and its legitimacy in the eyes of many subjects. Searching for an alternative present and future, hundreds of thousands of disillusioned and impoverished peasants joined in what became known as the Taiping Rebellion.

> *The Taiping's drive to "restore" the heavenly kingdom, imagined as a just and egalitarian order, appealed to the subordinate classes caught in the flux of social change.*

Beginning in 1850, the rebellion was led by a prophet, Hong Xiuquan (1813-1864), who established the "Taiping Heavenly Kingdom" (or "Heavenly Kingdom of Great Peace"). Its message of revitalization of a troubled land and its drive to "restore" the heavenly kingdom, imagined as a just and egalitarian order, appealed to the subordinate classes caught in the flux of social change. As in the Islamic world and other parts of sub-Saharan Africa, population increases—from 250 million in 1644 to over 400 million by the 1850s—had put considerable pressure on land and other resources. Moreover, the rising consumption of opium, grown in India and brought to China in increasing quantities by English traders, had produced further social instability and financial crisis in China. As social dislocation spread, banditry and rebellions became frequent. The ruling Qing dynasty turned to the gentry to maintain order in the countryside. But as the gentry raised its militia to put down secret societies and bandits, it whittled away at the authority of the Qing Manchu rulers. Faced with these changes, the Qing dynasty, already weakened by the humiliating Treaty of Nanjing (1842), imposed by Britain following the Opium War, struggled to maintain control. Before it could do so, the Taiping Rebellion shook the dynasty to its core.

The uprising drew upon China's long history of peasant revolts, kept alive over the centuries through the recitation of ballads and tales. Traditionally, these rebellions were rooted in popular religious sects. These sects frequently espoused visions that were egalitarian or millenarian (convinced of the imminent coming of a just and ideal society). Inspired by Daoist or Buddhist sources, they posed threats to the established order. In contrast to orthodox institutions, here women played important roles. In times of political breakdown, millenarian sects provided the organizational networks for transforming local revolts into large-scale rebellions. Thus did the Taiping Rebellion, which began as a local movement in southern China, tap into this millenarian tradition and spread rapidly. Drawing on a largely rural social base and asserting allegiance to Christianity, it claimed to herald a new era of economic and social justice. But the Taiping opposition to the Manchus and its vision of a just order did not entail the formation of a modern nation-state. Caught between the modern and the traditional, the Heavenly Kingdom sought to establish a millenarian polity based on the dictum that all were "brothers and sisters" under God.

THE DREAM

The story of the Taiping Rebellion begins with a complex and convoluted dream that inspired its founding figure, Hong Xiuquan. A native of Guangdong province in the southernmost part of the country, Hong first encountered Christian missionaries in the 1830s. He was then trying, unsuccessfully, to pass the civil service examination, which would have afforded him entry into the elite stratum and a potential career in the Qing bureaucracy. Disappointed by his poor showing, Hong began to have visions, including a dream in 1837 that led him to form the Society of God Worshippers in the 1840s, and subsequently to establish the Taiping Heavenly Kingdom in 1851.

In this dream, a ceremonial retinue of heavenly guards escorted Hong to heaven. The group included a cock-like figure, which he later identified as Leigong, the Duke of Thunder, a familiar figure in indigenous mythology. Upon reaching heaven, Hong's belly was slit open, and his internal organs were removed and replaced with new ones. As the operation for his renewal was completed, heavenly texts were unrolled for him to read and absorb. The "Heavenly Mother" then met and thoroughly cleansed him. She addressed him as "son," before bringing him in front of the "Old Father." Although not part of the heavenly bureaucracy, Confucius and women generals from the Song dynasty were also present. Upon meeting Hong, the "Old Father" complained that human beings had been led astray by demons, as demonstrated by the vanity of their shaven heads (a practice imposed by the Qing regime), their consumption of opium, and other forms of debauchery. The "Old Father" even denounced Confucius who, after being flogged and begging for mercy before Hong's heavenly "Elder Brother," was allowed to stay in heaven but forbidden to preach his teachings again. But the world was not yet free of demons. Thus, the "Old Father" instructed Hong to leave his heavenly family behind and return to earth to rescue human beings from demons.

How much of this account of Hong's dream has been embellished with hindsight we will probably never know. The differing extant versions date back at the earliest to the 1850s, when the Taiping Rebellion was already in full swing. What we do know is that Hong, after he failed the civil service examination for the third time in 1837, was afflicted with a strange "illness" in which he had visions of combating demons. He also took to proclaiming himself the Heavenly King. Relatives and neighbors thought he might have gone mad. Yet, after a burst of apparently outlandish behavior, Hong gradually returned to his normal state, resuming his studies and preparing himself for another attempt to pass the examination.

In 1843, after failing the examination for the fourth time, Hong immersed himself in a Christian tract entitled *Good Words for Exhorting the Age.* Reportedly, reading this tract enabled Hong to realize the full significance of his earlier dream. All the pieces suddenly fell into place. The "Old Father" in his dream, he came to understand, was the Lord Ye-huo-hua (a Chinese rendering of Jehovah), the creator of heaven and earth. Accordingly, the cleansing ritual foretold his baptism. The "Elder Brother" was, in turn, Jesus the Savior, son of God. He, Hong Xiuquan, was the younger brother of Jesus—God's other son. Just as Jesus had previously descended to save mankind, Hong was now being sent by God to rid the world of evil and demons. What was once a dream was now a prophetic vision.

> *Taiping policies were demanding and strict: the rules prohibited the consumption of alcohol, smoking of opium, or indulgence in sensual pleasure.*

THE REBELLION

Unlike earlier sectarian leaders whose rebellions tended to operate in secrecy before exploding onto the public arena, Hong chose a more audacious path. Once convinced of his vision, he began to preach his doctrines openly, baptizing converts and destroying Confucian idols and ancestral shrines. Such frontal assaults on the establishment testified to his conviction that he was carrying out God's will rather than engaging in heterodox activities. Converts were required to provide a statement, in writing, of their former transgressions before they could repent and proclaim their adherence to the godly path.

In addition to religious beliefs, material concerns fired the rebellion. Ending the Opium War in 1842, the Treaty of Nanjing had opened four more ports besides Canton (Guangzhou) along the southeastern coast of China to external trade. The city of Canton located about thirty miles south of Hong's home village and at the southern tip of the country, had long been both the center for regional commerce and the only port designated for

external trade. Since, after 1842, commodities that once were sent only to Canton began to be shipped to the other ports, the ensuing social and economic dislocation in the area near Canton created a sizeable reservoir of potential recruits to Hong's ranks. Indeed, many of Hong's early followers came from the marginal sectors of local society. Many were transport workers, miners, masons, pirates, militiamen, demobilized soldiers, as well as peasants. Despite the trauma of the Opium War, the anger of these rebels was directed not at the Europeans, but at the Qing government. The Taiping identified the Manchus as the "demons" and as the chief obstacle to the realization of God's kingdom on earth.

Taiping policies were demanding and strict: the rules prohibited the consumption of alcohol, smoking of opium, or indulgence in sensual pleasure. Men and women were to be segregated for administrative and residential purposes. At the same time, in a most drastic departure from the dynastic practice, women joined army units and could serve in the Taiping bureaucracy. Examinations were based on a translated version of the Bible and assorted religious and literary compositions by Hong. Finally, all land was to be divided among the families according to family size, with men and women receiving equal shares. Once each family's own need for sustenance could be met, the communities shared the remaining surplus. These were all radical departures from Chinese traditions of hierarchy and patriarchy and from common Chinese living arrangements and religious practices.

Initially, Hong's activities attracted scant attention from the authorities, but his anti-Qing message made imperial officials increasingly nervous. By 1850, Hong's movement had amassed a following of over 20,000, giving Qing rulers more cause for concern. They sent troops to arrest Hong and other rebel leaders. But they were repelled by Taiping forces, who then began to spread their rebellion beyond Hong's original base.

In 1851, Hong declared himself the Heavenly King of the Taiping Heavenly Kingdom. By 1853, the disciplined band of Taiping rebels had marched north and east from their original base, capturing major cities and swelling their ranks, as well as establishing a heavenly capital in the city of Nanjing (see Map 7-2). Upon capturing Nanjing, the Taiping cleansed the city of "demons," systematically killing all the Manchus—men, women, and children—they found.

But the rebels could not sustain their vision. Deadly struggles within the leadership, uncompromising codes of conduct, and the rallying of both Manchu and Han elites around the dynasty all contributed to the fall of the Heavenly Kingdom. Disturbed by the Taiping's repudiation of Confucianism and wanting to protect their property, local landowning gentry led militias against

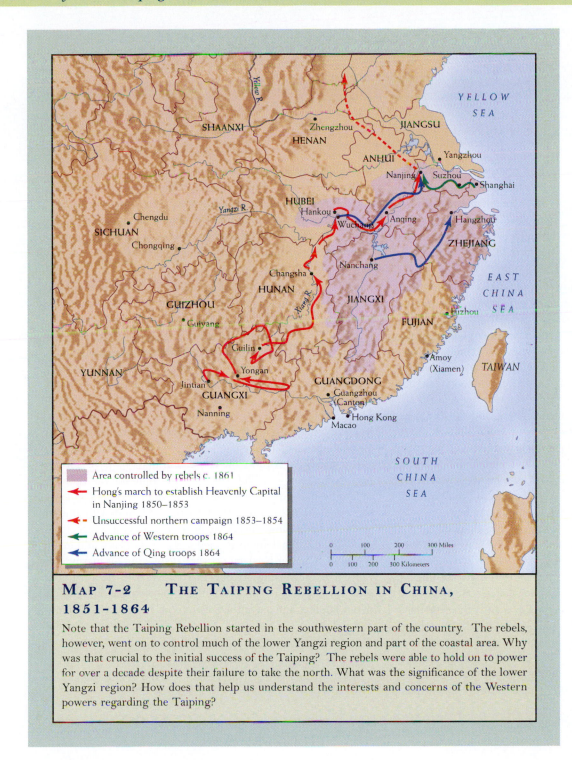

MAP 7-2   THE TAIPING REBELLION IN CHINA, 1851-1864

Note that the Taiping Rebellion started in the southwestern part of the country. The rebels, however, went on to control much of the lower Yangzi region and part of the coastal area. Why was that crucial to the initial success of the Taiping? The rebels were able to hold on to power for over a decade despite their failure to take the north. What was the significance of the lower Yangzi region? How does that help us understand the interests and concerns of the Western powers regarding the Taiping?

foreign-officered mercenary army eventually took part in its suppression. Hong himself perished as his heavenly capital fell in 1864. With the Qing victory imminent, few of the perhaps 100,000 rebels in Nanjing surrendered. They simply gathered themselves together, waiting for the Qing troops to deliver them from their earthly kingdom to a better place.

The slaughter of the Taiping rebels prepared the stage for a concerted attempt by imperial bureaucrats and elite intellectuals to rejuvenate the Qing state. Although the Taiping's millenarian vision vanished, the desire to reconstitute Chinese society and government did not. The rebellion, in that sense, continued to serve as an inspiration for reformers as well as for future peasant mobilizations.

Like its counterparts in the Islamic world and Africa, the Taiping based its critique of the old order on a promise to restore lost harmony. For all the differences of cultural and historical location, what Abd al-Wahhab, dan Fodio, Shaka, and Hong shared in common was the perception that the present world was unjust. Thus, they set out to reorganize their respective communities. Characteristically, these communities were caught up in the flux of change, and their reorganization into new polities involved confrontations with the established authorities. In this regard, the language of revitalization used by

the Taiping. Moreover, Western governments also opposed the rebellion. Despite the constant reiteration of the "brotherhood" of Christians, Western governments claimed that the Taiping's doctrines represented a perversion of Christianity and should be quashed. Although the rebellion's inception had so much to do with the disruptive forces unleashed by an expansive West, a

religious prophets in Islamic areas and China proved crucial, for it provided an alternative vocabulary of political and spiritual legitimacy. Although in non-Islamic Africa it was not religious revitalization that powered the creation of new polities, it still was an appeal to tradition—to communal solidarity and to the widespread tradition of "big men" in stateless societies. By

THE TAIPING ON THE PRINCIPLES OF THE HEAVENLY NATURE

In this excerpt from 1854, the Taiping leaders envisage a radically new community based on values that challenge the conventional modes of social organization of Chinese society. Inspired by their understanding of Christianity, the Taiping leadership confronted the central role of the family and ancestral worship in Chinese social life by urging all its followers to regard themselves as belonging to a single family. It also advocated the segregation of the sexes, despite its efforts to improve the lives of women in some of its other policy proclamations.

We brothers and sisters, enjoying today the greatest mercy of our Heavenly Father, have become as one family and are able to enjoy true blessings; each of us must always be thankful. Speaking in terms of our ordinary human feelings, it is true that each has his own parents and there must be a distinction in family names; it is also true that as each has his own household, there must be a distinction between this boundary and that boundary. Yet we must know that the ten thousand names derive from the one name, and the one name from one ancestor. Thus our origins are not different. Since our Heavenly Father gave us birth and nourishment, we are of one form though of separate bodies, and we breathe the same air though in different places. This is why we say, "All are brothers within the four seas." Now, basking in the profound mercy of Heaven, we are of one family. . . .

We brothers, our minds having been awakened by our Heavenly Father, joined the camp in the earlier days to support our Sovereign, many bringing parents, wives, uncles, brothers, and whole families. It is a matter of course that we should attend to our parents and look after our wives and children, but when one first creates a new rule, the state must come first and the family last, public interests first and private interests last. Moreover, as it is advisable to avoid suspicion [of improper conduct] between the inner [female] and the outer [male] and to distinguish between male and female, so men must have male quarters and women must

have female quarters; only thus can we be dignified and avoid confusion. There must be no common mixing of the male and female groups, which would cause debauchery and violation of Heaven's commandments. Although to pay respects to parents and to visit wives and children occasionally are in keeping with human nature and not prohibited, yet it is only proper to converse before the door, stand a few steps apart and speak in a loud voice; one must not enter the sisters' camp or permit the mixing of men and women. Only thus, by complying with rules and commands, can we become sons and daughters of Heaven.

At the present time, the remaining demons have not yet been completely exterminated and the time for the reunion of families has not yet arrived. We younger brothers and sisters must be firm and patient to the end, and with united strength and a single heart we must uphold God's principles and wipe out the demons immediately. With peace and unity achieved, then our Heavenly Father, displaying his mercy, will reward us according to our merits. Wealth, nobility, and renown will then enable us brothers to celebrate the reunion of our families and enjoy the harmonious relations of husband and wife.

Source: *The Principles of the Heavenly Nature*, in *Sources of Chinese Tradition*, 2nd ed., Vol. 2, compiled by Wm. Theodore de Bary and Richard Lufrano (New York: Columbia University Press, 2000), pp. 229–30.

mobilizing those eager to return to an imagined golden age, these prophets and charismatic leaders gave voice to those dispossessed by global change, while producing new, alternative ways of organizing society and politics. In China, political authorities crushed the Taiping Rebellion, but the desire to fashion a different order lived on and surfaced in later dissident political movements. In other regions, too, the new polities and communities endured to reconfigure their political and cultural landscapes.

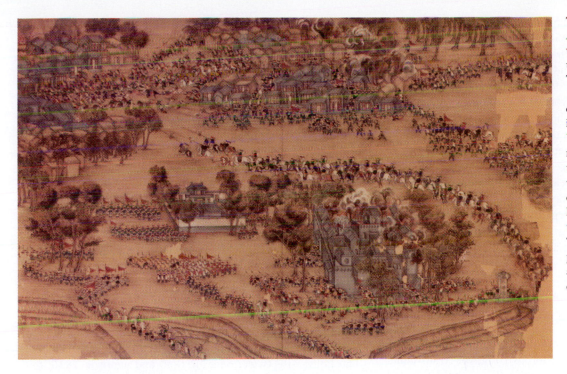

Taiping Northern Campaign.
A painting commemorating the victory of the Qing forces over the Taiping rebels during the Taiping's northern campaign of 1853–1855. After the Taiping established its heavenly capital in the city of Nanjing on the Yangzi River in 1853, its forces marched north to try to seize the Qing capital of Beijing. It would have undoubtedly changed the course of Chinese history and profoundly affected the rest of the world had the Taiping succeeded. The campaign, however, was a failure, and the Taiping rebels were driven back south.

UTOPIANS, SOCIALISTS, AND RADICALS IN EUROPE

→ *What forces fueled European radicalism?*

Europe and North America were the core areas of capitalist activity, nation-state building, and colonialism. But there, too, divergent conceptions of the political and social order challenged the main currents of thought and activity. Prophets of all stripes—political, social, cultural, and religious—propounded anti-establishment values and dreamed of alternative arrangements. Radicals, liberals, utopians, romantics, nationalists, abolitionists, and religious mavericks made plans for better worlds to come. They did so in the face of a new era of monarchical-conservative dominance after the Congress of Vienna in 1815. This conservative turn was especially pronounced in central Europe, where reestablished kings and aristocrats revived many of their privileges and much of their power. The restoration of old regimes, arranged by Austrian diplomat Clemens von Metternich (1773–1859), succeeded in

As a result of the innovations of the revolutionaries and the Napoleonic regime, there were now many different state forms and ideologies from which to choose.

turning back the clock only by ceaselessly tinkering with the gears. But opposition to the restored regimes was widespread, and radical voices confidently predicted the coming of a new day. When that new day would arrive and what that new world would look like remained, however, the stuff of dreams.

RESTORATION AND RESISTANCE

The social and political ferment of the Restoration period (1815–1848) owed a great deal to the ambiguous legacies of the French Revolution and the Napoleonic Wars. As a result of the innovations of the revolutionaries and the Napoleonic regime, there were now many different state forms and ideologies from which to choose. In the 1820s, 1830s, and 1840s, Europeans could also draw on a long tradition of religious radicalism, like that of the sixteenth- and seventeenth-century English Puritans and German Anabaptists, who sought to remake communities from the ground up. Predicting an apocalyptic end for those who lived under sinful and oppressive rulers, these radical dissenters had established principles of both violent and passive resistance that would be employed again and again in centuries to come. Europeans of the Restoration era also had utopian ideals at their beck and call; they could invoke the early egalitarian image of "Pansophia," an ideal republic of inquisitive Christians, united in the search for knowledge of nature as a means of loving God. Or they could refer to the utopian Enlightenment thinkers like William Godwin and the Marquis de Condorcet, men confident that mankind was already well on its way to scientific, political, and even biological perfection. The dislocations of the Napoleonic Wars offered an opportunity to reopen old debates—and old wounds—and, many hoped, to remake European society as a whole.

Critics of the old regime in the Restoration period appeared in many stripes, but all of them were shaped, in one way or another, by a combination of recent experience and older traditions. Reactionaries, liberals and radicals offered alternative visions to the world that Napoleon had left behind. Self-conscious "reactionaries" emerged at this time; their crusade was not just to restore privileges to kings and nobles, but also to reverse all the secularizing and democratizing concessions sovereigns had accorded their subjects during the revolutionary and Napoleonic periods. In Russia, for example, the Slavophiles touted what they regarded as nativist traditions and institutions against the excessively "westernizing" reforms introduced by Peter the Great and continued by his self-styled "enlightened despot" successors. Many Slavophiles were ardent monarchists. Their desire for a strong, yet "traditional" Russia brought them into conflict with the conservative, but modernizing, tsarist state.

The liberals, on the other hand, wanted their states to carry through the legal and political reforms envisioned in 1789, but not to attempt economic equalizing in the manner of the radical Jacobins. Liberals were eager to curb the states' restrictions on trade, destroy the churches' stranglehold on education, and enlarge the franchise, all the while preserving the free market, the Christian churches, and the rule of law. Proponents of liberalism, like John Stuart Mill, insisted on the individual's right to think, speak, act, and vote as he or she pleased, so long as no harm was done to people or property. Liberals feared the corruptibility of powerful states and held that the proper role of government was to foster civil liberties and promote legal equality. Thus, to sum up, the reactionaries wished for a return to privilege, the liberals for reforms that would not endanger order. Both could find elements to their taste in the post-Napoleonic world, and indeed, it was the rivalry between these two groups that defined much of the political landscape of the era before 1848.

> *The rivalry between the liberals and conservatives defined much of the European political landscape of the era before 1848.*

RADICAL VISIONS

Reactionaries and liberals did not form the only groups of importance at this time. In addition, there was the most discontented group of all—and the one with the greatest ambitions for grand-scale change—the radicals. The term "radicals" refers to those who favored the total reconfiguration of the old regime's state system: radicalism meant going to the root of the problem, continuing the revolution, not reversing it or stopping with reform. In general, radicals shared a bitter hatred for the status quo and an insistence on popular sovereignty, but beyond this consensus, there was much dissension in their ranks. If some radicals demanded the equalization, or even abolition, of private property, others, like Serbian, Greek, Polish, and Italian nationalists, were primarily interested in throwing off the oppressive overlordship of the Ottoman and Austrian empires and creating their own "nation-states." It was the radicals' threat of reopening the age of revolution that ultimately reconciled both liberals and reactionaries to preserving the status quo.

NATIONALISTS The least terrifying of the radicals, in the long run, proved to be the nationalists, though for those in power, nationalist uprisings like those of the Poles, Serbs, Greeks, and Italians, were unsettling enough (see Map 7-3). The Poles rose twice, once in 1830 and again in 1846; both times, Prussian, Austrian, and Russian oppressors bloodily put down their nationalist revolts. By contrast, the Greeks, inspired by religious revivalism as well as by enlightened ideas, managed to wrest independence from the Ottoman Turks after a long series of skirmishes (1821–1829). Invoking both the classical tradition and their membership in the community of Christians, Greek patriots won support among Europeans in their fight against the Muslim Ottoman empire. Interestingly, however, most of this support had to come in the form of private donations or volunteer soldiers. European rulers feared that sympathy for the oppressed Greeks would fan the flames of revolution at home. Still to counter the power of the Ottomans the Europeans sent their ships to the Mediterranean and defeated the Ottomans at Navarino in 1827. The Ottomans finally recognized Greek independence in 1829. In the new state, the Greeks could not resolve differences between those who wanted a small, essentially secular republic and those who wanted to reclaim Istanbul for Greek Orthodoxy, and they ended up inviting Otto, a Bavarian prince, to be the new king of Greece in 1832. The new Greek state had won its independence from the Ottomans, but it was neither the resurrected Athens nor the revivified Byzantium that the revolutionaries had envisioned.

Other nationalist movements were suppressed or at least slowed down with little bloodshed, and they gradually developed a more conservative character. In places like the German

MAP 7-3   CIVIL UNREST AND REVOLUTIONS IN EUROPE, 1819–1848
Civil unrest and revolution were endemic to Europe after the Congress of Vienna, with conservative governments fighting off liberal rebellions and demands for change. On the basis of this map, what parts of Europe would appear to have been politically stable and conservative and what parts rebellious? Can you explain the reasons for the stability of some parts of Europe and the instability of others? What countries were most heavily involved in suppressing civil unrest and revolutionary activity, and why did they do so? Can you explain why countries sent their troops to suppress revolutions where they did?

principalities, the Italian states, and the Hungarian parts of the Habsburg empire, secret societies comprised of young men—students and intellectuals—gathered to plan bright, republican futures. Regrettably for these patriots, however, organizations like "Young Italy," founded in 1832 by Giuseppe Mazzini (1805–1872) to bring about national unification and renewal, had little popular or foreign support. Censorship and a few strategic executions suppressed them. In this way, German, Hungarian, and Italian campaigns for national recognition were prevented from reaching the revolutionary stage. Nonetheless, all of these movements would ultimately succeed in the century's second

half, when conservatives and liberals in Western Europe recognized the advantages of permitting a tamer sort of nationalist fervor. Nationalism remained, however, a perilous force in central Europe, where minority groups like the Czechs, Serbs, and Poles ceaselessly campaigned for states of their own.

SOCIALISTS AND COMMUNISTS   Much more threatening to the ruling elite, however, were the radicals who believed that the French Revolution had not gone far enough. They longed for a new, grander revolution that would sweep away the Restoration's political *and* economic order. Early socialists and

The Peterloo Massacre. On August 16, 1819, local guardsmen fired on a crowd of peaceful protesters who had gathered on St. Peter's Field outside Manchester to advocate political and economic reforms. Eleven were killed, and hundreds injured, and the radical propagandists dubbed the event "the Peterloo Massacre," to suggest a parallel with the recent slaughter at Waterloo.

communists (the terms were more or less interchangeable) insisted that political reforms offered no effective answer to the more pressing "social question": what was to be done about the inequalities being introduced by industrial capitalism? The socialists worried in particular about the deleterious effects of the division of labor on the human personality and the growing gap between impoverished workers and newly wealthy employers. Thus, the targets of their criticisms were not only the political power brokers but also their own employers. They believed that the whole free market economy, not just the state, had to be transformed to save the human race from self-destruction. Liberty and equality, they insisted, could not be separated; aristocratic privilege along with capitalism ought both to be thrown on history's ash heap.

No more than a handful of radical prophets hatched revolutionary plans in the years after 1815. Yet, by no means were they the only participants in the many strikes, riots, peasant uprisings, and protest meetings of the era. Ordinary workers, artisans, women employed in textile manufacturing, and domestic servants all participated in attempts to answer "the social question" to their satisfaction. A few socialists and feminists campaigned for the social and political equality of the sexes. In Britain in 1819, Manchester workers at St. Peter's Field demonstrated peacefully for political reform—specifically increased representation in Parliament—but they were fired on by panicking guardsmen, who left 11 dead and 460 injured in an incident later dubbed the Peterloo Massacre. In 1839 and 1842, more than 3 million people, or nearly half the adult population of Britain, signed the People's Charter, which called for universal suffrage for all adult males, the secret ballot, equal electoral districts, and annual parliamentary elections. This mass movement, known as Chartism, like most such endeavors, ended in defeat. Parliament rejected the Charter each time.

Utopian socialism was the most visionary of all Restoration-era alternative movements, though not the most radical.

FOURIER AND UTOPIAN SOCIALISM Despite their many defeats, the radicals kept trying. Some sense of this age of revolutionary aspirations reveals itself in one European visionary with big grievances and even bigger plans, the "utopian socialist" Charles Fourier (1772–1837). "Utopian socialism" was the most visionary of all Restoration-era alternative movements, though not the most radical in either political or social terms. Utopians introduced planning, where the revolutionaries invoked violence, and they generally rejected the equalizing of conditions, fearing the suppression of diversity. Still, they dreamed of transforming states, workplaces, and human relations in a much more thorough way than their religious or political predecessors. Fourier, in particular, deserves to be classed among the most influential of Europe's prophet-visionaries.

Fired both by the egalitarian hopes and the cataclysmic failings of the French Revolution, Charles Fourier believed himself to be the scientific prophet of the new world to come. He was a highly imaginative, self-taught man who earned his keep in the cloth trade, an occupation that gave him an intense hatred for merchants and middlemen. Convinced that both the division of labor and repressive moral conventions destroyed mankind's natural talents and passions, Fourier concluded that a revolution grander than that of 1789 was needed. But this utopian transformation of economic, social, and political conditions, he thought, could be accomplished by organization, not by bloodshed. Indeed, Fourier, by 1808, believed that the thoroughly corrupt world was already on the brink of giving way to a new and harmonious age, of which he was, of course, the oracle.

First formulated in 1808, his "system" envisioned the reorganization of human communities into what he called phalanxes: in these harmonious collectives of about 1,500 to 1,600 people and 810 personality types, diversity would be preserved, but efficiency maintained; best of all, work would become enjoyable. All members of the phalanx, rich and poor, would work, if not necessarily at the same tasks. All, however, would work only in short spurts of no more than two hours, so as to make work more interesting and sleep, idleness, and profligacy less attractive. A typical rich man's day would begin at 3:30 A.M.; the first two hours would be spent eating breakfast, reviewing the previous day, and participating in an industrial parade. At 5:30, he would hunt; at 7:00 he would turn to fishing. At 8:00, he would have lunch and read the newspapers (though what news there might be in this world is hard to fathom). At 9:00, he would meet with horticulturists, and at 10:00 he would go to mass. At 10:30, he would meet with a pheasant breeder; later he would tend exotic plants, herd sheep, and attend a concert. Each man would cultivate what he wanted to eat and learn about what he wanted to know—as long, that is, as he could find fellows who shared this particular passion. As for unpleasant tasks, they would become less so because they would now be done in more comfortable settings, in warmed barns and spotless factories. Truly undesirable jobs, like sweeping out the stables or cleaning the latrines, would be done by hordes of young adolescents, who, Fourier argued, actually liked muck-

ing about in filth. This was by no means an Eden in which man lived without knowing what it was like to sweat; rather it was a workers' paradise in which comforts and rewards made working enjoyable.

Importantly, however, this would be a system of production and distribution run without merchants. Fourier intentionally excluded middlemen like himself from his plan for paradise. He believed that they corrupted civilization and introduced unnaturalness into the division of labor. Eliminate the middlemen, Fourier wrote, and corruption would disappear. This, like his critique of Adam Smith's invisible hand, would show up prominently in the work of Karl Marx and Friedrich Engels.

Fourier's writings finally gained popularity in the 1830s,

> *Fourier thought that a utopian transformation of economic, social, and political conditions would be accomplished by organization, not by bloodshed.*

though it was not his plans for the phalanx, but his critiques of the corruptions of commercial civilization that appealed to a generation of radicals across Europe. In Russia, his ideas attracted a liberal westernizer, Alexander Herzen (1812–1870), and they fired the imaginations of the Petrashevsky circle in St. Petersburg, to which the young writer Fyodor Dostoevsky (1821–1881) belonged; Dostoevsky and fourteen others were sentenced to death for their radical views, though their executions were called off at the last minute. In 1835–1836, both the young Italian nationalist Giuseppe Mazzini and the Spanish republican Joaquin Abreu published important articles on Fourier's thought. Karl Marx (1818–1883) read Fourier with great care; there are many remnants of utopian thought in Marx's work, including the passage in *The German Ideology*, in which he describes life in a communist society, "where nobody has one exclusive sphere of activity but each can become accomplished in any branch he wishes, society regulates the general production and thus makes it possible for me to do one thing today and another tomorrow, to hunt in the morning, fish in the afternoon, rear cattle in the evening, [and] criticize after dinner."

MARXISM Marx, indeed, proved to be the most consequential of Restoration-era radicals. University educated and philosophically radical, Marx took up a career in journalism. Required to cover legislative debates over property rights and taxation, he was induced to dabble in economics. His understanding of "capitalism," a term he was instrumental in popularizing, was greatly enhanced by his collaboration after 1845 with Friedrich Engels (1820–1895). Like Marx, Engels was a German-born radical, who in 1844, after spending two years observing conditions in the factories owned by his wealthy father in Manchester, England, published a hair-raising indictment of industrial wage-labor entitled *The Condition of the Working Class in England*.

THE COMMUNIST MANIFESTO

In January 1848, Karl Marx and Friedrich Engels prepared a party program for the Communist League, a German workingman's association. Published in French as The Communist Manifesto *on the eve of the June 1848 uprisings, the document foretold the inevitable overthrow of bourgeois-dominated capitalism by the working classes and the transition to socialism and ultimately to communism. The following excerpt gives the reader a sense of their certainty that history, driven by economic factors and class conflict, was moving inexorably toward the revolution of the proletariat. Marx and Engels defined the bourgeoisie as capitalists, owners of the means of production and employers of wage laborers, and they defined proletariats as wage laborers who had to sell their labor to live.*

A spectre is haunting Europe—the spectre of Communism. . . .

The history of all hitherto existing society is the history of class struggles. . . .

The modern bourgeois society that has sprouted from the ruins of feudal society has not done away with class antagonisms. It has but established new classes, new conditions of oppression, new forms of struggle in place of the old ones.

Our epoch, the epoch of the bourgeoisie, possesses, however, this distinctive feature: it has simplified the class antagonisms: Society as a whole is more and more splitting up into two great hostile camps, into two great classes directly facing each other: Bourgeoisie and Proletariat. . . .

The bourgeoisie . . . has put an end to all feudal, patriarchal, idyllic relations. It has pitilessly torn asunder the motley feudal ties that bound man to his "natural superiors," and has left remaining no other nexus between man and man than naked self-interest, than callous "cash payment.". . .

The need of a constantly expanding market for its products chases the bourgeoisie over the whole surface of the globe. It must nestle everywhere, settle everywhere, establish connexions everywhere. . . .

The bourgeoisie, by the rapid improvement of all instruments of production, by the immensely facilitated means of communication, draws all, even the most barbarian, nations into civilisation. The cheap prices of its commodities are the heavy artillery with which it batters down all Chinese walls, with which it forces the barbarians' intensely obstinate hatred of foreigners to capitulate. . . .

The weapons with which the bourgeoisie felled feudalism to the ground are now turned against the bourgeoisie itself.

But not only has the bourgeoisie forged the weapons that bring death to itself; it has also called into existence the men who are to wield those weapons—the modern working class—the proletarians. . . . These labourers, who must sell themselves piece-meal, are a commodity, like every other article of commerce, and are consequently exposed to all the vicissitudes of competition, to all the fluctuations of the market. . . .

But with the development of industry the proletariat not only increases in number; it becomes concentrated in greater masses, its strength grows, and it feels that strength more. . . . Thereupon the workers begin to form combinations (Trades Unions) against the bourgeois; they club together in order to keep up the rate of wages; they found permanent associations in order to make provision beforehand for these occasional revolts. Here and there the contest breaks out into riots.

Now and then the workers are victorious, but only for a time. The real fruit of their battles lies, not in the immediate result, but in the ever-expanding union of the workers. . . .

. . . What the bourgeoisie, therefore, produces, above all, is its own grave-diggers. Its fall and the victory of the proletariat are equally inevitable.

. . . The first step in the revolution by the working class is to raise the proletariat to the position of ruling class, to win the battle of democracy.

These measures . . . will be pretty generally applicable.

1. Abolition of property in land. . . .
2. A heavy progressive or graduated income tax.
3. Abolition of all right of inheritance. . . .
6. Centralisation of the means of communication and transport in the hands of the State. . . .

If the proletariat during its contest with the bourgeoisie is compelled, by the force of circumstances, to organise itself as a class, if, by means of a revolution, it makes itself the ruling class, and, as such, sweeps away by force the old conditions of production, then it will, along with these conditions, have swept away the conditions for the existence of class antagonisms and of classes generally . . .

Let the ruling classes tremble at a Communistic revolution. The proletarians have nothing to lose but their chains. They have a world to win.

Source: Karl Marx and Friedrich Engels, *The Communist Manifesto*, in *The Marx-Engels Reader*, 2nd ed., edited by Robert C. Tucker (New York: W. W. Norton & Co., 1978), pp. 473–83, 490–91, 500.

Together, Marx and Engels developed a materialist theory of history. What mattered in history, they argued, was the production of goods, and the ways in which society was organized into classes of producers and exploiters. History consisted of successive forms of exploitative production and rebellions against it. Capitalist exploitation of the wage worker was only the latest, and worst, version of endemic class conflict. In industrialized societies, capitalists owned the means of production (the factories and machinery) and exploited the wage workers, whose dignity was destroyed in producing the goods that the capitalists distributed and sold. Marx and Engels were confident, however, that the clashes between industrial wage workers—or proletarians—and capitalists would end in a colossal transformation of human society, and would usher in a brave new world of true liberty, equality, and fraternity.

It is essential to emphasize the comprehensive nature of Marx and Engels's critique of post-1815 Europe. They identified a whole class of the exploited—the working class. They believed that more and more people would fall into this class as industrialization proceeded and that the masses would not share in the rising prosperity that capitalists enjoyed, since wealth would be concentrated in the owners' hands. They predicted that there would be overproduction and underconsumption, which would lead to lower profits for capitalists and consequently to lower wages or unemployment for workers, and that this would ultimately lead to a proletarian revolution. This revolution would result in a "dictatorship of the proletariat" and the end of private property. With the destruction of capitalism, exploitation would cease, and the state, as an instrument of proletarian rule, would wither away.

In February 1848, hearing that revolution had broken out in France, Marx and Engels published *The Communist Manifesto*, calling on the workers of all nations to unite in overthrowing capitalism. They would be sorely disappointed, not to mention exiled, by the course of events. After 1850, Marx and Engels took up permanent residence in England, where they tried to perfect a "scientific" socialism and organize an international workers' movement. In the doldrums of mid-century, they turned to science and organization, but they never abandoned the romantic dream of total social reconfiguration. Nor would their many admirers and heirs forsake this alternative vision.

The revolutionary fervor of 1848 resulted in uprisings in France, Austria, Russia, Italy, Hungary, and Czechoslovakia, but the reactionary crackdowns that followed defied Marx's expectations. Still, the failure of the 1848 revolutions did not doom prophecy itself, nor diminish commitment to alternative social landscapes.

> *The revolutionary fervor of 1848 resulted in uprisings throughout Europe, but the reactionary crackdowns that followed defied Marx's expectations.*

INSURGENCIES AGAINST COLONIZING AND CENTRALIZING STATES

→ *How were the alternative movements in America and India similar and different?*

Outside Europe, in the Americas and in British India, the colonizing process mediated the power of industrial capitalism and centralizing states. Here, the Native Americans and Britain's colonial subjects experienced the challenge to their traditional worlds as alien encroachments. They responded by rising up in revolts and by offering alternative visions of political and social authority. But, while European radicals looked back to revolutionary legacies in imagining a transformed society, Native American insurgents and rebels in British India drew upon their traditional cultural and political resources to imagine new, local alternatives to alien impositions. Like the peoples of China, Africa, and the Middle East, the indigenous groups in the Americas and India met challenges to their political and cultural worlds with rebellion, prophecy, and charismatic leadership. Just as a dream in southern China and a prophetic vision in northern Nigeria brought displaced groups to the center stage of politics, so too were Native Americans and colonial Indian subjects emboldened by prophecies to defend local autonomy against challenges to the expanding Euro-American world. Mobilizing the common people as political actors, these struggles attempted to forge politically and culturally autonomous worlds in a time of historical change. Everywhere the insurgents spoke in the languages of the past, but the new worlds they envisioned nonetheless bore unmistakable marks of the present as well.

ALTERNATIVE TO THE EXPANDING UNITED STATES: THE SHAWNEE PROPHET

Like other native peoples threatened by an expansionist imperial power, the Indians of North America's Ohio Valley dreamed of a world in which intrusive colonizers disappeared. Taking such dreams as prophecies, many Indians flocked in the spring of 1805 to hear the revelations of a Shawnee Indian named

Tenskwatawa. A portrait of Tenskwatawa, the "Shawnee Prophet," whose visions stirred thousands of Indians in the Ohio Valley and Great Lakes to renounce dependence on colonial imports and resist the expansion of the United States. Like several other Indian prophets, Tenskwatawa's message raised hopes for a restoration of an older, better world. But Tenskwatawa's ability to rally Indians behind his vision faded after an American army destroyed his village.

Tenskwatawa (1768–1834). Facing a dark present and a darker future, they enthusiastically embraced the Shawnee Prophet's visions, which foretold how invaders would vanish if Indians returned to their customary ways and traditional rites. Thanks to the efforts of Tenskwatawa's brother, Tecumseh (1768–1813), the message of Indian renaissance soon circulated among Indian villages from the Great Lakes to the Gulf Coast. Thousands of followers renounced their ties to colonial ways and prepared to combat the expansion of the United States.

Tenskwatawa's visions—and the anti-colonial uprising they inspired—drew on a long tradition of such visions. From the first encounters with Europeans, Indian seers had periodically emerged to encourage native peoples to purge their worlds of colonial influences and to revitalize indigenous traditions. Often these prophets had aroused their adherents not only to engage in cleansing ceremonies but also to cooperate in violent, anti-colonial uprisings. In 1680, for example, previously divided Pueblo villagers in New Mexico had united behind the prophet Popé to chase Spanish missionaries, soldiers, and settlers out of that colony. In the wake of their military victory, Popé's followers destroyed all things European: wheat fields and fruit orchards were torched, livestock was slaughtered, and Catholic churches were ransacked. For a dozen years, the Indians of New Mexico reclaimed control over their lands, but divisions within native ranks soon returned and prepared the way for Spanish reconquest in 1692.

Seventy years later and half a continent away, the preachings of the Delaware shaman Neolin encouraged Indians of the Ohio Valley and Great Lakes to take up arms against the British, who, in the aftermath of the Seven Years' War, had assumed that their victory over the French amounted to a victory over all Indians as well. Taking exception to being treated as conquered peoples, Indians from various tribes rallied behind Neolin's vision of a world restored to pre-colonial conditions. In the months that followed, insurgents captured several British military posts and terrorized frontier settlers in western Pennsylvania and Virginia. Although the British were able to put down the uprising, imperial officials learned a lesson from this expensive conflict. They assumed a less arrogant posture toward Ohio Valley and Great Lakes Indians, and to preserve peace, they issued a proclamation that forbade colonists from trespassing on lands west of the Appalachian Mountains.

The British, however, proved incapable of restraining the flow of settlers across the mountains, and the problem became much worse for the Indians once the American Revolution ended. With the Ohio Valley transferred to the new United States, American settlers crossed the Appalachians and flooded into Kentucky and Tennessee. Still, despite this considerable migration, much of the territory between the Appalachians and the Mississippi, which Americans referred to as the "western country," remained an Indian country. North and south of Kentucky and Tennessee, Indian warriors more than held their own against American forces. As in previous anti-colonial campaigns, the visions of various prophets bolstered the confidence and unity of Indian warriors, who in 1790 and again in 1791 joined together to rout invading American armies. But the confederation of Indian warriors was defeated in a third encounter, in 1794, and their leaders were forced to surrender lands in what is now the state of Ohio to the United States.

> *From their first encounters with Europeans, Indian seers had periodically emerged to encourage their peoples to purge their worlds of colonial influences and to revitalize indigenous traditions.*

TENSKWATAWA'S VISION

In the first decade of the nineteenth century, the Shawnee Indian leader Tenskwatawa recalled an earlier, happier time for the Indian peoples of the Great Lakes and Ohio Valley before the coming of the Europeans. In this oration, Tenskwatawa recounts how Indians were contaminated and corrupted by contact with the "white men's goods" and urges them to spurn the ways of white Americans and return to the pure ways of a pre-colonial past. Nonetheless, Tenskwatawa's message itself reflects certain colonial influences.

Our Creator put us on this wide, rich land, and told us we were free to go where the game was, where the soil was good for planting. That was our state of true happiness. We did not have to beg for anything. Our Creator had taught us how to find and make everything we needed, from trees and plants and animals and stone. We lived in bark, and we wore only the skins of animals. . . .

Thus were we created. Thus we lived for a long time, proud and happy. We had never eaten pig meat, nor tasted the poison called whiskey, nor worn wool from sheep, nor struck fire or dug earth with steel, nor cooked in iron, nor hunted and fought with loud guns, nor ever had diseases which soured our blood or rotted our organs. We were pure, so we were strong and happy. . . .

For many years we traded furs to the English or the French, for wool blankets and guns and iron things, for steel awls and needles and axes, for mirrors, for pretty things made of beads and silver. And for liquor. This was foolish, but we did not know it. We shut our ears to the Great Good Spirit. We did not want to hear that we were being foolish.

But now those things of the white men have corrupted us, and made us weak and needful. Our men forgot how to hunt without noisy guns. Our women don't want to make fire without steel, or cook without iron, or sew without metal awls and needles, or fish without steel hooks. Some look in those mirrors all the time, and no longer teach their daughters to make leather or render bear oil. We learned to need the white men's goods, and so now a People who never had to beg for anything must beg for everything! . . .

And that is why Our Creator purified me and sent me down to you, to make you what you were before! As you sit before me I will tell you the many rules Our Creator gave me for you.

No red man must ever drink liquor, or he will go and have the hot lead poured in his mouth! . . .

Do not eat any food that is raised or cooked by a white person. It is not good for us. Eat not their bread made of wheat, for Our Creator gave us corn for our bread. . . .

The Great Good Spirit wants our men to hunt and kill game as in the ancient days, with the silent arrow and the lance and the snare, and no longer with guns.

If we hunt in the old ways, we will not have to depend upon white men, for new guns and powder and lead, or go to them to have broken guns repaired. Remember it is the wish of the Great Good Spirit that we have no more commerce with white men! . . .

Our Creator told me that all red men who refuse to obey these laws are bad people, or witches, and must be put to death. . . .

The Great Good Spirit will appoint a place to be our holy town, and at that place I will call all red men to come and share this shining power. For the People in all tribes are corrupt and miserable! In that holy town we will pray every morning and every night for the earth to be fruitful, and the game and fish to be plentiful again. . . .

Source: http:courses.smsu.edu/ftm922f/Documents/Prophet&Tecumseh. htm. Words of Tenskwatawa, in *Messages and Letters of William Henry Harrison*, edited by Logan Esarey (Indianapolis: Indiana Historical Commission, 1922).

The Shawnees, who had lost most of their holdings, were among the most bitter—and bitterly divided—of the Indian peoples living in the Ohio Valley. Some Shawnee headmen concluded that their people's survival now required that they cooperate with American officials and Christian missionaries. This strategy, they realized, entailed wrenching changes in Shawnee culture. Reformers, after all, insisted that Indian men give up hunting and take up farming, an occupation that the Shawnees and their neighbors had always considered "women's work."

What is more, the Shawnees were pushed to abandon communal traditions in favor of private property rights. And, of course, missionaries prodded Indians to quit their "heathen" beliefs and practices and become faithful, "civilized" Christians. For many Shawnees, these demands went too far, and worse, they promised no immediate relief from the dispossession and impoverishment that now marked their daily lives. Young men especially grew angry and frustrated.

Among the demoralized was a Shawnee Indian named

Tenskwatawa, whose story of overcoming personal failures through religious visions and embracing a strict moral code has uncanny parallels with that of Hong Xiuquan, the Taiping leader. In his first thirty years, Tenskwatawa could claim few accomplishments. He had failed as a hunter and as a medicine man, had blinded himself in one eye, and had earned a reputation as an obnoxious braggart. All this changed in the spring of 1805, however, after he fell into a trance and experienced a vision, which he vividly recounted to one and all. In this dream, Tenskwatawa encountered a heaven where the virtuous enjoyed the traditional Shawnee way of life and a hell where evildoers were punished and those who had consumed alcohol were forced to swallow molten metal. Additional revelations followed, and Tenskwatawa soon stitched these together into a new social gospel that urged disciples to abstain from alcohol and to return to traditional customs.

> *Like other prophets, Tenskwatawa exhorted Indians to reduce their dependence on European trade goods and to sever their connections to Christian missionaries.*

Like other prophets, Tenskwatawa exhorted Indians to reduce their dependence on European trade goods and to sever their connections to Christian missionaries. To these ends, Tenskwatawa urged his audiences to replace imported cloth and metal tools with animal skins and implements fashioned from wood, stone, and bone. So, too, livestock was to be banished, as Indian men again gathered meat by hunting wild animals, with bows and arrows instead of guns and powder. If Indians obeyed these dictates, Tenskwatawa promised, the deer, which "were half a tree's length under the ground," would come back in abundant numbers to the earth's surface. Likewise, Indians killed in conflict with colonial intruders would be resurrected, while evil Americans would depart from the country west of the Appalachians.

Like the Qing in responding to Hong's visions, American officials initially regarded Tenskwatawa as deluded, but harmless; their concerns grew, however, as the Shawnee Prophet gathered more and more adherents during the summer and fall of 1805. These converts came not only from among the Shawnees, but also from Delaware, Ottawa, Wyandot, Kickapoo, and Seneca villages. The spread of Tenskwatawa's message raised anew the specter of a pan-Indian confederacy. Hoping to undermine the Shawnee Prophet's claims to supernatural power, territorial governor William Henry Harrison (1773–1841) challenged Tenskwatawa to make the sun stand still. But Tenskwatawa one-upped Harrison. Having learned of an impending eclipse from white astronomers, Tenskwatawa assembled his followers on June 16, 1806. On schedule, and as if on command, the sky darkened. Claiming credit for the eclipse, Tenskwatawa's standing soared, as did the ranks of his disciples. Now aware of the growing threat, American officials tried to bribe Tenskwatawa, hoping that cash payments might dim

his vision and quiet his voice. Failing that, they wondered if one of the prophet's Indian adversaries might be encouraged to assassinate him.

In fact, Tenskwatawa had made plenty of enemies among his fellow Indians. His visions, after all, consigned drinkers to hell and singled out those who cooperated with colonial authorities for punishment in this world and the next. Indeed, Tenskwatawa condemned as witches those Indians who rejected his preaching and stuck instead to the teachings of Christian missionaries and American authorities. To be sure, Tenskwatawa's damnation of missionized Indians was somewhat ironic, for Christian doctrines certainly influenced his visions (as they had other native prophets). This was perhaps most apparent in Tenskwatawa's conception of a burning hell for sinners and in his crusade against alcoholic beverages.

Although Tenskwatawa's accusations alienated some Indians, his prophecies gave heart to many more, particularly once his brother, Tecumseh, began traveling to recruit others to their cause. Tecumseh had earned distinction as a warrior in the Indian confederacy's battles against American invaders in the 1780s and 1790s. On his journeys after 1805, Tecumseh did more than spread his brother's visions, he also wed them to the idea of a resurgent and enlarged Indian confederation. Moving around the Great Lakes and traveling across the southern half of the western country as well, Tecumseh preached the need for Indian unity. Always, he insisted that Indians resist any American attempts to get them to sell more land.

By 1810, Tecumseh had emerged, at least in the eyes of American officials, as even more dangerous than his brother. Impressed by Tecumseh's charismatic organizational talents, William Harrison warned that this new "Indian menace" was forming "an Empire that would rival in glory" that of the Aztecs and the Incas. Evidence that Tecumseh was receiving supplies from British posts north of the Great Lakes added to Harrison's sense of alarm.

In 1811, while Tecumseh was traveling among southern tribes, Harrison attacked Tenskwatawa's village, Prophet's Town, on the Tippecanoe River in what is now the state of Indiana. The resulting battle was evenly fought, but the Indians eventually gave ground and American forces burned Prophet's Town. That defeat discredited Tenskwatawa, who had promised that his followers would be protected from destruction at American hands. Spurned by his former disciples, including even his brother, Tenskwatawa fled to Canada.

Tecumseh soldiered on. Although he mistrusted the British, Tecumseh recognized that only a British victory over the Americans in the War of 1812 could check further American expansion. Commissioned as a brigadier general in the British army, Tecumseh recruited many Indians to the British cause, though his real aim remained the building of a pan-Indian union. But, on October 5, 1813, with the war's outcome in doubt and the pan-Indian confederacy still fragile, Tecumseh was killed at the Battle of the Thames.

The discrediting of Tenskwatawa and the death of Tecumseh damaged the cause of Indian unity; but a British betrayal dealt it a fatal blow. Following the end of the war in 1814, the British withdrew their support and left the Indians south of the Great Lakes to fend for themselves against land-hungry American settlers and the armies of the United States. By 1815, American citizens outnumbered Indians in the western country by a seven to one margin, and this gap dramatically widened in the next few years. Recognizing the hopelessness of military resistance, Indians south of the Great Lakes resigned themselves to relocation. During the 1820s, most of the peoples north of the Ohio River were removed to lands west of the Mississippi River. During the 1830s, the southern tribes were cleared out, completing what amounted to an ethnic cleansing of Indian peoples from the region between the Appalachians and the Mississippi. In the midst of these final removals, Tenskwatawa died, though his dream of an alternative to American expansion had faded for his people years earlier. Through the rest of the nineteenth century, however, other Indian prophets emerged, and their visions continued to inspire their followers with the hope of an alternative to life under the rule of the U. S. government. But like Wovoka and the Ghost Dancers in 1890, these dreams failed to halt the expansion of the United States and the contraction of Indian lands.

ALTERNATIVE TO THE CENTRAL STATE: THE CASTE WAR OF THE YUCATAN

As in North America, the establishment of an expansionist nation-state in Mexico sparked widespread revolts by indigenous peoples. The most protracted—and militarily the most successful of all rebellions in the modern history of the New World—was the Mayan revolt in the Yucatan. The revolt started in 1847, and its flames were not finally doused until the full occupation of the Yucatan by Mexican national troops in 1901.

The strength and endurance of the Mayan revolt stemmed in large measure from the unusual

The strength and endurance of the Mayan revolt stemmed in large measure from the unusual features of the Spanish conquest in southern Mesoamerica.

features of the Spanish conquest in southern Mesoamerica. Because this area was not a repository of precious metals or fertile lands, Spain and its rivals focused on central and northern Mexico and the Caribbean islands. As a result, the Mayan Indians escaped forced recruitment for silver mines or sugar plantations. This does not mean that global processes sidestepped the Indians, however. Production of dyes and foodstuffs for shipment to other regions drew the Yucatan into long-distance trading networks. Nonetheless, cultivation and commerce were much less disruptive to indigenous lives in the Yucatan than elsewhere in the New World. Indians there could enter exchange relations without losing their sovereign ways of life, which they fought to preserve.

The dismantling of the Spanish empire gave way to almost a century of political turmoil in Latin America. In-fighting among state leaders gave Indians an opportunity to advance their own political projects. They wanted guarantees of local autonomy for their villages, legal respect for their ways of holding property, and cultural sovereignty. In the Yucatan, civil strife gave the region autonomy by default, allowing Mayan ways to survive without much upheaval. Their villages remained the chief political domain, ruled by elders; their land was held collectively, the property of families and not individuals. Corn, a mere staple to white consumers, continued to enjoy sacred status in Mayan culture.

Local developments, however, encroached on the Mayan world. First, regional elites—mainly white, but often with the support of *mestizo* populations—bickered for supremacy so long as the central authority of Mexico City remained weak. Weaponry flowed freely through the peninsula, and some belligerents even appealed for Mayan support. At the same time, regional and international trade spurred the spread of sugar estates. This threatened traditional corn cultivation. Over the decades, plantations encroached on Mayan properties. Planters used several devices to lure independent Mayans to work, especially in the harvest. The most important, debt peonage, gave small cash advances to Indian families, which obligated fathers and sons to work for meager wages to pay off these debts. To boot, Mexico's costly wars, culminating in the showdown with the United States in 1846, drove tax collectors out to villages in search of revenues while army recruiters sought soldiers.

The combination of spiritual, material, and physical threats was explosive. When a small band of Mayans, fed up with rising taxes and ebbing autonomy, used firearms to drive back white interlopers in 1847, they sparked a war that took a half-century to complete. The rebels were primarily free Mayans who had not yet been absorbed into the sugar economy. They wanted to dismantle old definitions of Indians as a "caste"—a status that deprived Indians of rights to defend their sovereignty on equal legal footing with whites and that also subjected the Indians to special taxes. Thus, local Mayan leaders, like Jacinto Pat and Cecilio Chi, upheld a republican model in the name of formal equality of all political subjects and devotion to a spiritual order that did not distinguish between Christians and non-Christians. One Mayan explained the revolt thus: "If the Indians revolt, it is because the whites gave them reason; because the whites say they do not believe in Jesus Christ, because they have burned the cornfield."

Horrified, the local white elites reacted to the uprising with vicious repression. If they could not agree on who would rule locally, white potentates did agree on who should be excluded from the political arena: Indians. In fact, it was the whites who dubbed the ensuing conflict a "Caste War," seeking to present their cause as a struggle between forward-looking liberals and backward-looking Indians.

At first, whites and *mestizos* were no match for determined Mayans. Mayan forces took town after town. They especially targeted the emblems of their subservience. With relish they demolished the whipping posts that had previously been used for public humiliation and punishment of Indians. By July 1848, Indian armies controlled three-quarters of the peninsula and were poised to take the Yucatan's largest city, Mérida. Fear seized the embattled whites, who appealed for U.S. and British help, offering the peninsula for foreign annexation in return for military rescue from the Mayans.

In the end, good fortune, not political savvy, saved the Yucatan's whites. The farmers, who had picked up arms to defend their world, went back to being farmers. The planting season called. When rain clouds appeared, related the son of the Mayan leader Crecencio Poot, the Indians saw "that the time has come for us to make our planting, for if we do not we shall have no Grace of God to fill the bellies of our children." But by putting down their weapons and returning to their fields, Mayan farmers became vulnerable to military reconquest by Mexican armies. Furthermore, they were unaware of international changes: settlement of the war with the United States in 1848 enabled Mexico City to rescue local elites. With the help of a $15 million payment from Washington for giving up its northern provinces, Mexico could spend freely to build up its southern armies. The U.S. armies in Mexico offered to sell their stockpiles before demobilizing (thereby ensuring that much of the compensation wound up back in American hands). Within weeks, ships began arriving off the Yucatan coast bristling with arms and troops. The Mexican government soon fielded an army of 17,000 reinforced soldiers, and waged a scorched earth campaign to drive back the depleted Mayan forces. Jacinto Pat, when he heard that the white army's soldiers had boots, exclaimed, "Let's get out of here; the great rich of Mérida have come out to make war."

By 1849, the confrontation had entered a new phase in which Mexican troops engaged in mass repression of the Mayans. Mexican armies set Indian fields and villages ablaze. Upon capturing the city of Tekax, Mexican troops dragged prisoners to the main plaza, whipped them furiously, took them to the balcony of municipal buildings, and threw them over the railing to be impaled by soldiers with bayonets waiting below. Slaughtering Indians became a blood sport of barbaric proportion. Between 30 and 40 percent of the Mayan population perished in the war and its repressive aftermath. The white governor even sold captured survivors into slavery to Cuban sugar planters.

The white formulation of the caste nature of the war eventually became a self-fulfilling prophecy. Entire Mayan cities pulled up stakes and withdrew to more isolated districts protected by fortified villages. War between armies degenerated into guerrilla warfare between an occupying Mexican army and mobile bands of Mayan squadrons inflicting a gruesome toll on the invaders. As years passed, the war ground to a stalemate, especially once the U.S. indemnity ran out and Mexican soldiers began deserting in droves.

Warfare prompted a spiritual transformation that reinforced a purely Mayan identity against the invaders' "national" project. Thus, a struggle that began by demanding legal equality and relative cultural autonomy became a crusade for spiritual salvation and the complete cultural separation of the Mayan Indians. A particularly influential group under José María Barrera retreated to a hamlet called "Chan Santa Cruz" (Little Holy Cross). There, at the site where he found a cross carved into a mahogany tree, Barrera had a vision of a divine encounter. A swathe of Yucatan villages refashioned themselves as moral communities orbiting around Chan Santa Cruz. Leaders created a polity, with soldiers, priests, and tax collectors pledging their fealty to the Speaking Cross. At the top ruled a Tatich (Father), with an Interpreter of the Cross, called Tata Polin. As with the followers of Hong in China's Taiping Rebellion, Indian rebels forged a syncretic religion, blending Christian rituals, faiths, and icons with Mayan legends and beliefs. At the center was a stone temple, Balam Na (House of God), 100 feet long and 60 feet wide. Through pious pilgrimages to Balam Na and the secular justice of Indian judges, the Mayans soon governed their autonomous domain in the Yucatan, almost completely cut off from the rest of Mexico.

This alternative to Latin American state formation, however, faced formidable hurdles. Disease ravaged the people of the Speaking Cross. Once counting 40,000 inhabitants, the villages dwindled to 10,000 by 1900. A new crop was beginning to spread across the Yucatan: henequen. Used to bind bales for North

> *A struggle that began by demanding legal equality and relative cultural autonomy became a crusade for spiritual salvation and the complete cultural separation of the Mayan Indians.*

American farms and to stuff the seats of new automobiles, its production spread. And as profits from henequen production rose, white landowners began turning the Yucatan into a giant plantation. But Mayan villagers refused to give up their autonomy and rejected labor recruiters. Finally, the Mexican oligarchy, having resolved its internal disputes, threw its weight behind the strong-arm ruler, General Porfirio Díaz (ruled 1876–1911). The general sent one of his veteran commanders, Ignacio Bravo, to do what no other Mexican could accomplish: vanquish Chan Santa Cruz and drive Mayans into the henequen cash economy. When General Bravo finally entered the town, he found the once-imposing temple Balam Na covered in vegetation. Nature was reclaiming the territories of the Speaking Cross. Hunger and arms finally drove Mayans to work on white Mexican plantations; the alternative vision was now vanquished.

THE REBELLION OF 1857 IN INDIA

Like Native Americans, the peoples of nineteenth-century India could point to a long history of opposition to colonial domination. Armed revolts had been endemic since the onset of rule by the English East India Company. Nonetheless, the uprising of 1857 was unprecedented in its scale, and it posed a greater threat than had any previous rebellion. Marx, with the hope for revolution dashed in Europe, cast his eyes on the revolt in British India, eagerly following the events and commenting on them in daily columns for the New York *Daily Tribune*. Though led primarily by the old nobility and petty landlords, it was a popular insurrection with strong support from the lower orders of Indian society. The rebels appealed to bonds of local and communal solidarity, invoked religious sentiments, and reimagined traditional hierarchies in egalitarian terms. They did this to pose alternatives to British rule and the deepening involvement of India in a network of capitalist relationships.

When the revolt broke out in 1857, the East India Company's rule in India was a century old. During that time, the Company had become an increasingly autocratic power, its reach extending across the whole of the subcontinent. Mughal rule still existed in name, but the emperor lived in Delhi, all but forgotten, and without any effective power. For a while, the existence of several princely states with which the British had entered into alliances prevented the British from exercising complete control over the subcontinent. These princely domains enjoyed a measure of fiscal and judicial authority within the British empire. They also contained landed aristocrats who enjoyed the right to shares in the produce and main-

Though led primarily by the old nobility and petty landlords, the Indian Rebellion was a popular insurrection with strong support from the lower orders of Indian society.

tained their own militias. By the 1840s, however, the Company had come to see the princely powers and landed aristocracies as anachronisms. Lord Dalhousie, upon his appointment as the governor-general in 1848, immediately set about annexing what had been independent princely domains and stripping native aristocrats of their privileges. Swallowing one princely state after another, the British removed their erstwhile allies. The government also decided to collect taxes directly from peasants, displacing the landed nobles as intermediaries. In disarming the landed nobility, the British threw the retainers and militia of the notables into unemployment. Moreover, the Company's new systems of land settlement not only dispossessed the old gentry, they also eroded peasant rights and enhanced the power of moneylenders. Meanwhile the Company transferred judicial authority to an administration insulated from the indigenous social hierarchy.

The most prized object for annexation was the kingdom of Awadh in northern India (see Map 7-4). Founded in 1722 by an Iranian adventurer, it was one of the first successor states to have extracted a measure of independence from the Mughal ruler in Delhi. With access to the fertile resources of the Gangetic plain, its opulent court in Lucknow was known to be one place where Mughal splendor still survived. In 1765, the Company imposed a treaty on Awadh under which the ruler paid an annual tribute for the British troops stationed in his territory to "protect" his kingdom from internal and external enemies. The British constantly ratcheted up their demands for tribute and abused their position to monopolize the lucrative trade in commodities. But the more successful they were in exploiting Awadh, the more they longed to annex it completely. Thus, Dalhousie declared in 1851 that Awadh was "a cherry which will drop into our mouths some day."

In 1856, citing misgovernment and deterioration in law and order, the Company violated its treaty obligations and sent its troops to Lucknow to assume control of the province. Nawab Wajid Ali Shah, the poet-king of Awadh, whom the British saw as effete and debauched, refused to sign the treaty of abdication. Instead, he came dressed in his mourning robes to meet with the British official charged to take over the province. After pleading unsuccessfully for his legal rights under the treaty, he handed over his turban to the official and then left for Calcutta to argue his case before Dalhousie. There was widespread distress at the treatment meted out to the nawab. Dirges were recited, and religious men rushed to Lucknow to denounce the annexation.

The annexation of princely domains and the abolition of feudal privileges formed part of the developing philosophy and practices of European imperialism. To the policy of annexation,

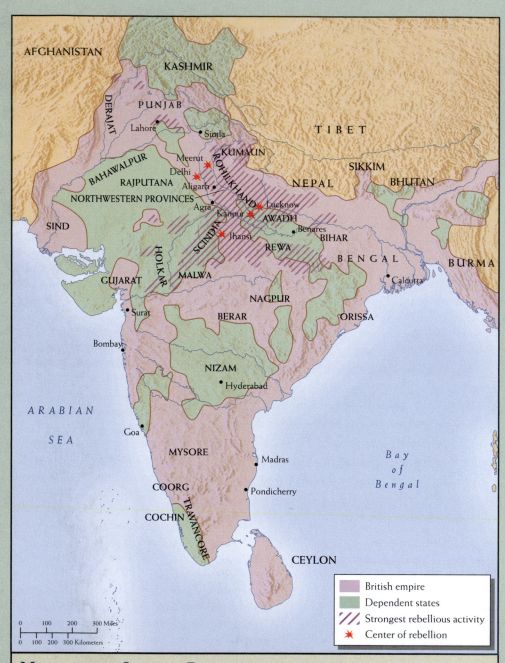

Dalhousie added an ambitious program of building railroads, telegraph lines, and a postal network to unify the disjointed territory into a single "network of iron sinew" controlled by the British. Dalhousie saw these infrastructures as key to developing India into a productive colony, a supplier of raw materials for British industry and a market for its manufactures. Accordingly, the first telegraph line was laid in India in 1851, followed by the opening of the first railway line in 1853. Mining and irrigation works were intended to make India a thriving colonial-capitalist economy under a watchful and strong modern state. Although the realization of this vision demanded the violation of British treaty obligations and the destruction of feudal regimes and privileges, the British considered this a small price to pay. When Dalhousie left India in 1856, he looked upon his tenure as governor-general with satisfaction and pride. He had forged the Company's far-flung territorial possessions into a unitary entity, and he had laid the foundations of a modern state. But he failed to gauge the smoldering disaffection among the dispossessed magnates and the exploited peasantry.

A year after Dalhousie's departure, India went up in flames. The spark that ignited the simmering discontent into a furious rebellion was the famous "greased cartridge" controversy. At the end of 1856, the British army, which consisted of many Hindu and Muslim recruits (sepoys), commanded by British officers, intro-

MAP 7-4   INDIAN REBELLION OF 1857

Why was the center of the Indian rebellion in northern India? The rebellion broke out first among the Indian soldiers of the British army. Can you think of any reasons why the largest concentrations of Indian troops would be in the northern part of the country? Can you speculate on why the rebellion was centered in the interior of the subcontinent rather than along the coasts? Referring to the map on the British in India in Chapter 6 (Map 6-3, p. 228), especially the map that shows the British empire in 1805, locate the primary areas of rebellion in relationship to the heart of the British empire and those territories that enjoyed some degree of autonomy at that time. Is it possible that British expansion into once autonomous princely states was a factor in the rebellion?

The Indian Sepoys. Pictured here are Indian soldiers, or sepoys, who were armed, drilled, and commanded by British officers. The sepoys were drawn from indigenous groups that the British considered to be "martial races." This illustration shows the Sikhs, designated as one such "race."

duced the new Enfield rifle to replace the old-style musket. To load the rifle, the soldiers were required to bite the cartridge open. Though manufacturing instructions stated that linseed oil and beeswax were to be used to grease the cartridge, a rumor circulated that cow and pig fat had been used. To bite into cartridges greased with cow and pig fat meant the violation of the religious taboos of Hindu and Muslim sepoys. They became convinced that there was a plot afoot to defile them and to compel their conversion to Christianity. A wave of rebellion spread among the 270,000 Indian soldiers, who greatly outnumbered the 40,000 British soldiers employed to rule over 200 million Indians.

The mutiny broke out on May 10, 1857, at the military barracks in Meerut. The previous day the native soldiers had witnessed eighty-five of their comrades being manacled and shackled in irons and marched off to the prison for refusing to load their rifles. The next day, all three regiments at Meerut mutinied, killed their British officers, and marched thirty miles south to Delhi, where they were welcomed by their comrades in regiments stationed there. Together, they "restored" the aging Bahadur Shah as the Mughal emperor, which lent legitimacy to the uprising. The revolt then spread rapidly to other garrisons, and soon turned from a limited military mutiny into a widespread civil rebellion. Peasants, artisans, day laborers, religious leaders, and landed gentry joined in open rebellion. While the insurgents did not eliminate the power of the Company, which managed to retain the loyalty of princes and landed aristocrats in some places, they did throw the Company into a crisis. The mutineers in Delhi issued a proclamation in August, declaring that, since the British were bent upon destroying the religion of both Hindus and Muslims, it was the duty of the wealthy and the privileged to support the rebellion.

To promote Hindu-Muslim unity, rebel leaders asked Muslims to refrain from killing cows in deference to Hindu sentiments.

Triumphant in Delhi, the rebellion spread to other parts of the subcontinent. In Awadh, proclamations in Hindi, Urdu, and Persian called on Hindus and Muslims to rise. On May 30, troops at the garrison in Lucknow, Awadh's capital, did just that. Seizing control of the town, rebels crowned a ten-year-old putative son of the deposed king as the new ruler, but his mother, the Begum Hazrat Mahal, emerged as the real force. The queen mother, however, accepted the condition laid down by the rebel army that the king be subordinate to the Mughal emperor in Delhi. The rebels then called upon all classes to unite in expelling the British. Gathering in Lucknow, people from the surrounding countryside and towns laid siege to the fortress in which the British had retreated along with their Indian followers. British troops tried to fight their way to Lucknow to relieve the besieged garrison. But as they tried to send in reinforcements, they had to fight the dispossessed magnates and peasants in the surrounding countryside village by village. Anti-British sentiments ran high as the rebels from everywhere, responding to the queen mother's call for help in the name of God, gathered in Lucknow to press the siege to victory. In November, the British evacuated the garrison, and Lucknow now belonged to the rebels.

Though the dispossessed aristocracy and petty landholders led the rebellion, leaders also appeared from below. Bakht Khan, who had been a junior noncommissioned officer in the Company army, became the commander-in-chief of the rebel forces in Delhi, replacing one of the Mughal emperor's sons who had been discredited in the eyes of the ordinary rebels. Devi Singh, a wealthy peasant, set himself up as a peasant king. Dressed in yellow, the insignia of royalty in the Hindu idiom, he constituted a government of his own, modeling it on the British

The Indian Rebellion of 1857. The 1857 rebellion was sparked by the mutiny of Indian sepoys in the British army. The rebellion left a deep impression on the British. This British engraving depicts a cavalry attack by the rebel soldiers.

administration. While his imitation of Company rule showed his respect for the British bureaucracy, he defied British authority by leading an armed peasantry against the hated local moneylenders. The call to popular forces also marked the rebel career of Maulavi Ahmadullah Shah, a Muslim theologian. He stood at the head of the rebel forces in Lucknow, leading an army composed primarily of ordinary soldiers and people from the lower orders. Claiming to be an "Incarnation of the Deity," and thus inspired by the divine will, he emerged as a prophetic leader of the common people. He voiced his undying enmity to the British in religious terms, calling upon Hindus and Muslims to destroy British rule and warning his followers against betrayal by landed magnates.

The presence of popular leadership points to the role of lower classes as historical actors. Though feudal chieftains often brought them into the rebellion, they made the insurrection their own. The organizing principle of their insurgency was the common experience of oppression. Thus, they destroyed anything that represented the authority of the Company: prisons, factories, police posts, railway stations, European bungalows, and law courts. Equally significant, the peasantry attacked indigenous moneylenders and local magnates who had purchased land at government auctions and were seen as benefiting from Company rule.

Vigorous and militant as the popular rebellion was, it was limited in its territorial and ideological horizons. To begin with, the uprisings were local in scale and vision. Peasant rebels attacked the closest seats of administration and sought to settle scores with their most immediate and visible oppressors. They did not carry their action beyond the village or collection of villages. Their loyalties remained intensely local, based on village attachments and religious, caste, and clan ties. Nor did popular militants seek to undo traditional hierarchies of caste and religion. Instead, peasant rebels sought validation from higher authorities, from the Mughal emperor and the divine will.

To the British, the initial mutinies and the wider revolts that followed smelled of a grand conspiracy. Unwilling to acknowledge their oppressive presence as the cause of the rebellion, British authorities attributed it to a plot. In 1856–1857, many officials reported that *chapatis* (the flat unleavened bread that was the staple diet in northern India) had been passing from village to village. Traditionally, the circulation of such objects was a ritual means of expelling an epidemic or some such misfortune from one's village. British officials now read the circulation of *chapatis* as evidence of an organized plot. There is no evidence that such a plot existed, but in an atmosphere charged with growing discontent in the countryside, it was just as possible to believe in Indian bread messages as it was to believe in British intentions to convert everyone to Christianity.

Convinced that the rebellion was the result of the plotting of a few, the British carried out their counterinsurgency with brutal vengeance. Villages were torched, and rebels were tied to cannons and blown to bits to teach Indians a lesson in power. Delhi fell in September 1857, and Lucknow was captured in March 1858. The British exiled the unfortunate Mughal emperor, Bahadur Shah, to Burma, where he died in 1858. The emperor's sons were murdered in cold blood. Most of the other rebel leaders were either killed in battle or captured and executed. By July 1858, the vicious pacification campaign had

THE INDIAN REBELLION OF 1857

The Indian leaders of the Rebellion of 1857 issued numerous proclamations. The Azamgarb Proclamation, excerpted below, is representative of these petitions. It was issued in August 1857 by the Emperor Bahadur Shah on behalf of the mutineers who had seized the garrison town of Azamgarb, sixty miles north of Benares. Like other proclamations, it attacks the British for subverting Indian traditions and calls on its followers to restore the pre-British order, in this case the Mughal empire.

It is well known to all, that in this age the people of Hindoostan, both Hindoos and Mohammedans, are being ruined under the tyranny and oppression of the infidel and treacherous English. It is therefore the bounden duty of all the wealthy people of India, especially of those who have any sort of connection with any of the Mohammedan royal families, and are considered the pastors and masters of their people, to stake their lives and property for the well being of the public. . . .

Several of the Hindoo and Mussalman chiefs, who have long since quitted their homes for the preservation of their religion, and have been trying their best to root out the English in India, have presented themselves to me, and taken part in the reigning Indian crusade, . . . Parties anxious to participate in the common cause, but having no means to provide for themselves, shall receive their daily subsistence from me; and be it known to all, that the ancient works, both of the Hindoos and the Mohammedans, the writings of the miracle-workers and the calculations of the astrologers, pundits, and rammals, all agree in asserting that the English will no longer have any footing in India or elsewhere. . . .

Section I—Regarding Zemindars. It is evident, that the British Government in making zemindary settlements have imposed exorbitant *Jumas*, and have disgraced and ruined several zemindars. . . . Such extortions will have no manner of existence in the Badshahi Government; but on the contrary, the *Jumas* will be light, the dignity and honour of the zemindars safe, and every zemindar will have absolute rule in his own zemindary. . . .

Section II—Regarding Merchants. It is plain that the infidel and treacherous British Government have monopolized the trade of all the fine and valuable merchandise, such as indigo, cloth, and other articles of shipping, leaving only the trade of trifles to the people, and even in this they are not without their share of the profits, which they secure by means of customs and stamp fees, &c. in money suits, so that the people have merely a trade in name. . . . When the Badshahi Government is established, all these aforesaid fraudulent practices shall be dispensed with, and the trade of every article, without exception, both by land and water, shall be open to the native merchants of India. . . .

Section IV—Regarding Artisans. It is evident that the Europeans, by the introduction of English articles into India, have thrown the weavers, the cotton dressers, the carpenters, the blacksmiths, and the shoemakers, &c., out of employ, and have engrossed their occupations, so that every description of native artisan has been reduced to beggary. But under the Badshahi Government the native artisan will exclusively be employed in the services of the kings, the rajahs, and the rich. . . .

Section V—Regarding Pundits, Fakirs and other learned persons. The pundits and fakirs being the guardians of the Hindoo and Mohammedan religions respectively, and the Europeans being the enemies of both the religions, and as at present a war is raging against the English on account of religion, the pundits and fakirs are bound to present themselves to me, and take their share in the holy war. . . .

Source: "Proclamation of Emperor Bahadur Shah," in *India in 1857: The Revolt Against Foreign Rule*, edited by Ainslie T. Embree (Delhi: Chanakya Publications, 1987), pp. 3–6.

achieved its object. Yet, in August, the British Parliament abolished Company rule and the Company itself and transferred responsibility for the governing of India to the crown. In November, Queen Victoria issued a proclamation guaranteeing religious toleration, promising improvements, and allowing Indians to serve in the government. She promised to honor the treaties and agreements with princes and chiefs and to refrain from interfering in religious matters.

Thus ended a rebellion to forge a popular alternative to the developing colonial order. Combining languages of religion, community, and the old order, the rebels cast the alternative order as a restoration of the old regime. Yet, the restoration was to be accomplished by popular action. It was the functioning of the subordinate groups as historical actors—their discontent, their mobilization, their destructive violence, their religious visions—that gave force to dreams for an alternative order. The insurgents rose up, not as a nation, but as a multitude of communities acting independently and often without coordination.

Their determination to find a new order shocked the British and threw them into a panic. Having crushed the uprising, the British resumed the work of transforming India into a modern colonial state and economy. But the desire for radical alternatives and traditions of popular agency, though vanquished, did not vanish.

Chronology

1804–1809	Dan Fodio leads revolt in West Africa
1804–1812	Popular uprising in Serbia against Ottomans
1805–1811	Preaching of Tenskwatawa (North America)
1812–1814	War of 1812 between Britain and U.S.
1813–1815	Wahhabis wage militant religious campaign
1814–1815	Congress of Vienna
1815–1817	Second Serbian uprising against Ottomans
1818–1828	Shaka creates Zulu empire
1819	Peterloo Massacre (England)
1820s–1830s	American Indians moved west of Mississippi River
1821–1829	Greek war for independence
1830	Revolutions in France, Belgium, Rhineland, Italy
1830	Revolution in Brazil
1830s	Revolt of Abd al-Qadir in Algeria
1831–1834	Revolutions in Poland, Spain, Italy
1832	Mazzini founds "Young Italy" movement
1839–1848	Chartism in England
1846–1847	Mexican War between U.S. and Mexico
1846–1848	Economic crisis in Europe
1847–1901	Yucatan Caste War (Mexico)
1848	Revolutions in France, Austria, Prussia, Italy
1849	Revolt in Algeria against French
1851–1864	Taiping Rebellion (China)
1856	British take over Lucknow in India
1857–1858	Indian Rebellion
1889–1890	Ghost Dance Movement (North America)

 CONCLUSION

The nineteenth century was a time of turmoil and transformation. As powerful forces reconfigured the world as a place for capitalism, colonialism, and nation-states, so too did prophets, charismatic leaders, radicals, peasant rebels, and anti-colonial insurgents arise to offer alternatives. Responding to specific circumstances and drawing upon particular traditions, the struggles of these men and women for a different political and cultural future opened up spaces for the ideas and activities of subordinate classes. Conventional historical accounts either neglect these struggles or fail to view them as a whole. These individuals were not just romantic, last-ditch resisters, as some have argued. Even after defeat, their messages remained alive within their communities. Nor were their actions isolated and aberrant events, for when viewed on a global scale, they bring to light a world that looks very different from the one that became dominant. To see the Wahhabi Movement in the Arabian peninsula together with the Shawnee Prophet in North America, utopians and radicals in Europe with the peasant insurgents in British India, and the Taiping rebels with the Mayans in the Yucatan, is to gain a glimpse of a world of marginalized regions and groups, a world that the more powerful endeavored to suppress but could not erase.

In this world, the prophets and rebel leaders usually cultivated power and prestige locally; the emergence of an alternative polity in one region did not impinge on communities and political organizations in others. As much as these radicals, prophets, charismatic leaders, and anti-colonial insurgents had in common, they envisioned widely different kinds of futures rooted in their particular contexts. Even Marx, who called the workers of the world to unite, was acutely aware that the call for a proletarian revolution applied only to the industrialized countries of Europe. Others had even more localized horizons. A world fashioned by movements for alternatives meant a world with multiple centers and divergent historical trajectories.

To see the world through the lenses of prophets and rebels across the nineteenth century is to realize that widely different inspirations and goals produced these movements. What gave force to a different mapping of the world was that common people were at the center of these alternative visions, and their voices, however muted, gained a place on the historical stage. Egalitarianism in different shapes and forms defined efforts to reconstitute alternative worlds. In Islamic regions, the egalitarianism practiced by revitalization movements was evident in their mobilization of all Muslims, not just the elites. Even charismatic military leaders in Africa, such as Shaka, for all their use of raw power, utilized the framework of community to build new polities. The Taiping Rebellion distinguished itself by seeking to establish an equal society of men and women in service of the Heavenly Kingdom. Operating under very different conditions, the European radicals imagined a society free from the hierarchical order of both aristocratic privileges and bourgeois property. Anti-colonial rebels and insurgents depended upon local solidarities and advanced alternative imagined moral communities. In so doing, these movements compelled ruling elites to adjust the way they governed. This challenge is discussed in the next chapter.

FURTHER READINGS

Anderson, David M., *Revealing Prophets: Prophets in Eastern African History* (1995). Good discussion of the prophets in eastern Africa.

Beecher, Jonathan, *The Utopian Vision of Charles Fourier* (1983). A fine biography of this important thinker.

Clancy-Smith, Julia, *Rebel and Saint: Muslim Notables, Populist Protest, Colonial Encounter (Algeria and Tunisia, 1800–1904)* (1994). Examines Islamic protest movements against Western encroachments in North Africa.

Clogg, Richard, *A Concise History of Greece* (1997). A good introduction to the history of Greece in its European context.

Dowd, Gregory E., *A Spirited Resistance: The North American Indian Struggle for Unity, 1745–1815* (1992). Emphasizes the importance of prophets like Tenskwatawa in the building of pan-Indian confederations in the era between the Seven Years' War and the War of 1812.

Guha, Ranajit, *Elementary Aspects of Peasant Insurgency in Colonial India* (1983). Not specifically on the Indian Rebellion of 1857, but includes it in its pioneering "subalternist" interpretation of South Asian history.

Hamilton, Carolyn (ed.), *The Mfecane Aftermath: Reconstructive Debates in Southern African History* (1995). Debates on Shaka's *Mfecane* movement and its impact on southern Africa.

Hiskett, Mervyn, *The Sword of Truth: The Life and Times of the Shehu Usman dan Fodio* (1994). A recent and authoritative study of the Fulani revolt in northern Nigeria.

Johnson, Douglas H., *Nuer Prophets: A History of Prophecy from the Upper Nile in the Nineteenth and Twentieth Centuries* (1994). Deals with African prophetic and charismatic movements in eastern Africa.

Michael, Franz, and Chung-li Chang, *The Taiping Rebellion: History and Documents*, 3 vols. (1966–1971). The basic source for the history of the Taiping.

Mukherjee, Rudrangshu, *Awadh in Revolt 1857–58* (1984). A careful case study of the Indian Rebellion.

Omer-Cooper, J. D., *The Zulu Aftermath: A Nineteenth Century Revolution in Bantu Africa* (1966). A good place to start in studying Shaka's *Mfecane* movement, which greatly rearranged the political and ethnic makeup of southern Africa.

Peires, J. B. (ed.), *Before and After Shaka* (1981). Discusses new elements in the debate over Shaka's *Mfecane* movement.

Reed, Nelson, *The Caste War of Yucatan* (1964). A classic narrative of the Caste War of the Yucatan.

Restall, Matthew, *The Maya World* (1997). Describes in economic and social terms the origins of the Yucatan upheaval in southern Mexico.

Rugeley, Terry, *Yucatán's Peasantry and the Origins of the Caste War* (1996). Explains the combination of economic and cultural pressures that drove the Mayans in the Yucatan to revolt in the Caste War.

Spence, Jonathan, *God's Chinese Son: The Taiping Heavenly Kingdom of Hong Xiuquan* (1996). A fascinating portrayal of the Taiping through the prism of its founder.

Wagner, Rudolf, *Reenacting the Heavenly Vision: The Role of Religion in the Taiping Rebellion* (1982). A brief, but insightful analysis of the religious elements in the Taiping's doctrines.

White, Richard, *The Middle Ground: Indians, Empires, and Republics in the Great Lakes Region, 1650–1815* (1991). A pathbreaking exploration of intercultural relations in North America that offers a provocative interpretation of the visions of Tenskwatawa and the efforts of Tecumseh to resist the expansion of the United States.

8

NATIONS AND EMPIRES, 1850–1914

n 1895, the Cuban patriot José Martí launched a rebellion against the last Spanish tocholds in the Americas. The anti-Spanish struggle continued until 1898, when Spain withdrew its last forces from Cuba and Puerto Rico. Martí hoped to bring freedom to a new Cuban nation and republican equality to all Cubans regardless of race or class. But if Martí's efforts helped secure freedom from the declining Spanish empire, he could not prevent Cuba's military occupation and political domination by the world's newest imperial power, the United States. Even while American involvement introduced new laws and investment into the former Spanish colonies, it frustrated the hopes of sovereign nation-states in the Caribbean.

Martí's hopes and frustrations found parallels around the world. After 1850, both nation-state building and imperial expansion changed the map of the world. This remapping stemmed, in the first place, from the great political and economic upheavals of the late eighteenth and early nineteenth centuries that had battered the old regimes. American revolutionaries, Haitian slaves, and Napoleon's armies had embraced the concept of popular sovereignty (of power residing in the people themselves) and challenged the legitimacy of kings and conservative elites. Simultaneously, new forms of production were bringing to the fore persons of wealth and merit to rival older aristocratic groups whose high status rested on the ownership of land. Close on the heels of these transformations came the upsurge

271

of charismatic leaders, radicals, peasant rebels, and anti-colonial insurgents who clamored for their alternative visions of power and community. These developments prepared the way for the rise of new rulers and elites in the second half of the nineteenth century, mainly in the Americas, Japan, and parts of Europe. These individuals embraced the nation-state organization at home and fostered territorial empires overseas.

NATION-BUILDING AND EXPANSION

> → *What was the relationship between nationalism and imperialism?*

During the second half of the nineteenth century, the ideology of nation-state building spread across the globe. The exponents of the nation-state claimed that the world's population could be divided up into "peoples" who shared a common past, territory, culture, and traditions, and who needed only a political expression of their own, namely the nation-state, to be joined together and freed from external overlords and to attain national well-being. This seemed such a natural process that little thought was given to how nation-states arose—they were simply supposed to well up from the people's longing for togetherness.

In practice, however, in many instances, the state created the nation rather than the other way around. The state did so by compelling diverse communities and regions to accept a unified network of laws, administration, time zones, national markets, and a single regional dialect as the "national" language. To overcome strong regional identities, the state broadened public education in the new national language

> *The exponents of the nation-state claimed that the world's population could be divided up into "peoples" who shared a common past, territory, culture, and traditions, and who needed only a political expression of their own, namely the nation-state.*

and imposed universal military service to build a national army. In this fashion, the state nurtured the notion that there was a one-to-one correspondence between a "people" and a nation-state. Those who spoke different languages became national minorities, often compelled to assimilate or face discrimination.

The new nation-state took on its clearest expression in the Americas, Japan, and parts of Europe. In the latter, two new polities—Germany and Italy—forced nations into existence through strategic conquests. Elsewhere on the continent, the nationalist example inspired central European and Balkan intellectuals living under the supranational Habsburgs and Ottomans to begin to envision consolidated national communities as autonomous regions within these large empires or as breakaway nation-states. The diversity of the many imagined nationalities within these empires, however, prompted imperial rulers to offer a supranational identity—with varying degrees of success. In the Russian empire, the ruling Romanovs tried to adapt their religiously and linguistically diverse realm into a nation-state through heavy-handed, if nonsystematic Russification. This could only be a stopgap measure, however, for as Russia embarked on further expansion of its vast realm into Central Asia, its land empire became even more diverse and more difficult to characterize as a single nation-state.

Whereas highly developed nation-states could readily acquire overseas territories without upsetting their national agendas at home—indeed, the popularity of overseas acquisitions helped nation-states domestically—the expansion of landed empires greatly complicated the challenge of creating a single "people" out of many ethnic and national groups. In those countries that could successfully forge a nation-state, state-led nation-building, territorial expansion, and imperialism went hand in hand. They were the means by which leaders attempted to make their countries strong. The rulers believed that national strength was measured not only by the unity and loyalty of the people, but also by the conquest of new territories

Focus Questions NATIONS AND EMPIRES

→ *What was the relationship between nationalism and imperialism?*
→ *How did the nation-building patterns compare among the U.S., Canada, and Brazil?*
→ *How did European nation-states forge national identities?*
→ *How did new materials and technologies transform industry and the global economy?*
→ *What were the motives for imperialism and the practices of colonial rulers?*
→ *How did expansionism affect Japan, Russia, and China?*

and the possession of the most modern forms of production. Thus did a large number of great powers—Germany, France, the United States, Russia, and Japan—seek to rival Britain by expanding and modernizing their internal industries (thereby kicking off a second industrial revolution) and by seizing adjacent or far-off colonies. By the century's end, conquest of new territory had become so important to the prestige of these states that they engaged in a veritable "scramble" to colonize peoples from Africa to the Amazon, from California to Korea.

Never before had there been such a rapid reshuffling of peoples and resources as in these decades, a time in which the nation-state and the territorial empire became the most highly desired form of political organization. As transportation costs declined, workers left their homes in search of better opportunities across the world. In large numbers, Japanese moved to Brazil, Indians to South Africa and the Caribbean, Chinese to California, and Italians to New York and Buenos Aires. At the same time, American capitalists began to invest outside the United States, and British investors reaped handsome profits by financing the construction of railroads in China and India. Raw materials from Africa and Southeast Asia flowed to the manufacturing nations of Europe and the Americas.

Imperial umbrellas facilitated this movement of labor, capital, and commodities. As mapmakers filled in the "empty spaces," labeling territory that had not been measured, mapped, or owned by Europeans, scholars and officials carried out studies of tribes and races. New schools taught the colonized the languages, religions, scientific practices, and cultural traditions of the colonizers, while publications and artifacts from the "mother country" circulated more widely, at least among the indigenous elites. Yet, empire-builders were not willing to extend to nonwhite inhabitants of their colonies the same rights as they conferred on inhabitants of their own nations; here, nation and empire were incompatible. Not only were the colonized prohibited from participating in government—as were the working classes, women, and Jews in Europe itself—colonial subjects were not considered members of the nation at all.

We begin the story of nation and empire with the Americas, where the quest for national self-rule had enjoyed its first successes and generated the desire for territorial aggrandizement. From the New World, we turn to the Old World, where nationalism and nation-building emerged as a more immediate response to the popular upheavals of the 1840s. In contrast to the American model, in which frontier territories, often by force, were incorporated into the nation, the expansion of Western European nations into Africa and Asia involved the erection of colonial systems. Nation-building and imperial expansion, however, were not confined to Europe and the Americas; at the other end of Eurasia, a similar rise in nationalist fervor and scramble

for possessions took place. Thus, a series of events drew three other states—Russia, China, and Japan—into rivalry and warfare over colonial domains in Asia.

EXPANSION AND NATION-BUILDING IN THE AMERICAS

> → *How did the nation-building patterns compare among the U.S., Canada, and Brazil?*

Freed from European control in the late eighteenth and early nineteenth centuries, the elites of the Americas set about creating political communities of their own. By the 1850s, they shared a desire to establish—at least nominally—inclusive political systems and expand territorial domains. This required two things: first, refining the tools of government to induct the "people" into public life with national laws and court systems, standardized money, and national political parties, and second, devising ways to occupy and settle hinterlands that previously belonged to the hemisphere's aboriginal populations. Once themselves European colonies, New World territories emerged as vibrant nation-states, based on growing material prosperity and industrialization.

While the decades after 1850 saw general expansion and development of nation-states throughout the world, the Americas witnessed the most thoroughgoing and complete assimilation of new possessions into old domains. Instead of treating peripheral areas as mere colonial outposts, American nation-state builders turned their conquered territories into new provinces. Indeed, with the help of rifles, railroads, schools, and land

With the help of rifles, railroads, schools, and land surveys, frontiers became lucrative and strategic possessions, central to the very fabric of North and South American societies.

surveys, frontiers became lucrative and strategic possessions, central to the very fabric of North and South American societies. For the indigenous peoples of these newly colonized territories, however, national expansion meant the loss of lands.

Not all conquests, colonizations, and national consolidations in the Americas were the same, however. The United States, Canada, and Brazil, to cite three examples, experienced differing processes of nation-building, territorial expansion, and economic development. Each of these three successfully incorporated frontier regions into national polities and economies, though they employed varying techniques for subjugating Indian peoples and administering new holdings. And while Brazil and Canada did not rival the economic power of the United States, by century's end they, too, had become durable nation-states.

"MANIFEST DESTINY"

In July 1845, the New York newspaper editor John L. O'Sullivan coined the phrase "Manifest Destiny" to explain how the "design of Providence" supported the territorial expansion of the United States. In this excerpt, O'Sullivan outlines the reasons why the United States was justified in annexing Texas and why it must soon do the same in supplanting Mexican rule in California. In the view of O'Sullivan and other ardent expansionists, the superiority of "Anglo-Saxon" civilization led to a fast increasing population that must inevitably take over the lands of lesser peoples. Cries of "Manifest Destiny" often accompanied American conquest and colonization of new territories.

. . . Texas has been absorbed into the Union in the inevitable fulfilment of the general law which is rolling our population westward; the connexion of which with that ratio of growth in population which is destined within a hundred years to swell our numbers to the enormous population of *two hundred and fifty millions* (if not more), is too evident to leave us in doubt of the manifest design of Providence in regard to the occupation of this continent. It was disintegrated from Mexico in the natural course of events, by a process perfectly legitimate on its own part, blameless on ours; and in which all the censures due to wrong, perfidy and folly, rest on Mexico alone. And possessed as it was by a population which was in truth but a colonial detachment from our own, and which was still bound by myriad ties of the very heart strings to its old relations, domestic and political, their incorporation into the Union was not only inevitable, but the most natural, right and proper thing in the world—and it is only astonishing that there should be any among ourselves to say it nay. . . .

California will, probably, next fall away from the loose adhesion which, in such a country as Mexico, holds a remote province in a slight equivocal kind of dependence on the metropolis. Imbecile and distracted, Mexico never can exert any real governmental authority over such a country. The impotence of the one and the distance of the other, must make the relation one of virtual independence; unless, by stunting the province of all natural growth, and forbidding that immigration which can alone develop its capabilities and fulfil the purposes of its creation, tyranny may retain a military dominion which is no government in the legitimate sense of the term. In the case of California this is now impossible. The Anglo-Saxon foot is already on its borders. Already the advance guard of the irresistible army of Anglo-Saxon emigration has begun to pour down upon it, armed with the plough and the rifle, and marking its trail with schools and colleges, courts and representative halls, mills and meeting-houses. A population will soon be in actual occupation of California, over which it will be idle for Mexico to dream of dominion. They will necessarily become independent. All this without agency of our government, without responsibility of our people—in the natural flow of events, the spontaneous working of principles, and the adaptation of the tendencies and wants of the human race to the elemental circumstances in the midst of which they find themselves placed. . . .

Source: John L. O'Sullivan, "Manifest Destiny," *Democratic Review* (July 1845), pp. 7–10, in Clark C. Spence, ed., *The American West: A Source Book* (New York: Thomas Y. Crowell Company, 1966), pp. 108–109.

THE UNITED STATES

Military might, fortuitous diplomacy, and the power of numbers enabled the United States to lay claim to a transcontinental territory. By the middle of the nineteenth century, hundreds of thousands of American citizens occupied the Pacific slope (see Map 8-1). The territorial expansion and economic development of the United States appears even more impressive given the deep cleavages of race and geography that beset the republic. From the American Revolution, the new nation had emerged as a barely united confederation of states. Indian resistance and Spanish and

Canadian Westward Expansion
- Settled before 1825
- Settled between 1825 and 1871
- Settled between 1871 and 1891
- Settled between 1891 and 1911
- Boundary of original Confederation, 1867
- Rupert's Land territories added to provinces, 1912

United States Westward Expansion
- United States, 1783
- Louisiana Purchase, 1803
- West Florida annexation, 1810, 1813
- East Florida ceded by Spain, 1819
- Acquired from Britain, 1818, 1842
- Texas annexation, 1845
- Oregon Country, 1846
- Ceded by Mexico, 1848
- Gadsden Purchase, 1853
- Acquired from Russia, 1867
- Annexed, 1894
- Railroad

MAP 8-1 U.S. AND CANADIAN WESTWARD EXPANSION, 1803–1912

The Americans and the Canadians expanded westward rapidly in the second half of the nineteenth century, aided greatly by railways. A close inspection of the map will enable you to understand the chronology of migration. Who led the westward migration—citizens of the United States or Canada? On the basis of your knowledge of the geography and history of the United States and Canada would you be able to guess what kinds of items were being carried from east to west and west to east? The railways carried people as well as commodities and were crucial in creating the major cities of the western United States and Canada. What were the major railway hubs of the western United States and Canada?

British rivalry hemmed in "Americans" (as they came to call themselves). At the same time, these disunited states also threatened to fracture into separate northern and southern polities, as questions of slavery versus free labor intruded into national politics.

The expansion of the United States offered a means to unite the country's citizenry and was promoted by some as necessary for safeguarding the independence and virtue of rising generations of white men. President Thomas Jefferson (1743–1826) had boldly predicted the independence of America's family farmers for a thousand years soon after he had procured the vast French Louisiana Territory from Napoleon (for a mere $15 million) in 1803. But expansion required the violent dispossession of Indian peoples and the invasion of Mexican territory. Not long after Jefferson concluded the Louisiana Purchase, ardent expansionists began to fix their attention on lands even further to the west of this area. Rallying to the rhetoric of Manifest Destiny, which maintained that it was God's will for the United States to "overspread" the North American continent, the most aggressive expansionists sought control of British lands in the northwest (in the Oregon country), and of the lands south and west of the Louisiana Territory (in the northern provinces of Mexico). A peaceful compromise was reached with Britain, but the United States went to war against Mexico in 1846, which resulted in the United States' acquiring almost half of Mexico's land. In a treaty with Mexico, the United States guaranteed the Mexican nationals who remained within the territory it had acquired equal rights with American citizens. In practice, however, Mexicans who became American citizens often lost their landholdings and suffered other forms of discrimination.

The myth of the frontier, with its belief that plentiful land existed for any white family that wished to establish an independent homestead, played a fundamental role in forging a new American identity. Yet, free land and (white) independence were not the only aspects of American identity—and about the other aspects many disagreed. In the southern plantation societies, to be American meant aristocratic honor, proper female behavior, and above all, the ownership of slaves. In the South, as in the North and the West, regional definitions of "the people" were often more inspiring than national definitions. The incoherence of the American "nation" condemned the federation to eventual bitter conflict—the worst ever witnessed in the Americas.

To defend their lifestyles—and their property—eleven southern states plunged the United States into a gruesome Civil War (1861–1865). This war transformed the United States more profoundly than any other event. The bloody struggle led to the abolition of slavery, and the attempts to extend voting and citizenship rights to the freed slaves qualified the Civil War as a second American Revolution. It gave the nation a new generation of heroes and martyrs such as the assassinated president, Abraham Lincoln. Lincoln had promised a new model of freedom for a nation reborn out of bloodshed. Its cornerstone would be the incorporation of the freed slaves as citizens of the United States. Alas, the biracial democracy of the post–Civil War era was short-lived. In the decades after the Civil War, counterrevolutionary pressure, spearheaded by the terrorism of the Ku Klux Klan, led to the denial of voting rights to African Americans and the restoration of (white) planter rule in the southern states.

> *The expansion of the United States offered a means to unite the country's citizenry and was promoted by some as necessary for safeguarding the independence and virtue of rising generations of white men.*

Nonetheless, the war ushered in an irreversible political transformation. The defeat of the South vanquished the chief proponents of states' rights and established the preeminence of the national government. After the Civil War, Americans learned to speak of their nation in the singular ("the United States is" in contrast to "the United States are"). With an invigorated nationalism came an enlarged national government.

Even more dizzying were the social and economic changes that flowed from the Civil War. Within ten years of the Civil War's end, the industrial output of the United States had climbed by 75 percent from its already high wartime levels. Symbolizing and stimulating this growth was the expansion of railroad lines. In 1865, the United States boasted 35,000 miles of track. By 1900, nearly 200,000 miles of track connected the Atlantic to the Pacific and crisscrossed the American territory in between. Increasingly, steam-powered machines supplanted human muscle as the engine of production, bringing dramatic improvements in output. Before the Civil War, it took sixty-one hours of labor to produce an acre of wheat; by 1900, new machinery cut the time to a little over three hours. On farms and in factories, mechanization boosted production, and rapid railroad transportation permitted the shipment of more goods at lower prices across greater distances. Wheat production, with the help of new technologies and the dispossession of numerous Great Plains Indians, jumped 250 percent in the last quarter of the nineteenth century.

Americans not only had huge successes in agriculture, they also had equally impressive industrial gains, so much so that the United States joined Britain and Germany atop the list of industrial giants. The Americans innovated in nearly all of the areas necessary for industrial success—technical education, inventions, factory routines, marketing, and above all, the mobilization of capital. In the United States (as in Germany), a potent instrument of capital accumulation appeared at this time—the limited-liability joint-stock company. Firms such as Standard Oil and U.S. Steel mobilized capital from shareholders, who left the running of these enterprises to paid managers. Intermediaries, like J. Pierpont Morgan, the New York financial titan who became the world's wealthiest man, loaned money and brokered big deals on the New York Stock Exchange. So great were the fortunes amassed by leading financiers and corporate magnates that by 1890 the richest 1 percent of Americans owned nearly 90 percent of the nation's wealth.

In spite of its awesome economic growth, the United States now faced an even more pernicious wedge dividing its "people"—the divisions of social class. As mechanized production churned out ever more goods, the threat of overproduction became a pressing concern. Farms and factories produced more than Americans needed or could afford to purchase. In the 1890s, the problem of overproduction plunged the American economy into a harsh depression. Millions of urban workers were thrown out of work, while those who kept their jobs suffered sharp cuts in their wages. Radical labor leaders called for the dismantling of the industrial capitalist order, and strikes proliferated. Discontent spread to the countryside as well, where declining prices and unfair railroad freight charges pushed countless farmers toward bankruptcy. Moreover, many Americans worried that the forge of national identity, the frontier, was vanishing. Indeed, in 1890, the U.S. Census Bureau pronounced the "American frontier" closed. The spread of the agrarian opposition of "Populists" and "Greenbacks" (political parties advancing the interests of farmers) reinforced the Jeffersonian image of a virtuous agrarian republic going sour. Ex-homesteaders and those for whom there were no good lands left to homestead were becoming disillusioned.

> *In spite of its awesome economic growth, the United States now faced an even more pernicious wedge dividing its "people"—the divisions of social class.*

One solution to the problem of overproduction and the threat of class unrest was to increase exports and create new frontiers abroad. Exports of agricultural and industrial commodities had, in fact, already more than tripled in value since the Civil War. Yet, even this increase did not absorb the surplus of goods, leading farmers and industrialists to demand greater access to foreign markets. To secure these, advocates of commercial expansion championed the creation of American colonies in overseas territories. By the 1890s, the rising sentiment for the acquisition of overseas possessions led the United States to go to war with Spain and to annex the Philippines.

By the end of the nineteenth century, the United States had become a major world power. It boasted an expanding economy, an ever more integrated nation after the Civil War, and a constitution that claimed to uphold equality of all members of the American nation. But there was no full agreement on what that equality should entail. Equality before the law? Equality of social classes? In the United States, territorial expansion and economic growth muted internal divisions but did not eliminate them.

CANADA

Canadians also built a new nation, enjoyed economic success, and followed an expansionist course. Like the United States, Canada had access to a frontier for growing agricultural exports. These lands also became the homes and farms of increasing numbers of European immigrants. Canada's path to nationhood was, however, different from that of its southern neighbor. Where the United States had to fight and win a war to gain independence, Canada's separation from Britain was a peaceful process. From the 1830s to the 1860s, the mother country gradually passed authority to the colony, leaving Canadians to grapple with the task of creating a shared national community.

That task was made more difficult by sharp internal divisions. The French population left behind after the British took the northern colony from France in 1763 wanted to keep their villages, their culture, their religion, and their language intact. They did not feel completely integrated into the new Canadian national entity. Nor were they eager to join the English-speaking Canadian population in expanding into new areas, for such migration threatened to dilute the French-Canadian presence. The English speakers were no more enthusiastic about creating an independent nation. Fear of being absorbed into the American republic reinforced Canadian loyalty to the British crown and made Canadians content with colonial status. Indeed, when Canada finally gained its independence in 1867, it was by an Act of Parliament in London and not by revolution. But even with nationhood granted, Canadians, including some prominent French speakers, promised to keep up their fealty, now in the form of a "dominion" within a British Commonwealth.

Without cultural or linguistic unity and bereft of an imperial overlord, the Canadians also used territorial expansion to fashion an integrated state for a "people." But they did so with a different twist from their neighbor to the south. In response to the United States' acquisition of Alaska and the movement of settlers onto the American plains, Canadian leaders realized that they had to incorporate their own western territories, lest these, too, fall into American hands (see Map 8-1). Since pioneers seemed unwilling to venture to these prairies of their own accord, the Canadian state became actively involved in promoting expansion. More so than the United States, the Canadian state lured potential farming emigrants from Europe and the United States with subsidized railway rates and the promise of fortunes to be made. It also offered attractive terms to railway companies to connect dispersed agrarian hinterlands with Montreal and Toronto and not with commercial cities in the United States.

Governments also played an important role in handling the inevitable friction with Indians. Frontier warfare threatened to drive away investors and settlers—who always had access to property south of the border. To prevent the kind of bloodletting among settlers and Indians that characterized the westward expansion of the United States, the Canadian government signed treaties with Indians to ensure strict separation between natives and newcomers. To keep settlers off Indian lands, the government created a special police force, the Royal Canadian Mounted Police (the "Mounties"), to patrol the territories.

Canadian expansion was hardly bloodless, however. Many Indians and mixed-blood peoples (*métis*) resented the treaties.

Moreover, the government was often less than honest in its dealings. As in the United States, the government's Indian policy sought to turn Indians into farmers, and then to incorporate them into Canadian society. And as in the United States, the Canadian government paid little heed to whether Indians or *métis* wished to become farmers or join the nation.

The combination of defensive expansionism, the need to accommodate French speakers, and the respect for at least some minimal degree of legality in dealings with Indians meant that the Canadian government emerged with fuller powers to intervene, regulate, and mediate than did the U.S. government. But if the state was relatively strong, the nation was comparatively weak. Without voluntary or forcible integration, Canadians entered the twentieth century without a strong sense of national identity. Expansionism helped Canada remain an autonomous state, but it did not solve the internal question of what it meant to belong to a Canadian nation.

SPANISH AMERICA AND BRAZIL

Latin America also engaged in nation-state building and joined the expansionist fervor. By the middle of the nineteenth century, the New World colonies south of the Rio Grande, like those to the north, had become liberal, capitalist societies. As in North America, Latin American regimes extended their territorial claims to vast hinterlands. But unlike in the United States and Canada, expansion and the creation of new provinces did not always create homesteader frontiers. Far more than in North America, the richest lands in Latin America went not to small farmers, but to large estate holders producing exports such as sugar, coffee, or beef. In addition, privileged elites monopolized political power more effectively than in North America's fledgling democracies. While territorial expansion and high rates of economic growth were Latin American hallmarks, these processes sidelined the poor, Indians, and blacks from participating fully in market or political life.

A major factor in the debate over how to create new republics in Latin America was the constant worry about Indian and peasant uprisings. Fearing insurrections, elites devised governing systems that protected private property and investments, while enabling the state and privileged individuals to curb the political rights of the poor and the propertyless. Likewise, the specter of slave revolts, driven home not just by events in Haiti, but by the constant daily rumors of rebellions, kept elites in a state of alarm. The Argentine liberal writer Domingo Faustino Sarmiento (1811–1888) captured the sentiment of many of his Latin American peers when he described the challenge of nation-state building as a struggle between elitist "civilization" and popular "barbarism."

Latin American statesmen, then, sought to build nation-states that excluded large swathes of the population from both the "nation" and the "state." Brazil provides a stark example of this process. Through the nineteenth century, rulers in Rio de Janeiro defused political conflict and allowed planters to retain the reins of power. Although the Brazilian government officially abolished the slave trade in 1830, it allowed illegal slave im-

ports to continue for another two decades. Finally, British pressure compelled Brazil to enforce the ban. The end of the slave trade, coupled with slave resistance, began to choke the planters' system by driving up the price of slaves. Sensing that the system of chattel labor was unraveling, slaves began to flee the sugar and coffee plantations en masse. Many in the army no longer supported the system and refused to hunt down runaway slaves. In the 1880s, even while laws upheld bonded labor, country roads in the state of São Paulo were filled with fugitive slaves looking for relatives or access to land. Finally, in 1888, the Brazilian emperor, with the support of some planters, abolished slavery. Brazil was the last American country to put an end to slavery. But, as in the United States, plantations remained. No land was redistributed. By importing European labor and retaining ex-slaves as gang-workers or sharecroppers, Brazilian elites found a new free labor force for their estates.

The Brazilian state was deliberately exclusive. The new constitution of 1891, establishing a federal system and proclaiming Brazil a republic, separated those who could be trusted with power from the rest. Previously, the political system had been remarkably open. Elections were contested, if often bloody, affairs. But with the abolition of slavery, the sudden enfranchisement of millions of freedmen threatened to flood the electoral lists with propertyless, potentially uncontrollable voters—many of them black. Politicians responded by slapping severe restrictions on suffrage and rigging rules to reduce political competition. By 1900, the Brazilian state was in the hands of local political bosses who shaped policies and practices to safeguard property.

Political stability proved good for Brazilian business. Although the state excluded the majority of citizens, it still wanted to create the illusion of an expansive territorial nation. The flag of the republic boasted the new slogan of "Order and Progress." At the inauguration of new railways, governors and capitalists, dressed in white and shaded with parasols, gathered to celebrate the opening of new frontier lands. Like Canada and the United States, the Brazilian state expanded its control over distant areas and incorporated them as provinces of the republic, despite the fact that they had been the home to Indians and others who held little affection for, never mind loyalty to, the new nation-state.

The largest land-grab occurred in the world's largest drainage watershed, the Amazon River basin, where the Brazilian state allocated giant concessions to capitalists to extract the rubber latex from the region. Rubber, when combined with sulfur, was the raw material for tire manufacturing for European and North American bicycle and automobile industries. As Brazil became the world's exclusive exporter of rubber, its planters, merchants, and workers prospered. Rich merchants became the lenders and financiers, not only to workers, but also to the landowners themselves. The mercantile upper crust of Manaus, the capital of the Amazon region, designed and decorated their city to reflect the bounty of their new fortunes. While the streets were still paved with mud, the town's potentates built a replica of the Paris Opera House, and Manaus was, for a time at least, a regular stopover for European opera singers on the New World circuit between Buenos Aires and New York. The rubber workers, called "tappers" because they

Opera House in Manaus. The turn-of-the-century rubber boom brought immense wealth to the Amazon jungle. As in many boom and bust cycles in Latin America, the proceeds from rubber flowed to a small elite, and soon crashed when the rubber supply outstripped the demand. But the wealth was sufficient to prompt the local elite to build temples of modernity in the midst of the jungle. Pictured here is the Opera House built in the rubber capital of Manaus. Typical of other works built by Latin American elites of the period, this one emulated the original built in Paris.

drew the oozing latex from taps sunk into the rubber plant, also benefited from the boom. Mostly either Indians or mixed-blood people, they remitted their wages to families living elsewhere in the Amazon jungle or on the northeastern coast of Brazil.

But the Brazilian rubber boom soon went bust. Part of the problem was rooted in the ecosystem: the land and vegetation could not tolerate a regimented, agrarian form of production. Leaf blight and ferocious ants destroyed all experiments at creating more sustainable rubber plantations. In addition, it was expensive to haul the rubber latex out of the jungle to the coast along the slow-moving Amazon River. In addition, Brazilian rubber faced severe competition from other rubber-producing regions of the world once a British scientist named Henry Wickham had smuggled rubber plant seeds out of Brazil in 1876. Following many years of experimenting with the plant at Kew Gardens in London,

British patrons transplanted a new blight-resistant hybrid to the British colony of Ceylon (present-day Sri Lanka). Competition increased supplies and reduced prices, bankrupting Brazilian producers. In the Amazon, merchants called in their loans, landowners forfeited their titles, and tappers returned to their subsistence economies. The Manaus Opera House fell into disrepair.

Throughout the Americas, nineteenth-century societies worked to adapt obsolete elite models of politics and to satisfy popular demands for inclusion. While the ideal was to construct nation-states that could reconcile underlying differences among their citizens and pave the way for economic prosperity, in fact, political autonomy did not bring prosperity, or even the right to vote, at all. As each nation-state gave in to the urge to expand its territorial boundaries, many new inhabitants of the nation were left out of the political realm.

Rubber Plantation Workers. *(Left)* Workers on rubber plantations draw latex from rubber plants by using taps that have been sunk into the rubber plant. *(Right)* The workers collect the latex in buckets and then take it to central collection points.

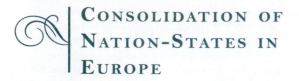

CONSOLIDATION OF NATION-STATES IN EUROPE

→ *How did European nation-states forge national identities?*

Nationalism was a product of the revolutionary era—of the ebbing of dynastic power after 1789 and of the popular upheavals of the 1830s and 1840s, especially the political revolutions of 1848. For a few heady months in 1848, some European states even belonged to "the people," with the creation of some republics and even talk of unifying the German- and Italian-speaking peoples into single states. And while this euphoric moment was brief, Europe's revolutions had lasting effects. Many rebels died, but still more fled into exile. This created a waiting pool of enemies of the restored regimes, enemies that kept alive revolutionary traditions.

The upheaval of 1848 also galvanized the conservatives. Austria got a new Habsburg emperor; Prussia kept its old king; elsewhere dukes and princes returned to their dominions. In a final blow to the hopes of many revolutionaries, Louis Napoleon (nephew of Napoleon) staged a coup against the French republic in December 1851. With the help of lower-middle-class conservatives and the army, he declared himself Emperor Napoleon III and ruled until 1870. Thus, in much of Europe, nationalism assumed a conservative quality by the second half of the nineteenth century, as middle-class liberals sided increasingly with conservatives rather than radicals. In Western Europe, mobilizing the "nation" became a means to preempt social revolution and strengthen the state. While the new nation-states of the post-1850 period were more than ever determined to create unified political communities, they were often faced with the reality of diverse linguistic and cultural populations inhabiting what they called their homelands. Nationalism had become an antagonistic worldview, in which diversity equaled weakness and opposition amounted to betrayal.

Everywhere, in the spring of 1848, the rebels had declared that the state belonged to the people. But in Europe after 1848, no one was sure who "the people" really were—and what sort of government they deserved. There was a general consensus among liberals that the nation should be sovereign. But what was the "nation"? For some, the nation was a collection of all those who spoke one language (for example, the Czechs). This did not work for the Irish, who spoke English, but who were predominately Catholics and wanted to be free from Anglican rule. For others, the nation was defined by a kind of ethnicity, and as the century wore on, writers increasingly began to suggest that com-munities were, or ought to be, defined by race. Confused and complicated as nationalism might appear, the idea had taken hold: the "nation" now seemed deeply rooted in the "natural" order of things, the authentic basis for a state. This longing for unified, homogeneous states spread throughout the continent despite the fact that most existing states were to some degree multinational, and many, such as Habsburg Austria, did not have a "dominant" or majority nationality around which to forge a nation-state.

Another legacy of 1848 was that the inheritors of the revolutionary traditions of 1789—the radicals and the liberals—once united, were now divided. In their brief months of victory, the two camps had discovered their incompatibility. The liberals found the radicals' demands for economic equalization and universal suffrage unacceptable. After the revolutions collapsed, the radicals and the urban working class more than ever seemed a dangerous threat to the middle-class liberals' cherished principles: property, respectability, free trade, family, and national patriotism. As a result, the liberals in France, as in Brazil, decided to work with, not against, the conservative, monarchical elites. Although this meant toning down plans for political reform, they believed that the chance to have the army on *their* side was worth the sacrifice.

It was the conservative elite, however, that learned most from the experience of 1848: they discovered that the legs had been kicked out from under traditional authority, and that henceforth they would need the support of the increasingly wealthy middle classes. Frightened by the political militancy of radicals, conservatives were in general happy to appease the liberals in order to fend off social revolution. One of the most sophisticated leaders of the post-1850 period, Louis Napoleon, realized that he could use universal (male) suffrage *against* radicalism. In many ways, he provided an example for other European nation-builders: popular suffrage and nationalism could blunt radicalism. After 1850, Italian and German nationalists took the lessons to heart.

> *In Western Europe, mobilizing the "nation" became a means to preempt social revolution and strengthen the state.*

UNIFICATION IN GERMANY AND IN ITALY

Two of Europe's fledgling nation-states came into being when the dynastic states of Prussia and Piedmont-Sardinia swallowed their smaller, linguistically related neighbors, creating the new German and Italian nation-states (see Map 8-2). In both regions, astute conservative prime ministers, Count Otto von Bismarck (1815–1898) of Prussia and Count Camillo di Cavour (1810–1861) of Piedmont, exploited radical, and especially liberal, nationalist sentiment to rearrange the map of Europe.

Clever strategists, Bismarck and Cavour used nationalist feelings and small-scale, limited wars to enlarge their states. Both were determined to build state power and to preserve monarchical and conservative rule. To these ends, they appealed

MAP 8-2   ITALIAN UNIFICATION AND GERMAN UNIFICATION, 1815–1871

Italian unification and German unification altered the political map of Europe as well as European balance-of-power arrangements. Who were the big winners and who were the big losers? How did Austria change as a result of these unifications, and how was France's place on the continent of Europe affected? Remembering that Prussia led the movement of unification in Germany and Piedmont led the unification of Italy, what were the most likely internal divisions in these two new countries?

to shared literary traditions and languages to paper over social, economic, political, and religious fault lines. They also used force to obtain their aims. In a famous address in 1862, Bismarck bellowed: "Not through speeches and majority decisions are the great questions of the day decided—that was the great mistake of 1848 and 1849—but through blood and iron." Taking his own advice, he accomplished the unification of the northern German states in the 1860s by war: with Denmark in 1864, Austria in 1866, and France (over the western provinces of Alsace and Lorraine) in 1870–1871. Italy also was united by means of a series of small conflicts, many of them intended to head off the establishment of some sort of republic.

These new, "unified" states were economically and militarily able to compete with Britain, France, and the United States, but they rejected democracy. In the new Italy, which was a constitutional monarchy not a republic, less than 5 percent of the 25 million people could vote. The new German empire (the Reich) was ruled by a combination of aristocrats and efficient bureaucrats. Liberals dominated in many localities, but only the emperor (the kaiser) could depose the prime minister, and Bismarck continued his illiberal reign for twenty-eight years, displaced only in 1890 by the new sovereign, Kaiser Wilhelm II (ruled 1888–1918), who proved to be even more illiberal than the Iron Chancellor.

The new German and Italian nation-states nonetheless had many internal problems. In Italy, Piedmontese liberals had hoped that centralized rule would transform southern Italy, making it a prosperous, commercial, and industrial region like their own. But southern notables, owing their wealth mainly to their large agricultural estates, had little interest in conforming to northern standards and customs. Germany contained many non-Germans—Poles in Silesia, French in Alsace and Lorraine, Danes in the provinces of Schleswig-Holstein—who became "national minorities" and whose rights remained in question. In addition, many non-Prussian Germans—Bavarians, Hanoverians,

WHAT IS A NATION?

The French linguist and ancient historian Ernest Renan (1823–1892) frequently embroiled himself in controversy. The piece below, from an 1882 essay entitled "What Is a Nation?" offers an explicitly republican model of nationhood (note that he is arguing with racial, religious, and dynastic interpretations of nationhood).

. . . The principle of nations is our principle. But what, then, is a nation? . . . Why is Switzerland, with its three languages, its two religions, and three or four races, a nation, when Tuscany, for example, which is so homogeneous, is not? Why is Austria a state and not a nation? In what does the principle of nations differ from that of races? . . .

Ethnographic considerations have . . . played no part in the formation of modern nations. France is Celtic, Iberic, and Germanic. Germany is Germanic, Celtic, and Slav. Italy is the country in which ethnography finds its greatest difficulties. Here Gauls, Etruscans, Pelasgians, and Greeks are crossed in an unintelligible medley. The British Isles, taken as a whole, exhibit a mixture of Celtic and Germanic blood, the proportions of which are particularly difficult to define.

The truth is that no race is pure, and that to base politics on ethnographic analysis is tantamount to basing it on a chimera. . . .

What we have said about race, applies also to language. Language invites union, without, however, compelling it. The United States and England, as also Spanish America and Spain, speak the same language without forming a single nation. Switzerland, on the contrary, whose foundations are solid because they are based on the assent of the various parties, contains three or four languages. There exists in man a something which is above language: and that is his will. The will of Switzerland to be united, in spite of the variety of these forms of speech, is a much more important fact than a similarity of language, often attained by vexatious measures. . . .

Nor can religion provide a satisfactory basis for a modern nationality. . . . Nowadays . . . everyone believes and practices religion in his own way according to his capacities and wishes. State religion has ceased to exist; and a man can be a Frenchman, an Englishman, or a German, and at the same time a Catholic, a Protestant, or a Jew, or practice no form of worship at all.

A nation is a soul, a spiritual principle. Two things, which are really only one, go to make up this soul or spiritual principle. One of these things lies in the past, the other in the present. The one is the possession in common of a rich heritage of memories; and the other is actual agreement, the desire to live together, and the will to continue to make the most of the joint inheritance. . . . The nation, like the individual, is the fruit of a long past spent in toil, sacrifice, and devotion. . . . To share the glories of the past, and a common will in the present; to have done great deeds together, and to desire to do more— . . . these are things of greater value than identity of custom-houses and frontiers in accordance with strategic notions. These are things which are understood, in spite of differences in race and language.

. . . The existence of a nation is . . . a daily plebiscite. . . . A province means to us its inhabitants; and if anyone has a right to be consulted in the matter, it is the inhabitant. It is never to the true interest of a nation to annex or keep a country against its will. The people's wish is after all the only justifiable criterion, to which we must always come back. . . .

Source: Ernest Renan, "What Is a Nation?," in *The Nationalism Reader*, edited by Omar Dahbour and Micheline R. Ishay (Atlantic Highlands, NJ: Humanities Press, 1995), pp. 143–55.

Saxons, and others—remained wary of a united Germany, believing that it signified Prussian Protestant rule. State authorities countered by mounting extensive "Germanizing" efforts, including using the North German Hamburg dialect as the national language, although the new state passed along considerable power to the old Germanic principalities, now incorporated into the unified Germany as federal lands and allowed them to keep their own regional institutions and symbols. Together, Bismarck and the liberals sought to root out Catholic resistance to basic Prussian institutions in a campaign of persecution known as the *Kulturkampf* (fight for culture). Hitting its zenith in the mid-1880s, this campaign resulted simply in the further alienation of southern Germans and the formation of a formidable Catholic political movement. Still, unification brought advantages, including brisk economic growth and Europe's most extensive programs of support for the sick, the disabled, and those injured at work—programs enacted by Bismarck to diminish socialism's appeal.

Kaiser Wilhelm I at Versailles. For the French, recently defeated in the Franco-Prussian War, insult was added to injury when the Prussian king, Wilhelm I, was proclaimed emperor (kaiser) of the newly united Germany in the palace of France's greatest king, Louis XIV, at Versailles. In 1919, the French would have their revenge, forcing the Germans to sign the humiliating Versailles Treaty in the same location.

Berlin, the capital of Prussia, became the capital of the German Reich. Kaiser Wilhelm II remarked in 1892 that "the glory of Paris robs Berliners of their sleep." But Berlin had over 1 million people in 1875; by 1910, there were 2 million. The Reichstag, a vast neoclassical parliament, was completed in 1894. In the 1890 elections, the Social Democratic Party garnered thirty-five seats in the Reichstag. By 1912, it had become the country's largest political party. Although the Socialist Party became less revolutionary as it assumed a leading role in the parliament, its electoral successes frightened conservatives and liberals. The new Germany, with its great might, was divided along class as well as regional and religious lines.

CONTRADICTIONS OF THE NATION IN EUROPE

Bismarck's wars of unification came at the expense of Habsburg supremacy in central Europe. In the wake of Germany's swift victory over the Austrian army in 1866, the Hungarian nobles who controlled the eastern areas of the Habsburg empire forced the weakened dynasts to grant them home rule in their "historic" lands. In the Compromise of 1867, the Habsburgs agreed that their state would officially be known as the Austro-Hungarian empire. But within the empire, especially the eastern areas, only about half the population were ethnic Hungarians.

The Hungarian elite proceeded to try to assimilate forcibly its many Slavs and other nationals. Czechs, Poles, and other Slavs also clamored for their own power-sharing "compromise" or national homeland in the now "dual" Austro-Hungarian state. In 1871, the Habsburg emperor, Francis Joseph (ruled 1848–1916), seemed prepared to accommodate the Czechs and move to a trilateral state. He was willing to do this over the objections of German speakers in the Czech lands, but his Hungarian partners scuttled the deal. The 1867 Compromise with Hungary had made other compromises impossible and inhibited any moves toward federalism (regional autonomy) in the empire as a whole. Still, multinationalism flourished in the imperial bureaucracy, the army officers' corps (whose members had to speak both German and the languages of the soldiers under their direct command), the upper administration of the Catholic Church, and in the highly cosmopolitan cities.

In France, too, events of the 1860s and 1870s compromised nationalist aspirations. Napoleon III dreamed of a France with restored grandeur—only to run headlong into expansionist Prussians. In the Franco-Prussian War of 1870–1871, Prussian troops delivered a swift and sound drubbing: in early September 1870, the German army broke through French defenses, captured the French emperor, and besieged Paris. Unprepared, Parisians had no food stocks, and were compelled to eat all sorts of things, including two zoo elephants. Under terrible conditions, and without effective leadership, the French capital resisted until January 1871, when the government signed a humiliating peace treaty. The Germans left in power an impotent provisional French government under the right-wing liberal Adolphe Thiers. Furious Parisians vented their rage and established a socialist "Commune," proclaiming the city a utopia for workers. The popular regime lasted until May 21, 1871, when Thiers's army stormed Paris. At least 25,000 Parisians died in the bloody mop-up that followed. Over the long term, the state turned its attention to building a strong sense of a French nation by expanding education and army service.

Even the British Isles—seen as the quintessential nation-state and the heartland of liberalism—suffered from national divisions. Its leaders wrestled with lower-class agitation and demands for independence that Irish nationalists made so powerfully in the British House of Commons that they interfered with the smooth functioning of Parliament. More rapidly and thoroughly than elsewhere (except France), however, England responded to these pressures by gradually extending political rights to all men. Free trade and progress became the dogmas of a middle class flush with new wealth generated by industry and empire. The long reign of the popular Queen Victoria (ruled 1837–1901), as well as England's prosperity, overseas conquests, and world power, increasingly bound both workers and owners to the nation. Yet, Ireland remained England's Achilles' heel. Here, English rule was neither democratic nor beneficent. The potato famine of 1845–1850 killed more than 1 million Irish and caused many more to emigrate. The English were widely condemned for their failure to relieve the suffering; this, on top of 300 years of repressive English domination, lay behind the birth of a mass movement for Irish "home rule."

INDUSTRY, SCIENCE, AND TECHNOLOGY

> → *How did new materials and technologies transform industry and the global economy?*

A powerful combination of industry, science, and technology shaped the establishment of nation-states in North America and Western Europe and reordered the relationships between different parts of the world. The industrial sector of the world economy expanded and became more advanced after 1850 as Western Europe and North America underwent a new phase of industrial development, known as the second industrial revolution. After the 1880s, Japan, too, joined the ranks of industrializing nations as its state-led program of industrial development started to pay dividends. These changes transformed the global economy and intensified rivalries among industrial societies. Although Britain had been the leader of the earlier phase of industrial expansion, it now had to contend with competition from the United States and Germany. Between 1870 and 1913, Germany's share of world industrial output rose from 13 percent to 16 percent. The United States' output soared from 23 percent to 36 percent and surpassed Britain's, which fell from 32 percent to 14 percent.

> The breakthroughs of the second industrial revolution ushered in new business practices, most importantly mass production and the creation of the giant integrated firm.

German companies led the way in creating laboratories where university-trained chemists and physicists conducted research to serve industrial production. The United States followed the German example in consummating a profitable marriage between scientific research and capitalist enterprise. Universities and in-house corporate laboratories produced swelling ranks of engineers and scientists, as well as patents.

The breakthroughs of the second industrial revolution ushered in new business practices, most importantly mass production and the creation of the giant integrated firm. No longer would relatively modest amounts of capital suffice, as they had in Britain a century earlier when a wealthy family or a few partners were able to accumulate enough capital to establish new firms and to support industrial schemes. Now large industrial banks were major providers of funds. In Europe and the United States, limited-liability joint-stock firms provided even more powerful means of raising capital on stock markets. Companies like Standard Oil, U.S. Steel, and Siemens mobilized capital from a large number of investors, called shareholders, who because of the new limited-liability laws were no longer personally responsible for the debts of their firms. The scale of these firms was awesome. U.S. Steel alone produced over half the world's steel ingots, castings, rails, heavy structural shapes—and nearly half of all its steel plates and sheets.

NEW MATERIALS, TECHNOLOGIES, AND BUSINESS PRACTICES

New materials and new technologies were vital in late-nineteenth-century economic development. For example, steel, which was more malleable and stronger than iron, became an essential ingredient for industries like shipbuilding and railways. The world output of steel shot up from 0.5 million tons in 1870 to 28 million tons in 1900. The miracle of steel was celebrated through the construction of the Eiffel Tower (completed in 1889) in Paris, an aggressively modern monument that loomed over Paris's picturesque cityscape, and which was double the height of any other building in the world at the time. Steel was part of a bundle of new innovations that included chemicals, oil, pharmaceuticals, and mass transportation vehicles like trolleys and automobiles.

A new source of cheap energy—electricity—also came into being, which slashed the costs of production and meant that manufacturers no longer had to be close to their energy source (previously factories needed to be near running water). Scientific research also became important to industrial development. The link between science and technology, which had remained episodic until now, became systematic and was institutionalized.

INTEGRATION OF THE WORLD ECONOMY

Not only did industrial change concentrate power within North Atlantic societies, it also reinforced their power on the world economic stage. The development of new products enabled Europe and the United States to increase their exports. At the same time, the new industrial wave intensified Europe's and North America's desires to control the importing of tropical and subtropical staples. While the North Atlantic societies were still largely self-sufficient in coal, iron, cotton, wool, and wheat—the major commodities of the first industrial revolution—the second industrial revolution rendered European and North American factories reliant on rubber, copper, oil, and bauxite, which were not available domestically. Equally important, large pools of money became available for investing overseas. London may have lost its industrial leadership, but it retained its dominance over the world's financial operations. By 1913, the British had the huge sum of £4 billion overseas—funds that generated an annual income of £200 million, or one-tenth of Britain's national income.

Finally, the enlarged and more integrated world economy needed workers for the fields, factories, and mines. This led to vast movements of the laboring population seeking new opportunities and an escape from poverty. Indians moved thousands of miles to work as indentured laborers in the sugar plantations in the Caribbean, Mauritius, and Fiji, and in South African mines and on East African railroads. Chinese laborers constructed railroads in California and worked on sugar plantations in Cuba. The Irish, Poles, Jews, Italians, and Greeks flocked to North America to fill its burgeoning factories. Italians in great numbers also moved to Argentina to harvest wheat and corn.

> *The enlarged and more integrated world economy needed workers for the fields, factories, and mines, leading to vast movements of the laboring population seeking new opportunities and an escape from poverty.*

New technologies of warfare, transportation, and communication eased global economic integration—and European domination. With steam-powered gunboats and breech-loading rifles, Europeans opened new territories for trade and conquest. At home and in their colonial possessions, imperial powers constructed networks of railroads that facilitated the movement of people and goods from the hinterland to the coasts. From there, steamships carried them across the seas. The completion of the Suez Canal in 1869 shortened ship voyages between Europe and Asia and lowered the costs of intercontinental trade. Information moved even faster than cargoes, thanks to the laying of telegraph cables under the oceans, supplemented by overland telegraph lines.

The integration of the world economy also produced a bumper crop of scientific and technological innovations. Although machines were the most visible new manifestations of Euro-American confidence that the universe could be mastered, perhaps the most momentous shift in the nineteenth-century conception of nature was the product of the travels of one scientist: Charles Darwin (1809–1882). Longing to see exotic fauna, Darwin abandoned his pursuit of a clerical career. In 1831,

he signed on for a four-year voyage on the *Beagle*, a surveying vessel bound for Latin America and the South Seas—a voyage made possible by Europe's imperial expansion and mastery of the sea. As the ship's naturalist, Darwin collected vast quantities of specimens and recorded observations daily. After his return to England in 1836, he became ever more convinced that the species of organic life were not fixed, but had instead evolved under the uniform pressure of natural laws, not by means of a special, one-time creation as described in the Bible.

Darwin's theory, finally articulated in his epoch-making *Origin of Species* in 1859, laid out the principles of natural selection. Inevitably, he claimed, populations grew faster than the food supply; this condition created an equally inevitable "struggle for existence" among members of a species, the outcome of which was that the "fittest" survived to reproduce, while the less adaptable or healthy did not. Darwin's *Origin of Species* dealt exclusively with animals (and mostly with birds), yet his readers immediately realized what his theory implied for humans.

A widespread and passionate debate began among scientists and laymen, clerics and anthropologists. Some read the doctrine of the "survival of the fittest" to mean that it was natural for the strong nations to dominate the weak. In the years that followed the publication of Darwin's treatise, Europeans would repeatedly suggest that they had evolved more than Africans and Asians, and that hence nature itself gave them the right to rule others. Some asserted that Darwinian doctrines justified the right of the ruling classes to dominate the rest. A whole set of beliefs known as Social Darwinism ratified the suffering of the underclasses in industrial society: it was unnatural, Social Darwinists claimed, to tamper with natural selection.

Suez Canal. The Suez Canal opened to world shipping in 1869 and reduced the amount of time it took to sail between Europe and Asian ports. Although the French and the Egyptians supplied most of the money and the construction plans and Egyptians were the main workforce, British shipping dominated canal traffic from the outset.

IMPERIALISM

> → *What were the motives for imperialism and the practices of colonial rulers?*

One of the reasons European believed themselves "the fittest" was their success in bringing others under their rule. Expansion seemed proof of national greatness. It also became a source of new lands and opportunities, a means of dealing with inequalities that persisted at home. Increasing rivalries among nations and increasing social tensions within them produced an expansionist wave in the last half of the nineteenth century. Although Africa became the primary focus of interest, a frenzy of territorial conquest overtook Asia as well. The period between the 1860s and the 1890s witnessed the French occupation of Vietnam, Cambodia, and Laos, and the British expansion in Malaya (present-day Malaysia) in the 1870s and 1880s. The competition to establish spheres of influence in China heated up in the 1890s. Real and perceived threats to India provoked the British to conquer

Imperialism became a source of new lands and opportunities, a means of dealing with inequalities that persisted at home.

Burma (present-day Myanmar) in the 1880s. Moreover, Britain and Russia engaged in a competition for imperial preeminence from their respective outposts in Afghanistan and Central Asia. Unlike in the Americas, where expansion involved the incorporation of new territories into enlarged nations as provinces, European imperialism in Asia and Africa turned far-flung territories into colonial possessions.

INDIA AND THE IMPERIAL MODEL

The pioneering model of European empire-building to enhance domestic grandeur and extend overseas markets was Britain's imperial regime in India. In India, British expansion did not lead to territorial incorporation, nor were colonial subjects supposed to become part of a national citizenry. The British experience of ruling India provided lessons to a generation of colonial officials in Africa and other parts of Asia.

In India, methods of rule also were responses to popular discontent. Having suppressed the Indian Rebellion of 1857 (see Chapter 7), authorities revamped the colonial administration. Indians were not to be appeased—and certainly not brought into British public life.

The Mem Sahib. This late eighteenth-century painting shows a British woman surrounded by her Indian servants. European women were addressed as Mem sahib—combining "Mem," a corruption of madam, and the Hindi honorific title "sahib." The decor of the room, including both European and Indian elements, and the scene itself present an image of imperial power in an exotic setting.

But they did have to be governed, and with an iron fist. So, immediately after suppressing the rebellion and replacing East India Company rule by crown government in 1858, the British set out to make India into a more secure and productive colony, vesting authority in Her Majesty's viceroy, who was responsible to the secretary of state for India, a member of the British Cabinet. As the colonial state expanded its reach over the next several decades, the British referred to their administration of India simply as "the Raj"—a term that literally means "rule"—and provided a system for the transformation of India from private exploitation into a nationally useful colony for Britain as a whole.

The most urgent task facing the British in India was that of modernizing the subcontinent's transportation and communication system and transforming the country into an integrated colonial state. These changes had begun under Lord Dalhousie, the governor-general of the Company. During his eight-year tenure, Dalhousie oversaw the development of India's modern infrastructure. When he left office in 1856, he boasted that he had harnessed India to the "great engines of social improvement—I mean Railways, uniform Postage, and the Electric Telegraph." A year later, northern India exploded in the 1857 rebellion. But the rebellion also demonstrated the military value of railroads and telegraphs. After the British suppressed the revolt, they took up the construction of public works with renewed vigor. The railways formed a key element in this project, attracting approximately £150 million of British capital during the nineteenth century. Though the capital came from British investors, Indian taxpayers paid off the debt through their taxes. Beginning with the opening of the first railway line in 1853, the subcontinent had 30,627 miles of railway track in operation by 1910, making the Indian railways the fourth largest railway system in the world.

The construction of other public works followed. Military engineers built dams across rivers to tame their force and to channel the water to irrigate lands; workers installed a grid of telegraph lines that made communication possible between distant parts of the subcontinent. As the nineteenth century progressed, the British planned and put into place one project after another to shore up the foundations of their rule.

These public works also had an economic purpose: India was to become a consumer of British manufactures and a supplier of primary staples like cotton, jute, tea, wheat, and vegetable oil seeds. The control of India's massive rivers allowed farmers to cultivate the rich floodplains, converting large areas into lucrative cotton-producing provinces. On the hillsides of the island of Ceylon and the northeastern plains of India, the British established vast plantations to grow tea, which was then marketed in England, especially by the firm Lipton's, as a healthier alternative to Chinese green tea. Independent farmers, indentured laborers, and others under various other property systems produced these staples. Peasant producers, however, rarely saw the full returns from their labors. India also became an important consumer of British manufactures, especially textiles, which was ironic given India's cen-

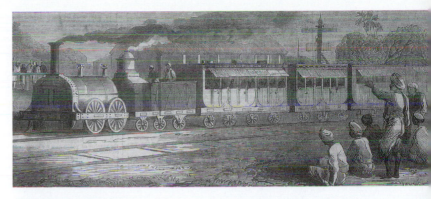

Sinews of the Raj. (*Top*) During the second half of the nineteenth century, the British built an extensive system of railroads to develop India as a profitable colony, and to maintain military security. This engraving shows the East India Railway around 1863. (*Bottom*) The British allowed several native princes to remain so long as they accepted imperial paramountcy. This photograph shows a road-building project in one such princely state. Officials of the Muslim princely ruler and British advisers supervise the workers.

turies-old tradition of producing and exporting cotton and silk textiles. In an effort to bolster sales, the British removed economic protections that benefited local textile producers—with only mixed results, as Indian entrepreneurs found ways to set up their own modern factories to rival British products.

India recorded a consistent surplus in its foreign trade through the export of agricultural goods and raw materials. But what India gained from its trade to the world it lost to Britain, its colonial master. India was forced to use its export surplus to pay for "home charges," such as interest on railroad loans, salaries to colonial officers on furlough in Britain, and the maintenance of imperial troops outside India. "Home charges" meant that India ended up balancing Britain's huge trade deficits with the rest of the world, especially the Americas. Favorable trade with India helped Britain retain its financial might and sustain the international gold standard.

Nonetheless, administrative programs had the effect of making India into a unified territory and enabling its inhabitants to regard themselves as "Indians." India had taken the first steps to becoming a "nation"—like Italy and the United States. There were, of course, profound differences: Indians lacked a single national language, and they were not citizens of their political community able to enjoy a semblance of sovereignty. Rather, they were colonial subjects ruled by outsiders.

DUTCH COLONIAL RULE IN INDONESIA

The Dutch, like the British, joined the parade of governments trying to modernize and integrate their colonies economically without integrating colonial peoples into the life of the nation at home. Decades before the British had taken control of India away from the East India Company, Holland had put an end to the rule of the Dutch East India Company over the archipelago of islands we now call Indonesia. Beginning in the 1830s, the Dutch government assumed direct administrative responsibility over Indonesian affairs. Holland's new colonial officials envisioned an even more completely regulated colonial economy than that of their British counterparts in India. For example, they ordered villagers to allocate one-third of their land for coffee bean cultivation. In return, the colonial government paid a set price (well below world market prices) and placed a ceiling on rents owed to landowners.

These policies—the rhetoric of "free trade" notwithstanding—had dreadful local consequences. Increased production of coffee beans, sugar, and tobacco led to a reduction of food production. By the 1840s and 1850s, famine spread across Java. In 1849–1850, over 300,000 Indonesians, like the Irish, perished from mass starvation. Surviving villagers voiced growing discontent, prompting harsh crackdowns by colonial forces. Back in Holland, the spectacle of colonial oppression proved embarrassing and prompted calls for reform. This led the Dutch government to introduce in the 1860s what it called an "Ethical Policy" for governing Asian colonies. This policy had the effect of reducing governmental exploitation and encouraging Dutch settlement of the islands and more private enterprise. For Indonesians, the replacement of government agents with private merchants meant little difference, however. In some areas, islanders put up fierce resistance. On the sprawling island of Sumatra, for instance, villagers armed themselves and fought off Dutch invaders. After decades of warfare, costing the lives of 4,000 Dutch soldiers, Sumatra was finally subdued in 1904, and the shipping of Indonesian staples, like sugar, tobacco, rice, tin, oil, and eventually tons of rubber, continued to bring large profits to the Dutch.

COLONIZING AFRICA

No continent felt the impact of European colonialism more powerfully than Africa. In 1880, the only two large European colonial possessions on the African continent were French Algeria and the two British-ruled South African states, the Cape Colony and Natal. By 1914, seven European states (Britain, France, Germany, Spain, Italy, Portugal, and Belgium) had carved almost all of Africa into colonial possessions (see Map 8-3). Only two corners remained independent: Liberia, thanks to American protection for this home for freed American slaves, and Ethiopia, because Emperor Menelik II (ruled 1889–1913) had harnessed a budding sense of Ethiopian national identity to a strong, well-disciplined army.

British and French forces occupied toeholds in Africa from earlier in the nineteenth century—the British in the south, the French in the north. The French had conquered Algeria in 1830 and then proceeded to expand their influence in Morocco, Tunisia, Senegal, and in Egypt, where they promoted the building of the Suez Canal (1859–1869). The canal opened a direct passage between the Mediterranean and the Red Seas and dramatically cut the costs of shipping to the Orient.

The British took the former Dutch colony of Cape Town after the Peace of 1815 ended the Napoleonic Wars. They immediately ran into trouble not just with Africans, but with fundamentalist Protestant Afrikaans speakers who had settled there under Dutch rule. Conflicts between the British and the Afrikaners (often referred to as the Boers) festered until the latter led a "Great Trek" to the interior in the 1830s to escape British rule, displacing the Bantu-speaking peoples who had previously occupied much of the area. Subsequent discoveries of diamonds and gold in the 1860s and 1880s only spurred the British to penetrate further into the interior of southern Africa, leading to more friction with Africans and Afrikaners.

With the example of French and British colonization of Africa, other Europeans rushed to the continent. As European powers joined the "scramble for Africa," Portugal called for an international conference to discuss claims to Africa. Promoted by Germany's Bismarck, this conference met in Berlin between 1884 and 1885, with delegates from Germany, Portugal, Britain, France, Belgium, Spain, Italy, the United States, and the Ottoman empire in attendance. They agreed to carve up Africa and to recognize the acquisitions of any European power that had achieved occupation on the ground.

The consequences for Africa of the European partition were devastating. Nearly 70 percent of the newly drawn borders failed to correspond to older demarcations of ethnicity, language, culture, and commerce, as Europeans knew little of the continent beyond its coast and rivers. They based colonial boundaries on European trading centers rather than on the location of the

> *The consequences of European partition of the continent for Africa were devastating, as the newly drawn borders failed to correspond to older demarcations of ethnicity, language, culture, and commerce.*

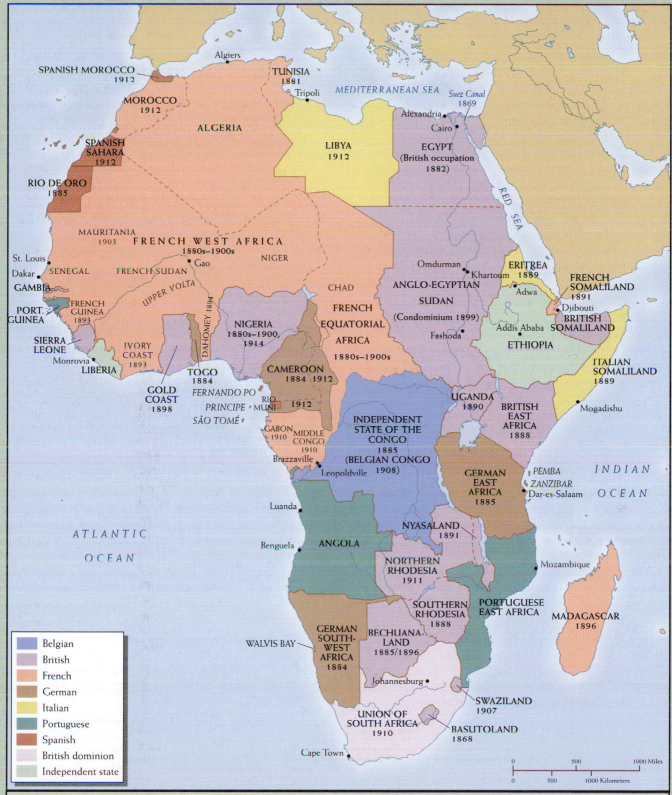

Belgian
British
French
German
Italian
Portuguese
Spanish
British dominion
Independent state

SPANISH MOROCCO
1912
Algiers
TUNISIA
1881
MEDITERRANEAN SEA
Suez Canal
1869
MOROCCO
1912
Tripoli
Alexandria
Cairo
SPANISH
SAHARA
1912
ALGERIA
LIBYA
1912
EGYPT
(British occupation
1882)
RIO DE ORO
1885
RED SEA
MAURITANIA
1903
FRENCH WEST AFRICA
1880s-1900s
St. Louis
Dakar
SENEGAL
Gao
NIGER
Omdurman
Khartoum
ERITREA
1889
FRENCH
SOMALILAND
1891
GAMBIA
FRENCH SUDAN
CHAD
ANGLO-EGYPTIAN
SUDAN
(Condominium 1899)
Adwa
Djibouti
BRITISH
SOMALILAND
PORT.
GUINEA
FRENCH
GUINEA
1893
UPPER VOLTA
NIGERIA
1880s-1900,
1914
FRENCH
EQUATORIAL
AFRICA
1880s-1900s
Addis Ababa
Fashoda
SIERRA
LEONE
IVORY
COAST
1893
DAHOMEY 1894
CAMEROON
1884 1912
ETHIOPIA
Monrovia
LIBERIA
GOLD
COAST
1898
TOGO
1884
UGANDA
1890
ITALIAN
SOMALILAND
1889
FERNANDO PO
PRINCIPE
SÃO TOMÉ
RIO
MUNI
1912
GABON
1910
MIDDLE
CONGO
1910
INDEPENDENT
STATE OF THE
CONGO
1885
(BELGIAN CONGO
1908)
BRITISH
EAST
AFRICA
1888
Mogadishu
Brazzaville
Leopoldville
GERMAN
EAST
AFRICA
1885
PEMBA
ZANZIBAR
Dar-es-Salaam
INDIAN
OCEAN
Luanda
NYASALAND
1891
ATLANTIC
OCEAN
Benguela
ANGOLA
NORTHERN
RHODESIA
1911
PORTUGUESE
EAST AFRICA
Mozambique
MADAGASCAR
1896
SOUTHERN
RHODESIA
1888
WALVIS BAY
GERMAN
SOUTH-
WEST
AFRICA
1884
BECHUANA-
LAND
1885/1896
Johannesburg
SWAZILAND
1907
UNION OF
SOUTH AFRICA
1910
BASUTOLAND
1868
Cape Town

0   500   1000 Miles
0   500   1000 Kilometers

MAP 8-3   PARTITION OF AFRICA, 1880–1939

The partition of Africa took place between the early 1880s and the outbreak of World War I. Which of the European powers gained the most territory in Africa? Lord Salisbury, prime minister of Britain, was criticized for allowing France to acquire so much territory. Why was he able to deflect this criticism by pointing out that a lot of the French territory was of little value? Cecil Rhodes wanted to acquire territory for the British that stretched from the Cape to Cairo, and Germany wanted a *Mittel Afrika* empire that connected lands on the Indian Ocean with lands along the Atlantic. Did they realize their ambitions, and if not, what powers blocked their successes?

Global Connections & Disconnections

DRAWING THE BOUNDARIES OF AFRICA

The political boundaries of contemporary Africa are largely those drawn by European colonizers. So far, the new African leaders have elected to change the names of their countries (Ghana for the Gold Coast and Zimbabwe for Southern Rhodesia, for example), but they have altered few of the boundary lines. Boundaries invariably connect and disconnect people. How well, then, did the European cartographers do? The easy, yet correct, answer is poorly. The European colonizers knew little about the geography of the interior of Africa, still characterized by them as "the dark continent," and were utterly lacking in information about Africa's ethnic groups, its long-distance trading networks, and its history. Lord Salisbury, who was British prime minister while the partition was underway, aptly summed up the problem: "We have been engaged in drawing lines upon maps where no white man's feet have ever trod; we have been giving away mountains and rivers and lakes to each other, only hindered by the small impediment that we never knew exactly where the mountains and rivers and lakes were."

Salisbury's statement reveals the European boundary-making dilemma. The colonizing powers had to lay down the basic lines of the partition—those that would separate British colonies from French and German colonies—even before their armies and colonial officials, let alone their mapmakers, had arrived on the scene. European knowledge of the interior of the continent did not extend much beyond the rivers and their basins, which had attracted much attention from earlier European travelers. European mapmakers accordingly drew the new boundaries to take account of river basins. Thus, for example, the Anglo-Egyptian Sudan and the Belgian Congo followed the river basins of the Nile and Congo Rivers. The results of such mapmaking were often catastrophic for later-day independent African states, as is clear in West Africa, where the French colony of Senegal completely surrounded the tiny British colony of Gambia (see Map A below). This geographical anomaly merely reflected pre-partition conditions, since the British had been preeminent on the Gambia River, and the French everywhere else.

But what a dilemma it has made for the modern leaders of Senegal and Gambia!

Nigeria is Africa's most populous state today, with a population of over 100 million. Its tangled postcolonial history of civil war, civil violence, and frequent military coups d'état is a direct result of the boundary-making decisions made by the British, French, and Germans as they divided up the Niger River basin area before World War I. The final arrangements turned large and powerful ethnic groups like the Ibo, Yoruba, and Hausa-Fulani peoples into bitter competitors for power in a single state. They also sliced apart large communities and even small villages that had long histories of dwelling together.

Contemporary Nigeria is surrounded by four states—Benin in the west, Niger and Chad in the north, and Cameroon in the east. The primary decisions about these borders were made between 1880 and 1900 at a time when the British, French, and Germans were only just pushing into the West African interior. These original boundaries were entirely geometrical, consisting of a series of straight lines and arcs, ignoring conditions on the ground. But they did have the advantage to the European powers of resolving the question of how far the individual European power's authority would extend. Only after the colonizers had drawn these lines did they set about the task of demarcating them on the ground and in detail. This entailed what the colonizers liked to refer to as boundary rectifications. But these could only be small adjustments; they could not overcome major problems that might have occurred as a result of the original boundary determinations. The results were altogether dismaying to many groups, such as the Mandara peoples of northeastern Nigeria and Cameroon (see Map B below). These peoples had formed a unified Islamic kingdom before the arrival of the European colonial powers; now they were split between Nigeria and Cameroon. This was not an unusual occurrence, and the number of African states that found themselves under two, or even in a few cases, three colonial administrations was quite substantial.

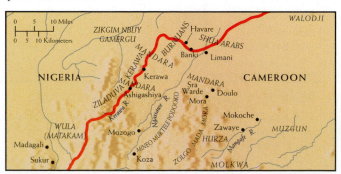

Map A

Map B

native populations. In West Africa, the Yoruba were split between the French in Dahomey and the British in southwestern Nigeria. Nigeria became an administrative nightmare, as the British endeavored to integrate the politically centralized Muslim populations of the north (Hausa, Fulani, and Kanuri) with the city-state Yoruba dwellers and small tribes of the Ibos of the south.

Several motives led the European powers into their frenzied partition of Africa. Although big European business magnates were not excited about Africa, except for Egypt and South Africa, where European investment was substantial and lucrative, smaller-scale European traders and investors were intrigued by the economic prospects on the western and eastern coasts of Africa. These smaller capitalist adventurers had some knowledge of the coastal areas, and harbored fantasies of great treasures locked in the vast uncharted interior of Africa. Politicians, publicists, and the reading public also took an in-terest in Africa. The writings of explorers like David Livingstone (1813–1873), a Scottish doctor and missionary, and Henry Morton Stanley (1841–1904), an American journalist, excited readers with accounts of Africa as a continent of unlimited economic potential and likely converts to Christianity.

The pursuit of money and converts provoked European nations to build or expand their empires by grabbing land in Africa. Europeans saw in empires a way to bring greatness to their respective nations. There was, of course, also the lure of building personal fortunes and reputations. In eastern Africa, Carl Peters (1856–1918) aspired to be the maker of a vast German colony, and he brought German East Africa into existence. In southern Africa, the British imperial apostle Cecil Rhodes (1853–1902) exclaimed that he would annex the planets if he could. Instead, he contented himself with bringing the Rhodesias, Nyasaland, Bechuanaland, the Transvaal, and the Orange Free State into

Europeans in Africa. (*Left*) Henry Morton Stanley was one of the most famous of the nineteenth-century explorers in Africa. He first made his reputation when he located the famous British missionary-explorer David Livingstone, feared dead, in the interior of Africa, uttering the famous words, "Dr. Livingstone, I presume." Stanley worked on behalf of King Leopold, establishing the Belgian king's claims to territories in the Congo and often using superior weaponry to cow African opponents. (*Right*) The ardent British imperialist, Cecil Rhodes, endeavored to bring as much of Africa as he could under British colonial rule. He had an ambition to create a swathe of British-controlled territory that would stretch all the way from the Cape in South Africa to Cairo in Egypt, as this cartoon shows.

the British empire. He was delighted that the Rhodesias bore his name, and in his later years, as his heart condition worsened, he worried about his legacy. "They can't change the name of a country, can they?" he anxiously wondered.

Even more committed to the imperialist project was Leopold II (ruled 1865–1909), king of the Belgians. Chafing at the prospect of being a minor monarch of a small European state with a population of 5 million, Leopold saw in empire a way to be a player on the world stage. As the Belgian people expressed little interest in imperial ventures, Leopold seized for himself a colonial state ten times the size of Belgium, dubbing his possession the Congo Independent State. Leopold's agent in the Congo was Henry Stanley, known to his adversaries locally as *bula matari*, the breaker of rocks. Stanley knew the Congo well, and he did not shrink from using overwhelming firepower to subdue local populations.

The Congo Independent State was unique in that it belonged to a single individual, the Belgian king. It remained Leopold's personal fiefdom until 1908, when gruesome news of the enslavement and slaughter of innocent Congolese began to leak out. Belgians were horrified, and international criticism mounted. Finally, the Belgian parliament took away Leopold's African property and made the Congo a Belgian colony.

While longing for national grandeur and personal fortunes drove many Europeans to Africa, others saw the continent as a grand opportunity for converting souls to Christianity. Europe's civilizing mission was an important motive in the scramble for African territory. In Uganda, northern Nigeria, and central Africa, missionaries went ahead of European armies, imploring the European statesmen to follow their lead.

Contrary to European assumptions, Africans did not passively wait around to be civilized; resistance, however, with few exceptions, proved futile. Africans faced two unattractive options. They could capitulate to the Europeans and seek through negotiations to limit the loss of their autonomy. Or they could fight. Only a few chose the course of moderation. Prempeh, the supreme ruler or Asantehene of the Asante, decided to spare his people a bloody confrontation with the British. But the British promptly exiled him to the Seychelles and ruled the people so imperiously that the remnants of the Asante army rose in revolt in 1900. For the most part, African leaders opted to fight to preserve their sovereignty. Lat Dior, a Muslim warlord in Senegal, refused to let the French build a railway through his kingdom. "As long as I live, be well assured," he wrote the French commandant, "I shall oppose with all my might the construction of this railway. I will always answer no, no, and I will never make you any other reply. Even were I to go to rest, my horse, *Malay*, would give you the same answer." Conflict was inevitable, and Lat Dior lost his life in a battle with the French in 1886.

In fact, only Menelik II of Ethiopia repulsed the Europeans. But Menelik had advantages that the other African resisters did not. He knew how to play off European rivals against each other, and in so doing managed to procure weapons from the French,

The Asante War. The caption for the cartoon reads, "The Asante War—Probable Results." The Asante kingdom in West Africa provided stiff resistance to British colonial rule. But the British prevailed, and, as this cartoon suggests, thought that they could make the African peoples avid consumers of British-manufactured items.

British, Russians, and Italians. He also had a united and powerful army that was reasonably well-equipped and dedicated to the Ethiopian cause. In 1896, his troops routed Italian forces at the Battle of Adwa, in which many Italians lost their lives or were captured, and the rest of the Italians scattered. Hereafter, Adwa became a celebrated moment in African history and its memory served to inspire many of Africa's later nationalist leaders.

> *The early years of European rule in Africa were full of pillage and plunder, carried out by Africa's new hunters and gatherers in pursuit of the continent's raw materials.*

Most resisters were not so fortunate. They misjudged the strength and determination of their adversaries and were ignorant of the disparity in the military technology of the Africans and the Europeans, especially the killing power of European breech-loading weapons and the Maxim machine gun (a weapon capable of firing many bullets a second). European military successes rested on more than superior weapons, however. The European armies also had better tactics and a more sustained appetite for battle. African military traditions were effective in fighting neighbors, but when it came to fighting well-equipped invaders, they were not. Africa's armies fought during the nonagricultural season, engaging in open battles so that the warriors could achieve quick and decisive results and then return to their agricultural duties. But on the open field, African forces were easy prey for European armies.

Some African forces did succeed in adapting their military techniques to the European challenge. Samori Touré (1830–1900) proved a stubborn foe for the French, employing guerrilla warfare and avoiding full-scale battles in the savannah lands of West Africa. From 1882 until 1898, Touré eluded the French. Dividing his 35,000-man army, Touré had one part take over territories not yet conquered by the French and there reestablish a fully autonomous domain. A smaller contingent of Touré's army conducted a scorched earth campaign in the regions from which it was retreating, leaving the French with parched and wasted new possessions. But these tactics only delayed the inevitable. The French finally defeated, captured, and sent Touré into exile in Gabon, where he died in 1900.

COLONIAL ADMINISTRATIONS

With so much African opposition, and so many European adventurers staking out their fiefdoms, how did imperial states establish colonial governments? The new colonial states continued to rely on superior firepower. Toward the end of Joseph Conrad's novel *Heart of Darkness*, first published in a magazine in 1899, the rapacious ivory trader, Kurtz, utters the words, "the horror, the horror" just before dying. Conrad's novel called attention to the butchery of Leopold's regime in the Congo and fueled a debate about the practice

of administration in Africa. The Congo, with its large loss of African life, may have been extreme. But it was not unique. The early years of European rule in Africa were full of pillage and plunder, carried out by Africa's new hunters and gatherers in pursuit of the continent's raw materials.

Once the euphoria of partition and conquest had worn off, power devolved to "men on the spot"—military adventurers, settlers, and avaricious entrepreneurs. Their main goal was to enrich themselves as fast as possible. Strong-willed individuals established near-fiefdoms in some areas. And Africans, like Native Americans, found themselves confined to territories where they could barely provide for themselves. To keep the colonized in their place and uphold such an invasive system, Europeans had to create permanent standing armies. They did not want to spend the money, however, on more European soldiers and administrators. Instead, the new governors armed their African supporters, who were bribed or compelled to join the side of the victors. They created the new African armies, like the *Force Publique* in the Congo, which bullied local communities into doing the bidding of the colonial authorities.

Having suppressed African revolts and subdued the civilian population, rulers had to create lasting administrations. As in India, the colonial powers in Africa laid the foundations for future nation-state organizations. By then, information trickling

Missionary School. Throughout colonial Africa, European missionary organizations dominated African education. Here, a missionary teacher oversees a class in Swahili in German East Africa just before the outbreak of World War I. Portraits of the German kaiser, Wilhelm II, and his wife are prominently displayed in the front of the classroom.

out of Africa left little doubt that the imperial governments were not realizing their goal of bringing "civilization" to the "uncivilized." To correct these failings, each European power implemented a new rationalized form of colonial rule, stripping the strongman conquerors of their absolute powers. Various terms described the policy: the Germans called their reformed system scientific colonization; the Belgians *dominer pour servir* (dominate to serve), the French *mission civilisatrice* (civilizing mission), and the British "native paramountcy."

However much the colonial administrative systems of the European states differed from each other, colonial rule was meant to satisfy three goals: First, the colony was to pay for its own administration; no mother country was willing to tax citizens at home to pay for colonial rule. Second, administrators on the spot had to preserve the peace; nothing brought swifter criticism or more rapid censure from the mother country than a colonial rebellion. Third, colonial rule was also to attract other European groups—missionaries, settlers, and merchants—who would help to promote economic growth in Africa and pay the expenses of colonial authority as well as generate income for African workers and European investors. These three goals were, of course, often incompatible, and would eventually undermine colonial polities in Africa.

For the moment, stabilized, rationalized colonies did begin to deliver on their economic promise. Early imperialism in Africa had been based on the export of ivory and wild rubber. When overexploitation depleted these resources at the turn of the century, the colonies in Africa turned to a new range of exports. From the tropical rain forests came cocoa, coffee, palm oil, and palm kernels, cultivated mainly by small-scale African farmers, who responded quickly to the prospects of growing these new products. In the highlands of East Africa, tea, coffee, sisal (used in cord and twine), and pyrethrum (a flower used to make insecticide) became the major exports, though these tended to be cultivated on European settler farms. Another important commodity was long-staple, high-quality cotton, grown in abundance in Egypt and the Anglo-Egyptian Sudan. From across Africa, as from India and Latin America, tropical commodities flowed to industrializing societies.

African resources generated new streams of wealth, though little of this found its way to African laborers. Much went to the colonial administrations, which derived their revenue mainly from import and export taxes. Another large slice went to the great European export-import firms. European banking and shipping companies also profited. Only after these groups had taken their share did the rest trickle down to the cultivators.

Thus, European colonial administrators saw Africa, like India, as fitting into the world economy in the comfortable

niche of exporter of raw materials and importer of manufactures. They expected Africa to profit from its incorporation into the world economy. But, in truth, the African workers gained little from participating in colonial commerce, while the price they paid in disruption to traditional social and economic patterns was substantial. Women took care of domestic needs, while men worked for wages or sold cash crops such as peanuts and cocoa at markets. Unable to contest the disadvantageous terms of trade enforced by public policy and private monopolies of export-import houses, African peasant producers benefited even less than European workers from the new scale and scope of world trade.

The disruptions to traditional life were particularly acute in southern Africa, where mining operations lured African men thousands of miles from their homes. Katanga and parts of South Africa were, in the opinion of one mining expert, "a geological scandal," so abundant were the deposits of gold, diamonds, and copper. With cash advances, European companies lured African workers from their villages to the mines, but indebted laborers often had difficulty paying off these loans. Meanwhile, it fell to women to take care of subsistence and cash crop production in the home villages. By the turn of the century, the gold mines of Witwatersrand in South Africa required a workforce of 100,000. Miners had to be drawn from as far away as Mozambique, the Rhodesias, and Nyasaland, as well as from South Africa itself. Work below ground was hazardous, and the health services were inadequate. Once aware of these conditions, workers often tried to flee. But their debts, as well as armed guards and barbed-wired compounds, kept them in the mines. In the diamond mines, workers were strip-searched before being discharged to prevent diamond smuggling. The companies made enormous profits for their European shareholders, while the workers toiled in dangerous conditions and barely eked out a living wage.

To the outside observer, the European empires of the late nineteenth century were solid and durable institutions, but in fact, European colonial rule was fragile. The staffing of imperial armies and administrations required the recruitment of many Africans. For all of British Africa, the only all-British force was 5,000 men, garrisoned in Egypt. Elsewhere in colonial territories, European officers commanded African military and police forces. The colonial civil services were equally thin on the ground and profoundly dependent on the participation of the colonized. Prior to 1914, the number of British administrative officers available for the whole of northern Nigeria was less than 500. These were hardly powerful—never mind permanent—foundations for statehood. It would not take much to destabilize the European order in Africa.

> *European colonial administrators saw Africa, like India, as fitting into the world economy in the comfortable niche of exporter of raw materials and importer of manufactures.*

Diamond Mine. The discovery of diamonds and gold in South Africa in the late nineteenth century led to the investment of large amounts of overseas capital, the mobilization of a large number of poorly paid and severely exploited African mine workers, and the South African War of 1899 to 1902, which resulted in the incorporation of the Afrikaner states of the Transvaal and the Orange Free State into the Union of South Africa.

THE AMERICAN EMPIRE

Imperial adventurism was not limited to European powers. In the United States, too, overseas expansion offered a means to create new frontiers and to restore prosperity to the American economy during the economic doldrums of the 1890s. Low agricultural prices and industrial overproduction spurred a quest for export markets. Expansion overseas also had the added virtue of bringing Americans together in a common purpose—to civilize others and secure the nation against bothersome neighbors who just happened to have darker skins. Echoing the rhetoric of Manifest Destiny from the 1840s, the expansionists of the 1890s claimed that Americans still had a divine mission to spread their superior civilization and their Christian faith around the globe. In the 1890s, however, America's new imperialists chose to emulate the European model of colonialism in Asia and Africa: colonies were to provide harbors for American vessels, supply raw materials to American industries, and buy the surplus production of American farms and factories. America's new territorial acquisitions were not intended for American settlement or destined for American statehood. Nor were their inhabitants to become American citizens, for nonwhite foreigners were deemed unfit for incorporation into the American nation.

The pressure to expand came to a head in the late 1890s, when the United States declared war on Spain and invaded the

> *In the United States, too, overseas expansion offered a means to create new frontiers and to restore prosperity to the American economy during the economic doldrums of the 1890s.*

Philippines, Puerto Rico, and Cuba. From 1895, Cuban patriots had slowly pushed back Spanish troops and had begun to occupy sugar plantations—some of which belonged to American planters. Concerned about the specter of social revolution off the shores of Florida, the American expansionists presented themselves as the saviors of Spanish colonials yearning for freedom, while at the same time safeguarding property for foreign interests in the Spanish-American War (1898). After easily defeating Spanish regulars in Cuba, American forces began disarming Cuban rebels and returning lands to their owners.

Although the Americans had claimed that they were intervening to promote freedom in Spain's colonies, they quickly forgot their promises. The United States quietly annexed Puerto Rico after minimal resistance. Cubans and Filipinos met American plans to make them into colonial subjects with insurrection. Bitterness ran particularly high among Filipinos who had been promised independence by American leaders if they joined in the war against Spain. Betrayed, Filipino rebels launched a war for independence in the name of a Filipino nation. In two years of fighting, over 5,000 Americans and perhaps 200,000 Filipinos perished.

Colonies in the Philippines and Cuba laid the foundations for a revised model of twentieth-century U.S. expansionism. The

"That wicked man is going to gobble you up, my child!"

Uncle Sam Leading Cuba. In the years before the Spanish-American War, cartoonists who wished to see the United States intervene on behalf of Cuba in the islanders' struggle for independence from Spain typically depicted Cuba as a white woman in distress. By contrast, in this and other cartoons following the Spanish-American War, Cubans were drawn as black, and usually as infants or boys unable to care for themselves and in need of the benevolent paternal rule of the United States.

earlier pattern had been to turn Indian lands into privately owned farmsteads and to expand the reach of the Atlantic market across the continent. This now yielded to a new era in which the nation's largest corporations, supported by the enlarged power of the American national government, aggressively intervened in the affairs of near and distant neighbors. Following the Spanish-American War, the United States regularly sent troops to many Caribbean and Central American countries. The Americans preferred to make these regimes into dependent client states, however, rather than making them part of the United States itself or converting them into formal colonies as the Europeans had done in Africa and Asia.

IMPERIALISM AND CULTURE

Overseas empires transformed Europeans and North Americans at home as well as colonial subjects abroad. The change did not stop at economic profits; it also redefined the meaning of belonging to a "British," "Belgian," or "American" nation. Ideas of

racial superiority associated with Social Darwinism gave Europeans the conviction that natural laws had destined them to lead "the civilizing mission." The idea that Europe had the power, and even the patriotic duty, to "civilize" the so-called backward world had old roots. What was novel in the late nineteenth century was the deployment of imperial images to buttress the legitimacy of the European nation-states. Many in Europe believed that empire would lift Europe out of the worries associated with regional and class friction and create a new sense of national purpose. David Livingstone, who went to Africa to "open a path for commerce and Christianity," helped to popularize the idea of the "civilizing mission." After he died in Africa in 1873, he was buried as a national hero in Westminster Abbey. Political pressure groups like the Imperial Federation League, the British Empire League, and the Primrose League celebrated imperial expansion; the Pan-German League made a similar case for German colonies; and the Comité de l'Afrique Française championed empire in France.

In Britain, the foremost colonial power, the cultural and political force of empire reshaped royalty itself, transforming Queen Victoria's image. Between 1861, the year of her husband's

The Civilizing Mission. This advertisement for Pears' Soap shamelessly tapped into the idea of Europeans bringing civilization to the people of their colonies. It said that use of Pears' Soap would teach the virtues of cleanliness to the "natives" and implied that it would even lighten their skin.

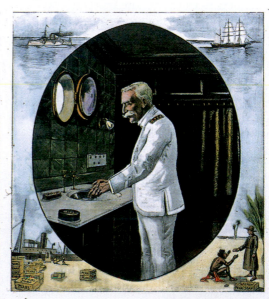

The first step towards lightening

The White Man's Burden

is through teaching the virtues of cleanliness.

Pears' Soap

is a potent factor in brightening the dark corners of the earth as civilization advances, while amongst the cultured of all nations it holds the highest place—it is the ideal toilet soap.

death, and 1876, the queen had made few public appearances. But after 1876, her image as a grieving and distant widow evolved into that of an imperial matriarch who ruled over her native subjects with nurturing care. The Tory prime minister, Benjamin Disraeli (1804–1881), orchestrated this transition by having her crowned, in 1877, empress of India. The event ushered in a regular ceremonial tradition to applaud British greatness overseas.

Imperial triumphs were widely celebrated. Once the invention of photographic film and the appearance of the Eastman Kodak camera in 1888 revolutionized the visual media, imperial images surfaced routinely in popular forms such as postcards and advertisements. These images recorded imperial achievements in transport, engineering, and architecture, showed contented colonial subjects, commemorated visits by royal figures, and celebrated colonial conquests. Imperial themes and myths were widely used in packaging materials, and tins of coffee, tea, tobacco, and chocolates featured pictures that highlighted the colonial origins of these commodities. Cigarettes often had names like "Admiral," "Royal Navy," "Fighter," and "Grand Fleet."

This glorification of colonial adventure elevated the importance of motherhood. Champions of empire argued that if the British population did not grow fast enough to fill the sparsely settled regions around the globe, the population of other nations would. Population was power, and the number of children provided an accurate measure of global influence. But the concern was not just for children, but particularly for healthy children. Wars in the colonies exemplified the need for an abundant and healthy soldiery. "Empire cannot be built on rickety and flat-chested citizens," warned a British member of Parliament in 1905. Another British ideologue touted the German example of patriotic mothers nurturing "a land devoted to the three Ks—*Kinder, Küche, Kirche* [Children, Kitchen, and Church]." Thus did the desire for healthy bodies also entail the idealization of domesticity as women's destiny and duty.

Just as motherhood was exalted, imperial cultures also touted a new model of adventurous boyhood. Elite British schools, which became the training ground for the colonial service, actively taught a sense of imperial mission and adventure. A boys' juvenile literature emerged in the 1880s. While earlier juvenile literature had spoken chiefly to audiences according to class, now it spoke to audiences organized on the basis of gender. Where girls' literature stressed domestic service, childrearing, and nurturing, boys' readings described exotic locales, depicted devious Orientals and savage Africans, and extolled daring colonial exploits. No one evoked this notion of empire as boyish adventure better than Rudyard Kipling (1865–1936) in his immensely popular novels and short stories. Born in India, Kipling was dispatched to an English boarding school at a young age. Compared with his carefree childhood in India, the public school provided a dreary, regimented experience, and it furnished him with an enduring subject matter—the interaction between youth and unpleasant authority. His most popular novel, *Kim* (1901), described the life of a thirteen-year-old

Irish boy, Kim, who goes "native," and then participates in a wondrous "Great Game," a spy adventure pitting the British against the Russians over Central Asia.

JAPAN, RUSSIA, AND CHINA

⇨ *How did expansionism affect Japan, Russia, and China?*

The challenge of integrating political communities and extending territorial borders was a problem not just for the nations of Western Europe and the United States. Other societies also aimed to overcome domestic dissent and to extend their command over larger domains. Japan, Russia, and China provide three contrasting models of expansionism; their differing forms of expansion led these societies to converge on—and eventually fight over—East Asian possessions.

JAPANESE TRANSFORMATION AND EXPANSION

Starting in the 1860s, Japanese rulers sought to recast their country to look less like an old dynasty and more like a modern nation-state. Since the early seventeenth century, the Tokugawa Shogunate had kept outsiders within strict limits and thwarted internal unrest. But an American officer, Commodore Matthew Perry (1794–1858), entered Edo Bay in 1853, leading a fleet of steam-powered ships. Other Americans, as well as Russian, Dutch, and British intruders, entered Japan's ports and forced its rulers to sign humiliating treaties, which opened Japanese ports, slapped limits on Japanese tariffs, and exempted foreigners from Japanese laws. Younger Japanese, especially among the military (samurai) elites, felt that Japan should respond by adopting, not rejecting, Western practices. In 1868, a group of these reformers toppled the Tokugawa Shogunate and promised to return Japan to its mythic greatness. When they forced the shogun to resign, Emperor Mutsuhito, known as the Meiji Emperor ("Enlightened Rule"), became the symbol of a new Japan. His reign, from 1868 to 1912, was referred to as the Meiji Restoration. By founding schools, initiating an active propaganda campaign, and revamping the army to create a single "national" fighting force, the new government put forward a new model of political community. The new nationalists stressed linguistic and ethnic homogeneity—as well as superiority compared to others. In this fashion, the Meiji leaders overcame age-old regional divisions, subdued local political magnates, and mobilized the country to face the threat of the powerful Europeans.

One of the Meiji period's remarkable achievements was the economic transformation of the island. In 1871, the government banned the feudal system and allowed peasants to become small landowners. Farmers subsequently improved their agrarian techniques, and saw their standard of living rise. Some business practices that underlay the economic transformation had taken shape under the shogunate, but the new government was far more activist. Under the slogan "rich country, strong army," it unified the currency around the yen, created a postal system, introduced tax reforms, laid telegraph lines, formed compulsory foreign trade associations, launched savings and export campaigns, established an advanced civil service system, began to build railroads, and hired thousands of foreign consultants. In 1889, the Meiji oligarchs introduced a constitution, based largely on the German model. The following year, 450,000 people—about 1 percent of the population—elected Japan's first parliament, the Imperial Diet. When the Japanese people resisted various initiatives, they were exhorted to "yield as the grasses before the wind."

The government also sold valuable enterprises to the people it knew best, creating private economic dynasties. By the 1890s, however, the government's role became more indirect, and private capital took greater initiative. Of the country's pow-

> *In contrast to American limited-liability firms, which issued shares on stock markets to anonymous buyers, Japan's version of managerial capitalism was a personal and family affair.*

erhouse family-holding companies such as Sumitomo, Yasuda, Mitsubishi, and Mitsui, only the last pre-dated 1868. The new giant firms were family organizations. Fathers, sons, cousins, and uncles participated, running different parts of large integrated corporations—some in charge of banks, some running the trade wing, and others overseeing factories. Women played a crucial role—not just as custodians of the home, but as cultivators of important family alliances, especially among potential marriage partners. In contrast to American limited-liability firms, which issued shares on stock markets to anonymous buyers, Japan's version of managerial capitalism was a personal and family affair.

As in many other emerging nation-states, expansion was a tempting prospect. It offered markets in which to sell goods and procure staples and a way to burnish the image of national superiority and greatness. Although the Japanese leaders modeled their expansionism on European practices, their overarching goal was to secure a sphere of influence against rivals.

Japanese ventures abroad were initially spectacularly successful. The Meiji moved first to take over the kingdom of the Ryūkyūs, located southwest of Japan (see Map 8-4). In 1872, the Meiji government made it clear that it intended to incor-

Economic Transformation of Japan. During the Meiji period, the government transformed the economy by building railroads, laying telegraph lines, founding a postal system, and encouraging the formation of giant firms known as *zaibatsu*, which were family organizations consisting of factories, import-export businesses, and banks. Here we see a raw-silk reeling factory that was run by one of the *zaibatsu*.

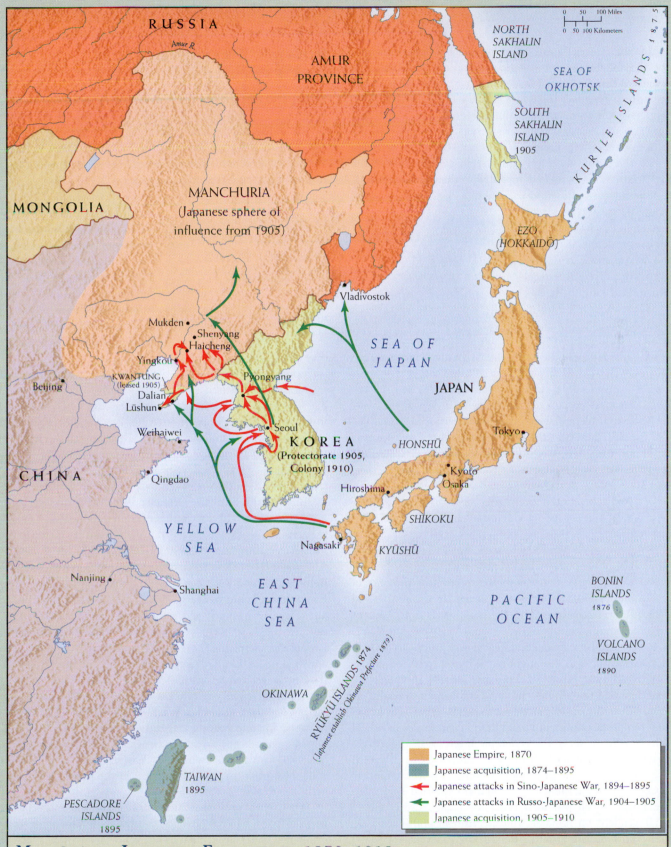

Legend:
- Japanese Empire, 1870
- Japanese acquisition, 1874–1895
- Japanese attacks in Sino-Japanese War, 1894–1895
- Japanese attacks in Russo-Japanese War, 1904–1905
- Japanese acquisition, 1905–1910

MAP 8-4 JAPANESE EXPANSION, 1870–1910

Follow the chronology and geography of Japan's expansion. Is there a "logic" to the process of Japanese expansionism? From acquiring Taiwan as a colony, to annexing South Sakhalin Island and Korea, to establishing a sphere of influence in Manchuria, in what ways does geography help us to understand the policies of Japan? What were Japan's objectives? How were they similiar to or different from European expansionism of the same period?

porate the kingdom fully into the Japanese polity—to the dismay of the inhabitants of the largest of the Ryūkyūs, the Okinawans. A small show of force, only 160 Japanese soldiers, was enough to establish the new Okinawa Prefecture in 1879. The Japanese annexed Okinawa, but treated it as a subordinate part of the nation. They regarded the people of the Ryūkyūs as an ethnic minority and refused to incorporate them into the nation-state on equal terms. Suspicious of the Ryūkyū aristocrats—who had appealed to the Chinese for military help against the annexationists—the Japanese conquerors refused to train a "native" governing class, as the British were doing in India and the Americans were doing in Puerto Rico. Meiji intellectuals insisted that the "backward" Okinawans were unfit for local self-rule and representation.

In 1876, the Japanese turned to the Asian mainland and fixed upon Korea, which put Meiji plans on a collision course with what the Chinese considered their sphere of influence. In a formal treaty, the Japanese recognized Korea as an independent state, opened Korea to trade, and were given extraterritorial rights. The Chinese worried that soon the Japanese would try to take over Korea. These fears were well-founded, for nationalist Japanese leaders regarded the peninsula, in the words of one of their German advisers, as "a dagger pointed at the heart of Japan." Japanese designs on Korea eventually brought on the Sino-Japanese War of 1894–1895 in which the Chinese suffered a humiliating defeat.

The Sino-Japanese War accelerated Japan's rapid transformation to a nation-state and colonial power with no peer in Asia. China was the big loser and was forced to cede the province of Taiwan to the Japanese. Japan also annexed Korea in 1910 and converted Taiwan and Korea into the twin jewels of its nascent empire. The colonial administration built transportation networks and created educational and health institutions to develop its colonies—while still keeping the colonized from top managerial and technical positions. Like the British in India, the Japanese regarded the peoples they had colonized as racially inferior and unworthy of the privileges that they enjoyed at home. Like other imperial powers of the day, the Japanese also expected their possessions to serve the economic interests of the metropolitan center. Japan, densely populated and short of land, wished these colonies to become granaries, sending rice to the mother country. Moreover, the Meiji regime further exploited Taiwanese sugar exports, which provided relief for a Japanese economy heavily dependent on imports. Indeed, Korean and Taiwanese farmers exported their produce to the rest of Asia, especially China. These staple-exporting regions thereby provided Japan with a source of foreign exchange to help defray its trade deficits, incurred as a result of massive imports to build up new industries.

RUSSIAN TRANSFORMATION AND EXPANSION

Russia also embarked on expansion in the late nineteenth century, both out of a sense of mission and as a defensive response to the expansion of countries along its immense border. An emerging Germany, a British presence in the Middle East and Persia, a consolidating China, and an ascendant Japan meant that Russia, too, would have to enlarge its domain. What is remarkable is how many expansionist fronts Russia opened simultaneously. Russians went southwest to the Black Sea, south into the Caucasus and Turkestan, and east into Manchuria (see Map 8-5). Success depended on adopting techniques akin to those used on the American frontier: annexing territories as provinces and establishing protectorates over the vulnerable peoples it conquered.

> *Russia's defeat in the Crimean War spurred the authorities on a course of aggressive modernization and expansion.*

Looking to expand to the west and the south, Russia invaded the Ottoman territories of Moldavia (present-day Moldova) and Walachia (present-day Romania) in 1853. The invasion provoked opposition from Britain and France, who joined with the Ottomans to defeat Russia in the Crimean War (1853–1856). The defeat exposed Russia's military weaknesses, including a lack of modern weapons and problems supplying troops over long distances without a railway system.

Russia's defeat in the Crimean War had a similar, yet even more immediate, effect than that of Commodore Perry's 1853 intrusion into Japan: it spurred the authorities on a course of aggressive modernization and expansion. In the 1860s, Tsar Alexander II (ruled 1855–1881) launched a wave of "Great Reforms." These were designed to make Russia more competitive without going too far politically. Autocratic rule remained, but officials revamped and reintegrated the society they oversaw. In 1861, a decree emancipated peasants from serfdom. Landowners kept the most fertile land, however, and the peasants had to pay large redemption taxes for the poor-quality land they received. Other changes included a reduction in military service from twenty-five years to six, schooling for the conscripts, and the beginnings of a mass school system to teach children reading and writing and Russian culture. Beginning in the 1890s, railroads spread and factories expanded, as did the steel, coal, and petroleum industries. Peasants who could not make ends meet often wound up working in the newly built factories or in the mines.

The reforms revealed a fundamental problem: officials were more interested in reforming society than in reforming the government. This caused many—liberals, conservatives, and malcontents alike—to question the state-led modernizing mission. In the press, courtrooms, and streets, men and women denounced the regime. Revolutionaries, forbidden from forming legal political parties, engaged in terror and assassination. In 1881, a ter-

→ *How did expansionism affect Japan, Russia, and China?*

MAP 8-5   RUSSIAN EXPANSION, 1801–1914

If you compare this map on Russian expansion with Map 4-7 in Chapter 4 (p. 151), you will see that the Russian empire continued to expand into vast territories in Eurasia. Did the territorial weight of the expanded Russian empire change? Did Russia become a predominantly European power or an Asian empire or both? About how many countries did Russia acquire borders with as a result of its expansion? Russia's ambition was to gain access to the sea, especially to warm-water ports. Which acquisitions helped it to realize this goal?

rorist bomb blew the tsar to pieces. In the 1890s, following yet another period of famine, the radical doctrines of Marxism gained popularity in Russia. Even aristocratic intellectuals, such as Count Leo Tolstoy, lamented their despotic government.

Yet, the shortcomings of internal reform did not interfere with the ambitions—and achievements—of Russian expansionists. Expansionism added to the domestic and international prestige of the regime. Thus, the 1860s conquest of

> *The shortcomings of internal reform did not interfere with the ambitions—and achievements—of Russian expansionists.*

Turkestan enabled Russia's military to boast of its prowess against an outgunned foe, and it reinforced the image of a great power able to defend its borders in Asia Minor, especially against the British. Moreover, as in the United States, the acquisition of new territories was seen as a means to defuse rural unrest by providing peasants with frontier lands. Russian peasants migrated to Turkestan after its conquest, and by 1916, agrarian newcomers made up over one-third of Turkestan's population. Even more important, Russian expansionists believed that they had to take over certain lands to prevent them from falling into the hands of rivals. Thus, for example, they conquered the highland people of the Caucasus Mountains to prevent the Ottomans and Persians from taking over this area on Russia's southern flank. And they butted heads with the British over the areas between Turkestan and British India, such as Persia (Iran) and Afghanistan, in a competition known as "The Great Game." While Russians moved to the lands they had conquered, however, they never made up the majority there. The new provinces still consisted of multiethnic and multireligious communities that were only partially integrated into the Russian state.

> *The Russian empire was huge, and its rulers were only partially effective at integrating its disparate parts into a political community.*

Perhaps the most impressive Russian expansion transpired in East Asia. Here Russian ambitions came into conflict with the Chinese, who had also sought to occupy and colonize the vast, underpopulated area of the Amur River basin (just north of Manchuria, with rich lands and mineral deposits and access to the Pacific Ocean). After wrestling with the Chinese between 1840 and 1860, the Russians eventually acquired land both north and south of the Amur River and in 1860 founded Vladivostok, a port on the Pacific Ocean. Deciding to put its money and efforts into exploiting these areas in Asia, the Russian government sold Alaska, its only overseas possession, to the United States (for $7.2 million) in 1867, and thus no longer had to overextend itself to govern and defend this territory in North America. To link the capital (Moscow) and the western part of the country

to its East Asian spoils, it began construction of the Trans-Siberian Railroad. When it was completed in 1903, after thirteen years of hard labor, the new railroad created an overland bridge between the east and the west. Russia then began to eye the Korean peninsula, on which Japan, too, had set its sights.

This was a huge empire—one-sixth of the world's land mass—and its rulers were only partially effective at integrating its disparate parts into a political community. In 1897, the Russian government took its first complete population census. Ethnographers and political authorities struggled to figure out what to call and how to classify all of the peoples inhabiting the empire. Should they be considered as nations or tribes? In the end, the census opted for the term "nationalities," recognizing 104 of them, speaking 146 languages and dialects. Ethnic Russians accounted for slightly more than half the population.

Counting and categorizing peoples formed part of the state's attempts to figure out how to govern this diverse realm. Russia did not follow Britain's policy in India, that is, creating a small but efficient bureaucracy and imposing law through a trained "native" elite. Rather, as in the United States, conquered regions were made full parts of the empire. But unlike the United States, Russia was suspicious of decentralized federalism, fearing that this would lead to secession. Moreover, Russia's tsars were terrified by the idea of popular sovereignty. They preferred the tried and true method of centralized autocracy. With the exceptions of two "protectorates," Bukhara and Khiva, and the Grand Duchy of Finland, no province enjoyed self-rule. The rest of the empire was divided into governorships ruled by appointed civilian or military governors who had varying powers, depending on the distance from Moscow and the national makeup of the population under their supervision.

Unlike the other transcontinental nation-empire, the United States, which displaced or slaughtered native populations during expansion, Russia faced a more daunting task of assimilating new peoples. State treatment of the empire's peoples was inconsistent, ranging from outright repression (Poles, Jews) to favoritism (Baltic Germans, Finns). In the western regions, linguistic "Russification" programs provoked opposition from those upon whom it was applied. In the south and east, Russians built cities and garrisons alongside the indigenous towns, leaving the local elites in place and trying to co-opt them. But this, too, had its limitations. Further, unlike the United States, which managed to pacify its borders with its weaker neighbors, Russia faced the constant suspicions of Persians and Ottomans, and the menace of British troops in Afghanistan that were sent to prevent Russia from cutting off the overland route to India. And in East Asia, a clash with expansionist Japan loomed on the horizon. Russia's expansionism meant that defending its borders was a constant fiscal drain and a heavy burden on the

The Trans-Siberian Railroad. Russia's decision to build an extremely costly railway across the rugged expanses of Siberia to the Pacific Ocean derived from a desire to expand the empire's power in East Asia and simultaneously to forestall British advances in Asia. The colossal undertaking, which claimed the lives of thousands of workers, reached completion just as Russia clashed militarily with Japan. The new railroad ferried Russian troops over very long distances to battles, such as the one at Mukden, in Manchuria, which was then the largest land battle in the history of warfare and observed by military attachés from all the great powers.

TWO FACES OF EMPIRE

"Russification" (forced assimilation) became one of the Russian empire's responses to the challenge of the nation-state idea. In 1863, the tsar prohibited publication of the Bible in the Little Russian (Ukrainian) language, alienating many otherwise loyal Slavic subjects. By contrast, most non-Christians, such as the Muslim peoples of newly annexed Turkestan (Central Asia), were exempted from Russification as they were considered "aliens" who should be ruled separately. Here, the bureaucracy prohibits use of Ukrainian in an 1876 Russification edict, while G. P. Fedorov of the Russian governor-general's office in Turkestan celebrates colonialism.

Russification in Ukraine In order to halt what is, from the state's point of view, the dangerous activity of the Ukrainophiles, it is appropriate to take the following measures immediately: 1. To prohibit the import into the empire of any books published abroad in the Little Russian dialect [Ukrainian], without the special permission of the Chief Press Administration. 2. To prohibit the printing inside of the empire of any original works or translations in this dialect, with the exception of historical documents. . . . 3. Equally to prohibit any dramatic productions, musical lyrics and public lectures (which at present have the charter of Ukrainophile demonstrations) in this dialect. 4. To support the publication in Galicia of the newspaper *Slovo*, hostile to Ukrainophilism, assigning it a small but permanent subsidy. . . . 6. To strengthen supervision by the local educational administration so as not to allow any subjects in primary schools be taught in the Little Russian dialect. . . . 7. To clear the libraries of all primary and secondary schools in the Little Russian provinces of books and pamphlets prohibited by paragraph 2. . . . 8. . . . To demand from the heads of these districts a list of teachers with a note as to their reliability in relation to Ukrainophile tendencies. Those noted as unreliable or doubtful should be transferred to Great Russian provinces. . . .

Colonialism in Turkestan Our battalion arrived in Tashkent four years after Turkestan had been annexed to the empire. Tashkent at that time looked more like a military settlement than the chief city of the region, that is the capital of Russian Central Asia. The majority of the inhabitants were soldiers, either resting after some campaign or else about to go out on a new expedition. Civilians and women were a rarity. Now, thirty-six years later, looking proudly at the path we have followed, I can see the colossal results achieved by the Russian government, always humane to the vanquished, but insistently pursuing its civilising mission. Of course, there have been many mistakes, there have been abuses, but this has not halted the rational and expedient intentions of the government. We went into a region which had a population alien to us. . . . They had for many centuries been accustomed to submitting humbly to the barbaric and cruel despotism of their rulers, but they nevertheless came to terms with their position because their rulers were of their own faith. . . . The fanatical mullahs began rumours amongst the mass of the population that, instead of true believer khans, they were to be ruled by heathens who would convert them to Christianity, put crosses around their necks, send them to be soldiers, introduce their own laws, revoke the Sharia [the fundamental law of Islam] and make their wives and daughters uncover their faces.

. . . Frequent outbursts, uprisings and disorders took place and repression followed. But at the same time the natives saw that the very first steps of the first Governor-General proved the complete falseness of the mullahs. . . . It was announced solemnly everywhere to the local population, that as subjects of the Russian monarch, the population would keep its faith, its national customs, its courts and its judges, that all taxes demanded by the previous collectors were illegal and burdensome in the extreme and would be revoked, and that instead just taxes would be imposed, and that the position of women would remain inviolable. All this of course soon calmed the population and an industrious people settled down to a peaceful life.

Source: Martin McCauley and Peter Waldron, *The Emergence of the Modern Russian State, 1855–1881* (Totowa, NJ: Barnes and Noble Books, 1988), pp. 209, 211–12.

population. To promote the image of a great Russian empire, rulers had to lean more heavily on the rural poor and to pursue more intensive modernization strategies, but all that generated instability. For the time being, however, the main threat, as far as Moscow was concerned, did not come from within Russia's borders. It came from the outside.

CHINA UNDER PRESSURE

While the Russians and Japanese scrambled to emulate European models of industrialism and imperialism, the Qing, in the wake of China's territorial expansion in the eighteenth century (see Chapter 6), were slower to mobilize against threats from the West. For a long time, the Chinese were not inclined to see the Europeans as serious threats. Through the early decades of the nineteenth century, Qing leaders consistently underestimated the challenges of European and American economic aggression. Historically, they were much more worried about internal revolts and overland threats from the dynasty's northern borders. This is why the Treaty of Nanjing's stipulations (following the Opium War of 1839–1842) calling for indemnities, the opening of a few extra ports, including Shanghai, and the cession of the sparsely populated island of Hong Kong to the British, seemed a small price to pay to satisfy the demands of these lesser aggressors. Into the 1850s and 1860s, the dynasts continued to be more concerned with dissenters from within. The Taiping Rebellion (1851–1864; see Chapter 7), having nearly toppled the regime, was the kind of threat that authorities most feared, given that it had weakened the central government, wasted agrarian lands, drained the treasury, created waves of refugees, and bolstered the power of local magnates. Many Qing officials still considered foreigners a minor—if noisy—nuisance.

A growing number of officials, however, recognized the superior armaments and technology of rival powers. Starting in the 1860s, reformist Chinese bureaucrats sought to adopt elements of Western learning and technological skills, but with the intention of keeping the core of Chinese culture intact. Collectively known as the "Self-Strengthening Movement," these measures included a variety of new ventures: arsenals, shipyards, coal mines, a steamship company to contest the foreign domination of coastal shipping, and schools for learning foreign ways and languages. The most interesting was the dispatch abroad of about 120 schoolboys under the charge of Yung Wing. Yung, having graduated from Yale University in 1854, was the first Chinese graduate of an American college and believed that Western education would greatly benefit Chinese students. Yung took his charges to Hartford, Connecticut, in the 1870s to attend school and live with American families. The experiment did not go well from the point of view of the Chinese authorities. In 1881, after the U.S. government refused to admit the boys into military academies, conservatives at the Qing court, dismayed by the travelers' liking for Christianity and aptitude for baseball, summoned the students home.

Yung Wing's abortive educational mission was not the only setback for the Self-Strengthening Movement. Skepticism about the wisdom of appropriating Western technology was rife among conservative officials. Some insisted that the introduction of machinery would only have an adverse effect on a country with as big a population as China's, since it would lead to unemployment. Even more adamant was the opposition to the construction of railways. Detractors maintained railways would simply facilitate Western military maneuvers and lead to an invasion of the country. Others complained that the crisscrossing tracks were an affront to aesthetic sensibilities and disturbed the harmony between humans and nature. The first short railway track ever laid in China was torn up in 1877 shortly after it was built. Indeed, there were a mere 288 kilometers of track in China prior to 1895, less than a tenth of the total boasted by the small island nation of Japan.

Even without the railways, however, the Chinese were on the move. The population explosion of the previous centuries and the increasing shortage of arable land forced many to head to the frontier areas, such as Manchuria or to Southeast Asia and beyond. In some cases these migrations facilitated the further consolidation of the polity. For example, the northwestern region of Xinjiang, which had been incorporated into the Qing empire in the eighteenth century, became a full-fledged province in 1884. Similarly, Taiwan, soon to be lost to Japan, earned provincial status the following year.

Although they did not acknowledge the usefulness of the railroad, the Chinese did take advantage of other new technologies to gain access to a wider range of information more quickly than ever before. That was particularly true for those residing in the coastal cities. By the early 1890s, there were about a dozen Chinese-language newspapers (as distinct from the foreign-language press) published in the major cities, with the largest ones based in Shanghai and having a circulation of 10,000 to 15,000 each. To avoid government intervention, these papers were careful to sidestep political controversy. Instead, they emphasized commercial news and often accepted literary contributions. In 1882, *Shenbao*, the newspaper with perhaps the largest circulation, made use of a new telegraph line to publish dispatches within China.

China's defeat at the hands of Japan in the Sino-Japanese War (1894–1895), sparked by quarreling over Korea, provided the impetus for the first serious attempt at comprehensive re-

> *Starting in the 1860s, reformist Chinese bureaucrats sought to adopt elements of Western learning and technological skills, but with the intention of keeping the core of Chinese culture intact.*

form by the Qing. Known as the "Hundred Days' Reform," the episode lasted only from June to September 1898. The force behind it was a thirty-seven-year-old scholar named Kang Youwei (1858–1927) and his twenty-two-year-old student Liang Qichao (1873–1929). The reformers argued that the Qing needed to go much beyond the Self-Strengthening Movement. Citing rulers such as Peter the Great of Russia and the Meiji Emperor of Japan as their inspiration, they urged Chinese leaders to develop a railway network, a state banking system, a modern postal service, and institutions to foster the development of agriculture, industry, and commerce.

If reformers wanted to accelerate change, their opportunity came in the summer of 1898 when the twenty-seven-year-old Guangxu Emperor decided to put into practice many of their ideas, including changes in the venerable civil service examination system. But the effort was short-lived. Conservative officials rallied behind Guangxu's aunt, the Empress Dowager Cixi, who emerged from retirement to overturn the reforms. The young emperor was put under house arrest. Kang and Liang fled for their lives and went into exile.

> *The reforms of the Self-Strengthening Movement were too modest, and they were poorly implemented.*

The reforms of the Self-Strengthening Movement were too modest, and they were poorly implemented. Marred by bureaucratic corruption and inept coordination, very few Chinese actually acquired new skills. The students who did acquire Western learning could not really exploit it, for the civil service examination, despite talk of modernizing, still was based on the Confucian classics and still opened the only doors to governmental service. The official governing elites were not yet ready to reinvent the principles of their political community, and they stuck instead to the traditional dynastic structure.

 CONCLUSION

Between 1850 and 1914, the majority of the world's people lived not in nation-states but in landed empires—the Ottoman, Habsburg, Russian, and Chinese—or in the colonies of nation-states, as in Africa, the Middle East, and South and Southeast Asia. But as many rulers and reformers around the world sought a new political framework to meet the crises of authority created by popular upheavals and economic transformations, the nation-state became an increasingly desirable form of governance. Strengthening state power went hand in hand with widening sovereignty and reordering the polity around the "nation."

The new ideal of "a people" united by territory, history, and culture was a fiction (an "imagined" reality) that was becoming increasingly powerful and popular around the world. Deepening and extending this imagined reality was a difficult matter. Official histories, national heroes, novels, poetry, and music helped, but central to the process of nation formation were the actions of bureaucrats. Asserting sovereignty over what it claimed as national territory, the state sought to "nationalize" diverse populations by creating a unified system of law, education, military service, and government. Toward the end of the nineteenth century, such projects of nation-building created strong states with greater capacities to act upon their subjects and to seize new territories.

Colonization beyond borders was an integral part of nation-building in many societies. States sought to establish the nation by undertaking territorial conquests, which they touted as nationalist endeavors. In Europe, the Americas, Japan, and, to some extent, Russia, the intertwined processes of nation-building and territorial aggrandizement were most effective. The Amazon, Okinawa, and most especially, the North American West became important provinces of integrated nation-states, populated with settlers and producing for "national" and international markets. By the end of the nineteenth century, the world saw the emergence of three great states, which a century earlier had played only bit parts on the world stage: the United States, Germany, and Japan. Russia, too, emerged as a world power—if standing on a less firm foundation.

It should be said, however, that these emerging "nations" did not wipe out local differences. Indeed, more often, national projects coexisted with subnational, local, and regional identities. Thus, Western Europeans had little interest in integrating already densely populated overseas colonial territories as provinces of their nation-states. Doing so would have threatened the very idea that nation-states were based on homogeneous communities. Besides, the imagined reality of such communities was under siege internally, as European and American "masses" and ethnic minorities clamored for their place alongside the "established" classes of the nation-state. This did not mean that a colony like India was divorced from Britain's sense of self or that Indonesia was an accidental possession for the Dutch. Quite the opposite: India and Indonesia were lucrative colonies, and they provided a yardstick by which the British and Dutch rulers measured their own glory. Ideologies of race and empire became woven into the fabric of national culture in Western Europe.

The drive to found nation-states and subordinate colonies provided an effective catalyst for integrating the global economy. More regions of the world became industrialized, and labor, commodities, and capital moved across the world more rapidly and in greater numbers than ever before. Nonetheless, labor, capital, and commodities were described in national terms—British capital, Chinese labor, German goods—and the system of imperial nation-states structured their movement. Thus, Indian laborers migrated to British possessions in Africa and the Caribbean; Britain used colonial control to fend off Japanese and German competition; and colonized and semicolonized territories became suppliers of raw materials for the North Atlantic imperial nation-states. The political division of the world into imperial nation-states and colonial outposts shaped the economic division of the world into industrialized and nonindustrialized societies.

One of the great ironies of this age was the unintended consequence of nation-building for societies that were also embarking on external expansion. The purported new openness and opportunities of national and even colonial cultures bred discontents. Self-determination could also apply to racial or ethnic minorities both at home and in the colonies. Armed with the rhetoric of progress and uplift, colonial authorities sought to subjugate distant people. But as the gap between rhetoric and rule yawned ever wider, colonial subjects embraced the language of the nation, and accused imperial overlords of betraying their own lofty principles. As the twentieth century opened, Filipino and Cuban rebels used Thomas Jefferson's Declaration of Independence to oppose American invaders, Koreans defined themselves as a "nation" crushed under Japanese heels, and Indian nationalists made colonial governors feel shame for violating their own conceits about English "fair play."

Chronology

1853	Commodore Perry "opens" Japan
1853–1856	Crimean War
1858	"The Raj" begins in India
1859	Publication of Darwin's *Origin of Species*
1860s	"Great Reforms" to modernize Russia
1860s–1890s	Self-Strengthening Movement (China)
1860s–1890s	French occupation of Vietnam, Cambodia, and Laos
1861–1865	U.S. Civil War
1867	Canada gains self-rule
1867	Russia sells Alaska to the U.S.
1868–1912	Meiji Era in Japan
1869	Opening of Suez Canal
1870–1871	Franco-Prussian War
1872	Japan takes over Ryūkyūs
1870s–1880s	British expansion in Southeast Asia
1877	Victoria crowned empress of India
1882	British occupy Egypt
1884–1885	Berlin Conference on Africa
1887–1889	Construction of the Eiffel Tower
1888	Brazil abolishes slavery
1891–1903	Russia constructs Trans-Siberian Railroad
1894–1895	Sino-Japanese War
1898	Spanish-American War
1910	Japan annexes Korea

FURTHER READINGS

Cain, P. A., and A. G. Hopkins, *British Imperialism: Innovation and Expansion, 1688–1914* (1993). An excellent discussion of British imperialism, especially British expansion into Africa.

Cronon, William, *Nature's Metropolis: Chicago and the Great West* (1991). Makes connections among territorial expansion, industrialization, and urban development.

Davis, John, *Conflict and Control: Law and Order in Nineteenth-Century Italy* (1988). A superb study of the north-south and other rifts after Italian political unification.

Friesen, Gerald, *The Canadian Prairies* (1984). The most comprehensive account of Canadian westward expansion.

Gluck, Carol, *Japan's Modern Myths: Ideology in the Late Meiji Period* (1985). A study of how states fashion useful historical traditions to consolidate and legitimize their rule.

Headrick, Daniel R., *The Tools of Empire: Technology and European Imperialism in the Nineteenth Century* (1981). A useful general study of the relationship between imperialism and technology.

Hine, Robert V., and John Mack Faragher, *The American West: A New Interpretive History* (2000). Presents an excellent synthesis of the conquests by which the United States expanded from the Atlantic to the Pacific.

Hobsbawm, Eric J., *Nations and Nationalism since 1780: Programme, Myth, Reality* (1993). The most insightful recent survey of the origins and development of nationalist thought throughout Europe.

Lee, Leo Ou-fan, and Andrew Nathan, "The Beginnings of Mass Culture: Journalism and Fiction in the Late Ch'ing and Beyond," in David Johnson, Andrew Nathan, and Evelyn Rawski (eds.), *Popular Culture in Late Imperial China* (1985), pp. 360–395. An important article on the emergence of a mass media market in late-nineteenth- and early-twentieth-century China.

Lieven, Dominic, *Empire: The Russian Empire and Its Rivals* (2000). A comparison of the British, Ottoman, Habsburg, and Russian empires.

Mackenzie, John M., *Propaganda and Empire* (1984). Contains a series of useful chapters showing the importance of the empire to Britain.

McClintock, Anne, *Imperial Leather: Race, Gender and Sexuality in the Colonial Contest* (1995). A study of the imperial relationship between Victorian Britain and South Africa from the point of view of cultural studies.

McNeil, William, *Europe's Steppe Frontier: 1500–1800* (1964). An excellent study of the definitive victory of Russia's agricultural empire over grazing nomads and independent frontier people.

Montgomery, David, *The Fall of the House of Labor: The Workplace, the State, and American Labor Activism, 1865–1925* (1987). An excellent discussion of changes in work in the late nineteenth century.

Myers, Ramon, and Mark Peattie (eds.), *The Japanese Colonial Empire, 1895–1945* (1984). A collection of essays exploring different aspects of Japanese colonialism.

Needell, Jeffrey, *A Tropical Belle Epoque: Elite Culture and Society in Turn of the Century Rio de Janeiro* (1987). Shows the strength of the Brazilian elites at the turn of the century.

Pan, Lynn (ed.), *The Encyclopedia of Chinese Overseas* (1999). A comprehensive coverage of the history of the Chinese diaspora.

Sperber, Jonathan, *The European Revolutions, 1848–1851* (1994). A survey of the movements that led to revolutions between 1848 and 1851, and the course of events that ensued across Europe.

Topik, Steven, *The Political Economy of the Brazilian State, 1889–1930* (1987). An excellent discussion of the Brazilian state, and especially of its elites.

Walker, Mack, *German Home Towns: Community, State, and the General State, 1648–1871* (1971, 1998). A brilliant, street-level analysis of the Holy Roman empire (the First Reich) and the run-up to the German unification of 1871 (the Second Reich).

Wasserman, Mark, *Everyday Life and Politics in Nineteenth-Century Mexico* (2000). Wonderfully captures the way in which people coped with social and economic dislocation in late-nineteenth-century Mexico.

Weeks, Theodore R., *Nation and State in Late Imperial Russia: Nationalism and Russification on the Western Frontier, 1863–1914* (1996). A good discussion of the Russian empire's responses to the concept of the nation-state.

Yung Wing, *My Life in China and America* (1909). The autobiography of the first Chinese graduate of an American university.

An Unsettled World, 1890–1914

In 1905 a young African man, Kinjikitile Ngwale, began to move among the different ethnic groups in the newly founded colony of German East Africa, inspiring his followers with a message of opposition to the German colonial authorities. In the tradition of visionary prophets (see Chapter 7), Kinjikitile claimed that by anointing adherents with specially blessed water (*maji* in Swahili), he could protect them from European bullets and drive the unwanted Germans from East Africa. Kinjikitile's reputation quickly spread, drawing followers to him and other like-minded prophets across 100,000 square miles of territory. Although the Germans executed Kinjikitile in 1905, they could not prevent his followers from taking part in a broad insurrection, called the Maji-Maji Revolt. The Germans brutally suppressed the uprising, killing between 200,000 and 300,000 Africans.

The Maji-Maji Revolt and its brutal suppression revealed an intensity of opposition to the world of nations and empires (described in Chapter 8) that surprised many at the time. Pressures against the dominant system came from two directions. In Europe and North America, cultural and social changes prompted a diverse group of critics who felt left out of the emerging nation-states, especially women, proletarians, and frustrated nationalists, to demand far-reaching reforms. In Asia, Africa, and Latin America, anti-colonial critics and exploited classes also expressed their opposition to the Euro-centered order.

European elites for the most part remained confident of their ability and right to dominate the rest of the world's population. Events like the Maji-Maji Revolt and other revolts that swept through Africa in the wake of Europe's scramble for colonies, however, suggested that colonial rule required more than promises of progress to colonial peoples. Progress, in their view, required order—and sometimes order demanded the application of brute force. Yet, resistance to European coercion led to doubts about Europe's imperial mission and the nature of "European civilization." Making matters worse, back home the social and economic dislocations of the last decades of the nineteenth century also produced discontent and social unrest. The rule of European elites now depended upon the dynamic forces of industrialization, global commerce, nation-building, science, and the ideals (if not practices) of freedom and equality. Would it last?

That this question arose at the turn of the nineteenth century was surprising, because people of European descent then occupied a commanding position in the world. Their share of the world's population stood at an all-time high of nearly 30 percent. Their proportion of the world's wealth was still greater. They had become the primary decision makers throughout the world. Looking to the future, they envisioned the twentieth century as a "European century." Yet, despite these hopeful prospects, European confidence and Europe's preeminence were hardly secure. Even as statesmen and artists extolled the achievements of European civilization, new developments at home and abroad unsettled their faith in the persistence of a Euro-centered world order.

At the end of the nineteenth century and beginning of the twentieth, economic, cultural, and political changes reverberated around the globe as never before. People reacted to these changes with a mixture of faith in progress and distress about it. Such reactions were a defining characteristic of the turn of the nineteenth century, but exactly what form the reaction took and what the consequences were varied from place to place.

Progress and Upheaval

> → *In what ways did progress lead to anxiety?*

The decades leading up to 1914 were a time of unprecedented possibility for some, and social disruption and economic frustration for others. They were also years of anxiety throughout the world. The rapid economic progress and opportunity that occurred led to challenges to the established order and the people in power. In Europe and the United States, left-wing radicals and middle-class reformers agitated for political and social change. Their reforming efforts resulted in a larger number of men participating in choosing their rulers and in programs to assist the poor, the unemployed, the sick, and the aged. In areas colonized by European countries and the United States, resentment was sometimes directed at colonial rulers and sometimes at indigenous elites, whose authority had already been eroded by imperial incursions. Even in nations such as China, which had not been formally colonized but whose state's autonomy had been compromised by less direct foreign intrusions, popular discontent fastened on the domination of Europeans. In China, Mexico, and Russia, angry peasants and workers, allied with frustrated reformers, toppled autocratic regimes.

In the late nineteenth century, whole new industries fueled high levels of economic growth, especially in the industrial countries and in those colonial and semi-colonial territories that

The decades leading up to 1914 were a time of unprecedented possibility for some, and social disruption and economic frustration for others.

Focus Questions AN UNSETTLED WORLD

→ *In what ways did progress lead to anxiety?*
→ *How did Africans and Chinese show their opposition to imperialism?*
→ *What were the sources of discontent around the world?*
→ *How was cultural modernism manifested in different fields?*
→ *How did conceptions about race and nation change in this era?*

exported vital raw materials to Europe and the United States. But the flowering of industrial capitalism also ushered in growing inequalities within industrial countries and especially between the industrial and nonindustrial regions of the world. Industrialization also enforced unwelcome changes in how and where people worked and lived. Rural peoples flocked into the cities, sometimes in response to expanding economic opportunities, but often in a desperate effort to escape widespread rural poverty. Urbanization tore at communal solidarities. Social problems abounded in the cities where differences between rich and poor were starkly displayed. The rich lived in beautiful homes and gave money to build opera houses, museums, and libraries; the poor were crowded together in unhealthy slums and barely had money to pay the rent and feed their children. The anxieties of the poor—as well as the not so poor—became particularly acute when economic downturns threw thousands into the ranks of the unemployed. This led to increased disillusionment with capitalism and the free market system.

Global economic changes caused profound social and economic transformations in the lives of women. Everywhere in the world, women became wage earners or took over primary responsibilities for the economic well-being of their households. Many of these domestic realignments threatened the traditional status of husbands and fathers. This was particularly true when women sought more independence and especially when they demanded enhanced political and legal rights. In the latter arena, some women made gains, though in general the opportunities for women to express their political voice remained limited.

Developments in the arts and sciences added to the feeling of unease. Scientific and technological progress enabled men and women to accomplish feats unimaginable a generation earlier. This facilitated the circulation of ideas around the world that paralleled the dispersion of goods and people. The uneven spread of scientific breakthroughs and economic advances and the use of knowledge and wealth to conquer and regulate lives led intellectuals to worry about the downside of progress. European and North American intellectuals began to worry that the world was less rational and the future much bleaker than Enlightenment thinkers had believed. Their writings were labeled modernism. Modernist ideas also circulated in colonial and semi-colonial areas, but for the Western-trained intelligentsia in these areas achieving political independence and understanding the challenge of the West had the highest priority.

In response to political upheavals, economic uncertainties, social disruptions, and modern ideas, personal and national identities came under scrutiny. Race became a central part of new identities and a justification for inequalities. In the effort to reimagine and revitalize nations, writers, artists, and political leaders created mythic histories to unify states. Such inventions

would prove crucial in the twentieth century's work of nation-building. But they also contributed to conflict between nations that in 1914 erupted in the Great War, an event that turned dislocation into catastrophe.

DISCONTENT WITH IMPERIALISM

> → *How did Africans and Chinese show their opposition to imperialism?*

In the decades before World War I, opposition to European colonial rule in Asia and Africa gathered strength. During the nineteenth century, Europeans had commenced colonial expansion quite sure of their "civilizing mission." True, a number of prophetic leaders had presented "alternative visions" that contested the supremacy of Europeans (see Chapter 7). Although these localist movements were quashed, opposition to European influence and dominance did not abate, and, in some cases, drew inspiration from these earlier movements. While European imperialists consolidated their hold over their colonial possessions, they found themselves suppressing unrest and uprisings in their colonies with more force and more bloodshed. As the cycle of resistance and repression escalated, many Europeans back home grew increasingly distressed and questioned the harsh means that were being used to control the colonies. By 1914, these questions were intensifying as colonial subjects were challenging imperial domination across Asia and Africa. In China, too, where Europeans were scrambling for new trading opportunities, though without formally seizing the reins of power, local populations were rising up against foreign control.

In the decades before World War I, opposition to European colonial rule in Asia and Africa gathered strength.

UNREST IN AFRICA

Last to be colonized, Africa witnessed many anti-colonial uprisings and scandals in the first decades of colonial rule (see Map 9-1). Violent conflicts embroiled not only the Belgians and the Germans, who ruled autocratically, but also the British, who often boasted that their colonial system was superior because it left traditional African rulers in place. These uprisings made thoughtful Europeans uneasy: why were Africans trying to overthrow regimes that had huge technological advantages in firepower and mechanical transport and that were supposed to be

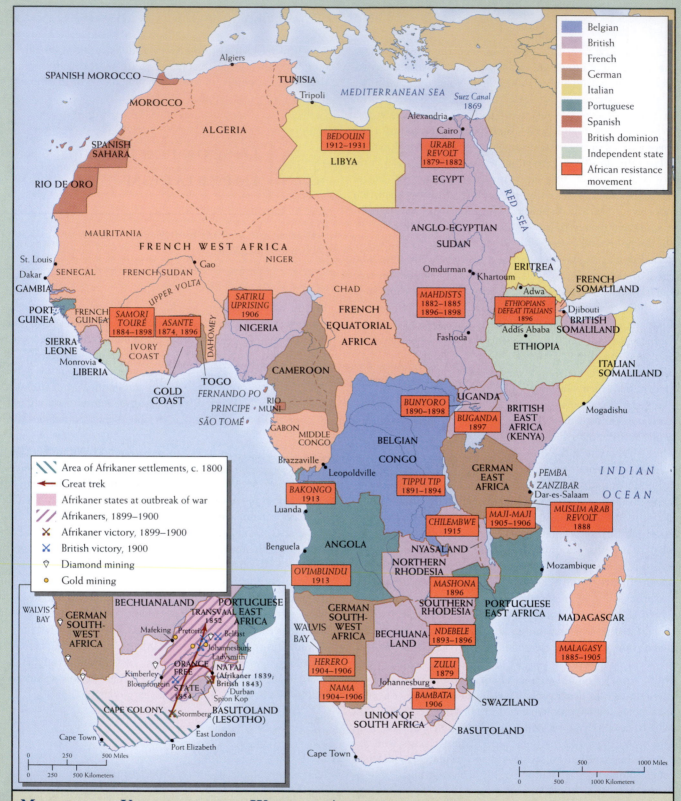

Legend (upper right):
- Belgian
- British
- French
- German
- Italian
- Portuguese
- Spanish
- British dominion
- Independent state
- African resistance movement

Inset legend (left):
- Area of Afrikaner settlements, c. 1800
- Great trek
- Afrikaner states at outbreak of war
- Afrikaners, 1899–1900
- X Afrikaner victory, 1899–1900
- X British victory, 1900
- ▽ Diamond mining
- ● Gold mining

Map labels:

SPANISH MOROCCO · MOROCCO · Algiers · TUNISIA · Tripoli · MEDITERRANEAN SEA · Suez Canal 1869 · Alexandria · Cairo

SPANISH SAHARA · ALGERIA · *BEDOUIN 1912–1931* · LIBYA · *URABI REVOLT 1879–1882* · EGYPT

RIO DE ORO · MAURITANIA · FRENCH WEST AFRICA · NIGER · CHAD · ANGLO-EGYPTIAN SUDAN · RED SEA · ERITREA · FRENCH SOMALILAND

St. Louis · Dakar · SENEGAL · FRENCH SUDAN · Gao · UPPER VOLTA · *SATIRU UPRISING 1906* · Omdurman · Khartoum · Adwa · *ETHIOPIANS DEFEAT ITALIANS 1896* · Djibouti · BRITISH SOMALILAND

GAMBIA · PORT. GUINEA · FRENCH GUINEA · *SAMORI TOURÉ 1884–1898* · *ASANTE 1874, 1896* · NIGERIA · FRENCH EQUATORIAL AFRICA · *MAHDISTS 1882–1885 1896–1898* · Fashoda · Addis Ababa · ETHIOPIA · ITALIAN SOMALILAND

SIERRA LEONE · IVORY COAST · DAHOMEY · Monrovia · LIBERIA · GOLD COAST · TOGO · FERNANDO PO · CAMEROON

PRINCIPE · RIO MUNI · SÃO TOMÉ · GABON · MIDDLE CONGO · *BUNYORO 1890–1898* · UGANDA · BRITISH EAST AFRICA (KENYA) · Mogadishu

Brazzaville · Leopoldville · BELGIAN CONGO · *BUGANDA 1897* · *TIPPU TIP 1891–1894* · GERMAN EAST AFRICA · PEMBA · ZANZIBAR · Dar-es-Salaam · INDIAN OCEAN

BAKONGO 1913 · Luanda · *CHILEMBWE 1915* · *MAJI-MAJI 1905–1906* · *MUSLIM ARAB REVOLT 1888*

Benguela · ANGOLA · NYASALAND · NORTHERN RHODESIA · Mozambique

OVIMBUNDU 1913 · GERMAN SOUTH-WEST AFRICA · *MASHONA 1896* · SOUTHERN RHODESIA · PORTUGUESE EAST AFRICA · MADAGASCAR

WALVIS BAY · BECHUANA LAND · *NDEBELE 1893–1896* · *MALAGASY 1885–1905*

HERERO 1904–1906 · *ZULU 1879* · SWAZILAND

NAMA 1904–1906 · Johannesburg · *BAMBATA 1906* · BASUTOLAND · UNION OF SOUTH AFRICA

Cape Town

Inset (southern Africa):
WALVIS BAY · GERMAN SOUTH-WEST AFRICA · BECHUANALAND · PORTUGUESE EAST AFRICA · TRANSVAAL 1852 · Mafeking · Pretoria · Belfast · Johannesburg · Ladysmith · Kimberley · ORANGE FREE STATE 1854 · NATAL (Afrikaner 1839; British 1843) · Durban · Bloemfontein · Spion Kop · CAPE COLONY · Stormberg · BASUTOLAND (LESOTHO) · Cape Town · East London · Port Elizabeth

0 · 250 · 500 Miles
0 · 250 · 500 Kilometers

0 · 500 · 1000 Miles
0 · 500 · 1000 Kilometers

MAP 9-1   UPRISINGS AND WARS IN AFRICA

The European partition and conquest of Africa was a violent affair. Referring to the map, with its dates of warfare, can you determine in which parts of Africa conquest took the longest and resistance was the most prolonged? The Ethiopian defeat of the Italians at the battle of Adwa in 1896 preserved that country's independence. Why were the Ethiopians able to do that which the other African opponents of European armies were not? Does the inset map of southern Africa help you to understand the factors that led to the South African War of 1899 to 1902?

bringing medical skills, literacy, and the fruits of European civilization? Some concluded that the Africans simply were too stubborn or too unsophisticated to appreciate Europe's generosity and would have to be forced along the path to progress. Others, shocked by colonial cruelty, called for reform. A few radicals even called for an end to imperialism.

African opposition to European conquest and colonial rule was too spirited to ignore. Across the continent, organized African armies and unorganized African villagers rose up to challenge the European conquest. The resistance of African villagers in the central highlands of British East Africa (Kenya) was so intense that the British had to mount savage punitive expeditions to bring the area under their control. But even after European powers had put down this early resistance, Africans continued to revolt against imperial authority. Uprisings were particularly common in areas where colonial rulers enacted programs that resulted in forced labor, increased taxation, and land appropriation. In northern Nigeria, in 1906, a mere three years after the British had conquered the area, an Islamic leader claiming to be the *mahdi*, or the chosen one, rallied people anew in opposition to the British and their African collaborators. Similar rebellions erupted in other colonies.

> The South African War brought a fundamental questioning of Britain's imperial ideology.

The most devastating of all of the wars and uprisings in colonial Africa occurred in South Africa. Unlike other conflicts on the African continent, this struggle pitted two white communities against each other: the British in the Cape Colony and Natal against the Afrikaners, descendants of the original Dutch settlers, who lived in the Transvaal and the Orange Free State. Although fought between two white regimes, the South African War (often called the Boer War; 1899–1902) involved the 4 million black inhabitants as fully as the area's 1 million whites. Its horrors particularly traumatized the British, who had come to see themselves as Europe's most enlightened and efficient colonial rulers. Cecil Rhodes, the leading politician in the Cape Colony, for example, had claimed that the British were "God's rulers," for his countrymen supposedly possessed an innate ability to govern the "less fortunate." The South African War brought a fundamental questioning of Britain's imperial ideology.

The bloody war's origins lay in the discovery of gold in the Transvaal. With exports amounting to £24 million per year during the 1890s, the Transvaal had become the richest state in Africa. The prospect that the mineral-rich Afrikaner Republics might become the powerhouse in southern Africa was more than British imperialists like Joseph Chamberlain, colonial secretary in London, and Cecil Rhodes could accept. They found ready allies in the non-Afrikaner, British population living in the Afrikaner Republics. Denied voting rights and subject to other forms of discrimination, these outsiders (*uitlanders*)

protested the Afrikaner governments' policies and pressed the British to intervene. For their part, Afrikaner leaders initiated a campaign of anti-colonial rhetoric that emphasized the rights of a free people to resist.

Fearing that war was inevitable, the president of the Transvaal, Paul Kruger, launched a preemptive strike against the British. In late 1899, Afrikaner forces crossed into South Africa. British glee at what they considered a fateful political blunder soon turned to frustration, even despair, as the fast-moving Afrikaner forces won early victories. Gradually, the British realized that the "Empire on which the sun never set" might actually lose this war. Horrified at the prospect, they committed new forces and, three years later, they managed to subdue the Afrikaners.

Ultimately the British won, bringing the two Afrikaner Republics of the Transvaal and the Orange Free State—with their vast gold reserves—into their empire. But the gains came at an enormous expenditure in men, matériel, and prestige. Recruiting nearly every able-bodied man and fighting a guer-

The South African War. Between 1899 and 1902, the Afrikaner states of the Transvaal and the Orange Free State fought a bitter struggle against British troops based in South Africa in a unsuccessful effort to maintain their political independence.

rilla campaign that broke all the rules of military manuals, the Afrikaners waged a war that cost Britain 20,000 soldiers and £200 million. The war dragged on longer than British military strategists thought possible. Britain's frustrated attempts to respond to Afrikaner hit-and-run tactics and contain the local civilian population led the British to start burning farms and to institute a terrifying innovation: the concentration camp. At one moment in the war, no fewer than 155,000 men, women, and children were being held in camps surrounded by barbed wire. Nor were the camps restricted to Afrikaners. The British also rounded up Africans whom they feared would side with the "anti-colonial" Dutch descendants. The suffering and loss in these camps were appalling; by war's end, 28,000 Afrikaner women and children, as well as 14,000 black Africans, had perished in these camps. These atrocities did not go unnoticed, however, as new technology in the form of newspaper reports and photographs brought the misery of the South African War back to Europe.

> *The atrocities did not go unnoticed as new technology in the form of newspaper reports and photographs brought the misery of the South African War back to Europe.*

The chill of revulsion that the South African War sent through Western public opinion deepened after Germany's African adventures went brutally wrong. Germany had established colonies in Southwest Africa (present-day Namibia), Cameroon, and Togo in 1884, and in East Africa in 1885. In German Southwest Africa, the Herero and San people resisted the Germans, and in German East Africa (modern-day Tanzania), the Muslim Arab peoples rebelled. Between 1904 and 1906, the fighting in German Southwest Africa escalated into a brutal, no-holds-barred conflict, during which the German commander General von Trotha issued a genocidal extermination order against the Herero population. Equally troubling was the Maji-Maji Revolt in German East Africa of 1905–1906, already described at the beginning of this chapter.

Numerous apologists for imperial violence tried to dampen public outcries. Journalists portrayed the Maji-Maji rebels as fanatics in the thrall of a demonic African witch doctor and the Afrikaners as uncouth ruffians who deserved what they got. The best-selling German novel by Gustav Frenssen, *Peter Moor's Trip to the Southwest* (1906), glorified the small-town Aryan hero who gives his all to defend noble German settlers against the barbarism of the Hereros. According to defenders, Leopold's Belgian Congo (described in Chapter 8) was an exception, created by an aging and dissolute monarch who had no scruples when it came to enhancing his wealth and political power. Besides, had not Belgian legislators stripped Leopold of his claims and then implemented a more humane version of African colonialism? The rationalizers from all the European powers argued that these incidents reflected unpleasant aberrations, and did not represent the real purpose and reality of empire—at least not *their* nation's empire. Thus, the British denounced the Belgians to tout their own enlightenment, while the French

spread gory images of German repression abroad to contrast with their own success at uplifting Africans. What all European rationalizers did was to portray Africans as either accepting subjects or as child-like primitives. For Europe's rationalizers, the message was simply to redouble their coercive efforts and, in many cases, the number of officials and garrisoned soldiers.

THE BOXER UPRISING IN CHINA

At the turn of the century, forces from within and without also unsettled China. Chinese turmoil differed from the anti-colonial unrest in Africa, but it was no less symptomatic of concern about European intrusions. The population, which exceeded half a billion, was outstripping the country's resources. Landlessness, poverty, and peasant discontent, constants in China's modern history, led many to mourn the decay of political authority. In response, Guangxu, the Qing Emperor, had tried to enact reforms in the summer of 1898 to deal with accumulating social problems. The reforms were intended to modernize industry, agriculture, commerce, education, and the military. But opponents blocked the emperor's designs. By September, Guangxu found himself under house arrest in the palace, while the Empress Dowager Cixi, around whom the conservatives rallied, actually ruled.

The breakdown of dynastic authority can be traced in large part to foreign pressure. China's defeat at the hands of Japan in the Sino-Japanese War of 1894–1895 (see Chapter 8) deeply humiliated the Chinese. That defeat also upset the tacit agreement among foreign powers to keep China open to trade with all. Although Japan, which acquired Taiwan as its first major colony, was the immediate beneficiary of the war, Britain, France, Germany, and Russia quickly scrambled for additional concessions from China. These European powers demanded that the Qing government grant them specific areas within China as their respective "spheres of influence" (see Map 9-2). The United States, prompted by a combination of ideology and self-interest, argued instead for maintaining an "open door" policy in which access would remain available to all traders. But the Americans also wished to force the Qing regime to assent to Western norms of political and economic exchange, and to convince the Chinese of the truth and superiority of Christian civilization. In response, some Chinese political and intellectual leaders developed an anti-European stance, while advocating the use of European ideas and technology to strengthen China itself.

The most explosive reaction to these internal and external problems originated within the peasantry and was known as the Boxer Uprising. Like colonial peoples in Africa, the Boxers employed violence against the unwelcome meddling of Europeans in their communities. As in the case of the Taiping Rebellion

MAP 9-2 FOREIGN SPHERES OF INFLUENCE IN CHINA, 1842–1907
Note the location of the different spheres of influence claimed by the foreign powers in China. What does this tell us about the dynamics of Western and Japanese imperialism in Asia in the nineteenth and early twentieth centuries? How can we explain the geography of the division? What were the factors that accounted for the way in which the different spheres were carved? What, indeed, was a "sphere of influence"? How was it different from a colony? What were "treaty ports"?

decades earlier (described in Chapter 7), the story of the Boxers was tied to missionary activities. In earlier centuries, Jesuit missionaries had sought chiefly to convert the court and the elites. By the mid-nineteenth century, evangelical revivals in Europe had made converting Chinese commoners seem a critical goal. In the decades after the Taiping Rebellion, Christian missionaries had streamed into China, impatient to make new converts in the hinterlands and confident of the backing of their governments. With the dynasty in a weakened state, Christian missionaries became more aggressive, often challenging local officials and the customary practices of Chinese communities.

An incident in 1897, in which Chinese residents killed two German missionaries, brought tensions to a boil. The missionaries had been attempting to "open" the city of Yanzhou (located in the northern province of Shandong, long a hotbed of unrest and rebellion) for Catholic proselytizing. In retribution for the deaths, the German government demanded the right to construct three cathedrals, to remove hostile local officials, and to seize the port of Jiaozhou. As tensions mounted between the Chinese and Western missionaries, martial arts groups in the region became increasingly politicized and began to attack the missionaries and converts, calling for an end to specific privileges for the

Cixi's Allies. The Empress Dowager Cixi emerged as the most powerful figure in the Qing court in the last decades of the dynasty, from the 1860s until her death in 1908. Highly able, she approved many of the early reforms of the Self-Strengthening Movement, but her commitment to the preservation of the Manchu Qing dynasty made her suspicious of more fundamental and wide-ranging changes. Here she is shown surrounded by court eunuchs. Early Qing rulers were very conscious of the danger of the meddling of eunuchs in court affairs. Yet, as a woman whose power relationships with orthodox officials were often ambivalent, Cixi was perhaps particularly compelled to ally herself closely with the eunuchs as a counterweight to the other official factions.

Christians. In early 1899, several of these groups joined together under the rubric "Boxers United in Righteousness," and adopted the slogan "Support the Qing, destroy the foreign." Rather like the African followers of Kinjikitile, the Boxers believed that their divine protection rendered them immune to all earthly weapons. As a Boxer put it, "We requested the gods to attach themselves to our bodies. When they had done so, we became Spirit Boxers, after which we were invulnerable to swords and spears, our courage was enhanced, and in fighting we were unafraid to die and dared to charge straight ahead."

The Boxer Movement especially flourished where natural disasters and harsh economic conditions spread suffering. In Shandong, where the movement began, there had been floods throughout much of the decade, followed by a prolonged drought in the winter of 1898. Idle, restless, and often hungry, peasants, boatmen, and peddlers turned to the Boxers for support. They were also receptive to the Boxers' message that the gods were angry due to the foreign presence in general and Christian activities in particular.

These indigent activists, many of them young men, swelled the ranks of the Boxers. Women also participated in the movement. The so-called "Red Lanterns" were mostly teenage girls and unmarried women, who announced their loyalty by dressing entirely in red garments. Though the Red Lanterns were segregated from the male Boxers—they worshipped at their own altars and practiced their martial arts at separate boxing grounds—they were important to the movement as a counter force that could destroy the power of Christian women. Indeed, one of the Boxers' greatest fears was that cunning Christian women would use their guile to weaken their spirits. Such a threat, however, could be countered by the "purity" of the Red Lanterns. The Red Lanterns, too, were believed to be able to carry out incredible feats: they could walk on water or fly through the air. Their magical power was said to provide critical assistance for the uprising.

As the movement gained momentum, the Qing vacillated between viewing the Boxers as a threat to order and embracing them as a potential force to check increasingly brazen

The Boxer Uprising in China. The Boxer Uprising was eventually suppressed by a foreign army made up of Japanese, European, and American troops that arrived in Beijing in August 1900. The picture here shows fighting between the foreign troops and the combined forces of Qing soldiers and the Boxers. After a period of vacillation, the Qing court, against the advice of some of its officials, finally threw its support behind the quixotic struggle of the Boxers against the foreign presence, laying the ground for the military intervention of the imperialist powers.

foreign encroachment. In the early part of 1900, Qing troops on occasion clashed with the Boxers in an escalating cycle of violence. By spring, however, it was clear that the Qing could not control the Boxers, tens of thousands of whom roamed the vicinities of Beijing and Tianjin. Embracing the Boxers' cause, the empress dowager declared war against the foreign powers in June 1900.

Acting without any discernible plan or leadership, the Boxers went after Christian and foreign symbols and persons. In addition to harassing and sometimes killing Chinese Christians in various parts of northern China, the Boxers attacked owners of foreign objects such as lamps and clocks. Railroad tracks and telegraph lines also became targets of destruction. In Beijing, the Boxers besieged the foreign embassy compounds within which were the foreign diplomats and their families. The Boxers also reduced the Southern Cathedral to ruins, then besieged the Northern Cathedral, where more than 3,000 Catholics and 40 French and Italian marines had sought refuge. They were rescued only with the arrival of a foreign expeditionary force.

In August 1900, a foreign army of 20,000 men crushed the Boxers. About half of the troops came from Japan; the rest came primarily from Russia, Britain, Germany, France, and the United States. Following the suppression of the uprising, the victors forced the Chinese to sign the punitive Boxer Protocol in September 1901. Among other punishments, it required the regime to pay an exorbitant indemnity in gold for damages to foreign life and property. The cost was about twice the annual income of the empire. The Protocol also authorized Western powers to station troops in Beijing.

The humiliating terms prompted the Qing to make a last-ditch effort to reform. The post-Boxer "New Policy" included the reorganization of the ministries and the army, an attempt to recentralize the government, the abolition of the old civil service examination system, and the promise of constitutional reform. But by then the Qing regime was so crippled that these abrupt reforms merely snapped the ties between the rulers and their subjects.

Although defeated, the Boxers' anti-Western uprising showed how much had changed in China since the Taiping Rebellion. Although primarily peasants from a relatively remote part of what was still an agrarian empire, the Boxers shared in the unsettledness generated by European inroads into China. The commercial and spiritual reach of Europeans, once confined to elites and port cities, had extended across much of China. While the Taiping Rebellion had mobilized millions against the Qing, the Boxers remained loyal to the dynasty and focused their wrath on foreigners and Chinese Christians. In the process, they demonstrated the possibility for mass political opposition to westernization.

> *Political and military tension increased among the European states as they competed for raw materials and colonial footholds.*

WORLDWIDE INSECURITIES

→ *What were the sources of discontent around the world?*

The protests against European intrusion in Africa and China were distant movements that most Europeans could in the end disregard. News of unrest in the colonies and in China did not lead many Europeans to lose faith in the superiority of European ways. Quite the contrary, it reinforced their belief in the inferiority of the other cultures. The imperial powers overcame their differences to join together to put down the Boxers in China. In Africa, unrest in a rival's empire was taken as a sign of poor management with the accompanying belief that colonial administration was better done in one's own empire. Anxiety here was primarily generated by the difficulty and costs of the "civilizing mission." A few did begin to worry about its ethics. At the same time, however, conflicts closer to home tore at European and North American confidence. These included political and military rivalries among the Western powers, the booms and busts of the expanding industrial economies, and the problems that developed as a result of uncontrolled urbanization (see Map 9-3).

IMPERIAL RIVALRIES COME HOME

Many internal factors fostered conflict among the Western powers, including France's smoldering resentment at its defeat in the Franco-Prussian War. But political and military tension increased among the European states as they competed for raw materials and colonial footholds. The Western powers built up their supply of weapons as well as ships and railroads to transport troops where needed. Yet, not everyone supported the military buildup. Many decried the money spent on massive new steam-powered warships. Others warned that new technologies of warfare, such as the machine gun, debased the honor of the soldier-citizen, making him into an anonymous mass executioner.

In the main, the creation of a European-centered world deepened rivalries within Europe and promoted instability across the continent. Competition accentuated the position of two powers in particular: Germany and Russia. The unifications of Germany and Italy at the expense of France and the Austrian empire had smashed the old balance of power in Europe. New alliances began to

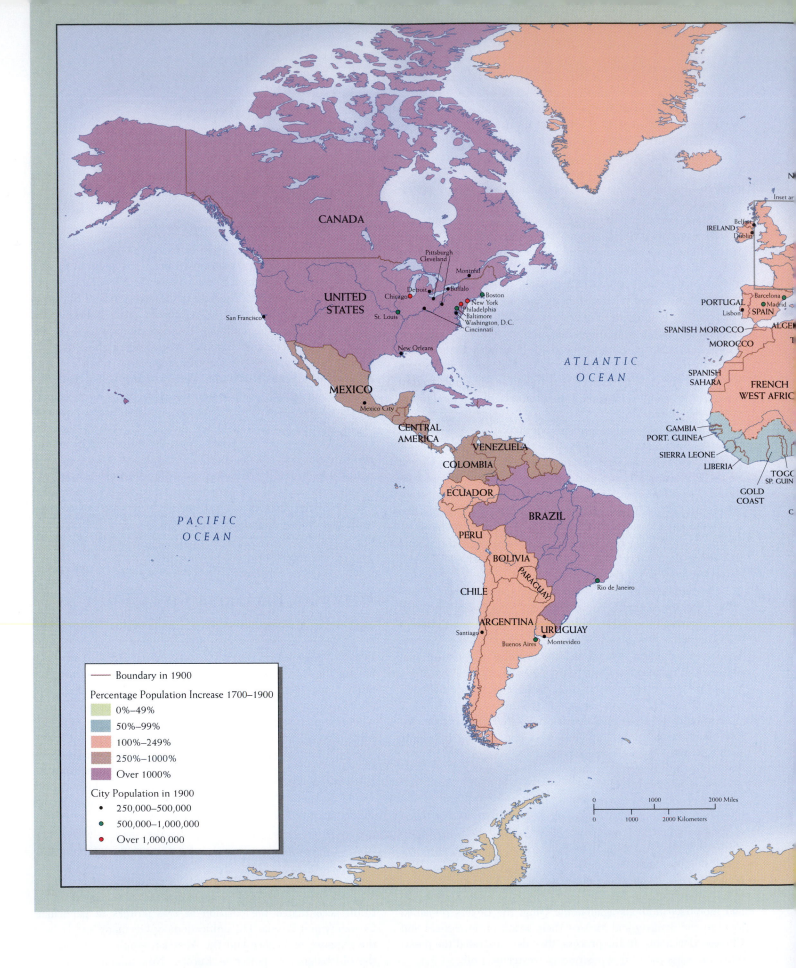

CANADA

Pittsburgh
Cleveland
Montreal

UNITED
STATES

Detroit
Buffalo
Chicago
Boston
New York
St. Louis
Philadelphia
Baltimore
Washington, D.C.
Cincinnati

San Francisco

New Orleans

ATLANTIC
OCEAN

IRELAND
Belfast
Dublin

PORTUGAL
Lisbon
Barcelona
Madrid
SPAIN

MEXICO

Mexico City

CENTRAL
AMERICA

SPANISH MOROCCO
MOROCCO
ALGE

SPANISH
SAHARA

FRENCH
WEST AFRIC

VENEZUELA

COLOMBIA

ECUADOR

PACIFIC
OCEAN

BRAZIL

PERU

GAMBIA
PORT. GUINEA

SIERRA LEONE

LIBERIA

GOLD
COAST

TOGO
SP. GUIN

BOLIVIA

PARAGUAY

CHILE

Rio de Janeiro

ARGENTINA

URUGUAY

Santiago

Buenos Aires
Montevideo

— Boundary in 1900

Percentage Population Increase 1700–1900

▪ 0%–49%

▪ 50%–99%

▪ 100%–249%

▪ 250%–1000%

▪ Over 1000%

City Population in 1900

• 250,000–500,000

• 500,000–1,000,000

• Over 1,000,000

| 0 | 1000 | 2000 Miles |

| 0 | 1000 | 2000 Kilometers |

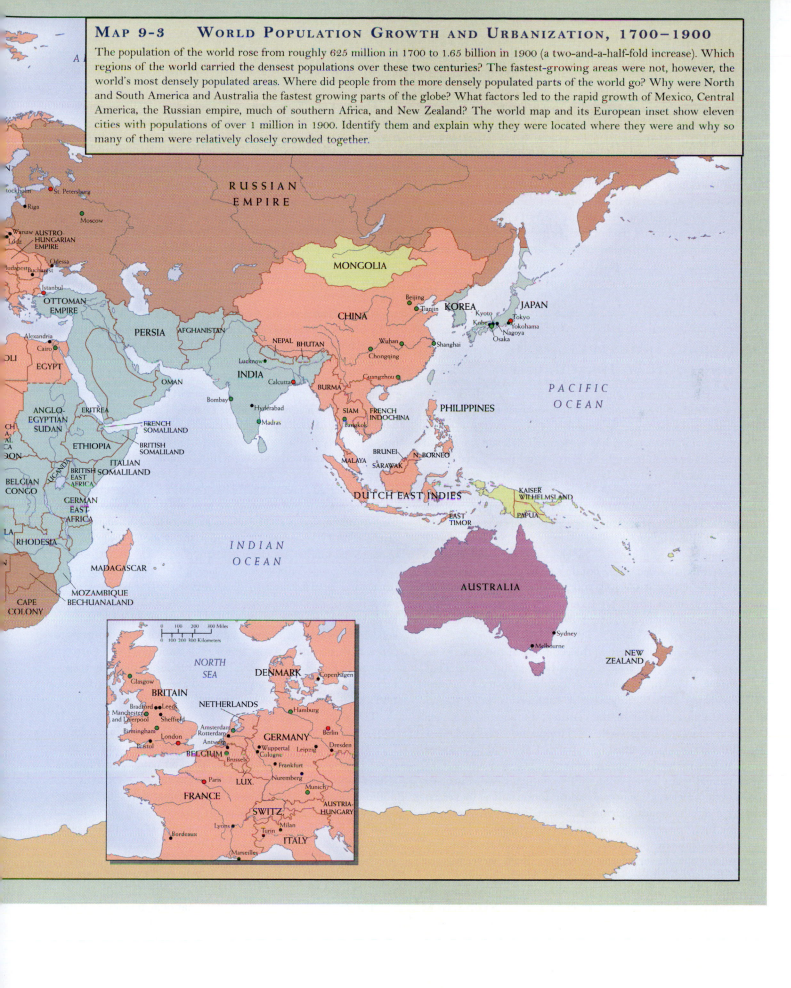

MAP 9-3   WORLD POPULATION GROWTH AND URBANIZATION, 1700–1900

The population of the world rose from roughly 625 million in 1700 to 1.65 billion in 1900 (a two-and-a-half-fold increase). Which regions of the world carried the densest populations over these two centuries? The fastest-growing areas were not, however, the world's most densely populated areas. Where did people from the more densely populated parts of the world go? Why were North and South America and Australia the fastest growing parts of the globe? What factors led to the rapid growth of Mexico, Central America, the Russian empire, much of southern Africa, and New Zealand? The world map and its European inset show eleven cities with populations of over 1 million in 1900. Identify them and explain why they were located where they were and why so many of them were relatively closely crowded together.

crystallize after 1890, as German-French hostility persisted, and German-Russian friendship broke down. This left Germany surrounded by foes: Britain and France to the west, Russia to the east. Adding to the instability among reigning great powers was the weakening of Europe's old empires, the Ottoman and the Habsburg. On the flanks of these empires were the Balkans, where a series of small wars and the rise of Slavic nationalism destabilized the area in the years between 1909 and 1913. Sensing conflict on the horizon, Britain, Germany, France, Austria-Hungary, and Russia entered into a massive arms race, investing much of their newfound prosperity in the very weapons that would destroy millions of their subjects after 1914.

FINANCIAL, INDUSTRIAL, AND TECHNOLOGICAL INSECURITIES

Economic developments helped make powers "great," but the same industrial and commercial dynamism upset the arrangements that had held societies together. Certainly those at the apex of the capitalist system had reason to celebrate the wealth that industrialism had brought to Europe and the United States in the nineteenth century. Living standards had never been higher in the West. But pride about wealth and growth coincided with laments about changes in national and international economies. To begin with, Americans and Europeans recognized that the small-scale, laissez-faire capitalism that Adam Smith had championed had given way by the close of the nineteenth century to an economic order dominated by huge, heavily capitalized firms. Gone, it seemed, was Smith's vision of a capitalist system of many small producers in vigorous competition with one another, all benefiting from efficient, but not exploitative, divisions of labor.

Instead of smooth progress, the economy of the West in the nineteenth century bounced between booms and busts. Thus, the industrial system was characterized by long-term business cycles of rapid growth, followed by counter-cycles of stagnation. In the last quarter of the century, the pace of economic change accelerated. Large-scale steel production, railroad building, and textile manufacturing expanded at breakneck speed, while waves of bank closures, bankruptcies, and agricultural crises ruined many small-holders. By century's end, European and North American economies were dominated as never before by a few large-scale firms that were, however, more efficient for the production of commodities like steel.

During this era, the power of the industrial magnate was matched by the power of the financier. These were years of heady international financial integration. More and more countries joined a world system of borrowing and lending; more and more countries embraced a set of economic rules governed by the gold standard. The hub of this world system was composed of the banks of London, which since the Napoleonic Wars had been a major source of capital for international borrowers.

The rise of giant banks and huge industrial corporations caused much alarm, for it seemed to signal an end to the age of free markets and competitive capitalism. In the United States, an entire generation of journalists cut their teeth exposing the skullduggery of financial titans and industrial magnates. These "muckrakers" portrayed the captains of finance like J. P. Morgan and John D. Rockefeller as plutocrats bent on amassing ever greater private power at the expense of working families and public authorities. In Europe, too, critics decried a similar trend toward economic monopolies or oligopolies in which lack of competition generated profiteering and created greater disparities of wealth between the owners of firms and the workforce.

Rather than longing for the return of truly free markets, many critics argued for reforms and regulations that would protect people from economic instability. Indeed, starting in the 1890s, the reaction against economic competition gathered steam. Producers, big and small, grew disenchanted with supply and demand mechanisms and sought to circumvent them. To cope with an unruly market, farmers created cooperatives, while big industrialists attempted to create their own monopolies, or cartels, in the name of improving "efficiency," correcting failures in the market, and heightening profits. At the same time, government officials, along with a new class of academic specialists, worried openly that modern economies were inherently unstable, often prone to produce too much, and thus liable to bankruptcy and crisis. The solution, according to many turn-of-the-century economists, was for the state to step in and manage the market's inefficiencies.

Banking especially seemed in need of closer government supervision. In many industrial societies, central banks already existed and, in London, the Bank of England had long since taken on the supervision of local and international money markets. But public institutions did not yet have the resources to protect all investments in times of economic crisis. Between 1890 and 1893, 550 American banks collapsed, and only the intervention of J. P. Morgan prevented the depletion of the nation's gold reserves.

The road to regulation, however, was hardly smooth. In 1907, a more serious crisis threatened. Once again, it fell to J. P. Morgan to rescue the dollar from financial panic. With a cigar clenched between his teeth, Morgan compelled financier after financier to commit unprecedented funds (eventually $35 million) to protect banks and trusts against depositors' panic. Morgan himself lost $21 million in this endeavor and emerged from the bank panic convinced that some sort of public oversight was needed. By 1913, the United States Congress, too, was persuaded, and it ratified the Federal Reserve Act, creating a series of boards to monitor the supply and demand of the nation's money.

The crisis of 1907 showed how national financial matters could quickly become international affairs. The sell-off of the shares of banks and trusts in the United States in that year also led American investors to withdraw their funds from other countries that relied on American capital. As a result, Canada, for instance, suffered a bank crisis of its own. For countries like Egypt and Mexico, far removed from each other geographically yet linked through international capital, the 1907 crisis also resulted in either withdrawal of investors' funds or a suspension of new investments and a string of bankruptcies. The head of Mexico's government, General Porfirio Díaz, tried to regain investors' confidence and their funds. But Mexico still fell into a severe recession in 1908–1909 as U.S. capital dried up. In turn, Mexicans lost faith in their economic—and political—system. Unemployed and subjected to new hardships, many Mexicans flocked to General Díaz's political opponents, who eventually lifted the flag of insurrection in 1910. A year later, the entire regime collapsed in revolution.

Just as financial circuits linked nations as never before, so, too, did industrialization, which now affected a larger share of the world's population. Backed by big banks, industrialists by century's end could afford to extend their enterprises, both physically and geographically. Heavy industries came to new places. In Russia, for example, which had lagged far behind the Western European nations in its economic development, industrial activity began to quicken. With loans from European (especially French, Belgian, and British) investors, Russia built railways, telegraph lines, and factories, and developed coal, iron, steel, and petroleum industries. The country's railroad mileage nearly doubled in the last decade of the nineteenth century. By 1900, Russia was producing half of the world's oil and a considerable amount of steel. Yet, industrial development remained uneven: southern Europe and the American South continued to lag behind northern regions. The gap was even more pronounced in colonial territories, which contained few industrial enterprises (aside from railroad building and mining).

By 1914, the factory and the railroad had become globally recognizable symbols of the modern economy—and of its positive and negative effects. Everywhere, the coming of the railroad to one's town or village was a big event: for some, it represented an exhilarating leap into the modern world; for others, a terrifying abandonment of the past. Ocean liners, automobiles, and airplanes, likewise, could be both dazzling and disorienting. Not surprisingly, the older conservative elite found technological development more worrying than did urban liberals, who increasingly set state policies.

For ordinary people, the new, industrial economy brought a mixture of benefits and costs. Factories produced cheaper goods, but they belched clouds of black smoke. Railways offered faster travel and transport, but they also ruined small towns unlucky enough to be left off the branch line. Machines (when operating properly) were more efficient than human and animal labor, but working with them often made workers feel that they had

been reduced to machines themselves. Indeed, the American Frederick Winslow Taylor (1856–1915) proposed a system of "scientific management" to make human bodies perform more like machines, maximizing the efficiency of workers' movements in order not to waste an instant of precious time. But what Taylor and an increasing number of industrial employers condemned as waste was to employees a more flexible way of working. Workers did not want to be managed, scientifically or otherwise. Moreover, giving up customary rhythms meant ceding control of the pace of production to employers. This was not something that workers welcomed, and labor's resistance to "Taylorization" led to a number of prominent strikes. For strikers, as for conservatives, the course of progress had clearly taken an unsettling turn.

URBANIZATION AND ITS DISCONTENTS

The city and city life also epitomized the modern era at the turn of the century. Large cities, of course, long pre-dated the late nineteenth century. Already in the thirteenth century, the Chinese city of Hangzhou probably had more than 1 million inhabitants. Still, in the last decades of the nineteenth century, urbanization reached unprecedented proportions (see Map 9-3). Although the majority of the world's population continued to live on and cultivate the land, the growth of cities and the flow of population from the countryside to the cities was a global phenomenon. Because cities were so closely associated with modernity, to celebrate or criticize them was to take an obvious stance on the question of "progress." Certainly, it was not hard to find things to criticize. Social problems pervaded urban life, as cities struggled to accommodate swelling numbers of domestic and international migrants. Yet, even as millions crowded into disease-ridden slums, cities also gained magnificent new cultural institutions, such as opera houses, museums, and libraries, that made urban life more refined—at least for those who had the leisure time and disposable income to patronize them.

Consider, for example, Buenos Aires, which underwent an ambitious makeover at the end of the nineteenth century. So successful was this overhaul that, by the early twentieth century, this Argentine city was hailed as the "Paris of South America." Indeed, models for the new boulevards of Buenos Aires had been lifted straight from the blueprints of Georges-Eugène Haussmann (1809–1891), the city planner who had "modernized" mid-century Paris. The architecture of preference in Buenos Aires was also Parisian, with ornate facades and marble pillars. Even in the sweltering South American summer, men in top hats and women in furs flocked to Buenos Aires' new Opera House, a replica of the Paris Opera House.

> *In the last decades of the nineteenth century, urbanization reached unprecedented proportions.*

At the Race Track: Buenos Aires 1904. Buenos Aires became one of the world's wealthiest cities by 1900. Pictured here is a scene at the race track in the Argentine capital, where, despite the heat, the elites sported suits, top hats, and fancy wear for their outing to the races. Notice how these spaces excluded the middle and working classes, but made room for elite women to join with men to hobnob.

Not all city dwellers benefited from urban redevelopment and beautification, as was illustrated by the situation in South America's other great city, Rio de Janeiro. Like Buenos Aires, Rio was transformed in the late nineteenth century. The Brazilian city's prefects demolished the sprawling downtown slums, staked out parks, and tree-lined thoroughfares, and erected a municipal theater, a national library, and a city hall. But for Rio's poor, the redesign pushed slums out of the inner city and into the surrounding hills. More time and money was now needed to get to work. When hygienists tried to demolish infested tenements and vaccinate Rio's slum dwellers against smallpox in 1904, the poor revolted, and they vented their accumulated grievances at the elite's modern urban installments. In days of rioting, they tore up the new paving stones to make barricades, destroyed marble statues, and smashed the recently installed electric lampposts. By the time troops restored order, downtown Rio de Janiero was in shambles.

Similar conflicts between rich and poor accompanied urban redevelopment in North American and European metropolises. King Leopold II of Belgium, for example, employed the enormous proceeds from his exploitation of the Congo to beautify his capital, Brussels. Imitating the "Haussmannization" of Paris, Leopold built parks and museums and widened the Avenue de Tervuren to create a grand approach to the city. But while the well-off applauded the beautification of Brussels, the downtrodden registered their discontent in a series of violent strikes that shook the city between 1886 and 1893.

THE "WOMAN QUESTION"

Adding to the unsettledness of the domestic situation was the turmoil about the politics of domesticity, or what was often called the "woman question." In Western countries, for most of the nineteenth century, an ethos of "separate spheres" had supposedly confined women's attention to domestic and private matters, while leaving men in exclusive charge of public life and economic undertakings. In practice, the proscription against women working outside the home for wages had never been rigidly enforced, except among the wealthiest families, who could afford such limits on women's activities. These restrictions were further breached as economic developments created new paid jobs for women. At century's end, women were increasingly employed as teachers, secretaries, typists, department store clerks, and telephone operators. These jobs offered women a greater degree of economic and social independence. They also required some education, which was increasingly open to women as well; by 1900, 40 percent of American college graduates were women, and many of these educated women entered formerly all-male professions. Others became involved in public life when they led efforts to improve the conditions of the urban poor and to expand the role of government in the regulation of economic affairs.

Probably the most important change in women's lives was the control that many began to assert over reproduction. Although many countries had made it a crime to advocate the use of contraceptive devices, women still found ways to limit the number of children they bore. At the opening of the twentieth century, the birthrate in America was half what it had been at the beginning of the nineteenth century. By having fewer children, families could devote more income to education, food, housing, and leisure activities. Naturally, too, declining birthrates, on top of improved medicine, meant that fewer women died in childbirth and more could expect to see their children reach adulthood.

> *Probably the most important change in women's lives was the control that many began to assert over reproduction.*

Still, these changes in women's social status did not translate readily into electoral reform at the national level. At mid-century, several women's suffrage movements had been founded, but these campaigns bore little immediate fruit. In 1868, women received the right to vote in local elections in Britain. Within a few years, Finland, Sweden, and some American states allowed single, property-owning women the right to cast their ballots, again only in local elections. Women

VIRAGOES OR TEMPLE COURTESANS?

The German avant-garde novelist Franziska von Reventlow occupied one of the more radical positions in the fragmented European women's movement. In the 1899 essay excerpted below, Reventlow attacked the feminist "viragoes" (aggressive women) who failed to understand that freedom for women did not mean making them into men. Instead of pressing for political and economic rights, Reventlow—who was herself notorious for her many affairs—advocated a return to the promiscuity permitted to special temple courtesans in Ancient Greece, and the freeing of women from oppressive work and the sensuality-killing conventions of middle-class Christian culture.

The most fanatical movement-women have put forward the claim: women can do everything men can do. . . . We don't want to deny that there are many achievements of which both sexes are equally capable. . . . But when it comes to heavy physical labor, that is a different question. One has only to look at these hard-working women of the lower classes, who, in addition [to their jobs] bring a child into the world every year, to see that the female body is not made for this, and that it in this way loses its form and gradually is ruined. . . .

The man has the role that he has been given by nature, he is everywhere the dominant, the attacker, in all areas of life, in all professions . . . [The woman] is not made for the harder things of this world, but for ease, for joy, for beauty. . . .

But perhaps a women's movement will arise in this sense, one that frees the woman as a sexual being, and which teaches her to demand what it is proper to demand, full sexual freedom, that is, full control over her body, which publicly sanctioned promiscuity will bring back. Please, no cries of indignation! The temple courtesans of antiquity were free, highly cultivated, and respected women, and no one took offense when they gave their love and their bodies to whom and as often as they like and at the same time took part in the intellectual life enjoyed by men. Instead of this, Christianity created monogamy—and prostitution. The latter is a proof that marriage is a flawed institution. While, by means of Christian moral education, there is an attempt to kill the sexual feelings of one part of womankind . . . at the same time, prostitution is institutionalized, and thereby another part of womankind is compelled to be polygamous in order to service men for whom marriage is unsatisfying . . .

To return to the women's movement: it is the declared enemy of all erotic culture, because it wants to make women into men. . . .

Darwin tells us that the English sheep breeders weed out the sexual mutants from their herds because they don't produce either beautiful wool or good mutton chops. Nature has already done the same among humans; the newest textbooks on anatomical pathologies show that hermaphrodites are dying out. The viragoes, who want to do away with our men, are for the most part just hermaphroditic ghosts who will soon be banished by the healthy erotic spirit of the new paganism whose triumph we await in the next century.

Source: Franziska von Reventlow, "Viragines oder Hetaeren," in *Autobiographisches: Novellen, Schriften, Selbstzeugnisse*, edited by Else Reventlow (translated by S. Marchand) (Frankfurt: Ullstein Verlag, 1986), pp. 236–49.

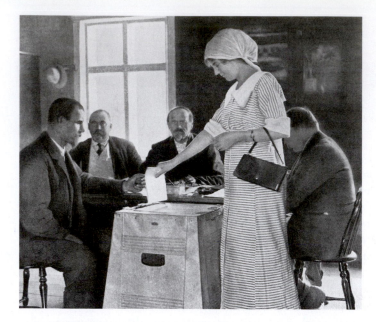

Woman Suffrage in Finland. The British and then the French introduced the concept of citizenship with universal rhetoric, but in practice the category of citizen was generally restricted to property-holding males. Only gradually were all men, and then women, recognized as citizens, with the right to own property, associate in public, and vote. Finland granted its women the right to vote in 1906, earlier than most countries. In the photo, the Finnish woman casts her ballot in the election of 1906.

obtained the right to vote in national elections in New Zealand in 1893, in Australia in 1902, in Finland in 1906, and in Norway in 1913. Despite these gains, male alarmists frequently portrayed women's suffrage and women's rights as the beginning of civilization's end.

> *Radicalized women, like radicalized men, met stiff repression wherever they challenged the established order.*

To be sure, most middle-class women were not seeking to make women equal to men. Many bourgeois women recoiled from the symbiotic relationships that existed in many countries between socialism and feminism. In Latin America, for example, anarchists championed a version of feminism, arguing that the abolition of private property would liberate women from their misery, and that the traditional family was a bourgeois convention.

Radicalized women, like radicalized men, met stiff repression wherever they challenged the established order. In 1903, China's Qiu Jin (1875–1907) left her husband and headed to Japan to study. There she was drawn to other radicals and made a name for herself by dressing in men's clothing, carrying a sword, and trying her hand at bombmaking. Returning to China in 1906, she founded the *Chinese Women's Journal* (*Zhongguo nübao*) and wrote articles urging women to fight for their rights and to leave home if necessary. She remained a radical and was executed by the Qing after she participated in a failed attempt to topple the dynasty in 1907.

In the colonial world, the woman question was a hotly debated issue, but there it was mainly argued among males. European authorities liked to boast that colonial rule improved the status of women. They cited examples of traditional societies' subordination of women in Africa and Asia and insisted that women fared better under European rule. They criticized the practices of veiling women in Islamic societies, binding women's feet in China, widow burning (*sati*) in India, and female genital mutilation in Africa as evidence of barbarism. Europeans believed that prohibiting such acts was a justification for colonial intervention.

And yet, women in Africa, the Middle East, and India found colonialism added to their burdens. As male workers were drawn into the export economy, formerly shared agricultural work fell exclusively on women's shoulders. In Africa, for example, the opening of vast new gold and diamond mines induced thousands of men to go to work in the mines, leaving women to fend for themselves. Similarly, the rise of large European-owned agricultural estates in Kenya and Southern Rhodesia depleted surrounding villages of male family members, who went to work on the estates. In these circumstances, women kept the local, food-producing economy afloat. Nor did colonial "civilizing" rhetoric improve women's political or cultural circumstances. European missionaries preached a cult of domesticity to Asian and African families, emphasizing that a woman's place was in the home raising children and that women's education should be different from that of men. Thus males overwhelmingly dominated the new schools that Europeans built. Customary law in colonial Africa, as interpreted by chiefs who collaborated with the colonial powers, favored men, and women were often deprived of landholding and other rights that they had enjoyed before the arrival of Europeans.

CLASS CONFLICT IN A NEW KEY

Capitalism's new dynamism, and especially its volatility, as we have seen, shook confidence in free market economies. Although living conditions for European and North American workers improved over time, increasing inequalities in income led to sharper conflicts between the classes. While most of these workers remained committed to peaceful agitation, some radicals gave up on capitalism and on the political process and turned to violence to achieve their aims. Often, especially in Eastern Europe and Russia, the conservative and closed character of political systems contributed to the growth of frustration—and

A CHINESE FEMINIST CONDEMNS INJUSTICES TO WOMEN

Although still a small minority, the Chinese feminists of the early twentieth century were vocal in their condemnation of the injustices inflicted upon women in China. In this famous essay from 1904 titled "An Address to Two Hundred Million Fellow Countrywomen," Qiu Jin compares the treatment of Chinese women to slavery. She also formulates a passionate indictment of the Chinese practices of preference for male children, footbinding, and arranged marriage. Typical of her generation, Qiu's feminism also bears a strong nationalistic streak as she ties the future of Chinese women to the fate of the Chinese nation.

Alas! The greatest injustice in this world must be the injustice suffered by our female population of two hundred million. If a girl is lucky enough to have a good father, then her childhood is at least tolerable. But if by chance her father is an ill-tempered and unreasonable man, he may curse her birth: "What rotten luck: another useless thing." Some men go as far as killing baby girls while most hold the opinion that "girls are eventually someone else's property" and treat them with coldness and disdain. In a few years, without thinking about whether it is right or wrong, he forcibly binds his daughter's soft, white feet with white cloth so that even in her sleep she cannot find comfort and relief until the flesh becomes rotten and the bones broken. What is all this misery for? Is it just so that on the girl's wedding day friends and neighbors will compliment him, saying, "Your daughter's feet are really small"? Is that what the pain is for?

But that is not the worst of it. When the time for marriage comes, a girl's future life is placed in the hands of a couple of shameless matchmakers and a family seeking rich and powerful in-laws. A match can be made without anyone ever inquiring whether the prospective bridegroom is honest, kind, or educated. On the day of the marriage the girl is forced into a red and green bridal sedan chair, and all this time she is not allowed to breathe one word about her future. . . .

When Heaven created people it never intended such injustice because if the world is without women, how can men be born? Why is there no justice for women? We constantly hear men say, "The human mind is just and we must treat people with fairness and equality." Then why do they greet women like black slaves from Africa? How did inequality and injustice reach this state? . . .

I hope that we all shall put aside the past and work hard for the future. Let us all put aside our former selves and be resurrected as complete human beings. Those of you who are old, do not call yourselves old and useless. If your husbands want to open schools, don't stop them; if your good sons want to study abroad, don't hold them back. Those among us who are middle-aged, don't hold back your husbands lest they lose their ambition and spirit and fail in their work. After your sons are born, send them to schools. You must do the same for your daughters and, whatever you do, don't bind their feet. As for you young girls among us, go to school if you can. If not, read and study at home. Those of you who are rich, persuade your husbands to open schools, build factories, and contribute to charitable organizations. Those of you who are poor, work hard and help your husbands. Don't be lazy, don't eat idle rice. These are what I hope for you. You must know that when a country is near destruction, women cannot rely on the men any more because they aren't even able to protect themselves. If we don't take heart now and shape up, it will be too late when China is destroyed.

Sisters, we must follow through on these ideas!

Source: Qiu Jin, "An Address to Two Hundred Million Fellow Countrywomen," in *Chinese Civilization: A Sourcebook* (2nd ed., revised and expanded), edited by Patricia Buckley Ebrey (New York: The Free Press, 1993), pp. 342–44.

INDUSTRIALIZATION AND WOMEN'S FREEDOM IN EGYPT

In this selection, taken from a 1909 lecture in Cairo open only to women, Bahithat al-Badiya (1886–1918) insists that female confinement is unnatural and absurd, and demands a place for women in the workplace. Here, the writer, an educated upper-class Egyptian woman, deplores the effect of traditional religious practices on women's freedom, but she also urges her country-women not to follow blindly in the path of the West.

Men say when we become educated we shall push them out of work and abandon the role for which God created us. But isn't it rather men who have pushed women out of work? Before, women used to spin and to weave cloth for clothes for themselves and their children, but men invented machines for spinning and weaving and put women out of work. . . . Since male inventors and workers have taken away a lot of our work should we waste our time in idleness or seek other work to occupy us? Of course, we should do the latter. . . . Obviously, I am not urging women to neglect their home and children to go out and become lawyers or judges or railway engineers. But if any of us wish to work in such professions our personal freedom should not be infringed. . . .

Men say to us categorically, "You women have been created for the house and we have been created to be bread-winners." Is this a God-given dictate? How are we to know this since no holy book has spelled it out? Political economy calls for a division of labor but if women enter the learned professions it does not upset the system. The division of labor is merely a human creation. . . . If men say to us that we have been created weak we say to them, "No it is you who made us weak through the path you made us follow." After long centuries of enslavement by men, our minds rusted and our bodies weakened. . . .

Men criticize the way we dress in the street. They have a point because we have exceeded the bounds of custom and propriety. . . . [But] veiling should not prevent us from breathing fresh air or going out to buy what we need if no one can buy it for us. It must not prevent us from gaining an education nor cause our health to deteriorate. When we have finished our work and feel restless and if our house does not have a spacious garden why shouldn't we go to the out-skirts of the city and take the fresh air that God has created for everyone and not just put in boxes exclusively for men.

Source: Bahithat al-Badiya, "A Public Lecture for Women Only in the Club of the Umma Party," in *Opening the Gates: A Century of Arab Feminist Writing*, edited by Margot Badran and Miriam Cooke (translated by Ali Badran and Margot Badran) (Indianapolis: Indiana University Press, 1990), pp. 228–38.

---

of radicalism. This was also the case in Latin America, where economic development was not accompanied by political democratization. Here, the middle classes, too, were largely shut out of politics until the rise of new parties offered fresh opportunities for political expression. Meanwhile, in Argentina, for example, workers found syndicalism (the organization of workplace associations for even the unskilled laborers), socialism, and anarchism appealing banners for urban protest.

In the Americas and in Europe, radicals of various persuasions adopted numerous new tactics for asserting the interests of the working class. In Europe, the franchise was gradually expanded in the hopes that the lower orders would prefer voting to revolution—and indeed, most of the new political parties that catered to workers had no desire to overthrow the state. Conservatives feared them nonetheless, especially as they began to achieve real electoral clout. The Labour Party, which was founded in Britain in 1900, quickly gained a large share of the vote; by 1912, the German Social Democratic Party had become the largest party in the Reichstag. But it was not the legally sanctioned parties that sparked the violent street protests and strikes, which grew exponentially in the last decades of the century. A whole array of syndicalists, anarchists, radical royalists, and revolutionary socialists sprang up in this period, making work stoppages, particularly in big cities like Paris, everyday affairs.

Although the United States did not see the emergence of similarly radical factions or successful labor parties, American workers were also organizing in larger numbers. The new power of the labor movement burst forth dramatically in 1894 when the newly organized American Railway Union launched a strike that spread across the nation. Spawned by wage cuts and firings in the wake of an economic downturn, the Pullman Strike (directed against the maker of railway sleeping cars, George Pullman) involved approximately 3 million workers. The strike's conclusion was, however, indicative of the enduring power of the status quo. After hiring replacement workers to break the strike, Pullman requested the intervention of federal troops to protect his operation. The troops arrived, infuriating strikers and precipitating violence, which led to a further crackdown by the government against the union. When its leaders were jailed, the strike by the American Railway Union against the Pullman Company collapsed.

A few upheavals from below did succeed—at least briefly. In 1905, in the wake of the Russo-Japanese War, in which the Russians were defeated by the Japanese, revolt briefly shook the tsarist state, forcing Nicholas II (ruled 1894–1917) to establish a fledgling form of representative government. The revolutionaries tried some new forms, most notably workers' soviets, which were groups of delegates representing particular industries. A wave of peasant uprisings ensued. Ultimately, however,

> *A whole array of radicalists sprang up in this period, making work stoppages in big cities like Paris everyday affairs.*

the army put down both urban and rural unrest, and autocracy was reestablished; the liberals, not to mention the radicals, were excluded from power.

Perhaps the most successful turn-of-the-century revolution occurred in Mexico. This was the century's first great peasant revolution, and it thoroughly transformed Mexico. Long in gestation, and fueled by the unequal distribution of land and by disgruntled workers, the Mexican Revolution erupted in 1910 when political elites openly split over the succession of General Porfirio Díaz after decades of his strong-arm rule. Dissidents balked when Díaz refused to step down, and peasants and workers rallied to the call to arms. What destroyed the Díaz regime and its powerful army were the swelling armies of peasants, farmers, cattlemen, and rural workers desperate for a change in the social order. From the north—led by the charismatic, if mercurial Pancho Villa—to the south—under the helm of the legendary Emiliano Zapata—rural folk helped topple the Díaz regime. In the name of providing land for the farmers and ending oligarchic rule, peasant armies defeated General Díaz's troops; they then proceeded to destroy many of Mexico's large estates. The fighting lasted for ten brutal years, at the cost of 1 million Mexicans, almost 10 percent of the country's population. But popular forces succeeded in the end in forcing new political leaders to accept their demands for democracy, respect for the sovereignty of peasant communities, and land reform. The Constitution of 1917 incorporated widespread reform. By 1920, as the revolution was winding down, an emerging generation of politicians recognized the power of a mobilized and militarized peasantry and began

The Pullman Strike. In 1894, in response to wage cuts and layoffs by the Pullman Company, the American Railway Union organized a nationwide strike that brought 3 million workers onto the picket lines. That year's labor unrest often turned violent, as in the incident pictured here, showing strikers setting fire to several hundred freight cars.

The Mexican Revolution. (*Left*) By 1915, Mexican peasants, workers, and farmers had destroyed much of the old elitist system. This was the first popular, peasant revolution of the twentieth century. Among the most famous leaders were Pancho Villa and Emiliano Zapata. They are pictured here in the presidential office in the capital. Villa took the president's chair jokingly. Zapata, carrying the broad hat typical of his people, refused to wear military gear, and glowered at the camera suspiciously. (*Right*) By the 1920s, Mexican artists and writers were putting recent events into images and words. Pictured here is one of the muralist Diego Rivera's paintings of the Mexican Revolution. Notice the nationalist interpretation: Porfirio Díaz's troops defend foreign oil companies and white aristocrats against middle-class and peasant (and darker-skinned) reformers who call for a "social revolution." Observe also the absence of women in this epic mural.

to implement deep-seated changes in Mexico's social structure. These leaders also realized that they needed to make their new regime ideologically appealing to popular folk. The revolution thus spawned a set of new national myths, based on the heroism of rural peoples, Mexican nationalism, and a celebration of the Aztec past.

Although the Mexican Revolution succeeded in toppling the old elite, elsewhere in Latin America the ruling establishment remained united and withstood assaults from below. Already in 1897, the Brazilian army had mercilessly suppressed a millenarian peasant movement in the eastern part of the country. Moreover, in Cuba, the Spanish and then the American armies crushed organized tenant farmers' efforts to reclaim land from sugar estates. In Guatemala, Mayan Indians lost land to coffee barons and their private troops.

The preservation of established orders did not rest on repression alone. By the century's end, left-wing agitators, muckraking reporters, and middle-class reformers began to achieve their goal of meaningful social improvements. Elites, unwilling to rely purely on force to stay in power, grudgingly agreed to gradual change. Unable to suppress the socialist movement, Otto von Bismarck, the German chancellor, defused the appeal of socialism by enacting social welfare measures in 1883–1884

> *By the century's end, reformers began to achieve their goal of meaningful social improvements.*

(as did France in 1904 and England in 1906). He pushed through legislation insuring workers against illness, accidents, and old age, and establishing maximum working hours. In the United States, it took lurid journalistic accounts of unsanitary practices in Chicago slaughterhouses—including tales of workers falling into lard vats and being rendered into cooking fat—to spur the federal government into action. In 1906, President Theodore Roosevelt signed a Meat Inspection Act that provided for government supervision of meatpacking operations. Ironically, this measure, though opposed vigorously by meatpackers, ultimately helped to restore the public's confidence in a much tarnished industry; in numerous other cases (banking, steel production, railroads), the enhancement of the federal government's supervisory authority served corporate interests as well.

These consumer and family protection measures were part of a broader reform movement, in the United States especially, but also elsewhere, dedicated to creating a more efficient society and correcting the unsavory consequences of urbanization and industrialization. At local and state levels, self-styled progressive reformers attacked corrupt city governments that had, in the eyes of mostly native-born reformers, fallen into the hands of immigrant-dominated "political machines." Other vices, such as gambling, drinking, and prostitution, all associated in reformers' minds with industrialized, urban settings, were also targeted by progressives. The creation of city parks became an obsession for urban planners, who hoped their greenery would serve as the "lungs" of the city and offer healthier (and less dangerous) forms of entertainment than houses of prostitution, gambling dens, and bars. In Europe and the United States, thousands of associations were formed in the hopes of tempering capitalism's excesses. From Scandinavia to California, the backers of old-age pensions and the proponents of public ownership of utilities put pressure on lawmakers, and they occasionally succeeded in changing state policies. Intervening in the market and attending to the needs of the poor, the aged, the unemployed, and the sick in ways never dreamed of in classical liberal philosophy, reform movements laid the foundations for the modern welfare state.

CULTURAL MODERNISM

→ *How was cultural modernism manifested in different fields?*

As revolutionaries and reformers wrestled with the problems of progress, intellectuals, artists, and scientists also revealed the age's insecurities and uncertainties. What we call "modernism,"

Sigmund Freud, at Work in His Study in Vienna. Freud surrounded himself not only with books but also with Egyptian figurines and African masks, expressions of universal artistic prowess—and irrational psychological drives.

the self-conscious sense of having broken with tradition, came to prominence in many fields, from physics to architecture, from painting to the social sciences. The movement largely originated from the experimental thinking shaped by turn-of-the-century anxieties. Emblematic of innovative conceptions was the work of Sigmund Freud (1856–1939), the Jewish physician in Vienna who pioneered insights into the power of the irrational. Modernist movements were also notably international as traffic in ideas and forms now passed in multiple directions. Egyptian social scientists read the works of European thinkers, while French and German painters flocked to museums to inspect artifacts from Egypt, as well as artworks collected from other parts of Africa, Asia, and Oceania. These museums, as well as numerous international exhibitions thet were held in the second half of the century, reflected a change in the meaning of "culture," which was gradually becoming less elitist and more democratic.

The European elites did not give up their opera houses and paintings, however, in favor of arts and entertainments that were popular among urban workers or colonized peoples. To the contrary, elite culture became even more elitist as modern musicians abandoned the comfort of harmonic and diatonic sound (the eight-tone scale standard in classical Western music at the time) and left representational art behind. Contemptuous of the popular press and of what they considered to be middle-brow forms of beauty, many artists sought to demonstrate their avant-garde, or cutting-edge, originality, spurning sales figures for loftier ambitions. "Art for art's sake" became the motto of some of these artists; their aim was to speak to posterity, not to the undiscriminating bourgeois public of the present.

Above all, modernism in arts and sciences replaced the certainties of the Enlightenment with the unsettledness of the new age. No longer confident about civilizing missions or urban and industrial "progress," artists and scientists struggled to make sense of a world in which older beliefs and traditional faiths had given way. What would come next, however, was unknown.

POPULAR CULTURE COMES OF AGE

By the late nineteenth century, the production and consumption of the arts, books, music, and sports were much different from what they had been a century earlier, thanks chiefly to new urban settings, technological innovations, and increased leisure time. As education, especially in America and Europe, became nearly universal, there were many more readers and museum-goers. At the same time, there were also new forms of cultural activity that were created by and for nonelite members of society. Lithographs and mass-produced engravings were bought by middle-class art lovers who could not afford original paintings; dance halls and vaudeville (a form of entertainment that included popular singers, dancers, and comedians) pleased millions who could not attend operas and formal dress balls. For the first time, sports began to attract mass followings, making soccer in Europe, baseball in the United States, and cricket in

India highly popular games that had middle- and working-class fans.

At the century's close, the press had emerged as a major form of popular entertainment and information. This was partly because publishers had begun to cater to specialized markets, offering different wares to different classes of readers—and because there were now many more who could read among the world's inhabitants, especially in Europe and the Americas. The "yellow press" was full of stories of murder and sensationalism that appealed to the urban masses. By the turn of the century, the English *Daily Mail* and the French *Petit Parisien* boasted circulations over 1 million. In the United States, urban masses, many of whom were immigrants, avidly read newspapers, some in English, some in their native languages. Here, too, newspapers like Joseph Pulitzer's *New York World* and William Randolph Hearst's *New York Journal* employed banner headlines, sensational stories, and simple language to reach out to readers with little education—or little English. Books, too, increased in number—and fell in price; penny novels about cowboys, murder, and romance became the rage. The Mexican printmaker and artist José Guadalupe Posada became a favorite source of what might be considered a forerunner of comics. In fliers, new songs, cooking recipes, and especially gory sensational news stories, Posada criticized the Díaz regime and revolutionary excess and parodied Mexican life in the country's popular penny press. His allegorical skeleton drawings, known as *calaveras*, issued for Mexico's celebration of the Day of the Dead, dwelled on popular themes of betrayal, death, and festivity.

By the turn of the century, the kind of culture one consumed had become a reflection of one's real (or desired) status in society, a central part of one's identity. For many Latin American workers, for example, reading one's own newspaper or comic strip was part of the business of being a worker. Argentina's socialist newspaper, *La Vanguardia*, was one of Buenos Aires' most prominent periodicals, read and debated at work and in the popular cafes of the city's working-class neighborhoods. Anyone seen reading the "bourgeois" paper, *La Prensa*, was heckled and ridiculed by proletarian peers.

The community of cultural consumers was now much enlarged from that of previous centuries, and writers, artists, and scholars were now subject to a much wider range of influences than ever before. As new forms and ideas trickled in, regions with rich cultural traditions and an elite class of producers, as in Europe and China, tried to adapt to the social, political, and economic changes all around them. Their attempts to confront the brave new world in the making resulted in a series of remarkable innovations, which have usually been described as "modernism."

> *By the turn of the century, the kind of culture one consumed had become a reflection of one's real (or desired) status in society, a central part of one's identity.*

EUROPE'S CULTURAL MODERNISM

In intellectual and artistic terms, Europe at the turn of the twentieth century experienced perhaps its richest age since the Renaissance. A desire to understand social and imperial maladies laid the foundations for the twentieth century's social sciences; the French scholar Emile Durkheim (1858–1917), for example, pioneered the field of sociology by studying what he took to be a characteristic affliction of his age, suicide. Seeking "talking cures" for neurotic or traumatized patients, Sigmund Freud discovered a substratum of the psyche he called "the unconscious." In 1896, the popular writer Gustave Le Bon (1841–1931) wrote a treatise on crowd behavior that became a classic in Europe and beyond; here he equated the unconscious volatility of crowds with the irrationality of women and "primitives." Le Bon's work, a true product of the century's end, gained great popularity, appealing to, among others, Benito Mussolini in Italy and Vladimir Lenin in Russia.

The work of artists reflected their ambivalence about the modern, as represented by the railroad, the big city, and the factory. While the left-leaning impressionists and realists of the mid-nineteenth century had largely celebrated progress, the painters and novelists of the century's end almost universally took a darker view. They turned away from enlightened clarity and descriptive prose in search of new, more mysterious and instinctual truths. In this epoch, the primitive came to symbolize both the romance of lost innocence and the terrors of the prerational mind. The term "primitivism" accurately reflects the ambivalence of this new appreciation for non-Western art. The painter who led the way in incorporating these themes into modern art was Pablo Picasso (1881–1973). The son of an impressionist painter, Picasso found in African art forms, notably masks and wood carvings, a shocking new way of expressing interior human sentiments. Against considerable conservative criticism, Picasso and his contemporaries claimed that African and Oceanic forms were both beautiful and more instinctual than overly refined Western forms.

Europeans began to see the world in a fundamentally different way, aided by the experience of non-Western visual arts. A way of seeing that was structured by classical and Christian images and forms, pervasive since the Renaissance, now began to seem at best banal, at worst lifeless and passé. The experience of seeing the artwork of other peoples was essential to this revolutionary change. But there were many other sources of this new vision, from anti-bourgeois attitudes among Bohemian (unconventional) artists, to a new machine aesthetic, to the desire to convey the content of dreams. And painting was certainly not the only art form in which contemporary observers registered the arrival of a modern style. In music, Arnold

Pablo Picasso. The great Franco-Spanish artist Pablo Picasso was one of the first artists to incorporate "primitive" artistic forms into his images. Here he is pictured with some of his ceramic work outside his studio at Vallauris, France.

Schönberg (1874–1951) invented the twelve-tone system in his *Five Piano Pieces* (c. 1921). World-famous dancers like Isadora Duncan (1877–1927) pioneered the expressive, free-form movements that laid the foundations for modern dance.

But the arts alone did not undermine older Christian, classical, and comfortable views of the world. Even science, in which the Enlightenment had placed so much faith, worked a disenchanting magic on the liberal, Victorian worldview. Darwinism claimed that progress could not be achieved without a "struggle for existence." James Clerk Maxwell (1831–1879), the Scottish physicist, described the law of entropy, which indicated that our universe was destined to die. Matter, Maxwell argued, is moved by heat, but as heat over time increasingly loses its ability to move particles, and as the universe has a fixed supply of energy, sooner or later, entropy—the inability of heat to do work—will set in, and an exhausted, chaotic universe will emerge. In Maxwell's wake, the pioneering physicists and mathematicians of the turn of the century took apart the Enlightenment's conviction that man could achieve full knowledge of, and control over, nature. Probabilities took the place of certainties in physics. Although most scientists continued to collect data with the conviction that they could and would plumb nature's depths, some of their foresightful colleagues began to question the arrogance expressed in this view.

From the time of the Enlightenment, Europeans had prided themselves on their "reason"; to be rational was to be civilized, and respectable, middle-class nineteenth-century men were thought to be exemplars of both of these high virtues. But in the late nineteenth century, faith in rationality began to falter; perhaps reason was *not* man's highest attainment, said some; perhaps reason was too hard for man to sustain, said others. Friedrich Nietzsche (1844–1900) might be said to characterize those who held that rationality without passion threatened to become machine-like idiocy. Sigmund Freud went further in the exploration of the world of passion, excavating the layers of the human subconscious, where all sorts of irrational desires and fears lay buried. For Freud, human nature was not as simple as it had seemed to the thinkers of the Enlightenment—humans were driven by sexual longings and childhood traumas, some of these so thoroughly repressed that they were revealed only as neuroses, in dreams, or in the course of extensive psychoanalysis (a therapy Freud invented). Neither Nietzsche (who went mad in 1889) nor Freud (who lived almost long enough to become respectable) was well-loved, certainly not among the nineteenth-century liberal elites. But in the new century, Nietzsche would be made the prophet for a wide range of anti-liberal, anti-rational causes, from nudism to Nazism, and Freud's dark vision, more than that of any other intellectual, would become central to the twentieth century's understanding of the self.

CULTURAL MODERNISM IN CHINA

What it meant to be "modern" was a question that was also debated beyond the borders of Western Europe and North America. In other parts of the world, too, the debate did not yield to a particular meaning. The Europeans provided one set of answers; intellectuals elsewhere, drawing on separate cultural traditions and confronted with different problems, often offered quite different answers. For example, the Chinese literati also became caught up in the debate about what it meant to be modern, and they articulated their own perspectives. As in Europe, Chinese artists and scientists at the turn of the century engaged in considerable experimentation and innovation, including selectively importing Western ideas and cultural forms. In the realm of literature, for instance, late Qing writers strove to produce narrative strategies that were recognizably new; their works explored the self, technology, and sexuality. As in the West, Chinese writers could now write for a wider and more diverse readership. By the end of the nineteenth century, there were more than 170 presses in China serving a potential readership of 2 to 4 million. Indeed, some have argued that the late Qing period should be described as a time of competing cultural *modernities*, in contrast to the post-Qing era, characterized by the self-conscious pursuit of a single, Western-oriented *modernity*. These forms of modernity were characterized by both critical reflection on Chinese traditions and ambivalent reactions to Western culture.

Consumers of late Qing literature were most likely to be urbanites, particularly in the treaty ports, the coastal cities that had been designated as centers of trade and residence for the growing foreign community. These cities typically boasted an environment that was both more economically vibrant and culturally fluid than the hinterlands. Not only was there an expanding body of readers, but the *nouveaux riches*, beneficiaries of the newly reconfigured treaty-port economy, now formed a group of patrons for the arts. In the latter half of the nineteenth century, for example, painters from different parts of the lower Yangzi region congregated in Shanghai to practice their craft. Collectively known as the Shanghai School, they symbolized the vitality of the artistic scene. The Shanghai painters adopted elements from both indigenous and foreign sources for their innovations in compositional structure, coloring, figural rendering, and spatial conception. Classically trained, they appropriated Western technical novelties into their artistic practice. One of the most famous earlier examples was the self-portrait of the artist Ren Xiong (1820–1857), an arresting image of the artist himself, bareheaded and legs apart, standing upright and staring straight at the viewer. Ren Xiong was not the only Chinese artist whose work embraced photography, although the effect of this new visual medium was usually most popular among professional effigy painters rather than scholarly artists.

> *What kind of balance should exist between Western thought and Chinese learning remained an issue that would haunt generations to come.*

Ren Xiong, Self-Portrait. This famous self-portrait of Ren Xiong was most likely produced in the 1850s. Ren Xiong was probably familiar with the then brand-new practice of portrait photography in the treaty ports. Although in some ways his self-portrait reproduced some old conventions of Chinese scholarly art, such as the unity of the visual image with a lengthy self-composed inscription, it is also clear that, through its rather unconventional pose and image, Ren Xiong had pointed to the establishment of a new kind of subject position characteristic of the trend of "cultural modernism" in China during this period.

Similarly, the fantasy novels of the late Qing period drew both on the authors' knowledge of Western science and on indigenous supernatural beliefs. Experimental writers turned out titles such as *The End of the World*, *Moon Colony*, and *The Future of New China*, some of which explicitly treated the question of Chinese-Western relations. The 1908 novel *New Era*, for example, put its opening scenes in the year 1999, by which time China had become a supreme world power and a constitutional monarchy. Depicting China at war with Western powers, *New Era* celebrated conventional military ventures and heroism, but it also introduced the readers to new inventions such as electricity-repellent clothing and bulletproof satin. More visionary still was the novel *The Stone of Goddess Nüwa*, published in 1905. Here the male author imagined a technologically advanced feminist utopia in which the female residents studied subjects ranging from the arts to physics, drove electric cars, and were nourished by purified liquid extracts of food from a breast-shaped device. Their mission was to save China by getting rid of corrupt male officials. As the authors of these fantasy novels combined the fanciful with the critical, their works sought to resolve the very real cultural tensions of their era and offered a new and provocative vision of China.

Yet, if Western science proved to be an inspiration for late Qing writers, its integration into Chinese culture was an intellectual challenge. Did being modern entail forsaking China's scholarly traditions, or could Western science exist alongside Chinese values? The nineteenth century had seen Christian missionaries, following in the footsteps of the Jesuits, use their scientific knowledge to attract followers. For example, John Fryer, an English missionary and translator, founded *The Science Journal* (*Gezhi huibian*) in 1876. Other publications in the same period included *The Universal Gazette* (*Wanguo gongbao*). Recognizing its utilitarian value, many Chinese scholars assisted missionaries in their efforts to promote Western science, although they continued to regard it mostly as a means of acquiring national wealth and power, rather than as a means of understanding the world. It is not surprising that they took this stance; Western visitors to China also tended to present science as little more than a means to material ends. The result was that while steamships, telegraphs, and railroads captured public attention, there was little interest in changing fundamental Chinese beliefs. Thus, although they recognized the need to incorporate new modes of knowledge into their repertoire, many members of the elite insisted that traditional Chinese learning remain the principal source of all knowledge. This was so even though they also lamented that in recent times traditional learning had often fallen victim to empty and superfluous studies. What kind of balance should exist between Western thought and Chinese learning, or indeed whether the ancient classics should retain their fundamental role, remained an issue that would haunt generations to come.

RETHINKING RACE AND REIMAGINING NATIONS

> ↦ *How did conceptions about race and nation change in this era?*

Ironically, in this world of huge population transfers and increasingly shared technological modernization, individuals and nations became passionate defenders of the idea that identities were deeply rooted and unchangeable. Although physical characteristics had always played *some* role in identifying persons, by the late nineteenth century, the Linnaean classifications developed in the eighteenth century (see Chapter 5) had become the means for ranking the worth of whole nations. As we saw in Chapter 8, race now defined who could belong to the nation and share in its rights and privileges; by the century's close, racial roots had also become a crucial part of cultural identity. This was the era, par excellence, of ethnographic museums, folkloric collectors, national essence movements, and racial genealogies; people wanted to know who they (and their neighbors) were—and, increasingly, this was defined by one's *biological* ancestry. Just as traditional ways of life and family ties were being disrupted by imperialism and extensive industrialization, inheritance took on new weight, both in cultural and in biological forms. Doctors, officials, and novelists described the genetic inheritance of madness, alcoholism, criminality, and even homosexuality; nationalists spoke of the uniqueness of the Slavic soul, the German mind, Hindu spirituality, the Hispanic race.

In the West, people had been constructing racial hierarchies since at least the Enlightenment. By the end of the nineteenth century, however, race was considered a more central part of individual identity, and science was used to sanction racial inequalities. Just as Darwin's generation had suggested the incompatibility of human races, the generation that followed discussed the existence of separate white, black, yellow, and red races. Doctors and anthropologists warned against racial mixing, suggesting that mixed types were more likely to become vagrants, prostitutes, homosexuals, or criminals, whose presence would debase and weaken national vitality. Discussions of race pervaded European and North American culture, where they served to justify the seizing of colonial territory and the subservience of African Americans. Race was now considered a biologically defined determinant of behavior and belonging, and it was on virtually everyone's lips, from China to India to England. The preoccupation with race testified to a worldwide longing for new, fixed roots—and unshakable hierarchies—in an age that seemed to be burning all its bridges to the past.

Nationalist and racial ideas had different configurations in different portions of the world. In Europe and America, debates about race and national purity evolved from a combination of fears about the loss of individuality and vitality in a techno-logical world, rising tensions between states, and fear of being defeated or overrun by the brown, black, and yellow peoples beyond the borders of "civilization." By contrast, in India, these ideas evolved as part of an anti-colonial discourse, and they were involved in the beginnings of popular political mobilization, particularly among the urban elite. This was also the case in China, Latin America, and the Islamic world, where discussions of identity were wrapped up with opposition both to Western domination and to corrupt indigenous elites. Especially in the colonial and semi-colonial world, the question of racial identity was very much a question about the coherence and endurance of the community, not about the races of man in general.

The result of these new voices and new fears produced a variety of new national movements, from China's anti-Qing campaign to India's Swadeshi Movement. At the same time, pan-ethnic movements attempted to go beyond the nation-state, proposing the creation of communities based on ethnicity. Although these projects were not realized then, the notion that political communities should be built on racial purity or draw on unsullied indigenous traditions did not die. They inspired later leaders, especially in the years between the two world wars. They also offered further evidence of just how unsettled the world was by the century's end, and how urgent the questions of identity and belonging had become.

NATION AND RACE IN NORTH AMERICA AND EUROPE

In the United States, where belief in progress had been strongest, the changing temper was particularly striking. Americans greeted the end of the century with a combination of chest-beating pride and shoulder-slumping pessimism. In the early 1890s, for example, Americans flocked to scores of extravagant commemorations of the four hundredth anniversary of Christopher Columbus's discovery. The largest of these was the Columbian Exposition in Chicago. At that world's fair and at smaller gatherings, Americans saw displays of the most modern machinery and celebrated the nation's marvelous destiny. And yet, even as Americans glorified the progress of their times, they worried about the present and future of their nation. Foremost among their anxieties was the fear that America had exhausted what had once been thought an infinite supply of new land and resources. The disappearance of the buffalo, the erosion of soils, and the depletion of once abundant timber stands by aggressive logging companies had worried some early conservationists, and that alarm became more intense with the 1890 announcement by the Census Bureau that the American frontier had "closed."

With the succession of Theodore Roosevelt (1858–1919) to the presidency in 1901, the concerns about conserving natural resources were translated into government policy. Fearing a world without conquerable frontiers, Roosevelt, like a growing number of his generation, agonized about the fate of market economies and the decline of America's pioneering ethos. The market, insisted Roosevelt and like-minded conservationists, could not be trusted to protect "nature." Instead, federal regulation, on a scale far beyond nineteenth-century imaginations, was necessary, leading to the creation in 1905 of the National Forest Service, with its cadre of scientifically trained officials to manage the development of millions of acres of permanent public lands. Roosevelt also feared that a nation dominated by impersonal corporations and populated primarily by urban-dwelling factory workers would lose its spirit of pioneer individualism. He worried in particular that modern comforts in post-frontier America would deprive men of the tests of rough-and-ready manhood that generations of pioneers had found in conquering Indians and taming the wilderness. To give Americans a chance to play pioneer, Roosevelt pushed for lands to be set aside as wildlife reserves and national parks, where he hoped that future generations would continue to experience what he extolled as "the strenuous life."

What white Americans did not, in general, agonize about was what the African-American intellectual W. E. B. Du Bois (1868–1963) predicted would be "the problem of the twentieth century," that is, "the problem of the color line." Rather, white

The Conservation Movement. Recognizing that certain vital resources were being rapidly depleted and concerned that urban men were losing the vitality of their pioneer forebears, a "conservation" movement gathered political strength in the last decades of the nineteenth century. Among the notable early victories for conservationists was the setting aside of California's Yosemite Valley as a national park.

Americans were busily drawing color lines, initiating new forms of racial discrimination where old forms (like slavery) had broken down. In the American West, virulent animosity toward Chinese workers culminated in the 1882 Exclusion Act, which prohibited almost all immigration from China. In the American South, where most of the nation's 7 million African Americans resided, a system of "Jim Crow" laws codified racial segregation and inequality.

The anxieties of white Americans intensified as more and more "swarthy" immigrants entered the United States. These people were primarily from southern and eastern Europe, but to the champions of "Anglo-Saxonism" these Europeans were not "white." Even more threatening were the darker peoples over whom the United States now ruled as colonial subjects in the Philippines, Puerto Rico, and Cuba. Talk of the demise of white America permeated elite conversations, and these fears built support for more restrictive immigration policies.

These conversations about race and national identities were not limited to North America. Across the North Atlantic, European elites engaged in similar discussions. For European elites, the final divvying up of Africa was in many respects equivalent to the closing of the American frontier. The Germans and Italians, in particular, complained bitterly about the lack of new territories on which to plant their flags. The French and British began to worry more about how their empires were to be preserved, especially as they became more aware of the anti-colonial sentiments that were seething in their domains.

Like Americans, Europeans also expressed concerns about trends at home. Intellectuals in Europe, as in the United States, suggested that mechanization deprived men of their vitality. At the same time, the spread of Darwinist theory provoked new anxieties about inherited diseases, racial mixing, and the dying out of white "civilizers." Concubinage and mixed offspring had always been part of European colonization, but as racial identities hardened, the consorting of white men with native women now seemed to threaten the moral fiber of the whole nation. A new discourse of virility arose, in part provoked by the increased involvement of doctors and scientists in the treatment of social problems. In the century's last decades, English and American schoolboys were encouraged to play sports, if not to be like pioneers, then at least to avoid becoming weak degenerates unable to defend the nation should the need arise. In addition, new medical attention was given to homosexuality, which was viewed as a disease and a threat to the future of Anglo-Saxon civilization. In France, the falling birthrate, especially after the loss of Alsace-Lorraine to Germany at the end of the Franco-Prussian War, convinced many officials, social scientists, and artists that their nation had entered a period of decadence, characterized by weak, sickly men and irrational women. Some tied decadence to what was termed "the Jewish Question." Especially in Austria, Germany, Russia, and France, reactionaries cooked up anti-Semitic diatribes. Perhaps because nothing else seemed stable and enduring, white, well-to-do male Europeans, like their American counterparts, looked to racial purity to shore up the civilizations they saw coming apart at the seams.

RACE-MIXING AND THE PROBLEM OF NATIONHOOD IN LATIN AMERICA

Latin American debates about identity were chiefly defined by the question of ethnic intermixing and the legacy of a system of government that, unlike much of the North Atlantic world, excluded rather than included the populace. Social hierarchies reaching back to the sixteenth century ranked white Iberians at the top, creole elites in the middle, and indigenous and African populations at the bottom. According to this formulation, the higher on the social ladder, the more likely the people were to be white. In fact, however, the "racial" order did not stick, since some Iberians occupied the lower ranks, while a few people of color did manage to ascend the ladder. Moreover, starting in the 1880s, the racial hierarchy was further disrupted by the deluge of poor European migrants to prospering Latin American countrysides or to booming cities like Buenos Aires in Argentina or São Paulo in Brazil. Latin American societies, then, did not easily become homogeneous "nations." Indeed, many Latin American observers began to wonder whether national identities could survive these transformations at all.

In an age of acute nationalism, the mixed racial composition of Latin Americans generated special anxieties. In the 1870s in Mexico, it was common to view Indians as obstacles to change. The demographer Antonio García Cubas, for example, stressed what he considered to be "the decadence and degeneration in general of the indigenous race and the few elements of vitality and vigor that it offers for the republic's progress." In Cuba and Brazil, observers made the same claims about blacks. Latin America, according to many modernizers, was being held back by its own people. The solution, argued some writers, was to attract white immigrants and to implement educational programs that would uplift Indians, blacks, and people of mixed descent. Thus, many intellectuals joined the crusade to modernize and westernize their populations.

For their part, Latin American leaders began to exalt a mythic past and to celebrate bygone glories as a way to promote a strong sense of national selfhood. In Mexico, General Díaz placed the bell that Father Hidalgo had tolled on September 16, 1810, to mark the beginning of the war against Spain, in the National Palace in Mexico City. In the month of that centennial in 1910, a series of grand processions wound through the

Diego Rivera's History of Mexico. This is one of the most famous works of Mexican art history, a portrait of the history of Mexico by the radical nationalist painter Diego Rivera. In this chapter and in previous chapters we have illustrated parts of this mural. In stepping back to view the whole work, which is in the National Palace in Mexico City, we can see how Rivera envisioned the history of his people generally. Completed in 1935, this work seeks to show a people fighting constantly against outside aggressors, from their glorious pre-conquest days (lower center), winding like a grand epic through the conquest, colonial exploitation, the revolution for independence, nineteenth-century invasions from France and the U.S., to the popular 1910 Revolution. It culminates in an image of Karl Marx, framed by a "scientific sun"—pointing to a future of progress and prosperity for all, as if restoring a modern Tenochtitlán of the Aztecs. This work captured many Mexicans' efforts to return to the indigenous roots of the nation and to fuse them with modern scientific ideas.

capital. Many of these parades celebrated Aztec grandeur, thereby creating a mythic arch from the greatness of the Aztec past to the triumphal story of Mexican independence—and thence to the benevolence and progress of the Díaz regime. As the government glorified the Aztecs with pageants, statues, and pavilions, however, it continued to ignore modern Aztec descendants, who lived in squalor.

It was in these years that some thinkers began to celebrate a pre-modern basis of national identities. For some, especially in Mexico, and eventually in the Andes, the pre-Spanish past became a crucial foundation stone of the nation-state. The young Mexican writer José Vasconcelos (1882–1959) grew disenchanted with the brutal rule of Díaz and his westernizing ambitions. Nonetheless, he endorsed Díaz's celebration of the Indian past—for his own purposes. Mexicans, he believed, were capable of a superior form of civilization. He insisted that if they were less driven by material concerns, their combined Aztec and Spanish Catholic origins could create a spiritual domain of even higher achievement. Mexico's greatness flowed not in spite of, but because of, its mixture. Vasconcelos's inspiration was itself mixed. He drew on European spiritualism to expose the false illusions of material freedoms. At the same time, Indian philosophy inspired him to believe that what he described as the Anglo civilization was bound to give way to a moral and aesthetic successor. He argued that this new civilization would eventually be governed by a "Cosmic Race." It is telling that Vasconcelos, who would soon emerge as one of Latin America's leading writers and the founder of Mexico's modern school system, still clung to biological explanations of culture and national identity.

SUN YAT-SEN AND THE MAKING OF A CHINESE NATION

The turn to an authentic and usable past that characterized Latin American thought at the end of the century paralleled the development in China of a literature that emphasized the power and depth of Chinese culture—in obvious contrast to the Qing empire's failing political power and social instability. Here, writers invoked race to emphasize the superiority of the Han Chinese. Here, too, the increasing pace of change generated the desire to trace one's roots back to secure foundations. And here, as well, traditions were reinvented in the hope of saving the Chinese soul threatened by modernity.

In China, as elsewhere, the reformulation of identities was a matter both for scholars and for political mobilizers. By the century's end, prominent members of both groups had abandoned their commitment to the preservation of the old order.

Yet, most were not prepared to seek a solution in the wholesale adoption of Western norms and practices. In these attempts at salvaging and selective borrowing, combining traditions and values from home and abroad, the modern Chinese intelligentsia and modern Chinese nationalism were born.

The challenge of nation-building was symbolized, most spectacularly, by the endeavors of one man, Sun Yat-sen (1866–1925), though he was part of an emerging generation of critics of the old regime. Like his European counterparts, Sun dreamed of a reconstituted political community along "national" lines. Born into a modest rural household in the Canton region in southern China, Sun studied medicine in the British colony of Hong Kong in the late 1880s. A man of forceful personality and grand ambitions, he turned to politics at the time of the Sino-Japanese War of 1894–1895. The Qing government spurned his offer of service to the Chinese cause, an act that not only embittered Sun, but convinced him of the decrepitude of China's rulers. Shortly thereafter, he set up an organization based in Hawaii to advocate the Qing downfall and the cause of republicanism. The cornerstone of his message was Chinese, or more specifically, Han, nationalism.

Sun blasted the feeble rule by outsiders, the Manchus, and trumpeted the image of a virile, sovereign political community of "true" Chinese. No ruler, he argued, could enjoy legitimacy without the nation's consent. Accordingly, Sun articulated a vision of a new China free of Manchu rule, moving gradually toward a democratic form of government and an economic system based on vaguely defined processes for equalizing land rights. In this fashion, China would join the world community of nation-states and have the will and power to defend its borders against aggressors.

Sun's nationalism did not catch on immediately in China itself, in part because the Qing regime persecuted all dissenters, executing them or forcing them into exile. This persecution prevented the organization of popular protest in China. But his ideas fared much better among the huge population of overseas Chinese. Between 1845 and 1900, population pressure, shortage of cultivable land, and the social turmoil of the mid-nineteenth century forced an estimated 400,000 Chinese to seek new homes in the United States, Canada, Australia, and New Zealand. A similar number went to the West Indies and Latin America, and close to four times as many settled in Southeast Asia. In the United States alone, the Chinese population reached 107,488 in 1890, in spite of harsh restrictions that sought to exclude Chinese laborers from immigrating. In the United States and elsewhere, the Chinese immigrants were overwhelmingly male workers who came from southern and southeastern parts of China. Often victims of discrimination in their adopted homelands, members of these communities applauded Sun's brand of racial national-

> *In these attempts at salvaging and selective borrowing, combining traditions and values from home and abroad, the modern Chinese intelligentsia and modern Chinese nationalism were born.*

Sun Yat-sen. Through the medium of clothing, these two images of Sun Yat-sen, the man generally known as the "father of the Chinese nation," epitomize the changes and the evolving cultural ambiguities of China in the late nineteenth and early twentieth centuries. *(Left)* As a young man studying medicine in the British colony of Hong Kong in the late 1880s, Sun and his friends are seen here in the conventional Qing garb of Chinese gentlemen. *(Right)* Two decades later in early 1912, Sun and the officials of the new republic appeared in public donning full Western-style jackets and ties. Clothing, like so many other parts of the cultural arena in China during this period, had become a contested ground in the battle to forge a new nation's identity.

ism and democratic ideas. In addition, Chinese students who were studying abroad, including a growing number of young women, found inspiration in Sun's message.

Sun's nationalist and republican call resonated more powerfully as the Qing empire grew weaker in the first decade of the twentieth century. Defeat at the hands of the Japanese was especially humiliating, coming as it did from those whom the Chinese had historically considered a "lowly" folk. The Manchu court realized that reforms were necessary, and set about overhauling the administrative system and the military and enacting constitutional reforms. Yet, these changes came much too late and satisfied no one. The old elites grumbled. The new stratum of urban merchants, entrepreneurs, and professionals, who were benefiting from the recent socioeconomic changes and the opportunities of doing business with westerners, regarded the government as outmoded. Peasants and laborers resented the high cost of the reforms, which seemed to help only the rulers and not the ruled. A mutiny, sparked in part by the government's nationalization of China's railroads and low compensation to native Chinese investors, that broke out in the city of Wuchang in central China in October 1911, quickly spread to other parts of the country. Sun Yat-sen wrapped up his travels in the United States and hurried home. Few people rallied to the emperor's cause, and the Qing dynasty collapsed. The emperor, who was a six-year-old child, abdicated in February 1912. In the provinces, coalitions of gentry, merchants, and military leaders ran the government. A dynastic tradition of more than two thousand years had come to an abrupt end.

Soldiers Cutting Manchu Queues. The queue was initially the hairstyle of the Manchus. It was forcibly imposed upon the Han Chinese after the establishment of the Qing regime in the seventeenth century. With the founding of the republic in 1912, the new government regarded cutting the queue as an important symbolic gesture for its citizens, both as a final defiance of the authority of the old regime as well as an embrace of modernity. The irony was that, over the centuries, many Chinese had come to accept the queue as an integral part of their own cultural identity, and its often involuntary cutting, as shown in this picture, turned out to be a traumatic event for many in the early republic.

China would soon be reconstituted, and Sun's ideas, in particular those regarding race, would play a central role in the configuration of the new state. The original flag of the republic, for example, consisted of five colors. These were meant to represent the five major racial groups that made up the citizenry: red for the Han, yellow for the Manchus, blue for the Mongols, white for the Tibetans, and black for the Muslims. But Sun was never really comfortable with this "multiracial" flag, believing that there should only be one Chinese race. The existence of the different groups in China, he argued, was simply the result of incomplete assimilation, a problem that the modern nation, having replaced an outmoded imperial dynasty, now had to confront.

> *Now it was possible to speak of "India" as a single unit, which also made it possible for anti-colonial thinkers to imagine seizing and ruling India by themselves.*

NATIONALISM AND INVENTED TRADITIONS IN INDIA

British imperial rule persisted in India, but the turn of the century saw cracks widen in the colonial edifice. The consolidation of colonial administration, the establishment of railways and telegraphs, the growth of Western education and ideas, and the development of colonial capitalism had transformed and unified the territory, not only for the purposes of commerce and transportation, but also in people's minds. Now it was possible to speak of "India" as a single unit, which also made it possible for anti-colonial thinkers to imagine seizing and ruling India by themselves. A new form of anti-colonial resistance emerged, one that differed from the peasant rebellions of the past. Unlike earlier visionaries and local opposition movements, the proponents of resistance at the beginning of the twentieth century talked of Indians as "a people" who had a "national" past as well as "national" traditions.

The leaders of the nationalist opposition were Western-educated intellectuals from colonial cities and towns. The origin of this group went back to the early nineteenth century when Western education was first introduced. By 1900, nearly half a million Indians had some form of Western education. Though they formed less than 1 percent of the Indian popula-

Symbols of Imperial Power. George V, king of England and emperor of India, with his wife, Queen Mary, at a *durbar* (ceremony) in Delhi, the capital city of India, in 1911. Using the symbols of imperial power to show the pomp and splendor of the British Raj, the British rulers receive homage from their imperial subjects and thereby cement the ties between England and India.

A MUSLIM WOMAN DREAMS OF SECLUDING MEN FROM THE WORLD

Though international in its breadth, the women's movement took on very different concerns and causes in different national contexts. In the Muslim world, many women demanded the end to their seclusion and the right to appear in public without being fully veiled. In this selection, Rokeya Sakhawat Hossain (1880–1932), a Muslim Bengali woman, uses satire to underline the injustices and inefficiencies of confining women to the zenana *(the harem). In Hossain's story, originally published in 1905 in* The Indian Ladies Magazine, *an English journal in Madras, India, the heroine dreams of the perfections of a world turned upside down, in which women, not men, fill the streets and lock away the men.*

One evening I was lounging in an easy chair in my bedroom and thinking lazily of the condition of Indian womanhood. I am not sure whether I dozed off or not. But, as far as I remember, I was wide awake. I saw the moonlit sky sparkling with thousands of diamondlike stars, very distinctly.

All of a sudden a lady stood before me; how she came in, I do not know. I took her for my friend, Sister Sara. . . .

I used to have my walks with Sister Sara, when we were at Darjeeling. Many a time did we walk hand in hand and talk lightheartedly in the botanical gardens there. I fancied Sister Sara had probably come to take me to some such garden, and I readily accepted her offer and went out with her.

When walking I found to my surprise that it was a fine morning. The town was fully awake and the streets alive with bustling crowds. I was feeling very shy, thinking I was walking in the street in broad daylight, but there was not a single man visible.

Some of the passersby made jokes at me. Though I could not understand their language, yet I felt sure they were joking. I asked my friend, "What do they say?"

"The women say you look very mannish."

"Mannish?" said I. "What do they mean by that?"

"They mean that you are shy and timid like men."

"Shy and timid like men?" It was really a joke. . . .

"I feel somewhat awkward," I said, in a rather apologizing tone, "as being a *purdahnishin* woman I am not accustomed to walking about unveiled."

"You need not be afraid of coming across a man here. This is Ladyland, free from sin and harm. Virtue herself reigns here.". . .

I became curious to know where the men were. I met more than a hundred women while walking there, but not a single man.

"Where are the men?" I asked her.

"In their proper places, where they ought to be."

"Pray let me know what you mean by 'their proper places.'"

"Oh, I see my mistake, you cannot know our customs, as you were never here before. We shut our men indoors."

"Just as we are kept in the *zenana*?"

"Exactly so."

"How funny." I burst into a laugh. Sister Sara laughed too.

"But, dear Sultana, how unfair it is to shut in the harmless women and let loose the men. . . . Why do you allow yourselves to be shut up?"

"Because it cannot be helped as they are stronger than women."

"A lion is stronger than a man, but it does not enable him to dominate the human race. You have neglected the duty you owe to yourselves, and you have lost your natural rights by shutting your eyes to your own interests."

"But my dear Sister Sara, if we do everything by ourselves, what will the men do then?"

"They should not do anything, excuse me; they are fit for nothing. Only catch them and put them into the *zenana*."

Source: Rokeya Sakhawat Hossain, *Sultana's Dream and Selections from The Secluded Ones,* edited and translated by Roushan Jahan (New York: The Feminist Press at the City University of New York, 1988), pp. 7–9.

tion, they came to occupy the center stage in colonial India because they enjoyed access to the official world and were familiar with European knowledge and history. The intelligentsia used this knowledge to develop characteristically modern cultural forms. It turned colloquial languages into standardized, literary forms for writing novels and dramas. Hindi, Urdu, Bengali, Tamil, Malayalam, and other languages developed as modern vernaculars, with the aid of a lively print culture in different Indian languages. The publication of journals, magazines, newspapers, pamphlets, novels, and dramas increased rapidly. The development of this print culture created networks of exchange and communication throughout the territorial boundaries of British India.

The development of print cultures went hand in hand with the growth of a new public sphere where the intelligentsia discussed and debated social and political matters. By the 1860s and the 1870s, voluntary associations had begun to proliferate in big cities. The urban professionals who ran these associations began to coordinate their efforts, and eventually established a political party in 1885, the Indian National Congress. Lawyers, prominent merchants, and local notables dominated the early leadership of the Congress. Deeply committed to constitutional methods, the Congress leadership composed long, well-reasoned petitions demanding greater representation of Indians in administrative and legislative bodies. They penned sharp critiques of the government's economic policies and wrote essays proposing policies to encourage India's industrialization.

> *The critical question for nationalists was: Could India both be a modern nation and retain its Indian identity?*

Underlying political nationalism, expressed in the formation of the Indian National Congress, was cultural nationalism. The nationalists claimed that Indians might not be a single "race," but they were at least a unified people because they possessed a unique culture and a common colonial history. Of course, such a claim was not peculiar to India; everywhere nations were imagined in a similar fashion, forging new national identities for societies in the midst of economic and political transformations. But nationalism in India, unlike in Europe, developed with an acute awareness of Indians as colonial subjects. The nationalists criticized the West in order to differentiate their movement from Western visions of a modern world. The critical question for nationalists was: Could India both be a modern nation *and* retain its Indian identity? How could India be distinguished from the West while at the same time being modern?

Like their Latin American counterparts, Indian intellectuals delved into the past and rewrote the histories of the ancient empires and kingdoms as pasts of the nation. The "recovery" of traditions became the intelligentsia's consuming concern, its means to establish a modern Indian identity without adopting the subordinate role assigned to Indians by British colonizers. In this way, they disseminated the idea of the nation-state, which had not had an integrated, national history prior to colonization. To press the claims of Indians as a people with a unifying religious creed, intellectuals reconfigured Hinduism so that it resembled Western religion. While traditional Hinduism did not possess a singular textual authority, a monotheistic God, an organized church, or an established creed, nationalist Hindu intellectuals combined the diverse range of philosophical texts, cultural beliefs, social practices, and Hindu historical traditions into a synthetic creation that they then identified as the authentic Hindu religion. In this formulation, Indianness was "revived" not "invented." Similarly, other late-nineteenth-century Indian revivalists explored the roots of a national culture in the subcontinent's past. Some delved into ancient manuscripts to discover Indian contributions to astronomy, mathematics, algebra, chemistry, and medicine, and advocated the development of a national science. In the fine arts, intellectuals constructed an imaginary line of continuity to the glorious past to formulate a vivid notion of a specifically Indian art and aesthetics.

Reviving the past opened the way for creative accommodations of indigenous and modern cultures, but in the process of fashioning these hybrid forms, revivalists also produced a narrowed definition of Indian traditions. As the Hindu intelligentsia looked back, it identified Hindu traditions and the pre-Islamic past as *the* sources of India's culture. Other contributors to the Indian mosaic's cultural past were forgotten. Indeed, the history of "India" was increasingly identified with the history of Hinduism; the Muslim past, in particular, enjoyed no prominent role in this movement.

Hindu revivalism became a powerful political force during the closing years of the nineteenth century, when the nationalist challenge to the colonial regime took a decidedly militant turn. New leaders arose who disdained constitutionalism and called for militant methods of agitation. The British decision to partition Bengal in 1905 into two provinces—one predominantly Muslim, and the other with a Hindu majority—prompted militants to take to the streets in protest and to urge the boycott of British goods. Rabindranath Tagore, the famous Bengali poet and future Nobel laureate, was inspired to compose stirring nationalist poetry. To promote self-reliance, the activists formed voluntary organizations, called Swadeshi (meaning "one's own country") Samitis. These organizations championed the creation of indigenous enterprises for the manufacture of soap, cloth, medicine, iron, and paper, as well as the establishment of schools to impart nationalist education. Few of these experiments were successful, but the efforts nonetheless reflected the nationalist desire to assert the autonomy of Indians as a people.

Rabindranath Tagore. The Bengali writer, philosopher, and teacher Rabindranath Tagore (1861–1941) became the poet laureate of the Swadeshi Movement in Bengal in 1903–1908. The first Asian Nobel laureate, he became disenchanted with nationalism, viewing it as narrow-visioned and not universalistic. The photo shows Rabindranath Tagore reading to a group of his students in 1929.

Marshaling cultural resources, reconfiguring society, and inspiring popular participation in the anti-partition agitation, the Swadeshi Movement swept aside the old moderate leadership of the Indian National Congress and installed a new, radical leadership. The leadership achieved notable successes in broadening the nationalist agitation. No longer was nationalism just an ideology for the few: by century's end, it had become a broad-based movement. Though the people did not topple the colonial regime, the experience of Indian mass mobilization was enough to shake the confidence of the British rulers, who found themselves having to resort to coercive measures to keep the colony intact. When the movement slipped into a campaign of terrorism in 1908, the government responded by imprisoning militant leaders. But the colonial administrators also annulled the partition of Bengal in 1911.

Although the nationalists did not view their movement as a Hindu campaign, Hindu symbols figured prominently in the language of Indian nationalism. This is not surprising, for as the idea of India as a nation took shape, regional, linguistic, and religious identities were being mobilized by Western-educated elites, and these identities were part of the process that made India thinkable as a nation. Intellectuals representing Hindu,

but also other ethnic, linguistic, and religious groups living in India, notably Bengalis, Tamils, and Muslims, were using religious revival and the exploitation of new media (for example, the print culture of newspapers and journals) to unite and mobilize their communities. While the appeal to ethnic and religious identification was central to these mobilizing efforts, the goal was modern and secular—as was demonstrated by the founding of the Indian National Muslim League in 1906. Rather than spreading the Islamic religion, this group was dedicated to the advancement of the *political* interests of Muslims.

Late-nineteenth-century Indian nationalisms posed a different kind of challenge to the British than the suppressed 1857 rebellion. The insurgents of 1857, too, had spoken in the idiom of religion, but they had proclaimed an alternative order; they had wanted to preserve local identities against the encroachment of the modern state and the colonial economy. Millennialism had fired the rebels as they strove to build a social and political order based on bonds of kinship, locality, religion, and traditional authority. Nationalist leaders, by contrast, drew on traditional forms, but imagined a modern national community. Invoking religious and ethnic symbols and idioms, they formed modern political associations and intended to operate as rational political actors in a "national" public arena. Unlike the insurgents of 1857, they did not seek a radical alternative to the colonial order; rather, they fought for the political rights of Indians as a secular, national community. In these new nationalists, British rulers discovered an enemy not so different from themselves.

THE PAN MOVEMENTS

India and China were not the only places where activists dreamed of founding new states. Indeed, across the continents, groups had begun to imagine new communities based on ethnicity. Some of these transcended a single ethnicity, looking to religion as a basis for unity. Pan movements sought to link people across state boundaries and included such diverse movements as pan-Asianism, pan-Islamism, pan-Africanism, pan-Slavism, pan-Turkism, pan-Arabism, pan-Germanism, and Zionism. The grand aspiration of all of these groups, however, was the rearrangement of borders so that dispersed communities would be united. But such remappings posed a threat to existing states, which made these movements extremely dangerous in the eyes of the rulers of the Russian, Austrian, and Ottoman empires, as well as of the overseers of the British and the French colonial empires.

Within the Muslim world, intellectuals and political leaders begged their co-religionists to put aside sectarian and political differences so that they could unite under the banner of

> *The grand aspiration of all "pan" groups was the rearrangement of borders so that dispersed communities would be united.*

GERMAN AND EGYPTIAN UNIVERSITIES

In the late eighteenth and early nineteenth centuries, sweeping reforms transformed the universities of German-speaking Europe. No longer polishing schools for aristocrats, these centers for higher learning became the preeminent institutions for the collection and dissemination of knowledge. Taking the place of salons, courts, and royal societies (see Chapter 5), the universities now determined which subjects were worthy of study and which were not. The ideal of the German universities was to combine research with teaching in such a way that each complemented the other; and both would be protected from the interference of the state or the market. The new German universities were so successful in producing pathbreaking scholarship that other Europeans and Americans looked to them as models for organizing higher learning and promoting scholarship.

These new institutions were places where researchers, students, and teachers exchanged ideas and information, supposedly on an equal basis (though in practice, one still had to be male, and middle class or above, to be able to attend courses there). For most of the nineteenth century, they were dominated by humanists, those who studied languages (especially classical languages), history, philosophy, and religion. Proficiency in Latin and ancient Greek was particularly prized, for educated Europeans still looked to classical antiquity for the origins of their advanced "civilization," as opposed to what was seen as the non-culture of the Americas and Africa and the decadent culture of Asia. This focus on the classics produced a wealth of important studies and insights—but it was extremely narrow. And by the century's end, these institutions were under siege, both from within and from without.

From within, the natural scientists and specialists in *modern* subjects (such as the social sciences, modern European history and languages) claimed a greater share of the university's budget and curriculum. Their demands suited Germany's modernizing aims, and by the end of the century a recognizably "modern" set of laboratories, lecture courses, and scholarly institutes had become central to the mission of the university. The universities were more reluctant to attend to the demands of women and workers, who insisted that they, too, should be allowed to attend courses. Ultimately, some accommodations were made, but not until the 1920s did these outsiders really make their presence felt. Increasingly, too, it was argued that the universities should increase their attention to non-European subjects, especially in order to prepare businessmen and state officials for service in the colonies. In 1910, the Hamburgisches Kolonialinstitut was founded for

this purpose, which it should be noted, departed radically from the universities' aim to exclude the state and the marketplace from the domain of pure knowledge. In 1919, when Germany was forced to give up its colonies, the Kolonialinstitut was closed, to be replaced by a new institution on the old model: the University of Hamburg.

As the university became the hallmark of modern learning, the colonial and semi-colonial areas of the world struggled to adapt their traditional scholarly institutions to it. In Egypt the approach to higher learning followed two pathways. On the one hand, a group of Egyptian reformers sought to create afresh a university that replicated the institutions of higher learning in Europe. They agitated in favor of a purely secular and modern Egyptian University, finally overcoming the opposition of British officials, who had argued that Egypt was not yet ready for a full-scale university. In 1908, the Egyptian University came into being. It proved an immediate success, attracting the cream of Egypt's student population, and it was staffed in its early days by top European academics. Its curriculum was hardly different from the curriculum found in the European and North American universities, on which it was so carefully modeled.

The second pathway proved more difficult. Egypt's religiously trained elite, not wishing to be left behind, adapted Egypt's, and indeed the Islamic world's, leading center of higher religious learning, al-Azhar, to modern purposes. Founded in the tenth century during the Fatimid conquest of Egypt, the mosque of al-Azhar had become by the Ottoman era in the sixteenth century the leading center of learning throughout the Islamic world as well as a venerable place of worship, attracting Islamic scholars from all over the world. But the secular and westernizing tendencies that swept through Egypt in the nineteenth century threatened to render it irrelevant. In response, its advocates sought to bring it up to date. Al-Azhar's most energetic reformer, the noted Islamic modernist Muhammad Abduh, who had studied there as a youth, introduced modern and secular subjects alongside traditional religious subjects. The reformers altered the curriculum, improved the training of the faculty, regularized the course work, instituted regular examination procedures, and expanded the library. In short, they introduced many of the features of the modern Western university while retaining the traditional training in Islamic learning. Indeed, they gave al-Azhar a new breath of life, enabling it to retain an important place in the hierarchy of Egyptian schools in the twentieth century.

Islam in opposition to European incursions. The leading spokesman for pan-Islamism was the well-traveled and intellectually nimble Jamal al-Din al-Afghani (1839–1897). Born in Iran and given a Shiite upbringing, he nonetheless called on Muslims around the world to overcome their Sunni and Shiite differences so that they could make common cause against the West. Afghani called for unity and action, for an end to corruption and stagnation, and for the acceptance of the true principles of Islam. During a sojourn in Egypt, in the 1870s, Afghani joined with a young Egyptian reformer, Muhammad Abduh (1849–1905), to inspire a proto-nationalist and Islamic protest against Europe. Later, in 1884, Afghani and Abduh, from exile in Paris, published a pan-Islamic newspaper, *al-Urwah al-Wuthqa (The Indissoluble Bond)* that popularized Afghani's call for a union of all Islamic countries. In the latter years of his life, Afghani made his way to Istanbul, where he supported the pan-Islamic ambitions of Sultan Abdul Hamid II, who made the defense of Islam one of the devices to thwart European schemes to divide up the Ottoman empire.

The pan-Islamic appeal only added to the confusion of Muslims as they confronted the West. Arab Muslims living as Ottoman subjects had multiple identities and many calls on their loyalties. Should they support the Ottoman empire as a means to defend themselves from European encroachments? Or should they embrace the Islamism of Afghani? At this stage, most opted to work within the embryonic nation-states that were arising in the Islamic world, looking to a Syrian or Lebanese identity as the way to deal with the West and gain autonomy. But Afghani and his disciples had struck a chord in Muslim culture, and their Islamic message has long retained a powerful appeal.

Pan-Germanism, to cite another example of a movement that crossed national boundaries, found followers across central Europe, where it often competed with a pan-Slavic movement that threatened to unite all the Slavs against their Austrian, German, and Ottoman overlords. This area had traditionally been ruled by German-speaking elites, who owned the land farmed by Poles, Czechs, Russians, and other Slavs. German elites began to feel increasingly uneasy as Slavic nationalisms, spurred by the mid-century revivals of traditional Czech, Polish, Serbian, and Ukranian languages and cultures, became more popular. Even more threatening to the German elites was the fact that the Slavic populations were growing faster than the German. As pogroms in the Russian empire's borderlands in the 1880s drove a large number of eastern European Jews westward, German resentment toward these new arrivals also increased.

What made pan-Germanism a movement and an ideology, however, was the intervention at this point of a former liberal, Georg von Schönerer (1842–1921). In 1882, Schönerer, outraged by the Habsburg empire's failure to favor Germans, founded the League of German Nationalists, a group composed of several hundred students, artisans, teachers, and small businessmen. Schönerer detested the Jews, defining them by their "racial characteristics," rather than by their religious practices.

When he was elected to the Austrian upper house, he attempted to pass anti-Jewish legislation modeled on the American Chinese Exclusion Act of 1882. Schönerer's subsequent campaigns in the 1890s to promote the interests of Germans within the Habsburg empire were designed to break what he believed to be Austria's anti-German dependency on the pope. Ultimately, he aimed for German Austria to unite with the Germans in Bismarck's empire, thus forming a huge, racially unified state to dominate central Europe. Although Schönerer's plans were too radical for the majority of German Austrians (most of whom were Catholic), his anti-Semitism was revived in a milder form by Viennese mayor Karl Lueger in the late 1890s.

The rhetoric of pan-Germanism accustomed central Europeans to thinking of themselves as members of a German *race*, their identities fixed by blood rather than defined by state boundaries. This, too, was very much the lesson of pan-Slavism. Both led fanatics to take actions that were dangerous to existing states; the organization of networks of radical southern Slavs, for example, unsettled Serbia and Herzegovina (annexed by the Austrians in 1908). Indeed, it was a Serbian proponent of plans to carve an independent Slav state out of Austrian territory in the Balkans who assassinated the heir to the Habsburg throne, Archduke Francis Ferdinand, in June 1914. By August, the whole of Europe had descended into mass warfare, bringing the subjects of much of the rest of the world directly or indirectly into the conflict as well. Eventually, the war would realize the pan-Slav, pan-German, and anti-Ottoman Muslim nationalist longing to tear down the Ottoman and Habsburg empires. The irony was that the post-1918 situation, in which these multinational empires were divided into polities based essentially on race, would prove to be far more unstable and unsettled even than the world at the turn of the century.

CONCLUSION

Ever since the Enlightenment, Europeans had put their faith in "progress." Through the nineteenth century, educated elites took pride in their improvements—as evidenced in booming industries, bustling cities, and burgeoning colonial empires. And yet, at century's end, many came to question that faith. Urbanization and industrialization, the signatures of the age, seemed more disrupting than uplifting, more disorienting than reassuring. Moreover, the burdens of colonial rule, especially the resistance of colonial people to what was termed the "civilizing mission," only fueled doubts about the course of progress.

Perhaps nothing was so unsettling to the ruling elite as the realization that "the people" were not only against them, but were developing the means to unseat them. In colonial settings, nationalists learned how to mobilize large populations. In Europe, charismatic socialist and right-wing leaders found the means to challenge liberal political power. By contrast, old elites, whose politics relied on closed-door negotiations between "rational" gentlemen, were unprepared to deal with modern popular ideas and identities.

Nor were they able to control the pace and scope of change. The expansion of empires had drawn more people into an unbalanced global economy, one that enriched many landowners, financiers, and industrialists. Everywhere, new disparities in wealth appeared—especially in Africa, Asia, and Latin America, where traditional peasant economies had to conform to an integrated world market. Moreover, the increased scale of enterprise produced its own dangers within Europe and North America. The size and power of industrial operations threat-

Chronology

1882	Chinese Exclusion Act (U.S.)
1882	British invasion of Egypt
1883–1884	Social welfare laws (Germany)
1885	Indian National Congress established
1886	Discovery of gold in the Transvaal
1890s–1910s	Labor unrest in West
1892	Columbian Exposition in Chicago
1894	Pullman Strike (U.S.)
1894–1895	Sino-Japanese War
1899–1900	Boxer Uprising (China)
1899–1902	South African (Boer) War
1900	Paris Exhibition
1900	British Labour Party founded
1904	Social welfare laws (France)
1904–1906	Herero Revolt (Africa)
1904–1905	Russo-Japanese War
1905	British partition of Bengal (India)
1905	Revolt in Russian empire
1905–1906	Maji-Maji Revolt (Africa)
1906	Indian National Muslim League founded
1906	Social welfare laws (England)
1906	Women vote in national elections (Finland)
1907	Financial Panic
1910–1920	Mexican Revolution
1911	Chinese Republican Revolution
1912	Abdication of the last Qing emperor
1914	World War I begins

ened small firms and made individuals seem insignificant. So, too, cities seemed too big and too dangerous. All these social and economic challenges stretched the capacities of gentlemanly politics.

Yet, the anxieties of the age also stimulated a burst of creative energy. Western artists borrowed non-Western images and vocabularies. At the same time, non-Western intellectuals and artists looked to the West for inspiration, even as they formulated anti-Western ideas. The process of exchange, and the dislocations of modern experience, propelled writers and scholars to look more deeply into the past, as well as to fabricate utopian visions of the future. As some explored the darker, mysterious sides of human character, others developed new means of escaping convention and tradition.

We have seen in this chapter how revivals and dislocations, as well as cultural and political movements, participated in this process of reformulating identities; in concluding it, we should reiterate the incomplete nature of this process. For, while economic, social, and cultural changes "unsettled" the European-centered world, they also intensified the struggles among European powers. Thus, this order was most unstable at its own center—Europe itself. And in the massive conflict that brought a definitive end to the late-nineteenth-century faith in progress, Europe would ravage itself. The Great War would give rise to an age of even more rapid change—and even more violent consequences.

FURTHER READINGS

Chatterjee, Partha, *The Nation and Its Fragments* (1993). One of the most important recent works on Indian nationalism by a leading scholar of "Subaltern Studies."

Cohen, Paul, *History in Three Keys: The Boxers as Event, Experience, and Myth* (1997). An exploration of the various problems regarding the historical reconstruction of the Boxer episode.

Conrad, Joseph, *Heart of Darkness* (1899). First published in a magazine in 1899, this novella contained a searing critique of King Leopold's oppressive and exploitative policies in the Congo and was part of a growing concern for the effects that European empires were having around the world, and especially in Africa.

Dikötter, Frank, *The Discourse of Race in Modern China* (1992). Traces the lineage of racial thought in Chinese history.

Esherick, Joseph, *The Origins of the Boxer Uprising* (1987). The definitive account of the episode.

Everdell, William R., *The First Moderns: Profiles in the Origins of Twentieth-Century Thought* (1997). A rich account of the many faces of "modernism," focusing particularly on science and art.

Gay, Peter, *The Cultivation of Hatred* (1994). A provocative discussion of the violent passions of the immediate pre–Great War era.

Gilmartin, Christina, Gail Hershatter, Lisa Rofel, and Tyrene White (eds.), *Engendering China: Women, Culture, and the State* (1994). Analyzes politics and society in modern China from the perspective of gender.

Hochschild, Adam, *King Leopold's Ghost: A Story of Greed, Terror, and Heroism in Colonial Africa* (1998). A well-written account of the violent colonial history of the Belgian Congo under King Leopold in the late nineteenth century.

Katz, Friedrich, *The Life and Times of Pancho Villa* (1998). A recent work on the Mexican Revolution that shows how Villa's armies destroyed the forces of Díaz and his followers.

Kern, Stephen, *The Culture of Time and Space 1880–1918* (1986). A useful study of the enormous changes in the experience of time and space in the age of late industrialism in Europe and America.

Meade, Teresa, *"Civilizing" Rio: Reform and Resistance in a Brazilian City, 1889–1930* (1997). A wonderful study of cultural and class conflict in Brazil.

Pick, Daniel, *Faces of Degeneration: A European Disorder, c. 1848–c. 1918* (1993). A study of Europe's fear of social and biological decline, particularly focusing on France and Italy.

Sarkar, Sumit, *The Swadeshi Movement in Bengal* (1973). A comprehensive study of an early militant movement against British rule.

Slotkin, Richard, *Gunfighter Nation: The Myth of the Frontier in Twentieth-Century America* (1992). Probes the unsettled character of American culture at the turn of the century in ways that illuminate the beginnings of American imperialism.

Trachtenberg, Alan, *The Incorporation of America: Culture and Society in the Gilded Age* (1982). A provocative synthesis of changes in the American economy, society, and culture in the last decades of the nineteenth century.

Wang, David Der-wei, *Fin-de-Siècle Splendor: Repressed Modernities of Late Qing Fiction, 1849–1911* (1997). A fine work that attempts to locate the "modern" within the writings of the late Qing period.

Wohl, Robert, *The Generation of 1914* (1981). A useful discussion of the nation-by-nation peculiarities of the generation that went to war in 1914.

Womack, John, Jr., *Zapata and the Mexican Revolution* (1968). A major work on the Mexican Revolution that discusses peasant struggles in the state of Morelos in great detail.

Chapter

10

OF MASSES AND VISIONS OF THE MODERN, 1910–1939

The last of the guns of the Great War (later dubbed World War I) fell silent not on the bloody battlefields of Europe but in a remote corner of East Africa. It took a full day for news that the powers had signed an armistice on November 11, 1918, to reach that part of East Africa where African soldiers, under British and German officers, were locked in a deadly struggle for the possession of German East Africa. It was altogether fitting that this war, which had begun as a European balance-of-power war but had rapidly become a world conflagration, came to a close outside of Europe. The East African campaigns were particularly lethal. Here, the German general Paul von Lettow-Vorbeck, with never more than 10,000 African soldiers, used hit-and-run guerrilla tactics to thwart the efforts of more than 300,000 British-led African soldiers. Thousands of African soldiers died in these East African battles, or from disease and inadequate medical attention, though they did so beyond the spotlight of international opinion. But while the African theater shared in the destruction of the Great War, the conflict and its aftermath fostered here, as well as elsewhere in the colonized world, universalistic notions of freedom and self-determination and a growing disillusionment with European rule.

Raging from August 1914 to November 1918, World War I shook the foundations of the nineteenth-century European-centered world. Although most of the major battles were fought on European soil, the conflict involved large numbers of American, African, and Asian soldiers who were ferried across the oceans to join European soldiers for the killing and maiming that occurred on European battlefields. Significant military campaigns also took place in Turkey, Egypt, Syria, and sub-Saharan Africa. This war was the first modern war to extend beyond soldiers and to involve whole societies. The scale and spread of the war accelerated mass production and consumption and inflamed disputes over how to manage mass societies. After the war, leaders and masses grappled with how to deal with the new forms of production, consumption, culture, and politics that had come into being during the war and that engaged not just elite individuals but entire societies.

In politics especially, the emergence of mass society put liberal regimes on the defensive as workers, peasants, women, and colonial subjects of all classes and ethnicities demanded more rights and better lives. The challenge to liberal governance became even more pressing once economic depression spread during the 1930s. In that decade, the success of autocratic regimes threw into doubt the future of liberalism, capitalism, and democracy. At the end of the 1930s, when the Second World War erupted, the nineteenth-century liberal credo extolling limited government and individual initiative seemed to many to be a thing of the past. Certainly, it did not seem a system upon which to build a desirable—or even viable—modern society.

ECONOMIC AND POLITICAL MODERNITIES

> → *What were the different forms of political modernity?*

When people spoke of "modernity," of "being or becoming modern" in the 1920s and 1930s, they disagreed on what it meant and on how to achieve or manage it. Most did agree, however,

that in economic terms modernity entailed the development of mass production and mass consumption. Here, the automobile, especially Henry Ford's Model T, exemplified the potential of economic modernism—in theory at least, an efficient and accessible mode of mass transportation. In the realm of culture, a variety of new technologies for communication and entertainment also stood for modernity. Available to the many, as opposed to an elite few, at least in the United States and parts of Europe, the gramophone, the cinema, and the radio represented the promises of modern mass culture.

This was about as far as any consensus got. When it came to political issues there was much dispute. Some wanted a strong hand to help stabilize weak states; others wanted more democracy to fill the vacuum left by the war's discrediting of monarchical and colonial rule. Then, when the Great Depression hit in the 1930s, and it became clear that U.S.- and Europe-centered markets could not provide prosperity for *all*, there arose an even more intense debate over the organization of modern mass society. By the 1930s, three competing visions for how to be modern had emerged in various parts of the world: liberal, authoritarian, and anti-colonial.

The first political vision of modernism reworked a form of old nineteenth-century liberalism, confronting the economic failings of the interwar years without sacrificing capitalism or parliamentary democracy. The United States was the leading example of the liberal perspective. As the pacesetter in the mass production and consumption of automobiles and the leader in new forms of popular entertainment, it had emerged in the 1920s as the great international symbol of being modern. But the Great Depression of the 1930s undermined faith in American-style institutions. As hard times and unemployment spread across the United States, the American model based on linking capitalism and democracy no longer seemed to be working for the people. Around the world, and even in the United States, citizens turned to alternative systems that they hoped would better deliver the benefits and promises of modernity. Although many turned away from the liberal perspective, the system survived in the United States, parts of Western Europe, and several Latin American nations. It did so, however, only thanks to far-reaching economic reforms that dramatically expanded the power of the state.

Focus Questions OF MASSES AND VISIONS OF THE MODERN

- → *What were the different forms of political modernity?*
- → *In what ways did the Great War change the world?*
- → *How does mass culture differ from elite culture?*
- → *How are mass production and consumption related?*
- → *How did different political systems respond to economic, political, and social disorder?*

For many contemporaries, however, these reforms did not seem to match the astonishing successes of the second political vision for becoming modern, that of the authoritarian regimes. Formed in the crucible of World War I and furthered during the Great Depression of the 1930s, authoritarian regimes subordinated the individual to the state, commanded most aspects of the production process, used censorship and terror to enforce loyalty among their citizenry, and exalted the virtues of an all-powerful leader. Authoritarianism appealed to radicals at opposite ends of the conventional political spectrum. It was manifested in both right-wing dictatorships (Italian fascist, German Nazi, and Japanese militarist) and a left-wing dictatorship (the Soviet Union). Needless to say, these regimes differed radically. In common, however, they shared in the rejection of parliamentary democracy, believing instead that forceful authoritarian rule more effectively delivered the benefits and promises of modernity.

The third variant, "anti-colonialism," also rejected the liberal order, primarily because of its connection to colonialism, though its exponents did not usually repudiate democracy or even private enterprise. Resentful of European rulers who preached democracy but practiced despotism, anti-colonial leaders looked first to oust their colonial rulers and then to find their own path to modernity. Their view of the modern advocated political independence from the West but favored some mixing of Western ideas and institutions with indigenous traditions. Yet, in working to create unified national communities out of disparate colonial subjects, nationalists in India, China, the Middle East, and Africa had to confront their own internal conflicts, as well as the hostility of the colonial powers.

THE GREAT WAR

> → *In what ways did the Great War change the world?*

Few events were more decisive in drawing men and women all over the world into national and international politics than the Great War. For over four years, millions of soldiers from Europe, as well as from its dominions and colonies, killed and mutilated one another with horrifying efficiency. Such carnage damaged European claims to civilized superiority and encouraged colonial subjects to break from imperial masters. Among Europeans, too, the unsettling effects of World War I razed—or at least threatened to raze—the hierarchies that defined prewar society. Above all, the war made clear how much the power of the state now depended on the support of the people.

Few events were more decisive in drawing men and women all over the world into national and international politics than the Great War.

The causes of the war were complex. Disputes over colonial territories produced tension in the prewar period, to which were added disputes about the southeastern corner of Europe. As the Ottoman empire slowly retreated from the Balkans, the rival ambitions of Austria-Hungary and Russia came to the fore. Even more dangerous was the rivalry between Great Britain and Germany. Through most of the nineteenth century, Britain had been the preeminent power in Europe. In 1871, the year of German unification, Britain accounted for almost one-third of world economic output. By the end of the century, however, German industrial output had surpassed Britain's, and Germany had begun building a navy to challenge British control of the world's seas. For the British, this was an impermissible affront; for the Germans, it was a logical step in their expanding ambitions.

International insecurity and rivalry led the great powers to construct political and military alliances. Germany joined Austria-Hungary to form the Central Powers; Britain affiliated itself with France and Russia in the Triple Entente (later called the Allies after Italy joined in 1915). The alliance of the French and Russians with the British meant that Germany faced the need to prepare for and fight a two-front war. Well-armed and secretly pledged to defend their partners, the rivals lacked only a spark to set off open hostilities. That came in August 1914, when Archduke Francis Ferdinand, the heir to the Habsburg throne, was assassinated in Sarajevo, the capital of Bosnia. In murdering the archduke, the assassin hoped to trigger an independence movement that would detach South-Slav territories from the Austro-Hungarian empire (see Chapter 9). This led to a cascade of diplomatic events over the next six weeks, culminating in intensified preparations for war by every major power in Europe. The world war that followed did, in fact, lead to the dismemberment of Austria-Hungary, but at the cost of millions of lives.

THE FIGHTING

The declarations of war were greeted with jubilation by populations that anticipated a short conflict culminating in a swift triumph for their side. Dreams of glory inspired tens of thousands of men to rush to enlist. But the fighting did not go as expected. The initial German advance through neutral Belgium in a grand "wheeling motion" stalled thirty miles outside of Paris (see Map 10-1). The Germans had intended to encircle Paris and defeat France with a single blow, but they were stopped by the Allies at the Battle of the Marne in September 1914 and forced to retreat. A stalemate ensued. Instead of a quick war, vast land armies, employing defensive techniques, dug trenches along the Western Front—from the

MAP 10-1   WORLD WAR I: THE EUROPEAN AND MIDDLE EASTERN THEATERS

Most of the fighting in World War I, despite its designation as a world war, occurred in Europe. Although millions of soldiers fought on both sides, the actual territorial advances were relatively small. Did the armies of the Central Powers or the Allies gain the most territory during the war? Which countries had to fight a two-front war? Can you identify the capital cities that were overrun by enemy powers and the capital city that was almost overrun in the early months of war in 1914 and then again in 1918?

Trenches in World War I. The anticipated war of mobility turned out to be an illusion; instead, armies dug trenches filled with foot soldiers and machine guns. To advance entailed walking into a hail of machine gun fire. Life in the trenches meant cold, dampness, rats, disease, and boredom.

English Channel through Belgium and France to the Alps—installing barbed wire and setting up machine gun posts. Neither side could gain much territory and the troops became immobilized. Anything but gallantry and glory, life in the trenches was a mixture of boredom, dampness, dirt, vermin, and disease, punctuated by the terror of being ordered to "go over the top" to attack the enemy's entrenched position. Doing so meant running across a "no man's land" in which machine guns mowed down all but a few attackers.

Meanwhile, Russian troops advanced into East Prussia and Austria-Hungary along the Eastern Front. Although the Russians managed to defeat Austro-Hungarian troops in Galicia and to score some initial victories in eastern Germany, they suffered a terrible defeat at Tannenberg in East Prussia once the Germans threw in well-trained divisions that were better-armed and provisioned than the Russian troops.

By 1915, the war had ground to a gruesome standstill. Along the Western Front, neither the Allies nor the Central Powers were able to advance. On the Eastern Front, the Russians had been driven back and had lost much of Poland. At Ypres in 1915, the Germans tried to break the stalemate by introducing poison gas, which at first caused panic, but the advantage was nullified by equipping soldiers with gas masks. On July 1, 1916, the British launched an offensive along the Somme River. By November, when the futile offensive was halted, approximately 600,000 British and French and 500,000 Germans had perished. For all of these casualties, the battle lines had hardly budged. Attempts to win by opening other fronts, like the Allied invasion of Turkey at Gallipoli in 1915 and fronts in

the Middle East and in Africa, failed and added to the war's carnage (see Map 10-2).

The death toll forced governments to call up more men than ever before. Nearly 70 million men worldwide fought in the war, including almost the whole of Europe's young adult male population. From 1914 to 1918, 13 million served in the German army, almost one-fifth of Germany's total population in 1914. In Russia, more than 15 million men, mostly peasants, took up arms. The British mobilized 5.25 million troops, almost half the prewar population of men aged fifteen to forty-nine, and in France, around 8 million served, nearly 80 percent of the prewar fifteen- to forty-nine-year-old population.

Mass mobilization breached gender boundaries as well. Tens of thousands of women served in auxiliary units at or near the front as doctors, nurses, and technicians. Even more women were mobilized on the home front. In Britain more than 1 million women replaced men in a variety of previously male occupations. In France, nearly 700,000 women worked in munitions plants, while German women made up more than one-third of the workforce at the great Krupp Armament works.

In the four full years of the war, military deaths exceeded 8 million. Another 20 million soldiers were wounded. Casualties, however, were not restricted to those in the armed forces. Naval blockades and aerial bombardments extended combat zones to civilian areas. Civilian populations also suffered from food shortages. These left them susceptible to epidemic diseases, like influenza, which demobilizing soldiers introduced into their communities and which claimed more than 100,000 lives in Europe, and perhaps as many as 15 million in India.

Gallipoli. In April 1915 the British and the French landed a huge force of 450,000 troops on the Gallipoli peninsula, a daring operation directed at Istanbul, to protect colonial possessions, reestablish direct communications with Russia, and knock Germany's ally, the Ottomans, out of the war. After a year of battle and about 150,000 killed, the French and British gave up and left in January 1916.

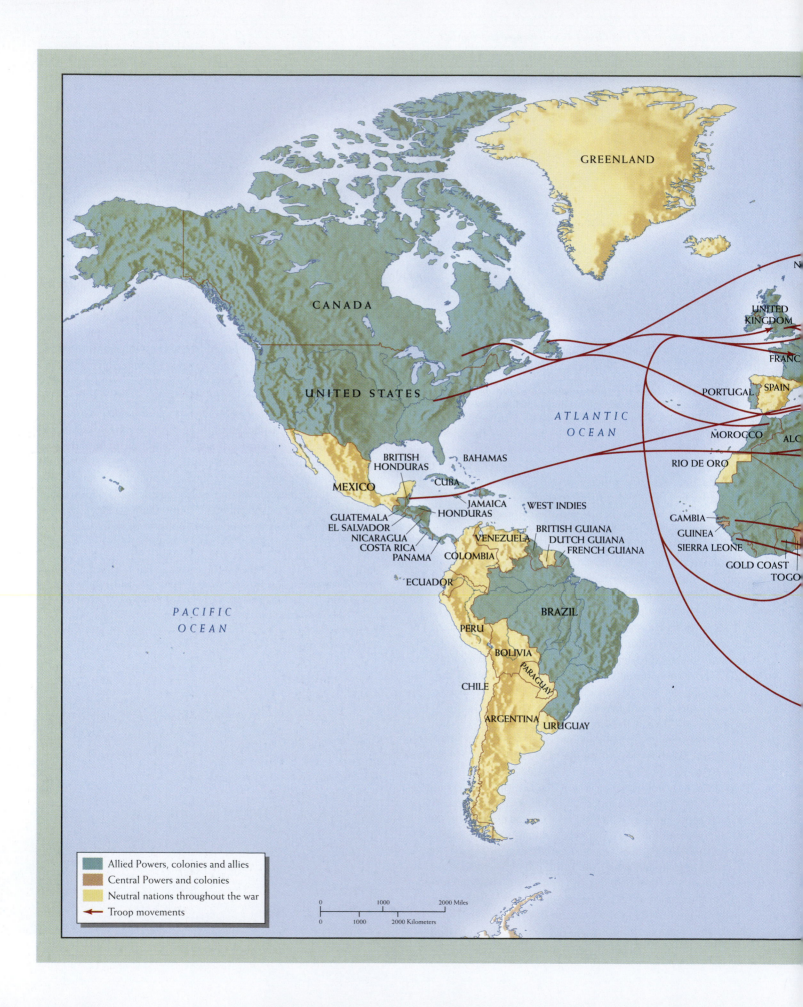

GREENLAND

CANADA

UNITED STATES

*ATLANTIC
OCEAN*

UNITED
KINGDOM

FRANC

PORTUGAL   SPAIN

MOROCCO   ALC

RIO DE ORO

BRITISH
HONDURAS   BAHAMAS

MEXICO   CUBA

JAMAICA
HONDURAS   WEST INDIES

GUATEMALA   BRITISH GUIANA
EL SALVADOR   VENEZUELA   DUTCH GUIANA
NICARAGUA   FRENCH GUIANA
COSTA RICA   COLOMBIA
PANAMA

ECUADOR

GAMBIA
GUINEA
SIERRA LEONE

GOLD COAST
TOGO

BRAZIL

PERU

*PACIFIC
OCEAN*

BOLIVIA

PARAGUAY

CHILE

ARGENTINA   URUGUAY

	Allied Powers, colonies and allies
	Central Powers and colonies
	Neutral nations throughout the war
→	Troop movements

0   1000   2000 Miles

0   1000   2000 Kilometers

ARCTIC OCEAN

FINLAND

DEN

RUSSIA

POLAND

STRIA-
NGARY

ROMANIA
BULGARIA

OTTOMAN
EMPIRE

REECE

PERSIA   AFGHANISTAN

JAPAN

CHINA

BYA

EGYPT

ARABIA

TIBET

ANGLO
EGYPTIAN
SUDAN

INDIA

BURMA

SIAM

PACIFIC
OCEAN

GERMAN
PACIFIC
POSSESSIONS
(lost 1914)

OON

ETHIOPIA

BRITISH
EAST
AFRICA

UGANDA

GERMAN
EAST
AFRICA

NORTHERN
RHODESIA

SOUTHERN
RHODESIA

INDIAN
OCEAN

AUSTRALIA

SOUTH
AFRICA

NEW
ZEALAND

MAP 10-2   WORLD WAR I: THE GLOBAL THEATER

This map helps us to understand the ways in which World War I was a world conflict. Outside of Europe, where did the fighting occur and for what reasons? How, for instance, did British and French colonial troops help the home governments during the war? Where did Indian troops fight? What role did the troops located in German colonies play in the war?

EMPIRE AND WAR The horrors of war, like the spread of influenza, reached across continents (see Map 10-2). The sprawling Ottoman empire sided with the Central Powers, battling British- and Russian-led forces in Egypt, Iraq, and the Caucasus. In 1915–1916, Ottoman forces massacred or deported between 800,000 and 1.3 million Armenians, who were said to be collaborating with the Russians. In East Asia, Japan declared war on Germany and seized German possessions in China. To increase their military forces, the British and French conscripted colonial subjects. India provided 1 million soldiers to the Allies. More than 1 million Africans fought in Africa and Europe for their colonial masters, and another 3 million were made to transport war supplies. Around 60,000 Indians and 150,000 Africans lost their lives, and a greater number were wounded. Even the scantily populated British dominions of Australia, New Zealand, and Canada dispatched over a million loyal young men to fight for the empire.

> The Romanov regime of Russia was the first empire destroyed by the war.

As the bloody war dragged on, despair and disillusionment turned into revolt and revolution. In British-ruled Nyasaland, a mission-educated African, John Chilembwe, directed his compatriots to refuse British military demands and to stand up for the new ideal, "Africa for the Africans." The British, who received 40 percent of their wartime human and material resources from colonies and dominions, suppressed the insurrection and executed the rebel leader. Yet, Chilembwe's death did not stop the growing desire of the colonized to undo their bonds to the mother country.

Controlling the masses proved even more difficult in Europe. In 1916, after the second winter of deprivation, antiwar demonstrations broke out in Europe. The next year, strikes roiled Germany, France, Britain, Italy, and Russia. Meanwhile, in an effort to break the stalemate on the battlefield, Allied commanders introduced new weapons such as the tank to counteract the omnipresent machine guns, which took so huge a toll on the soldiers. Unfortunately, neither civilian protest nor new armaments could stop the war's devastation. At a result, Europe's postwar leaders would reap a bitter harvest of anger, sorrow, and despair.

THE RUSSIAN REVOLUTION The war destroyed entire empires. The first to go was the Romanov regime of Russia. In February 1917, Tsar Nicholas II was forced to abdicate under pressure from his generals, who wanted to quash the unrest in the capital which, they believed, was threatening the war effort along the Eastern Front. Some members of the Duma, the Russian parliament, formed a provisional government, and in factories, garrisons, and towns, grassroots councils (soviets) were established. The irony of Russia's February Revolution was that the military and civilian elites, acting to restore order, seemed to sanction and encourage mass revolution. With the removal of the tsar, millions of peasants seized land, soldiers and sailors mutinied at the front and departed for home, and nationalities declared autonomy or independence from the crumbling Russian empire.

In October 1917, with the tsar gone but the war still going on, left-wing revolutionaries calling themselves Bolsheviks decided the time was right for full-scale revolution. Led by Vladimir Lenin (1870–1924) and Leon Trotsky (1879–1940), the Bolsheviks took advantage of the weakness of the government and drew on their support among the workers' soviets and troops in the capital. Arresting the members of the provisional government and claiming power in the name of the soviets, the Bolsheviks proclaimed a socialist revolution. In March 1918, Soviet Russia signed the Treaty of Brest-Litovsk, a separate peace acknowledging German victory on the Eastern Front, which had collapsed once the Russian troops gave way to German occupation. For protection, the Bolshevik leadership relocated the capital from Petrograd to Moscow, and set up what they called a dictatorship of the proletariat, whose fortunes, for the moment, remained unclear. It was Lenin who insisted upon accepting the peace treaty and loss of vast territories and safeguarding "the socialist revolution" at all costs. A child of modest privilege and a law-school dropout, he had spent

Petrograd Workers. The July 1917 demonstrations were among the largest in the Russian empire during that turbulent year of war and revolution. In the photo, marchers carry banners, "Down with the Ministers-Capitalists," and "All Power to the Soviets of Worker, Soldier and Peasant Deputies."

most of the years prior to 1917 in foreign exile, participating in small revolutionary discussion circles and writing voluminously. After the abdication of Nicholas II, Lenin managed to return to Russia, thanks to the Germans, who sent him on a special train across front lines to foment further chaos against their military foe. Neither the Germans nor Lenin's comrades foresaw how he would spearhead the creation of a new state out of the Russian empire's ruins.

THE FALL OF THE CENTRAL POWERS With the withdrawal of Russia from the war, the Germans were able to concentrate their forces on the Western Front. In March 1918, after signing the peace treaty with the Russians, German troops began several offensives to break through Allied lines, but they were unable to take Paris because of logistical problems and a lack of reserves. They now also found themselves faced by the United States, which had declared war on Germany in 1917. With fresh U.S. troops added to the fray, the Allies were able to turn the tide at the Second Battle of the Marne in July 1918 and to force the Germans to retreat into Belgium. There were mass surrenders of German troops in the field, and a soldiers' strike against the war, as hunger and influenza became too much for them to bear. By the fall of 1918, Germany was on the verge of civil war, as the Allied blockade led to food shortages. Many Germans feared—and some prayed—that the Russian Revolution would spread eastward. With defeat and civil strife in the offing, the Central Powers fell in succession. Bulgaria withdrew from the war in September; Turkey surrendered in October; and nationalist rebellions in Austria-Hungary diverted troops from the war front. Faced with a massive strike wave, German generals agreed to an armistice in November 1918. Kaiser Wilhelm II (ruled 1888–1918) stepped down and fled to the Netherlands; the German empire became a republic. The last Habsburg emperor, Charles I (ruled 1916–1918), also abdicated, and Austria-Hungary dissolved into several new states. With the dissolution of the Ottoman empire, the war added a fourth dynasty to its list of casualties.

> *With the dissolution of the Ottoman empire, the war added a fourth dynasty to its list of casualties.*

THE PEACE SETTLEMENT AND THE IMPACT OF THE WAR

To decide the fate of vanquished empires and the future of the modern world, the victors convened a peace conference at Versailles, France, in January 1919. What they devised, however, was a punitive treaty, largely dictated by the leaders of Britain and France. It assigned Germany sole blame for the war and forced it to pay reparations. In addition, the victorious states took over Germany's colonies. Arab lands of the dissolved Ottoman empire fell under French (Lebanon and Syria) or British (Iraq and Palestine) "mandates." The Russians, once part of the Allies, were not invited.

The American president, Woodrow Wilson, had originally hoped to make a "peace without victory," but he finally accepted the punitive treaty. Still, Wilson held out hope that the postwar world might be a more harmonious and peaceful one in which a newly organized League of Nations would bring the blessings of liberal freedom to all mankind. Realizing the ideal of self-determination that Wilson had proclaimed during the war, 60 million people in Central and Eastern Europe emerged after the Versailles Treaty as inhabitants of new nation-states. But such idealism had its limits. Under the empires, polyglot communities had lived under single multiethnic states. Under the new national states, suddenly more than 25 million Central and Eastern Europeans found themselves as ethnic minorities or completely stateless (see Map 10-3). The limits were even more telling when it came to establishing the rights of non-Europeans, for the "peacemakers" at Versailles were not prepared to extend self-determination beyond Europe.

What idealism survived the peacemaking process was further blasted when the U.S. Senate, reflecting a resurgence of isolationism among Americans, turned down the Versailles Treaty and kept the United States out of the League of Nations. The League was also weakened by the absence of Russia. Indeed, for Britain, France, Japan, and the United States, the isolation of "Red" Russia became a postwar priority.

The war also ushered in many changes invisible on the world map. It altered relations among classes, contributed to the making of mass societies, and shook up gender relations. Demobilization hit working women hard; when soldiers hobbled home, women were laid off from many of the jobs they had assumed during the war. Still, women did not retreat entirely back into their homes. In Russia, women gained the vote in 1917. The following year, the struggles of suffragists, who were campaigning for the right of women to vote, bore partial fruit as women thirty years and older were enfranchised in Britain. In Germany, women won the vote in 1919; in the United States, they gained it in 1920. France, however, held out against this trend until 1944. Nonetheless, in France, as in these other nations, women came out of the war claiming new privileges. Increasingly, young, unmarried women, went out in public unescorted, dressed as they saw fit, and maintained their own apartments. Such behavior shocked cultural conservatives, who called for a return to prewar norms. But these sermons did not impress young women—or men—sick of war, critical of established authority, and determined to enjoy the new, modern world.

Legend:
- Republic of Turkey after Treaty of Lausanne 1923
- French mandate
- British mandate
- British colony
- British influence

MAP 10-3 OUTCOMES OF WORLD WAR I IN EUROPE, NORTH AFRICA, AND IN SOME OF THE MIDDLE EAST

The political map of Europe and the Middle East changed greatly after the peace treaty of 1919. Comparing this map with Map 10-1(p. 350), the European theater of war, identify the new European countries that came into existence after the war. What happened to the Ottoman empire and what powers gained control over the old territories of the Ottoman state? How did Germany and Austria-Hungary fare in the peace arrangements?

MASS CULTURE

> → *How does mass culture differ from elite culture?*

Representative of the new, modern world were new forms of mass communication and entertainment. These, too, were at least partially wartime products. To mobilize populations for total war, leaders disseminated propaganda as never before. Through public lectures, theatrical productions, musical compositions, and (censored) newspapers, they attempted to unify and energize the masses. Thus did the war politicize cultural activities, while broadening the audience for nationally oriented information and entertainment. Together with the expanding impact of the new media, the war was instrumental in launching "mass culture."

> *Together with the expanding impact of the new media, the war was instrumental in launching "mass culture."*

Postwar mass culture was distinctive in several ways. First, it differed from elite culture (opera, classical music, paintings, literature; see Chapter 5). Thanks to rising incomes and leisure time, nonelites, lumped together as "the masses," now had more time and money to spend on entertainment and diversion. To be sure, elite culture did not disappear after World War I, and the masses (who were receiving more education) were increasingly interested in elite culture, but high culture gave way to the tastes of the working class and middle class. Second, mass culture relied on new technologies, of which film and radio were the most important. The embrace of these new media allowed images and ideas to spread much more widely than had the penny press or lithographs of the nineteenth century. This meant that cultural products could now reach the population of an entire nation. Mass culture, then, could be synonymous with national culture, which gave it immense commercial and political potential. Accordingly, during the 1920s and 1930s, advertisers and politicians strove to manipulate the new media to their own ends.

RADIO

Radio entered its golden age after the First World War. Invented at the beginning of the twentieth century, radio had made little impact prior to 1914. But during the 1920s, powerful transmitters were introduced, permitting stations to reach much larger audiences. The establishment of networks of stations allowed for the broadcast of nationally syndicated entertainment programs. Radio broadcasts, entering directly into the home, gave listeners a sense of intimacy with newscasters and stars, despite the fact that the programs were being sent out to millions of people. Consumers were addressed as personal friends and drawn into the lives of serial heroes. Special programs targeted children and women, making radio listening something for the whole family. To enjoy radio culture, one needed no previous education—even the illiterate could enjoy programs such as *The Lone Ranger*. By the end of the 1920s, nearly two-thirds of the homes in the United States had at least one radio.

Radio offered a means to mobilize the masses for political purposes. Authoritarian regimes especially depended on radio to get their message out. The Italian dictator Benito Mussolini pioneered the radio address to the nation. Later, Nazi propagandist Joseph Goebbels used this format with great regularity and effect. In Japan, too, radio became a tool to promote the right-wing government's goals. But even dictatorships could not exert total control over mass culture. Though the Nazis believed jazz to be racially inferior music, they could not prevent young Germans from tuning in to foreign radio broadcasts or smuggling records over the borders.

FILM AND ADVERTISING

Like radio, film had deep, if unpredictable, effects on societies and politics. For traditionalists, "Hollywood," which had emerged by the 1920s as the movie-making capital of the world, became synonymous with vulgarity and decadence. Indeed, modern sexual mores were on display on the silver screen—and often also in the back rows of darkened theaters. Like radio, film was also put to political ends. Here, again, anti-liberal

Charlie Chaplin in *Modern Times*. In 1936, Charles (Charlie) Chaplin directed and starred in *Modern Times*. In the film, originally titled *The Masses*, Chaplin played a factory worker whose travails on and off the assembly line offered a darkly comic view of mass production and modern politics in the 1930s. In this still photo from the film, Chaplin is shown caught in the immense machinery and wending his way through the gears like film through a projector.

governments took the lead, with the German film-maker Leni Riefenstahl's movie of the Nazi Nuremberg rally of 1934, *Triumph of the Will*, serving as the most notable example of propagandistic cinema. Yet, even in the most politicized places, producers created movies to please the masses, not just to indoctrinate them. *Triumph of the Will* was an artistic, as well as propagandistic, triumph. In Soviet Russia, film studios produced Hollywood-style musicals alongside didactic pictures about Bolshevik triumphs.

These media furthered the cause of commercial capitalism. During the 1920s, radio and film grew into big businesses, and with the expansion of product advertising, they promoted other enterprises as well. Especially in the United States, advertising emerged as a major industry, with commercials on radio becoming the preferred means for shaping national consumer tastes. Increasingly, too, American-produced entertainment, radio programs, and cinematic epics reached an international audience. Thanks to new media, America and the world began to share mass-produced images and fantasies.

> *Unlike the nineteenth century's liberal vision, assembly-line workers were joining the middle class and devoting their leisure hours not to quiet edification but to jazz and motoring.*

The war reshuffled the world's economic balance of power, destroying much of Europe's wealth, while playing a significant role in the rise of the United States as the world's economic powerhouse. As the American share of world industrial production climbed above one-third in 1929, roughly equal to that of Britain, Germany, and Russia *combined*, people around the globe came to look to the United States as a "working vision of modernity," in which not only production but also consumption boomed. During the 1920s, mean household income rose by 25 percent in the United States, so that "average" Americans enjoyed an unprecedented prosperity. This was a modern condition quite unlike the nineteenth century's liberal vision: assembly-line workers were joining the middle class and devoting their leisure hours not to quiet edification but to jazz and motoring.

MASS PRODUCTION OF THE AUTOMOBILE

The most outstanding example of the relationship between mass production and consumption in the United States was the motor car, which more than any other product came to symbolize the machine age—and the American road to modernization.

MASS PRODUCTION AND MASS CONSUMPTION

> → *How are mass production and consumption related?*

The same factors that contributed to the emergence of mass culture played a crucial role in enhancing production and consumption on a mass scale. Even more than its role in stimulating mass culture, World War I paid perverse tribute to the power of industry. Machine technologies were used to make war materials with abundant and devastating effect. Never before had armies had so much firepower at their disposal. In 1809, at the Battle of Wagram, Napoleon won the largest battle ever waged in Europe at that point, using to devastating effect his artillery, which discharged 90,000 shells over the two days of the battle. By way of contrast, at the bloody Battle of Verdun in 1916, 1,400 German guns fired off 100,000 rounds of shells per hour over the full twelve hours of the battle. To sustain the military production that supplied such large amounts of ammunition to the soldiers in the field, millions of men and women went to work in factories at home and in the colonies. Producing huge quantities of identical guns, gas masks, bandage rolls, and boots, these factories gave a broad cross-section of the world's population a feel for the modern world's demands for greater volume, faster speed, reduced cost, and standardized output.

Car Assembly Line. Mass production was made possible by the invention of the electric motor in the 1880s, and it enacted three principles: the standardization of core aspects of products, the subdivision of work on assembly lines, and the replacement of manual labor by machinery as well as by reorganizing flow among shops. The greatest successes occurred in the auto plants of Henry Ford, shown here in 1930. With each worker along the line assigned a single task, millions of automobiles rolled off the Ford assembly line, and millions of Americans became owners of automobiles.

BRUCE BARTON'S GOSPEL OF MASS PRODUCTION

In 1925, the journalist (and, later, advertising executive) Bruce Barton published The Man Nobody Knows, *which became a best-seller. In the book, Barton interpreted the life and teachings of Jesus as a gospel for success in modern business. In the excerpt below, Barton uses Henry Ford, whose Model T automobile reigned as the era's marvel of mass production, to show the profitable connections between religion and commerce.*

"If you're forever thinking about saving your life," Jesus said, "you'll lose it; but the man who loses his life shall find it."

Because he said it and he was a religious teacher, because it's printed in the Bible, the world has dismissed it as high minded ethics but not hard headed sense. But look again! . . .

What did Henry Ford mean, one spring morning, when he tipped a kitchen chair back against the whitewashed wall of his tractor plant and talked about his career?

"Have you ever noticed that the man who starts out in life with a determination to make money, never makes very much?" he asked. It was rather a startling question; and without waiting for my comment he went on to answer it: "He may gather together a competence, of course, a few tens of thousands or even hundreds of thousands, but he'll never amass a really great fortune. But let a man start out in life to build something better and sell it cheaper than it has ever been built or sold before—let him have *that* determination, and, give his whole self to it—and the money will roll in so fast that it will bury him if he doesn't look out.

"When we were building our original model, do you suppose that it was money we were thinking about? Of course we expected that it would be profitable, if it succeeded, but that wasn't in the front of our minds. We wanted to make a car so cheap that every family in the United States could afford to have one. So we worked morning, noon and night, until our muscles ached and our nerves were so ragged that it seemed as if we just couldn't stand it to hear anyone mention the word automobile again. One night, when we were almost at the breaking point I said to the boys, 'Well, there's one consolation,' I said, 'Nobody can take this business away from us unless he's willing to work harder than we've worked.' And so far," he concluded with a whimsical smile, "nobody has been willing to do that." . . .

Source: Bruce Barton, *The Man Nobody Knows: A Discovery of the Real Jesus,* in Loren Baritz, ed., *The Culture of the Twenties* (Indianapolis: Bobbs-Merrill, 1925), pp. 241–42.

Before World War I, the automobile had been a rich man's recreational toy. Around the turn of the century, dozens of small companies manufactured automobiles, yet total annual production did not reach 200,000 cars. Then came Henry Ford, who founded the Ford Motor Company in 1903. Five years later, he began production of the Model T, a car that at $850 considerably reduced the price at which comparably powerful vehicles were selling. Soon popular demand far outstripped supply. Seeking to make more cars faster and cheaper, Ford used mechanized conveyors to send the auto frame along a track or line. In this assembly line, each worker was assigned one simplified, repetitive task to perform. By standardizing the manufacturing process, subdividing work, and substituting machinery for manual labor, Ford's assembly line brought a new efficiency to the mass production of automobiles.

By the 1920s, at Ford's River Rouge factory near Detroit, a finished car rolled off the assembly line every ten seconds. Although many of Ford's workers complained about speedups and being turned into "cogs" in a depersonalized labor process, managers properly credited the system with boosting output

and reducing costs. The effects reverberated across the nation and throughout the economy. River Rouge alone employed 68,000 workers, making it the largest factory in the world. In addition, millions of cars required millions of tons of steel alloys, as well as vast amounts of glass, rubber, textiles, and petroleum. Cars also needed roads to drive on and service stations to keep them running. Altogether, nearly 4 million jobs were connected directly or indirectly to the automobile, an impressive total in a labor force of 45 million workers.

After World War I, the ownership of automobiles became more affordable and more common among Americans. By the 1920s, assembly-line mass production had dropped the price of the Model T from $850 to $290. Ford further expanded the market for cars by paying his own workers $5 per day— approximately twice the average manufacturing wage in the United States. He understood that without mass consumption there could be no mass production. Whereas in 1920 Americans owned 8 million motor cars, a decade later, ownership nearly tripled to 23 million. The spread of the automobile in the 1920s seemed to demonstrate that mass production worked.

THE GREAT DEPRESSION

Not all was easy listening or smooth motoring in the United States or in other countries where mass societies were taking root in the 1920s. During that decade, many primary producers of foodstuffs, coal, and ores faced sagging prices because of overproduction. By the late 1920s, staple prices were declining in proportion to manufactured goods, and farmers throughout the United States, Canada, Australia, and Latin America were complaining bitterly about their dwindling fortunes compared to their urban cousins. The world economy was on a downward spiral that was much worse than previous panics because of the scale and interconnectedness of postwar economies.

On Black Tuesday, October 24, 1929, the American stock market collapsed, plunging not only the American economy but also international financial and trading systems into crisis and leading the world into the "Great Depression." The causes of the Great Depression went back to the Great War, which had left European nations in deep debt as they struggled to rebuild their economies and to pay off war debts. To restore stability after the war, Europeans borrowed heavily from the United States, the world's largest lender of capital. When wobbly governments and small investors defaulted on their loans, the United States' Federal Reserve managers reacted by raising interest rates. One by one, financial institutions, starting with banks in central Europe, began to collapse. As banks fell, other lenders scrambled to call in their loans. Companies, governments, and private borrowers were soon floating in a sea of debt. The panic then spread to the world's stock markets, where investors had been purchasing stocks for much more than they were worth and investing in risky speculative ventures. This led to the Wall Street crash of 1929, which was followed by a wave of bank closures.

> *The world economy was on a downward spiral that was much worse than previous panics because of the scale and interconnectedness of postwar economies.*

Financial turmoil produced a major contraction of world trade. Striving to protect workers and investors at home from the influx of cheap foreign goods, governments raised tariff barriers against foreign inputs. After the United States enacted the first protective tariffs, one by one, other governments around the world abandoned free trade in favor of protectionism. Manufacturers cut back production, laid off millions of workers, and often went out of business. By 1935, world trade had shrunk to one-third of its 1929 level. Primary producers felt the harshest effects. Their international markets shut down almost completely. The world prices for Argentine beef, Chilean nitrates, and Indonesian sugar all dropped sharply. The anvil of shrinking markets and the hammer of drastic shortages of credit pounded industries and farms across the world.

The Great Depression soon spawned some rethinking of the tenet that markets should govern themselves. More than anything else, the Depression exposed the fallacies of laissez-faire liberalism. By the late 1930s, the exuberant embrace of mass production as the means to modern happiness had given way to a new conviction that state intervention to regulate the economy was critical to prevent disaster. Many governments

Stock Traders after the Crash. On October 24, 1929, the American stock market crashed. Here traders are pictured congregating outside the New York Stock Exchange, a neoclassical temple that became an international symbol of capitalism, on what came to be known as "Black Tuesday." As stock values plummeted, panic gripped Wall Street and soon spread across the nation. The market crash was followed by even more devastating bank runs as the Great Depression overtook the world.

launched make-work projects, such as building highways and dams. Some even found militarization a way to prime the market with demand for manufactures. In 1936, the Cambridge University economist John Maynard Keynes published one of the landmark treatises in economic thought, *The General Theory of Employment, Interest, and Money*. In it, Keynes argued that the market could not always adjust to its own failures and that sometimes the state had to step in to manage the economy and to stimulate it by increasing the money supply and creating jobs for those in need. While the "Keynesian Revolution" took years to transform economic policy and to produce what became known as the "welfare state," governments were already becoming aware that to save world capitalism public authorities had to be brought in to manage markets more effectively. Indeed, many governments by the 1930s had given up on "free market" capitalism, and on its political counterpart—liberalism.

MASS POLITICS: COMPETING VISIONS OF BECOMING MODERN

> → *How did different political systems respond to economic, political, and social disorder?*

In the West, events and ideas around 1900 raised doubts about the liberal order, unsettling class, gender, and colonial relations. In many ways, World War I challenged the liberal dream of technological progress, free markets, and societies guided by the educated few. During the war, peasants and colonial subjects had fought and died for their imperial nations, and women had suffered extreme hardships on the home front. They all sacrificed for the nation and believed the promise that they would share in the modern world's prosperity. After the Great War, the masses, tired of waiting for the wealth to trickle down, demanded an end to political and economic systems that provided special privileges to middle- and upper-class white men. Politics became a noisy and dangerous business, often conducted in the street, instead of in genteel chambers. Everywhere (except in the United States), socialism gained enormous numbers of new adherents. In Soviet Russia, the Bolsheviks began to construct a new society whose rules defied capitalist principles. On the right, too, mass movements imperiled the stability of liberal democracies (as in Germany, Italy, and Spain). Moreover, the liberal empires (especially Britain and France) faced new challenges from colo-

After World War I, politics became a noisy and dangerous business, often conducted in the street, instead of in genteel chambers.

nial subjects, who now exposed the emptiness of European claims of providing freedom and progress for all.

The Great Depression weakened the support for liberal capitalist parliamentary regimes. Several, like the Weimar Republic in Germany, collapsed. Even in the United States, many people, especially the millions thrown out of work during the Great Depression, lost faith in the constitutional government and market economy that were the foundations of liberal modernity. By 1934, Italians had a fascist state, Germany was ruled by Nazis, and the governments of Austria, Hungary, Romania, and Poland were in the hands of right-wing dictators. In 1920, almost all of Europe's states were briefly parliamentary democracies; by 1939, on the eve of the Second World War, only a few such regimes remained.

Authoritarian solutions to problems like mass unemployment grew more and more popular, especially as the Communist Soviet Union, Nazi Germany, fascist Italy, and militaristic Japan projected images of national strength and pride. Outside Europe, anti-colonial movements gathered steam; here, too, it was clear that liberal models could not cope with the scale and diversity of the new politics. Thus, by the late 1930s, the states that retained democracy and capitalism in some form appeared weak and vulnerable; dictators seemed to be riding the wave of the future, and the colonies threatened to go their own separate ways.

LIBERAL CAPITALISM UNDER PRESSURE

In Europe of the 1920s, anxiety about modernization, already a feature of the pre-1914 years, spread. The slaughter of millions during the war added to the disenchantment with the course of modernity. A "primitivist" aesthetic flourished during the 1920s and 1930s, as elite Europeans looked longingly for supposedly pristine worlds that their own corrupting civilization had not destroyed. The popularity of Josephine Baker, the African-American dancer who performed nude, "wild" dances on the Parisian stage, was just one expression of this failing confidence in Europe's urban-industrial society. So, too, was the best-seller status achieved by Oswald Spengler's 1919 pessimistic world history, *The Decline of the West*, whose title seemed to capture the trajectory of liberal modernity in Europe.

The demands of fighting a total war had offered European states the opportunity to experiment with illiberal policies. The war brought both the suspension of parliamentary rule and government efforts to manage industry and distribution. States on both sides of the conflict produced nationalist propaganda and jailed those who opposed the war. Governments regulated and organized both production and, through rationing, consumption. Wartime organization of the economy went furthest in Germany, where it was called "war socialism" (and became an inspiration to Soviet Russia). Above all, the war revolutionized the size and scope of the state. The British established a Munitions Ministry that grew from 20,000 to 65,000 bureaucrats. State budgets in prewar France had peaked at around 5 billion francs, but in 1918, the French budget was 190 billion francs.

BRITISH AND FRENCH RESPONSES TO ECONOMIC CRISES Liberal elites, especially in Britain, wished to return to free market policies at the end of the war. But newly politicized masses (including women) were no longer willing to wait patiently for the free market to provide for them. Soldiers and workers insisted that the states for which they had fought respond to their needs—for jobs, for housing, and for compensation for war wounds. Many who tired of waiting for the liberals to provide benefits turned to socialism, communism, or radical right-wing movements. Recurrent economic crises, especially the Great Depression, swelled the ranks of antiliberalism and forced all but the most die-hard liberals to rethink their ideas. By 1930, Britain had given up on free trade, and other nations were avidly seeking economic self-sufficiency.

Britain and France were the two major states to retain their parliamentary systems, but even here, old-fashioned liberalism was clearly on the run. In Britain, the working class now began to muscle its way into government. The Labour Party first came to power briefly in 1923, and then again from 1929 to 1931. In 1931, during the Depression, Britain got its first "national government" of all three parties, Liberal, Conservative, and Labour. But this coalition, as well as the parties individually, proved unable to bring the country out of the economic crisis. Strikes were increasingly common at home, while strife rippled across the empire, leading Britain to give independence to what became the Republic of Ireland in 1922. Despite these problems, the English retained their commitment to parliamentarianism and capitalism. There was more resistance here to both left- and right-wing radicalism than on the European continent.

Economic, political, and social disorder was more pronounced in France, which had to deal with the deaths of 10 percent of its young men and the destruction of large areas of its territory during the war. Governments changed often. In 1932–1933, six cabinets came and went over the course of just nineteen months. Against the threat of a rightist coup, a broad coalition of the moderate and radical left, including the French Communist Party, formed a "Popular Front" government (1936–1939). It pushed through the right of collective bargaining, a forty-hour workweek, two-week paid vacations, and minimum wages.

THE AMERICAN NEW DEAL Even in the United States, the land of plenty, liberalism faced challenges from those who found it threatening to traditional values. And when the Great Depression shattered the nation's fortunes, the fears grew more widespread, as did the pressure to create a more secure political and economic system.

In contrast to postwar Europe, where labor parties and socialist movements were on the upswing, the 1920s saw a conservative tide sweep across American politics. Calling for a "return to normalcy," by which he meant a retreat from the government activism of the Progressive Era, Warren Harding won the presidency in 1920 with a resounding 60 percent of the popular vote. Four years later, Calvin Coolidge, whose remark that the "business of America is business" reflected his antipathy for government interference with the workings of free enterprise, scored an even greater landslide. With the election of Herbert Hoover in 1928, Republicans continued their string of presidential triumphs.

Trumpeting prosperity, Republican leaders tended to dismiss or downplay criticisms of American capitalism. While Republican officials paid lip service to the virtues of family farming, they did little to alleviate the immense hardships of the 1920s for rural dwellers. In this decade, while others prospered, rural folk, who still made up just under half of all Americans, suffered as farm incomes stagnated or fell. In contrast to the modern amenities enjoyed by city dwellers, fewer than one in ten farmhouses boasted indoor plumbing and only one in five had electricity.

Left behind for the most part as well was the nation's African-American population. In the rural American South, where most blacks lived, "Jim Crow" laws enforced social segregation, economic inequality, and political disenfranchisement. Like rural whites, millions of blacks quit the countryside and moved to northern cities in the years after World War I. In New York, Chicago, and other metropolises, the migrants found some relief from the legal barriers that had restricted their opportunities and reduced their rights. But social and economic discrimination continued to hold African Americans down and to restrict their residences to emerging urban ghettos. Still, within black neighborhoods, most famously New York City's Harlem, a vibrant cultural scene emerged. The "New Negro Movement," or "Harlem Renaissance," as it was variously called, gave voice to black novelists, poets, painters, and musicians, many of whom used their art to protest racial subordination.

With the beginning of the Great Depression came broader and deeper challenges to liberal modernity. By the end of 1930, more than 4 million American workers had lost their jobs. While President Hoover resisted relief measures and insisted that individual thrift and self-reliance, not government handouts, would restore prosperity, the economic situation steadily worsened. By 1933, industrial production had dropped a staggering 50 percent since 1929. One in four workers was unemployed, and those who remained on the job suffered drastic wage and salary cuts. Across the country, joblessness and bankruptcies swelled the ranks of the hungry and the homeless. The hard times were even more severe in the countryside, where farm income plummeted by an additional two-thirds between 1929 and 1932.

Bread Lines. In the early 1930s, the Great Depression left millions of American workers unemployed, making the prosperity of the "roaring twenties" a distant memory and leading not only to widespread suffering but to a crisis of confidence and legitimacy in capitalism and its institutions. Prior to the establishment of government relief programs under the "New Deal," many of the unemployed had no choice but to depend on private charities for handouts and to spend long hours waiting for food on bread lines, such as this one in lower Manhattan.

In the 1932 presidential election, a Democrat, Franklin Delano Roosevelt (1882–1945), defeated the discredited Republican, Hoover, in a landslide. Roosevelt had been vague about his plans to stimulate economic recovery, offering contradictory prescriptions while pledging to establish a "new deal" and "to try something." Although the ideological bearings of the New Deal remained murky after Roosevelt's inauguration, the new president certainly fulfilled his promise of "bold, persistent experimentation." Indeed, in his first hundred days in office, Roosevelt pushed through Congress legislation to provide relief for the jobless and to rebuild the shattered economy. Among the experiments were a Federal Deposit Insurance Corporation to guarantee bank deposits up to $5,000, a Securities and Exchange Commission to monitor the stock market, and a Federal Emergency Relief Administration to help states and local governments assist the needy. Taking state intervention a step further, a National Recovery Administration for industrial planning was also established, though this was declared unconstitutional by the Supreme Court. These early efforts were followed in 1935 by the Works Progress Administration, which put nearly 3 million people to work building roads, bridges, airports, and post offices. That same year, the Social Security Act inaugurated old-age pensions and insurance for the unemployed.

Never before had the federal government of the United States expended so much on social welfare programs or inter-vened so directly in the workings of the national economy. And yet, despite these varied efforts, the Depression lingered. Two years into the New Deal, national unemployment remained around 20 percent. The next two years offered signs of recovery, but, just as Roosevelt began his second term, another contraction shrank the economy. Unemployment again climbed—from 7 million in 1937 to 11 million in 1938.

The persistence of hard times opened the New Deal to acidic attacks from both the left and right. Emboldened labor leaders, resurgent radicals, and populist demagogues claimed that the New Deal was not addressing the problems of the poor and the unemployed. But Roosevelt continued to plot a moderate course. The New Deal did not substantially redistribute national income. Likewise, while the Roosevelt administration established public agencies to build dams and to oversee the irrigation of arid lands and the electrification of rural districts, these were the exceptions to the rule. Privately owned enterprises continued to dominate American society. Roosevelt's aim was not to destroy capitalism but to save it. In this regard, the New Deal succeeded. Although the United States was hit hardest among industrial powers by the worldwide economic collapse, the New Deal staved off authoritarian solutions to modern problems.

AUTHORITARIANISM AND MASS MOBILIZATION

Like the liberal systems they challenged, authoritarian regimes came in various stripes. On the right arose dictatorships in Italy, Germany, and Japan. These differed from one another in important respects, though all shared an antipathy to the left-wing dictatorship of the Soviet Union. And needless to say, the Soviets had no liking for the fascists. Yet, all the postwar dictatorships, on both the right and left, were forged principally in opposition to the liberal democracies, whose "decadence" they claimed to have transcended. In place of liberal inertia, these regimes professed their success in mobilizing the masses to create dynamic yet orderly societies. All also had charismatic leaders, who personified the prestige, power, and unity of the societies over which they ruled.

Although dismissive of liberal democracy, postwar dictators insisted that they had the support of the people. True, they demanded much of the people, treating society as a mass conscript army that needed to be commanded if the problems of liberal capitalism were to be overcome. But their demands, the leaders maintained, would result in rebuilt economies, restored order, and renewed national pride. In addition, dictators gained support by embracing, to varying degrees, public welfare programs. Thus, in the short run, authoritarians claimed to protect the people's well-being better than did liberal regimes and vowed to deliver on all of modernity's promises—prosperity, national pride, technology—without having to endure any of its costs—class divisions, unemployment, urban-industrial squalor, the breakdown of morals. For a time, a large number of the globe's inhabitants believed them.

THE SOVIET UNION   The most enduring blow against liberal capitalism was struck in Russia, where liberalism had never had deep roots. In October 1917, with World War I still going on and the empire in chaos, the most radical of Russia's political parties, the Bolshevik Party, seized power in the capital. Their coup d'état aroused opposition inside and outside the country. Fearing the spread of socialist revolution, Britain, France, Japan, and the United States sent armies to Russia to subvert or at least contain Bolshevism. After the Bolsheviks executed the tsar and his family in July 1918, they rallied support for their cause by defending the homeland against its invaders. They also mobilized to fight a vicious civil war (1918–1921) that pitted an array of disunified forces (former supporters of the tsar as well as some social democrats and large independent peasant armies) against the Bolsheviks and their supporters (many soldiers, sailors, workers, and state functionaries). Their armed opponents came close but failed to dislodge the Bolsheviks from the Muscovite core of the former Russian empire.

It was precisely in the all-out mobilization against those whom they labeled the Whites, or "counterrevolutionaries," that the Bolsheviks, calling themselves the Reds, began to rebuild state institutions. The civil war also provided an impetus for Bolshevik-led armies to reconquer, in the name of revolution, many of the former tsarist lands that had seceded from the empire.

The need to requisition grain from the peasantry as well as the military operations that covered much of the country weighed heavily on the population and interfered with the harvest. From 1921 until 1923, Russia suffered from a severe famine. Some 7 to 10 million people died from hunger and disease. To revive the economy in the early 1920s, the Bolsheviks enacted dozens of decrees (collectively known as the New Economic Policy) that grudgingly sanctioned private trade and private property. In 1924, with the country still recovering from the civil war, the undisputed leader of the revolution, Lenin, died. Lenin had suffered a series of strokes in 1922, but until that time no one had done more to shape the institutions of the revolutionary regime, including creating expectations for a single ruler. After skillfully eliminating his rivals, especially Trotsky, Joseph Stalin (1879–1953) emerged as the new leader of the Communist Party and the Soviet Union.

Stalin and the Soviet leadership understood history as moving in the stages defined by Karl Marx, from feudalism to capitalism to socialism and to communism. But before achieving communism, a final stage in which there would be a classless society and a withering away of the state, they believed that the Communist Party would first have to build socialism. Yet, since

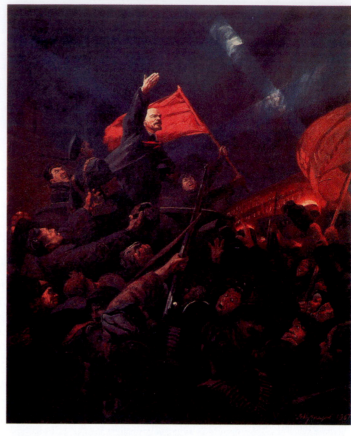

Lenin. Vladimir Lenin died just six years and three months after the October 1917 revolution, but he lived on in his writings and images, such as in this painting by Pavel Kuznetsov. Artists and propagandists helped make Lenin a ubiquitous icon of the new Soviet order.

> *Yet, since socialism as a fully developed social and political order did not exist anywhere in the 1920s, no one was quite sure how it would work in practice.*

socialism as a fully developed social and political order did not exist anywhere in the 1920s, no one was quite sure how it would work in practice. During the 1930s, the leadership moved aggressively to resolve this dilemma by defining Soviet or revolutionary socialism in opposition to capitalism. Since capitalism had "bourgeois" parliaments serving the interests of the rich, socialism, as elaborated by the Bolshevik leaders, would have "soviets" of worker and peasant deputies. Since capitalism had unregulated markets, which led to inefficiency and unemployment, socialism would have economic planning and full employment. Because capitalism permitted the "exploitation" of private ownership, socialism would outlaw private trade and private property. In short, socialism would eradicate capitalism and then attempt to invent socialist forms in housing, culture, values, dress, and even modes of reasoning.

The efforts to build a noncapitalist society were by design violent, and they began in the countryside, where the majority of the population lived. Peasants had long been organized in village communes, owning the land together, while working it individually. Stalin wanted to combine the farms into larger units, called collectives, that would be owned and worked collectively and that would be run by regime loyalists. Tens of thousands of enthusiastic urban activists and Red Army soldiers, under the slogans of "class warfare" and liquidation of the class of "kulaks" (supposedly better-off peasants), led a drive to establish these new collective farms and to compel the farmers working on them to sell all of their grain and livestock at state-run collection points for whatever price the state was willing to pay. The collectives also became dependent on the state for obtaining their seed, fertilizers, and farm equipment.

In protest, many peasants burned their crops, killed their livestock, and destroyed their farm machinery. These protesters, derided as kulaks even if they were dirt poor, were deported to remote areas of the country. Villages were given quotas for deportation, and often those selected were the people who had slept with someone's wife or stolen someone's milk; thus, "class warfare" was likely to be based on personal animosities, greed, ambition, and vengeance. In the midst of this turmoil, harvests again declined, and a second famine between 1931 and 1933 claimed another 3 to 5 million lives. When the dust settled, the collectivized peasants were permitted to have "household plots," on which they could grow their own food, and could even take some of it to legally sanctioned peasant markets.

For the cities, in the late 1920s, the leadership announced the beginning of a frenzied Five-Year Plan to "catch and overtake" the leading capitalist countries. Millions of enthusiasts as well as deported peasants set about building a new socialist (noncapitalist) urban utopia, founded upon advanced technology, almost all of it purchased from the Depression-mired capitalist countries. In just a few years, more than 10 million people moved to cities, where they helped build or rebuild hundreds of giant factories, as well as hospitals and schools. A number of the Soviet projects were intended to demonstrate the audacity of the new regime: huge hydroelectric dams, automobile and tractor factories, heavy machine-building plants. These stood as symbols of the promise of Soviet-style modernity, which eliminated unemployment, then the scourge of liberal capitalist societies.

The Soviet authorities also embarked upon what they called building socialism in the borderlands. In 1922, the Union of Soviet Socialist Republics (U.S.S.R.) was formed. It joined the nominally independent states of Ukraine, Belorussia (Belarus), and the Transcaucasian Federation with Soviet Russia to form a single federal state. The U.S.S.R. also included a number of republics, eventually fifteen (see Map 10-4), all of which acquired borders and their own institutions, though they were subject to centralized rule from Moscow. A policy of "nativization" of the Union republics fostered native-language schools and the development of local elites. In the 1930s, the collectivization and mass arrests devastated the peasants and nomads as well as the officials of the republics, but industrialization and urbanization helped to consolidate the power of local elites who advanced the cause of the Union and socialism.

The Soviet political system grew more despotic as the state bureaucracy expanded its size and reach. The political police grew the most, partly as a result of their role in forcing peasants into collectives and organizing mass deportations. During the early 1930s, as the ranks of the party grew, ongoing "loyalty" verifications also led to the removal or "purge" of members from the rolls, even when they professed absolute loyalty. Whatever the reason for expulsions, initially most former party members were not arrested. All that began to change in the mid-1930s. From 1936 to 1938, both public and closed trials of supposedly treasonous "enemies of the people" resulted in the execution of around 750,000 people and the arrest or deportation of several million more. They were sent to forced labor camps, collectively known as the Gulag, which spread across the country. Such purges decimated the Soviet elite—party officials, state officials, intelligentsia, army officers, and eventually even members of the police who had enforced the terror.

Behind this mass terror stood the Soviet leader, Joseph Stalin, who relentlessly built up a personal dictatorship. Although Stalin initiated the mass terror against the elite, his motives remain unclear. Neither he nor the regime was threatened, and the loyalty of the leaders was not in doubt. What is clear is that the political police, given sizeable arrest quotas, often exceeded them. In addition, millions of ordinary people helped to implement the terror. Some reluctantly turned in neighbors; some did so to try to save themselves; many showed fanatical zeal in fingering "enemies." In the end, the terror, like the regime's grandiose rule more generally, was actualized by the pettiest of motives, to avenge wrongs, assuage hunger, satisfy greed, but also by a desire to play one's part in the violent crusade of building

Collectivized Agriculture. Soviet plans for the socialist village envisioned the formation of large collectives supplied with advanced machinery, thereby transforming peasant labor into an industrial process. The realities behind the images of smiling farmers—such as in this poster, exhorting "Let's Achieve a Victorious Harvest"—were low productivity, enormous waste, and often broken-down machinery.

MAP 10-4   THE SOVIET UNION

The Union of Soviet Socialist Republics came into being after World War I. How did the Russian republic (RSFSR) dominate the Soviet state? How did the territorial boundaries of the Russian Soviet Federative Socialist Republic compare with the older Russian empire of the nineteenth century as shown in Map 8-5 (p. 301)? What were the larger Soviet republics besides that of the Russian republic? Could these other republics be described as "borderlands"?

socialism in a hostile world. Indeed, it appears that most inhabitants of the Soviet Union accepted the upheaval and mass arrests as a response to internal and external opposition and as a method for creating a new world. Moreover, despite the staggering losses, the elite continually expanded because the planned economy had a voracious need for officials and administrators.

ITALIAN FASCISM   Long before the Soviets could boast any accomplishments, disillusionment with the costs of the Great War, along with inspiration drawn from the Bolshevik takeover in Russia, had begun to alter the political situation in capitalist societies. In Italy, for example, the mass strikes, occupations of factories, and peasant land seizures swept through the country in 1919 and 1920. In response to this disorder, rightists, under the leadership of Benito Mussolini (1883–1945), seized power.

In 1919, Mussolini, a former socialist leader, sought to organize disaffected veterans into a mass political movement that he called fascism. His early programs mixed nationalism with social radicalism and revealed a yearning to sweep away all the institutions discredited by the war. Fascist supporters demanded the annexation of "Italian" lands in the Alps and on the Dalmatian coast, called for female suffrage, an eight-hour workday, a share of factory control for workers, a tax on capital, land redistribution, and a constituent assembly—in short, a populist program.

The fascists believed in the value of direct action and attracted much attention and numerous followers. Their direct-action shock troops wore black shirts and loose trousers tucked into high black leather boots, and saluted with a dagger thrust into the air. In 1920, the squads received money from landown-

Mussolini. Benito Mussolini liked to puff out his chest, particularly when appearing in public. *Il Duce* pioneered the leader's radio address to the people, and he encouraged fascist versions of the mass spectacles that also became common in Soviet Russia.

ers and factory owners to beat up socialist leaders, and it was at this point that Italian fascism became fully identified with the right. Still, the fascists saw themselves as champions of the little guy, of peasants and workers, as well as of war veterans, students, and white-collar types. By 1921, the squads numbered 200,000.

In 1922, Mussolini announced a march on Rome. The march was a colossal bluff, an exercise in psychological warfare—but it worked. Dressed in their black shirts, his followers intimidated King Victor Emmanuel III (1900–1946), who opposed fascist ruffians but feared bloodshed, and thus withheld use of the well-equipped army against the lightly armed marchers. When the Italian government resigned in protest, the monarch invited Mussolini to become prime minister, despite the fact that the fascists had won only 35 seats out of 500 in the 1921 elections.

The 1924 elections, in which the fascists won 65 percent of the vote, were conducted in an atmosphere of intimidation and fraud. Mussolini dealt with other challenges by mobilizing his squads and carrying out police crackdowns on the liberal and socialist opposition. A series of decrees transformed Italy from a constitutional monarchy into a dictatorship. By the end of 1926, all parties except that of the fascists were dissolved.

Mussolini's dictatorship came to terms with big business and the church, thus falling short of the social revolution that the fascist rank and file desired. Nonetheless, it was skilled at using parades, films, the radio, and visions of recapturing Roman imperial grandeur to boost support during the troubled times of the Depression. The cult of the leader, *Il Duce*, also provided

cohesion and uplift. As the first anti-liberal, anti-socialist alternative, Italian fascism served as a model for other countries.

GERMAN NAZISM In Germany, too, fear of Bolshevism and anger over the punitive peace imposed after the war helped to propel the right to power. Here, the dictator was Adolf Hitler (1889–1945), whose rise to power, like Mussolini's, was anything but easy or inevitable. Throughout 1918, and for several years thereafter, Germany was in political ferment, marked by the appearance of many small political groups. In Munich in January 1918, a nationalist workers' organization was formed, dedicated to winning workers over from socialism to nationalism. In 1920, a young demobilized corporal was ordered by the army high command to infiltrate and observe this new nationalist group. That corporal, Adolf Hitler, the son of an Austrian customs official, soon came to dominate the nationalist workers' movement, whose name he changed to the National Socialist German Workers' Party (*National-Sozialisten,* or Nazis). Unlike Mussolini, the young Hitler was never a socialist. The first Nazi party platform, set forth in 1920, combined nationalism with anti-capitalism and anti-Semitism. The program also called for the abrogation of the Versailles Treaty. It was an assertion of Germany's grievances against the world and of the small man's grievances against the rich.

The Nazis came to public attention with the "Beer Hall Putsch" in 1923. That year, the French occupied the industrial Ruhr Valley to obtain German reparation payments that had not been forthcoming, and German communists made an attempt to seize power in the provinces of Saxony and Thuringia. Making their own grab for power, Hitler and his associates invaded a meeting of Bavarian leaders in a Munich beer hall to force them to support the Nazis. The army, however, fired on the Nazis and arrested Hitler. He was sentenced to five years in prison for treason, though he served less than a year. While in prison, he wrote an autobiography, *Mein Kampf (My Struggle)* (1925), which sold widely.

Although the Nazi Party received only 2.6 percent of the vote in 1928, it started to build up support when it broadened its appeal to small farmers, shopkeepers, and clerks. The Nazis' fortunes grew as Germany's economy sagged. As more and more people lost their jobs and saw their savings wiped out by hyperinflation, they lost faith in the leaders of Germany's Weimar Republic and looked to more radical political alternatives. Fearing the growing popular support of both the Communist and Socialist Parties and convinced that he could control Hitler, Germany's eighty-five-year-old president, Field Marshal Paul von Hindenburg (1847–1934), appointed Hitler chancellor (prime minister) in January 1933. Initially, Hitler pledged that the government would be dominated by traditional conservatives. Thus, like Mussolini, Hitler came to power "peacefully" and legally. True, troops of young men (the "brown shirts," who grew from 100,000 in 1930 to 1 million in 1933) kept up the pressure in the streets with marches, mass rallies, confrontations, and beatings. But Hitler was invited to become

Hitler. Adolf Hitler, perhaps better than other dictators, staged mass rallies and projected an image of dynamism and collective will, which he claimed to embody.

chancellor by the existing elites, who feared a Bolshevik-like revolution.

Once in power, Hitler's first steps were to heighten the impression that there was a Communist conspiracy to take power. The burning of the Reichstag building in Berlin on February 27, 1933, provided the opportunity. Without any real evidence, the Nazis blamed the fire on the Communists, and a young, deranged Dutch Communist was arrested. A decree on February 28 suspended civil liberties "as a defensive measure against the Communists." Hitler then proposed an "Enabling Act," so that he could promulgate laws on his authority as chancellor, without the parliament.

The Enabling Act that was passed on March 23, 1933, freed Hitler from the parliament and also from the traditional conservative elites who had agreed to make him chancellor. In May, the offices, banks, and newspapers of trade unions were seized, and their leaders were arrested. The Socialist and Communist Parties were outlawed; other parties of the center were dissolved. By July 1933, the Nazis were the only legal party. Hitler, who became a German citizen only in 1932, soon became dictator of Germany. He moved aggressively to curb dissent, ban strikes, and stamp out anti-Nazi protests. The Nazis filled the prisons with political opponents and built the first concentration camps (initially to house political prisoners) when the jails overflowed. They also unleashed a campaign of persecution against the Jews, excluding them from the civil service and the professions, forcing them to sell their property, depriving them of citizenship, and forbidding them to marry or have sex with Aryans (so-called "pure Germans").

Hitler Youth. Youth became a special target of Nazi recruitment and socialization, just as under the Italian fascists and the Soviet Communists. This poster, called "Youth of the Future," depicts a boy waving a Nazi flag.

Der Jugend die Zukunft

CULT OF THE DYNAMIC LEADER

Nazi political theorists offered no apologies for dictatorship. On the contrary, like their Soviet, Italian, and Japanese counterparts, they bragged about it as the most efficacious form of mobilizing the energies of the masses and directing the state. The Führer, or Leader, stood above the Nazi party and all government institutions, and embodied the supposed will of the German nation. The Führer also decided who belonged, or did not belong, to the nation. Even though Nazi administration proved to be chaotic, the Führer and the idea of dictatorship were popular. The following excerpt, taken from the writings of Ernst Rudolf Huber, Germany's major constitutional expert of the 1930s, elaborated on the awesome powers that were being conferred on Hitler as Führer.

The office of Führer has developed out of the National Socialist movement. In its origins it is not a State office. This fact must never be forgotten if one wishes to understand the current political and legal position of the Führer. The office of Führer has grown out of the movement into the Reich, firstly through the Führer taking over the authority of the Reich Chancellor and then through his taking over the position of Head of State. Primary importance must be accorded to the position of "Führer of the movement"; it has absorbed the two highest functions of the political leadership of the Reich and thereby created the new office of "Führer of the Nation and of the Reich." . . .

The position of Führer combines in itself all sovereign power of the Reich; all public power in the State as in the movement is derived from the Führer power. If we wish to define political power in the *völkisch* Reich correctly, we must not speak of "State power" but of "Führer power." For it is not the State as an impersonal entity which is the source of political power but rather political power is given to the Führer as the executor of the nation's common will. Führer power is comprehensive and total; it unites within itself all means of creative political activity; it embraces all spheres of national life; it includes all national comrades who are bound to the Führer in loyalty and obedience. Führer power is not restricted by safeguards and controls, by autonomous protected spheres, and by vested individual rights, but rather it is free and independent, exclusive and unlimited.

Source: Ernst Rudolf Huber, *Führergewalt*, in *Nazism 1919–1945: A History in Documents and Eyewitness Accounts*, edited by J. Noakes and G. Pridham (Exeter, England: University of Exeter Press, 1984), pp. 198–99.

Although some in Germany opposed Hitler's illiberal activism, the Nazis won popular support for restoring order and reviving the German economy. In 1935, Hitler repudiated certain provisions of the Versailles Treaty and began a vast rearmament program, which absorbed the unemployed. The Nazis transformed economic despair and national disgrace into fierce national pride and impressive national power. Ownership of the economy remained in private hands, but the state directed and coordinated it. It also financed public works like reforestation and swamp drainage projects, organized leisure, entertainment, travel and vacations for low-income people, and built highways and public housing. Nazi rhetoric about nationalism and anti-Semitism persisted, but so did full employment and social welfare programs.

> *In contrast to Mussolini's vague ideological goals, Hitler had grand aspirations to impose racial purity and German power in Europe, and perhaps beyond.*

With internal foes disciplined or silenced and the economy revived, Germany reemerged as a great power with expansionist aspirations. Hitler called his state the "Third Reich" (the first being the Holy Roman empire and the second the empire created by Bismarck in 1871). He claimed that the Third Reich would last 1,000 years, just like the Holy Roman empire. In contrast to Mussolini's vague ideological goals, Hitler had grand aspirations to impose racial purity and German power in Europe, and perhaps beyond. As the song went, "Today Germany, tomorrow the whole world."

MILITARIST JAPAN Unlike other authoritarian regimes, Japan's power and pride were not wounded during World War I. To the contrary, because wartime disruptions greatly reduced

European and American competition, Japanese products found new markets in Asia. Japan managed to expand production, exporting munitions, textiles, and consumer goods to Asian and also Western markets. During the war, the Japanese gross national product (GNP) grew 40 percent, and the country built the world's third largest navy. Like the United States, Japan had been a debtor nation in 1913, but it became a creditor by 1920. After the war, the nation continued on what seemed a successful road to modernity. Between 1910 and the 1930s, Japan experienced a twelvefold increase in manufacturing and a threefold increase in the production of raw materials. Having suffered a devastating earthquake and fire in 1923, Tokyo was rebuilt with steel and reinforced concrete, symbolizing the new, modern Japan.

Initially, postwar Japan seemed headed down the liberal road. When Japan's Meiji Emperor, a symbol of national power and prosperity, died in 1912, his third son took over and ruled from 1912 to 1926, overseeing the rise of mass political parties. These eclipsed the oligarchic rule of the Meiji era. Suffrage was expanded in 1925 to all males over twenty-five, increasing the electorate from around 3 million to 12.5 million.

Still, this democratization was accompanied by new repressive measures. Although the Meiji Constitution remained in effect, a Peace Preservation Law, passed the same year that male suffrage was enacted, specified up to ten years' hard labor for any member of an organization advocating a basic change in the political system

> *Russia, Italy, Germany, and Japan all rejected parliamentary rule as ineffective and sought to revive their countries' power through authoritarianism, violence, and the cult of the leader.*

or the abolition of private property. The law served as a club against the mass leftist parties, such as the Japanese Communist Party, which was founded in 1922.

Japan veered still further from the liberal road after Emperor Hirohito succeeded his enfeebled father in 1926. In Japan, as in Germany, a major catalyst in the eventual shift to dictatorship was the Great Depression. Japan's trade with the outside world had more than tripled in value between 1913 and 1929, but after 1929 China and the United States imposed barriers on Japanese exports. The demand for silk and cotton goods also dropped precipitously. These measures contributed to a 50 percent decline in Japanese exports. At the same time, unemployment surged.

Such turmoil invited calls for stronger leadership, which military commanders were eager to provide. Already the leaders of Japan's armed forces were beyond civilian control. In 1927 and 1928, the army flexed its muscles by twice forcing prime ministers out of office. New "patriotic societies" echoed the call for order. Professing dedication to the emperor and nation, these squads used violence to intimidate political enemies. Violence culminated in the assassination of Japan's prime minister in 1932, accompanied by an uprising of young naval officers and army cadets. This coup failed, but it further eclipsed the power of the political parties.

During the 1930s, militarism and expansionism became dominant themes in the Japanese press. In 1931, a group of Japanese army officers arranged an explosion on the Japanese-owned South Manchurian Railroad, using this as a pretext for taking over Manchuria. The following year, the Japanese formed the puppet state of Manchukuo, adding Manchuria to its Korean and Taiwanese colonies (see Map 10-5). At home, "patriots" continued their campaign of terror against uncooperative businessmen and critics of the military, while intimidating others into silence. As in Italy and Germany, the Japanese state took on a sacred aura. This was done through promotion of an official religion, Shintō, "the way of the gods," and of the emperor's divinity. By 1940, the clique at the top dissolved all political parties into the Imperial Rule Assistance Association, ending even the semblance of parliamentary rule.

COMMON FEATURES Communist Russia, fascist Italy, Nazi Germany, and militarist Japan may seem too diverse to be compared. But, in fact, they shared many traits and, to some extent, imitated one another. All four rejected parliamentary rule as ineffective, and sought to revive their countries' power through authoritarianism, violence, and the cult of the leader.

In the economic sphere, all were convinced that modern economies required state direction. In Japan, the government fostered the emergence of huge business conglomerates, known as *zaibatsu*. The two largest *zaibatsu*, Mitsui and Mitsubishi, were probably the biggest private economic empires in the world. The Italians encouraged big business to form cartels. In Germany, the state also looked to the private sector as the vehicle of economic growth, but it expected entrepreneurs to support Germany's racial, anti-democratic, and expansionist ambitions. The most thorough form of economic coordination took place in the Soviet Union, which enthusiastically adopted American-style mass production, while eliminating private enterprise. Instead, the Soviet state owned and managed all the country's industry, with separate government ministries overseeing the manufacture of different products. Here, as elsewhere, state-organized labor forces replaced independent labor unions.

Employing mass organizations for state purposes was a second common feature of the four authoritarian regimes. Russia, Italy, and Germany had single mass parties; the Japanese had various rightist groups until a merger occurred in 1940. All sought to rally the young, often with dynamic youth movements, such as the Hitler Youth and the Union of German Girls, the Soviet Communist Youth League, and the Italian squads marching to their anthem *Giovinezza* (Youth).

Legend:
- Japanese acquisitions as of 1895
- Japanese acquisitions, 1905–1910
- Japanese area of influence before 1914
- Japanese attack, 1914
- Occupied by Japan after 1918
- Occupied by Japan, 1920–1925
- Japan forms puppet state of Manchukuo, 1932
- Occupied by Japan, 1933

MAP 10-5   THE JAPANESE EMPIRE IN ASIA

Japan aspired to become a great imperial power like the European states and succeeded in creating a far-flung set of colonies and spheres of influence before the outbreak of World War II. What were the main territorial components of the Japanese empire? How far did the Japanese succeed in extending their political influence throughout East Asia? Comment on the Japanese political involvement in China.

Three of the four states adopted large-scale social welfare policies for members of the national community. Only the Japanese failed to enact innovative social welfare legislation, but the Home Affairs Ministry eagerly enlisted helpmates among civic groups, seeking to co-opt the new middle classes to raise savings rates and improve childrearing. The Nazis emphasized full employment, built public housing, and provided assistance to families in need as long as they were racially Aryans. The Italian National Agency for Maternity and Infancy, created in 1925, provided services for unwed mothers and infant care. The Soviet authorities proclaimed social welfare as one of the fundamental tenets of the socialist revolution. Unemployment benefits ended when the government announced the end of unemployment in 1930. Still, the state created or extended programs to deal with disability, sickness, old age, death, maternity, and retirement. Unencumbered by private property interests, the Soviet state had ceased to think of welfare assistance as a stopgap in cases of social breakdown; instead, it was viewed as an ongoing, comprehensive program that distinguished socialism from capitalism.

A fourth common feature of the dictatorships was their ambivalence about women in public roles. Most propaganda emphasized women's traditional place in the home and their duty to produce healthy offspring for the nation. The state targeted them in campaigns aimed at higher rates of reproduction. It rewarded mothers who had many children, and it restricted abortion. State officials were eager to honor new mothers as a way to repair the loss of so many young men during the Great War. Yet, women were also entering professional careers in greater numbers. Monetary losses that middle-class families suffered during the war, coupled with a rise in the number of single women, compelled many women to become primary wage earners. In Italy, the fascist authorities were forced to accept the existence of *la maschietta*—the new woman, or flapper, who wore short skirts, bobbed her hair, smoked cigarettes, and engaged in freer sex. In Japan, she was called the *mogā* or *modan gāru* (modern girl), and though her presence provoked considerable negative comment, the authorities could not suppress the phenomenon. The Soviets offered the most glaring case of contradictory behavior. In 1918, they declared men and women equal, legalized (and subsidized) abortion, and eased divorce laws. The state changed its mind, however, and in 1935–1936, new laws made divorce nearly impossible, drove abortion underground, and rewarded "hero mothers" of multiple children. But the rapidly industrializing Soviets had by far the highest percentage of women in the paid workforce.

Finally, the four dictatorships used violence and terror against their own citizens, colonial subjects, and "foreigners" living within their state borders. Violence was not an external element but was viewed as an essential lever for remaking the socio-political order. To be sure, the extent of that violence varied greatly. The Italians and the Japanese were not shy about arresting political opponents, particularly in their colonies, but it was the Nazis and the Soviets who filled concentration camps with those deemed to be enemies of the state. In Germany, repression meant that almost every German Jew faced systematic persecution.

Still, brutal as all these regimes were, they were founded on mobilizing popular support for their schemes. Their successes in mastering the masses were apparent enough at home. Across Europe and the Americas, these accomplishments drew envious glances even from those still trying to stay on the liberal road. Given the power projected by dictatorships, above all, by Nazi Germany and the Soviet Union, it is not surprising that they attracted imitators. British and French fascists and Communists, though they never came to power, formed national parties and proclaimed their support for foreign models. Numerous admirers of Hitler, Lenin, and Stalin could also be found among politicians, intellectuals, and labor organizers in Latin America and the United States. Often, admirers saw what they wanted to see rather than the realities in the political and economic systems of Germany and the Soviet Union. They also sometimes admired the methods of mass mobilization and mass violence, which they hoped to use for their own ends. This was particularly true of anti-colonial movements.

THE HYBRID NATURE OF LATIN AMERICAN CORPORATISM

Latin American nations were subject to the same pressures that produced liberal and authoritarian responses to modern problems in Europe, Russia, and Japan. But here leaders devised solutions to their problems that had elements of both authoritarianism and democracy. The Latin American countries had stayed out of the fighting in the First World War, but their export economies had

> *In Latin America, leaders devised solutions to their problems that had elements of both authoritarianism and democracy.*

suffered. As trade plummeted, popular confidence in oligarchic political regimes fell, while radical agitation rose. During the war years, trade unionists in the port of Buenos Aires took control of the city's docks, and the women of São Paulo's needle trades inspired Brazil's first general strike. Bolivian tin miners also took up the banner of protest and, inspired by events in Russia, they proclaimed a full-blown socialist revolution.

The Great Depression brought even more severe challenges to the status quo from workers' groups. More than in any other region of the world, the Depression hammered at the trading and financial systems of Latin America. Responding to the Depression's destruction, Latin American governments, with the enthusiastic backing of people from the middle classes, na-

SAMBA: MASS CULTURE FROM THE BOTTOM UP

Although the instruments of the new mass media originated in Europe and North America and were more widely dispersed in these societies, African, Asian, and Latin American audiences also gained access to them. Radio especially helped to diffuse distinctly regional cultural products throughout Latin America. The evolution and dissemination of the musical and dance form known as samba in Brazil illustrates the ways in which mass culture could emerge in poorer societies and then spread upward to elite consumers and outward across national borders. Samba originated in Rio de Janeiro's shantytowns as a mixture of popular Spanish fandangos and the 2/4 meter of slave songs. Samba's lyrics extolled the freeing of the slaves in 1888 and the benevolence of the old monarchs. But mostly samba celebrated the idea that life was not all squalor, despite the dreadful conditions of the shantytowns. Samba was not high culture (though many in the elite had joined the audiences and even the dance troupes by the 1920s), and it was not the culture of any race or ethnic group (though it had African roots). Nor was it simply popular culture. Rather, it became a mass culture uniting the people of Rio de Janeiro and soon thereafter other parts of Brazil, and eventually it found an international audience as well.

What transformed the samba musical form from a local into a national and then international mass cultural phenomenon was the invention of the phonograph and long-playing records. These allowed samba to be broadcast on the new medium, radio. In Brazil, the phenomenally popular *Casé Program* on radio was exclusively dedicated to broadcasting popular music. In 1936, the national *Hour of Brazil* radio program featured the songs of the greatest samba school, Mangueira, in a special broadcast to Germany. The movie house, too, aided in the dissemination of samba. Brazilian samba musical films brought fame to a Portuguese-born dancer, Carmen Miranda, whose fruit-decorated hats made her a household symbol of the tropics in the United States. Records and radio also spread the tango of Argentina, boleros of Mexico, and salsa, the New York musical creation of Cuban and Puerto Rican emigrés that became a mass phenomenon in the Spanish Caribbean by the 1930s.

The content and influence of musical mass culture were internationalized, but music and dance were also instrumental in fostering "national" cultures in Latin America. Songs and artists transcended physical barriers and regional accents, and as such, they did the work of nation-building, creating cultural links between disparate people. Samba took on new political implications during the 1920s when dance organizations began to create "schools" to instruct neighbors and to raise funds to help with public works in the face of the Brazilian state's neglect. By the 1930s, samba schools were often the largest benefactors of schools, roads, and utilities in Rio de Janeiro. They also became patronage machines for local political bosses competing for the support of clienteles. For many years, the Brazilian government banned these organizations as potentially subversive, although they continued to operate illegally. But President Getúlio Vargas, aware that prohibition was politically costly and eager to induct the schools into his own political network, legalized the schools in 1935 and allowed them to occupy an ever more prominent place in the capital's cultural landscape. Thereafter, the annual festival of Mardi Gras evolved from a boisterous parade and religious celebration to an occasion for Rio's proliferating samba schools to strut their colorful and highly choreographed stuff. The belated efforts by the authorities to harness samba for their own purposes demonstrated its power as a mass culture from and for the people.

tionalist intellectuals, and urban workers, created an economic model that looked toward domestic rather than foreign markets as an engine of growth. The state, as in the United States and much of Europe, was called upon to play a more interventionist role in market activity.

In Latin America after the war, elites had to do something to keep order in a mass age. The solution devised by ruling elites was to establish new mass parties and encourage interest groups to associate with them. Collective bodies, like trade unions, peasant associations, and even organizations for minorities like blacks and Indians, all operated with state sponsorship. This form of modern politics, often labeled corporatist, used such social and occupational groups as trade unions, chambers of commerce, and business firms to create a bridge between the ruling elites and the rank and file of the population.

Consider, for example, Brazil, where the old republic collapsed in 1930. In its place, a new coalition, led by a skilled civilian politician, Getúlio Vargas (1883–1954), sought to create a strong political following by enacting socially popular reforms. Vargas dubbed himself the "father of the poor" and encouraged workers to organize. The government began to build schools across Brazil. Vargas made special efforts to appeal to Brazilian blacks, who had been left out of public life since the abolition of slavery. To reinforce his paternalistic image, he legalized many proscribed Afro-Brazilian practices and pledged support for samba schools (organizations that taught popular dances like the samba but that also raised funds to help with public works). Being a good patriarch also meant providing for Brazilian women and families. Accordingly, Vargas tinkered with maternity and housing policies. His Constitution of 1934 made Brazil one of the first Latin American countries to enfranchise women (although they had to be able to read, just as did male voters). And like a good patriarch, Vargas presented himself as the builder of a new nation. He paved roads, erected monuments to national heroes, and invoked a mild nationalist discourse to condemn the old elites who had betrayed the country to serve the interests of foreign consumers and investors. Although Vargas also arranged foreign funding and technical transfers to build steel mills and factories, he did it to create domestic industry so that Brazil would not be so dependent on imports.

Ruling as a patriarch meant squelching political rivals and dissent and building new lines of obedience. When he revamped the constitution in 1937, Vargas banned competitive political parties and created forms of national representation along "corporatist" lines. Each social sector or class would be represented by its function in society (for example, as workers, industrialists, or educators), and each one would pledge allegiance to the all-powerful state. Although his opponents complained vociferously about losing their democratic rights, Vargas also created rights for hitherto excluded groups like trade unions, who now could use their corporatist representatives to press for their collective demands. To bolster the system, he employed a small army of modern propagandists who used billboards, loudspeakers, and the radio to broadcast the benevolence of father Vargas.

ANTI-COLONIAL VISIONS OF MODERN LIFE

The debates that raged in Europe and the Americas over liberal democratic or authoritarian solutions to modern problems engaged peoples in the colonial and semi-colonial regions of the world as well. But here there was a larger concern: What was to be done about colonial authority? In Asia, the goal of most of the educated members of these communities was to roll back the European and American imperial presence. On this issue, leaders in these territories were in agreement. In Africa, on the other hand, where the European colonial presence was more recent and claimed to be more benign, intellectuals were still trying to discern the real meaning of colonial rule. Were the British and the French sincerely committed to African improvement, as they claimed to be? Or were they obstacles to the well-being of the peoples of the continent?

The First World War left Europe crippled, but in possession of more colonies than ever before. Ottoman territories, in particular, wound up in Allied hands. Great Britain emerged from the war with an empire that now straddled one-quarter of the earth. The spoils of war included vast oil fields in the Middle East, which had formerly been held by the Ottoman empire, and mineral-rich possessions in what had been German Africa. Christened as the British Commonwealth of Nations in 1926, the Commonwealth conferred "dominion status" on Britain's white-settler colonies in Canada, Australia, and New Zealand. This meant independence in internal and external affairs in exchange for continuing loyalty to the crown. But no such privileges were extended to possessions in Africa and India, where nonwhite peoples made up the vast majority. To justify the discriminatory practices applied to nonwhite colonial subjects, the British fell back on an old line: nonwhite peoples were not yet ready for self-government.

In Asia and Africa, then, the search for modern alternatives to colonial control began, first of all, with demands for power sharing or even outright full political independence. Otherwise divided, the intelligentsias of different countries agreed that the only sure path to the future required an end to their colonial or quasi-colonial status. Thus, anti-colonialism served as the preeminent vision of educated and literate Asians and Africans during the years between World War I and World War II. To overcome the contradictions of European liberalism, they proposed various incarnations of nationalism.

Not far beneath the surface of the Asian and African nationalist movements were profound disagreements about how nations should be governed once they gained independence and about how citizenship should be defined. For many of the educated elite, the democratic ethos of the imperial powers had great attraction. For others, the radical authoritarianism of fascism and communism, with their promises of rapid and guided change and a quick transit to the modern world, had much appeal. Whatever their political preferences, the majority of literate colonials, including those with secular, Western educations, also looked to their own religious and cultural traditions as sources for political mobilization and organization. Muslim,

> *In Asia and Africa, the search for modern alternatives to colonial control began first with demands for power-sharing and then with outright full political independence.*

Hindu, Chinese, and African values became vehicles for galvanizing the rank and file around the nation. The colonial figures involved in political and intellectual movements, whose visions for modern change derived in part from Western modernity, still insisted that their views were different from those that existed in Europe; the new societies they sought to establish were going to be modern *and* at the same time retain their indigenous characteristics.

The diversity of nationalist and anti-colonial movements depended on a variety of factors. Whether an area had been formally colonized (India and Africa), or was a semi-colonial territory (China), or was an area threatened by colonization (Turkey) was important. Equally relevant was the duration of the colonial experience.

AFRICAN STIRRINGS Africa contained the most recent territories to come under the control of the European powers, and as such, anti-colonial nationalist movements were just getting under way. The fate of the continent remained very much in the hands of Europeans. After 1918, however, African peoples probed more deeply for the meaning of Europe's imperial presence.

There was some room, albeit very confined, for voicing African interests under colonialism. The French—the world's second largest colonial power, which, like Britain, had emerged from the war with an expanded empire—had long held to a vision of "assimilation" of *its* colonial peoples, whatever their race and religion, to French culture. In France's primary West African colony, Senegal, four coastal cities had elected one delegate to the French National Assembly. In this long-standing tradition, voters sent delegates of mixed African and European ancestry. That practice lasted until 1914, when Blaise Diagne, an African candidate, ran for office and won, invoking his African origins and garnering the African vote. The electorate was small, no more than 5,000 in all, and Diagne's presence in the French Assembly posed no serious challenge to the French empire. But his election signaled the potential for political change. So did his bold, if quickly rebuffed, call in 1918 for granting all Africans the vote. Yet, Diagne's example of the incorporation of the African population into the French polity did not spread elsewhere in French colonial Africa. The British were no more accommodating to demands for local elections and fully desegregated schooling. Assimilation remained a policy without practice.

Excluded from representative bodies, Africans began to experiment with various forms of protest. For example, in southeastern Nigeria in 1929, Ibo and Ibibio women responded to a new tax by refusing to have contact with the local colonial chiefs, a form of action they referred to as "sitting on a man." Moving beyond boycotts of local officials, women burned down chiefs'

huts, as well as European and Lebanese trading establishments to protest their exploitation.

Opposition was still not massive in Africa. Such protests ran up against not only colonial administrators but also urban-based and Western-educated African elites, who often embraced European products and manners, built Western-style homes, drove automobiles, wore Western clothing, and consumed Western foods. Yet, even this relatively privileged group began to reconsider its relationship to colonial authorities. In Kenya, immediately after World War I, a small contingent of mission-educated Africans, mainly Kikuyu speakers living in or near Nairobi, demanded that the British correct what they regarded as clear violations of Britain's obligations to them. Led by Harry Thuku, they called on the British to provide more and better schools and to return lands they claimed European settlers had stolen from them. Although they enlisted the support of liberal missionaries in drafting their petitions, their pleas for change fell on deaf ears. In 1922, Thuku was arrested and placed in detention. Although defeated in this instance, the young, educated nationalists drew important lessons from their confrontation with the authorities. They now viewed colonialism in a more combative light. Their new spokesperson, Jomo Kenyatta (1898–1978), turned away from missionary and colonial sources and invoked precolonial Kikuyu traditions as a basis for resisting colonialism. In Kenyatta's brilliant ethnographical description of the precolonial Kikuyu peoples, entitled *Facing Mt. Kenya*, published in 1937, Kenyatta invoked African traditional ways as an antidote to Europeanization.

IMAGINING AN INDIAN NATION As Africans began to explore the use of modern politics against Europeans, in India opposition was taking on a still more advanced form. The war and its aftermath led to full-blown challenges to British rule. Indeed, the Indian nationalist challenge to the British provided inspiration and methods for other anti-colonial movements.

For over a century, Indians had heard British authorities extol the virtues of parliamentary government, yet they, like other colonial peoples, were excluded from participation. In 1919, the British did enlarge the franchise in India, but the reforms brought voting rights to only 3 percent of the population. They also granted more power to Indians in local self-government. Again, however, giving Indians limited responsibility for local taxation and administration did not satisfy nationalist strivings. During the 1920s and 1930s, the nationalists, led by Mohandas Karamchand (Mahatma) Gandhi (1869–1948), transformed the Indian National Congress into a mass party and laid the foundations for an alternative, anti-colonial movement.

Before returning to India in 1915, Gandhi had studied law in England and had worked in South Africa on behalf of Indian

> *The Indian nationalist challenge to the British provided inspiration and methods for other anti-colonial movements.*

immigrants. Upon his return, he assumed leadership in what were then local struggles. He also spelled out the moral and political philosophy of *satyagraha*, or nonviolent resistance, which he first developed while he was in South Africa. His message to Indians was simple: Develop your own resources and inner strength, control the instincts and activities that encourage participation in colonial economy and government, and you shall achieve *swaraj* (self-rule). Faced with Indian self-reliance and self-control pursued nonviolently, eventually the British would have to leave.

> *With his wooden staff in hand, the sixty-one-year-old Gandhi reminded European journalists of a modern-day Moses.*

A crucial event in rising Indian opposition to British rule was a massacre on April 13, 1919, of Indian civilians who were protesting British policies at Amritsar in the Punjab. The incident, in which British general Reginald Dyer ordered soldiers to fire on the protesters, left 379 Indian civilians dead and more than 1,200 wounded. As news of the massacre spread, many Indians were infuriated, and were more so when they learned that British authorities were unwilling to punish General Dyer.

This and other conflicts with state officials spurred the nationalists to oppose cooperation with government officials, to boycott the purchase of goods made in Britain, to refuse to send their children to British schools, and to withhold their taxes. Gandhi added his voice to the protest movement, calling for an all-India *satyagraha*. He also formed an alliance with Muslim leaders and began turning the Indian National Congress from an elite organization of wealthy lawyers and merchants into a mass organization open to anyone who paid dues, even the illiterate and poor.

When the Depression struck India in 1930, Gandhi singled out a seemingly harmless commodity, salt, as a testing ground for his ideas on civil disobedience. Every Indian used salt, whose production remained a heavily taxed government monopoly. Thus, salt symbolized the Indians' subjugation to an alien government. To break the colonial government's monopoly, Gandhi began a march from his *ashram* (commune) in western India to the coast to gather sea salt for free. Accompanied by seventy-one followers chosen to represent different regions and religions of India, Gandhi walked 240 miles to the sea. News wire services and mass circulation newspapers in India and around the world reported on the drama of the Salt March. Photographs of Gandhi walking determinedly to the sea circulated widely at the time. With his wooden staff in hand, the picture of the sixty-one-year-old Gandhi, dressed in coarse homespun garments and leading the march of volunteers, reminded European journalists of a modern-day Moses. Indeed, a religious aura enveloped the march as Gandhi and his followers conducted themselves as disciplined

Gandhi and the Road to Independence. *(Left)* Gandhi launched a civil disobedience movement in 1930 by violating the British government's tax on salt. Calling it "the most inhuman poll tax the ingenuity of man can devise," Gandhi, accompanied by his followers, set out on a month-long march on foot covering 240 miles to Dandi on the Gujarat coast. The picture shows Gandhi arriving at the sea, where he and his followers broke the law by scooping up handfuls of salt. *(Right)* Gandhi believed that India had been colonized by becoming enslaved to modern industrial civilization. Indians would achieve independence, he argued, when they became self-reliant. Thus, he made the spinning wheel a symbol of *swaraj*, and handspun cloth the virtual uniform of the nation.

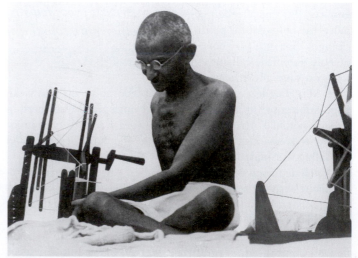

INDIA AND SELF-GOVERNMENT

The following excerpt is from Mohandas (Mahatma) Gandhi's Hind Swaraj, *a widely read pamphlet that he wrote in 1909 to explain his views on why India needed self-government. Gandhi wrote it as a dialogue between a newspaper editor and a reader. He assumed the role of the editor and criticized modernity as represented by modern Western civilization, which was based on industry and materialism. Set against modernity was his imagined civilization of India—one that derived from religion and that drew on harmonious village life. According to him, India demanded modern nationhood so that it could return to its age-old civilization.*

READER: . . . I would now like to know your views on Swaraj. . . .

EDITOR [Gandhi]: It is quite possible that we do not attach the same meaning to the term. You and I and all Indians are impatient to obtain Swaraj, but we are certainly not decided as to what it is. . . .

Why do we want to drive away the English?

READER: Because India has become impoverished by their Government. They take away our money from year to year. The most important posts are reserved for themselves. We are kept in a state of slavery. They behave insolently towards us, and disregard our feelings.

EDITOR: Supposing we get self-government similar to what the Canadians and the South Africans have, will it be good enough?

READER: . . . We must own our navy, our army, and we must have our own splendour, and then will India's voice ring through the world.

EDITOR: . . . In effect it means this: that we want English rule without the Englishman. You want the tiger's nature, but not the tiger; that is to say, you would make India English, and, when it becomes English, it will be called not Hindustan but Englistan. This is not the Swaraj that I want.

READER: Then from your statement I deduce that the Government of England is not desirable and not worth copying by us.

EDITOR: . . . If India copies England, it is my firm conviction that she will be ruined.

READER: To what do you ascribe this state of England?

EDITOR: It is not due to any peculiar fault of the English people, but the condition is due to modern civilisation. It is a civilisation only in name. Under it the nations of Europe are becoming degraded and ruined day by day.

READER: . . . I should like to know your views about the condition of our country.

EDITOR: . . . India is being ground down not under the English heel but under that of modern civilisation. It is groaning under the monster's terrible weight. . . . India is becoming irreligious. Here I am not thinking of the Hindu, the Mahomedan, or the Zoroastrian religion, but of that religion which underlies all religions. We are turning away from God.

READER: You have denounced railways, lawyers and doctors. I can see that you will discard all machinery. What, then, is civilisation?

EDITOR: . . . The tendency of Indian civilisation is to elevate the moral being, that of the Western civilisation is to propagate immorality. The latter is godless, the former is based on a belief in God. So understanding and so believing, it behooves every lover of India to cling to the old Indian civilisation even as a child clings to its mother's breast.

READER: . . . What, then, . . . would you suggest for freeing India?

EDITOR: . . . Those alone who have been affected by Western civilisation have become enslaved. . . . If we become free, India is free. And in this thought you have a definition of Swaraj. It is Swaraj when we learn to rule ourselves. . . . Passive resistance is a method of securing rights by personal suffering; it is the reverse of resistance by arms. When I refuse to do a thing that is repugnant to my conscience, I use soul-force. For instance, the government of the day has passed a law which is applicable to me. I do not like it. If, by using violence, I force the government to repeal the law, I am employing what may be termed body-force. If I do not obey the law, and accept the penalty for its breach, I use soul-force. It involves sacrifice of self.

Source: M. K. Gandhi, *Hind Swaraj and Other Writings*, edited by Anthony J. Parel (Cambridge: Cambridge University Press, 1997), pp. 26–91.

and Spartan pilgrims. Thousands of people who had gathered en route were moved by the sight of the frail apostle of non-violence encouraging them to embrace independence from colonial rule. The air thickened with tension as observers speculated on the British reaction to Gandhi's arrival at the sea. After nearly three weeks of walking, Gandhi finally waded into the surf, picked up a lump of natural salt, held it high, confessed that he had broken the salt law, and invited every Indian to do the same.

Inspired by Gandhi's example, millions of Indians found ways to violate the salt monopoly and to further challenge British rule by joining strikes, boycotting foreign goods, and substituting indigenous handwoven cloth for imported textiles. Many Indian officials in the colonial administration resigned from their jobs to demonstrate solidarity with Gandhi's vision. The colonizers were taken aback by the mass mobilization. Yet, British denunciations of Gandhi only added to his personal aura and to the anti-colonial crusade that he embodied. By insisting that Indians follow the dictates of their conscience, though always in nonviolent forms of protest, by exciting the masses through his defiance of colonial power, and by using symbols like homespun cloth as a counter to foreign, machine-spun textiles, Gandhi strengthened Indian national awareness and instilled in the people a sense of pride and resourcefulness.

> *Hindu symbols and a Hindu ethos colored the fabric of Indian nationalism woven by Gandhi and the Indian National Congress Party.*

Unlike the charismatic authoritarians who came to power in Italy, Germany, and Russia, Gandhi did not aspire to dictatorial power, and his program met opposition from within the anti-colonial movement itself. Many in the Indian National Congress Party did not share Gandhi's communitarian vision. Cambridge-educated Jawaharlal Nehru (1889–1964), for example, believed that only by embracing science and technology could India develop as a cosmopolitan, modern nation. Still, Gandhi's idea of forming the nation through self-reliance and sacrifice enthralled Nehru.

Less enamored were radical activists who wanted a revolution, not peaceful protest. In the countryside, these radicals scorned Gandhi's appeals to use nonviolence, and they sought to organize peasants to overthrow colonial domination. Other activists sought to bring the growing industrial proletariat into mass politics by organizing trade unions. Their stress on class conflict ran against Gandhi's ideals of national unity.

Religion, too, threatened to fracture Gandhi's hope for anti-colonial unity. The Hindu-Muslim alliance crafted by nationalists in the early 1920s began to splinter. Differences arose not over the religious rights of the Muslims but over who represented them and what political arrangements were necessary to assure them of their political rights. The gulf widened after the elections held under the Government of India Act of 1935, which conceded substantial provincial autonomy and enlarged the franchise to encompass 10 percent of the population. The Indian National Congress Party swept the elections in most provinces, except the two Muslim-majority states of Bengal and the Punjab. But because the Muslim votes went to provincial parties rather than to the national Muslim party (the Muslim League), the Congress Party rebuffed overtures from the League's leader, Muhammad Ali Jinnah (1876–1948). In response, Jinnah set about making the Muslim League the sole representative of the Muslims. In 1940, the League passed a resolution demanding independent Muslim states in provinces where they constituted a majority, on the grounds that Muslims were not a religious minority of the Indian nation, but a nation themselves.

Hindus also sought to claim a political role on the basis of religious identity. Movements to revitalize Hinduism, which in the nineteenth century had focused on theological and philosophical matters, began organizing Hindus as a religious nation. The most extreme expression of this trend was the formation of the *Rashtriya Swayamsevak Sangh* (RSS)—the National Volunteer Organization—in 1925. Openly admiring the Nazis' anti-liberal nationalism, the RSS campaigned to organize Hindus as a militant, modern community. Instead of reviling Jews, the RSS spewed hatred at Muslims. Although the RSS remained a fringe group, the influence of Hindu culture on Indian nationalism was broad. Hindu symbols and a Hindu ethos colored the fabric of Indian nationalism woven by Gandhi and the Indian National Congress Party.

A further challenge came from women. Long-standing nineteenth-century efforts to "uplift" women escalated during the interwar period into a demand for women's rights. The demand for women's suffrage appeared as early as 1917, and the formation of the All India Women's Conference (AIWC) in 1927 completed the shift from social reform to political rights. The AIWC activists took up issues relating to women workers, health, employment, education, and literacy, and demanded that legislative seats be reserved for women. The Indian National Congress Party, however, elevated its nationalist agenda above women's demand for a change in male-female power relations, just as it had done in dealing with the lower castes and the relations between Hindus and Muslims.

In 1937, the British belatedly granted India provincial assemblies, a bicameral national legislature, and a self-governing executive. By then, however, the people of India were deeply politicized. The Congress Party, which helped bring the masses onto the political stage to overthrow British rule, struggled to contain the different ideologies and new political institutions, such as labor unions, peasant associations, religious parties, and communal organizations. Confronted with the economic power of property-owners, the party searched, too, for a path to eco-

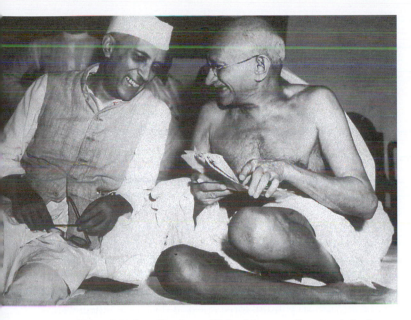

Gandhi and Nehru Sharing a Light Moment. Despite their divergent views on modernity, Gandhi was personally close to Nehru, who was his chosen political heir.

nomic modernization that suited Indian conditions and values. On one side, Gandhi looked back to the supposed harmony of self-sufficient village communities, envisioning independent India as an updated collection of village republics organized around the benevolent authority of patriarchal households. On the other side, his fellow nationalist, Nehru, hoped for a far-reaching socioeconomic transformation powered by science and planning. Both, however, believed that India's traditions of collective welfare and humane religious and philosophical practices set it apart from the modern West.

CHINESE NATIONALISM Unlike India and Africa, China was never formally colonized. But its sovereignty was compromised by the presence of substantial "concession areas" established by various foreign powers on Chinese soil. Foreign nationals who lived in China enjoyed many privileges, including the right to be tried by their own consuls and to be immune from Chinese law. Furthermore, huge indemnities imposed upon the Qing government had robbed China of its customs and tariff autonomy. Thus, the Chinese nationalists' vision of a modern alternative echoed that of the Indian nationalists. They, too, saw ridding the nation of foreign domination as the initial condition of national fulfillment. To many, the 1911 revolution, as the fall of the Qing dynasty came to be known, symbolized the first

> *To many, the 1911 revolution, as the fall of the Qing dynasty came to be known, symbolized the first step toward transforming a large and crumbling agrarian empire into a modern nation.*

step toward transforming a large and crumbling agrarian empire into a modern nation.

Despite high hopes for the new government, the new republic could not establish its legitimacy. For the most part, the government remained in the hands of a loose alliance of military, gentry, and merchant elites and was hobbled by factional and regional conflicts. In March 1912, shortly after the abdication of the emperor, a military strongman, Yuan Shikai (1859–1916) forced the nationalist leader Sun Yat-sen (1866–1925) to concede the presidency to him. While Sun had organized his followers into a political party, called the Guomindang, Yuan dismissed all efforts to further democracy and halted China's first electoral experiment by dissolving the parliament in 1913. Only Yuan's death in 1916 ended his attempt to establish a new personal dynasty.

The republic endured another blow when the Versailles Treaty awarded Germany's old concession rights in the Shandong peninsula to Japan. On May 4, 1919, thousands of Chinese students demonstrated in Beijing. The events triggered widespread agitation, as protests quickly spread to other cities, with students for the first time openly appealing to workers and merchants to join their ranks. In what became known as the May Fourth Movement, workers went on strike and merchants closed shops. Across the country, the Chinese boycotted Japanese goods.

As the Guomindang tried to rejuvenate itself, it looked to the new waves of social agitation by students and workers as well as the Russian Revolution for inspiration. In 1923, Sun reached agreement with the Russians and admitted Chinese Communists to the Guomindang as individual members. Under the banner of anti-imperialism, the newly reorganized party sponsored mass organizations of worker unions, peasant leagues, and women's associations.

In 1926, one year after the death of Sun, amid a renewed tide of anti-foreign agitation, Chiang Kai-shek (1887–1975), who seized control of the party following Sun's death, launched a military campaign, the Northern Expedition, to reunify the country under the Guomindang. Although Chiang's success was only partial, he was able to establish a new national government with its capital in Nanjing. In April 1927, however, Chiang broke with the Soviets and the Chinese Communists, whom he viewed as more threat than ally. Furthermore, his regime, despite its anti-imperialist platform, was generally careful to honor the treaty rights and concessions gained by the foreigners in the late Qing.

Still, Chiang acknowledged the need for change if China was to succeed as a modern nation. He believed that the Chinese masses had to be mobilized behind the nation. The New Life Movement, launched with a torchlight street parade in early

Chiang. Riding the current of anti-imperialism, Chiang Kai-shek, shown here in military garb in a picture taken in 1924, led the Guomindang on a military campaign in 1926–1928 and seized power, establishing a new national government based in Nanjing.

1934, best exemplified his aspiration for a new Chinese national consciousness. Drawing on diverse ideas—from Confucian precepts to Social Darwinism—and fascist practices, the New Life Movement was supposed to instill discipline and moral purpose to a unified citizenry. Among the measures were dress codes for women, condemnation of casual sexual liaisons, and campaigns against spitting, urinating, or smoking in public.

PEASANT POPULISM IN CHINA: THE WHITE WOLF
To many of the Guomindang leaders, the vast majority of the peasant population represented a backward class. Thus, the Guomindang leadership failed to see the revolutionary potential of the countryside, a failure that the Chinese Communists would later exploit. Nonetheless, the countryside was alive with grassroots movements, such as that of the "White Wolf."

From late 1913 to 1914, Chinese newspapers were filled with reports about a roving band of armed men, led by a mysterious figure known as White Wolf, who, in a large part of northern and central China, terrified many members of the elite with his almost magical power. Rumored to have close to a million followers, it is unlikely that the band, even at its height, had more than 20,000 members. But the mythology surrounding White Wolf was so widespread that the movement's impact was felt well beyond its physical presence.

Popular myth depicted White Wolf as a Chinese Robin Hood with the mission to restore order. The band's proclaimed objective was to rid the country of the injustices of Yuan Shikai's government. Raiding major trade routes and market towns, White Wolf's followers quickly gained a reputation for robbing the rich and aiding the poor. It was said that once the band captured a town, "cash and notes were flung out to the poor." Such stories won the White Wolf army followers in rural China,

The Guomindang leadership failed to see the revolutionary potential of the countryside, a failure that the Chinese Communists would later exploit.

where local peasants joined temporarily as fighters and then returned home when the band moved on.

Although the White Wolf army lacked the power to restore order to the Chinese countryside, its presence reflected the changes that had come to China and suggested those still to come. The White Wolf army struck areas where inhabitants were feeling the effects of the new market forces. In the northwestern province of Shaanxi (Shensi), for example, where the band made its most famous march, markets that were once alive with trade in Chinese cotton now awaited camels carrying cotton bales shipped from Fall River, Massachusetts. That the Guomindang never managed to bridge the differences between themselves and a rural-based movement such as the White Wolf army showed the limits of their nationalist vision. It was left to the Chinese Communists, who had fled to the countryside to escape Chiang's persecution, to take up the challenge. The Communists learned that the passivity and vulnerability of the peasants were illusions and that the rural population could be turned into a mass political force, a lesson that served them well during the subsequent war and Japanese occupation in the 1930s and 1940s.

A POST-IMPERIAL TURKISH NATION Of all the anticolonial nationalist and modernizing movements of the 1920s and 1930s, none was more politically successful or more thoroughly committed to Western models than that of Mustafa Kemal Ataturk (1881–1938), who created the modern Turkish nation-state. Until 1914, the Ottoman empire was a colonial power in its own right. But having fought on the losing German side, it collapsed. The Treaty of Sèvres, which ended the war between the Allies and the Ottoman empire, reduced the sultan's realm to a part of Anatolia. Some of its former territories, such as those in southern Europe, became independent states; others, such as those in the Middle East, became colonies of the British and the French. Elites in the former Ottoman military feared that the rest of the empire would be colonized. Although as Ottoman loyalists, many of these military men had resisted Turkish nationalism, they now embraced the cause. What made modern Turkish nationalism so successful was its ability to convert the mainstay of the old regime, the army, to the goal of creating a Turkish nation-state. These men, in turn, sought to mobilize the Turkish masses and to launch a state-led drive for modernity.

In the wake of the Ottoman empire's resounding defeat in World War I, survival of even a truncated Turkey had not been assured. But harnessing a groundswell of popular opposition to the European powers, Mustafa Kemal, an Ottoman army officer and military hero, organized a military offensive in the summer of 1920 and reconquered most of Anatolia and the area

Ataturk. In the 1920s, Mustafa Kemal, known as Ataturk, introduced the Latin alphabet for the Turkish language as part of his campaign to modernize and secularize Turkey. He underscored his commitment to change by being photographed while giving instruction.

civil and political affairs. The Turkish elite replaced the Muslim religious law with the Swiss civil code, instituted the Western (Christian) calendar, and abolished the once-powerful dervish religious orders. They also eliminated Arabic and Persian words from Turkish and substituted the Roman script for Arabic letters. Polygamy was proscribed. Wearing the fez (a brimless cap) was criminalized, and Turks were instructed to wear European-style hats. The veil, though not outlawed, was denounced as a relic. In 1934, the government enfranchised Turkish women, granted them property rights in marriage and inheritance, and allowed them to enter the professions. Schools, too, were taken out of the hands of Muslim clerics, placed under the control of the state, and, along with military service, became the chief instrument for making the masses conscious of belonging to a Turkish nation. Yet, many villagers did not accept Ataturk's non-Islamic nationalism, remaining devoted to Islam and resentful of the prohibitions against dervish dancing.

In emulating Europe, Kemal borrowed Europe's anti-liberal models. Inspired by the Soviets, Kemal inaugurated a five-year plan for the economy, though the emphasis on centralized coordination was not tied to the abolition of private property. During the 1930s, Turkish nationalists drew on Nazi examples by advocating racial theories that posited Central Asian Turks as the founders of all civilization. And in another move characteristic of authoritarian dictators, Kemal occasionally rigged parliamentary elections, while using the police and judiciary to silence his critics.

THE MUSLIM BROTHERHOOD IN EGYPT Elsewhere in the Middle East, where France and Britain expanded their holdings at the Ottomans' expense, anti-colonial movements borrowed from European models, while putting their own stamp on nation-making and modernization campaigns. In Egypt, for example, British occupation pre-dated the fall of the Ottoman empire by several decades, but here, too, the First World War energized the forces of anti-colonial nationalism. When the war ended, Sa'd Zaghlul (1857–1927), an educated, upper-crust Egyptian patriot, pressed for an Egyptian delegation to be invited to the peace conference at Versailles. There, he hoped to present Egypt's case for national independence. Instead, British officials arrested and exiled him and his most vocal supporters to Malta. When news of this action came out, the country burst into revolt. Rural rebels broke away from the central government, proclaiming local republics. Villagers tore up railway lines and telegraph wires, the symbols of British authority.

around Istanbul. The French and Italians decided to come to terms. The British, too, unable to convince their dominions to lend troops for more fighting, negotiated. Thus, in 1923, Turkish leaders signed a new treaty, the Peace of Lausanne, abrogating punitive reparations and expanding the original borders inscribed in the Treaty of Sèvres. Turkish negotiators relinquished claims to Arab lands and several Aegean islands. A vast, forcible exchange of populations took place. Approximately 1.2 million Greek speakers left Turkey to settle in Greece, and 400,000 Turks moved from Greece to Turkey.

In forging a Turkish nation, Kemal looked to construct a European-like secular state and to eliminate Islam's hold over civil and political affairs.

With the empire broken up, Kemal and his followers moved to build a state based upon Turkish national consciousness. That meant first deposing the sultan in 1922. Two years later, the new leaders abolished the office of the Ottoman caliphate and proclaimed Turkey a republic, whose supreme authority would be lodged in an elected House of Assembly. Later, after Kemal insisted that the people should adopt European-style surnames, the assembly conferred on Kemal the mythic name "Ataturk," father of the Turks.

In forging a Turkish nation, Kemal looked to construct a European-like secular state and to eliminate Islam's hold over

After defusing the conflict, British authorities tried to mollify Egyptian sensibilities. Their half-hearted efforts helped at first, but then aggravated tensions. In 1922, Britain proclaimed Egypt independent, though it retained the right to station

British troops on Egyptian soil. Ostensibly, this provision was adopted to protect traffic through the Suez Canal and foreign populations residing in Egypt, but it also enabled the British to continue to influence Egyptian politics. Two years later, elections took place, and Zaghlul's new nationalist party, the Wafd, took office. But the British prevented the Wafd from exercising real power.

This subversion of independence and democracy in Egypt provided an opening for anti-liberal variants of anti-colonialism

to arise. During the Depression years, a fascist group, called Young Egypt, garnered wide appeal. So did an Islamic group established in 1928, the Muslim Brotherhood, which attacked liberal democracy as a facade for middle-class, business, and landowning interests. The Muslim Brotherhood was anti-colonial and anti-British, but its members considered mere political independence insufficient. Egyptians, they argued, must also renounce the blandishments of the West, whether they be those of liberal capitalism or godless communism, and return to a purified form of Islam. For the ideologues of the Muslim Brotherhood, Islam offered a complete way of life. A "return to Islam" through the nation-state created yet another model of modernity for colonial and semi-colonial peoples.

Chronology

1912	Abdication of Qing emperor (China)
1914	The Great War begins
1917	Bolshevik Revolution
1917	U.S. enters W.W. I
1918	Dissolution of German, Austro-Hungarian, and Ottoman empires
1918–1921	Russian Civil War
1919	Treaty of Versailles ends W.W. I
1919	Massacre at Amritsar (India)
1919	May Fourth Movement (China)
1922	Ottoman sultan deposed
1922	Republic of Ireland established
1922	Mussolini and fascists march on Rome
1924	Mustafa Kemal leads Turkey to nationhood
1926	British Commonwealth of Nations established
1928	Chiang Kai-shek becomes leader of China
1928	Muslim Brotherhood established (Egypt)
1929–1938	Collectivization in Russia
1929	Great Depression begins
1930	Getúlio Vargas becomes leader of Brazil
1930	Gandhi's March to the Sea
1933–1941	American "New Deal"
1932	Japan annexes Manchuria
1933	Hitler becomes dictator of Germany
1936–1939	Popular Front rules France
1936–1939	Purges in the Soviet Union

CONCLUSION

The Great War and its aftermath accelerated the trend toward mass society and the debate over how to organize it. Mass society meant production and consumption on a staggering scale. Politics and culture were no longer the exclusive province of a small number of elite men and women. For rulers around the globe, satisfying the populace became a pressing concern. Indeed, it became the central problem of the postwar decades, with competing programs vying for pride of place in the new, broader, public domain.

Most of the programs fell into three categories: liberal, authoritarian, and anti-colonial. The first, liberalism, was a holdover from the nineteenth century—and to varying extents, it defined the political and economic systems in Western Europe and the Americas. Resting on faith in free enterprise and representative democracy (with a restricted franchise), liberal regimes had already been unsettled before the Great War. Turn-of-the-century reforms had broadened electorates and brought government oversight and regulation into private economic activity. But during the Great Depression, dissatisfaction again deepened. Only far-reaching reforms, introducing greater regulation and more aggressive government intervention to provide for the welfare of the citizenry, saved capitalist economies and the democratic political systems to which they were attached from collapse.

Still, through the 1930s, liberalism was in retreat. Authoritarianism seemed better positioned to satisfy the masses while claiming to represent the cutting edge of modernity. Dictatorial regimes challenged liberalism from both the left and right of the political spectrum. While authoritarians differed about the faults of capitalism, they joined in the condemnation of electoral democracy. Authoritarians mobilized the masses to put the interests of the nation above the individual. That mobilization often entailed brutal repression of large portions of the population, and yet the grand crusade seemed also to restore pride and purpose to the masses.

In the colonial and semi-colonial world, the tribulations of liberalism and the triumphs of authoritarianism, especially those of Soviet communism and German Nazism, were closely watched by those searching to escape from the domination of European empires. In Asia and Africa, anti-colonial leaders confronted diverse situations. In common, however, they faced the challenge of how to eliminate foreign rule while turning colonies into nations and subjects into citizens. Some anti-colonial intellectuals and leaders looked to the liberal West for models of nation-building. But for some in Asia and Africa, liberalism was discredited because it was associated with colonial rule. Instead, socialism, fascism, and a return to religious traditions offered more compelling models for the anti-colonial crusade.

The competition among democratized liberalism, radical authoritarianism, and anti-colonial nationalism was not purely intellectual. It entailed geopolitical rivalry among the great powers, and it involved the fate of the existing empires. Yet, while the age of mass production and mass politics was marked by political upheavals and economic dislocations, it was tame compared to what was about to erupt in 1939—the Second World War.

FURTHER READINGS

Bergère, Marie-Claire, *Sun Yat-sen* (1998). Originally published in French in 1994, this is a judicious and most recent biography of the man generally known as the father of the modern Chinese nation.

Brown, Judith, *Gandhi: Prisoner of Hope* (1990). A biography of Gandhi as a political activist.

De Grazia, Victoria, and Ellen Furlough (eds.), *The Sex of Things: Gender and Consumption in Historical Perspective* (1996). Pathbreaking essays on how gender affects consumption.

Dumenil, Lynn, *The Modern Temper: America in the 1920s* (1995). A general discussion of American culture in the decade after World War I.

Fainsod, Merle, *Smolensk under Soviet Rule* (1989). The most accessible and sophisticated interpretation of the Stalin revolution in the village.

Friedman, Edward, *Backward Toward Revolution: The Chinese Revolutionary Party* (1974). An insightful look at the failure of liberalism in early republican China through the prism of the short-lived Chinese Revolutionary Party.

Gelvin, James, *Divided Loyalties: Nationalism and Mass Politics in Syria at the Close of Empire* (1998). Offers important new insights into the development of nationalism in the Arab world.

Horne, John (ed.), *State, Society, and Mobilization during the First World War* (1997). Essays on what it took to wage total war among all the belligerents.

Johnson, G. Wesley, *The Emergence of Black Politics in Senegal* (1971). A useful examination of the stirrings of African nationalism in Senegal.

Kennedy, David M., *Freedom from Fear: The American People in Depression and War, 1929–1945* (1999). A wonderful narrative of turbulent years.

Kershaw, Ian, *Hitler*, 2 vols. (1998–2000). A masterpiece combining biography and context.

Kimble, David, *A Political History of Ghana* (1963). An excellent discussion of the beginnings of African nationalism in Ghana.

Kotkin, Stephen, *Magnetic Mountain: Stalinism as a Civilization* (1995). Recaptures the atmosphere of a time when everything seemed possible, even creating a new world.

LeMahieu, D. L., *A Culture for Democracy: Mass Communication and the Cultivated Mind in Britain Between the Wars* (1988). One of the great works on mass culture.

Lyttelton, Adrian, *The Seizure of Power: Fascism in Italy, 1919–1929* (1961). Still the classic account.

Marchand, Roland, *Advertising the American Dream: Making Way for Modernity 1920–1945* (1985). An excellent discussion of the force of mass production and mass consumption.

Mazower, Mark, *Dark Continent: Europe's Twentieth Century* (1999). A wide-ranging overview of Europe's tempestuous twentieth century.

Nottingham, John, and Carl Rosberg, *The Myth of "Mau Mau": Nationalism in Kenya* (1966). Dispels the myths in describing the roots of nationalism in Kenya.

Thorp, Rosemary (ed.), *Latin America in the 1930s* (1984). An important collection of essays on Latin America's response to the shakeup of the interwar years.

Tsin, Michael, *Nation, Governance, and Modernity in China: Canton, 1900–1927* (1999). An analysis of the vision and social dynamics behind the Guomindang-led revolution of the 1920s.

Vianna, Hermano, *The Mystery of Samba* (1999). Discusses the history of samba, emphasizing its African heritage as well as its persistent popular content.

Wakeman, Frederic, Jr., *Policing Shanghai 1927–1937* (1995). An excellent account of Guomindang rule in China's largest city during the Nanjing decade.

Winter, J. M., *The Experience of World War* (1988). A comprehensive presentation of the many sides of the twentieth century.

Young, Louise, *Japan's Total Empire: Manchuria and the Culture of Wartime Imperialism* (1998). An innovative case study of Japanese imperialism and mass culture with broad implications.

Chapter

11

THE THREE-WORLD ORDER, 1940–1975

In February 1945, the three leaders of the Allied war coalition—President Franklin Delano Roosevelt of the United States, Prime Minister Winston Churchill of the United Kingdom, and Premier Joseph Stalin of the Soviet Union—met in the Black Sea resort city of Yalta in Russian Crimea to make preparations for the postwar order. By then, Germany, Italy, and Japan were losing the war. The three men had different visions of how a war-torn world should be reconstructed. Roosevelt anticipated a world of independent states, kept at peace by an international body. He had no interest in restoring the old European empires, which he believed had been ruled selfishly with little commitment to a civilizing mission. New nations then should take the place of old empires. Roosevelt had high hopes that China would emerge under the guidance of Chiang Kai-shek as the leader of Asia after the anticipated downfall of the Japanese empire. The American president requested that the Soviet Union enter the Pacific war on the American side, and Stalin agreed. But Britain's Churchill had no intention, as he so aptly put it after the war, of presiding over the liquidation of the British empire. Finally, just what Stalin wanted was not clear, though the Soviet leader's negotiations at Yalta left no doubt that he intended to secure influence in Eastern Europe and Asia and to weaken Germany so that

385

it could never again menace the Soviet Union. In short, as the end of the war approached, these contrasting visions of the post-war world order threatened to usher in a contentious era.

The First World War had shocked the European-centered world, but the Second World War destroyed it. When the fighting finally stopped in August 1945, empires had been destroyed or were set for dismantling by colonial independence movements. The nation-state more than ever had emerged as the prevailing political organization. Moreover, the reach of the state had been expanded as it took on new functions related to postwar reconstruction. Meanwhile, with the end of the war and the weakening of the former great powers, a new three-world order began to emerge. Heading the "First World" was the United States. Leading the "Second World" was the Soviet Union. Allies during World War II, the United States and the Soviet Union became postwar enemies. Their rival blocs—capitalist and Communist—were locked in a "cold war." Caught in between were formerly colonized and semi-colonized people lumped together as the "Third World."

Competing Blocs

> → *What challenges did each world order face?*

The roots of the division of the world into three blocs lay in the breakup of Europe's empires and the demise of European world leadership. The destruction of Europe and the defeat of Japan left a power vacuum, which the United States and the Soviet Union rushed to fill. The United States and the Soviet Union both believed that their respective ideologies—liberal capitalism and communism—had universal application. In the new world order, they were superpowers—so called because of their size, their possession of the atomic bomb, and the fact that each embodied a model of civilization applicable to the whole world. As both nations expanded their spheres of influence, they engaged in an arms race that threatened world peace. Bitter rivalry dominated world politics for several decades.

While the capitalist and Communist blocs embarked on a cold war, in which no direct war was fought between the two, in the Third World the conflicts got very hot indeed. In Asia and Africa, anti-colonial leaders capitalized on European weakness and Japanese defeat to intensify their campaigns for independence. Winning popular support by mobilizing deep-seated desires for justice and autonomy, they were able to sweep away foreign rulers and assert their claims for national independence. Latin America, too, joined this effort to achieve progress and nationhood. But newfound political freedom did not easily translate into economic development or social equity. Moreover, as the two superpowers looked for allies and clients, they militarized rival states and factions within the Third World. Still, the Third World continued to nurture powerful movements for national liberation and social transformation.

While each superpower touted its own achievements, each also had to confront internal problems. The United States maintained that its booming industrial economy, abundant consumer goods, liberal democracy, and entertaining popular culture were proof of the superiority of capitalism. Yet, the United States also wrestled with deep-rooted racism that diminished the appeal of the American way of life for nonwhite peoples. And it became involved in unpopular wars to stop the spread of communism, most notably in Vietnam. The Soviet Union celebrated its own economic prowess and social welfare policies. But its continued authoritarianism, its millions of political prisoners, and its use of military force to crush reform efforts within the Soviet bloc undermined communism's allure.

By the 1960s and the early 1970s, tensions were beginning to appear in the three-world order. The United States and the Soviet Union faced discontent within their societies and opposition within their respective blocs. At the same time, the rising economic might of Japan and the other Pacific economies, the emerging clout of oil-rich states, and the specter of radical revolution in Africa, Asia, and Latin America suggested a shift in the balance of wealth and power away from the First and Second Worlds, if not toward the Third.

Focus Questions THE THREE-WORLD ORDER

→ *What challenges did each world order face?*

→ *How was World War II a total war?*

→ *How did the U.S. try to contain the spread of communism?*

→ *In what cases and why did decolonization involve large-scale violence?*

→ *What were the successes and failures of each world order?*

→ *What were the major fissures that developed in the three-world order?*

WORLD WAR II AND ITS AFTERMATH

→ *How was World War II a total war?*

The seeds for World War II grew out of unresolved problems connected to the Great War. World War I had not been, as many had prophesied, "the war to end all wars." It became instead merely the *First* World War after the *Second* World War began in 1939. Especially influential were the resentments bred by the harsh provisions and controversial new state boundaries set out in the treaties signed at the war's end. World War II was also an outgrowth of the aggressive ambitions and racial theories of Germany and Japan, who sought to impose their theories of racial hierarchy (master and inferior races) through conquest and coerced labor. By the late 1930s, German and Japanese ambitions to expand and to become colonial powers, like Britain, France, and the United States, brought these conservative dictatorships (along with Italy, these were the Axis Powers) into conflict with France, Britain, the Soviet Union, and eventually the United States (the Allied Powers). Germany sought to end reparations payments imposed after World War I and demanded the right to rearm itself.

Even more than its predecessor, World War II was a true world conflict and was devastatingly total. Fighting took place in Europe, Africa, and Asia, the Atlantic and the Pacific, and the Northern and Southern Hemispheres. Warring nations mobilized millions of people into armed forces and placed enormous demands on civilian populations. Noncombatants had to produce far more to support the war effort, and they had to consume far less.

> *Even more than its predecessor, World War II was a true world conflict and was devastatingly total.*

Moreover, as aerial bombardment of cities resulted in colossal numbers of civilian casualties, the new total war erased the old distinction between soldiers and civilians.

In addition to refashioning the nature of modern war, World War II completed the decline of European world dominance that World War I had set in motion. The unspeakable acts of barbarism perpetrated during the war, including the Nazi genocides directed against Jews and others, robbed Europe of its lingering claims as a superior civilization. In the war's wake, anti-colonial movements demanded national self-determination from exhausted and battered European powers.

THE WAR IN EUROPE

Although Hitler had annexed Austria and parts of Czechoslovakia in 1938, World War II officially began in Europe in September 1939, with Germany's invasion of Poland and the British and French decision to oppose it. Hitler's early success in the air and on the battlefield was staggering. He overran Poland, France, Norway, Denmark, Luxembourg, Belgium, and Holland. Within less than two years, the Germans controlled virtually all of Western Europe (see Map 11-1). Only Britain escaped Axis control, though Nazi airplanes strafed British cities with bombs. In the east, Germany had a nonaggression pact with the Soviet Union, but in June 1941, the German army invaded the Soviet Union with 170 divisions, 3,000 tanks, and up to 4 million men—an unprecedented invasion force. Here, as elsewhere, the Germans fought what was called a *blitzkrieg*, or lightning war, of tank-led assaults followed by motorized infantrymen (and then foot soldiers). Already by October 1941, the Germans had conquered Romania, Hungary, Bulgaria, Yugoslavia, and the western portion of the Soviet Union and had reached the outskirts of Moscow. The Soviet Union seemed on the verge of a monumental defeat.

The Nazi war was also a crusade to create a "new order" based on race. Nazi occupation policies were monstrous and created massive social, economic, and political upheavals throughout Europe. In general, occupied civilian populations were terrorized and displaced on a mass scale. Some 12 million foreign laborers were forcibly transported to Germany during the war. There, they received lower wages (or none at all) and lived in more deprived conditions than did the German population. To enforce his policies, Hitler established puppet governments, which complied with deportation orders against Jews and dissidents. Hitler's police and the puppet states turned Europe into a giant police state and spawned both collaborators and resistance fighters. Even within the resistance movements, however, there were many different points of view—from nationalists, who opposed German domination, to Communists, who wanted to defeat both fascism and capitalism; here, the seeds for many postwar enmities were sown.

In the east, the tide turned against the Germans and their collaborators after the ferocious battles of Stalingrad in 1942–1943 and Kursk in 1943. Once the Soviet army blunted the initial German assault, it launched a massive counter-offensive. This was the beginning of the end of the German war effort on the Eastern Front, but the full retreat would take another two years as the Soviets drove Hitler's army slowly westward. Before 1944, the Soviets bore the brunt of the fighting, although the British attacked the Nazis in the air and on the sea and, along with American troops, they stopped a German advance across North Africa into Egypt. The D-Day landing of Western Allied forces in Normandy on June 6, 1944, however, brought the Germans face to face with American and British troops determined to fight their

MAP 11-1 WORLD WAR II: THE EUROPEAN THEATER

The Axis armies enjoyed great success during the early stages of World War II. What were the territorial boundaries when the Axis Powers reached their greatest extent? When did the military balance begin to turn against Germany and Italy? Which countries were not allied with, occupied by, or dominated by the Axis in 1940? What areas were the primary sites of conflict, destruction, and casualties during the war in Europe?

way to Germany itself. On April 30, 1945, as Soviet and Anglo-American forces converged on Berlin, Hitler committed suicide in his concrete bunker. On May 7, 1945, Germany surrendered unconditionally. Still, the question of what the European map would look like after this terrible, "total" war was unresolved.

The war in Europe had devastating human and material costs. This was particularly the case in Eastern Europe, where the Germans had plundered and murdered the local populations. Fighting on the Eastern Front leveled more than 70,000 Soviet villages and obliterated one-third of the Soviet Union's wealth. Soviet military deaths numbered 7 million, about half the total

The Devastation of War. *(Left)* In November 1942, Nazi troops had entered the streets of Stalingrad, some 2,000 miles from Berlin. Hitler wanted to capture the city not only to exploit the surrounding wheat fields and the nearby oil of the Caucasus, but also for its very name. With handheld flamethrowers and sometimes just their fists, Soviet troops finally drove out the Germans in February 1943, leaving behind a pile of rubble. *(Right)* In the Battle of Britain, Nazi warplanes strafed British cities in an effort to break British morale. But the devastating bombing raids, such as this one in Coventry in November 1940, helped rally the British, who refused to capitulate.

of all combatants (by contrast, the Germans lost 3.5 million men). Estimates of Soviet civilian deaths range from 17 to 20 million. Bombing of British cities, such as London by the German *Luftwaffe*, inflicted a heavy toll on civilians and buildings, as did Allied bombing of war plants and German cities like Dresden and Berlin. By the end of the war, Poland had lost 6 million people, and Great Britain had lost 400,000. Tens of millions in the east and west were left homeless.

> *Around six million—two-thirds of all European Jews—died, many from gassing, others from starvation or exhaustion.*

Europe's Jews paid an especially high price. Hitler had long talked of "freeing" Europe of all Jews. At the outset of the war, the Nazis herded Jews into ghettos and labor camps, seizing their property. But as the army moved eastward, more and more Jews came under German control. At first, the Nazi bureaucrats contemplated deportation, perhaps to the island of Madagascar. But transporting "subhumans" was ruled out as too costly and complicated, and already by 1940, special troops in the east had begun mass shootings of Communists and Jews. This, however, was seen as a waste of ammunition. Accordingly, shootings gave way to the use of mobile gas vans. By the fall of 1941, Hitler and the S.S. (the *Schutzstaffel*, a security police force) began to plan a series of killing centers. The largest of these concentration camps was a complex known as Auschwitz-Birkenau in Poland. Cattle cars shipped Jews from all over Europe to the new extermination sites, where the latest tech-

nology was used to kill men, women, and children. Around 6 million—two-thirds of all European Jews—died, many from gassing, others from starvation or exhaustion. The Nazis also turned their mass killing apparatus against gypsies, homosexuals, Communists, and Slavs, with deportations to the death camps continuing to the very end of the war.

THE PACIFIC WAR

Like the war in Europe, the conflict in the Pacific transformed the military and political landscape (see Map 11-2). The war broke out when Japan's ambitions to obtain access to vital Southeast Asian oil and rubber supplies and to become a major colonial power in the area ran squarely into American opposition. Japan's expansionist aims became clear in 1931 when its forces invaded and occupied Manchuria in northern China and intensified when it launched an offensive against the rest of China in 1937. Although the Japanese captured a large amount of Chinese territory, they were not able to force China's complete submission. But the invaders exacted a terrible toll on the Chinese population. The most infamous of Japanese atrocities was the "Rape of Nanjing," in which the aggressors indiscriminately slaughtered at least 100,000 civilians and raped thousands of women in the Chinese capital between December 1937 and February 1938.

Legend:
- Japanese Empire, 1 Dec. 1941
- Ally of Japan
- ······ Furthest line of Japanese advance, July 1942
- *Date* Japanese attack or capture
- *Date* Allied attack or capture
- ← Allied offensive
- ← Japanese offensive
- ← British offensive
- ← Chinese-U.S. offensive
- ← Chinese offensive
- ← Soviet offensive
- ← Japanese naval victory
- ← U.S. naval victory
- ✹ Conventional bombing
- ✸ Nuclear bombing
- ✳ Japanese battle victory
- ✳ U.S. battle victory

MAP 11-2   WORLD WAR II: THE PACIFIC THEATER

Like Germany and Italy, the Japanese experienced stunning military successes in the early years of the war. Can you explain why Japan was so successful militarily at this time? Against whom did the Japanese wage war in the Pacific? How well did the European empires in Asia fare during the war in the Pacific? Which of the European colonies in Southeast Asia and South Asia fell under Japanese rule and which were spared? What were the areas of heaviest fighting and damage in the war?

Japanese Aggression. *(Left)* The Battle of Shanghai, which took place between August and November of 1937, was a brutal campaign that marked the beginning of what turned out to be World War II in Asia. Claiming to be "protecting" China from the aggressions of European imperialists and expecting a relatively easy victory, the Japanese found themselves met instead with surprisingly stiff resistance from Chinese troops under Chiang Kai-shek. Here we see Japanese marines parading through the streets of the city after they finally broke through Chinese defenses. About a quarter of a million Chinese soldiers, or close to 60 percent of Chiang's best-trained troops, were killed or wounded in the campaign, a blow from which Chiang's regime never fully recovered. The Japanese sustained over 40,000 casualties. *(Right)* Japanese troops are pictured celebrating a victory over the Americans on Bataan, in April 1942. Only the stalemate of the Battle of the Coral Sea (south of New Guinea) halted the run of Japanese victories. With the defeat of the Japanese at the Battle of Midway in June 1942, the United States finally began to turn the tide of the Pacific War.

Events in Europe opened opportunities for further Japanese expansion in Asia. Germany's swift occupation of Western Europe left the colonies of defeated nations at the mercy of Japanese forces. After concluding a pact with Germany in 1940, the Japanese proceeded to occupy French Indochina in 1941 and made demands on the Dutch East Indies for oil and rubber. Now the chief obstacle to further expansion in the Pacific was the United States. Japanese leaders, however, remained divided over the advisability of going to war with the United States. This issue was resolved when a group of military officers led by General Tōjō Hideki (1884–1948) assumed the leadership of the Japanese government in 1941. Hoping to strike the United States before it was prepared for war and before the Americans could prevent Japan from seizing resource-rich territories in Southeast Asia, the Japanese launched a full-scale surprise air attack on the American naval base at Pearl Harbor in Hawaii on December 7, 1941. As the United States entered the war, Germany and Italy, under the terms of the Tripartite Pact of 1940, also declared war on America.

In the months after Pearl Harbor, Japan's expansion shifted into high gear. During 1942, the Japanese military achieved spectacular successes, racking up victory after victory over the tottering Western armies. With French Indochina already under their control, the Japanese turned against the American colony of the Philippines and against the Dutch East Indies, both of which fell in 1942. By coordinating their army, naval, and air force units and using tactical surprise, the Japanese were able to seize a huge swathe of Asian territory that included British-ruled Hong Kong, Singapore, Malaya, and Burma, while threatening the British empire's hold on India as well.

Japan christened its new empire the Greater East Asia Co–Prosperity Sphere, dressing its aggression in the garb of anti-colonial, pan-Asianism. In practice, however, the Japanese made huge demands on Asians for resources, developed their own myth of Japanese racial purity and supremacy, and treated Chinese and Koreans with brutality.

Asians under Japanese dominion soon discovered that "Asia for Asians" was an empty slogan. During the war, Japan put up to 4 million Koreans to work for its empire, while forcibly importing another 700,000 Korean men as laborers. Up to 200,000 young women, most but not all from Korea, were pressed into service as prostitutes, euphemistically referred to as "comfort women," for Japanese soldiers.

Like the Germans in their war against Russia, the Japanese could not sustain their military successes against the United States. By the middle of 1943, U.S. forces had thrown the Japanese on the defensive. Fighting from island to island, American troops under General Douglas MacArthur (1880–1964) recaptured the Philippines, and a combined force of British, American, and Chinese troops returned Burma to Britain. The Allies then moved toward the Japanese mainland. By the summer of 1945, American bombers had all but devastated the major cities of Japan. At sea, the Japanese navy was no match for American warships, and its soldiers scattered across Asia found themselves abandoned without supplies and support. Yet, Japan did not surrender. Anticipating that an invasion of Japan would cost hundreds of thousands of American lives, Harry Truman (1884–1972), recently elevated to the American presidency following the death of Franklin Roosevelt, decided to unleash the Americans' secret weapon. On August 6, 1945, an American plane dropped an atomic bomb on the city of Hiroshima, killing and maiming over 100,000 people. Three days later, the Americans dropped a second atomic bomb, on Nagasaki. Five days after this second attack, Emperor Hirohito announced Japan's surrender.

THE BEGINNING OF THE COLD WAR

> → *How did the U.S. try to contain the spread of communism?*

The Second World War left much of Europe in ruins. Charred embers lay where great cities had once stood. Major bridges lay crumbled at the bottom of rivers; railway lines were twisted scrap; sunken ships blocked harbors. Industrial and agricultural production plummeted, leading to widespread scarcity and hunger. Millions had died; tens of millions more were wounded, displaced, widowed, and orphaned. "What is Europe now?" mused British prime minister Winston Churchill at the war's end. "A rubble heap, a charnel house, a breeding ground of pestilence and hate."

REBUILDING EUROPE

The task of political rebuilding was daunting. The old order, which had either collaborated with fascists or crumpled before their armies, was discredited. By contrast, communism gained new appeal—many underground resisters were Communists, and their credo promised a clean slate. Some Eastern Europeans, knowing little of Stalin's crimes, wanted Soviet help to create proletarian paradises. After the horrors of fascism, some form

Nagasaki after the Dropping of the Atomic Bomb. *(Left)* A view of Nagasaki, less than half a mile from "ground zero" after the atomic bomb struck in August 1945. A few reinforced concrete buildings still stand. *(Right)* Thousands of victims of the atomic blast were immediately crushed or burned to death. Many survivors later succumbed to the effects of horrendous burns and radiation poisoning.

Postwar Planning at Yalta. The "Big Three" allies confer at the Black Sea resort of Yalta in February 1945. On the left is British prime minister Winston Churchill, at the center is American president Franklin Roosevelt, and on the right is Soviet premier Joseph Stalin. At Yalta, the Allied leaders made plans for the end of the war.

of socialism seemed to offer the potential to create powerful, modern, egalitarian societies in Europe.

Europe's leftward tilt alarmed U.S. policymakers. They feared that the Soviets would use their ideological influence to establish a Communist bloc and that Stalin might lay claim to Europe's possessions overseas, thereby creating Communist regimes outside Europe. By threatening capitalism from Eastern and Western Europe, Stalin went from being America's ally to being its enemy. American and British governments had mistrusted Stalin during the war, but they had depended on the Soviet Union's strength against Germany. With a common enemy gone, however, misgivings quickly evolved into a decision to hold the line against further Soviet influence. An American journalist coined and popularized the term "cold war" in 1946 to describe the new struggle.

President Truman advocated a policy of containing Soviet communism. America's policy soon faced a test in Germany, which had been partitioned into British, French, American, and Soviet zones of occupation after the war. Although Berlin, the capital city, was technically in the Soviet occupation zone, postwar agreements stipulated that it was to be jointly administered by all four powers. In 1948, the Soviets attempted to seize Berlin for themselves by blocking all routes to the capital. The Allies responded by launching a massive effort to keep Berlin from falling to the Soviets; by transporting supplies in planes to the Western zone of Berlin, the Berlin Airlift managed to keep the population from capitulating to the Soviets. This crisis lasted for almost a year, until Stalin allowed trucks to roll through the Eastern zone in May 1949.

Stalin and his successors did not, however, relax their hold on Eastern Germany, and in 1949, a line drawn through occupied Germany split the territory into two hostile states: the democratic Federal Republic of Germany in the west, and the

The Berlin Airlift. In the summer of 1948, a new currency was issued for the united occupation zones of West Germany. It began to circulate in Berlin at exchange rates that were much more favorable than the Eastern zone's currency, and Berlin seemed poised to become an outpost of the West inside the Soviet Eastern occupation zone. The Soviets responded with a blockade of Western traffic into Berlin; the West countered with an airlift, forcing the Soviets to back down in May 1949, but hastening the formation of two Germanies.

Communist German Democratic Republic in the east. In 1961, the easterners built a wall around West Berlin to insulate the east from capitalist propaganda and halt a flood of emigrés fleeing communism. The Berlin Wall emerged as the symbol of a divided Europe and the cold war.

U.S. policymakers wanted to shore up democratic governments in Europe. Hoping to prevent Western European voters from electing Communist governments, Truman proclaimed the Truman Doctrine, which promised American military and economic aid where needed. Containing the spread of communism meant securing a capitalist future for Western Europe, a job that fell to Truman's Secretary of State, General George C. Marshall. He launched the Marshall Plan, an ambitious program through which, between 1948 and 1952, the United States provided over $13 billion in grants and credits to reconstruct Europe. Earmarked for the purchase of technology and capital goods, the money facilitated an economic revival. U.S. policymakers hoped the aid would dim communism's appeal by fostering economic prosperity, muting class tensions, and integrating Western European nations into an alliance of capitalist democracies.

Stalin saw the Marshall Plan, along with the formation in 1949 of the North Atlantic Treaty Organization (NATO), a military alliance between countries in Western Europe and North America, as direct threats to the Soviet Union. He believed that the Soviet Union, having sacrificed millions of its people to the war against fascism, deserved to be the dominant influence in Eastern Europe. Soviet troops had occupied the Eastern European nations at the end of the war, and both Communists and leftist members of other parties formed Soviet-backed coalition governments. With the continuing Soviet military presence, the Communists established dictatorships in Bulgaria, Romania, Hungary, and Czechoslovakia in 1948. It was with these Communist nations that the Soviets, responding to NATO, formed the Warsaw Pact, a military alliance of their own, in 1955. With Warsaw Pact nations of Eastern Europe facing off against NATO's forces in Western Europe (see Map 11-3), the 1950s and 1960s produced a series of tense confrontations, which brought the world to the brink of an atomic Third World War.

THE NUCLEAR AGE

The cold war changed military affairs for good. When the Americans dropped atomic bombs on Japan, they had a decisive technological edge. In 1949, however, the Soviets tested their first nuclear bomb—and shocked the West. Thereafter, each side rushed to stockpile nuclear weapons and to update its military technologies. In so doing, they shifted from explosives using nuclear fission to nuclear fusion. The weapon that destroyed

> *The Berlin Wall emerged as the symbol of a divided Europe and the cold war.*

Hiroshima, a fission bomb, was calculated in kilotons (each kiloton was the equivalent of 1,000 tons of TNT). Fusion, or hydrogen, bombs became calculated in megatons (one *million* tons of TNT, or 1,000 kilotons). Moreover, the bombs on both sides became physically smaller, could be launched and propelled independently on missiles, and carried in mobile units either on land or at sea—or even under the sea, as the Americans demonstrated in deploying their nuclear-powered Polaris submarine. Thus, more devastating weapons became almost impossible to detect. By 1960, it was possible that an all-out nuclear war might lead to the destruction of the world—without a soldier firing a single shot. This changed the rules of the game. Each side possessed the power to rain total destruction on the other, a circumstance that caused great anxiety but also inhibited direct confrontations. Proxy wars, such as the Korean War, became the norm.

The confrontation between capitalist and Communist blocs turned into open military struggle in Asia where, in contrast to Europe after World War II, no well-defined Soviet and American spheres of influence came into being. In East and Southeast Asia, the postwar settlement was murky, and the area remained a war zone into the 1980s. After the war, the French wanted to restore their Indochinese empire, but they met fierce resistance from Vietnamese nationalists. China descended into a civil war that was won by the Communists, with American-backed remnants fleeing to the island of Taiwan. Korea was divided at the thirty-eighth parallel, having been liberated from the Japanese by the Americans from the south and the Soviets from the north.

In June 1950, Soviet-backed troops from North Korea invaded U.S.-backed South Korea, setting off the Korean War (see Map 11-4). Claiming this was a violation of the Charter of the United Nations, which had been established in 1945 to safeguard world peace and protect human rights, President Truman ordered American troops to drive back the North Koreans. The U.N. Security Council (made up of eleven member nations) declared North Korea the aggressor and sent troops from fifteen nations to restore peace. Within a year, the invaders had been routed and were near collapse. When U.N. troops advanced to the Chinese border, Stalin maneuvered his Communist Chinese allies into rushing to the rescue of the Communist regime in North Korea and driving the South Koreans and the U.N. forces back to the old boundary. Across the Korean isthmus, Communist and American-led U.N. troops waged a seesaw war. The fighting continued until July 1953, when an armistice divided the country at roughly the same spot as at the start of the war. Nothing had been gained. Losses, however, included 33,000 Americans, at least 250,000 Chinese, and up to 3 million Koreans.

The Korean War energized America's anti-Communist commitments. No longer did elected officials hesitate about the need

MAP 11-3   NATO AND WARSAW PACT COUNTRIES

The cold war divided Europe into two competing blocs—those that joined with the United States in the North Atlantic Treaty Organization (NATO) and those that were linked to the Soviet Union under the Warsaw Pact. Can you explain why the dividing line existed where it did? How important were financial and military factors in accounting for who aligned with the Americans and who aligned with the Soviets? Which countries were the largest recipients of American Marshall Plan aid and why? Where would you expect the European sites of cold war tensions to be the most intense?

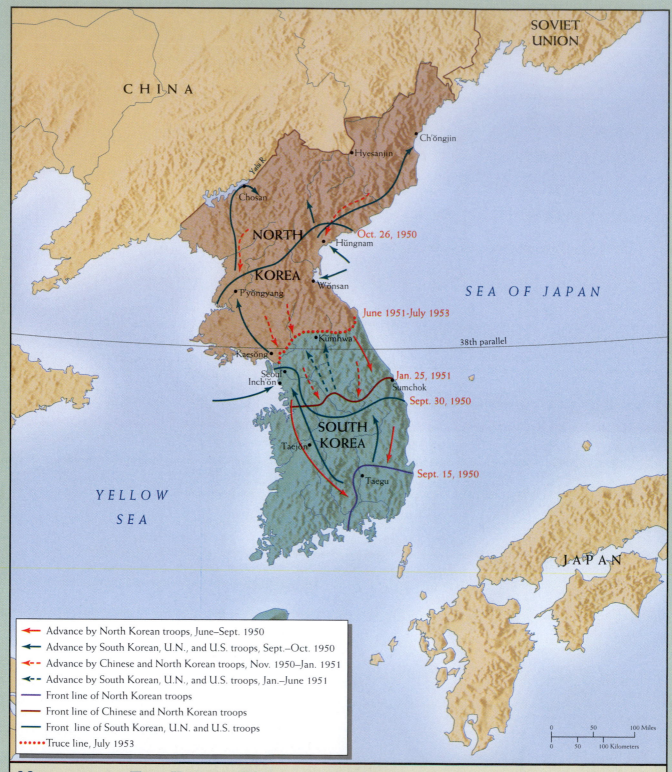

Legend

- → Advance by North Korean troops, June–Sept. 1950
- → Advance by South Korean, U.N., and U.S. troops, Sept.–Oct. 1950
- ◄- - Advance by Chinese and North Korean troops, Nov. 1950–Jan. 1951
- ◄- - Advance by South Korean, U.N., and U.S. troops, Jan.–June 1951
- — Front line of North Korean troops
- — Front line of Chinese and North Korean troops
- — Front line of South Korean, U.N. and U.S. troops
- •••• Truce line, July 1953

Map labels: SOVIET UNION, CHINA, Ch'ŏngjin, Hyesanjin, Yalu R., Chosan, NORTH KOREA, Oct. 26, 1950, Hŭngnam, SEA OF JAPAN, Wŏnsan, P'yŏngyang, June 1951–July 1953, 38th parallel, Kumhwa, Kaesŏng, Seoul, Inch'ŏn, Jan. 25, 1951, Sumchok, Sept. 30, 1950, SOUTH KOREA, Taejŏn, YELLOW SEA, Taegu, Sept. 15, 1950, JAPAN

Scale: 0 50 100 Miles / 0 50 100 Kilometers

MAP 11-4   THE KOREAN WAR

Examine carefully the geography of the Korean peninsula and its surrounding areas. How does that help us explain the outbreak of the Korean War? Apart from the Koreans themselves, who were the major protagonists of the conflict and why? In what specific ways was the Korean War a product of the larger geopolitical trends in post–World War II Asia and the world? How were the Korean conflict and its consequences similar to or different from postwar political developments in other parts of the world?

to contain Soviet communism at any cost. NATO forces were rapidly increased, reaching 7 million by 1953. While Japan was demilitarized at the end of World War II, and some militarists and ultranationalists were purged, U.S. policy shifted as Japan was seen as a bulwark against communism. Although Japan renounced war in its new postwar constitution, a 1951 treaty with the United States stipulated that the Japanese could rearm for self-defense and that American troops could be stationed in Japan. Moreover, the United States resolved to rebuild Japanese economic power. Like West Germany, Japan went from being the enemy in the Second World War to being a valued ally. American aid and investment—though never matching the scale of the Marshall Plan—helped blunt any leftist drift in war-torn Japan.

DECOLONIZATION

> → *In what cases and why did decolonization involve large-scale violence?*

The unsettling of all empires during the war inspired colonial peoples to reconsider their political futures. Rid of the Japanese, the peoples of liberated Asian territories had no desire to restore colonial or even quasi-colonial rule. In Africa, too, the years after World War II brought increasing pressure for decolonization. As it became apparent that the European-centered world was no more, anti-colonial nationalism surged after 1945. Drawing on the lessons in mass politicization and mass mobilization of the 1920s and 1930s, anti-colonial leaders set about dismantling the European order and creating a world of their own.

The process of decolonization and nation-building followed three broad patterns: civil war, negotiated independence, and incomplete decolonization. The first can be identified principally in China, where the ousting of the Japanese occupiers led to a civil war, culminating in a Communist triumph. Here, national independence was associated with a socialist revolution. The second pattern was negotiated independence, as in the Indian subcontinent and much of Africa. Algeria and South Africa exemplify the third pattern, in which the presence of sizeable European settler populations complicated the path from colony to nation.

THE CHINESE REVOLUTION

Although the Japanese defeat left China politically independent, some of its leaders, notably the Chinese Communists, looked askance at any restoration of the prewar regime. Their campaign formed part of a more general worldwide movement to achieve autonomy from the Western powers. Painfully aware of China's long semi-colonial subordination, the Communists vowed to free themselves from colonialism. After all, it was the feeble pro-

The Long March. In China, the Long March of 1934–1935 has been commemorated by the ruling Communists as one of the most heroic episodes in the party's history. This picture shows some of the Communist partisans trudging across the rugged terrain of snow-covered mountains in the western province of Sichuan in 1935. Despite their tremendous efforts, the ranks of the party were decimated by the end of the 6,000-mile journey from the southeastern to the northwestern part of the country—less than one in eight succeeded in reaching their destination.

Western regime that had allowed the Japanese to seize Manchuria. The triumph of the Chinese Communists in 1949 had been in the making for decades. Back in 1927, the Nationalist regime of Chiang Kai-shek had driven outgunned Communist forces from China's cities into remote, mountainous refuges. There, the Communists had established so-called red bases, or soviets, and there Mao Zedong (1893–1976) had emerged as the leader of the largest soviet. In late 1934, under attack by Chiang's Nationalist forces, Mao and his associates abandoned their base and embarked on an arduous, year-long 6,000-mile journey through some of the world's most rugged terrain. Often covering more than twenty miles per day, they finally retreated to the distant northwest of the country (see Map 11-5). This great escape, subsequently glorified in Communist lore as the Long March, was costly. Of the approximately 80,000 persons who started the journey, fewer than 10,000 made it to their destination. Fortunately for the Communists, the Japanese invasion

MAP 11-5   THE LONG MARCH, 1934–1935

Follow the routes of the Long March. Note that the Chinese Communists traveled all the way from the southeastern part of the country to the northwest. Why did the Communists take this particular route? The Long March was triggered by a struggle for power between the Guomindang (Nationalists) and the Communists within China, but how was the conflict related to developments in the international political arena in the mid-1930s? How would you describe the political conditions in China at the time? Why was the Long March a significant episode in world history?

diverted Nationalist troops and offered Mao and the survivors a chance to regroup.

When the Japanese seized China's major cities but were unable fully to control the countryside, the Communists were able to expand their support among the peasantry, whom they had been organizing for decades. In contrast to other Marxist theorists who thought that waging a successful "class struggle" required primarily the allegiance of the industrial proletariat, Mao urged his followers to recruit China's vast rural populace. They moved in behind Japanese lines and established their own governing apparatuses, particularly in the northern part of the country. To foster anti-Japanese unity, the Communists deemphasized land redistribution. Instead, they used rent reduction, carefully designed electoral systems, graduated taxes, mutual aid, cooperative farming, and anti-Japanese propaganda to gain popular support. Mao's emphasis on a peasant revolution, a deviation from orthodox Marxist belief in the urban proletariat, proved immensely effective. Not only did he build support for his cause, but his success served as inspiration to many later revolutionaries in largely agrarian societies, notably Ho Chi Minh (1890–1969) in Vietnam and Fidel Castro (1926–   ) in Cuba.

As part of their critique of the oppressiveness of traditional China, the Communists promised women that liberation would apply to them too. As early as 1931, Mao's rural base had promulgated a new marital law forbidding arranged marriages

MAO ZEDONG "ON NEW DEMOCRACY"

Many twentieth-century Chinese political and intellectual leaders, including the Communists, believed that the rejuvenation of China would necessitate a change of its culture. The key question, then, was what to embrace and what to discard. Here we find Mao in 1940 explicating the New-Democratic culture—nationalistic, scientific, and mass-based—that he regarded as a transitional stage to communism. He cautions against the uncritical wholesale importation of Western values and practices, including Marxism, and emphasizes instead the specific conditions of the Chinese revolution.

New-Democratic culture is national. It opposes imperialist oppression and upholds the dignity and independence of the Chinese nation. . . . China should absorb on a large scale the progressive cultures of foreign countries as an ingredient for her own culture; in the past we did not do enough work of this kind. We must absorb whatever we today find useful, not only from the present socialist or New-Democratic cultures of other nations, but also from the older cultures of foreign countries, such as those of the various capitalist countries in the age of enlightenment. However, we must treat these foreign materials as we do our food, which should be chewed in the mouth, submitted to the working of the stomach and intestines, mixed with saliva, gastric juice, and intestinal secretions, and then separated into essence to be absorbed and waste matter to be discarded—only thus can food benefit our body; we should never swallow anything raw or absorb it uncritically. So-called wholesale Westernization is a mistaken viewpoint. China has suffered a great deal in the past from the formalist absorption of foreign things. Likewise, in applying Marxism to China, Chinese Communists must fully and properly unite the universal truth of Marxism with the specific practice of the Chinese revolution; that is to say, the truth of Marxism must be integrated with the characteristics of the nation and given a definite national form before it can be useful; it must not be applied subjectively as a mere formula. . . .

Communists may form an anti-imperialist and anti-feudal united front for political action with certain idealists and even with religious followers, but we can never approve of their idealism or religious doctrines. A splendid ancient culture was created during the long period of China's feudal society. To clarify the process of development of this ancient culture, to throw away its feudal dross, and to absorb its democratic essence is a necessary condition for the development of our new national culture and for the increase of our national self-confidence; but we should never absorb anything and everything uncritically. . . .

Source: Mao Zedong, Selected Works, in *Sources of Chinese Tradition*, 2nd ed., vol. 2, edited by Wm. Theodore de Bary and Richard Lufrano (New York: Columbia University Press, 2000), pp. 422–23.

and allowing either partner to initiate divorce proceedings. The Communists also promised improvements in health care and access to education. These measures helped to mobilize support for Communist plans. Indeed, the growth of the Communist Party during the war years was spectacular. Party membership swelled from a mere 40,000 in 1937 to over a million in 1945, at which time, about 100 million people, or between a fifth and a sixth of the total population, lived under the jurisdiction of the Communists.

> *In 1949, Mao proclaimed that China had "stood up" to the world and had experienced a "great people's revolution," providing much hope in the Third World.*

After Japan surrendered to end World War II in August 1945, the civil war between the Nationalists and the Communists resumed. But the Communist forces now had the numbers, the guns, and the popular support to launch assaults on Nationalist strongholds. By contrast, although the Nationalist government had weapons and financing from the United States and control of the cities, it had never fully recovered from its demoralizing defeat at the hands of the Japanese. In the post–World War II civil war, having lost popular support and running a corrupt governmental machine, it proved no match for the invigorated Communists. Faced with the Communist victory, the Nationalist leaders escaped and set up a rival Chinese state on the island of Taiwan.

In 1949, Mao proclaimed that China had "stood up" to the world and had experienced a "great people's revolution." In subsequent years, many of Mao's ventures proved disastrous failures, but the Chinese model of an ongoing people's revolution provided much hope in the Third World.

NEGOTIATED INDEPENDENCE IN INDIA AND AFRICA

In India and much of colonial Africa, independence came with little bloodshed. The British, realizing that they would be unable to rule India after World War II without strong doses of coercion, bowed to the inevitable and withdrew. Much the same happened in Africa, even though the British and French colonial officials were aware that there were few educated Africans and that African territories were much less ready for independence than India.

The Founding of the People's Republic of China. *(Left)* Mao Zedong standing atop the reviewing stand at Tiananmen Square as he declared the founding of the People's Republic of China on October 1, 1949. It was a time of anticipation and optimism. Although most Chinese knew little about the Communist Party, many had high hopes for a new, independent, and liberated China. *(Right)* With red flags flying, the enthusiastic crowd celebrated the dawn of a new era.

INDIA   Unlike China, where the path out of semi-colonial domination involved first a war against Japan and then a prolonged civil war ending in a "people's revolution," the Indian subcontinent achieved political independence without an insurrection. But after that mostly nonviolent achievement, India veered dangerously close to civil war. In British India, anti-colonial elites in the Indian National Congress Party negotiated a peaceful transfer of power from British to indigenous rule. Within the Congress leadership, however, there was much disagreement about what kind of state an independent India should have. Should it, as Gandhi wished, be constructed as a nonmodern utopia of self-governing village communities, or should it emulate Western and Soviet models with the goal of establishing a modern nation-state? Even more pressing was the question of relations between a Hindu majority and the Muslim minority.

> *In India, even more pressing than modernization was the question of relations between a Hindu majority and the Muslim minority.*

For the most part, the Congress leadership continued to exercise tight control over the mass movement that it had mobilized in the 1920s and 1930s. Even Gandhi remained skeptical of leaving the initiative to the common people, believing that they had not assimilated the doctrine of nonviolence. Accordingly, Gandhi and the Congress leadership worked hard to convince the British that they, the middle-class leaders, spoke for the nation. At the same time, the threat of a mass peasant uprising with more radical aims (as was occurring in China, where Mao was organizing the peasants into a revolutionary force) encouraged the British to hasten negotiations for a transfer of power.

As negotiations for independence moved forward, Hindu-Muslim unity deteriorated. Whose culture would define the new nation? Insofar as an Indian nationalism existed in the later nineteenth century, it was based on the culture and symbols of the Hindu majority. Yet, this movement masked the multiplicity of regional, linguistic, caste, and class differences *within* the Hindu community, just as Muslim movements overlooked divisions within their ranks. Now, however, the real prospect of defining "India" created a grand contest between newly self-conscious communities. Riots broke out between Hindus and Muslims in 1946, which increased the mutual distrust between Congress and Muslim League leaders. With the British playing their usual divide and rule role, Muhammad Ali Jinnah, the leader of the Muslim League, demanded that British India be partitioned into separate Hindu and Muslim states if there were no constitutional guarantees for Muslims. The specter of civil war haunted the proceedings, as outgoing colonial rulers decided to divide the subcontinent into two states, India and Pakistan.

On August 14, 1947, Pakistan gained independence; a day later, India did the same. The euphoria of decolonization, however, was drowned in a frenzy of brutality. In the days after independence, perhaps as many as 1 million Hindus and Muslims killed one another. Fearing further violence, 12 million Hindus and Muslims left their homes to relocate in the new country where they would be in the majority. Distraught by the violent rampage, Gandhi fasted, refusing sustenance until the killings stopped. The violence abated. This was perhaps Gandhi's finest hour. But while his actions prevented the violence from turning into all-out war, animosity and fanaticism remained. Less than six months later, on January 30, 1948, a Hindu zealot shot Gandhi dead as he walked to a prayer meeting.

Had Gandhi lived, he would not have approved of the direction independent India took. Already before his death, he had begun to voice his disapproval of industrialization and equipping the Indian state with army and police forces. But India's first prime minister and leader of the Indian National Congress Party, Jawaharlal Nehru, and other Congress leaders were committed to the goal of state-directed modernization. Inspired by Soviet-style planned development, on the one hand, and by Western democratic institutions, on the other, Nehru strove to establish a "socialistic pattern of

Jawaharlal Nehru. Nehru, the leader of independent India, sought to combine a "mixed economy" of private and public sectors with democracy to chart an independent path for India. The photo shows him at a public meeting in 1952.

NEHRU ON BUILDING A MODERN NATION

The following excerpt was written by Jawaharlal Nehru in 1940 and documents the centrality that planning occupied in the desire to build a modern nation. Although the idea of planning was derived from the Soviet experience, Nehru did not wish India to adopt communism; he saw planned development as a scientific instrument for achieving rapid economic growth and fundamental social changes. Planning would avoid the excesses and inequalities of capitalism and provide a "third way"—equally distanced from both communism and capitalism.

The octopus of war grips and strangles the world and the energy of mankind is more and more directed to destroying what man has built up with infinite patience and labour. Yet it is clear that war by itself cannot solve any problem. It is by conscious, constructive and planned effort alone that national and international problems can be solved. In India many people thought, with reason, that it was premature to plan, so long as we did not have the power to give effect to our planning. The political and economic freedom of India was a prerequisite to any planning, and till this was achieved our national and international policy would continue to be governed, as heretofore, in the interests of the City of London and other vested interests. And yet we started, wisely I think, a National Planning Committee and we are trying, even in these days of world conflict and war, to draw up a picture of planned society in the free India of the future.

Our immediate problem is to attack the appalling poverty and unemployment of India and to raise the standards of our people. That means vastly greater production which must be allied to juster and more equitable distribution, so that the increased wealth may spread out among the people. That means a rapid growth of industry, scientific agriculture and the social services, all co-ordinated together, under more or less state control, and directed towards the betterment of the people as a whole. The resources of India are vast and if wisely used should yield rich results in the near future.

We do not believe in a rigid autarchy, but we do want to make India self-sufficient in regard to her needs as far as this is possible. We want to develop international trade, importing articles which we cannot easily produce and exporting such articles as the rest of the world wants from us. We do not propose to submit to the economic imperialism of any other country or to impose our own on others. We believe that nations of the world can co-operate together in building a world economy which is advantageous for all and in this work we shall gladly co-operate. But this economy cannot be based on the individual profit motive, nor can it subsist within the framework of an imperialist system. It means a new world order, both politically and economically, and free nations co-operating together for their own as well as the larger good.

Source: Jawaharlal Nehru, A Note to the Members of the National Planning Committee, May 1, 1940, in *Jawaharlal Nehru: An Anthology*, edited by Sarvepalli Gopal (Delhi: Oxford University Press, 1980), pp. 306–307.

---

society" based on a mixed economy of public and private sectors. Declaring that he wanted to give India the "garb of modernity," he asked Indians to consider hydroelectric dams and steel plants the temples of modern India. Such a vision allowed Nehru, until his death in 1964, to guide Indian modernization along a third path.

AFRICA FOR AFRICANS Within a decade and a half of Indian independence, most of the African states also gained their sovereignty. Except for the southern part of the African continent, where minority white rule persisted, the old colonial states disappeared, replaced by indigenous rulers. One reason for this rapid decolonization was the power gained by the nationalist movements during the interwar period. These years had taught a generation of nationalist critics of colonial rule to rely upon

themselves and to seek mass support for their political parties. World War II, then, swelled the ranks of anti-colonial political parties, as many African soldiers came to expect tangible rewards for serving in imperial armies.

The postwar years also saw large numbers of Africans flock to the cities in search of a better life. Expanding educational systems produced a wave of primary and secondary school graduates. Like the new urban dwellers, these educated young people became disgruntled when attractive employment opportunities were not forthcoming. These three groups—the ex-servicemen, the urban unemployed or underemployed, and the educated—became the shock troops of the nationalist agitation that began in the late 1940s and early 1950s (see Map 11-6).

Faced with rising nationalist demands, European powers agreed to decolonize. The new world powers, the Soviet Union

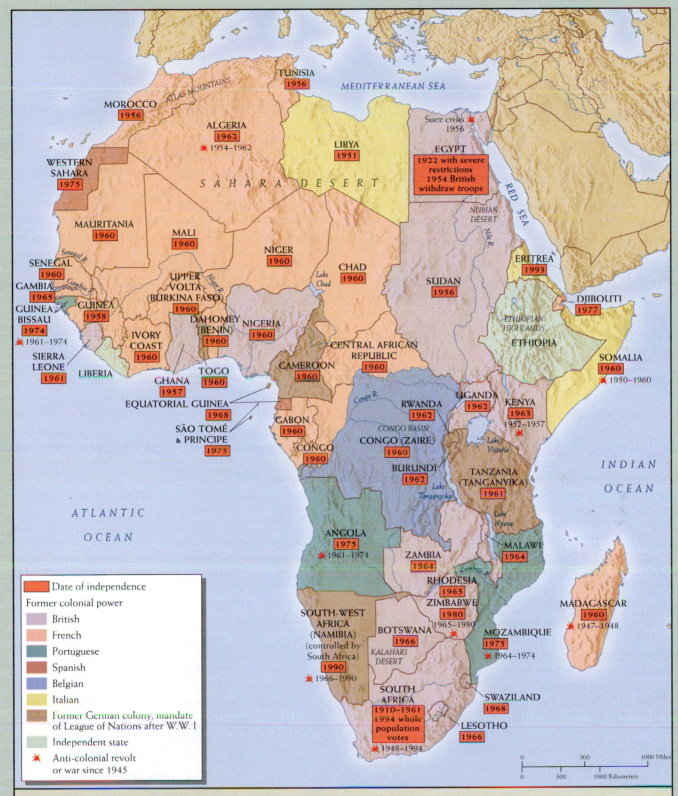

MOROCCO 1956
TUNISIA 1956
MEDITERRANEAN SEA
ALGERIA 1962 ★ 1954–1962
LIBYA 1951
Suez crisis 1956 ★
EGYPT 1922 with severe restrictions 1954 British withdraw troops
WESTERN SAHARA 1975
ATLAS MOUNTAINS
SAHARA DESERT
NUBIAN DESERT
RED SEA
Nile R.
MAURITANIA 1960
MALI 1960
NIGER 1960
CHAD 1960
SUDAN 1956
ERITREA 1993
DJIBOUTI 1977
Senegal R.
SENEGAL 1960
GAMBIA 1965
Gambia R.
GUINEA BISSAU 1974 ★ 1961–1974
GUINEA 1958
UPPER VOLTA (BURKINA FASO) 1960
Niger R.
DAHOMEY (BENIN) 1960
NIGERIA 1960
CENTRAL AFRICAN REPUBLIC 1960
ETHIOPIAN HIGHLANDS
ETHIOPIA
SIERRA LEONE 1961
LIBERIA
IVORY COAST 1960
GHANA 1957
TOGO 1960
CAMEROON 1960
SOMALIA 1960 ★ 1950–1960
EQUATORIAL GUINEA 1968
SÃO TOMÉ & PRINCIPE 1975
GABON 1960
Congo R.
Congo Basin
RWANDA 1962
UGANDA 1962
KENYA 1963 1952–1957
CONGO 1960
CONGO (ZAIRE) 1960
BURUNDI 1962
Lake Victoria
Lake Tanganyika
TANZANIA (TANGANYIKA) 1961
INDIAN OCEAN
Lake Nyasa
ATLANTIC OCEAN
ANGOLA 1975 ★ 1961–1974
ZAMBIA 1964
MALAWI 1964
Zambezi R.
RHODESIA 1965 ZIMBABWE 1980 1965–1980 ★
MADAGASCAR 1960 ★ 1947–1948
SOUTH-WEST AFRICA (NAMIBIA) (controlled by South Africa) 1990 ★ 1966–1990
BOTSWANA 1966
KALAHARI DESERT
MOZAMBIQUE 1975 ★ 1964–1974
SWAZILAND 1968
SOUTH AFRICA 1910–1961 1994 whole population votes ★ 1948–1994
LESOTHO 1966

Date of independence
Former colonial power
British
French
Portuguese
Spanish
Belgian
Italian
Former German colony, mandate of League of Nations after W.W. I
Independent state
★ Anti-colonial revolt or war since 1945

0   500   1000 Miles
0   500   1000 Kilometers

MAP 11-6   DECOLONIZATION OF AFRICA

African decolonization, like such developments elsewhere, occurred after World War II, largely in the 1950s, 1960s, and 1970s. Identify those countries that gained their independence in the first wave of decolonization, and explain why they gained independence before other states in Africa did. The southern part of the continent became independent later than the rest of Africa. Why was this so? Can you explain why anti-colonial revolts occurred only in a minority of the colonies, and why these territories were caught up in political violence?

Kwame Nkrumah. West Africa's leading nationalist, Kwame Nkrumah, mobilized the peoples of the Gold Coast behind his Convention Peoples Party and, through electoral successes, convinced the British to confer independence on the Gold Coast, which was renamed Ghana, in 1957.

and the United States, for their own reasons, also favored decolonization. Given this background, decolonization in most of Africa was a rapid and relatively sedate affair. In 1957, the Gold Coast (renamed Ghana) became tropical Africa's first independent state. At the handing-over ceremonies, the British governor, James Arden-Clarke, and the Ghanaian prime minister, Kwame Nkrumah (1909–1972), took turns praising each other for the smooth transition from colonial rule to self-government. Other British colonial territories followed in rapid succession, so that by 1963 all of British-ruled Africa except for Southern Rhodesia was independent.

In each of these colonial possessions, charismatic nationalist leaders took charge of populist political parties and became the leaders to whom the British turned over power. Many of the new rulers of Africa had obtained Western educations but were committed to returning Africa to the Africans. Nkrumah had studied in American universities before returning to Africa. The Nigerian nationalist, Nnamdi Azikiwe (1904–1996), was also a graduate of American colleges and universities as well as a newspaper editor and businessman. Others, too, returned from Western schools, organizing new political parties, establishing nationalist newspapers, and appealing to the masses, especially the youth who had flocked to the cities after the war.

Decolonization in much of French-ruled Africa followed a similarly smooth path, though the French were initially more resistant than the British. Immediately after World War II, the French planned to respond to growing anti-colonial sentiments, not by giving states more autonomy, as the British had, but by drawing protesting territories closer to France. Believing their empire to be eternal and their culture unrivaled, the French treated decolonization as assimilation. Instead of negotiating independence, the French tried first to accord fuller voting rights to their colonial subjects, even allowing Africans and Asians to send delegates to the French National Assembly. In the end, however, the French electorate had no desire to share their assemblies and the privileges of French citizenship with overseas populations. Thus, under the leadership of Charles de Gaulle (1890–1970), France dissolved its political ties with French West Africa and French Equatorial Africa in 1960, having already given the protectorates in Morocco and Tunisia their independence in 1956. Algeria, always regarded as a integral part of France overseas, was a different matter. Its independence did not come quickly or easily (see p. 408).

Among the leaders of African independence, the sense of creating something new—different from the existing patterns in the world—was strong. For men like Nkrumah of Ghana, Azikiwe in Nigeria, and Julius Nyerere (1922–1999) in Tanzania, Africa's pre-colonial traditions would enable the continent to move from colonialism right into a special African form of socialism, without going through the depredations of capitalism. The so-called "African personality," they claimed, was steeped in communal solidarities and able to embrace the values of social justice and equality, while rejecting the naked individualism that Africans felt lay at the core of European culture.

The figure who most brilliantly articulated the idea of African uniqueness was Senegal's first president and leading nationalist, Léopold Sédar Senghor (1906–2001). A prize pupil in the French colonial educational system, Senghor had gone on

Léopold Sédar Senghor. Senghor combined intellectual acuity with political savvy. An accomplished poet and essayist and one of the founders of the Negritude movement among Francophone intellectuals, he became Senegal's leading nationalist politician and first president when the country gained full independence in 1960.

SENGHOR'S VIEW OF POLITICAL INDEPENDENCE

One of the most striking visions of African independence as a third way separate from Western capitalism and Soviet communism came from the pen of Léopold Sédar Senghor, a Senegalese nationalist leader, who became the first president of Senegal. The first excerpt, drawn from his essay "African Socialism," published in 1959, differentiates the socialism of Africa from Marxism, while the second document, taken from a speech that Senghor delivered at Oxford University in 1961, develops the idea of "Negritude," or black civilization, as a way of thinking and acting that was markedly different from but not inferior to European cultural forms.

African Socialism In the respective programs of our former parties, all of us used to proclaim our attachment to socialism. This was a good thing, but it was not enough. Most of the time, we were satisfied with stereotyped formulas and vague aspirations, which we called scientific socialism—as if socialism did not mean a return to original sources. Above all, we need to make an effort to rethink the basic texts in the light of Negro African realities. . . .

Can we integrate Negro African cultural values, especially religious values, into socialism? We must answer that question once and for all with an unequivocal "Yes." . . .

We are not Communists for a practical reason. The anxiety for human dignity, the need for freedom—man's freedom, the freedoms of collectivities—which animate Marx's thought and provide its revolutionary ferment—this anxiety and this need are unknown to Communism, whose major deviation is Stalinism. The "dictatorship of the proletariat," which was to be only temporary, becomes the dictatorship of the party and state by perpetuating itself. . . .

The paradox of socialistic construction in Communist countries—in the Soviet Union at least—is that it increasingly resembles capitalistic construction in the United States, the American way of life, with high salaries, refrigerators, washing machines, and television sets. And it has less art and freedom of thought. Nevertheless, we shall not be won over by a regime of liberal capitalism and free enterprise. We cannot close our eyes to segregation, although the government combats it; nor can we accept the elevation of material success to a way of life.

We stand for a middle course, for a *democratic socialism* which goes so far as to integrate spiritual values, a socialism which ties in with the old ethical current of the French

socialists. . . . In so far as they are idealists, they fulfill the requirements of the Negro African soul, the requirements of men of all races and countries. . . .

A third revolution is taking place, as a reaction against capitalistic and Communistic materialism—one that will integrate moral, if not religious, values with the political and economic contributions of the two great revolutions. In this revolution, the colored peoples, including the Negro African, must play their part; they must bring their contribution to the construction of the new planetary civilization. . . .

"What Is Negritude?" . . . Assimilation was a failure; we could assimilate mathematics or the French language, but we could never strip off our black skins or root out black souls. And so we set out on a fervent quest for the "holy grail": our collective soul. And we came upon it. . . .

Negritude is the *whole complex of civilized values—cultural, economic, social, and political—which characterize the black peoples*, or, more precisely, the Negro-African world. All these values are essentially informed by intuitive reason, because this sentient reason, the reason which comes to grips, expresses itself emotionally, through that self-surrender, that coalescence of subject and object; through myths, by which I mean the archetypal images of the collective soul; and, above all, through primordial rhythms, synchronized with those of the cosmos. In other words, the sense of communion, the gift of mythmaking, the gift of rhythm, such are the essential elements of Negritude, which you will find indelibly stamped on all the works and activities of the black man. . . .

Source: Léopold Sédar Senghor, "African Socialism" and "What Is Negritude?" in *The Ideologies of the Developing Nations*, edited by Paul Sigmund (New York: Frederick A. Praeger, Publisher, 1959), pp. 240–44, 248–49.

to the Sorbonne in Paris, where he had come into contact with other black intellectuals. There, they had developed the idea of "Negritude" as a statement of the virtues of the black identity in an environment that emphasized the primacy of France and the inferiority of non-French ways. The exponents of Negritude claimed that people of African descent were more humane and had stronger communal feelings than Europeans, who were cold and excessively analytical.

Negritude did not reject Western culture, however. Senghor, for example, promised to "assimilate" that which was good from France but not to be "assimilated" into French culture. The validation of African culture and the African past by the Negritude poets was part of a more general effort by African leaders and intellectuals to identify indigenous cultural resources for charting an independent place, a third way, for Africa in the modern world.

> *Contrary to Zionist assertions, a substantial Arab population already lived in Palestine, and the Palestinian Arabs joined their Arab neighbors to oppose a Jewish political entity.*

VIOLENT AND INCOMPLETE DECOLONIZATIONS

Although decolonization in most of Africa and Asia ultimately occurred through peaceful transfers of power, there were notable exceptions. In Palestine, Algeria, and southern Africa, the presence of European immigrant groups impeded negotiations and created violent conflicts that aborted any peaceful transfer of power—or left the process incomplete. In Vietnam, the process was also violent and delayed, though the problem was not the intransigence of European colonists. Instead, it stemmed first from France's desire to reimpose its imperial control, and then from the power politics of cold war competition. In this last respect, Vietnam's struggle foreshadowed the fate of much of the Third World: newly independent nations finding their pursuit of a "third way" thwarted by superpower demands that client states stick close to the capitalist or Communist line.

PALESTINE, ISRAEL, EGYPT In Palestine, Arabs and Jews had been on a collision course from the moment that the British promulgated the Balfour Declaration in 1917. Before World War I, a group of European Jews, known as Zionists, had argued that only an exodus from existing states to their place of origin in Palestine could lead to Jewish self-determination. Championed by Jewish intellectuals like Hungarian-born Theodore Herzl (1860–1904), Zionism combined a yearning to realize the ancient biblical injunction to return to the holy lands with a fear of European anti-Semitism and anguish over increasing Jewish assimilation. Zionists advocated the creation of a Jewish state, and they won a crucial victory during World War I when the British government, under the Balfour Declaration, promised a homeland for the Jews in Palestine. This

encouraged the immigration of Jewish settlers into the country. At the same time, however, it also guaranteed the rights of indigenous Palestinians.

The immigration of Jews to Palestine set the stage for a conflict between fledgling Jewish and Arab nations. Contrary to Zionist assertions, a substantial Arab population already lived in Palestine, and the Palestinian Arabs joined with their Arab neighbors to oppose a Jewish political entity. In due course, they proclaimed their own right to self-determination as Palestinians. When Hitler came to power in Germany, European Jews looked to Palestine as a haven, but the British, increasingly mindful of Arab opposition and the strategic oil wealth of the Arab states, vacillated over supporting Zionist demands for greater immigration. How the conflicting aspirations of Jewish settlers and indigenous Palestinians were to be reconciled was not clear to anyone. Moreover, the pressure to allow more immigration increased after World War II as hundreds of thousands of survivors of the Nazi concentration camps clamored for entry into Palestine. The Arabs resented the presence of the Jews, who continued to buy land and to displace farmers who had lived on the land for generations.

In 1947, the British announced that they would end their role administering Palestine as a mandate (first of the League of Nations, then of the United Nations) in one year's time and leave negotiations over the fate of the area to the United Nations.

Ben Gurion Declares the Creation of the State of Israel.
Standing beneath a portrait of Theodore Herzl, the founder of the Zionist movement, David Ben Gurion, the first Israeli prime minister, proclaimed independence for the state of Israel in May 1948.

The U.N. tried to resolve the conflict by voting in November 1947 to partition Palestine into Arab and Jewish territories. When the British withdrew their troops on May 15, 1948, a Jewish provisional government proclaimed the establishment of the state of Israel. Although the Jews were delighted to have an independent state, they were dismayed by the small size of their country, its indefensible borders, and the fact that it did not include all of the lands that had belonged to ancient Israel. For their part, the Palestinians were shocked at the partition, and they looked to their better-armed Arab neighbors to take back Israeli territories.

The ensuing Arab-Israeli War of 1948–1949, the first of many such conflicts, shattered the legitimacy of Arab ruling elites. Arab states entered the war poorly prepared to take on the newly established, but well-run and enthusiastically supported Israeli Defense Force. When the United Nations finally negotiated a truce be-

Nasser became the chief symbol of a pan-Arab nationalism that swept across the Middle East and North Africa.

tween the combatants, Israel had extended its boundaries, and more than 1 million Palestinians had become refugees, living in makeshift camps in surrounding Arab countries.

One of the groups most embittered by their defeat were young officers in the Egyptian army who plotted to overthrow a regime that they felt had not yet shed its colonial subordination. Though Egypt had acquired its legal independence from Britain in 1936, the plotters believed that the nation's sovereignty was being squandered by incompetent leaders like King Faruq (Farouk; ruled 1936–1952), whom they condemned as corrupt and decadent. Among the disaffected officers, Gamal Abdel Nasser (1918–1970) had distinguished himself in battle, and he became the head of a secret organization of junior military officers that called itself the Free Officers Movement. Nasser and his like-minded colleagues debated the maladies of Egyptian society and devised a program to transform it. The Free Officers had ties with Communists and numerous other dissident groups, including the Muslim Brotherhood, which favored a return to Islamic rule.

Fearing that King Faruq would strike before they had a chance, the young officers launched a successful coup d'état in the early hours of July 26, 1952. Within a week, they forced Faruq to abdicate and to leave the country. Within three months, they enacted a far-reaching land reform scheme that deprived the large estate owners of lands in excess of 200 acres. They expropriated all of the lands belonging to the royal family, some 180,000 acres, and redistributed these estates to the landless and small-holders, who instantly became ardent supporters of the new regime. The Revolutionary Command Council, the executive body of the new regime, consolidated its power through such reforms but also through political changes like dissolving parliament, banning political parties, and enacting a new constitution. It turned against its rivals for power, banning the Communists and the Muslim Brotherhood and stripping the old elite of most of its wealth.

Israel viewed Egypt's resurgence with suspicion, fearing that a strengthened Egypt would become the focal point of Arab opposition to the Zionist state. Nasser nationalized the Suez Canal Company—an Egyptian company, mainly run by French businessmen and experts—in July 1956. In response, in October 1956, the Israelis as well as the British and the French invaded Egypt. The invaders seized territory along the Suez Canal, but they had to agree to a ceasefire before they were able to control all of it. Opposition by both the United States and the Soviet Union forced the invaders to withdraw, providing Nasser with a spectacular diplomatic triumph. As Egyptian forces reclaimed the canal, Nasser's reputation as leader of the Arab world soared. He became the chief symbol of a pan-Arab nationalism that swept across the Middle East and North Africa and especially through the camps of Palestinian refugees.

The Anglo-Egyptian Treaty. The photo shows Egyptian president Gamal Abdel Nasser signing the Anglo-Egyptian Treaty with the British minister of state in 1954. This agreement ended the stationing of British troops on Egyptian soil and specifically called for the withdrawal of British troops stationed at the Suez Canal military base. Shortly after the last British soldiers left Egypt in early 1956, however, Britain invaded the country in a vain effort to block Nasser's nationalization of the Suez Canal Company and to topple the Egyptian leader from power.

THE ALGERIAN WAR OF INDEPENDENCE Arab nationalism's appeal was particularly strong in Algeria, where a sizeable French settler population (the *colons*) also stood in the way of a complete and peaceful decolonization. Even as decolonization proceeded in many French colonies, French leaders claimed that Algeria was an integral part of metropolitan France, an overseas department that was juridically no different from Brittany or Normandy. With nearly 1 million European inhabitants, Algeria's *colon* population ranked second on the African continent only to the 4 million Europeans in South Africa. Although the *colons* constituted a minority to the nearly 9 million indigenous Arab and Berber peoples, they held the best land and lived in wealthy residential quarters in the major cities. In addition, although all of Algeria was supposed to be a part of France and entitled to the rights and privileges of the French citizenry, in fact the *colons* reserved these advantages to themselves.

As elsewhere, anti-colonial nationalism in Algeria gathered force after the Second World War. When French settlers refused to share their privileges and when the French military responded to anti-colonial demands with harsh countermeasures, the movement for independence gained strength. The Front de Libération Nationale (FLN), as the leading nationalist party called itself, used violence to provoke its opponents and to force the local population to decide whether to support the nationalist cause or to rally to the side of the *colons*. The full-fledged revolt that erupted in 1954 pitted the FLN troops and guerrillas against thousands of French troops. Atrocities and terrorist acts were perpetrated on both sides.

The war dragged on for eight years (1954–1962), at a cost of as many as 300,000 lives. At home, French society was torn asunder; many French citizens had come to accept the myth that Algeria was not a colonial territory but part of France itself. The *colons* ceaselessly reiterated this point, insisting that they had emigrated to Algeria in response to government promises and that yielding power to the nationalists would be a betrayal. The negotiations to end the war began only after an insurrection led by *colons* and army officers had caused the Fourth Republic to fall in 1958 and brought Charles de Gaulle to power. Concluding that France could not continue to squander resources on colonial wars, De Gaulle negotiated a peace accord with the Algerian nationalists.

Although the final agreement, signed at Evian on March 18, 1962, contained elaborate protections for the European settlers of Algeria, these proved unnecessary. In June, shortly after handing over power to the Algerian nationalists of the FLN, more than 300,000 *colons* left. By the end of 1962, over nine-tenths of the European population had departed. At independence, then, Algeria had a population mix no different from that of the other countries of North Africa.

EASTERN AND SOUTHERN AFRICA The bloody conflict in Algeria highlights one of the harsh realities of African decolonization. The presence of European settlers prevented the smooth transfer of power. Even in British-ruled Kenya, where the European settler population had never exceeded 20,000, a violent war of independence broke out between European settlers and African nationalists. Employing secrecy and intimidation, the Kikuyu peoples, Kenya's largest ethnic group, organized a revolt against British colonial rule and in favor of independence. This uprising, known as the Mau-Mau Revolt, which began in 1952, forced the British to fly in troops to suppress it, but the rebellion ultimately persuaded the British government to concede independence to a black majority in Kenya in 1963. Jomo Kenyatta (1898–1978), a nationalist leader who had been jailed by the British, became its first president. Decolonization proved even more difficult in the southern third of the African continent, where the political independence of Portuguese Angola, Portuguese Mozambique, and British Southern Rhodesia (present-day Zimbabwe) had to wait until the 1970s.

South Africa defied the "wind of change" and black majority rule even more successfully. The largest and wealthiest settler population in Africa resided in South Africa, where more than 4 million white residents fervently resisted the stirrings of black power. After winning the elections of 1948, the Afrikaner-dominated National Party enacted an extreme form of racial segregation known as apartheid. Apartheid laws stripped Africans, Indians, and colored persons (those of mixed descent) of their few political rights. Racial mixing of any kind, including mixed marriage, was forbidden, and schools were strictly segregated. The Group Areas Act, passed in 1950, divided the country into separate racial and tribal areas, and required Africans to live in their own racial areas, called "homelands." Pass laws prohibited Africans from traveling outside their homelands without special work or travel passes.

> *Apartheid laws stripped Africans, Indians, and colored persons (those of mixed descent) of their few political rights.*

The ruling party tolerated no protest. Nelson Mandela (1918–   ), one of the leaders of the African National Congress (ANC), campaigned for an end to discriminatory legislation and was harassed, detained, and tried by the government on numerous occasions, even though he urged peaceful resistance. After the Sharpeville massacre in 1960, in which the police killed demonstrators who were peacefully protesting the pass laws, Mandela and the ANC decided to oppose the apartheid regime with violence. Responding to Sharpeville, the government announced a state of emergency, banned the ANC, and arrested those of its leaders who had not fled the country or gone underground. A South African court sentenced Mandela to life imprisonment and sent him to the most notorious of the South African prisons, Robben Island, in 1962. Other black leaders were tortured, and some were beaten to death. Despite such human rights violations, the whites still retained external support.

Through the 1950s and 1960s, Western powers, especially the United States, saw South Africa as a bulwark against the spread of communism in Africa. The same concern to contain communism also drew the United States into support for another unpopular regime—and eventually war—in Vietnam.

VIETNAM Vietnam had come under French rule in the 1880s. After putting down all armed resistance, the French proceeded to establish a highly centralized administration. By the 1920s, approximately 40,000 Europeans lived among and ruled over roughly 19 million Vietnamese. To promote an export economy of rice, mining, and rubber, the colonial rulers granted vast land concessions to French companies and local collaborators, while leaving large numbers of landless peasants.

The colonial system also gave rise to a new intelligentsia. Primarily schooled in French and Franco-Vietnamese schools, educated Vietnamese worked as clerks, shopkeepers, teachers, and petty officials. Yet, their educational achievements did not open many opportunities for advancement in the French-dominated colonial system. Discontented, the educated turned from the traditional ideology of Confucianism to modern nationalism. The Vietnamese intellectuals overseas, most notably Ho Chi Minh, took the lead in imagining a new Vietnamese nation-state.

Ho had left Vietnam at an early age and found his way to London and Paris. In Paris in the interwar period, he became acquainted with the writings of Marx, Engels, and Lenin, and he discovered not only an ideology for opposing French injustice and exploitation, but also a vision for turning the common people into a political force. He was a founding member of the French Communist Party and went to the Soviet Union, where he extended his knowledge of classical Marxism and Leninism. Returning to Vietnam, he founded the Indochinese Communist Party. After the Japanese occupied Indochina, he traveled to China, where he embraced the idea of an agrarian revolution and established the Viet Minh, a liberation force, in 1941. Back in Vietnam, the Communist-led Viet Minh became a powerful nationalist organization as it mobilized the peasantry.

When the French tried to restore their rule after Japan's defeat in 1945, Ho appealed to the United States (for whom he had been an intelligence agent during the war) for diplomatic and moral support, citing the American Declaration of Independence as an inspiration for Vietnam. His appeals fell on deaf ears, and the Viet Minh declared independence. War with France followed (1946–1954). In the ensuing combat, Ho and the Viet Minh relied on guerrilla tactics to undermine French positions. They were most successful in the north, but even in the south their campaign bled the French. Finally, in 1954, the Battle of Dien Bien Phu resulted in a decisive victory for the anti-colonial forces. At the Geneva Peace Conference, Vietnam (like Korea) was divided into two zones, north and south. Ho controlled the north, while a government with French and American support was installed in the south—with a promise of popular elections for future reunification that was not fulfilled because of American opposition.

Though the French had departed, decolonization in Vietnam was incomplete. North Vietnam supported the Viet Cong—Communist guerrillas—who were determined to overthrow the non-Communist government in South Vietnam and to unite the north and south. Determined to contain the spread of communism in Southeast Asia, the United States began smuggling arms to the regime in the south. During the early 1960s, under President John F. Kennedy, U.S. involvement steadily escalated beyond that of an advisory role. In 1965, large numbers of American troops entered the country to fight on behalf of South Vietnam, while Communist North Vietnam turned to the Soviet Union for supplies. Over the next several years, the United States introduced more and more soldiers. Yet, even the deployment of 500,000 troops in Vietnam could not prevent the spread of communism in Southeast Asia.

 THREE WORLDS

→ *What were the successes and failures of each world order?*

The Second World War made the Soviet Union and the United States into superpowers. Possessing nuclear weapons, superior armies, and industrial might that gave them the clout to dominate other nations, they vied for influence around the globe. As decolonization spread, the two cold war belligerents offered new leaders their models for economic and political modernization.

Ho Chi Minh. A leader and symbol of Vietnam's anti-colonial struggles, Ho spent his early years in France, the Soviet Union, and China, and he founded the Indochinese Communist Party in 1930. His formation of the League for the Independence of Vietnam, or Viet Minh, in 1941 set the stage for his rise at the end of World War II. Here he is shown attending a youth rally in October 1955, just over a year after the decisive victory of his forces at Dien Bien Phu, which resulted in the ousting of the French from Vietnam.

On one side, the United States, together with its Western European allies and Japan, had developed democratic forms of governance and a dynamic capitalist economy capable of producing an immense quantity of ever-cheaper consumer goods. The Soviet Union, on the other side, was ruled by the Communist Party, which trumpeted its egalitarian ideology and its remarkably rapid transition from a "backward" to a highly industrialized nation as worthy of emulation. Both the First World and the Second World expected other nations, including those in the decolonized Third World, to adopt their models wholesale.

The decolonized, however, often had ideas of their own. With the Communist takeover in 1949, China had freed itself from semi-colonial status, and Mao soon broke from Soviet direction. Other newly decolonized nations in Asia and Africa had inherited underdeveloped economies and could not leap into capitalist or Communist industrial development. Moreover, in various corners of the globe, decolonization remained incomplete. Most problematic for Third World nations was the widening scope of the cold war. In Europe, First and Second Worlds coexisted uneasily alongside one another, but in the Third World, the conflict often turned hot—and bloody. And even at peace, Third World nations found their search for alternative models of development confined by the strings that the superpowers attached to their support.

THE FIRST WORLD

As the cold war spread in the early 1950s, Western Europe and North America became grouped together as the First World, or what its champions referred to as "the free world." Later on, Japan joined this group. Building on the principles of liberal modernism, which had been salvaged by the New Deal and by victory in World War II, the First World sought to organize and administer the world on the basis of capitalism and democracy. Yet, in its struggle against communism, the free world sometimes aligned itself with Third World dictators, thereby sacrificing its commitment to freedom and democracy to political expediency.

WESTERN EUROPE   The reconstruction of Western Europe after World War II was by most measures a spectacular success. By the late 1950s, the economies of most nations in Western Europe were thriving, thanks in part to massive postwar American economic assistance through the Marshall Plan. Improvements in agriculture were particularly impressive. With increased mechanization and the use of pesticides, fewer farmers fed more people. In 1950, for example, each French farmer produced enough food for seven people; in 1962, one farmer could feed forty. Industrial production also boomed, doubling between 1948 and 1951, and again by 1960. As real wages rose, consumer goods that had been luxuries before the Second World War—refrigerators, telephones, automobiles, and indoor plumbing—became commonplace. Prosperity also allowed gov-ernments in Western Europe to expand social welfare systems. By the end of the 1950s, Western European nations had brought education and health care within the reach of virtually all citizens.

Western Europe's economic recovery blunted the appeal of socialist and Communist political programs. Moreover, the cold war tempered anti-fascist reckonings, putting stability first. Although the victors convened war crimes trials that resulted in the conviction of a number of prominent Nazis, the fear was that a thorough de-Nazification would deprive Germany of political and economic leaders, leaving it more susceptible to Communist subversion.

THE UNITED STATES   While Europe lay in ruins after the Second World War, the United States entered a period of prolonged economic expansion that raised the standard of living of virtually every segment of the population. Thanks to steadily rising incomes, Americans could afford more consumer goods than ever before. These were almost always items manufactured within the United States, for "American made" was synonymous

Levittown. The decades after the Second World War saw a massive shift of the American population away from the cities and to the suburbs. To satisfy the demand of Americans for single-family homes, private developers, assisted by favorable government policies, constructed thousands of new communities on the outskirts of urban centers. Places like Long Island's Levittown (pictured here), made affordable by the standardization of design and construction, enabled many middle-class Americans to fulfill their dreams of home ownership. But the flight of the white middle class to the suburbs brought turmoil to inner cities that were increasingly inhabited by poor and nonwhite populations.

with quality and efficiency. Home ownership became more common, especially in the burgeoning suburbs to which millions of Americans moved in the decades after World War II. Stimulating this suburban development was a "baby boom" that reversed more than a century of declining birthrates. In the 1950s, these child-rich suburbs came to epitomize the abundance of American life. Indeed, in contrast to the gloomy outlook of the 1930s, in the 1950s Americans basked in unprecedented prosperity and broadcast their faith in capitalism's future. "Progress," proclaimed actor turned General Electric spokesman Ronald Reagan, "is our most important product." This progress, predicted one sociologist, would soon turn the United States into a "wantless" society.

Yet, even as suburbanites basked in the unparalleled affluence that they credited to free enterprise, anxieties about the future of the free world abounded. Terrified by Stalin's demands at Yalta and by rumors of Soviet sympathizers and spies operating within the government of the United States, President Harry Truman spoke frequently and ominously of the specter of communism that haunted the postwar world. In the wake of the Soviet Union's explosion of an atomic bomb, the Communist Revolution in China, and the outbreak of the Korean War, anti-Communist rhetoric became shriller still. No individual exploited the anti-Communist hysteria more effectively than the Republican senator from Wisconsin, Joseph McCarthy. In 1950, he commenced a campaign to uncover closet Communists in the State Department and in Hollywood. Televised congressional hearings gave the Wisconsin senator a forum to broadcast his views to the entire nation. Though by the end of 1954, the tide had turned decisively against him, "McCarthyism" persisted in American foreign policy, where almost all elected officials, not wanting to risk being labeled "soft" on communism, voted to spend more money on American armies and armaments.

Postwar American prosperity did not benefit all citizens equally. During the prosperous 1950s, nearly a quarter of the American population lived in what the government designated as poverty. But progress emboldened those living on the margins to demand more. Many African Americans, a group disproportionately trapped below the poverty line, participated in an increasingly powerful movement for equal rights and the end of racial segregation. In the courts, the National Association for the Advancement of Colored People (NAACP) won a series of victories that mandated the desegregation of schools with "all deliberate speed." Boycotts, too, became a weapon of a growing civil rights movement, with Martin Luther King, Jr. (1929–1968) rising to prominence after leading a successful strike against injustices in the bus system of Montgomery, Alabama. Here and in subsequent campaigns to overturn white supremacy, King borrowed his most effective weapon, the commitment to nonviolent protest and the appeal

During the prosperous 1950s, nearly a quarter of the American population lived in what the government designated as poverty.

Anti-Communist Hysteria. As the cold war heated up, anti-Communist fervor swept across the United States. Leading the charge against the "Communist conspiracy" within the United States was the Wisconsin senator Joseph McCarthy, who is pictured here with his aide, the attorney Roy Cohn.

to conscience, from Gandhi. As the civil rights movement grew, officials in the federal government gradually came to support programs for racial equality. Eager not to destabilize the existing order, however, President Dwight D. Eisenhower (1890–1969) used federal power to enforce court-ordered desegregation only with great reluctance.

After the war, the United States symbolized the promise and potential of liberal capitalism. Want could be reduced and individual rights upheld. Not even the excesses of anti-Communist crusaders would destroy this image. In the United States and elsewhere, the market economy, increasing rights for all, and electoral democracy became heartfelt principles of citizenship in the First World.

THE JAPANESE "MIRACLE" Unquestionably, one of the most impressive triumphs for the Western liberal capitalist vision was the emergence of Japan, America's enemy during World War II, as an economic powerhouse after the war. The war had ended with Japan's unconditional surrender in 1945, its dreams of dominating East Asia dashed, and its homeland devastated. As in war-devastated Europe, socialism and communism were enticing options for rebuilding the country and meeting basic needs. Yet, by the middle of the 1970s, Japan (like West Germany), once a dictatorship, had emerged as a politically stable civilian regime with a dynamic, thriving economy. As in the case of Germany, Japan owed some of this momentous change to American military protection, investment, and transfers of technology. Japan, therefore, exemplified the benefits of being incorporated into the First World.

American military protection, especially from any Communist threat, spared the Japanese from the rising military expenditures of Western nations and of Soviet-bloc states. Even more important was economic support. To facilitate recovery, the United States opened its enormous domestic market to Japanese goods. Initially, Japanese goods were rather primitive, but over time, thanks to a skilled labor force and design expertise, they became more and more sophisticated. Indeed, to replace the country's physical plant, which had been largely destroyed during the war, the Americans transferred considerable technology to Japan. These transfers helped Japan rebuild its industries from top to bottom with a greater percentage of up-to-date equipment than any other country except perhaps West Germany. To enhance the rebuilding effort, the Japanese government guided much of the country's economic development through directed investment, working partnerships with private firms, and protectionist policies. To promote an export-driven economy, the government encouraged its citizens to save, not spend. At the same time, it erected import barriers that allowed specially targeted industries to take off without foreign competition.

Together, these factors resulted in, if not a miracle, then at least an unprecedented boom. Already in the 1950s, Japan's economy was surging upward at a rate of nearly 10 percent per year. No country in the world had experienced that kind of sustained growth before, yet Japan maintained its phenomenal run through the 1960s and into the 1970s.

The Second World

The scourge of the Second World War and the shadow of the cold war fell even more decisively—and gloomily—on the Soviet Union, which with its satellites constituted the Second World. Having suffered more deaths and more damage than any other industrialized nation during the war, the Soviet Union was determined to insulate itself from future aggression from the West. That meant turning Eastern Europe into a bloc of Communist buffer states. Just as American leaders had warned of Communist plots to undermine the free world, so, too, Soviet leaders were suspicious of American actions, seeing them as part of a concerted effort to destroy socialism. Under siege, or so they thought, the Soviets used coercion at home and in Eastern Europe to enforce their conception of state socialism.

THE APPEAL OF THE SOVIET MODEL For many who had seen capitalism and democracy flounder in the 1920s and

1930s and experienced the devastation wrought by fascist militarism, the Soviet model had appeal. Its egalitarian ideology and success in achieving rapid industrialization made it seem a worthy alternative to capitalism. Here, there was no private property and thus, in Marxist terms, no exploitation. Workers "owned" the factories and worked for themselves. The Soviet state claimed to assure full employment, and Soviet ideologues boasted that a state-run economy would be immune from upturns and downturns in business cycles. Freedom from exploitation, combined with security, was contrasted with the capitalist model of owners hoarding profits and firing loyal workers when suddenly they were not needed.

Enthusiasts of the Soviet system pointed to the protections afforded workers. The state gave a high priority to inexpensive mass transit and subsidized travel by rail, and later, airplane. In addition, the state granted women paid maternity leave and guaranteed them their jobs when they returned. Health care was technically free, and education was made universally available. Under the tsarist regime, less than half the Russian

Stalin and Soviet Propaganda. Amid the brick-by-brick reconstruction efforts following World War II, a 1949 Soviet poster depicts a youth in red scarf with a fatherly Stalin and the slogan: "May Our Motherland Live Long and Flourish."

population was literate; by the 1950s, the literacy rate soared above 80 percent, and it would eventually reach nearly 100 percent—the highest in the world. The entire Soviet population went to school, learning geography, literature, history, and especially the sciences. Indeed, the Soviet Union encouraged students to take up science from an early age. True, these policies did not provide material abundance of the sort that First World nations were enjoying. But if consumer goods were often scarce, they were cheap. Likewise, while it sometimes took ten years or more to obtain a small home through waiting lists at work, when one's turn finally came, the apartment carried only a nominal annual rent and could be passed on to one's children.

> *By the time of Stalin's death in 1953, the vast Gulag system confined several million people behind barbed wire.*

Critical to the attractiveness of the Soviet system was its victory in World War II and the fact that few ordinary people in the Soviet Union knew how their counterparts lived in the capitalist world. Government censors skewed news about the First World to present a negative picture. At the same time, they suppressed unfavorable information about the Soviet Union and the Communist bloc. Yet, even when people in the Soviet Union learned about the prosperity of Western Europe and the United States, usually from Western films and radio, they often clung to the idea that the Soviet Union remained the more just society. Theirs, they believed, was a land without a gulf between rich and poor, indeed, with no racial or class divisions at all. If members of the Soviet elite lived in privileged circumstances, evidence of their luxurious lifestyles was concealed from the public. Indeed, socialism's internal critics did not typically seek to overthrow the system and restore capitalism. Rather, they wanted the Soviet regime to live up to its promises and introduce reforms that would create what was termed "socialism with a human face."

REPRESSION OF DISSENT Few outside the Soviet sphere knew just how inhuman the face of Soviet communism was, and few within knew the extent of the brutality. In the wake of the war, rather than a hoped-for relaxation of political controls and a rumored de-collectivization (that is, the restoration of private peasant ownership in impoverished villages), the Kremlin leadership tightened its grip. Surviving soldiers who had been prisoners of war in Germany and civilians who had been slave laborers for the Germans and had somehow managed to survive captivity were sent to special screening camps, simply because they had been abroad; many disappeared. Women and youths who had experienced the German occupation were kept under suspicion. By the time of Stalin's death in 1953, the vast Gulag (or labor camp complex) confined several million people behind barbed wire.

Stalin's successors had to face the questions: What was to be done with so many prisoners? How could the existence of the labor camp system as a whole be explained? This problem became acute when a series of strikes rocked the camps, often led by veterans from World War II. In February 1956, the new party leader, Nikita Khrushchev (1894–1971), delivered a speech in which he attempted to separate Stalin's crimes from true communism. Given at the final, closed session of the Communist Party's Twentieth Congress, this "secret" speech was never published in the Soviet Union, but it was widely discussed among party members and distributed to party organizations abroad. The crimes that Khrushchev revealed came as a terrible shock.

The repercussions, especially in Eastern Europe, were immediate and far-reaching. Eastern European leaders interpreted Khrushchev's speech as an endorsement for political liberation and economic experimentation. Right away, Polish intellectuals began a drive to revive prewar institutions and break free from the Communist ideological straitjacket. In June 1956, Polish workers joined the intellectuals, and a general strike occurred in Poznan, first over bread and wages, then in protest against Soviet occupation. Emboldened by the events in Poland, Hungarian intellectuals and students held demonstrations demanding an uncensored press, free elections with genuine alternative parties, and the withdrawal of Soviet troops. The Hungarian Party leader, Imre Nagy (1896–1958), joined with the rebels.

But the seeming liberalization promised by Khrushchev's speech proved short-lived. Rather than let Eastern Europeans stray too far or allow the Soviet people to call for changes, the Soviet leadership crushed dissent. In Poland, the security police massacred strikers. In Hungary, on the morning of November 4, 1956, tanks from the Soviet Union and other Warsaw Pact members invaded the country, overthrew Nagy, and installed a new government that was expected to smash all "counterrevolutionary" activities. After these revolts, Hungary and Poland did win some economic and cultural autonomy—in Poland, for example, the collectivization of agriculture ended, and the Catholic Church resumed its spiritual and educational role, while in Hungary a small private sector emerged—but unquestionably, the Second World remained very much the dominion of the Soviet Union.

The crackdown in 1956 did not stamp out the tensions within Eastern Europe or the Soviet Union. Intellectuals, when given some freedom, demanded more, eliciting new repression. Many Soviet youths evinced what the authorities considered to be dangerous apolitical attitudes and a taste for unorthodox dress and behavior. In the republics of the Soviet Union, nationalists clamored for greater rights and more liberal language policies to combat the central government's efforts to spread the Russian language and Russian culture. Sporadic worker strikes over living conditions and price rises were ruthlessly suppressed.

ADVANCES AND LEADERSHIP The ability to use force at home and in Eastern Europe was only part of what made the Soviet Union a superpower. Taking advantage of the Soviets' excellent education system, students from Third World countries went to the Soviet Union to be trained as engineers, scientists, army commanders, and revolutionaries. Soviet science won worldwide admiration. That was particularly so in 1957, when the Soviets launched Sputnik, the first satellite, into space.

The Sputnik launch confirmed the Soviet Union's superpower status. With a vast military arsenal, an impressive system of education, and a fully employed population, the Soviet Union seemed very much on the rise. The updated 1961 Communist Party program predicted euphorically that within twenty years the Soviet Union would surpass the United States and eclipse the First World.

The Western powers looked to two new instruments of global capitalism, the World Bank and the International Monetary Fund (IMF), to provide crucial economic guidance in the Third World.

THE THIRD WORLD

In the 1950s, French intellectuals coined the term "Third World" (*tiers monde* in French) to describe the efforts of countries seeking a "third way" between Soviet communism and Western capitalism. By the early 1960s, the term had come to identify a large bloc of countries from Asia, Africa, and Latin America. What they shared in common was that all, at one time or another, had been subjected to European and North American domination and now believed that they could create more just and humane societies than those that existed in the First and Second Worlds. This search for anti-colonial forms of modernity had been underway at least since the end of World War I. After World War II, the time had come, many thought, to realize long-thwarted dreams. The exuberant hopes were eloquently captured by the African-American writer Richard Wright, who attended a meeting of the leaders of decolonized nations in 1955. "Only brown, black, and yellow men who had long been made agonizingly self-conscious, under the rigors of colonial rule, of their race and their religion could have felt the need for such a meeting. There was something extra-political, extra-social, almost extra-human about it."

Flush with their recently gained freedom, the leaders of the newly independent nations believed that they could build strong democratic polities, like those in the West, and also promote rapid economic development, as the Soviet Union had done. All of this could be achieved without experiencing the empty materialism that they believed characterized Western capitalism or the state oppression of Communist regimes. The early 1960s were years of heady optimism in the Third World. Ghanaian prime minister Kwame Nkrumah trumpeted pan-Africanism as a way for the African continent to place itself on a par with the rest of the world. Egyptian president Gamal Abdel Nasser boasted that his democratic socialism was neither Western nor Soviet-inspired and that Egypt would retain its neutrality in the cold war struggle. Indian prime minister Jawaharlal Nehru blended democratic politics and vigorous state planning to promote India's quest for political independence and economic autonomy.

LIMITS TO AUTONOMY Charting a "third way" between the West and the Soviet Union proved difficult, both economically and politically. Both the Soviets and the Americans saw the Third World as "underdeveloped," and Americans especially sought to ensure that market structures and private property established the girders for modernization. The Western powers looked to two new instruments of global capitalism, the World Bank and the International Monetary Fund (IMF), both created in 1944 at Bretton Woods, New Hampshire, to provide crucial economic guidance in the Third World. Originally designed to help restore order in Europe, these institutions quickly turned their attention to promoting economic development in the Third World. The World Bank funded loans for projects to lift poor societies out of poverty, while the IMF supported the monetary systems of these new governments when they experienced economic woes. Yet, while World Bank money financed programs to provide electricity to Indians and roads in Indonesia, and the IMF propped up the economies of Ghana, Nigeria, and Egypt, to mention only a few of its clients, they also intruded on the autonomy of these states.

Another force that threatened Third World economic autonomy was the multinational corporation. In the rush to transfer advanced technology from the First to the Third World, Africans, Asians, and Latin Americans struck deals with multinationals to import their know-how. Owned primarily by American, European, and Japanese entrepreneurs, these firms expanded cash cropping and plantation activities and established manufacturing branches around the globe. But large foreign corporations impeded the growth of indigenous business firms in developing countries. To critics, multinationals merely remitted the profits from their overseas ventures to stockholders in the United States, Western Europe, and Japan. Although the world's nations were more economically interdependent than ever before, it was still clear that the West made the decisions—and reaped most of the profits.

Whether dealing with the West or the Soviet Union, Third World leaders found their options limited. During the cold war, neither the United States nor the Soviet Union welcomed neutral parties. To create more client states, the Soviet Union backed Communist insurgencies around the globe, while the

United States supported almost any leaders who declared their anti-communism. To contain Communist expansion, the United States formed military alliances. Following the 1949 creation of NATO, similar regional arrangements were made in Southeast Asia (SEATO) in 1954 and in the Middle East (the Baghdad Pact) in 1955. These organizations brought many Third World nations into American-led alliances and allowed the United States to establish military bases in foreign territories. For its part, the Soviet Union countered by positioning its forces in friendly Third World countries.

One of the major consequences of the proliferation of military alliances was the militarization of many Third World countries. Nowhere was this development more apparent or more threatening to economic development than on the African continent. In the colonial era, African states had spent little on their military forces. All of this came to an abrupt halt when they became independent and were swept up in the cold war. Civil wars, like the one that tore apart Nigeria between 1967 and 1970, yielded opportunities for the great powers to wield influence. When the West refused to sell weapons to the Nigerian government so it could suppress the breakaway eastern province of Biafra, the Soviets supplied MIG aircraft and other vital weapons. A similar situation occurred in Egypt, which was Africa's most strategic region both to the West and the Soviets. After the founding of Israel, the new military rulers in Egypt insisted that their country never again be caught militarily unprepared. Keenly aware of the West's support for Israel, the Egyptians turned to the Soviet bloc. The arms race between Egypt and Israel left the region bristling with the most modern weaponry, including surface-to-air missiles and the most expensive military jets, some of which were even flown by Soviet pilots.

Thus, the Third World nations discovered that, having shrugged off the colonial yoke, they now confronted a new series of "neo-colonial" problems. How were they to apply liberal or socialist models within the context of national traditions? How were they to deal with economic relations that seemed to reduce their autonomy and limit their development? And how, finally, might they escape being puppets of the West or the Soviet Union? Facing these difficult questions, frustrations and disenchantment grew about the prospects for an alternative way to modernity.

By the middle of the 1960s, as the euphoria of decolonization evaporated and new states found themselves mired in debt and dependency, many Third World nations fell into dictatorship and authoritarian rule. Although some of these dictators continued to speak about forging a "third way," they did so mainly to justify their corrupt regimes. They had forgotten the democratic commitments that the term had initially implied. For the most part, they also had allowed themselves to be drawn into the cold war, the better to extract arms and assistance from one or the other superpower.

> By the middle of the 1960s, many Third World countries fell into dictatorship and authoritarian rule.

THIRD WORLD REVOLUTIONARIES AND RADICALS

It was against this background of blasted expectations that Third World radicalism emerged as a powerful force. Recalling the attempts of the early leaders of new nations to find a "third way," revolutionary movements in the late 1950s and the 1960s sought to transform their societies. But while some Third World radicals seized power, they, too, had trouble cracking the existing world order.

For inspiration, Third World revolutionaries drew especially on the pioneering writings of Frantz Fanon (1925–1961). Born in the French Caribbean colony of Martinique, Fanon was educated there and in France, fought with the Free French during World War II, and was trained as a doctor and psychiatrist in Lyon, France. While serving as a psychiatrist in French Algeria, he became deeply aware of the psychological damage of European racism and published a powerful book, *Peau Noire, Masques Blancs* (*Black Skin, White Masks*), in 1952. He subsequently joined the Algerian Revolution and became a radical theorist of liberation. His *The Wretched of the Earth*, published in 1961, shortly before his death, urged Third World peoples to achieve a collective catharsis through violence against their European oppressors. *The Wretched of the Earth* also offered a scathing critique of those Third World nationalists who wished merely to replace European masters without undertaking radical social transformations. Fanon's books became popular among radicals in the Third World who were inspired by his vision for decolonizing the mind as well as society.

While Fanon moved people with his writings, others did so by organizing radical political organizations and undertaking revolutionary social experiments. One model was Mao Zedong. In 1958, Mao introduced a program that he called the Great Leap Forward. True to his vision of an ongoing people's revolution, the Great Leap Forward was an audacious attempt to unleash the people's energy. It organized China into 24,000 basic social and economic units, called communes, of roughly 30,000 persons. Peasants left their fields and took up industrial production in their own backyards. The campaign was supposed to catapult China past the developed countries. But the experiment was a dismal failure. The communes failed to feed the people, and the industrial goods were of inferior quality. China took an economic leap backward. Some 20 million perished from famine and malnutrition, forcing the government to abandon the experiment. After the Great Leap Forward, Mao retreated from the day-to-day administration of the government.

Fearing that China's revolution was losing spirit, Mao reasserted his authority in 1966 and launched the Great

The Cultural Revolution in China. *(Left)* Public mass rallies played a key role in the mobilization strategy of the Chinese Communist Party. During the Cultural Revolution, scenes like the ones shown here from the northeastern province of Heilongjiang were common throughout the country. *(Right)* In their campaign to cleanse the country of undesirable elements, the Red Guards often turned to the familiar tactic of public denunciation as a way to rally the crowd. Here, a senior provincial party official of Heilongjiang is made to stand on a chair wearing a dunce's cap, while his young detractors nearby chant slogans and wave their fists in the air.

Proletarian Cultural Revolution. To break the opposition that had grown up during the Great Leap Forward, Mao turned against his longtime associates in the Communist Party, appealing to China's young people to reinvigorate the revolution. Brought up to revere Mao, these young people enthusiastically responded to his call to action. Organized into "Red Guards," over 10 million of them journeyed to Beijing to participate in eight huge rallies in Tiananmen Square between August and November 1966. Chanting, crying, screaming, and waving the little red book of Mao's quotations, they pledged to cleanse the party of its corrupt elements and to carry out Mao's will by thoroughly remaking Chinese society from top to bottom.

With the collusion of the army, the young revolutionary warriors set out to rid society of the "four olds"—old customs, old habits, old culture, and old ideas. They ransacked homes, libraries, museums, and temples. Classical texts, artworks, and monuments were declared to be feudal poison and were destroyed. With its rhetoric of struggle against American imperialism and Soviet revisionism, the Cultural Revolution also took on a xenophobic cast. Knowledge of a foreign language was enough to compromise a person's revolutionary credentials. The Red Guards attacked government officials, party cadres, or just plain strangers on the streets in an escalating cycle of violence. As the process intensified, family members and friends were pressured to denounce each other, and all were required to demonstrate purity and prove themselves faithful followers of Chairman Mao. With the chaos mounting, the army asserted itself in late 1967, moving in to quell the disorder and to reestab-

lish control. To forestall further political disruption in the urban areas, the government created an entire "lost generation" when, between 1967 and 1976, it deprived some 17 million former Red Guards and students of their formal education and relocated them to the countryside "to learn from the peasants."

Given the costs of the Great Leap Forward and the Cultural Revolution, many of Mao's revolutionary policies were hard to celebrate; but radicals in much of the Third World were unaware of these costs and found the style of rapid and massive—if deeply undemocratic—uplift of the populace attractive. At least rhetorically, such policies aimed to transform poor countries within a generation.

Most Third World radicals did not go as far as Mao, but they still dreamed of overturning the social order. In Latin America, such dreams excited those who wished to free their nations from the influence of U.S.-owned multinational corporations and from the power of local elites. Within the Americas, the United States had long flexed its political and economic muscle. Into the 1950s, no European state, the Soviet Union included, dared infringe on this sphere of American influence. Within Latin America, however, discontent bred calls for reform and, when these were repressed or went unheeded, for revolution.

Reform programs in Latin America addressed a variety of concerns. Seeking to free Latin American economies from U.S. domination, economic nationalists urged greater protection for domestic industries and sought to curb the might of multinationals. Liberal reformers emphasized the need to democratize political systems and to redistribute land, lest discontent blossom into full-blown revolutions like China's. But when liberals and nationalists joined forces, as in Guatemala in the early 1950s, their reforms met resistance from local conservatives and from the United States. In Guatemala, the banana-producing American multinational United Fruit Company, which was the largest landowner and controlled the country's railroads and its major port, opposed land reform. Still, the progressive and nationalist regime of Jacobo Arbenz (1913–1971) persevered with its plans for agrarian reform and proposed taking over uncultivated land owned by the United Fruit Company. Despite Arbenz's intention of compensating the company for its land, the U.S. Central Intelligence Agency (CIA) plotted with sectors of the Guatemalan army to put an end to reform, culminating in a coup d'état in 1954.

In the midst of the cold war, the United States effectively warned other wayward governments that Washington would not brook assaults on its national and security interests. Across Latin America, foreign—mainly American—power was synonymous with the impossibility of gradual reform. In 1954, the year of the Guatemalan coup, the Brazilian populist president Getúlio Vargas killed himself after writing to his people that he could not protect Brazilians against "domination and looting by international economic and financial groups."

In Cuba, as reformers predicted and feared, the failure to address political, social, and economic concerns brought on a revolution. Ironically, this rebellion occurred in the country most tied to the United States. Since the Spanish-American War of 1898, Cuba had been ruled by governments better known for their compliance with U.S. interests than with popular sentiment. In 1933, during the crisis resulting from the Great Depression,

Sergeant Fulgencio Batista (1901–1973) emerged as a strongman, and in 1952 he led a military coup that deposed a corrupt civilian government and made him dictator. The Batista dictatorship did little to clean up public affairs, while continuing to bend to the wishes of North American investors. Although sugar planters and casino operators prospered, middle- and working-class Cubans did not. The latter demanded a voice in politics and a new moral bond between the people and their government. Especially at the University of Havana, students became exponents of revolution. In 1953, a group of young men and women launched a botched assault on a military garrison. One of the leaders, a young law student named Fidel Castro, gave a stirring speech at the rebels' trial, which made him a national hero. After he was freed from prison in 1955, he fled to Mexico. Several years later, he returned with a small band of armed comrades and started organizing guerrilla raids.

Batista's fortunes nose-dived when, to his great surprise, the U.S. Congress suspended military supplies and aid. Deprived of American support, his regime crumbled in 1958. Entire regiments of his army defected to the rebels. On New Year's Day 1959, at a party at one of Havana's sumptuous hotels, Batista announced that he was leaving Cuba. He and his entourage fled to the airport to escape, and within days, young guerrillas took control of the capital.

As Castro began to consolidate his hold on power, his regime grew increasingly more radical. He elbowed aside rivals and seized control of the economy from the wealthy elite, who fled in droves to exile in southern Florida and elsewhere. Even before Castro's full intentions were apparent, American

Fidel Castro and Cuba's National Liberation. *(Left)* In the 1950s and 1960s, national liberation movements became increasingly radical. The Cuban Revolution of 1958–1959 was a powerful model for many young rebels. Pictured here are the icons, Fidel Castro and Che Guevara, discussing guerrilla strategy in the Cuban highlands. *(Right)* No sooner did Cuban rebels force a decisive break with the United States in 1959 than they discovered that they needed outside support to survive. The Soviet Union, eager to lay a toehold for communism so close to the United States, began to provide heavy economic and military subsidies to their Caribbean ally. Pictured here are Fidel Castro, leader of the Cuban Revolution, grasping the raised arm of Nikita Khrushchev (bedecked with three Order of Lenin medals) atop the Lenin mausoleum for the May Day parade in 1963. The turn of events in Cuba mostly surprised the Soviet inner circle but soon imbued them with a sense that socialism could recapture its revolutionary élan, especially in the Third World.

RADICALIZING THE THIRD WORLD: CHE GUEVARA

The Cuban Revolution was a turning point in the making of the Third World. After 1959, the Castro regime championed liberation for the Third World from the First World, and embraced socialism as a radical solution to underdevelopment. By rejecting the power of capitalist industrial societies, Castro and his followers thereby promoted revolution, and not reform, as a way to achieve Third World liberation. The symbol of this new spirit of revolution was Castro's closest lieutenant, Ernesto "Che" Guevara (1928–1967). Che wanted to unite the Third World as a socialist, postcolonial bloc, and thereby to undermine the capitalist world led by the United States.

"El Che," as he was known, grew up in Argentina and traveled widely around Latin America as a student. Shortly after receiving his medical degree in 1953, he set off once again, arriving in Guatemala in time to witness the CIA-backed overthrow of the progressive Jacobo Arbenz government in 1954. Thereafter, Guevara became increasingly bitter about American influences in Latin America. He joined Castro's forces and helped topple the pro-American regime of Fulgencio Batista in Cuba in 1958. After 1959, he held several posts in the Cuban government, but he grew increasingly restive for more action. Latin America, according to Guevara, should become the source of "many Vietnams" and should challenge the world power of the United States. Soon his casual military uniform, his patchy beard, his cigar, and his moral energy became legendary symbols of revolt.

The image of the guerrilla fighter as savior appealed to young people around the world. Che Guevara published a manual in 1960, *Guerrilla Warfare,* to instruct radicals on how to mount a successful revolution. Although Mao Zedong and North Vietnamese general Vo Nguyen Giap had also published blueprints for peasant-based revolutions, Che was able to draw on the more recent and successful experiences of the Cuban struggle. If Cuba could radicalize the Third World, any underdeveloped society could. Che told his radical readers to blend in with the urban and especially the rural poor to create a "people's army" and to strike blows at the weakest points in the established order. He enjoined men in particular to lead the crusade to show the poor that their misery could be reversed through heroic violence. Women, too, had a role to play in revolution. According to Guevara, they could cook for, nurse, and serve as helpmates for fighters. For all of Guevara's radicalism, he did not transcend conventional models of relations between the sexes. Not surprisingly, the image of the armed freedom fighter for Third World liberation appealed mainly to young men.

The idea of revolution as a way to overcome underdevelopment and free Third World societies spread beyond Latin America. Che became Castro's envoy to world meetings and summits of Third World state leaders, where he celebrated the Cuban road to freedom. The Soviet premier Nikita Khrushchev recognized the power of Che's message and in 1961 proclaimed his support for all "wars of national liberation." Che himself exported his model to Africa, seeking to link Africa and Latin America in a common front against American and European capitalism. Che led a group of Cuban guerrillas to join Congolese rebels under Laurent Kabila to fight the CIA- and South African-backed regimes in south-central Africa. The expedition failed, presaging the difficulties of throwing badly prepared rebels against armies trained in counterinsurgency techniques. Che, disgusted at Kabila's ineptitude and cowardice, withdrew, though Cuban forces remained involved in African struggles into the 1980s.

Che relocated to Latin America, where he believed that "many Vietnams" might be created. He set up his center of operations in highland Bolivia in 1966, among South America's poorest and most downtrodden Indians. "We have to create another Vietnam in the Americas with its center in Bolivia," he proclaimed. Guevara did not, however, know the local Indian language, and he had little logistical support. He and his two dozen fighters launched their continental war in absolute isolation. It took little time for the Bolivian army and CIA operators to surround and capture the small band of exhausted rebels. After a brief interrogation, Bolivian officers ordered that the guerrilla commander be killed on the spot. The executioner first shot the fighter's arms and legs; with Che agonizing on the ground, biting his fist to stifle his cries, another bullet penetrated his thorax. As Che's lungs filled with blood, he died.

Third World governments blocked radical options just as they had done with Che Guevara's movement. Only in Nicaragua—twenty years after Castro's victory—would rebels ever take control, and this exception had more to do with the degree of despotism exercised by the ruling Somoza family than with the appeal of radicalism. In Africa and Asia, too, Third World revolution became a rarity. Militaries in Latin America, Asia, and Africa learned to fight guerrillas with new technology and new counterinsurgency techniques. And all too often, poor people found guerrilla commanders as despotic as their governments.

leaders began to plot his demise. Castro replied by announcing a massive redistribution of land and eventually the nationalization of foreign oil refineries. Outraged, the United States put an end to all aid and sealed off the American market to Cuban sugar. Then, in April 1961, the CIA mounted an invasion by Cuban exiles, landing at the Bay of Pigs. A fiasco from the start, the invasion not only failed to overthrow Castro, it further radicalized Castro's ambitions for Cuba. At this point, Castro declared himself a socialist and openly courted the support of the Soviet Union. Within two years of coming to power, Cuban revolutionaries had consolidated a regime that openly defied the United States and aligned itself with the Soviet Union.

It was over Cuba and its radicalizing revolution that the world came closest to nuclear Armageddon in the Cuban Missile Crisis of 1962. To deter any further U.S. attacks, Castro appealed to the Soviet Union to install nuclear weapons in Cuba—ninety miles off the coast of Florida. When U.S. intelligence detected the weapons in October 1962, President John F. Kennedy ordered a blockade of Cuba, just as a flotilla of weapons-bearing Soviet ships was heading toward Havana. For several weeks, the world was paralyzed with anxiety as Kennedy, Khrushchev, and Castro matched threats. In the end, Kennedy succeeded in getting the Soviets to withdraw their nuclear missiles from Cuba.

If radicals could make a revolution ninety miles off the coast of the United States, what did this spell for the rest of the hemisphere? In Washington, many feared that revolution might become infectious. To combat the germ of revolution, the Kennedy administration unveiled the Alliance for Progress in 1961. Under this program, American advisers fanned out across Latin America to dole out aid and offer blueprints on how to reform local land systems and how to teach the populace the benefits of liberal capitalism.

To most Latin American radicals, these were Band-Aid solutions. Instead, inspired by the Cuban Revolution, many citizens wanted to take matters into their own hands. In Colombia and Venezuela, peasants seized estates; in Argentina, workers occupied factories. And in Chile, a leftist alliance led by President Salvador Allende (1908–1973) showed increasing strength at the ballot box, finally triumphing in 1970.

Reacting to the rising tide of revolutionary insurgency, the United States and its allies in the region bolstered their own counterinsurgency program. Under the guidance of American advisers, Latin American militaries were trained to root out radicalism. They learned that gaining the support of civilians, usually the most indigent, was the key to defeating the guerrillas; by targeting civilians, rather than the armed combatants, counterinsurgent forces were able to isolate and destroy guerrilla campaigns. Even Salvador Allende's democratically

> *During the 1960s, American society lost some of the confidence and much of the contentment that had characterized it in the previous decade.*

elected socialist government in Chile was not spared; the CIA and U.S. policymakers aided General Augusto Pinochet's military coup (in which Allende died) against the regime in 1973 and looked the other way while the junta butchered political opponents. By 1975, rebel forces had been liquidated in Argentina, Uruguay, Brazil, Mexico, Bolivia, and Venezuela. Elsewhere, they hunkered down in isolated hamlets. Where civilian governments failed to keep stability, militaries took over, not just to topple weak governments, but to rule directly.

TENSIONS IN THE THREE-WORLD ORDER

> → *What were the major fissures that developed in the three-world order?*

Third World radicalism raised hopes, but it did not alter the existing balance of global wealth and power. Still, through the 1960s and into the early 1970s, it exposed vulnerabilities in the three-world order. So did the continuation of the Vietnam War, which revealed the limits of American power and opened fissures within the First World. As antiwar and civil rights movements mushroomed, the United States experienced social unrest on a scale not seen since the Great Depression of the 1930s. In the Second World, too, division and dissent challenged the Soviet Union's hold on world communism. In Eastern Europe, satellite states sought more flexible orbits, while Mao's China charted a course at odds with Soviet designs. Finally, in the 1970s, the rising fortunes of oil-producing nations and of Japan introduced new problems in the relations within and between worlds.

TENSIONS IN THE FIRST WORLD

During the 1960s, American society lost some of the confidence and much of the contentment that had characterized it in the previous decade. Although the economy continued to grow impressively until the early 1970s, prosperity no longer translated into complacency. First, there was the assassination of President Kennedy in 1963, and then there was the violence that accompanied African-American struggles for equality. In 1964, resistance to the civil rights movement turned lethal. In Mississippi that year, three civil rights workers were murdered, and two dozen African-American churches were bombed and burned. In response, some African Americans turned away from the goal of integration and abandoned the commitment to nonviolent civil disobedience. Race riots rocked American cities and radicalized black nationalists. The 1960s also brought increasingly angry resistance to the war in Vietnam. College campuses became the staging grounds for massive antiwar protests that ruptured the cold war consensus.

Ironically, these protests occurred even as prosperity continued and government actions ameliorated legal and economic inequalities. In the wake of Kennedy's assassination, the new president, Lyndon Johnson, forwarded a bold plan to insure civil rights and end poverty. The passage of the Civil Rights Act of 1964, banning segregation in public facilities and outlawing racial discrimination in employment, marked an important step in correcting legal inequality. The following year, the Voting Rights Act afforded millions of previously disenfranchised African Americans an opportunity to exercise equal political rights. Addressing economic inequities, the Johnson administration secured significant increases for a range of social programs. Between 1965 and 1970, federal spending on social security, health, education, and assistance to the poor doubled. Aided by impressive economic growth, Johnson's War on Poverty made considerable strides. In the second half of the 1960s, the poverty rate in the United States was nearly halved. Belatedly, the United States was catching up with Western European societies in constructing an expanded welfare state that preserved free enterprise while protecting citizens from the excesses of capitalism.

Legacies of racism and inequality were not easily overcome, however. In spite of Supreme Court decisions, most schools remained racially homogeneous. This was true not only in the South but across the United States, as white flight to the suburbs left inner-city neighborhoods and schools to racial minorities. Within these cities, frustration over discrimination and lack of economic opportunity led to violence: Riots in Watts, Newark, and Detroit killed scores of people and destroyed large sections of these communities. Within the African-American community, militant voices, like those of Malcolm X (1925–1965) and the Black Panthers, became more prominent. Instead of integration into white society, these radicals advocated black separatism, and instead of Americanism, they espoused pan-Africanism. Nonetheless, although black division and white backlash derailed the momentum of the civil rights movement, they did not reverse the gains made in erasing legal discrimination and political inequality.

African-American struggles against segregation and injustice inspired Native Americans, Mexican Americans, homosexuals, and women to initiate their own campaigns for equality and empowerment. Women came to question a life built around taking care of home and family. Historians often point to the introduction of the birth control pill in 1960 and the 1963 publication of Betty Friedan's *The Feminine Mystique* as watershed moments in American women's history. Within a year of the pill's arrival on the market, 1 million women in the United States were using this contraceptive. The availability of oral contraception allowed women to delay and limit childbearing and to have sex with less fear of pregnancy. This freedom helped unleash a sexual revolution. The pill alone, however, did not

Students at Woolworth's Lunch Counter. During the 1950s and 1960s, African Americans demanded the end of racial segregation in the United States. Borrowing the tactics of nonviolent civil disobedience championed by Mohandas Gandhi, civil rights protesters staged "sit-ins" across the southern United States, as in this photograph of black and white students seated together at a segregated Woolworth's lunch counter in Jackson, Mississippi. Protesters peacefully defied laws that prohibited African Americans from being served at "white" establishments.

liberate women. Friedan's best-seller blasted the myth of middle-class domestic contentment, describing the idealized 1950s suburban home as a "comfortable concentration camp" from which women must escape. In fact, the number of married women in the paid workforce was slowly rising, as was the number of college-educated women. But despite these educational attainments, working women discovered that their compensation and opportunity for advancement lagged far behind those of men.

The civil rights and women's movements of the early 1960s led many white college students to question the ideals of American society, but what turned this questioning into massive resistance was the escalation of the war in Vietnam. As the United States increased the number of its troops in Vietnam in the 1960s, it started to conscript more and more men into the armed services. Tens of thousands of young Americans fled the country to escape the draft. Upwards of 250,000 simply did not register for conscription, while another 100,000 burned their draft cards. As the decade progressed, protesters took to the streets of college towns around the country, and they descended upon Washington, D.C., as well. In April 1965, 25,000 people gathered for an antiwar protest in front of the White House, and two years later, a march on the Pentagon drew four times that number. After President Richard Nixon (1913–1994) sent American troops into Cambodia in 1970 to root out North Vietnamese soldiers who were hiding there, students at over

500 campuses rose in protest. Across the country, protesters occupied buildings and closed down universities. At Kent State University in Ohio, National Guardsmen, who had been called out to stop the protests, killed four students. The United States finally agreed to withdraw its troops from Vietnam in 1973, and Saigon (present-day Ho Chi Minh City) and South Vietnam fell to the Communists in 1975, but not before the divisions created by the war had put a great strain on the First World.

TENSIONS IN WORLD COMMUNISM

The unity of the Communist world also came under increasing pressure. As early as 1948, Yugoslavia had broken free of the Soviet embrace and embarked on its own road to building socialism. Other satellites within the Soviet bloc had more trouble freeing themselves. In 1956, Poland and Hungary were forced back in line. Twelve years later, Czechoslovakia experienced the "Prague Spring," in which Communist authorities experimented with policies to create a democratic and pluralist "socialism with a human face." Workers and students rallied behind the reformist government of Alexander Dubček (1921–1992), calling for more freedom of expression, more autonomy for workers and consumers, and more debate within the ruling party. Once again, Soviet tanks crushed this "counterrevolutionary" movement. As the Russian tanks rolled into Prague, the Czech capital, one desperate student doused himself with gasoline and lit a match—his public suicide a gesture of defiance against Communist rule. Thereafter, the Prague Spring served as a symbol for dissenters. Underground reading groups proliferated in cities across Eastern Europe; many Russians renewed their faith in Orthodox Christianity, returning to their prerevolutionary religion. Many dissidents were kicked out of the Soviet Union. The most famous by the early 1970s was the great Russian novelist Alexander Solzhenitsyn (1918–   ). His masterwork, *The Gulag Archipelago*, became a best-seller in the West and repudiated the notion that socialism could be reformed by a turn away from Stalin's policies. Yet, very few people in the Soviet Union were able to obtain copies of Solzhenitsyn's exposé, which had been published abroad.

Still, not all forms of Communist rule were eliminated. During the 1950s and 1960s, "national communism" became the rule throughout Eastern Europe, even in countries that had been disillusioned by Soviet invasions. National variations were also observable within the Soviet Union, where Moscow conceded some autonomy to the Communist Party machines of its fifteen republics—in exchange for fundamental loyalty. Cracks in the Soviet model, particularly in Eastern Europe, became points of tension and unease. The possibility of rupture became a reality in China. After

> *During the 1950s and 1960s, "national communism" became the rule throughout Eastern Europe, even in countries that had been disillusioned by Soviet invasions.*

the Chinese Revolution of 1949, Marxist ideology as well as a shared antipathy toward the United States had helped cement the Sino-Soviet alliance. By the late 1950s, the Soviet Union had contributed large amounts of military and economic aid to China. But the Chinese increasingly sought to define their own brand of Marxism, which the Soviets would not tolerate. And whereas the Soviets became interested in a lessening of tensions with the United States, the Chinese preferred to accentuate confrontation and to build their own nuclear weapons. Another key factor in the split was personal. At the beginning of China's Communist Revolution, Mao Zedong had had little choice but to defer to Stalin, who even pushed for and received extraterritoriality rights in China for Soviet advisers. But after Stalin died in 1953, Mao had little interest in deferring to Nikita Khrushchev. A split developed in 1960.

After the split, the Chinese aggressively presented themselves as a peasant-socialist alternative to the Soviet model of development, especially for Third World countries. The fissure raised China's profile throughout Asia and even reverberated into Eastern Europe. In the 1960s, Romania achieved a measure of autonomy in foreign policy by playing off China and the Soviet Union. Albania declared its allegiance to China. African nations, interested in Soviet aid, increased their demands with subtle hints that they might consider deepening ties with China. It was clear that the Second World, too, was no monolith.

TENSIONS IN THE THIRD WORLD

In contrast to the First and Second Worlds, the Third World was never unified by economic, military, or political alliances. While the common history of domination and the shared search for a third way provided some basis for mutual action, the cold war polarized Third World nations, pushing states to choose between alignment with the First World or the Second. Nonetheless, the rise of radicalism nourished new hopes for unifying and empowering the Third World.

Collaboration among Third World countries was difficult at best and unrewarding at most. One such attempt was the formation of a consortium of Third World oil exporters—Algeria, Ecuador, Gabon, Indonesia, Iran, Iraq, Kuwait, Libya, Nigeria, Qatar, Saudi Arabia, the United Arab Emirates, and Venezuela—to form a cartel, the Organization of Petroleum Exporting Countries (OPEC) in 1960. Through the 1960s, the cartel had little impact in raising oil revenues, even though several members did nationalize their oil fields. But after the fourth major Arab-Israeli war broke out, in the fall of 1973, OPEC's Arab members decided to pressure Israel's First World allies by halting oil exports to them. Overnight, the embargo lifted oil prices from $3 to $10 per barrel, a bonanza that enriched all oil

Chronology

1937	Japan invades China
1939	Britain and France declare war on Germany after Germany's invasion of Poland
1941	U.S. enters World War II
1944	World Bank and IMF established
1945	World War II ends
1945–1949	Nationalists fight Communists in China
1947	India and Pakistan gain independence
1948–1949	Berlin Blockade and Airlift
1948–1952	Marshall Plan
1948–1949	Arab-Israeli War
1948	Apartheid begins in South Africa
1949	NATO alliance formed
1949	Communist victory in China
1950–1953	Korean War
1950s–1960s	African nations gain independence
1950s–1960s	American civil rights movement
1954	Vietnamese defeat French
1954	CIA overthrow of Guatemalan government
1954–1962	Algerian War
1955	Warsaw Pact formed
1956	Egypt nationalizes the Suez Canal Company
1956	Soviet crackdown in Hungary
1957	Soviets launch Sputnik
1958–1961	China's Great Leap Forward
1958–1959	Cuban Revolution
1960	Creation of OPEC
1962	Cuban Missile Crisis
1966	China's Cultural Revolution
1968	Prague Spring in Czechoslovakia
1973	Arab oil embargo
1975	Fall of Saigon and end of Vietnam War

producers and led to an oil crisis in the West. To many, the bulging treasuries of OPEC nations seemed like the Third World's revenge. Here were Saudi Arabian princes, Venezuelan magnates, and Indonesian ministers dictating world prices to industrial consumers. American secretary of state Henry Kissinger later wrote that the oil embargo "altered irrevocably the world as it had grown up in the postwar period." Kissinger meant that the oil embargo confounded the cold war's balance of power by introducing a new set of powerful, nonallied players onto the stage.

But the realignment was not as thorough as Kissinger thought—or feared. Third World producers of other raw materials tried to duplicate OPEC's model, but these associations failed to control the market as effectively as the oil nations. OPEC's members also had trouble maintaining their control. During the 1970s, new discoveries in the North Sea, Mexico, and Canada reduced the pressures on the large oil-consuming states to be more fuel efficient as new supplies began to flood the oil market. With supply up, prices fell. To make up for lost revenue, various OPEC states raised their own production, putting further downward pressure on prices.

Nor did oil revenues do much to overcome the poverty and dependency of the Third World as a whole. To the contrary, most revenue surpluses from OPEC simply flowed back to First World banks or were plowed into real-estate holdings in Europe and the United States. Some of it was in turn re-loaned to the world's poorest countries in Africa, Asia, and Latin America, at high interest rates, to pay for more expensive imports—including oil! Moreover, the biggest bonanza from rising oil prices went to multinational petroleum firms whose control over production, refining, and distribution allowed them to reap enormous profits.

For all the talk in the mid-1970s of changing the balance of international economic relations between the world's rich and poor countries, fundamental inequalities were not redressed. For those nations that appeared to break out of the cycle of poverty, like South Korea and Taiwan, their successes did not result from the workings of international markets. Rather, the states regulated markets, nurtured new industries, educated the populace, and required multinationals to work more collaboratively with native firms. These were exceptions that proved the general rule: the international economy reinforced existing structures.

 CONCLUSION

The three-world order arose on the ruins of European empires, and that of their Japanese counterpart. First, the Soviet Union and the United States emerged as superpowers. Second, World War II affirmed the nation-state rather than the empire as the primary form for organizing communities; the formation of new nations completed this process. Third, in spite of the rhetoric of individualism and the free market, the war and the postwar reconstruction greatly enhanced the reach and functions of the modern state. Never before had the state enjoyed as great a role as in the postwar economies and societies of the Soviet Union and its Eastern European satellites, and of Western Europe and the United States. In the Third World, too, the leaders of new nations saw the state as the primary instrument for promoting economic development and creating nations.

The organization of the world into three blocs lasted into the mid-1970s. This arrangement fostered the economic recovery of Western Europe from the political and economic wounds inflicted by the war. Recovery was linked to a cold war alliance with the United States, where an economic boom was accompanied by anti-Communist hysteria. The cold war also cast a shadow over the citizens of the Soviet Union and Eastern Europe. Gulags and political surveillance became the lot of the people, while the Soviets and their satellite regimes mobilized resources for military purposes. The Third World, squeezed by its inability to reduce poverty, on the one hand, and superpower rivalry, on the other, struggled to pursue a "third way." While some states managed to maintain democratic institutions and promote economic development, many tumbled into dictatorships and authoritarian regimes. It was in this context that Third World revolutionaries took to radical programs of social and political transformation, seeking paths different from both Western capitalism and Soviet communism. Though not successful, they brought to the surface the considerable tensions in the three-world order. These tensions intensified in the late 1960s and the early 1970s as the Vietnamese Communists defeated the United States, the oil crisis struck the West, and protests against the existing order escalated in the First and Second Worlds. Thirty years after the war's end, the world order forged after 1945 was beginning to give way.

FURTHER READINGS

Anderson, Jon Lee, *Che Guevara: A Revolutionary Life* (1997). A sweeping study of the radicalization of Latin American nationalism.

Chatterjee, Partha, *Nationalist Thought and the Colonial World: A Derivative Discourse?* (1986). An influential interpretation of the ideological and political nature of Indian nationalism and the struggle for a postcolonial nation-state.

Crampton, R. J., *Eastern Europe in the Twentieth Century and After* (2nd ed., 1997). Comprehensive overview covering all Soviet-bloc countries.

Dower, John W., *Embracing Defeat: Japan in the Wake of World War II* (1999). A prize-winning study of the transformation of one of the war's vanquished.

Gao Yuan, *Born Red: A Chronicle of the Cultural Revolution* (1987). A gripping personal account of the Cultural Revolution by a former Red Guard.

Gordon, Andrew (ed.), *Postwar Japan as History* (1993). Essays covering a wide range of topics on postwar Japan.

Hargreaves, John D., *Decolonization in Africa* (1996). A good place to start when exploring the history of African decolonization.

Hasan, Mushirul (ed.), *India's Partition: Process, Strategy and Mobilization* (1993). A useful anthology of scholarly articles, short stories, and primary documents on the partition of India.

Iriye, Akira, *Power and Culture: The Japanese-American War, 1941–1945* (1981). A discussion that goes beyond the military confrontation in Asia.

Jackson, Kenneth T., *Crabgrass Frontier: The Suburbanization of the United States* (1985). An insightful and influential consideration of the movement of the American population from cities to suburbs.

Jalal, Ayesha, *The Sole Spokesman: Jinnah, the Muslim League and the Demand for Pakistan* (1985). A study of the high politics leading to the partition of British India.

Keep, John L. H., *Last of the Empires: A History of the Soviet Union, 1945–1991* (1995). A detailed overview of the core of the "Second World."

Morris, Benny, *Righteous Victims: A History of the Zionist-Arab Conflict, 1881–1999* (2000). On the Arab-Israeli War of 1948.

Overy, Richard, *Russia's War: Blood Upon the Snow* (1997). An up-to-date narrative about World War II's decisive Eastern Front.

Patterson, James T., *Grand Expectations: The United States, 1945–1974* (1996). Synthesizes the American experience in the postwar decades.

Patterson, Thomas, *Contesting Castro* (1994). The best study of the tension between the United States and Cuba. Culminating in the Cuban Revolution, it explores the deep American misunderstanding of Cuban national aspirations.

Ruedy, John, *Modern Algeria: The Origins and Development of a Nation* (1992). Gives the history of the Algerian nationalist movements and provides an overview of the Algerian war for independence.

Saich, Tony, and Hans van de Ven (eds.), *New Perspectives on the Chinese Communist Revolution* (1995). A collection of essays reexamining different aspects of the Chinese Communist movement.

Schram, Stuart, *The Thought of Mao Tse-tung* (1989). Standard work on the subject.

Wright, Gordon, *The Ordeal of Total War, 1939–1945* (1968). A superb treatment of the many dimensions of the war in Europe.

Zubkova, Elena, *Russia after the War: Hopes, Illusions, and Disappointments, 1945–1957* (1998). Uses formerly secret archives to catalogue the devastation and difficult reconstruction of one of the war's victors.

GLOBALIZATION

At the dawn of this new millennium, it is no longer necessary, as it was in the thirteenth century, to posit an imaginary traveler able to traverse all of the continents. Today, many people move around the world with ease and speed, spanning in a matter of hours the distances that it took Marco Polo and Ibn Battuta years to cover. Even those who do not travel still have the wider world brought into their homes via books, newspapers, televisions, and computers. Consider two very different, contemporary, settings: a fishing village in the Amazon River basin and the cosmopolitan sprawl of Los Angeles. Picture a sixty-four-year-old fisherman in an Amazonian village trying to teach his eleven children their parents' tongue, Cocama-Cocamilla, but to no avail. All his kids speak Spanish instead. "I tried to teach them," he notes. "It's like paddling against the current." Seven centuries ago, over 500 languages were spoken in the Amazon River basin. Today, only 57 languages survive there; and probably around half are doomed to extinction. Evidently, one effect of globalization is to reduce global diversity. But globalization can also lead to increasing local diversity. For example, Los Angeles, once the emblem of white, suburban America, today has become a cacophonous city of over 100 languages, from Hmong to Russian to Spanish.

Whole families, even whole groups, as well as goods and ideas, now cross over the boundaries that once divided religious, ethnic, and national communities. This is one aspect of what we call globalization, the major force for producing world integration. While not entirely new, the forces of globalization have had greater significance since the 1970s. These forces include new technologies, cultures, economic exchanges, and political movements that cross national borders with greater ease than ever before.

Yet, while this flow of capital, goods, people, and ideas across national boundaries weaves the world's population more tightly together, it has also produced different effects and experiences around the world. Most people do not travel in airplanes. Many move in response to local conflicts, political chaos, religious persecution, or simply in hopes of escaping poverty. In contrast to jet-setting global adventurers, these migrants often slip across borders in the dark of night or travel literally as human cargo inside containers. Billions of others continue to live in worlds set apart from the technological wonders—and economic opportunities—of the global age. Many are deprived of the benefits of the new integration. Thus, while globalization has created possibilities for some, it has also led to a deepening of income and power disparities between and within different regions of the world.

> *From the end of the three-world order emerged a new architecture of power that organized the world into a unified marketplace with virtually unhindered flows of capital, commerce, culture, and labor across borders.*

the twenty-first century is that the new forces driving global integration—and inequality—are no longer the large political empires that dominated the last centuries. Already by the middle of the twentieth century, the European empires that had ruled so much of the world during the nineteenth century had lost their sway. The cold war and decolonization movements that had dominated so many of the events immediately after World War II and had given rise to the three-world order had ceased to matter. The structures of power in the First World, under such stress in the 1970s, did not crack. But those in the Second World did. The cold war ended with the implosion of the Soviet bloc. The Third World also splintered, with some areas and regions becoming highly advanced, while others became mired in deeper poverty. From the end of the three-world order emerged a new architecture of power that organized the world into a unified marketplace with virtually unhindered flows of capital, commerce, culture, and labor across borders. By 2000, most of the world's societies had endorsed electoral systems and adopted some form of market economy.

The United States has promoted these changes, and globalization has looked to some like "Americanization." The United States has unquestionably emerged as the most influential society in the world, with its music, food, principles of representative government, and free markets spreading to most corners of the globe. Yet, the process has not run one way. The world has also come to America and shaped the texture of American society: the people living in the United States, their patented inventions, sports stars, and musical inspirations have been increasingly imported from elsewhere.

Nor has the United States been immune from the transnational forces that have challenged the power of the nation-state itself. In the United States, as elsewhere, globalization has increasingly functioned through networks of investment, trade, and migration that have operated relatively independently of nation-states. In the process, globalization has shaken

 GLOBAL INTEGRATION

> → *How has globalization changed the nation-state?*

The full impact and final consequences of our era's globalization remain unknown to us. What is clear at the beginning of

Focus Questions GLOBALIZATION

→ *How has globalization changed the nation-state?*

→ *What were the major obstacles to globalization?*

→ *What are the agents of globalization?*

→ *What are the characteristics of the New Global Order?*

→ *How has citizenship in the global world created new problems and responses?*

deep-rooted forms of political and social identification, from ecclesiastical to military authority. Nation-states have faced great difficulty commanding the imaginations of political communities: members of societies often identify more strongly with local, subnational, or even international movements or cultures. To be sure, nation-states remain essential for establishing democratic institutions and protecting human rights, but supranational institutions like the International Committee of the Red Cross, the European Union, and the International Monetary Fund often impinge on their autonomy.

Both the U.S. and the Soviet Union shared something of a common crisis: fatigue from the strains and costs of the cold war and an economic challenge from East Asia.

From the beginning of time, access to resources and the education to use them profitably have never been equitably distributed within and between societies. This remains so today—indeed, in many ways, economic and educational inequalities have increased. In the meantime, political rights have gradually been extended to more and more of the globe's inhabitants—though by no means to all. Thus, in 2002, there still exist worlds together and worlds apart, though these are dramatically different from those that existed in 1300.

REMOVING OBSTACLES TO GLOBALIZATION

> → *What were the major obstacles to globalization?*

In the mid-1970s, a set of political practices and institutions associated with the three-world order began to crumble. By the end of the 1980s, the Second World had begun to disintegrate. The collapse of the Soviet Union brought the cold war to an end. At the same time, the First World gave up the last of its colonial possessions, and the remnants of white settler supremacy crumbled. But as this occurred, the Third World's dream of a "third way" also vanished. As empires withdrew from the world historical stage, they revealed a world integrated by ties other than forced loyalties to imperial masters.

ENDING THE COLD WAR

A world divided between two hostile factions after World War II limited the prospects for the global exchange of peoples, ideas, and resources. The many regional conflicts of the cold war era (Vietnam, Afghanistan, Nicaragua) were costly for the countries caught in the ideological crossfire. Vietnam became a battleground for Russian, Chinese, and American ambitions. This war

spilled over into Laos and Cambodia, dragging these countries to ruin along with Vietnam. China attracted several client states in the struggle for influence in the Third World and within the Communist bloc. In Afghanistan, Moscow propped up a puppet regime, only to get drawn into a bloody war against Islamic guerrillas financed and armed by the United States. In Central America, U.S. president Ronald Reagan and his advisers opposed the victory of the left-leaning Nicaraguan "Sandinista" coalition in 1979. In the 1980s, the United States pumped millions of dollars to the "Contras" (opponents of the Sandinistas) and also lent military and monetary assistance to other Central American anti-Communist forces (although many Americans opposed such actions and even brought those involved to trial for overstretching their authority). Thus, for much of the world, the cold war was a real confrontation with tremendously high costs for local powers.

But the struggle was costly to the superpowers as well. The 1970s and 1980s saw the largest peacetime accumulation of arms in world history. Despite efforts to halt the arms buildups with endless rounds of treaties and summits, both the United States and the Soviet Union stockpiled their nuclear and conventional weaponry. To top things off and to add yet more to American military expenditures, in 1983 Reagan unveiled the Strategic Defense Initiative ("Star Wars" as some called it), a master plan to use satellites and space missiles to insulate the United States from incoming nuclear bombs. For both sides, though, military spending sprees brought economic troubles. Americans found themselves swapping old Fords for cheaper and more reliable Toyotas; in the Soviet Union, the civilian infrastructure decayed and life expectancies began to decline.

The cracks on either side of the Iron Curtain began to appear in the 1970s. The KGB and, to a lesser extent, the CIA, began producing secret memos questioning whether the Soviet bloc could sustain its global position. Stalemate in Afghanistan, a war that Soviet censors acknowledged only obliquely, destroyed the myth of the mighty Soviet armed forces. Mothers of Soviet soldiers protested the Kremlin's adventures abroad. The Eastern European satellites became dependent on Western European loans and consumer goods. At the same time, the Western alliance also faced internal tensions. In Europe and North America, the anti-nuclear movement rallied millions to the streets. Western industrialists worried about Japanese competition, as Japan had made great economic strides since it plowed its money into rapid industrialization rather than arms. Political leaders also grappled with distressingly high unemployment rates. Thus, both sides shared something of a common crisis: fatigue from the strains and costs of the cold war and an economic challenge from East Asia.

In the end, the Soviet bloc buckled—and then, with startling rapidity, collapsed (see Map 12-1). Moscow capitulated, ending the cold war, because it could no longer compete. Planned economies employed the entire population. But they failed to fill department stores with consumer goods for the masses. Socialist health care and benefits lagged behind those of the capitalist welfare states, especially of neighboring Western Europe; authoritarian political structures were based on deception and coercion rather than on elections and civic activism.

The catalyst in socialism's defeat proved to be Poland. A critical turning point was the naming of the Polish archbishop of Cracow as Pope John Paul II (1920–) in late 1978. The first non-Italian pope in 455 years, John Paul opposed Soviet socialism. In 1979, he made a pilgrimage to his native Poland, holding enormous outdoor masses; in 1980 he helped inspire and supported a series of mass strikes at the Gdansk shipyard, which led to the formation of the Soviet bloc's first independent trade union, Solidarity, led by the electrician Lech Walesa (1943–). As Communist Party members defected to its side, the union became a society-wide movement calling itself "civil society"; it aimed not to reform socialism (as in Czechoslovakia in 1968) but to abolish it. A crackdown by the Polish military and police in December 1981 put most of Solidarity's leadership in prison and drove the movement underground, but the KGB secretly reported that Solidarity would eventually triumph.

In 1985, instability mounted when Mikhail Gorbachev (1931–) became general secretary of the Soviet Communist Party and launched an effort to reform the Soviet system along the lines of the 1968 Prague Spring—permitting contested elections for Communist Party posts, relaxing censorship, sanctioning civic associations, legalizing small nonstate businesses, granting state firms autonomy, and encouraging the republics to be responsible for their affairs within the Union. Gorbachev's attempts to

The Berlin Wall. The breaching of the Berlin Wall in late 1989 spelled the end of the Soviet bloc. Decades of debate over whether communism could be reformed turned out to be moot. In the face of competition from the richer, consumer-oriented West, communism collapsed.

create "socialism with a human face" were combined with dramatic arms control initiatives to ease the superpower burden on the Soviet Union. He began a withdrawal from Afghanistan and informed Eastern European leaders that they could not count on Moscow's armed intervention to prop up their regimes.

Having set out to improve socialism, however, Gorbachev instead destabilized it. Civic groups called not for reform of the system but for its liquidation. Eastern Europe declared its intention to leave the Soviet orbit, and the leaders of the many Union republics pushed for independence. Gorbachev commanded more than 5 million loyal troops, 40,000 nuclear weapons, 44,000 tons of chemical weapons, and stockpiles of biological weapons, but rather than cracking down to save the regime or even wreaking global havoc out of spite, he let everything go. Some factions within the Communist Party and the Soviet military objected to Gorbachev's initiatives and tried to restore the crumbling system. A gang of hard-liners, including the chiefs of the KGB, military, and some top party officials, belatedly tried to preserve what was left of the crumbling system. They staged a disorganized coup in August 1991. The former Communist Party boss of Moscow and president of the Russian republic, Boris Yeltsin (1931–), however, rallied the opposition and faced down the hard-liners. Under Yeltsin, Russia, like Ukraine and the other republics of the Soviet Union, became a refuge for the beleaguered Soviet elites, who abandoned the cause of the Union and socialism and became preoccupied with dividing up state property among themselves.

When Communist regimes collapsed, the European and

Lech Walesa. A Polish electrician from the Lenin Shipyard in the Baltic port city of Gdansk, Lech Walesa spearheaded the formation of Solidarity, a mass independent trade union of workers who opposed the Communist regime that ruled in their name. He later went on to be elected president of post-Communist Poland.

→ *What were the major obstacles to globalization?*

MAP 12-1 COLLAPSE OF THE COMMUNIST BLOC IN EUROPE

The Soviet Union's domination of Eastern Europe began to falter in the 1980s and came to an end in the 1990s. The political map of Eastern and Central Europe took on a different shape. Identify the new states that came into being in the 1990s. In what part of Eastern and Central Europe did the collapse of the Communist bloc produce the most political instability and conflict? Can you speculate on why this was so? The political reordering involved the unification of previously separate countries and the breakup of previously unified states. Identify the countries that were newly unified and those that broke apart. Try to account for why some merged and others fragmented.

TIDAL PULL OF THE WEST: EAST GERMANY DISAPPEARS

After Soviet premier Mikhail Gorbachev instituted a series of reforms to save socialism, dissenters in Eastern Europe saw their chance to throw off Russian dominance. The Berlin Wall was the most visible symbol of Soviet oppression. Here journalist Ann Tusa recalls the November 1989 press conference that accidentally led to the opening of the Berlin Wall (first erected in 1961). As both the Wall and East Germany fell, Russia kept its nearly 400,000 troops that were on East German soil confined to their barracks.

At about 7 o'clock on the evening of November 9, 1989, some 300 journalists from all over the world are crammed into a room in East Berlin for a routine press conference. . . . For the first time since the foundation of a separate Communist East German state in 1946, the German Democratic Republic, there have been massive demonstrations against the regime. . . . The Communist Party's only response so far has been to shuffle the men at the top . . .

East Germans, who have not known a free election since 1933, have been voting with their feet. From January to October 1989, some 200,000 people had left their country. By early November the figure was up to 250,000—and that was out of a total population of 16.7 million. At first, many East Germans went out on "holiday visas" to Iron Curtain countries, then claimed asylum in West German embassies in Warsaw, Budapest or Prague. Thousands more have driven or walked round the East German frontiers looking for an undefended crossing or a guard with a blind eye, wriggled across, then headed for Austria and a refugee camp. . . .

The November 9 press conference is handled by Günter Schabowski. . . . This evening he feeds the press a startling hint that there might soon be free elections. Good story. Everyone wants to go out and file it. But then Schabowski turns up a sheet from the bottom of the pile of papers on his table. "This will be interesting for you." And in a style that suggests it is all news to him, slowly reads aloud: "Today the decision was taken to make it possible for all citizens to leave the country through the official border crossing points. All citizens of the GDR can now be issued with visas for the purposes of travel or visiting relatives in the West. This order is to take effect at once. . . ."

The news is broadcast on an East German television bulletin at 7:30 P.M. The station's switchboard is immediately jammed with callers. "Is it true? I can't believe it." They always believed West German television, though, and it is soon flashing the announcement. A few East and West Berliners go to the Wall to see what is happening. . . . Then at 10:30 a discussion program on Sender Freies Berlin, the West Berlin television station, is interrupted by a live broadcast from the Wall. No preamble, just shots of a small crowd milling round a checkpoint, then a man runs toward the camera: "They've opened the crossing at Bornholmer Strasse." After that the news spreads like wildfire, by radio, television, telephone, shouts in the street. The trickle across the Wall swells to a flood. That weekend 2 million East Germans are reckoned to have stood in West Berlin. One reaction is common to them all: "We've seen the West on TV, of course. But this is real."

. . . The fatal piece of paper had been hurriedly swept up as he left for the press conference. It had never been intended for publication. It was a draft based on a recent Politburo decision: unable to control the tide of refugees, thrashing around for ways to quiet the demonstrators on the streets, they had decided that in their own good time they would ease travel restrictions, having first made arrangements for a limited issue of visas under carefully controlled circumstances.

Source: Ann Tusa, "A Fatal Error," in *Media Studies Journal*, Fall 1999, pp. 26–29.

Asian political maps changed dramatically. Old states disappeared, and many more were born. In Asia, although division between North and South Korea remained, Vietnam was united and, along with China, opened its country to Western capitalism. In Europe, however, East Germany ceased to exist; its remnants were folded into West Germany in 1990, shortly after the Berlin Wall came down in 1989. Gone was the original dividing line that froze the antagonisms between East and West. Soon followed the voluntary dissolution of the Soviet empire into independent states (see Map 12-2). But the end of Soviet-style socialism and of the Soviet Union was not entirely peaceful. In Moldova (formerly referred to as Moldovia and sandwiched between Ukraine and Romania), Tajikistan (which bordered Afghanistan), and across the Caucasus, regional wars

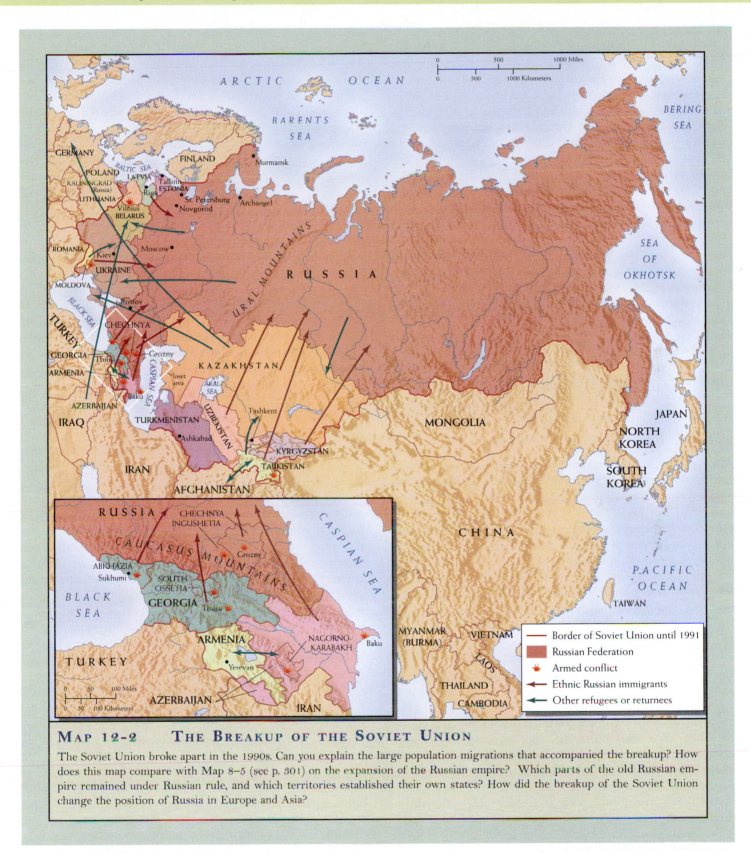

MAP 12-2 THE BREAKUP OF THE SOVIET UNION

The Soviet Union broke apart in the 1990s. Can you explain the large population migrations that accompanied the breakup? How does this map compare with Map 8–5 (see p. 301) on the expansion of the Russian empire? Which parts of the old Russian empire remained under Russian rule, and which territories established their own states? How did the breakup of the Soviet Union change the position of Russia in Europe and Asia?

broke out over pent-up grievances and the spoils of the Soviet era. But the worst carnage took place in the former Yugoslavia, where the collapse of communism took the form of a violent tug of war between manipulative leaders playing to ethnic fears. Serbs and Croats, in particular, engaged in savage struggles over territories in the Balkans. The overcoming of the

East-West political divide did not lead to peace and prosperity in the former East, but with a few exceptions (such as Poland), to political and economic stagnation and disenchantment. Despite newly opened borders, the old gap between East and West widened, for the collapse and cannibalization of Soviet-era structures continued well beyond 1989–1991.

By historical standards, the cold war had been relatively brief, spanning four decades. But communism had played a major role in the military conflicts and unprecedented modernization of two of Eurasia's largest societies, Russia and China, and it exercised an important influence on a third, India. Communism was, as one historian observed, a heavy-metal ideology. For the lighter stuff, it was ill-suited; it could not keep up the cold war fight *and* deliver a universal good life to its citizenry *and* survive in a more competitive world economy.

> Communism, a heavy-metal ideology, was ill suited for the lighter stuff. It could not keep up the cold war and deliver a universal good life to its citizenry and survive in a more competitive world economy.

AFRICA AND THE END OF WHITE RULE

Although the two decades that followed the end of World War II saw the dismantling of most of Europe's formal empires, remnants of colonial rule remained in the southern part of Africa (see Map 11-6 on p. 403). Here, whites held firmly to the centuries-old notions of innate white racial superiority over non-European peoples. Final decolonization meant that self-rule would return to all of Africa.

The last fortresses under direct European control were the Portuguese colonies of southern and western Africa, which, dating to the fifteenth century, had been the first European colonies on the continent. But, by the mid-1970s, efforts to suppress African nationalist movements had exhausted Portugal's resources. Demoralized and fed up, Portuguese officers pushed aside the dictatorship founded by Antonio Salazar (1889–1970) and began the Portuguese experiment with democracy in 1974–1975. The African nationalist demands for freedom led to a hurried Portuguese withdrawal from Guinea-Bissau, Angola, and Mozambique. Thus did formal European colonialism in Africa come to an end.

But white rule still prevailed elsewhere in Africa. In Rhodesia, a tiny white minority clung to power and resisted all international pressure to give way to black rule. In the end, independent African neighbors helped support a liberation guerrilla movement under Robert Mugabe. Surrounded, Rhodesian whites finally capitulated. Mugabe swept to power with massive electoral support in 1979. The new constitutional government renamed the country Zimbabwe, depriving the long-deceased British expansionist Cecil Rhodes of having a country bearing his name.

The final outpost of white rule was South Africa, where a European minority was much larger, richer, and more entrenched than elsewhere on the continent. Here, international firms were much more reluctant to enforce any boycott on the racist regime. For the United States, South Africa's large army was a useful tool to fight Soviet allies in other parts of southern Africa. The Afrikaner-led National Party seemed invulnerable to international economic and cultural pressures, and it used ruthless tactics in dealing with its internal critics. Yet, in the countryside and cities, defiance of white rule was growing. Africans not only lobbed rocks and Molotov cocktails at tanks, they also organized mass strikes in the country's multinational-owned mines. At the same time, pressures from abroad were mounting. South African athletes were banned from the Olympics starting in 1970. American students insisted that their universities "divest" themselves of companies that had investments in South Africa. As international pressures increased, foreign governments, including the United States, applied economic sanctions against South Africa. Around the world, a swelling chorus demanded that Nelson Mandela, the imprisoned leader of the African National Congress (ANC), be freed.

The white political elite eventually realized that it could not maintain apartheid without becoming a pariah police state and that it was better to negotiate new arrangements than to endure years of internal warfare against a majority population and international ostracism. In Nelson Mandela, South Africa's white rulers found a man of exceptional integrity and political savvy. Mandela had every right to be vengeful. He had spent more than two decades in prison, much of it at hard labor. But he looked beyond past injustices to settle the transition to full democracy. Besides, he was aware that, with the country veering toward civil war, only a negotiated change would preserve South Africa's industries, wealth, and educational system.

In 1990, President F. W. de Klerk (of the National Party) released Mandela from prison and legalized the ANC and the Communist Party of South Africa. The ensuing negotiations between the ANC and the National Party produced South Africa's first free, mass elections in April 1994. These resulted in an overwhelming victory for the ANC, with Nelson Mandela elected as president. Majority rule had finally come to South Africa, and for the first time in many centuries, Africans ruled over all of Africa.

Still, the leaders of politically independent Africa did not deliver on many of their promises. Decolonized Africa was beset by immense problems. New political rulers faced the arduous task of building coherent and stable political communities where

The End of Apartheid. *(Left)* Nelson Mandela, running for president in 1994 as the candidate of the African National Congress, is shown here casting a ballot in the first all-races election in South Africa. This election brought an end to apartheid and saw the African National Congress take control of the Republic of South Africa under Mandela's presidency. *(Right)* After the overwhelming electoral triumph of Nelson Mandela in South Africa's first free and democratic election, F. W. de Klerk, leader of the once powerful Afrikaner-dominated National Party, shakes hands with his successor.

artificial colonies had previously existed. In their effort to do so, Africans set out to destroy the vestiges of colonial political structures and to erect new African-based public institutions. Turning colonial subjects into citizens of nation-states was not easy, however, for it often created local contests for political power. Ethnic and religious rivalries, held in check to a degree in the colonial period, burst forth at independence. Civil wars erupted, and military leaders were drawn into politics. Coups d'état became common, and the ruling elements increasingly kept themselves in power by using the resources of the state to reward their clients and to punish their enemies. By the 1990s, the continent was aflame with civil strife—armed conflicts that started with the cold war and lasted well after it ended.

UNLEASHING GLOBALIZATION

> ↠ *What are the agents of globalization?*

With many of the political and ideological obstacles to international integration dissolving, capital, commodities, people, and culture crossed borders with ever-greater freedom. Most states of the world moderated restraints on the flow of resources, ideas, and individuals across borders, changing, for example, tariff and immigration laws. While trade, foreign investment, migration, and cultural borrowing have long been

hallmarks of modern history, the global age has changed the sheer scale of these activities. Nonetheless, as we shall also see, never have there been so many inequities in access to and distribution of the fruits of globalization.

FINANCE AND TRADE

The increased flow of goods and capital across national boundaries was already well underway in the 1970s, but the end of the cold war removed many impediments to globalization. During the 1990s, even the strongest of nation-states, such as the United States, were affected by economic globalization.

Major transformations started to occur in the world's financial system in the 1970s. America's budget and trade deficits prompted President Richard Nixon to take the dollar off the gold standard in 1971, an action that facilitated global financial transfers. One by one, the yen, the lira, the pound, the franc, and other national currencies cut their ties to the American dollar. Gone were centuries of "hard" money, anchored to silver or gold, or fixed to a solid reserve currency, like the British pound or American dollar. With the end of any fixed standard for money, international financial affairs enjoyed greater freedom from national regulators and found fresh business opportunities. A new system of informal management of money across borders replaced an older system of formal management within borders. Where formal management of world financial relations existed, it was exercised increasingly by international authorities such as the Bank for International Settlements and the International Monetary Fund to monitor world financial relations.

World Tourism. One of the signs of increasing globalization is the importance of world tourism. By the thousands, travelers venture to remote corners of the world, bringing with them many of the components of world consumerism. This image of the ancient Inca capital (Cuzco) in the Andes conveys how old colonial architecture gets combined with the latest of modern financial services (such as the Visa card).

The primary agents of this heightened global financial activity were some old actors: banks. Based mainly in London, New York, and, increasingly, in Tokyo, commercial banks became conduits for large amounts of mobile capital looking for lucrative ventures. The revenues from oil producers provided a large injection of cash into the global economy in the 1970s. At the same time, banks joined forces to issue mammoth loans to developing nations.

The banks found important academic allies whose treatises laid out the economic rules of financial and fiscal sobriety for a global economic environment. These intellectuals were primarily North American–trained economists who were schooled in a new framework of economic thinking, one that minimized the welfare concerns that had been so fundamental to the Keynesian approach. This younger generation of economists emphasized the power of unfettered markets and profit motivations as the cornerstone of capitalist economic development. Employed in banks and ministries around the world, they argued that the old regulatory and interventionist policies of nation-states prevented rather than promoted economic growth. Working as advisers in many governments, but especially under Margaret Thatcher in Britain and Ronald Reagan in the United States, these economists effectively guided public policy to deregulate market life.

Changes in the international financial sector now made it easier for investors to transact business. They could also buy each other out with much less government intrusion. In the United States, for instance, deregulators broke down old barriers to the integration of commercial and investment banking and spawned a transformation in world banking.

No international financial organization, however, played a more decisive role than the International Monetary Fund (IMF). As the 1980s unfolded, the IMF emerged as a central player, especially in response to what was called "the debt crisis" in Third World and Eastern-bloc countries. Throughout the 1970s, European, Japanese, and North American banks had loaned money on very easy terms to cash-strapped Third World and Eastern-bloc borrowers. But what was once good business soon turned sour. In 1982, a wave of defaults threatened to overrun Latin America in particular. Through the 1980s, international banks and the IMF kept heavily indebted customers solvent. The IMF offered short-term loans to governments on condition that recipients adopt new fiscal and financial ways and compel civilian populations to tighten their belts. Latin Americans pioneered the process of merging their domestic markets with international ones. Trade barriers crumbled; state enterprises became private firms; and foreign investors called the former debtors "emerging markets." Eastern Europe and Asia followed suit in the 1990s, and emerging market mania buoyed a boom in international finance.

New technologies and institutions enabled many more financial investors and traders to participate in these integrated networks of world finance. The Internet and online trading accelerated the mobility—and volatility—of capital across borders. For instance, in the United States, the amount of American investment abroad in bonds and equities soared nearly tenfold between 1980 and 1990 and expanded even more in the following decade. Volatility soon created problems, however. In the 1990s, currency devaluations in Mexico, Russia, and across East Asia shocked financiers. Panicky investors pulled their money out of risky holdings, leaving entire continents gasping for financial oxygen.

Globalization increased commercial, as well as financial, interdependence. There was a nearly tenfold increase in the total value of world trade between 1973 and 1998, and it grew faster in Asia. In 1960, trade accounted for 24 percent of the world's gross domestic product (GDP); by 1995, the share had climbed to 42 percent. Where an American would once have worn American-made clothes (Levi's), driven an American car (a Ford), and watched an American television (Zenith), such was not necessarily the case by century's end. More and more, consumers bought goods and services provided by foreigners and sold a greater share of their own output abroad. This pattern had always been true of smaller countries and regions like Central America or southern Africa. But in the 1980s, it intensified, with Hong Kong and Singapore prospering thanks to expanding world trade.

International trade not only made people more interdependent, but it also shifted the international division of labor. After the Second World War, Europeans and North Americans had dominated manufacturing, while Third World countries

Japanese Market in Los Angeles. After the enactment of a new immigration law in 1965, the influx of millions of immigrants from Latin America and Asia profoundly altered the ethnic composition of the population of the United States. Nowhere was the change more evident than in Los Angeles, where by the year 2000 the foreign-born accounted for 40 percent of the population. Immigrants brought a new cosmopolitanism to cities like Los Angeles, where the foods of the world were readily available at diverse restaurants and markets.

concentrated on raw materials. By the 1990s, this was no longer the case. Brazil became a major airplane maker, South Korea exported millions of automobiles, and China emerged as the world's largest source of textiles, footwear, and, increasingly, electronics.

The most remarkable global shift involved the rise of East Asian industry and commerce. Manufactured goods, including high-technology products, were now built on the eastern fringe of Eurasia as often as on its western fringe. Building on its postwar "miracle" (see Chapter 11), Japan blazed the Asian trail. Between 1965 and 1990, its share of world trade doubled to almost 10 percent. China, too, began to flex its economic muscle. When Deng Xiaoping (1905–1997) took power in 1978, China was already a growing economy. Under Deng, China started to become an economic powerhouse for Asia. For the next two decades, China chalked up astounding 10 percent annual growth rates, swelling its share of world GDP from 5 percent to 12 percent.

For East Asia as a whole, the share of world exports also doubled in the same period, to 22 percent, with smaller countries like Singapore, Taiwan, South Korea, and Hong Kong becoming mini-powerhouses. By the early 1990s, these countries and Japan also became major investors abroad. Japan alone was the world's largest foreign investor. Overall, East Asia's share of world production rose from 13.6 percent to 25.3 percent between 1965 and 1989. By contrast, over the same period, the U.S. share shrank from 38.6 percent to 35.4 percent, and Europe's share decreased from 33.5 percent to 30.6 percent.

Industrialization of previously less developed countries, combined with lower trade barriers, increased the pressures of world competition on national economies. Some areas responded to global competition by creating regional blocs. In North America, a great deal of trade and finance flowed back and forth across the U.S.-Canadian border. By the 1980s, fearing competition from inexpensive Asian manufactures, the two North American countries decided to admit Mexico into the trading bloc, to encourage plants to locate within the continent. They negotiated a North American Free Trade Agreement (NAFTA) in the early 1990s. The most complete process of regional integration took place in Europe. Europeans slashed trade barriers and harmonized their commercial policies toward the rest of the world. In December 1991, the Maastricht Treaty won the approval of most European states, which paved the way for creating a single European currency, the euro. Maastricht became, in effect, the constitution for the European Union, which was to be a fully integrated trading and financial bloc with its own bureaucracy and elected representatives.

Trade integration and interdependence coincided with a transformation in what was traded. Pharmaceuticals, computers, software, and services from insurance to banking have become ever more important exports and imports. High technology, in particular, occupies an ever greater share of the manufacturing and exports of the world's richest countries. Between 1970 and 1993, as a share of exports, high-tech shipments abroad rose from 16 percent to 21 percent in Germany, 20 percent to 37 percent in Japan, and 26 percent to 37 percent in the United States. Since the 1970s, the most important contributors to cutting-edge technologies have been information sciences and the production and distribution of goods and services requiring a highly skilled labor force.

Competition and the shift to the production of sophisticated goods has had enormous effects on world incomes. For the "rich" countries as a whole, about half of total GDP is based on the production and distribution of these goods and services, giving them a competitive advantage over other countries. In general, where global incomes are lower and people are less educated, the share of knowledge as a contributor to wealth is also lower. Poor nations remain, with few exceptions, locked in the production of low-tech goods and the export of raw materials. Between 1976 and 1996, as the share of high-tech goods in total world trade doubled from 11 percent to 22 percent, the share of primary products shrank from 45 percent to under 25 percent. Increasingly, technology and knowledge now divide the world into affluent, technically sophisticated countries and poor, technically underdeveloped regions.

MIGRATION

Not only do capital and products flow across borders, but the migration of peoples also knits our world together. Migration has been a constant feature of world history. But in the twentieth century, and especially after the 1970s, the movement of peoples within and across national boundaries became more widespread (see Map 12-3). True, the relative numbers did not

East Europeans 1918–1919

East Europeans 1918–1919

Russian Jews to USA 1980s and 1990s

European Jews to USA 1930s

West Indians to Britain

Spaniards to Mexico 1936

1950–

CANADA

UNITED
STATES

ATLANTIC
OCEAN

1950–

1960–

MEXICO

CUBA
1960–1980

BELIZE

HAITI

GUATEMALA

NICARAGUA

COLOMBIA

GREAT
BRITAIN

FRAN

SPAIN

1950

MOROCCO

ALGERIA

1970

IVORY
COAST

1970

PACIFIC
OCEAN

BRAZIL

1980

ARGENTINA

Foreign-born people as percentage of
total population (latest available year)

- Less than 1.5%
- 1.5%–2.9%
- 3.0%–7.5%
- More than 7.5%
- Data not available
- Migration

0   1000   2000 Miles

0   1000   2000 Kilometers

MAP 12-3 WORLD MIGRATION, 1918–1998

The world's population continued to grow and to change locations in the twentieth century. Compare the areas of most rapid population growth in Map 9–3 (pp. 318–19) with those parts of the world that, according to this map, had the highest proportion of foreign born. Can you identify the overlap countries? The migration arrows in this map show the directions in which populations were moving. Which parts of the world were the sending areas, which were the receiving territories, and why was this the case? Explain the factors that led Australia, New Zealand, Indonesia, Saudi Arabia, South Africa, Libya, France, and Canada to have the largest proportion of foreign born. Do these factors tend to be the same for all of these countries, or are they specific to each country? Some of the migrations occur over long periods of time, like Europeans to Australia and New Zealand from 1918 onward, while others are limited to one or two years, like the emigration out of Vietnam in 1975. The one- or two-year migrations were usually related to highly specific events. Can you identify and then explain these one-year or two-year-long migrations?

Poles and Baltic peoples to Siberia 1939–1940

RUSSIA

1930s and 1940s

Russian Jews to Israel 1980s and 1990s

AND
1918–1922
UKRAINE
1945
1922
TURKEY
GEORGIA 1922
1945–
ISRAEL
1947
AFGHANISTAN 1979
PAKISTAN
1947
BANGLADESH
CHINA
NORTH KOREA
1950–1954
SOUTH KOREA
JAPAN
YA
EGYPT
1980
1947–
SAUDI ARABIA
1970
INDIA 1972
1947
HONG KONG
to Canada
PACIFIC OCEAN
1970–
Falashas to Israel 1991
SUDAN mid 1980s
THAILAND
VIETNAM
to UK
to USA
ETHIOPIA 1980s
to Western Europe and USA
1975
MALAYSIA
1975
1975
RWANDA 1994
CONGO
to France
Southeast Asians to Australia 1970s
INDONESIA
TANZANIA
MOZAMBIQUE
INDIAN OCEAN
BOTSWANA 1960–
1960–
AUSTRALIA
SOUTH AFRICA
Europeans to Australia/New Zealand 1918–
NEW ZEALAND

reach the scale of demographic reshuffling of Europeans to the Americas from 1880 to 1914. Although after 1970, fewer Europeans were on the move, more Asians, Africans, and Latin Americans had become mobile. Indeed, one of the important destinations was Europe. By 2000, there were 120 million migrants scattered across 152 countries, up from 75 million in 1965. The vast majority of these migrants left poorer countries for richer destinations.

Who went where and why? To a large extent, migratory flows conformed to the contours of existing political relations. Where North America and Europe had colonies or dependencies, their political withdrawal left tracks for migrants to follow. Indians and Pakistanis moved to Britain. Dominicans, Haitians, and Mexicans went to the United States. Algerians and Vietnamese moved to France. And where emerging rich societies cultivated close diplomatic ties, these relations opened migratory gates. This was the case, for instance, of Germany's relationship with Turkey, Japan's with South Korea, and Canada's with Hong Kong. And in most cases, economic factors were what propelled migrants across national borders.

International migration was often an extension of regional and national migration, from poorer, rural areas to urban centers. In Nigeria, for example, rural-urban migration intensified after 1970. In 1900, Nigeria's capital, Lagos, had a population of 41,847. At the century's end, it had more than 10 million people, with predictions that it would grow to 20 million by 2025. The key to Lagos's boom in the 1970s was its black gold: oil. When OPEC sent oil prices soaring after 1973, money poured into Nigeria. The government kept most of it in the capital. That, in turn, encouraged people from the countryside to move to Lagos. This rural-urban migration increased Lagos's population by 14 percent per year in the 1970s and 1980s. No government, least of all a new, weakly supported one like Nigeria's, could cope with such a huge population influx. Electricity supplies failed regularly. There were never enough schools or teachers or textbooks. But the city burst with the vitality of the new arrivals, prompting one new immigrant to exclaim: "It's a terrible place; I want to go there."

The search for opportunities that sent people from the countryside to the cities also pushed them across national borders. Just as money and jobs in cities stimulated movement from rural areas to urban areas, so, too, did global inequities stimulate mass movements from less developed to more developed nations. Although many corporations relocated their manufacturing plants in poorer countries, where unskilled labor was abundant and government regulations were few, these jobs remained less attractive than even the lowest wage positions available in richer nations. Thus,

the possibility for better wages—and the hope for better lives—inspired millions to leave their homelands.

As in earlier times, some internal and international migrants moved for only temporary sojourns. At least that was the original intent. In the 1950s and 1960s, southern Europeans moved northward, but when Spain, Portugal, Greece, and Italy also became wealthy societies, not only did the exodus decline, but these countries became magnets for Middle Eastern, North African, and more recently Eastern European migrants. Europeans' strong identification with their nations did not permit the easy integration of foreigners. Nor did European states support the permanent settlement of immigrants. Most of the migrants from Asia and Africa went initially to Europe in search of "temporary" jobs and were known as guest workers.

In Japan, too, immigrants were not easily incorporated into public life. Tokyo's policy in the 1970s resembled the European guest worker program in Europe. Discouraging permanent settlement and immigration, Japan encouraged mainly itinerant workers to move to the country, yet its economy required increasing numbers of these sojourners. Indeed, Japan's deep reluctance to integrate migrants has led to dire labor shortages—as late as 1998, only 1.1 million foreigners had registered as residents in Japan.

After Japan, the economic boomers of Hong Kong, Taiwan, and Malaysia all became hosts for temporary migrants. The result was that millions of guest workers moved to these destinations, but after years of living in prosperous Asian and European cities, migrants sank ever deeper roots, especially once their children began to enter schools. This created a new challenge in host societies that were accustomed to thinking of national communities as ethnically homogeneous. At times, the discrimination and exclusion ran high and led to violent backlashes. Governments also grappled with the challenge of extending citizenship rights to newcomers.

One society that had far fewer problems integrating migrants and that attracted the lion's share of international migrants was the United States. For a long time a magnet for Europeans, the United States enacted an immigration reform in 1965 that threw open its gates to the world's migrants. Latin Americans, and especially Mexicans, accounted for the largest single source of migrants to the United States. By 2000, 27 million immigrants lived in the United States, accounting for almost 10 percent of the population—double the share in 1970. The profile of migration also changed dramatically. In 1970, there were more Canadians or Germans living in the United States than Mexicans. In the ensuing thirty years, the Mexican influx rose tenfold, and by 2000 accounted for almost one-third of the

> *Global inequities stimulated mass movements from less developed to more developed countries.*

immigrants in the United States. The numbers migrating from Asia also surged, accounting for over 40 percent of all immigrants to the United States in the 1990s.

As the world came to the United States, it transformed American cities. Nowhere was the changing ethnic composition of American cities more vivid than in Los Angeles, which had been the "whitest" of major American cities until it became the destination for millions of migrants after the 1965 Immigration Act. By the end of the twentieth century, two out of five Los Angelenos were foreign-born, and more than 40 percent of residents were Latino. Likewise, the proportion of Asians jumped fivefold. The percent of African Americans showed a similar rise beginning in 1930, though much of this expansion took place before 1965.

Americans continue to grapple with the challenge of bridging the widening gap between where one lives and one's nationality, between residence and citizenship. This issue has been fraught with tensions, as some longtime residents of the southwestern states, in particular, object to spending tax dollars on non-English-speaking immigrants. The arguments in Los Angeles over schools and health care for resident noncitizens have been part of a global debate. In Argentina, 200,000 undocumented Peruvians, Bolivians, and Paraguayans also live without rights as citizens. Even more staggering, between 3 and 8 million migrants have moved from Mozambique, Zimbabwe, and Lesotho to South Africa. In some Middle Eastern countries, like Saudi Arabia and Kuwait, the share of foreign-born workers tops 70 percent of the workforce. In general, migrants have been only partially accommodated, while many have been fully excluded from the mainstream of host societies. Thus, even though population movements have flowed across political, kinship, and market networks, the great demographic reshuffling resulting from globalization has heightened national concerns about the ethnic makeup of political communities.

Finally, forced migrations have remained a hallmark of the modern world. But rather than migration of slaves from Africa, the more recent involuntary flows have been of refugees fleeing civil war and torture. Many have not been able to migrate far, and they have been left to suffer for weeks, months, or years in refugee camps on the periphery of the violence. It is hardly surprising that the greatest concentration of refugees has occurred on the poorest continent—Africa. Those Africans who have not been able to make their way to the wealthier areas of the world have often been caught up in ethnic and religious conflicts that have resulted in vast refugee camps, where people live through the generosity of host governments and international contributions.

> *Americans continue to grapple with the challenge of bridging the widening gap between where one lives and one's nationality, between residence and citizenship.*

CULTURE

Migrations and new technologies have contributed to the creation of a more global entertainment culture as well. In this domain above all, globalization is often equated with Americanization. Yet, the American entertainments that have spread around the world have themselves been shaped by artistic practices from diverse parts of the globe, as one mass culture meets another. On the global scale, there was less diversity in 2000 than in 1300; but on the level of the individual's everyday experience, the potential for experiencing cultural diversity—if one could afford the technology to do so—was greatly increased.

NEW MEDIA Technology has played an important part in the diffusion of entertainment. In the 1970s, cassette tapes became the dominant circulating medium for popular music, sidelining the long-playing record and the short-lived eight-track tape. Cassette tapes could be illegally mass reproduced at home by bootleggers who disregarded copyright laws and sold them cheaply to young consumers. Television was another globalizing force. American producers bundled old dramas and situation comedies to stations around the world. Finally, films created global cultural linkages. American movie distributors sent movies to theaters around the world and made videocassettes of movies that were distributed (and also illegally copied) worldwide. But Americans were not the only entertainment exporters. Brazilian soap operas began to penetrate Spanish-language American TV markets in the 1980s, often inducing Mexican viewers to rush home from work to catch the latest episode. Latin American television shows and music were distributed in the United States in areas that had large Spanish-speaking populations. Bombay also produced its fair share of programs for viewers of British television. Movies and actors from New Zealand, Australia, France, Italy, China, and Iran found audiences in Europe and the United States.

In the early 1980s, a new form of television programming took off: cable. Once again, the United States pioneered the medium. But the innovation also caught on elsewhere. Increasingly, viewers had access to dozens, even hundreds, of specialized channels, challenging the dominance of the traditional "national" networks. Cable TV networks like MTV were devoted to pop music and introduced music videos, which popularized performers who had learned that a "rock video" was both a musical and a visual product.

Television's globalizing effects were especially evident in sports. In many parts of the globe, American sports made particularly deep inroads. This included the increasing number of foreigners participating in American sports, and more important, the increasing television time devoted to the broadcast of American games in other countries. The National Basketball Association (and the athletic footwear firm Nike) was particularly successful in its international marketing, and in the process made Michael Jordan the world's best-known athlete, and perhaps the world's best-known person, at the end of the twentieth century. Soccer (known as football outside the United States) became an international passion, with devoted national followings for national teams. Indeed, by the 1980s, soccer was becoming *the* world sport, and its fate was decided increasingly by television ratings. The organizers of the 1986 World Cup in Mexico insisted that big soccer matches be held at midday so that games could be televised live at prime time in Europe. As the players grumbled about having to play under the scorching sun, the president of the World Soccer Federation (FIFA), Brazilian magnate João Havelange, told them to stop complaining and just play soccer.

GLOBAL CULTURE Technology was not the only driving force of world cultures. Migration was also important. As people moved around, they brought with them their musical tastes, and they borrowed from other cultures they encountered. Reggae, born in the 1960s among Jamaica's Rastafarians, became a hit sensation in London and Toronto, where large West Indian communities had moved in the 1960s and 1970s. Reggae lyrics and realist imagery invoked a black countercultural sensibility and a redemptive call for a return to African roots. Soon, Bob Marley and the Wailers, Reggae's flagship band, played to audiences around the world. In the northeast of Brazil, where African culture began to emerge from the depths of decades of official and unofficial disdain, Bob Marley became a folk hero.

Bob Marley. In the 1970s, more and more young Europeans and North Americans began to listen to music imported from the Third World. Among the most popular was Jamaican-based Reggae, and its most renowned artist, Bob Marley. Marley's music combined rock and roll with African rhythms and lyrics about freedom and redemption for the downtrodden of the world.

In Soweto, South Africa, populated by black workers, he was also a symbol of resistance. Reggae propelled a major shift in black American music. In broadcasting Reggae, DJ's began to merge sounds and chant lyrics over a beat, a "talkover" form of music that also would be used in "rap" music. This was a disruptive concept in the late 1970s, but by the late 1980s, rap became a dance hall favorite—and a nonconventional provocation. Rap lyrics emulated Reggae realism by focusing on black problems, but they also pushed the countercultural messages into a new domain of controversies involving gang worldviews. On the world stage, Latino rappers used lyrical interventions to stress more multicultural themes, often in "Spanglish." Asian rap dispensed with the notion that the genre was the property of any ethnicity or race at all and stressed that rap was a new musical form that enabled cross-cultural sharing.

The effects of migration on global music have also been evident in Latin American transformations of North American genres. "Latin" music came into its own thanks to Latin American migrants to the United States. In New York and New Jersey, Puerto Ricans and Dominicans made boogaloo, salsa, and merengue popular. In Los Angeles, Mexican *corridos* (ballads) became pop hits. In the 1980s, East Los Angeles produced its own local rock sensation, "Los Lobos," a Chicano band that fused Mexican popular tunes with Californian themes. Their best-selling albums often had bilingual lyrics.

What reinforced cross-cultural borrowing was not just the medium of production and distribution of entertainment across borders, but also the message. Increasingly, world popular culture was youth culture. Often, what was appealing about television and music was its generational opposition. In Egypt, one of the most popular TV serials, *The School of Troublemakers*, carried a resolutely anti-establishment message. It showed schoolboys challenging the authority of their teachers and reveling in the chaos that they created. In Argentina, rock and roll was crucial to the counterculture during the military dictatorship of the 1970s and 1980s. "Charlie" García urged his Buenos Aires audiences to defy authorities by daring to dream of a different order. Indeed, in countries where public cultures were squashed underfoot by repressive regimes, pop culture was very often counterculture. In East Germany, before the fall of the Berlin Wall, rappers denounced the ruler Eric Honecker and his generation as a bunch of senile plutocrats.

National governments, especially ministers of culture, did not take these challenges lightly. In some countries, resistance to "Americanization" targeted the cultural exports of the United States. French leaders took a particularly active stance against the spread of American cultural influences and against the threat of English to the national and international prominence of the French language. The French were not the only worried parties. Through the 1980s, the mullahs of Teheran denounced the depravity of American materialism and secularism.

At the same time that American influences were spreading around the globe, world cultures were transforming American entertainment. Rap and hip-hop, the musical genres of the

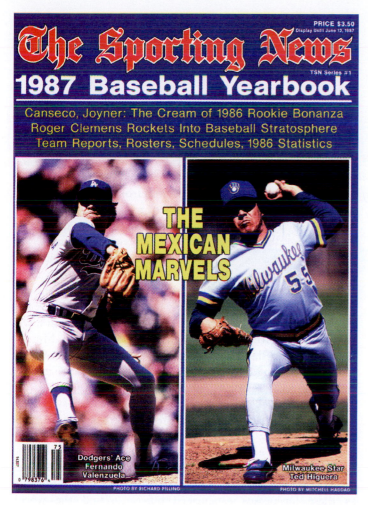

PRICE $3.50
Display Until June 12, 1987

The Sporting News

TSN Series #1

1987 Baseball Yearbook

Canseco, Joyner: The Cream of 1986 Rookie Bonanza
Roger Clemens Rockets Into Baseball Stratosphere
Team Reports, Rosters, Schedules, 1986 Statistics

THE MEXICAN MARVELS

Dodgers' Ace
Fernando
Valenzuela

Milwaukee Star
Ted Higuera

PHOTO BY RICHARD PILLING

PHOTO BY MITCHELL HADDAD

Hispanic Baseball Players. Like many other aspects of American life, the "national pastime," baseball, underwent a significant internationalization after 1965. Illustrative of both the increasing presence and popularity of players from Latin America and Asia on major league teams was the "Fernando-mania" generated by the Los Angeles Dodgers pitcher Fernando Valenzuela in the early 1980s.

1990s, derived partly from Caribbean and Hispanic influences, and even owed some of their theatrics to kung fu movies. The same globalizing effects could also be seen in sports. Consider the staple of American identity: baseball. Compared with basketball, baseball has lagged in its global marketing, but rosters of major league teams have taken on a more global cast. Since the 1960s, the number of Latin Americans playing in North American professional leagues has increased steadily. Most notable in the 1980s, perhaps, was the Mexican pitcher Fernando Valenzuela, whose exploits as a member of the Los Angeles Dodgers made him a hero to that city's Mexican population and to people in his native land as well. The Dodgers also took the lead in reaching for Asian talent. In the 1990s, as Los Angeles became home to a growing Asian immigrant population, the Dodgers added the Japanese pitcher Hideo Nomo

to the team. In many respects, "Nomo-mania" repeated the "Fernando-mania" of the previous decade, the difference being that Nomo's greatest acclaim came among Asian Americans in Los Angeles and among his countrymen in Japan.

LOCAL CULTURE   World cultures may have become more integrated and homogeneous, but they did not completely efface national and local cultures. Indeed, technology and migration often reinforced the appeal of "national" cultural icons, as national celebrities gained popularity, too, among immigrant groups abroad. New technology, like cassette tapes, made these stars known to more and more people. In Egypt, the most popular singer of the Nasser years was Umm Kalthum, who in 1975 was given a state funeral, the likes of which had rarely been seen. She was the favorite of the middle classes of her era—and the radio was her main medium. Egypt's more liberal economic and cultural policies under Nasser's successor, President Anwar al-Sadat, created new national pop stars. Some, like Muhammad Abd al-Wahhab, artfully blended Western and Eastern musical themes. Educated in *Quranic* schools, where he developed a talent for chanting the *Quran*, he caught on with a local touring group as a youngster and eventually became a big singing attraction. When he fused his *Quranic* vocals and chants with Western synthesizers and beats, he went from attraction to sensation.

As with the globalization of commerce and finance, transborder cultural exchanges did not become ruleless free-for-alls. Culture obeyed the rules, less of national regulators and censors, and, increasingly, of the global marketplace. China was the main exception to this dominance of the global cultural marketplace. There censors preserved strong, though not complete, control over local consumers. But even China was not immune, as its new entrepreneurs and urban youth became increasingly enthusiastic participants in the global cultural marketplace. In soccer, teams, leagues, and the world federation (FIFA) fought increasingly for corporate sponsors. The players, wanting a piece of the action, threatened to form a union in 1994, only to be rebuked by managers. Market rules also dictated behavior in the world music industry. The great difficulty of local bands breaking into larger markets has always been part of the reality of pop music. Bands in Liverpool resorted to Beatles-lookalike tactics to garner the attention of producers. Moreover, women often found it difficult to compete with men in the music industry, as in other industries.

The market for world cultures was increasingly competitive, and competition created more room for acceptable performance. Since the 1970s, competition in the world cultural markets registered some breakthroughs. Without a doubt, the most important was the triumph of black performers (Bob Marley, Whitney Houston), black athletes (Pelé, Michael Jordan), and black writers (Toni Morrison, Chinua Achebe), not just among white consumers, but among world consumers. Competition also shattered some sexual biases. Female performers like Madonna became popular icons. So did gay performers, starting with the

Village People, whose campy multicultural anthem "YMCA" disturbed fundamentalists but created a space for a new generation of homosexual or bisexual artists like Britain's Boy George, the American Melissa Etheridge, and the Turkish pop sensation Bulent Ersoy. Of course, beyond Europe and North America, flirting with sexual conventions had its limits. In the Middle East, female video artists continued to wear veils—but they still swung their hips.

The globalization of culture since the 1970s has introduced world consumers to a set of common icons—athletic, musical, and performing. In this sense, globalization has created an increasingly homogeneous world culture. Mass culture from the United States has been an especially important purveyor of products to the rest of the world. At the same time, however, local cultures have become increasingly diverse. Relatively homogeneous national cultures, often dominated by mature men representing the ethnic majority, have given way to a wide variety of entertainers and expressions. Artists and entertainers have crossed gender, racial, generational, and international boundaries with unprecedented ease and have been able to break loose of often confining local cultures. Nowhere has this been more true than in the United States, where other cultures have refashioned national tastes and have even challenged the idea that there is a shared "American" culture at all.

> *Within fifteen years, the computer revolution had moved from hardware to software to a fully interactive form of communications and storage with the clarity and resolution of a television.*

COMMUNICATIONS

Migration, money, and markets are not the only ties that have created human networks among world societies; a technological revolution in communications has played an even more important role. By the 1970s, satellites relayed telecommunications into living rooms around the world. Television brought the world home—but it was still a one-way technology. It was not interactive. Starting in the 1970s and early 1980s, however, engineers based primarily in California's Santa Clara Valley between San Francisco and San Jose, in what became known as "Silicon Valley," began to tinker with the idea of computers for personal use. At first, these were big, underpowered machines with little memory. But with the invention of the silicon chip, the computer weighed less and gained enormous memory power. On the heels of this hardware revolution, a software revolution enabled people to process words, run businesses, play games, and eventually communicate with each other from computer terminal to computer terminal.

Computer technology helped create new networks of interactive communications. In the late 1980s, while working in Switzerland, a British physicist named Tim Berners-Lee devised a means to pool the data he had stored on various computers. Hitherto, electronic links existed only between major universities and research stations. Berners-Lee figured out how to make data more accessible by creating a "World Wide Web." With each use and each connection, and as people entered more data, however, the Web grew more and more crowded. Pretty soon it was clear that users could get lost and tangled in unfamiliar electronic syntax. In the early 1990s, the first commercial browsers were developed to aid in navigating the so-called Internet. Within fifteen years, the computer revolution had moved from hardware to software to a fully interactive form of communications and storage with the clarity and resolution of a television. By the mid-1990s, people were communicating across global networks more easily than with neighbors and more inexpensively than with local phone calls.

The change created a whole new generation of wealth. Old stalwart CEOs from the top industries, like General Motors, Royal Dutch Shell, or Merck, were soon dwarfed monetarily by Michael Dell (a hardware maker), Bill Gates (a software maker), and Jeff Bezos (creator of Amazon.com). Accordingly, a boom in shares of Internet firms, known as dot-coms, swept the world's stock markets. In 2000, Gates's Microsoft had a market capitalization that was the size of Spain's robust GDP (c. $600 billion), IBM's exceeded Colombia's (c. $200 billion), and America Online's (AOL) surpassed that of the Philippines (c. $200 billion). Money from these companies flowed globally, as these businesses established offices around the world. Software and Internet technologies have enormous economies of scale, and they are thus prone to monopolization. Monoliths have emerged by means of takeovers of smaller companies. Two capitalist titans in particular, Gates of Microsoft and Jim Clark of Netscape, began to compete for mastery of the Internet in federal courts, each lashing out against the other's fetters to trade.

Hardware, software, and the Internet were by no means purely American innovations, however. Within a few years of their invention, personal computers were made in Mexico, and computer chips were mass-produced in Taiwan. The brains behind the Internet were less likely to be Ivy League graduates than students from Indian institutes of technology, especially the one located in Bombay. Originally devised as engineering schools to create the knowledge needed to modernize India, these institutes trained a whole generation of pioneering computing engineers, many of whom resettled in Silicon Valley in the United States. By 1996, Indians had taken half of the 55,000 temporary work visas issued by the U.S. government for high-tech employees. Roughly half the Silicon Valley start-up companies in the late 1990s were the brainchildren of Indian entrepreneurs.

But while this revolution gave people new means to communicate, share, and sell information, it also reinforced hierarchies between the haves and the have-nots. Great swathes of the world's population living outside the big cities were left beyond the reach

Global Connections & Disconnections

BOMBAY/MUMBAI

Bombay, more than any other Indian city, has always been connected to the world economy. Acquired by the Portuguese in the sixteenth century, who then transferred its control to the East India Company, Bombay developed as a colonial creation. Composed of seven islands joined by lands taken back from the sea, Bombay developed as a port city for colonial commerce, becoming an economic powerhouse during the nineteenth century. It profited from the cotton trade, developed a vibrant textile industry, attracted migrants, and took on a cosmopolitan image. The twentieth century brought it unprecedented growth as Indian-owned economic institutions achieved dominance and nationalist politics won popular support. After India's independence in 1947, Bombay came to epitomize the modern face of the nation, and its heterogeneous population became the ur (prototypical) symbol of the Indian melting pot.

Beginning with the 1980s, however, the nature and effects of integration into the world economy started to change. The cotton textile industry, which had served as Bombay's economic backbone since the late nineteenth century, went into a steep decline. Industrial employment fell sharply, the era of the trade unions ended, and the share of the informal sector of household enterprises, small shops, petty subcontractors, and casual laborers, along with the financial services sector of banking and insurance, rose. Economic liberalization transformed Bombay further, removing hurdles against the entry of foreign businesses and integrating the city into the global economy.

Even as Bombay continues to be a part of the nation, it now occupies, as do other global cities, a strategic place in transnational geography. It serves as a center for the servicing and financing of international trade, investment, and corporate office functions. The global constitution of Bombay is evident in the increasing presence in the city of financial institutions, trading organizations, insurance companies, telecommunications corporations, and information technology enterprises with worldwide operations. Forces of change can be observed even in its vibrant film industry, which produces roughly 120 films a year. Its trademark is spectacular melodramatic fantasies. But since the 1980s, Bombay films are increasingly addressed to a global, not only national, audience of Indians. In addition, many of the most successful and glossy productions can be characterized as "placeless," that is, the narrative is not pinned down to a definable place but situated in a global locale. Reflecting its increasingly global location, Bombay cinema has acquired the moniker "Bollywood" in recent years.

A striking effect of the concentration of global economic operations in the city is the high economic value that these activities command. Finance, banking, telecommunications, software industry, and corporate headquarter operations generate profits and offer remunerations to employees on a much richer scale than other sectors of the economy. On the other hand, low-skilled and unskilled workers, lacking union organization, receive low wages. The city still attracts a large number of poor migrants who live in slums, when they are lucky to have a roof over their heads, or call the pavements their "home." The gap between the rich and the poor, which has always been legendary in Bombay, has grown alarmingly. A tiny, rich elite connected to the global economy is dwarfed by millions who eke out a miserable living. This inequality also affects governance. The government is asked to protect global capital from the encroachment of squatters and pavement dwellers, and municipal services have been increasingly deployed to clear illegally constructed slums.

Globalization has also affected the very name of the city and sparked a contest over the identity of its residents. In January 1996, Mumbai became the official name of Bombay, which serves as the capital of the Maharashtra province. The government represented the renaming as an act of indigenizing the colonial name. The political party then in power in Maharashtra was the Shiv Sena, a nativist regional party named after the seventeenth-century Maratha chieftain Shivaji, who was an adversary of the Mughal empire. Since its inception in 1966, the Shiv Sena has campaigned militantly for the reservation of jobs and economic opportunities for Marathi speakers, who constitute a little over 40 percent of the city's heterogeneous population of 15 million. It was only in the 1980s, however, that the Shiv Sena grew rapidly. The timing is significant because it was then that the city's economy and society began to change dramatically. As the industrial economy and trade unions gave way to the service sector and unorganized labor, and as globalization uprooted identities located in the framework of the secular nation-state, a space opened for alternative mobilizations. It was in this context that the Shiv Sena emerged triumphant. It did so, not by opposing economic globalization, but by utilizing the social and political fluidity produced by deindustrialization and globalization to win support for its nativist and Hindu chauvinist ideology. Bombay's cosmopolitan image went up in smoke in 1992–1993, when the Shiv Sena directed and led pogroms against the city's Muslim residents.

Bombay/Mumbai today manifests the contradictory, conflictual, and uneven effects of globalization. The society is sharply divided, economic disparities are great, and its politics is a cauldron of conflicting identities. These are the local forms in which globalization is experienced in this vast and influential city.

Computers and India. Programmers trained by Indian educational institutions became ubiquitous in the computer industry worldwide, and many became successful as entrepreneurs in the Silicon Valley.

of the Internet. According to World Bank calculations, in the late 1990s, countries with low-income economies had, on average, 26 phone lines per 1,000 people; countries with high-income economies had 550 per 1,000 people. In 1996, the ratio of Internet users in countries with rich economies versus countries with poor economies was over 10,000:1. The real losers were the billions living in rural areas or towns neglected by state and private communications providers. The have-nots were poor not just because they had no capital but because they had no access to knowledge and to the new communications media. The result was a widening gap between rich and poor. In 1870, the average American made nine times what the average African earned; by 1990, an American earned forty-five times the income of someone in Chad or Ethiopia. Thus, globalization has had the paradoxical effect of integrating the world's peoples ever more tightly while at the same time intensifying the disparities among them.

CHARACTERISTICS OF THE NEW GLOBAL ORDER

> ❖ *What are the characteristics of the New Global Order?*

By 2000, population migrations, international banking, expanded international trade, and technical breakthroughs in communications had created a world not only radically different from that which existed in 1300 but one that would hardly have been recognizable to the inhabitants of the world at the beginning of the twentieth century. All these factors have contributed to increasing integration and to the creation of new power arrangements within and between societies. Around the world, globalization has had a number of clearly recognizable social and economic characteristics. The world's population has expanded dramatically, requiring greater industrial and agricultural output that has come from all parts of the world. Families have changed dramatically, and people are living longer. Decent education and good health determine one's status in society as never before. In general, while giving people access to an unimaginable array of goods, services, and culture, globalization also has deepened world inequalities, widening age-old divisions between the rich and the poor, the haves and the have-nots.

THE DEMOGRAPHY OF GLOBALIZATION

It took 160 years (1800–1960) for the world's population to go from 1 billion to 3 billion; in the next 40 years (1960–2000), it jumped from 3 billion to over 6 billion. Behind this steepening curve were two important developments: the decline in mortality, especially among children, and an increase in life expectancies.

Population growth was hardly equal across the globe (see Map 12-4). In Europe, population growth peaked around 1900, and it only moved upward gradually from 400 million to 730 million during the twentieth century, with little increase after the 1970s. In North America, population quadrupled over the same century but rose mainly because of immigration. The population booms in the twentieth century occurred in Asia (400 percent), Africa (550 percent), and Latin America (700 percent). China and India each passed the billion-person mark. What is more, increases were greatest in the cities. By the 1980s, the world's largest cities were no longer European and North American, but Asian, African, and Latin American. Greater Tokyo-Yokohama had 30 million inhabitants, while Mexico City had 20 million, São Paulo 17 million, Calcutta 15 million, Cairo 16 million, and Jakarta 12 million people.

In richer societies, population growth has been the slowest. For some, like Italy, the growth rate declined to zero. More recently enriched societies like Korea, Taiwan, and Hong Kong have also had fewer births. The societies that did not see their birthrates decline by the same rate—much of Africa, southern Asia, and impoverished parts of Latin America—had great difficulty raising income levels. But even among the poor nations, birthrates have declined since the 1970s.

The most remarkable turnaround in fertility rates occurred in China, the world's most populous country. In the 1950s and 1960s, the annual growth rate of the Chinese population was in excess of 2 percent. In the 1980s, it was down, according to the official count, to just above 1.4 percent. The demographic shift did not occur by choice. After 1979, China tried to enforce "one-child family" policy, with rewards for compliance and penalties for transgression. Cash subsidies, preferential access to

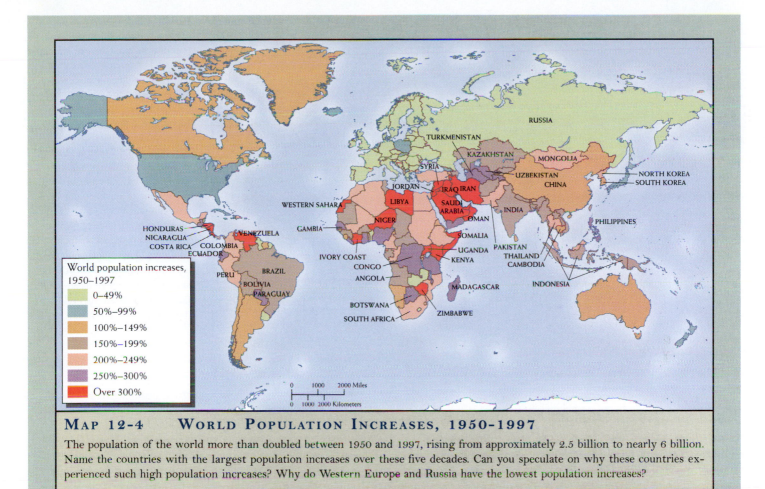

MAP 12-4   WORLD POPULATION INCREASES, 1950-1997

The population of the world more than doubled between 1950 and 1997, rising from approximately 2.5 billion to nearly 6 billion. Name the countries with the largest population increases over these five decades. Can you speculate on why these countries experienced such high population increases? Why do Western Europe and Russia have the lowest population increases?

nurseries and kindergartens, priority in medical care, and the promise of favored treatment in the allocation of housing, education, and employment were used as inducements in the one-child campaign.

In general, however, the decline in family size resulted from choice not coercion. In rich countries, more and more women chose to defer having children. Education, career prospects, and birth control devices—the contraceptive "pill" in particular—created incentives for women to pursue other ways of life before starting a family. One important part of this change was to make love a precondition to marriage and family formation. While this had been a romantic ideal for centuries, reality now conformed more completely to the ideal.

> *In general, the decline in family size resulted from choice not coercion, as more and more women in rich countries chose to defer having children.*

FAMILIES   The legal definition of families has become more fluid than at any time in modern history. Here again, the change reflects women's choices and the relationship between love and marriage. First, couples have chosen to end their marriages at historically unprecedented rates. In the United States, for example, the divorce rate doubled between 1970 and 1998—at the end of the twentieth century, one in two marriages ended in divorce. In Belgium and Britain, fewer than half of all marriages now survive. So, too, in China the divorce rate has been soaring in recent years. In a large city such as Beijing, it is reportedly close to 25 percent, double the 1990 rate. Notably, more than 70 percent of the divorces are initiated by women.

As marriages became more short-lived, new forms of child-rearing proliferated. In the United States, out-of-wedlock childbirths accounted for one-third of all births in the late 1990s; only about half of American children now live in households with both parents (compared with nearly three-quarters of children in the early 1970s). Europeans, too, including the

Family Planning in China. To control China's burgeoning population, the Chinese government tried to enforce a "one-child family" policy after 1979. While the policy has generally been effective, its impact tends to vary in different places and times, and disparity can often be found between urban and rural areas. Recent market reforms, moreover, have further eroded the extent of government control. Shown on this giant billboard from the city of Wuhan in 1996 is a propaganda slogan that says "Family planning is the need of mankind." Beneath the slogan is the image of an ideal family, with its single child being, significantly, a girl.

supposedly more traditional Italians and Greeks, are also abandoning nuclear family conventions. And in those European countries where divorce remains difficult, more and more couples are opting to live together without getting married.

AGING   Longer lifespans have also affected family fortunes. More infants are surviving childhood and growing to be old— in some areas very old. Along with other industrialized nations, the population of the United States has "grayed" considerably. Fewer children and longer-living adults have resulted in a marked increase in the median age of the American population. In 1970, half of all Americans were twenty-eight or under. By 1990, the median age had risen to thirty-four. Likewise, the percentage of Americans over the age of sixty-five had grown: from 8 percent in 1950 to 13 percent in 1990. In Western Europe and Japan, graying rates were even more marked. In Japan, the birthrate has plummeted, and the citizenry has been aging at such a rate that it is de-populating. From a population of 127 million in 2000, estimates forecast a decline to 105 million by 2050.

The aging of the world's population has presented new challenges for families. For centuries, being a parent meant providing for children until they could be self-sufficient. Old age, the

> *As societies have aged, the retirees have turned to society's savings to survive.*

years of relatively unproductive labor, was brief. Communities and households absorbed the cost of caring for the elderly. Household savings, if any, became family bequests to future, not older, generations. But as societies have aged, retirees have turned to society's savings to survive. Public and private pension funds have swollen to accommodate the need for future pools of money for the retired. In Germany, over 30 percent of the government's social policy spending has been earmarked for the state pension fund. Chinese demographers have warned that the one-child family threatens to create an unbalanced population structure. In a society in which the safety net is still largely assumed by the family, many worry that each able-bodied person may potentially have to support two parents and four grandparents.

In Africa, where publicly supported pension funds are rare, the aged face more dire futures. In an earlier age the elderly, especially men, were thought to be the fount of wisdom. Colonial rule and the postcolonial world, however, elevated the position of the young, especially those who had acquired Western educations and were able to earn Western-style livings. Then, in the 1970s, as birthrates began to soar, the demand on family resources to care for infants and children rose, at the very moment in which society's resource base began to shrink. The elderly could no longer work, but neither could they rely on the household's support.

HEALTH   The distribution of contagious diseases also exemplifies the inequities of the globalized world. On the surface, the spread of diseases would suggest that historically little has changed. After all, the Black Death of the fourteenth century was a pan-Eurasian epidemic, while after 1492 the spread of European maladies catastrophically reduced Native American populations across the Americas. It remains true that microbes have no respect for national, linguistic, or religious borders. But still, the incidence of world diseases reveals a great deal about how human lives have changed. Public health regulations, antibiotics, and vaccination campaigns have reduced the spread of contagions. By the late twentieth century, not only did nutrition and healthy habits count, as they always had, but so did access to medicines. What used to be universal afflictions in 1300, 1500, and 1850, were becoming more peculiar to particular peoples. Water treatment and proper sewerage, for example, had banished cholera from most urban centers by the middle of the twentieth century. In recent decades, however, its deadly impact has again reached across Asia, and into the eastern Mediterranean, parts of Latin America, and much of sub-Saharan Africa. Since the 1970s, Africa has suffered widespread and frequent outbreaks of the disease. The crucial cause of the re-spread of cholera was the failure of urban

> *By the late twentieth century, not only did nutrition and healthy habits count in reducing the spread of contagious diseases, but so did access to medicines.*

developers to keep sanitation systems growing apace with the demand for water. Thus, diseases proliferated where urban squalor was most acute—in cities with the greatest post-1970s population growth.

The global redistribution of sickness has become more than a matter of combating old diseases. In the 1970s, entirely new diseases appeared and began to devastate the world's population. This is best exemplified by a disease called Acquired Immunodeficiency Syndrome (AIDS), which can be transmitted through contact with the semen or blood of an infected person. AIDS, in time, compromises the ability of the infected person's immune system to ward off disease. First detected by a drug technician at Atlanta's Centers for Disease Control and Prevention in early 1981, AIDS was initially stigmatized as a "gay cancer" (at the outset appearing primarily in homosexual men) and received little attention. As the disease spread to heterosexuals and public awareness about it increased, a new campaign urged the practice of safe sex, control of blood stocks, and restrictions on sharing hypodermic needles. In Europe and North America, where the campaigns intensified in the late 1980s and new drugs were developed to keep the virus under control, AIDS rates began to stabilize, though in its first two decades, AIDS killed 12 million people, 2.6 million in 1999 alone.

Moreover, although doctors developed new treatments, these are very expensive, leaving the poor and disadvantaged

AIDS Treatment and Education. *(Left)* At the Thirteenth International AIDS Conference in Durban, South Africa, in July 2000, AIDS activists express their displeasure at the high prices and unavailability of life-saving drugs for most of those in the Third World who are affected by AIDS. *(Right)* African governments have not tackled the problem of AIDS in their severely affected continent with the energy that it warrants. Pictured here, however, a doctor seeks to impress on the youth of a local community how they should conduct their social and sexual lives in light of the AIDS crisis.

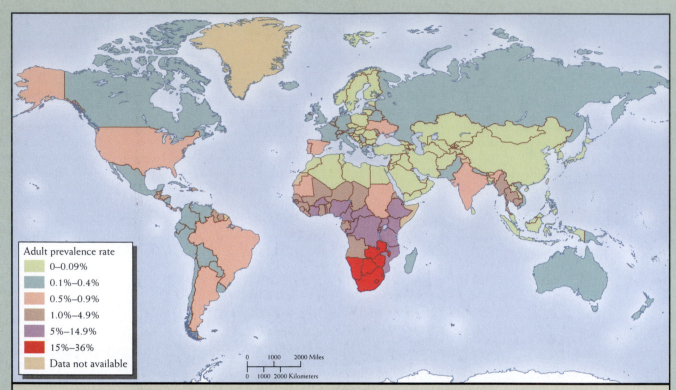

Map 12-5   HIV Infection across the World, 1999

Adult prevalence rate
- 0–0.09%
- 0.1%–0.4%
- 0.5%–0.9%
- 1.0%–4.9%
- 5%–14.9%
- 15%–36%
- Data not available

HIV, which leads to AIDS, has spread across the whole world, further evidence of global interconnectedness in the late twentieth century. Why do the highest infection rates occur in Africa south of the Sahara? Why are Egypt, North Africa, and much of the rest of the Islamic world, despite their close connections with Africa below the Sahara, thus far little affected? The outbreak of HIV began in Africa. Identify those countries outside the African continent that have high rates of infection, and explain why this is so.

still vulnerable to infection. By 2000, 33 million people had AIDS, the vast majority in poor countries, and even more were infected with HIV, the human immunodeficiency virus that causes AIDS (see Map 12-5). No less than two-thirds of those with AIDS lived in Africa below the Sahara. In Botswana, a quarter of the adult population was infected. In India, 7 million carried the virus; in China, the figure topped 1 million.

The expense of medical care was not the only factor in explaining the geographical and demographic prevalence of AIDS. Schooling and literacy played an important role in health promotion, especially in AIDS prevention. Better education led to safer sexual practices. Around the world, more educated men and women have shown higher use of condoms. One Tanzanian survey showed that 20 percent of women with four to five years of education insisted that their sexual partners use condoms, whereas only 6 percent of women with no education insisted on the use of condoms during sex with a casual partner.

EDUCATION Access to decent education has increasingly separated the haves from the have-nots. Moreover, because educational opportunities have often tilted in favor of men, schooling has also shaped differences between males and females. In sub-Saharan Africa and in India, for example, where men typically receive more formal education than women, literacy rates in these two regions are 63 and 64 percent for men, and only 39 and 40 percent for women. Both the generally low levels of literacy overall, and the depressed levels for women in particular, continued to be major impediments to each region's efforts to combat poverty. Gender bias is also present in rich societies. For decades, however, women and girls have pressed for equal access, with some astounding results. In the United States, women are now spending more time in school as well as more time in the workforce than they did in the past. By the late 1980s, more than half of all college degrees were granted to women (up from 38 percent in 1960). Even more dramatic has been the rising proportion of women among those earning postgraduate degrees (up from 3 percent to 35 percent). In China, women have made even more enormous strides, although they have also continued to hit roadblocks. Ironically, with the recent market reforms, women's access to basic education has regressed, as families, particularly in the rural areas, have reverted to the practice of spending their limited resources educating sons rather than daughters. Thus, in 2000, as many as 70 percent of China's 140 million illiterates were female.

EDUCATION AND INEQUALITY: WHY GENDER MATTERS

In the 1970s, aid agencies recognized that reducing world poverty means improving educational opportunities. International organizations urged national governments to plow resources into schools. The results were stunning. But a disparity appeared: the beneficiaries were mainly boys. So, since the 1980s, aid organizations, influenced by the growing strength of world feminism, have been especially active in trying to channel educational opportunities to girls. In this World Bank study, researchers found that development among the poor improves not just with better education, but especially with better education for girls.

Evaluations of recent initiatives that subsidize the costs of schooling indicate that demand-side interventions can increase girls' enrollments and close gender gaps in education. A school stipend program established in Bangladesh in 1982 subsidizes various school expenses for girls who enroll in secondary school. In the first program evaluation girls' enrollment rate in the pilot areas rose from 27 percent, similar to the national average, to 44 percent over five years, more than twice the national average. . . . After girls' tuition was eliminated nationwide in 1992 and the stipend program was expanded to all rural areas, girls' enrollment rate climbed to 48 percent at the national level. There have also been gains in the number of girls appearing for exams and in women's enrollments at intermediate colleges. . . . While boys' enrollment rates also rose during this period, they did not rise as quickly as girls'.

Two recent programs in Balochistan, Pakistan, illustrate the potential benefits of reducing costs and improving physical access. Before the projects there were questions about whether girls' low enrollments were due to cultural barriers that cause parents to hold their daughters out of school or to inadequate supply of appropriate schools. Program evaluations suggest that improved physical access, subsidized costs, and culturally appropriate design can sharply increase girls' enrollments.

The first program, in Quetta, the capital of Balochistan, uses a subsidy tied to girls' enrollment to support the creation of schools in poor urban neighborhoods by local NGOs. The schools admit boys as long as they make up less than half of total enrollments. In rural Balochistan the second program has been expanding the supply of local, single-sex primary schools for girls by encouraging parental involvement in establishing the schools and by subsidizing the recruitment of female teachers from the local community. The results: girls' enrollments rose 33 percent in Quetta and 22 percent in rural areas. Interestingly, both programs appear to have also expanded boys' enrollments, suggesting that increasing girls' educational opportunities may have spillover benefits for boys.

Source: World Bank, *World Development Report, 2000–2001.*

WORK Although women were holding jobs outside the home in increasing numbers, they faced obstacles to full equity at work. Limited by job discrimination and by burdens of child-rearing, women's participation in the workforce reached a fairly stable level by the 1980s. Roughly one-quarter to one-half of adult women across the world worked for a cash income. In Russia and Mexico, middle-class women opted for professional careers. Like their cousins elsewhere, they often encountered informal obstacles to many careers and found themselves channeled into feminized professions, such as nursing, teaching, and marketing. The percentage of women at the top of the corporate pyramid was considerably smaller than their overall participation in the labor force or even than their college graduation rates. In 1995, the Chinese government claimed that Chinese women had made better advances than their U.S. counterparts—it stated that there were more Chinese women (10 percent) than American women (3 percent) in senior managerial posts, defined as directors of enterprises or institutes. Still, Chinese women graduates consistently complained of discrimination in the job market. In 2000, some 60 percent of China's unemployed were women, and the number was growing. Women around the world have faced difficulties breaking through the "glass ceiling"—a seemingly invisible barrier to advancement. Consequently, while income disparities between men and women have narrowed, a significant gap persists.

Working outside the home has created problems for handling work inside the home. Who would take care of the children? Jamaican and Filipino women migrated by the thousands in the 1970s and 1980s to Canada and Australia to work as nannies to raise money to send back home, where they had often left their own children. In South Africa and Brazil, domestic servants and nannies came from local sources. They were doing the jobs that once belonged to middle- and upper-class homemaking women, women who now wanted the same rights as men: to parent *and* to work.

FEMINISM The deeply ingrained inequality between men and women prompted calls for change. Feminist movements arose mainly in Europe and in North America in the 1960s to call attention to the unequal treatment of men and women. The movement started to become global in the 1970s. In 1975, the first truly international women's forum was held in Mexico City. But becoming global did not necessarily imply running roughshod over local customs. Across the world, what feminists called for was not the abolition of gender differences, but equal treatment—equal pay and equal opportunities for obtaining jobs and advancement.

Women took increasingly active stances against discrimination. Across the world, countries passed laws to combat it in government and in the workplace. Indeed, as economic integration across borders intensified with regional trade pacts, usually negotiated by men in the interest of male-owned and male-run firms, women struggled to ensure that economic globalization did not cut them out of new opportunities. For instance, after Argentina, Uruguay, Paraguay, and Brazil negotiated the Mercosur free trade pact, the traffic across South American borders soared. But as trade grew, so did the governments' efforts to monitor the illegal commerce and foster licit trade along new highways and across new bridges. One kind of illicit commerce was conducted by women, who for generations had transported goods back and forth across the river separating Argentina and Paraguay. At the Argentine-Paraguayan border, customs officers tried to stop this transport. In response, in the mid-1990s, Argentine and Paraguayan women locked arms to occupy the new bridge that male truckers used to ship Mercosur products, protesting the increasing restrictions on their age-old enterprise.

This rising tide of global feminism culminated in a conference in Beijing in September 1995. More than 4,000 government delegates from more than 180 countries met there for the Fourth World Conference on Women, the largest gathering of its kind, to produce "a platform for action" on policies regarding women's rights in politics, business, education, and health. More impressive, alongside the official conference, there was a parallel conference for close to 30,000 representatives at the Non-Governmental Organizations (NGOs) Forum for Women. These grassroots activists represented 2,000 NGOs from literally every corner of the globe. Despite the persistent harassment of the Chinese security apparatus, which was suspicious of any discussions that touched on issues of human rights, the representatives were able to exchange ideas, plan strategies, and coordinate programs on how to improve the living and working conditions of women. What emerged from the conference were associations and groups that were ready and determined to lobby for the rights of women and girls around the world.

PRODUCTION AND CONSUMPTION IN THE GLOBAL ECONOMY

The growth of the world's population, the desire for more education and better health, the entry of women into paid employment, and the promise of rising standards of living have resulted in the accelerated production and consumption of the world's resources at an astonishing rate. The most immediate challenge is how to feed all these mouths (roughly 90 million additional people per year by the end of the 1990s).

AGRICULTURAL PRODUCTION Changing agrarian practices have made a huge difference in increasing food production. Starting in the 1950s, chemistry increased outputs dramatically. The "green revolution," largely involving the use of nonfarm inputs such as chemical fertilizers, herbicides, and pesticides, produced dramatically larger harvests. Then, in the 1970s, biologists took over, offering genetically engineered crops that multiplied yields at an even faster rate.

But these agrarian breakthroughs were far from evenly distributed across the globe. American farmers have been the biggest innovators, and hence the greatest beneficiaries. American farms, for example, by century's end produced approximately one-ninth of the world's wheat and two-fifths of its corn. From this output, American exports accounted for about one-third of the world's international wheat trade and four-fifths of all corn exports. At the heart of the innovation was political power—farmers had the clout to force officials to maintain roads, to subsidize credit and prices, and to mop up surplus supply. Asian rice farmers made impressive innovations, too. In Taiwan and Korea, chemical and biological breakthroughs allowed rice yields to jump by 53 and 132 percent respectively between 1965 and 1985. Indian wheat farmers also deployed chemical fertilizers and new seed varieties and built irrigation systems to double their output. Indeed, the Ganges River basin is now able to feed an ever larger urban population. The most miraculous transformation occurred in China in the wake of the reforms of Deng Xiaoping. Beginning in the late 1970s, the Chinese government began to break up some of the old collective farms and to restore the primacy of the individual household as the basic economic unit in rural areas. In the wake of the reforms, the value of agricultural output surged by an average rate of 9 percent per year between 1978 and 1986.

Other agricultural producers also replied to world demand, but in some areas their added production had disruptive consequences. While biology and chemistry allowed some farmers to get more out of their land, other farmers simply opened up new lands to cultivation. This pattern of extensive land use was, in many respects, cheaper, and involved less reliance on nonfarm inputs. Moreover, it reflected the relative weakness of small farmers who, bereft of access to credit, seed, and especially land, had to go where land was cheap to make their living. In Java, farmers cleared the sloping forest land to make way for coffee. In southern Colombia, peasants moved into semitropical woodlands to cultivate coca bushes (the source of cocaine) at profits that other cultivators could not expect to realize. The most notorious frontier expansion took place in the Amazon River basin. Populations began flocking to the Amazon frontier, largely from impoverished areas in northeastern Brazil. They cleared (by fire) cheap land, staked their claims, and, like nineteenth-century American homesteaders, tried to move up the social ladder by cultivating crops and raising livestock. But the promise of bounty started to fail: the soils were poor and easily eroded, and their land titles provided little security, especially once large speculators moved into the area. So the frontiersmen pulled up their stakes and moved further inland to repeat the cycle. By the 1980s, the migrants to the Amazon River basin had burned away much of the jungle in clearing the area, contaminated the biosphere, reduced the world's stock of

> *Food shortages, rare in Africa before the 1970s, thereafter increased in frequency and duration, wiping out large numbers of the sub-Saharan population.*

diverse plant and animal life, and fostered social conflict in the Brazilian hinterland between the haves and the have-nots.

Breadbaskets were not always able to keep pace with exploding populations, however. This was especially true in Africa from the 1970s onward, when the continent became a major importer of foodstuffs because domestic food production could not keep pace with population growth (see Map 12-6). Food shortages, rare in Africa before the 1970s, thereafter increased in frequency and duration, wiping out large numbers of the sub-Saharan population. The protruding ribs on African children became a clichéd image of the continent, as the first and second generations of the "green revolution" largely bypassed Africa. What explained Africa's famines? As the Indian Nobel Prize–winning economist Amartya Sen observed, famines—and their increasing frequency—are not "natural" disasters; they are man-made. Food shortages in Africa stemmed in large measure from governments that ignored the rural sector and its politically unorganized farmers. Unable to persuade the government to raise the prices that were paid for their crops, the farmers lacked incentives to expand their production. Food shortages were also byproducts of global inequities. African countries, compelled to earmark hefty chunks of their economies to agrarian exports to pay for debts incurred in the 1970s, were unable to produce enough foodstuffs domestically and became food importers.

NATURAL RESOURCES   While American farmers produce a large share of the world's food, Americans also consume a high proportion of the globe's natural resources. Take water, a resource that Americans use at a per capita rate three times the world's average. Indeed, extensive water consumption for irrigation was crucial to the growth of California's agricultural sector, the most productive and profitable in the world. Gathering more water also allowed a desert metropolis like Los Angeles to grow; only rarely have the city's residents questioned the environmental costs of their water use.

Energy consumption presents a similar story—though here, America's enormous appetite for fossil fuels has generated a domestic debate about reliance on foreign sources and the pollution of the environment. In the United States and Canada, attempts to curb energy consumption have met with little success, and the United States has grown more dependent on imported oil.

Dependence on foreign sources of precious fuel have locked oil importers into recurring clashes with oil exporters. In the 1970s, the Organization of Petroleum Exporting Countries (OPEC) established an effective cartel to raise the price of crude oil (see Chapter 11). The cartel crumbled in the 1980s, in part because new oil fields emerged elsewhere in the world,

Saving the Amazon. The rise of an international environmental movement in the 1970s led to alliances with local indigenous and environmental leaders, especially in the Amazon. One of the most popular figures advocating the rights of indigenous people, and with them the need to protect imperiled jungles, was the British pop sensation Sting. Here he is pictured alongside one of the Amazon's foremost Indian leaders, Bep Koroti Paiakan.

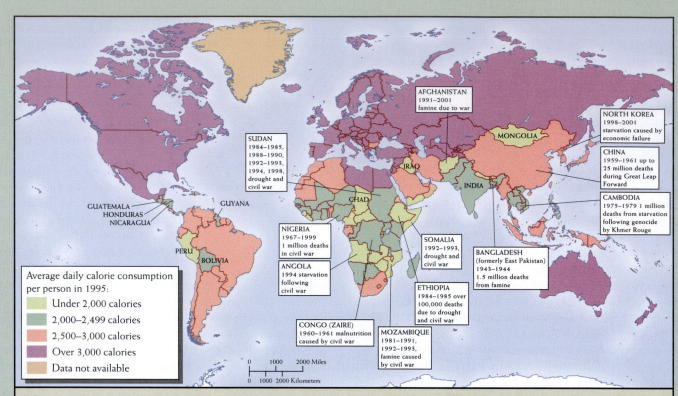

MAP 12-6   FOOD CONSUMPTION AND FAMINE SINCE THE 1940S

There is perhaps no better indicator of the division of the world into rich and poor, haves and have-nots than this map on food consumption and famine. Which parts of the world have had the most difficulty in feeding their populations? There have been many famine crises over the last six decades, and this map helps to identify the immediate, if perhaps not the long-run, causes. What are some of those immediate causes? How much are they due to human agency, and how much to climate and other matters over which human beings have little control?

increasing supply, and because internal struggles divided the exporters. The most bitter conflict was the savage war fought in the mid-1980s between Iran and Iraq, followed by the Iraqi invasion under Saddam Hussein of neighboring Kuwait in 1990 to seize its vast oil fields. Iraq was poised to assume a dominant status in the area, and thus to have a considerable measure of control over oil policies. The conquest of Kuwait would have given it control over about 7 percent of world oil supplies and nearly 20 percent of its known reserves. Only its neighbors, Saudi Arabia and Iran, would have been larger oil exporters, and Iraq would have been in a position to menace both of them. The Americans were quick to respond to restore the regional balance of oil power. Rallying a large coalition of other nations, the Americans and their allies built up a substantial military force to participate in Operation Desert Storm. The 1991 Gulf War, which ended with Iraq's expulsion from Kuwait, restored an order in which the global distribution of power favored oil consumers over producers and preserved a regional balance of power.

ENVIRONMENT The consumption of water, oil, and other natural resources increasingly became matters of international concern in the last decades of the twentieth century. So did problems associated with pollution control and the disposal of waste products. Part of this internationalization resulted from the recognition that environmental issues could not be handled by separate national exertions. Air and water, after all, do not stop flowing at political boundaries.

As Canadians saw their northern lakes fill up with "acid rain" (precipitation laced with heavy doses of sulfur, mainly from coal-fired plants), they urged their southern neighbor to curb emissions. Reciprocal agreements between Canada and the United States were signed in the 1980s. Europeans, beset by their own acidification, also negotiated regional environmental treaties. But some polluters simply moved overseas, to poorer and less politically powerful nations. As the West cleans up its environment, the rest of the world may end up paying the price.

Likewise, the problems associated with the greenhouse effect and global warming, as well as ocean pollution and the

→ *How has citizenship in the global world created new problems and responses?*

decline in biological diversity, cross all man-made borders. Successive rounds of international meetings have addressed these threats inconclusively. It is difficult to enforce an international solution on all national authorities when the forces of globalization are compelling some of them to rely on energy-intensive industries, which generate massive emissions, in order to produce exports to pay off their debts. In 1992, the world's governments flocked to the first Earth Summit in Rio de Janeiro. But much eco-friendly fanfare yielded only ineffective accords.

The relationship between power and resources has been especially stark in dealing with contaminants. Increasing numbers of automobiles, and the attendant carbon fumes, are presenting serious air pollution problems in the world's cities. In Los Angeles, Tokyo, Mexico City, and Jakarta, city dwellers choke and splutter their way through most days. But where environmentalists have acquired political power, they are forcing regulators to curb emissions. Starting in the late 1960s, Japanese local governments slapped pollution controls on filthy coal plants. Japan pioneered what one historian has called an "environmental miracle," spreading its regulations to many contaminating activities. By 1978, Japanese cars discharged only 10 percent as much pollution as in 1968. In 1987, Japan banned leaded gas altogether. But controls on fossil fuel emissions were dependent on power and wealth. It was much harder to impose restrictions in societies for whom high energy use was deemed a necessity of economic life. Even the Japanese pioneers of clean fuel were polluters in other spheres. With increasing controls at home, Japanese industrialists went abroad to unload Japanese hazardous waste. U.S. industrialists did the same, sending hazardous waste to Mexico. Argentina and Canada sent their nuclear detritus not abroad but to poor provinces desperate for jobs.

Environmental problems took on a new urgency after Soviet authorities revealed the meltdown of a nuclear reactor in Chernobyl in 1986. Initially, Communist authorities tried to cover up the mess, but when the fallout reached Sweden, they had to accept responsibility for the debacle. The delayed response was disastrous for Ukraine and Belarussia (present-day Belarus) which, relatively powerless under a centralized authoritarian regime, had no political voice to cry out for help from the contamination.

CITIZENSHIP IN THE GLOBAL WORLD

→ *How has citizenship in the global world created new problems and responses?*

Globalization has distributed its benefits unequally. In general, those with access to better education and more opportunities

Chernobyl and Protest. *(Left)* Among the victims of the 1986 explosion at the Chernobyl power plant, history's worst nuclear meltdown, were firefighters, such as the man pictured here, sent in to put out the blaze. A concrete sarcophagus meant to seal the reactor, in present-day Ukraine, continues to leak. *(Right)* The accident at Chernobyl tragically turned Mikhail Gorbachev's *glasnost*, or openness, into more than a slogan, and it became a rallying cry, along with environmental ruin more generally, for the populace, which hoped for political change and improvements in daily life.

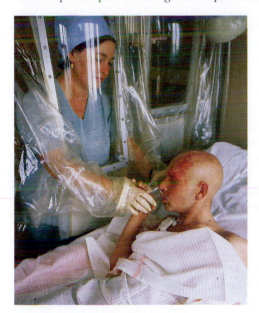

have embraced the new order with enthusiasm and have profited from the border-crossing freedoms it has permitted. For the majority of the world's population, however, the new power structure has not been so kind. Finding little opportunity in the globalized world, the disadvantaged have often expressed their discontent by invoking older religious and nationalist ideals. As globalization fosters human rights, environmental and labor standards, and women's rights across the globe, critics have claimed that the language of international rights and standards promotes neocolonial power in the form of a new "civilizing mission."

In particular, globalization has posed massive problems for the political organization that many had expected to emerge triumphant once empires had dissolved—the nation-state. Since the nineteenth century, nation-states were supposed to play the primary role in defining the rights of citizens. The rapid movement of ideas, goods, capital, and people across national boundaries has undercut the authority and legitimacy of even the most powerful and long-standing nations. Accordingly, other political spheres have emerged to define and defend citizens. After the 1970s, people came to understand that international organizations often had more influence over their lives than did their own national governments. Supranational organizations have become increasingly important in shaping the meaning of citizenship. This has been true especially in the Third World, where nation-states have struggled hardest to come to terms with globalization. In the end, however, local and regional forces have made an enormous difference. Globalization has implied greater integration of the world's societies, but it has not meant that all societies look the same. The world may be increasingly together, but in decisive ways, it is still apart.

> *After the 1970s, people came to understand that international organizations often had more influence over their lives than did their own national governments.*

SUPRANATIONAL ORGANIZATIONS

A variety of international bodies have come into existence since the end of World War II for the purpose of facilitating global activities. Although these organizations have often successfully dealt with crisis situations, they also have impinged on the autonomy of all but the most powerful states. Most prominent and powerful of the financial organizations are the World Bank and the International Monetary Fund (IMF). They have provided vital economic assistance to poorer nations, financing and providing essential technical information for some of the largest development programs in the Third World, as well as handling financial crises that could have brought on a new world depression. The World Bank provided funds for the large Volta River Project in Ghana to create an electrical power grid, as well as a system of national parks in the Philippines to help indigenous people manage rain forests, coral reefs, and other threatened ecological zones. Nonetheless, it has tied its financial assistance to demands that recipient governments implement far-reaching economic reform packages, which are often resented. Not infrequently, World Bank and IMF-imposed programs have required local governments to abolish subsidies for essential foodstuffs, leading to riots and demands to defy these international groups as agents of a new kind of imperialism.

Another set of supranational bodies, called non-governmental organizations (NGOs), has also stepped forward in the last several decades of the twentieth century. Many have sought to champion human rights around the world or to call attention to environmental problems that cross national boundaries. Others, like the International Committee of the Red Cross, an older organization once dedicated mainly to war relief, have become more active in peacetime, sheltering the homeless or providing food for famine victims. What has united NGOs has been not so much their goals but how they have pursued them: autonomously from state power. NGOs have created a layer of international forces that rival the political power of nation-states. They have joined other international organizations, like the United Nations or the International Monetary Fund, to make up a set of actors operating on a worldwide scale.

There was a reason why international NGOs reached a new level of influence in the 1970s: most of the world's nation-states at that time were still not democracies. Of the 121 countries in the world in 1980, only 37 were democracies, accounting for only 35 percent of the world population. People found it difficult to rely on authoritarians to uphold their rights as citizens. So much of the lofty language of the United Nations—like the 1948 Universal Declaration of Human Rights, "the Magna Carta for Mankind," in Eleanor Roosevelt's words—rang hollow. Indeed, the United Nations itself was a latecomer to enforcing human rights provisions, largely because its own members were the self-same authoritarians.

NGOs, then, took the lead in trying to make the language of human rights stick. The brutality of the military regimes in Latin America inspired the emerging network of international human rights organizations to take action. After the overthrow of Chile's Salvador Allende in 1973, solidarity groups proliferated to protest against the new military junta's harsh repression. When the Argentine military began killing tens of thousands of innocent civilians in 1976, and news of their refined torture techniques began to leak out, human rights movements again took action. Prominent among them was a relatively small organization called Amnesty International. Formed in 1961 by a British lawyer, Peter Benenson, to defend the cause of prisoners of conscience (detained for their beliefs, color, sex, ethnic origin, language, or religion), Amnesty International catalogued these

Bosnia in the Midst of War. Despite extensive destruction and perpetual sniper fire, the multiethnic population of Sarajevo refused to abandon their city. With the help of U.N. soldiers and aid workers, they kept alive the hope for the peaceful coexistence of Muslims, Serbs, and Croats in Bosnia.

human rights violations across the world. From these efforts, it went on to become one of the most influential and largest human rights organizations in the world. Moreover, even American foundations saw the importance of NGOs. The biggest of them all, the Ford Foundation, initiated support for human rights groups and research. By the 1990s, there was an extensive network of associations informing the public, lobbying governments, and pressuring the United Nations to keep its word.

VIOLENCE

International organizations and NGOs can play only a limited role in preserving peace and strengthening human rights. The end of the cold war left entire regions in such political turmoil that even the most effective humanitarian agencies could not prevent mass killings, as became terrifyingly apparent in the Balkans in the 1990s. In the territorial remains of Yugoslavia, Serbs, Croats, Bosnians, ethnic Albanians, and others fought for control. Former neighbors, fueled by the heated rhetoric of opportunistic leaders, no longer saw themselves as citizens of pluralistic political communities. Instead, demagogues trumpeted the superiority of ethnically defined states. Serbians took up arms against their Croat neighbors, and vice versa. International agencies moved in to try to bolster public authority. They, too, failed as Yugoslavia's ethnic mosaic imploded into an ugly civil war.

The Balkan tragedy was not an exception. Indeed, by the late twentieth century, with the end of the cold war and in-

creasing economic integration among nations, most warfare was conducted, not between states, but within them, with devastating consequences for innocent civilians. Between 1989 and 1992, eighty-three armed conflicts erupted. All but three were civil wars, and 90 percent of the casualties were civilian. By 1995, the world had 42 million displaced people; another 160 million were victims of disasters; and 2 billion lived in conditions of abject poverty.

The most gruesome political violence in the global age has occurred in Africa—where nation-states capable of upholding stability and the rule of law for all citizens have been weakest. In Africa, the tension has often been expressed as a conflict between ethnic groups. The crisis of African agriculture, its inability to sustain growing populations, and conflicts over unequal access to important resources like education, have exacerbated underlying ethnic rivalries. Droughts, famine, and corruption have led the rivalries to explode into riots and killings, or even to bitter civil war and the breakdown of centralized authority. In Rwanda, for example, the majority Hutus (agrarian people, often very poor) and the minority Tutsis (herders, often with better education and more wealth), after living side by side and intermarrying for many generations, began to slaughter one another. Some resentful Hutus blamed the Tutsis for all their woes. As tensions mounted, the United Nations dispatched 2,500 peacekeeping troops. Moderate Hutus urged peaceful coexistence, only to be shouted down by government forces in command of radio stations and a mass propaganda machine. Alerted to the impending problem, the Clinton administration blocked the U.N. Security Council in 1993 and 1994 from taking emergency actions. The international forces, fearing a clash, withdrew their troops, leaving a rump force. International involvement was thus downright destructive; the decision first to get involved, then to disengage, gave the Hutu government a green light to wipe out opponents. In one hundred days of carnage in 1994, Hutu militias massacred 800,000 Tutsis and moderate Hutus. This was not, as many proclaimed, the militarization of ancient ethnic rivalries: many Hutus were butchered as they tried to defend friends, relatives, and neighbors. Meanwhile, the refugee crisis that ensued, first of terrorized Tutsis, then of fleeing armed Hutus, destabilized a dozen African neighbors, and heightened tensions in Burundi and the Congo. The civil war in Rwanda sent riptides across eastern and central Africa, creating a whole new generation of conflicts.

Some societies, however, have endeavored to put political violence behind them. In some of the most heinous cases of human rights abuses, in Argentina, El Salvador, Guatemala, and South Africa, the transition to democracy has compelled elected rulers to establish inquiries to look into past violations. These "truth" commissions have been vital instruments for creating a new aura of legitimacy for democracies, and for promising to uphold the rights of individuals to live free from arbitrary authority. In South Africa, many blacks backed the new president Nelson Mandela, but they also demanded a reckoning with the punitive experience of the apartheid past. To avoid a backlash against the former white rulers, the South African leadership opted to record the events of the past rather than avenge them. Truth, the new leaders argued, would be powerful enough to heal old wounds. The Truth and Reconciliation Commission, under the chairmanship of Nobel Peace Prize winner Bishop Desmond Tutu, called on all who had been involved in political crimes, whites as well as blacks, to come before its tribunal and speak the truth. Although the truth alone did not fully settle old scores in South Africa, a more open discussion of the importance of basic liberties helped create new legitimate bonds between public authority and citizens.

Remarkably, democracy and peace swept into the war-torn Balkans in 2001. A ruthless Serbian government under Slobodan Milosevic had been spreading terror throughout the region, seizing neighboring territories where Serbian people had lived alongside other peoples for many centuries and purging or "cleansing" Serbia itself of other ethnicities. To drive out unwanted populations and to silence his critics, Milosevic relied on power and fear as his followers systematically tortured and killed entire populations. As matters worsened, the NATO countries and the European Union placed sanctions on Serbia and accused Milosevic of numerous human rights abuses carried out over his ten years in power. When he refused to relent, NATO bombed Serbian targets. Finally, the Serbian people voted Milosevic out of office in September 2000, and in April 2001 he was arrested and extradited to The Hague's International Criminal Tribunal, where he faces charges of crimes against humanity and war crimes.

But while democracy and human rights often act as bulwarks against political violence and terror, their efficacy is questionable when the perpetrators of terror are nonstate actors. This problem became apparent to anyone watching television on September 11, 2001. On the morning of that day, terrorists hijacked several commercial airliners and slammed them into the World Trade Center towers in New York and the Pentagon building in Washington, D.C., killing thousands in cold blood. Almost instantly, people across the globe saw on television screens the awesome, almost surreal images of the hijacked aircrafts crashing into the towers, their tanks of jet fuel erupting into flames that engulfed the skyscrapers. This was followed by shocking pictures of the icons of New York's famous skyline crumbling into a heap of ash, concrete, and twisted metal. The brutal attack was a reminder of the world's interdependence. The assault, allegedly masterminded by the self-styled Islamic leader Osama bin Laden, sitting thousands of miles away in Afghanistan, and carried out by a worldwide terrorist network, put the United States on notice that it was not invulnerable.

But why the United States? Was it, as President George Bush insisted, because the terrorists hated the freedom and democracy of the United States? Or was terrorism a reaction to the humiliation and powerlessness that many people in the world, particularly Muslims, felt in the face of America's global economic and political domination and its support of Israel? More importantly, how was the United States to combat political violence and warfare that emanated not from rival nation-states but from secretive, internationally organized groups?

RELIGIOUS FOUNDATIONS OF POLITICS

Secular concerns for human rights and international peace have not been the only foundations for politics after the cold war. In many regions, people have sought to give a new role to religion to define the moral fabric of political communities. Indeed, very often, religion has provided a way to reimagine the nation-state, just as globalization has been undermining national autonomy.

> *In many regions, people have sought to give a new role to religion to define the moral fabric of political communities.*

In India, Hindu nationalism has offered a communal identity for a country rapidly transformed by the forces of globalization. In the 1980s, India freed market forces, privatized state firms, and withdrew from its role as welfare provider. Economic reforms under the ruling Congress Party sparked economic growth, creating in the process Asia's largest, best-educated, and most affluent middle class. But these changes also widened the gap between the rich and the poor. Lower classes and castes formed political parties to challenge the dominant position of traditional elites. With established hierarchies and loyalties eroding under the pressure of economic change, right-wing Hindu nationalists argued that religion could now fill the role once occupied by a secular state. Arguing that the ideology of "Hindutva" (Hinduness) would bring the succor that secular nationalism had failed to give, Hindu militants aggressively promoted the idea of India as a nation of Hindus (the majority), with minorities relegated to a lesser status in the political community.

The chief political beneficiary of the politics established by economic liberalization was a Hindu nationalist party, the Bhartiya Janata Party (BJP), or Indian People's Party. The BJP was the political arm of an alliance of Hindu organizations devoted to establishing the Indian nation-state as a Hindu state. Until the mid-1980s, the BJP and other like-minded parties were influential, though not dominant, players in Indian politics. By the late 1980s, however, they rose to dominance, relentlessly advancing an anti-minority (chiefly anti-Muslim) ideology. Claiming that the state had consistently and systematically "appeased" the minorities and trampled on the rights of the majority, they called upon Hindus to overthrow "pseudo secularism." This communal ideology proved to be a winning formula in competitive electoral politics, and by the mid-1990s, a BJP coalition came to power under the leadership of A. B. Vajpayee, reducing the century-old Congress Party to an ineffectual opposition party. Hindu nationalists sought to transform the secular nation-state into a moral community, but without challenging the economic forces of globalization.

In some cases, religion provided a way to resist what has been seen as American-dominated globalization. One of the most spirited challenges to globalism arose in the Islamic Middle East. Significant segments of the people of that region believed that the modernizing and westernizing programs being enacted in their region were leading their societies toward rampant materialism and unchecked individualism. The critics included traditional clerics and young Western-educated elites whose job prospects seemed bleak and those who had become convinced that the promise of modernization had failed. Having criticized modernizing processes since the nineteenth century, Islamic conservatives flourished once more in the 1970s, as global markets and social dislocations undermined the moral foundations of secular leadership.

The most explosive and revolutionary of the Islamic movements took place in Iran, where clerics organized opposition against the shah and forced him from power in 1979. The revolt seemed to pit unequal forces against each other: a cadre of religious officials possessing only pamphlets, tracts, and tapes against the military arsenal and the vast intelligence apparatus that served the Iranian state. Shah Mohammad Reza Pahlavi had enjoyed unstinting U.S. technical and military support since the Americans had helped to place him on the throne of Iran in 1953. His bloated army and police force, as well as brutally effective intelligence service, had crushed all challenges to his authority. The shah also had benefited from infusions of oil revenues after 1973. Yet, the maldistribution of income, the oppression of a police state, and the public ostentation of the royal family fueled widespread discontent. As the discontent rose, so did the levels of repression. And as repression intensified, so did the impression that the government had abandoned the people. The most vociferous critique of the shah's rule came from Islamic quarters, mullahs who found in the Ayatollah Ruhollah Khomeini a courageous and obdurate leader. Khomeini used his traditional Islamic education and his training in Muslim ethics to attack the shah and to accuse his government of gross violations of Islamic norms. He also identified the shah's ally, America, as the great Satan. With opposition mounting, the shah fled the country in January 1979. In the shah's wake, Khomeini returned from exile and established a theocratic state ruled by a council of Islamic clerics. Although some Iranians grumbled about many aspects of this return to Islam—the reduced status of women, the arbitrariness of the leaders, the rupture in relations with the West, and failure to institute democratic procedures—they prided themselves on having inspired a revolution based on principles other than those drawn from the West.

The search for moral foundations of politics in the global age has not been restricted to non-Western societies. Indeed, in the United States, religion became an even more powerful force in politics after the 1970s. Organized religion has long loomed large in the United States, especially compared with its relatively less important place in other developed nations. A poll taken in the mid-1970s, for example, found that 56 percent of

American Hostage Crisis in Iran. Having restored the shah in a clumsy 1953 coup by the CIA, the United States was stunned in 1979 by Iran's Islamic Revolution, which overthrew the shah and brought the exiled cleric Ayatollah Ruhollah Khomeini to power. After radical students captured the U.S. embassy, as well as fifty-three hostages, an American rescue raid failed, leading to celebration by Iranians, as shown here.

Americans rated religious faith as "very important" to them. By contrast, only 27 percent of Europeans made the same claim. Since the 1970s, the membership and activism of conservative, fundamentalist Protestant churches have eclipsed more liberal mainline denominations. Insisting on the literal interpretation of the Bible, Protestant fundamentalists have long railed against secularizing trends in American society. In recent years, this traditionalist crusade has grown more fervent and has taken up a broad range of cultural and political issues. In particular, religious conservatives, predominantly evangelical Protestants, but including some Catholics and Orthodox Jews, have attacked many of the social changes that emerged from liberation movements of the 1960s. Shifting sexual and familial relations have been sore points for these religious conservatives, but the real diatribe has been reserved for public rulers who, by legalizing abortion and supporting secular values, have abandoned the moral purpose of authority.

DEMOCRACY

New sources of power and new social movements have drastically changed politics in the global age. Increasingly, international organizations have played a decisive role in defining the conditions of democratic citizenship.

Perhaps most remarkable is how much democracy has spread since the 1970s. In South Africa, Russia, and Guatemala, elections decided the fate of politicians. In this sense, the world's societies have embraced the idea that people have a right to choose their own representatives. Nevertheless, democracy has not triumphed everywhere. An important holdout has been China. Mao died in 1976, and within a few years, his successor, Deng Xiaoping, began to open the nation's economy to market forces. But Deng and other leaders in the Chinese Communist Party resisted opening the political system to multi-party competition. Instead of capitalism and Western-style democracy, Chinese officials maintained that China should follow its own path to modernity.

By the late 1980s, economic reforms had produced spectacular increases in production and rising standards of living for most of China's people. But the widening gap between rich and poor, together with increasing public awareness of corruption within the party and the government, triggered popular discontent. Worker strikes and slowdowns, peasant unrest, and student activism spread. On April 22, 1989, some 100,000 people gathered in Tiananmen Square at the heart of Beijing, in silent defiance of a government ban on assembling, under the pretext of honoring the recent death of a reformist official. The following month brought an even greater show of defiance. Television cameras and journalists of the world converged on China to cover the historic official visit of Soviet leader Mikhail Gorbachev. Several hundred students, flanked by thousands of their supporters, began a hunger strike at the foot of the Monument to the Heroes of the Revolution at the center of the square. They demanded the opening up of the political system to democratic reform. Tiananmen Square was now their stage and the world their audience. Within days, the strike spread to other cities. In Beijing, well over a million people filled the city center in what was perhaps the largest mass rally since the founding of the People's Republic in 1949. Even as dehydrated strikers were rushed to the hospitals, a carnivalesque atmosphere pervaded the square, as the students sang and danced to rock songs and folk ballads.

The regime responded by declaring martial law on May 19. Two huge protest demonstrations of over a million participants each followed, and residents erected barricades to defend the city against the troops that had begun to descend upon the capital. As the momentum of the protest began to wane, a twenty-eight-foot icon, in part inspired by the Statue of Liberty, was unveiled at the square on May 30, capturing the imagination of

Tiananmen Square. This white plaster and styrofoam statue, inspired in part by the Statue of Liberty and dubbed the Goddess of Democracy, was created by students at the Central Academy of Fine Arts in Beijing in the spring of 1989. It was brought to Tiananmen Square and unveiled at the end of May in an attempt to reinvigorate the Democracy Movement and the spirits of the protesters. For five days it captured the attention and imagination of millions of viewers around the world, until it was toppled by a tank on the morning of June 4 and crushed as the Chinese People's Liberation Army cleared the square of its democracy advocates.

the crowd and the attention of the cameras. But by then the government had assembled its loyal troops to crush the movement. In a night of terror that began at dusk on June 3, the People's Liberation Army turned their guns against the people. Most students in the square were able to negotiate a safe passage; those who lost their lives—estimates vary from about 2,000 to 7,000—were the nameless people who picked up Molotov cocktails, sticks, or bricks in a heroic, if futile, attempt to repel the occupying troops.

The Chinese government, unlike its Eastern European counterparts, weathered the storm. The government continued to suppress unofficial social organizations, to control access to information, including that obtained over the Internet, and to crack down on dissidents. But the Chinese government could not completely control the forces of globalization. Some organizations, like the quasi-religious group Falun Gong, managed to elude authorities and even to use the Internet to enlist international support and membership. At the dawn of the twenty-first century, signs of change are also apparent. A visible urban entrepreneurial class has emerged, whose top echelon conducts its global businesses over increasingly ubiquitous cellular phones. Rural dwellers, particularly from the southeastern coast, pay what little they have to be smuggled abroad, at great risk and often with lethal consequences, so that they can make a better living in America or Europe. Within China, tens of millions of people live a transient existence, with tens of thousands daily leaving the countryside for the cities. There they often become the victims of economic and social exploitation, to say nothing of police and other government abuse. Existing at the margins of the new prosperity, they, too, serve as reminders of the uneven and unsettling effects of globalization.

In Mexico, democracy has finally triumphed, as the single party that dominated the country for seventy-one years was finally defeated with the election of Vicente Fox in July 2000. Until that time, Mexican rulers had combined patronage and rigged elections to stay in office. By the 1980s, corruption and widespread abuse permeated the system. The abuse of democratic rights fell hardest on poor communities, especially hitting provinces where there were large numbers of indigenous people, as in the state of Chiapas in the south. Chiapas, an impoverished area with a significant population of Mayan descendants, encountered great difficulties coping with the challenges of social and economic change in the 1980s. From Mexico City, the president stripped Indians of their right to communal land and let the ruling party run Chiapas like a fiefdom. By the early 1990s, Chiapas was seething with discontent and demanding material betterment, cultural recognition of Indian rights, and local democracy. One group of rebels, called the Zapatistas in

Protests in Mexico. *(Left)* After generations of oppression and exclusion, peasants of Chiapas, in southern Mexico, called for democracy and respect for their right to land. When Mexican authorities refused to bend, peasants took up arms. While they knew that they posed no military threat to the Mexican army, the Zapatista rebels shrewdly used the world media and international organizations to embarrass the national political establishment into allowing reforms. *(Right)* Among the great Mexican muralists of the twentieth century, David Alfaro Siqueiros most advocated class struggle and most ridiculed the ruling classes. In this 1957 mural image, *The People in Arms*, Siqueiros portrays Mexican peasants as they pick up arms in 1910 to fight for a new order. Paintings such as these provided a popular repertoire for resistance and rebellion against injustice, and provided inspiration for movements such as the Chiapas Rebellion in the 1990s.

INDIGENOUS PEOPLE IN MEXICO SPEAK OUT

In late 1993, peasants of Chiapas, a southern state of Mexico, rejected the false promises of the national government. Mostly Indians living in the Lacandon jungle region, they had seen their land rights taken away and lived under the boot of oppressive authorities. On January 1, 1994, they finally took up arms against the government, protesting official abuses and calling for a restoration of the principles of the Mexican Revolution: land for the hungry, democracy, and an end to centuries of neglect and oppression of Indians across the Americas. They formed an organization, the Zapatista Army for National Liberation (EZLN—known familiarly as the Zapatistas, recalling the name of the hero of the 1910 Revolution). Vastly out-armed, the EZLN mounted a brilliant public relations campaign and enlisted massive international support. Here is an excerpt from their official declaration of war against the Mexican government.

We are a product of 500 years of struggle: first against slavery, during the War of Independence against Spain led by the insurgents; afterward to avoid being absorbed by American imperialism; then to promulgate our constitution and expel the French Empire from our soil; and later the Porfirista dictatorship denied us just application of the Reform laws, and the people rebelled, forming their own leaders; Villa and Zapata emerged, poor men like us, who have been denied the most elemental preparation so as to be able to use us as cannon fodder and pillage the wealth of our country, without it mattering to them that we have nothing, absolutely nothing, not even a decent roof over our heads, no land, no work, no health care, no food, or education; without the right to freely and democratically elect our authorities; without independence from foreigners, without peace or justice for ourselves and our children.

But TODAY WE SAY, ENOUGH! We are the heirs of those who truly forged our nationality. We the dispossessed are millions, and we call on our brothers to join in this call as the only path in order not to die of hunger in the face of the insatiable ambition of a dictatorship for more than 70 years led by a clique of traitors who represent the most conservative and sell-out groups in the country. They are the same as those who opposed Hidalgo and Morelos, who betrayed Vicente Guerrero, the same as those who sold over half our territory to the foreign invader, the same as those who brought a European prince to rule us, the same as those who formed the dictatorship of the Porfirista "scientists," the same as those who opposed the Oil Expropriation, the same as those who massacred the railroad workers in 1958 and the students in 1968, the same

as those who today take everything from us, absolutely everything.

To prevent this, and as our last hope, after having tried everything to put into practice the legality based on our Magna Carta, we resort to it, to our Constitution, to apply Constitutional Article 39, which says:

"National sovereignty resides essentially and originally in the people. All public power emanates from the people and is instituted for the people's benefit. The people have, at all times, the unalienable right to alter or modify the form of their government."

Therefore, according to our Constitution, we issue this statement to the Mexican federal army, the basic pillar of the Mexican dictatorship that we suffer, monopolized as it is by the party in power and led by the federal executive that is presently held by its highest and illegitimate chief, Carlos Salinas de Gortari.

In conformity with this Declaration of War, we ask the other branches of the Nation's government to meet to restore the legality and the stability of the Nation by deposing the dictator. . . .

PEOPLE OF MEXICO: We, upright and free men and women, are conscious that the war we declare is a last resort, but it is just. The dictators have been applying an undeclared genocidal war against our people for many years. Therefore we ask for your decided participation in support of this plan of the Mexican people in their struggle for work, land, housing, food, health care, education, independence, liberty, democracy, justice, and peace. . . .

Source: General Council of the EZLN, *Declaración de la Selva Lacandona,* 1993 (www.ezln.org, January 1, 1994).

honor of the hero of the Mexican Revolution, rose up against Mexico City on January 1, 1994. In response, the government prepared to crush the insurgents. What no one anticipated was how supranational forces would play a role in helping local democracy. Cable News Network set up a caravan to broadcast the clash to world living rooms; rebel leader Subcommander Marcos, meanwhile, set up a web site, whose humor and wit immediately attracted thousands of "hits." Thereafter, international news media flooded Chiapas, filming parading Indians waving flags and pronouncing victory. Mexico City, deeply embarrassed, asked local church authorities to help negotiate peace and to lead a special commission to hear the concerns of the villagers. In 2000, national elections toppled the ruling party, including its representatives in the state of Chiapas, and Mexico dismantled its one-party ruling system.

 CONCLUSION

In the thirteenth century (and much earlier, too), people ventured over long distances, to trade, to explore, and to convert souls; yet, communications technology was rudimentary, making long-distance mobility and exchange expensive, rare, and sometimes perilous. The vast majority organized their livelihoods and identified themselves with local places. The world was much more a series of communities set apart than a world bound together by culture, capital, and communication networks.

By the end of the twentieth century, that balance had changed. Food, entertainment, clothing, and even family life appeared more and more similar than ever before. To be sure, local differences have not been obliterated. In 2000, the local lives on, and in some cases has been revived, thanks to the challenges to the authority of nation-states. No longer does the nation-state or any single level of community life define collective identities. At the same time, worldwide purveyors of cultural and commercial resources offer local communities the same kinds of products, from aspirin to Nike shoes. Exchanges across local and national boundaries have become easier. The world is more together than apart.

New technologies, new methods of production and investment, and, above all, the greater importance of personal health and education for human betterment have created new possibilities and greater inequalities. Indeed, in contrast to the world in 1300, or in 1800, the degrees of disparity between the haves and the have-nots in 2000 could scarcely have been imagined.

For, as humanity has learned to harness new technologies to accelerate and intensify exchanges across and within cultures, a larger and larger gulf has separated those who participate in the networks of globalization and enjoy its fruits from those who languish on the margins. Thus, as the world has become more integrated, and grown more together, it has also grown apart along ever-deeper lines. These disparities also have produced divergent and different political and cultural forms, despite the collapse of the three-world order.

Chronology

1979–1980	American hostage crisis in Iran
1979–1989	Soviet war in Afghanistan
1979	Nicaraguan Revolution
1981	AIDS first detected
1983	Strategic Defense Initiative authorized (U.S.)
1985	Gorbachev becomes general secretary of Communist Party (Soviet Union)
1986	Chernobyl nuclear accident (Soviet Union)
1989	Berlin Wall falls
1989	Tiananmen Square demonstrations (China)
1989	Eastern European Communist regimes topple
1989–2001	Secession wars in former Yugoslavia
1990	Germany reunited
1990	Mandela released from prison
1990–1998	Civil war in Rwanda (Africa)
1991	Dissolution of Soviet Union
1991	Gulf War (Middle East)
1991	Maastricht Treaty (Europe)
1992	North American Free Trade Agreement (NAFTA) negotiated
1992	Earth Summit (Rio de Janeiro)
1994	Chiapas Revolt begins (Mexico)
1994	Free elections in South Africa
1995	Fourth World Conference on Women (Beijing)
2001	Civilian airliners crashed into World Trade Center and Pentagon (U.S.)

FURTHER READINGS

Bakhash, Shaul, *The Reign of the Ayatollahs: Iran and the Islamic Revolution* (1984). Provides good historical background on the events that resulted in the overthrow of the shah.

Davis, Deborah (ed.), *The Consumer Revolution in Urban China* (2000). A look at the different aspects of the recent, profound social transformation of urban China.

Davis, Mike, *City of Quartz: Excavating the Future in Los Angeles* (1990). Offers sometimes prescient, sometimes polemical, and always provocative reflections on the recent history, current condition, and the possible future of Los Angeles.

Davis, Mike, *Ecology of Fear: Los Angeles and the Imagination of Disaster* (1998). More on Los Angeles, with special attention to the connections between environmental problems and social inequities.

Dutton, Michael, *Streetlife China* (1999). A fascinating portrayal of the survival tactics of those inhabiting the margins of society in today's China.

Eichengreen, Barry, *Globalizing Capital: A History of the International Monetary System* (1996). An insightful analysis of how international capital markets changed in the period from 1945 to 1980.

Guillermoprieto, Alma, *Looking for History: Dispatches from Latin America* (2001). A collection of articles by the most important journalist reporting on Latin American affairs.

Han Minzhu (ed.), *Cries for Democracy: Writings and Speeches from the 1989 Chinese Democracy Movement* (1990). A collection of documents from the events leading up to the June 4th Incident of 1989.

Hancock, Graham, *Lords of Poverty: The Power, Prestige, and Corruption of the International Aid Business* (1989). An exposé of the many downsides of humanitarianism in the age of globalization.

Herbst, Jeffrey, *States and Power in Africa: Comparative Lessons in Authority and Control* (2000). Explores the political dilemmas facing modern African polities.

Honig, Emily, and Gail Hershatter, *Personal Voices: Chinese Women in the 1980's* (1988). A record of Chinese women during a period of rapid social change.

Keddie, Nikki R., *Roots of Revolution: An Interpretive History of Modern Iran* (1981). Provides good historical background on the Iranian Revolution.

Klitgaard, Robert, *Tropical Gangsters* (1990). On the contemporary world's symbiosis between corrupt native elites and international agencies.

Kotkin, Stephen, *Armageddon Averted: The Soviet Collapse, 1970–2000* (2001). Places the surprise dissolution of the Soviet Union firmly in the context of shifts in the post–World War II world.

Mamdani, Mahmood, *Citizen and Subject: Contemporary Africa and the Legacy of Late Colonialism* (1996). Discusses the political problems of modern Africa in light of the legacy of colonialism.

Patel, Sujata, and Alice Thorner (eds.), *Bombay: Metaphor for Modern India* (1997). Articles on the politics and economy of the city of Bombay.

Portes, Alejandro, and Rubén G. Rumbaut, *Immigrant America* (2nd ed., 1996). A good comparative study of how immigration has transformed the United States.

Van Der Wee, Hermann, *Prosperity and Upheaval: The World Economy, 1945–1980* (1986). Describes very well the transformation and problems of the world economy, particularly from the 1960s onward.

Winn, Peter, *Americas: The Changing Face of Latin America and the Caribbean* (1992). A useful portrayal of Latin America since the 1970s.

Each word is divided into syllables, with the stress on the syllable that is capitalized. Where all syllables are capitalized, each syllable gets equal stress. Where there is an apostrophe rather than a hyphen separating two syllables, it represents a slurring together of the two syllables. Below is a key to how the vowel sounds are being represented in this guide.

a	as in bat, hat
ah	as in bar, father
aw	as in awful, law
ay	as in date, same
eh	as in bet, set
ee	as in easy, teeth
eye	as in fine, shine
ih	as in if, stiff
o	as in door, or
oh	as in go, show
oo	as in jewel, tool
ow	as in cow, house
uh	as in but, abrupt

Abbasid (uh-BAH-sid)
Akbar (ak-BAHR)
al-Jabarti (AHL juh-BAHR-tee)
Alafin (uh-LAY-fihn)
Apartheid (uh-PAHR- tayd)
Asante (uh-SHAHN-tee)
Asantehene (uh-SHAHN-tee-hee-nay)
Atahualpa (ah-tuh-WAHL-puh)
Aurangzeb (AW-rahng-zehb)
Azikiwe, Nnamdi (uh-ZEE-kee-way, nih-NAHM-dee)
Aztlan (ahz-TLAN)

Babur (BAH-boor)
Bahia (buh-HEE-uh)
Benguela (ben-GAY-luh)
Bukhara (boo-KAHR-uh)

Cajamarca (ka-huh-MAHR-kuh)
Caliph (KAY-luhf)
Caravanserai (kar-uh-VAN-suh-reye)
Caravel (KAR-uh-vehl)
Caudillo (kaw-DEEL-yoh)
Ceausescu, Nicolae (chow-SHEHS-koo, nee-kaw-LEYE)
Ceuta ((SAY-oo-tuh)
Ceylon (say-LAHN)
Chiang Kai-shek (CHANG KEYE-SHEHK)
Chiapas (chee-AH-pahs)
Chinggis Khan (CHIHNG-GIHS KAAHN)
Cixi (TSSUH-SHEEH)
Cohong (CO-HOHNG)
Conquistador (kohn-KEE-stuh-dor)
Creole (KREE-ohl)
Crimea (kreye-MEE-uh)
Cuauhtémoc (kwow-TAY-mahk)
Curacao (koo-rah-SOW)
Cuzco (koos-COH)

Dahomey (DUH-hoh-mee)
Daimyo (DEYEM-YOH)
Deng Xaioping (DEHNG SHOW-PIHNG)
Devshirme (dev-sheer-MEE)
Dhow (DOW)
Dhimmi (dihm-MEE)
Dior, Lat (DEE-or, LAT)
Djerba (JER-buh)
Dongyang (DONG-YAHNG)
Dubcek, Alexander (DOOB-chehk, ah-lehk-SAHN-der)

Entrepot (AHN-truh-poh)
Eritrea (er-ah-TREE-uh)

Fang Xiaoru (FOHNG SHEE'OWW-ROO)
Faruq (fuh-ROOK)
Fatehpur Sikri (FAH-tah-poor SEEK-ree)

Fatimid (FAT-uh-mid)
Feringis (FEH-RING'GEES)
Fluitschips (FLOOT-shihps)
Fodio, Usman dan (FOH-dee-oh, OOS-mahn dan)
Foshan (FOH-SHAHN)
Fujian (FOO-JEE'EN)
Fulani (FOO-lah-nee)

Gallipoli (guh-LIHP-uh-lee)
Gangetic (gan-GEH-teek)
Gautama, Siddhartha (GOWT-uh-muh, si-DAHRT-uh)
Geisha (GAY-shuh)
Gezhi Huibian (GEH-JEH HWAY-BEE'EN)
Gouges, Olympe de (GOOJ, Oh-LEEMP-deh)
Guaman Poma de Ayuala (Gwah-MAHN poh-MAH day ah-WAY-lah)
Guan Yu (GWAHN-YEW)
Guangdong (GWOHNG-DONG)
Guangzhou (GWOHNG-JOH)
Guevara, Che (guh-VAHR-uh, CHAY)
Gujarat (goo-juh-RAHT)
Guomintang (GWOH-MIHN-DAHNG)

Hadith (hah-DEETH)
Hagia Sophia (HAY-jee-uh SOH-fee-uh)
Haiti (hay-TEE)
Hangzhou (HAHNG-JOH)
Hausa (HOW-suh)
hijra (HIJ-ruh)
Hind Swaraj (HIHND swuh-RAHJ)
Ho Ao (HEH OWW)
Hohenzollern (HOH-uhnt-SAWL-uhrn)
Homs (HOHMS)
Hongwu (HOHNG-WOO)
Hong Xiuquan (HOHNG SHEE'OH-CHEW'EN)
Hormuz (hohr-MOOZ)
Huang Liuhong (HWOHNG LEE'OH-HONG)
Huayi tu (HWAH-YEE TOO)
Huitzilopochtli (wee-tsee-loh-POCKT-lee)

Ibn Battuta (IB-uhn ba-TOO-tuh)
Ibn Khaldun (IB-uhn KAHL-dun)
Imam (ih-MAHM)
Imre Nagy (EEM-ray Nazh)
Iroquois (eer-uh-KWOY)

Jajiellons (YAH-hyuh-lohn)
Jahangir (JUH-hahn-geer)
Janissaries (JAN-ih-sayr-ees)
Jati (JAH-tee)
Jenne (Jeh-NAY)
Jiaozhou (JEE'OWW-JOH)
Jihad (jee-HAHD)
Jingdezhen (JING-DUH-JUN)

Jinsei (JIN-SAY)
Jizya (JIHZ-yuh)
Jurchens (JUHR-CHENZ)

Kabuki (KA-BOO-KEE)
Kaifeng (KEYE-FUNG)
Kang Youwei (KAHNG YOH-WAY)
Kanun (kah-NOON)
Karakorum (kohr-uh-KOHR-uhm)
Khalji, Ala-ud din (kuhl-JEE, AL-LAH-ood dihn)
Khanbaliq (KAHN-bah-LEEK)
Khomeini, Ayatollah Ruhollah (KOH-may-nee, EYE-ah-toh-lah ROO-hohl-lah)
Khruschev, Nikita (kroosh-SHAWF, nih-KEE-tah)
Khurasan (kor-uh-SAHN)
Kinsai (KEEN-SA'EE)
Kong Qiu (KOHNG CHEE'OH)
Kubilai (KOOH'BUH'LEYE)
Kshatriyas (KSHAHT-ree-uhs)

Lahore (luh-HOR)
Lesotho (luh-SOH-toh)
Liadong (LYOU-DONG)
Li Zicheng (LEE ZUH-CHUNG)
Liang Qichao (LEE'ANG CHEE-CHOWW)
Lin Zexu (LINN ZEH-SHOO)
Loyola, Ignatius (loy-OH-luh, ihg-NAY-shuhs)

Macao (MAH'KOWW)
Madrasa (muh-DRAH-suh)
Mahdi (MAH-dee)
Maluku (mah-LOO-koo)
Mamluk (mam-LOOK)
Manchukuo (MAN'CHOO'GWOH)
Mansa Musa (MAHN-suh MOO-suh)
Mao Zedong (MOWW ZEH-DONG)
Maraghah (mah-rah-GAH)
Mecca (MEK-kuh)
Meerut (MAY-ruht)
Mehmed (MEH-med)
Meiji (MAY-JEE)
Melaka (muh-LAH-kuh)
Metis (MAY-teez)
millet (MIL-leht)
Mitsui (MIH-TSUH-EE)
Mfecane (um-fuh-KAHN-uh)
Moctezuma (mon-teh-ZOOM-ah)
Motoori Norinaga (MOH-TOH-OREE NO-REE-NA-GA)
Modan gāru (MOH-DAN GAA-ROO)
mufti (MOOF-tee)
Mustafa Ali (moos-TA-fa A-lee)
Mutsuhito (MOO'TSUH-HEE-TOH)

Najd (NA-jid)

Ndebele (nih-duh-BAY-lay)
Negritude (NEH-grih-tood)
Nehru, Jawaharlal (NAY-roo, ja-WAH-hahr-lahl)
Nguni (nih-GOO-nee)
Ngwale, Kinjikitile (nih-guh-WA-lay, kihn-jih-KEE-tih-lay)
Nkrumah, Kwame (nih-KROO-muh, KWAH-mee)
Nüwa (NEW-WAAH)
Nyerere, Julius (NEE-yer-ay, JOO-lee-uhs)

Oxus (OX-us)

Palmares (PAL-muh-ruhs)
Pat, Jacinto (PAT, Ya-SIHN-toh)
Perestroika (PAYR-eh-stroy-kuh)
Poot, Crecencio (POOT, kree-SEHN-see-oh)
Potosi (poh-toh-SEE)
Punjab (POON-jahb)
Purdahnishin (puhr-DAH-nuh-shihn)

Qadi (KA-dee)
Qadiriyya (ka-duh-REE-yuh)
Qianlong (CHEE'EN-LOHNG)
Qing (CHIHNG)
Qiu Jin (CHEE'OH JIHN)
Qizilbash (kih-zihl-BAHSH)
Quanzhou (CHEW'EN-JOH)
Quechua (KECH-wuh)
Quetzalcoátl (keht-sahl-koh-AHT-l)
Quran (kor-AHN)

Rajput (RAHJ-poot)
Recife (re-SEE-feh)
Reconquista (ray-kohn-KEE-stah)
Ren Xiong (RUHN SHEE'OHNG)
Ricci, Matteo (REE-CHEE, mah-TAY-oh)
Rwanda (roo-WAHN-duh)
Ryūkyū (REE-YOO-K'YOO)

Saffavid (SAH-fah-vihd)
Samarkand (SAM-uhr-kahnd)
Samurai (SAM-uhr-eye)
Sangh, Rashtriya Swayasevak (SUHNGH, RAHSH-TREE-yuh swuhm-SWAY-uhk)
São Tomé (SOW TOH-may)
Satyagraha (suh-TYAH-gruh-huh)
Selim (say-LEEM)
Sepoy (SEE-poy)
Shaanxi (SHAHN-SHEE)
Sharia (shah-REE-uh)
Shiism (SHEE-ihz-uhm)
Shiite (SHEE-eyet)
Sichuan (SEHCH-WAHN)
Singh, Devi (SIHNGH, DAY-vee)
Sokoto (SOH-koh-toh)

Solzhenitsyn, Alexander (sohl-zhuh-NEET-sihn, ah-lehk-SAHN-der)
Sufi (SOO-fee)
Suleiman (SOO-lee-mahn)
Sunni (SOON-nee)
Suzhou (SUH-JOH)

Taiping (TEYE-ping)
Tanzimat (TAN-zee-mat)
Tecumseh (tuh-CUM-suh)
Tenochtitlán (tehn-osh-teet-LAHN)
Tenskwatawa (ten-SKWAH-tuh-wah)
Tiananmen (TEA'EN'AN'MUN)
Tippecanoe (tip-ee-kah-NOO)
Tlaxcala (tlah-SKAHL-uh)
Tokugawa Ieyasu (TOH-KOO-GAH-WAH EE'EH-YAH-SUH)
Topkapi (TOP-ka-pee)
Tsetse (TSEHT-see)

Uighur (WEE-GOOR)
Ulama (OO-luh-mah)
Usman dan Fodio (OOS-mahn dan FOH-dee-oh)

Vaishyas (VEYES-yuhs)
Vedas (VAY-duhs)
Vizier (vi-ZEER)

Wafd (WAHFT)
Wahhabi (wuh-HAHB-bee)

Walesa, Lech (WAH-lehn-sah, LEHK)
Wanguo gongbao (WAN-GWOH GOHNG-BOWW)
Wanli (WAN-LEE)
Wokou (WOH-KOH)
Wovoka (wah-VOH-kah)
Wu Sangui (WOO SAN-GWAY)
Wu T'ing-chü (WOO TING-CHEW)

Xinjiang (SHIN-JEE'ANG)

Yangzi (YAHNG-ZUH)
Yanzhou (YEN-JOH)
Ye-huo-hua (YEH-HWOH-HWAH)
Yingtian (YING-TEE'EN)
Yongle (YOHNG-LEH)
Yoruba (YOUR-uh-bah)
Yuan Shikai (YEW'EN SHIH-KYE)
Yunnan (YUN'NAN)

Zacatecas (sah-kah-TEH-kas)
Zaghlul, Sa'd (ZAHG-lool, SAHD)
Zaibatsu (ZA'EE-BAH-TSUH)
Zedong, Mao (ZEH-DONG, MOWW)
Zexu, Lin (ZEH-SHOO, LINN)
Zheng He (JUNG HEH)
Zhongguo Nübao (JUNG-GWOH NEW-BOWW)
Zhu Di (JOOH DEE)
Zhu Yijun (JOOH YEE-JUNE)
Zhu Yuanzhang (JOOH YEW'EN JAHNG)
Zimbabwe (zihm-BAHB-way)

World political map and world satellite map appearing in frontmatter courtesy The National Geographic Society Image Collection.

PRIMARY SOURCE DOCUMENTS

CHAPTER 1: p. 17: *Ibn Battuta in Black Africa*, pp. 58-59, edited by Said Hamdum and Miriam Cooke. Copyright © 1994 Markus Wiener Publishers. Reprinted by permission of Markus Wiener Publishers, Princeton. *The Travels of Marco Polo*, pp. 57-58, translated by Ronald Latham, Penguin Classics, 1958. Copyright © Ronald Latham, 1958. Reproduced by permission of Penguin Books, Ltd. **p. 19:** *The Travels of Ibn Battuta*, pp. 618, 747-48, translated by H. A. R. Gibb. Copyright © Cambridge University Press. Reprinted with the permission of Cambridge University Press. **p. 29:** *The Travels of Marco Polo*, pp. 213-14, translated by Ronald Latham, Penguin Classics, 1958. Copyright © Ronald Latham, 1958. Reproduced by permission of Penguin Books, Ltd. *The Travels of Ibn Battuta*, pp. 900-901, translated by H. A. R. Gibb. Copyright © Cambridge University Press. Reprinted with the permission of Cambridge University Press. **p. 34:** *The Travels of Marco Polo*, pp. 252-53, translated by Ronald Latham, Penguin Classics, 1958. Copyright © Ronald Latham, 1958. Reproduced by permission of Penguin Books, Ltd. *The Travels of Ibn Battuta*, pp. 876-80, translated by H. A. R. Gibb. Copyright © Cambridge University Press. Reprinted with the permission of Cambridge University Press.

CHAPTER 2: p. 54: Ahmet Karamustafa, *God's Unruly Friends: Dervish Groups in the Islamic Later Middle Period, 1200-1550*, Chapter 6, pp. 6-7. Copyright © University of Utah Press. Reprinted courtesy The University of Utah Press. **p. 57:** *Sources of Indian Tradition*, pp. 536-38, edited by William Theodore de Bary. Copyright © 1958 Columbia University Press. **p. 61:** Reprinted with the permission of The Free Press, a division of Simon & Schuster, Inc., from *Chinese Civilization: A Sourcebook*, Second Edition, revised and expanded, pp. 205-206, edited by Patricia Buckley Ebrey. Copyright © 1993 by Patricia Buckley Ebrey. **p. 67:** *The Black Death*, pp. 153-54, translated and edited by Rosemary Horrox. Copyright © 1994 Manchester University Press.

CHAPTER 3: p. 111: Tien-Tse Chang, *Sino-Portuguese Trade from 1514 to 1644: A Synthesis of Portuguese and Chinese Sources*, pp. 51-52. Copyright © 1933 by Brill Academic Publishers Inc. Reproduced with permission of Brill Academic Publishers Inc, in the format Textbook via Copyright Clearance Center.

CHAPTER 4: p. 129: "Claudia the Witch," in *Tales of Potosi*, pp. 117-21, edited by R.C. Padden. Copyright © 1975 by Brown University, reprinted by permission of University Press of New England. **p. 143:** Excerpt from *A Complete Book Concerning Happiness and Benevolence*, pp. 190-91, by Huang Liu-Hung, translated and edited by Djang Chu © 1984 The Arizona Board of Regents. Reprinted by permission of the University of Arizona Press.

CHAPTER 5: p. 169: Al Idrisi map, Giraudon/Art Resource; Iranian map, Private collection, courtesy of the owner and D. A. King; photo by Christies of London. **p. 175:** The *Huayi tu* map, Reprinted by permission of the Needham Research Institute; Chinese wheel map, Courtesy the British Library, London. **p. 181:** Waldseemüller map, Reprinted by permission of the Rare Books Division, The New York Public Library, Astor, Lenox, and Tilden Foundations; Mercator projection, courtesy Wychwood Editions.

CHAPTER 6: p. 225: *Napoleon in Egypt: al-Jabarti's Chronicle of the French Occupation, 1709*, pp. 24-29, translated by Schmuel Moreh. Reprinted by permission of Markus Wiener Publishers, Princeton.

CHAPTER 7: p. 250: *Sources of Chinese Tradition*, 2nd ed., Vol. 2, pp. 229-30, edited by William Theodore de Bary and Richard Lufrano. Copyright © 2000 by Columbia University Press. Reprinted with the permission of Columbia University Press. **p. 256:** "Manifesto of the Communist Party," from *The Marx-Engels Reader*, 2nd ed., by Robert C. Tucker. Copyright © 1978, 1972 by W. W. Norton & Company, Inc. Used by permission of W. W. Norton & Company, Inc.

CHAPTER 8: p. 282: "What Is a Nation?" in *The Nationalism Reader*, edited by Omar Dahbour and Micheline R. Ishay. Copyright © 1995 The Humanities Press. Reprinted by permission of Oxford University Press. **p. 303:** *The Emergence of the Modern Russian State, 1855-1881*, by Martin McCauley and Peter Waldron. Copyright © 1988 by Barnes and Noble Books.

CHAPTER 9: p. 323: Franziska von Reventlow, "Viragines oder Hetaere" in *Autobiographisches, Novellen, Schriften, Selbtzeugnisse*, edited by Else Reventlow, translated by Suzanne Marchand. Reprinted with the permission of Suzanne Marchand. **p. 325:** Reprinted with the permission of The Free Press, a division of Simon & Schuster, Inc., from *Chinese Civilization: A Sourcebook*, Second Edition, revised and expanded, pp. 342-44, edited by Patricia Buckley Ebrey. Copyright © 1993 by Patricia Buckley Ebrey. **p. 326:** *Opening the Gates: A Century of Arab Feminist Writing*, pp. 228-38, edited by Margot Badran and Miriam Booke. Copyright © 1990 Indiana University Press. Reprinted with the permission of Indiana University Press. **p. 339:** Rokeya Sakhawat Hossain, *Sultana's Dream: A Feminist Utopia and Selections from the Secluded Ones*, translation copyright © 1988 by Roushan Jahan, by permission of the Feminist Press at the City University of New York, www.feministpress.org

CHAPTER 10: p. 359: Reprinted with the permission of Simon & Schuster, Inc., from *The Man Nobody Knows* by Bruce Barton, pp. 241-42. Copyright © 1925 by The Bobbs-Merrill Co., Inc.; copyright renewed © 1952 by Bruce Barton. **p. 369:** Ernest R. Huber, "Fuhrergewalt," in *Nazism 1919-1945: A Documentary Reader, Volume 2: State Economy and Society 1933-1939*, pp. 198-99, edited by J. Noakes and G. Pridham, new edition 2000. Copyright © 2000, 1984 University of Exeter Press. Reprinted with the permission of University of Exeter Press. **p. 377:** Mohandas Gandhi, *Hind Swaraj and Other Writings*, pp. 26-91, edited and translated by Anthony J. Parel. Copyright © Cambridge University Press. Reprinted with the permission of Cambridge University Press.

CHAPTER 11: p. 399: *Sources of Chinese Tradition*, 2nd ed., Vol. 2, pp. 422-23, edited by William Theodore de Bary and Richard Lufrano. Copyright © 2000 by Columbia University Press. Reprinted with the permission of Columbia University Press. **p. 402:** *Jawaharlal Nehru: An Anthology*, pp. 306-307, edited by Sarvepalli Gopal. Copyright © 1980 Oxford University Press. Reprinted by permission of Oxford University Press. **p. 405:** Léopold Sédar Senghor, *African Socialism*, translated by Mercer Cook. Copyright © 1959 American Society of African Culture. Reprinted in *The Ideologies of the Developing Nations*, pp. 240-44, 248-49, edited by Paul Sigmund, Greenwood/Praeger Publishers.

CHAPTER 12: p. 430: Ann Tusa, "A Fatal Error," in *Media Studies Journal*, Fall 1999, pp. 26-29. Copyright © 1999. Reprinted by permission of *Media Studies Journal*. **p. 449:** World Development Report

2000-2001. Copyright © World Bank. Reprinted by permission of the World Bank. **p. 460:** Ejercito Zapatista, Declaracion de la Selva Lacandona, Today We Say Enough!, January 1, 1994. Open for public use; no permission required by the EZLN.

ART AND PHOTOS

CHAPTER 1: opener p. 2: Bibliothèque Nationale de France, Paris; **p. 9:** Schalkwijk/Art Resource, NY; **p. 12:** Werner Forman Archive/ Art Resource, NY; **p. 13:** Bibliothèque Nationale de France, Paris; **p. 14:** The Granger Collection; **p. 16:** The Granger Collection; **p. 18:** Sheldan Collins/Corbis; **p. 24:** ©1998 North Wind Picture Archives; **p. 25:** Réunion des Musées Nationaux/Art Resource; **p. 26:** North Wind Picture Archives; **p. 30:** ©1998 North Wind Picture Archives.

CHAPTER 2: opener p. 42: Scala/Art Resource, NY; **p. 45:** The Granger Collection, New York; **p. 51:** The Topkapi Palace Museum, Istanbul, Turkey/Giraudon/Art Resource; **p. 52:** ©Yann Arthus-Bertrand/Corbis; **p. 53:** *(top)* Stapleton Collection, UK/The Bridgeman Art Library International Ltd.; *(bottom)* Library of the Topkapi Palace Museum, folio 31b, photograph courtesy of Talat Halman; **p. 60:** The Granger Collection, New York; **p. 64:** The Jan Adkins Studio; **p. 68:** Bibliothèque Nationale de France, Paris; **p. 73:** Scala/Art Resource, NY; **p. 75:** Museo di Firenze com'era Firenze/Scala/Art Resource, NY.

CHAPTER 3: opener p. 78: Courtesy Wychwood Editions; **p. 82:** *(left)* By permission of The British Library (15226.b.19); *(right)* By permission of The British Library (15226.b.19); **p. 83:** Réunion des Musées Nationaux/Art Resource, NY; **p. 84:** *(top)*Service Historique de l'Armee de Terre, Vincennes, France/Giraudon/Art Resource, NY; *(bottom)* interoz.com; **p. 85:** Palazzo Ducale, Venice, Italy/Scala/Art Resource, NY; **p. 86:** Photograph by Erich Lessing/Art Resource, NY; **p. 88:** Biblioteca Estense, Modena,Italy/Scala/Art Resource, NY; **p. 89:** ©1994 North Winds Picture Archives; **p. 96:** *(left)* The Granger Collection, New York; *(right)* Nicolas Sapieha/Art Resource, NY; **p. 98:** *(left)* Schalkwijk/Art Resource, NY; *(right)* The Granger Collection, New York; **p. 99:** Angelo Cavalli/Superstock; **p. 101:** The Granger Collection, New York; **p. 104:** *(left)* The Granger Collection, New York; *(right)* Rare Books Division, New York Public Library, Astor, Lenox and Tilden Foundations; **p. 107:** Bildarchiv Preussischer Kulturbesitz; **p. 112:** Rijksmuseum, Amsterdam; **p. 114:** Réunion des Musées Nationaux/Art Resource, NY.

CHAPTER 4: opener p. 118: Réunion de Musées Nationaux/Art Resource, NY; **p. 124:** The Granger Collection, New York; **p. 130:** *(top)* The Granger Collection, New York; *(bottom left)* North Wind Picture Archives; *(bottom right)* Bibliothèque Nationale de France, Paris/Giraudon/Art Resource, NY; **p. 131:** *(left)* ©1989 North Wind Picture Archives; *(right)* Private Collection/The Bridgeman Art Library; **p. 134:** *(left)* Entwistle Gallery, London/Werner Forman/Art Resource, NY; *(right)* Rare Books Division, New York Public Library, Astor, Lenox and Tilden Foundations; **p. 135:** The Newberry Library; **p. 137:**

Reproduced from *Traditions and Encounters* (McGraw Hill, 2000); **p. 140:** Chester Beatty Library and Gallery of Oriental Art, Dublin/ The Bridgeman Art Library; **p. 142:** The Palace Museum, Beijing; **p. 147:** Réunion des Musées Nationaux/Art Resource, NY; **p. 150:** The British Museum/The Fotomas Index; **p. 153** *(bottom left)* Chester Beatty Library and Gallery of Oriental Art, Dublin/The Bridgeman Art Library; *(top right):* British Museum, London/E.T. Archives, London/SuperStock; **p. 154:** Amsterdam Historical Museum; **p. 155:** Anne S. K. Brown Military Collection, Brown University Library; **p. 157:** *(top)* Chateau de Versailles, France/The Bridgeman Art Library; *(bottom)* Private Collection/The Bridgeman Art Library; **p. 158:** By permission of Lord Dalmeny.

CHAPTER 5: opener p. 162: The Palace Museum, Beijing; **p. 165:** Topkapi Palace Museum, Istanbul, A3592, photograph courtesy of Talat Halman; **p. 166:** Topkapi Palace Museum, Istanbul; **p. 167:** *(left)* Topkapi Palace Museum, Istanbul/Werner Forman Archive/Art Resource, NY; *(Right)* Victoria & Albert Museum, London/Art Resource, NY; **p. 168:** Dr. Laurence Lockhart, Cambridge, England; **p. 169:** *(left)* Giraudon/Art Resource; *(right)* Private Collection, courtesy of the owner and D. A. King, contributor; photo by Christies of London; **p. 170:** Reproduced by the kind permission of the trustees of the Chester Beatty Library and Gallery of Oriental Art, Dublin; **p. 171:** Scala/Art Resource, NY; **p. 173:** Reproduced from *World Civilizations* (Addison Wesley Longman, 2001); **p. 174:** Courtesy Peabody Essex Museum, Salem MA; **p. 175:** *(left)* The Needham Research Institute; *(right)* The British Library, London; **p. 177:** *(top)* The British Library, London/The Bridgeman Art Library; *(bottom)* Réunion des Musées Nationaux/Art Resource, NY; **p. 179:** The Fotomas Index; **p. 181:** *(top left)* Courtesy Wychwood Editions; *(bottom right)* Rare Books Division, The New York Public Library, Astor, Lenox and Tilden Foundations; **p. 184:** Musée des Beaux-Arts, Rouen/SuperStock; **p. 185:** Private Collection/The Bridgeman Art Library; **p. 186:** Private Collection/The Bridgeman Art Library; **p. 189:** E.T. Archives, London/SuperStock; **p. 190:** The Granger Collection, New York; **p. 191:** The Granger Collection, New York; **p. 192:** Natural History Museum, London/The Bridgeman Art Library.

CHAPTER 6: opener p. 202: Lauros-Giraudon/The Bridgeman Art Library; **p. 202:** Collection of The New-York Historical Society; **p. 204:** Musée de la Ville de Paris, Musée Carnavalet/ Giraudon/Art Resource, NY; **p. 206:** Bibliothèque Nationale de France, Paris; **p. 208:** Lauros-Giraudon/The Bridgeman Art Library; **p. 210:** *(left bottom)* The Granger Collection, New York; *(top right)* North Wind Picture Archives; **p. 213:** The Granger Collection, New York; **p. 214:** Private Collection/The Bridgeman Art Library; **p. 216:** Reproduced from Michael Crowder's *West Africa: An Introduction to Its History* by courtesy of the publishers, Addison Wesley Longman; **p. 217:** The Granger Collection, New York; **p. 221:** The Granger Collection, New York; **p. 222:** The Granger Collection, New York; **p. 224:** Novosti/The Bridgeman Art Library; **p. 226:** Hulton/Bettmann/Corbis; **p. 229:** Courtesy of the director, National Army Museum, London; **p. 231:** The Palace Museum, Beijing; **p. 232:** *(top)* The British Library, London/The Bridgeman Art Library; *(bottom)* North Wind Picture Archives; **p. 233** Roy

Miles Fine Paintings/The Bridgeman Art Library; **p. 234:** © The National Maritime Museum Picture Library, London.

CHAPTER 7: opener p. 238: Harvard-Yenching Library, Harvard University; **p. 245:** The British Library, London; **p. 246:** National Archives, Zimbabwe; **p. 251:** Harvard-Yenching Library, Harvard University; **p. 254:** Bildarchiv Preussischer Kulturbesitz; **p. 258:** The Granger Collection, New York; **p. 265:** Corbis; **p. 266:** The Granger Collection, New York.

CHAPTER 8: opener p. 270: Tsuneo Tamba Collection, Yokohama/Laurie Platt Winfrey, Inc.; **p. 279:** Dmitri Kessel/TimePix; **p. 279:** *(left)* Hulton Getty/Archive Photos; *(right)* Hulton Getty/Archive Photos; **p. 283:** Schloss Friedrichsruhe, Germany/The Bridgeman Art Library; **p. 285:** © Archive Photos/PictureQuest; **p. 286:** The Art Archive; **p. 287:** *(top)* Illustrated London News/Mary Evans Picture Library; *(bottom)* Nizam's Good Works Project - Famine Relief: Road Building, Aurangabad 1895-1902, from Judith Gutman, *Through Indian Eyes*, Private Collection; **p. 291:** *(left)* Hulton Getty/Liaison; *(right)* The Warder Collection; **p. 292:** North Wind Picture Archives; **p. 293:** Ullstein Bilderdienst; **p. 295:** Illustrated London News, 1872/Mary Evans Picture Library; **p. 296:** *(top)* ©1999 North Wind Picture Archives; *(bottom):* © 1997 North Wind Picture Archives; **p. 298:** Tsuneo Tamba Collection, Yokohama/Laurie Platt Winfrey, Inc.; **p. 302:** Sovfoto/Eastfoto/PictureQuest.

CHAPTER 9: opener p. 308: SuperStock; **p. 313:** Private Collection/The Bridgeman Art Library; **p. 316:** *(top)* Photo by Hsun-ling, Freer Gallery of Art and the Arthur M. Sackler Gallery Archives, Smithsonian Institution, Washington, D.C.; *(bottom)* SuperStock; **p. 322:** ArchivoGeneral de la Nación, Buenos Aires, Documentos Fotográficos, Argentina; **p. 324:** Bettmann/Corbis; **p. 327:** © 2000 North Wind Picture Archives; **p. 328:** *(left)* Culver Pictures; **p. 328:** Sean Sprague/Mexicolore/The Bridgeman Art Library International Ltd; **p. 329:** Sigmund Freud Copyrights/Mary Evans Picture Library; **p. 331:** Bettmann/Corbis; **p. 332:** The Palace Museum, Beijing; **p. 334:** Bettmann/Corbis; **p. 335:** Schalkwijk/Art Resource, NY; **p. 337:** *(top left)* The Warder Collection; *(top right)* The Warder Collection; *(bottom right)* Harlingue-Viollet; **p. 338:** The Illustrated London News Picture Library; **p. 341:** E.O. Hoppé/Corbis.

CHAPTER 10: opener p. 346: The Illustrated London News Picture Library; **p. 351:** *(top)* The Imperial War Museum; *(bottom)* Hulton Getty/Archive Photos; **p. 354:** Sovfoto/Eastfoto; **p. 357:** SuperStock; **p. 358:** Culver Pictures; **p. 360:** Hulton Getty/Archive Photos; **p. 363:** SuperStock; **p. 364:** SuperStock; **p. 365:** Private Collection/The Bridgeman Art Library International Ltd; **p. 367:** The Illustrated London News Picture Library; **p. 368:** *(top)* Unattributed photograph in *The Hitler Album*/Mary Evans Picture Library; *(bottom)* TRH Pictures; **p. 376:** *(left)* The Illustrated London News Picture Library; *(right)* Private Collection/The Bridgeman Art Library; **p. 379:** Dinodia Picture Agency, Bombay; **p. 380:** Modern China Rare Photograph Library, *Sun Yat-Sen and the Guomindang Party* (The Commercial Press, Ltd., 1994); **p. 381:** Stock Montage, Inc.

Index